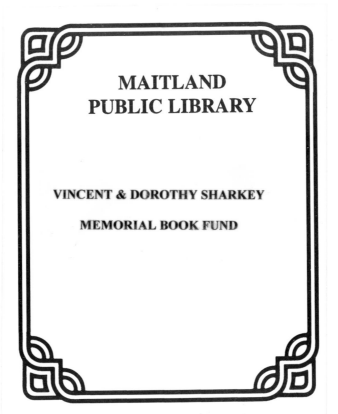

The
Patagonian
Hare

Claude Lanzmann

The Patagonian Hare
A Memoir

TRANSLATED FROM THE FRENCH

BY FRANK WYNNE

FARRAR, STRAUS AND GIROUX   NEW YORK

Farrar, Straus and Giroux
18 West 18th Street, New York 10011

Grateful acknowledgment is made for permission to reprint material from
Arthur Rimbaud's *A Season in Hell & The Drunken Boat*, translated by Louise Varese,
copyright © 1945, 1952, 1961. Reprinted by permission of New Directions Publishing
Corporation. All rights reserved.

Library of Congress Cataloging-in-Publication Data
Lanzmann, Claude.
   [Lièvre de Patagonie. English]
   The Patagonian hare : a memoir / Claude Lanzmann ; translated from the French by
Frank Wynne. — 1st American ed.
   p. cm.
   ISBN 978-0-374-23004-3 (alk. paper)
   1. Lanzmann, Claude.   2. Motion picture producers and directors—France—
Biography.   3. Journalists—France—Biography.   I. Wynne, Frank.   II. Title.

PN1998.3.L385 A3 2012
791.4302'33092—dc23
[B]

            2011048058

www.fsgbooks.com

1   3   5   7   9   10   8   6   4   2

Cet ouvrage publié dans le cadre du programme d'aide à la publication bénéficie du
soutein du Ministère des Affaires Etrangères et du Service Culturel de l'Ambassade
de France représenté aux Etats-Unis.
This work received support from the French Ministry of Foreign Affairs and the
Cultural Service of the French Embassy in the United States through their
publishing assistance program.

The publisher wishes to thank Georgia de Chamberet for her help.

For my son Felix

For Dominique

In the deep mid-afternoon, he stood illuminated by the sun like a holocaust on the graven plates of sacred history. Not all hares are alike, Jacinto, nor was it his fur that marked him out from other hares, believe me, nor his Tartar eyes, nor the peculiar shape of his ears. It was something that went far beyond what we humans call personality. The countless transmigrations his soul had endured had taught him, at the moments indicated to him by the complicity of God or some brazen angels, to render himself visible or invisible. For five whole minutes at noon he would stop at the same spot in the field, ears pricked, listening to something.

The deafening thunder of a waterfall that sets birds to flight, or the crackle of a forest blaze that terrified even the most foolhardy beast, would not have caused his eyes to dilate. The inconstant clamour of the world that he remembered, peopled with prehistoric animals, with temples that looked like withered trees, with futile, misbegotten wars, made him more temperamental and more cunning. One day he stopped as usual at the hour when the sun, at its zenith, poured down like lead on the trees, preventing them from casting shadows, and he heard barking, not of one dog, but of many, hurtling madly through the undergrowth. In a bound, the hare crossed the path and began to scurry away, the dogs giving chase, pell-mell, behind him. 'Where are we headed?' cried the hare in a voice that quavered like a lightning flash. 'To the end of your life,' howled the dogs in dogs' voices.

The Golden Hare, Silvina Ocampo

Preface

I have written a lot, pen in hand, throughout my life. And yet I dictated this book in its entirety, for the most part to the philosopher Juliette Simont, my assistant editor at *Les Temps modernes* and a very dear friend, and, when Juliette was occupied with her own work, to my secretary, Sarah Streliski, a talented writer. This is because I have experienced a strange and, I believe, somewhat rare adventure. Unlike most of the friends of my generation, who persist in clinging proudly to their pens and their spidery scrawl, I discovered, when I was given a computer shortly after my film *Shoah* was released in 1985, the extraordinary and entertaining possibilities of this machine, which I slowly learned to use and later mastered, if not all the possibilities it afforded, at least those features that were useful to me. When I was dictating, with Juliette next to me, both sitting before a large screen, I found it wonderful to see my thoughts immediately objectified, perfect in every word, with no deletions, no rough drafts. Gone were the problems I have always had with my own handwriting, which, in spite of the comments of those who thought it beautiful, to my eyes changed according to my mood, agitation or tiredness. I have often been sickened by my handwriting, which I found, to quote a remark by Sartre about his own, 'sticky with all my juices' – and he wrote so much that he must have known what he was talking about. And yet some insurmountable impediment had prevented me from fully embracing modernity. Moving directly from longhand to computer – having utterly avoided the typewriter – I found that I made very slow progress when working alone; I typed with one finger, I managed to objectify my thoughts, but what was sufficient for a police report was not practical for the work I envisaged, my hunt-and-peck typing disrupted the rhythm of my thoughts and killed the momentum. If I wanted successfully to conclude that terrifying task I had been grumbling about for so many years now, I needed an extension of myself, I needed other fingers. These belonged to Juliette Simont. But Juliette's role was not limited to typing. I have been told a thousand times by a thousand different people that I ought to write the story of my life, that it was rich, multi-faceted and unique, and it deserved to be told. I agreed, I wanted to do it, but after the colossal effort that had gone into making *Shoah*, I was not sure I had the strength for such a massive undertaking. It was at this point that Juliette began typing or, what amounts to the same thing, insisting that I do something and stop prevaricating. And so one day I effortlessly dictated the first page to her, but waited months before moving on to page two, other urgent tasks taking precedence. I returned to it, but have been working on it seriously only for the past two years. While I dictated, Juliette was infinitely patient, respectful of my pensive, often lengthy silences, and her own silent, companionable presence itself inspired me. It is hardly surprising, therefore, that I express my gratitude.

I am also grateful to Sarah, who proved to be as patient as Juliette, and to my first readers, Dominique, Antoine Gallimard, Éric Marty and Ran Halévi, whose favourable reception encouraged me.

The
Patagonian
Hare

Chapter 1

The guillotine – more generally, capital punishment and the various methods of meting out death – has been the abiding obsession of my life. It began very early. I must have been about ten years old, and the memory of that cinema on the rue Legendre in the 17th *arrondissement* in Paris, with its red velvet seats and its faded gilt, remains astonishingly vivid. A nanny, making the most of my parents' absence, had taken me, and the film that day was *L'Affaire du courrier de Lyon* [*The Courier of Lyons*], with Pierre Blanchar and Dita Parlo. I have never known or tried to discover the name of the director, but he must have been very proficient, for there are certain scenes that I have never forgotten: the attack on the Lyon courier's stagecoach in a dark forest, the trial of Lesurques, innocent but condemned to death, the scaffold erected in the middle of a public square, white, as I remember it, the blade swooping down. Back then, as during the Revolution, people were still guillotined in public. For months afterwards, around midnight, I would wake up, terror-stricken, and my father would get up, come into my room, stroke my damp forehead, my hair wet with anxiety, talk to me and calm me. It was not just my head being cut off: sometimes I was guillotined lengthwise, in the way a pit-sawyer cuts wood, or like those astonishing instructions posted on the doors of goods wagons that, in 1914, were used to send men and animals to the front: 'men

40 – horses (lengthwise) 8', and which, after 1941, were used to send Jews to the distant chambers of their final agony. I was being sliced into thin, flat slivers, from shoulder to shoulder, passing through the crown of my head. The violence of these nightmares was such that as a teenager and even as an adult, fearful of reviving them, I superstitiously looked away or closed my eyes whenever a guillotine was depicted in schoolbooks, historical writing or newspapers. I'm not sure that I don't still do so today. In 1938 – I was thirteen – the arrest and confession of the German murderer Eugen Weidmann had all of France on tenterhooks. Weidmann had murdered in cold blood, to steal and leave no witnesses, and, without needing to check, I can still remember the names of some of his victims: a dancer, Jean de Koven, a man named Roger Leblond, and others whom he buried in the forest of Fontainebleau, in the aptly named Bois de Fausses-Reposes – the Woods of False Repose. The newsreels, in great detail, showed the investigators searching the coppices, digging up the bodies. Weidmann was condemned to death and guillotined before the prison gate at Versailles in the summer before the war. There are famous photographs of the beheading. Much later I decided to look at them, and did so at length. His was the last public execution in France. Thereafter, the scaffold was erected inside the prison courtyard, until 1981 when, at the instigation of François Mitterrand and the then Minister of Justice, Robert Badinter, the death penalty was abolished. But, at thirteen, however, Weidmann, Lanzmann – the identical endings of his name and mine seemed to portend for me some terrible fate. Indeed, as I write these words, even at my supposedly advanced age, there is no guarantee that it will not still be so. The death penalty might be reinstated, all it would take is a change of regime, a vote in parliament, a *grande peur*. And of course the death penalty survives in many places: to travel is dangerous. I remember discussing it with Jean Genet, because of the dedication of *Notre-Dame-des-Fleurs* [*Our Lady of the Flowers*] to a young man, guillotined at the age of

twenty – 'Were it not for Maurice Pilorge, whose death continues to poison my life . . .' – and also because Weidmann's name opens the book: 'Weidmann appeared to you in a five o'clock edition, head swathed in white strips of cloth, a nun and yet a wounded airman . . .', and mentioning my abiding fear that I would die by the so-called *bois de justice* [the guillotine]. He replied brusquely, 'There's still time.' He was right. He didn't much like me; I felt exactly the same about him.

I have no neck. I have often wondered, during nocturnal moments of acute bodily awareness spent anticipating the worst, where the blade would have to fall to behead me cleanly. I could think only of my shoulders and my aggressively defensive posture, forged gradually night after night by the nightmares that followed the primal scene of Lesurques' death, which transformed them into a fighting bull's *morillo*, neck muscles so impenetrable the blade glances off, sending it back to its point of origin, each rebound weakening its original power. It is as though, over time, I had drawn in on myself so as to leave for the blade of *la veuve* – the widow, as Madame Guillotine is colloquially known – no convenient place and no opportunity for it to make one. In the boxing world, they would say I grew up in a 'crouch', with a curvature of the torso so marked that an opponent's fists slide off without the punches truly hitting home.

The truth is that throughout my whole life, and without a moment's respite, the evening before an execution (if I was aware of it, as I frequently was during the Algerian War), and the day after in the case of a non-political capital punishment, were nights and days of distress during which I compelled myself to anticipate or relive the last moments – the hours, the minutes, the seconds – of the condemned men, regardless of the reasons for the fatal verdict. The warders' felt slippers whispering along death row; the sudden clang of cell-door bolts slammed back, the prisoner, haggard, waking with a start, the prosecutor, the lawyer, the chaplain, the 'be brave', the glass of rum, the handover to the executioner and his aides and the sudden lurch to naked violence, the brutal acceleration of the final sequence: arms lashed behind the back, ankles crudely hobbled with a length of rope, shirt quickly slit with scissors to expose the neck, the prisoner manhandled, shouted at, then hauled, feet dragging along the ground, to the door, now suddenly thrown open, overlooking the machine, standing tall, waiting, in the ashen dawn of the prison courtyard. Yes, I know all these things. With Simone de Beauvoir I would be summoned to the offices of Jacques Vergès around nine o'clock at night where he would inform us that an Algerian was to be executed at dawn in some prison – Fresnes or La Santé in Paris, Oran or Constantine in Algeria – and we would spend the night trying to find someone who might contact someone else, who in turn might dare to disturb the sleep of Général de Gaulle, plead with him to spare this poor wretch to whom he had already refused clemency, consciously sending him to the scaffold. At the time, Vergès was head of a collective of lawyers from the *Front de libération national* (FLN) who practised what they called '*la defense de rupture*', refusing to recognize the legitimacy of the French courts' jurisdiction over the Algerian combatants, which resulted in some of their clients being more speedily dispatched to the guillotine. Very late one night, under the cold eye of Vergès, Le Castor (as Simone de Beauvoir was nicknamed) and I, gripped by the same sense of extreme urgency, managed to reach François Mauriac. A man was about to die, he had to be saved, what had been done might yet be undone. Mauriac understood everything, but he also knew that one did not wake de Gaulle and that, in any case, it would make no difference: it was too late, unquestionably. To Vergès, who was well aware of the futility of our attempts, our presence in his offices on the eve of these executions was a political strategy. One to which we consented, given that, from the first, we had militated in favour of Algerian independence, but to me the sense of the irreversible won out over everything else, becoming unbearable as the fatal hour approached. Time divided and negated itself like a gallop seen in slow motion: this scheduled death was endlessly about to take place. As in that space where Achilles can never catch up with the tortoise, so the minutes and seconds were infinitely subdivided, bringing the torment of imminence to its apogee. Vergès, notified of the execution by telephone, put an end to our waiting and in the early hours of morning, in the rain, de Beauvoir and I regularly found ourselves defeated, empty, without any plan, as though the guillotine had also decapitated our future.

When, in order to demoralize his own people and discourage further plots against him, Hitler ordered that the conspirators of 20 July 1944 be executed one after another, it became clear that the speed at which the executioners would have to work would compromise the precision and the concentration required for the ancient method of beheading by axe, the standard means of capital punishment in Germany. On 22 February 1943, the heroes of *die Weisse Rose* (the White Rose) – Hans Scholl, his sister Sophie and their friend Christoph Probst – died in their twenties beneath the executioner's axe in Stadelheim Prison, Munich, after a summary trial lasting barely three hours, conducted by the sinister Roland Freisler, the Reich's public prosecutor who had come specially from Berlin. Immediately the verdict was announced, they were put to death in a dungeon in Stadelheim, and Hans, as he laid his head on the block still red with his sister's blood, cried, 'Long live freedom!' Even today I cannot call to mind those three handsome, pensive young faces without tears welling in my eyes: the seriousness, the dignity, the determination, the spiritual force, the extraordinary courage of the solitude that emanates from each of them, all speak to their being the best, the honour of Germany, the best of humanity. The 20 July conspirators were the first to die by the German guillotine: unlike its French counterpart – slender, tall and spectacular, lending itself both to being elegantly draped and to literature – the German version is squat, ungainly, four-square, easy to set up in a low-ceilinged room; consequently the blade, which has no time to pick up speed, is enormously heavy, and I am not sure that, like ours, it has a bevelled edge: its efficacy is due entirely to its weight. It was Freisler once again who acted as prosecutor at the trial of the 20 July conspirators in Berlin. In fact, he held every role: public prosecutor and presiding judge, he made the opening statements, questioned the witnesses and summed up against the accused. Their trial was filmed for Nazi propaganda purposes, to edify the public and ridicule those about to be guillotined.

Fouquier-Tinville during the Reign of Terror, Vychinsky, the prosecutor of Stalin's show-trials in Moscow, the Czech prosecutor Urválek, barking like a dog at the Slánský trial, Freisler – they all descend from the same stock of bureaucratic butchers, unfailing in their service to their masters of the moment, affording the accused no chance, refusing to listen to them, insulting them, directing the evidence to a sentence that was decided before the trial began. In the footage of the 20 July trial Freisler can be seen, his face convulsed in feigned fury, cutting short the élite aristocratic officers and generals of the *Wehrmacht*, who are busy hiking up their trousers, which, having neither belt nor buttons, keep slipping comically to their knees, as the prosecutor moves from outrage to threats of contempt of court. But no one is laughing: the tortures suffered by the poor wretches before the trial, and the knowledge, etched on their faces, that they will die in the coming hours, set their features into unutterably tragic masks in which incomprehension vies with despair. The account of their beheading, in a dungeon in Moabit Prison in Berlin (which still stands, in the Alte Moabit district), is appalling: Freisler's victims had to queue up to die, hands bound, ankles fettered by their own trousers, they were suddenly seized by the stocky executioner's aides, who directed them either to right or to left – using an SS technique perfected elsewhere – for two guillotines were operating side by side beneath the low ceiling, amid screams of terror, the last shouts of defiance, amid the stench of blood and shit. In Moabit, there is no place for the beautiful – too beautiful – travelling shot the director Andrzej Wajda offers in his film *Danton*, where, in the midst of the Reign of Terror, Danton returns from Arcis-sur-Aube where he has spent several nights of passion with his mistress, arriving at the place de Grève at dawn, his barouche describing a perfect arc around the quiescent guillotine, elegantly draped in a long ribbon of night that, since it does not hide it completely, allows the '*Indulgent*' a glimpse of the bevelled edge of the naked blade, a grim forewarning. Alejo Carpentier's description, in the magnificent opening pages of *El Siglo de Las Luces* [*Explosion in a Cathedral*] is – no pun intended – of a different calibre: there Victor Hugues, a *Commissaire* of the Republic, former public prosecutor at Rochefort and a fervent admirer of Robespierre, brings with him to the Antilles both the decree – enacted on 6 Pluviôse, Year II – that will abolish slavery, and the first guillotine: 'But the empty doorway stood in the bows, reduced to a mere lintel and its supports, with the set-square, the inverted half-pediment upended, the black triangle with its bevel of cold steel suspended between the uprights . . . Here the Door stood alone, facing into the night . . . its diagonal blade gleaming, its wooden uprights framing a whole panorama of stars.'

So many last glances will haunt me forever. Those of the Moroccan generals, colonels, captains, accused of having fomented – or of not having foreseen – the 1972 attempted coup against Hassan II of Morocco and his guests at Skhirat palace, who were driven to their place of execution in covered lorries open at the back. Sitting on facing benches, they stare at one another, and the photographer captured the moment when, in the dazzling sunlight, they see the firing squad that is to execute them. It is an unforgettable photograph, published in *Paris Match*, which captured what Cartier-Bresson called the 'decisive moment': we do not see the firing squad; instead we see the eyes of those who see it, who are about to die in a hail of bullets and who know it. In spite of fables of peaceful passing from life to death, such as Greuze's painting, *The Death of a Patriarch*, or La Fontaine's tale of '*Le Laboureur et ses enfants*' ['The Labourer and

His Children'], every 'natural' death is, first and foremost, a violent death. But I never felt the absolute violence of violent death more than I did as I looked at that photograph, that *snapshot*. In that searing intensity, whole lives were laid bare before our eyes: these men were privileged, well-to-do members of the regime, they did not choose to risk their lives, unlike the heroes of the Resistance who, refusing the blindfold, stood to attention before the rifles and remained valiant even as the guns rang out. Why do I remember one face, one name so particularly – one I would never think to verify – Medbouh? He was, I believe, a general and devoted to his king, but the savagery and the vast spectre of the crackdown would not spare him. It is sweltering hot, sweat beads on his forehead, the irreparable is about to occur, and Medbouh's last glance, frantic with fear and disbelief, evokes the greatest pity.

Another last glance, also from *Paris Match*: that of a hard-faced young Chinese girl screaming her revolt before the judges at the moment that she learns she has been condemned to death. Face contorted, torn between pain and refusal as policemen's hands grab her and drag her away. In China, she knows, executions take place very quickly after sentence is pronounced, and the series of photographs published by *Paris Match* bears witness to the inexorable sequence of moments leading to her death. In the next photograph we see a second hand that, with overpowering force, pushes her head down to expose her neck but also to compel her to die in the position of a penitent. And, since executions there take place in public, to serve as an example, the last photographs show the pistol firing into the back of her neck and her battered, martyred body slowly slipping to the ground. Barely thirty minutes have elapsed between verdict and death. Other photographs, other films regularly reach us from China, all equally terrifying: a line of young men in black prison uniforms shot one by one, through the back of the neck, by a police executioner in white gloves wearing a peaked cap and full dress uniform, who forces each man's head into the same penitent posture, as though the death penalty were the supreme act of re-education.

Still in China, the same China, the China of today. In Nanjing there is a Chinese Yad Vashem, solemn, simple, poignant, which commemorates the great massacre of 1937, in which the Japanese Imperial army, the moment they had captured the city, murdered 300,000 civilians and soldiers, killing in a thousand different ways, each more inhumane than the last. The goal was to terrorize the entire country and, beyond that, the whole of South-east Asia, all the way to New Guinea. They achieved that goal. Wandering through Nanjing Massacre Memorial Hall with the curator who, in his humility, his calm, his lack of bombast in the face of the crushing weight of evidence, his reverence, the present incarnation of ancient suffering, ineluctably reminded me of the Israeli survivors in Kibbutz Lohamei HeGeta'ot in Galilee or at Yad Vashem during my preliminary research for *Shoah*, once again I realized that there is a universality of victims, as of executioners. All victims are alike, all executioners are alike. In Nanjing, to train the Japanese army rabble, bayonets fixed, in hand-to-hand combat, realism was pushed so far as to lash live targets to stakes as instructors gave detailed demonstrations of how and where the bayonet should be thrust: the throat, the heart, the abdomen, the face, all in front of the petrified faces of the guinea-pigs. Accounts and photographs bear this out, they show the faces of soldiers moving from crude laughter to rage and back again as they plunged their bayonets into the victims' bodies. Those lashed to the next stakes awaited their turn, which came as soon as the previous targets breathed their last. The soldiers did not train on corpses; the dead feel no pain.

Through a long tradition, a punctilious codification, the Japanese became masters in the technique – the art, they call it – of beheading by sabre (something that can also be seen at the Nanjing Memorial), and organized contests between their most skilled men. How to describe, beneath the yellow summer uniform of the Mikado's troops, its curious peaked cap framing with neck-cloths of floating fabric, the astonishing musculature of the swordsmen, steel bands of muscle that seem to be part of the sabre itself in that very moment when, gripped firmly in both hands, brandished high and vertical, it is about to sweep down a mere fraction of a fraction of a second later? Everything happens so quickly that the sabre passes through the neck while the head remains in place: it has no time to fall. What pride, what pleasure in a perfect execution, what smile of satisfaction on the face of the contest winners when, in the minutes after the competition, full of themselves, they posed beside the headless bodies, the bodiless heads.

And yet it is not in Nanjing, but 8,000 kilometres to the south, in Canberra, Australia, that, for me, was the culmination of horror. In Canberra there is a remarkable war museum, the Australian War Memorial, that is like no other in the world. Perhaps it is because Australia is not populous that every life is precious to them, and also because they have never fought a war in their own country, but only in distant lands. During World War I the Australian Expeditionary Force lost – who still remembers? – tens of thousands of men at Gallipoli, in the Dardanelles and on the French front. Between 1939 and 1945, on every front and in every branch of the army, many more selflessly spilled their blood to liberate Europe and Asia from barbarism. In Canberra, in one of the halls of the museum devoted to World War II, I could not tear my eyes from an extraordinary photograph, the work of two artists in the Japanese army: the photographer himself and the executioner. In an incredibly daring, low-angle shot, the photographer has succeeded in framing both executioner and his victim, a tall Australian, on his knees, arms pinioned, wearing a white blindfold. He has a chinstrap beard, his upper body is erect, his neck as long as a swan's, his head barely bowed, hieratic, his face a mask of ecstatic suffering, like those in El Greco's *Burial of the Count of Orgaz*. Above him, in the upper part of the frame, in the yellow uniform I have already described, the killer, face tensed in a rictus of concentration, arms raised to heaven, hands, white-knuckled, gripping the hilt of his sabre, which forms the apex of this devastating trinity. But though it may begin its trajectory on the vertical, it is on the horizontal that the blade will come to rest, having traced a perfectly controlled arc through space. Such is the mastery. Next to the two photographs of the Australian prisoner, one taken before the beheading, one after, is a letter, preserved like a precious relic, the letter that the executioner wrote to his family in Japan from the theatre of war in New Guinea, in which he gives details of his feat, boasting about the singular skills he required and marshalled to accomplish it (an English translation hangs next to the ideograms of the Japanese original).

But having spoken of the muscular backs of the swordsmen, having mentioned El Greco, I immediately think of Goya, the Goya of *Los fusilamientos del tres de mayo*, which I have so often stood and gazed upon in the Prado, turning away each time only with great difficulty, as though to walk away were to relinquish some supreme, some ineffable knowledge, utterly offered, utterly hidden. And yet in this remarkable painting everything is said, everything can be read, everything can be seen: the impenetrable wall formed by the serried backs of the Saxon fusiliers of the Grande Armée, black shakos pulled down over their eyes, swords slapping against their thighs, calves sheathed in black gaiters, left legs thrust forward, bent slightly in the classic position of a rifleman at drill, bayonets fixed, the barrels of their rifles perfectly aligned. The executioners are anonymous, all we can see are their backs weighed down with the trappings of an expeditionary troop, while the angle of their shakos tilted down over the sights of their weapons makes it clear that they are oblivious to the dazzled, dazzling faces of those they are gunning down. Between killers and victims, the light source, a square lantern, is set directly on the ground, its blazing light illuminating the night-time assassination with a vivid, surreal glow. The genius of Goya is that in the foreground, facing the lantern, the shakos, the rifles, standing

11

out against the shadows and the hills of Príncipe Pío, and the vague intimation of the city beyond, it is the truly preternatural whiteness of the central figure's shirt itself that seems to illuminate the whole scene. Two rival light sources are at war, that of the victims and that of their killers, the former so bright, so intense that it transforms the lamp into a dark lantern. Around the man wearing this shirt of light, the *morituri* seem grey or black, stooped, shrunken, hunched as though to offer no purchase to the bullets. A huddled mass climbs the steep narrow path to the place of execution. Suddenly, as they reach the summit, they see it all: the bloody corpses of the companions who went before them, the others, fatally wounded, already falling, and facing them, the firing squad relentlessly taking aim at each new group as it arrives. So as not to see, not to hear, they cover their eyes, their ears in a final posture of denial and of supplication. But in the centre, in the midst of those who have been shot, who are falling, at the absolute heart of it all, is he towards whom everything converges; kneeling yet huge, all the more huge because he is kneeling, in the instant before being hit, his shirt of light still immaculate, the man in white gazes, wide-eyed, upon his imminent death. How to describe him? How to depict his chest magnified, offered up to the gun barrels, its incredible whiteness, like an armour for his final hour? How to describe his mad, bulging eyes beneath the coal black of his eyebrows, his arms up, flung wide, not vertically, not crosswise but out at an angle, in a last gesture of bravado and sacrifice, of rebellion and helplessness, of despair and pity? How to convey his mute proffering, the message to his executioners written on his face, in every line of his body? In 1942, 130 years later, at the fortress of Mont Valérien in Paris, joining the ranks of those heroes of the night, the Communist Valentin Feldman addressed his unforgettable last words to the German riflemen about to execute him: 'Imbeciles, it is for you that I die!'

Why is there no end to this? Twenty years pass, and we find ourselves crossing the place de l'Alma towards the Spanish Embassy, fiercely guarded by a police cordon, to plead, although we have no illusions, for Julián Grimau, sentenced to death for trumped-up crimes supposedly dating back to the Civil War. In reality it was because he was a militant member of the clandestine Communist Party of Spain, a membership he proudly and publicly avowed when he was arrested, before he threw himself from a second-storey window during his interrogation. Cruelly tortured, in spite of his broken wrists, Grimau was hurriedly executed in the dead of night, by the light of car headlamps in the courtyard of the Campamento military barracks in Madrid a few hours after our demonstration in Paris. It was 20 April 1963. El Caudillo was fiercely stubborn and, until he was in his final death throes – as we know, he was kept alive with tubes and wires for months as all Spain held its breath – he continued to send men to their deaths. On 2 March 1974 the Catalan anarchist Salvador Puig Antich was executed by the garrotte in Modelo Prison in Barcelona. This method of meting out capital punishment was codified as the *garrotte vil*, which can be simply translated as the 'infamous garrotte', but '*vil*' in French can also be translated as 'base' or 'lowly': the condemned man dies sitting in a high-backed chair, his feet and hands clamped in vices, making it impossible for him to move; his neck is circled with an iron collar tightened by a screw at the back of the chair – slowly or quickly according to the cruelty or the professionalism of the executioner – crushing the carotid artery and then the spine. There is a specifically Catalan variation of the *garrotte vil*, where the collar is fitted with a spike that pierces the back of the neck as it crushes. Puig Antich was the last man to be garrotted under Franco, and for him too we protested in vain. The death penalty was abolished in Spain in 1978, so there is an end to this sometimes, somewhere.

Even as I write, the death penalty still flourishes throughout the world. I have said nothing of the anti-abolitionist states in the United States of America, each clinging to its own singular inhumanity, whether it be the electric chair, lethal injection, the gas chamber, the gallows. Nor have I said anything about the Arab countries, about the Saudi executioners who arrive ceremoniously at the place of execution in their white Mercedes, while the prisoner, already kneeling, head slightly bowed, waits for the white flash of the curved blade to behead them in public. They at least are experts, capable of competing with the Japanese executioners I spoke of earlier. Today, the time of the butchers has come (and I ask actual butchers to forgive me, for they practise the most noble of professions and are the least barbarous of men): why have we not been allowed to see the appalling images of hostages put to death under Islamic law in Iraq or in Afghanistan? Pathetic amateur videos shot by the killers themselves, which aim to terrorize – and succeed. Was this any reason to censor such images in the name of some dubious code of ethics, whose sole effect was to hush up an unprecedented qualitative leap in the history of global barbarism, to cover up the arrival of a mutant species in the relationship between man and death? And so these videos circulate clandestinely, and very few of us have been able to witness the true extent of the horror, struggling not to look away.

This is what happens: the film opens with a litany of verses from the Qur'an, which appear on screen as they are recited. As in pornographic films, there is no editing, no connection between the shots, which shift abruptly: suddenly the Tribunal appears, framed against a black background that fills the whole screen. In the foreground, kneeling, ankles shackled, hands tied, is the accused. Behind him, the Grand Judge and his assistants, tall, black-hooded phantoms, Kalashnikovs slung across their chests, meeting at the sternum, barrels pointing upward. The Grand Judge alone speaks. He does so in a deep, droning voice, he reads or does not read, it depends. He goes on speaking for some time, his voice becoming more furious, more sententious, a performance that culminates (he literally 'makes himself' angry) as the moment approaches when sentence is pronounced and carried out. The accused, whether or not he understands Arabic, knows that his fate is sealed, that at the end of the grandiloquent sequence of justifications adduced for the verdict, his life will be taken. Does he know how it will happen? Does he sense it? In the twenty or so 'films' I have managed to watch – all of them repulsive – I will retain only one. During the black-robed prosecutor's long, furious tirade, the hostage remained completely motionless: no movement, unblinking, his gaze vacant, staring into space, as though he had already left this life and must now suffer the worst so that he could rejoin himself. Utter resignation. He is still a young man, his hair is curly but his face is gaunt, and he has clearly already suffered the most terrible physical and psychological agony, the hellish torture of experiencing hope before losing it forever. He shows no sign of fear, he is the embodiment of fear, made rigid by fear. As soon as the last word of the sentence is uttered, the Grand Judge, who has been standing directly behind the prisoner, brings his right hand to his belt and draws a huge butcher's knife, brandishing it in front of the camera, shouting 'Allahu akbar' as he simultaneously seizes the prisoner by the hair and throws him to the ground, while one of the hooded henchmen grabs his ankles so he cannot struggle. It is with this butcher's knife that he will behead the prisoner, but not before forcing the poor man to look into the camera, to look at us. And so, several times during the procedure, we will see the eyes of the prisoner roll wildly in their orbits. But a human neck, even one emaciated by starvation, is not composed entirely of soft tissue: there is cartilage, cervical vertebrae. The killer is tall and heavily built, but even he has trouble finding a clear path for the blade. So he begins to use it like a saw, sawing for as long as necessary, through the spurts and spatters of blood, an unbearable to-and-fro motion that forces us to live through, right to the end, the slitting of a man's throat, like an animal, a pig or a sheep. When the head is finally severed from the body, the hand of the masked sawyer signs his work by displaying the head, placing it facing us, on the headless trunk; the eyes roll back one last time, indicating, to our shameful relief, that it is over.

But the camera keeps filming, the hooded men have left the scene, a clumsy zoom shot frames the head and the torso, which now fill the screen, alone, in close-up, for a long moment, for our edification and our instruction. The face of the dead man and of the living man he was are so alike that it seems unreal. It is the same face, and it is barely believable: the savagery of the killing was such that it seemed it could not but bring about a radical disfigurement.

Chapter 2

Just as I took my place in the endless cortège of those guillotined, hanged, shot, garrotted, among all the tortured in the world, so too I am that hostage with the vacant eyes, this man waiting for the blade to fall. You must understand that I love life madly, love it all the more now that I am close to leaving it – so much so that I do not even believe what I have just said, which is a statistical proposition, a piece of pure rhetoric that finds no response in my flesh, in my bones. I cannot know what state I shall be in nor how I shall behave when the last bell sounds. What I do know is that this life I love so irrationally would have been tainted by a fear of equal magnitude, the fear that I might prove cowardly if I had to lose that life through one of the evil acts described above. How many times have I wondered how I would react under torture? And every time my answer has been that I would have been incapable of taking my own life as Pierre Brossolette did, as André Postel-Vinay attempted to do, when, with sudden determination, like Julián Grimau, he jumped from the second-storey of the Prison de la Santé as he was brought in for questioning, and as many less famous but no less heroic people such as Baccot have done. I need to talk about Baccot because he is always with me; I am, in a certain sense, responsible for his death. It was in late November 1943, after class, in the boarders' quadrangle of the Lycée Blaise-Pascal in Clermont-Ferrand. Though

Baccot was studying for his *baccalauréat* in philosophy while I was already in *Lettres supérieures*, he knew that since we had returned to school that autumn I had been leading the Resistance at the Lycée. In fact, I had set up the Resistance network from scratch. I had become a member of the *Jeunesses communistes* during the summer and since coming back to school had recruited about forty boarders – *khâgneux* (preparing for the École normale supérieure), *taupins* (preparing for the École polytechnique) and *agros* (studying agronomy) – into the nucleus of the *Jeunesses communistes*, with whose help I had recruited 200 others into a mass organization – the FUJP, *Forces unies de la jeunesse patriotique* – controlled, unbeknownst to them, by the *Parti communiste français* (PCF). Such was the policy of the clandestine Communist Party at the time. Baccot, to whom I had barely spoken before then, faced me squarely, dark eyes blazing beneath his bushy eyebrows, his hair pushed back to reveal the cliff-face of his forehead; he was thick-set, stocky and exuded a concentration, a dark force. 'I want to join the Resistance,' he said simply, 'but the stuff you're doing doesn't interest me. I know there are action groups out there, that's what I want to join.' I asked him how old he was. 'Eighteen.' I was not even older than him! I said, 'You know what action groups mean, you know the risks?' He knew, he understood. I told him, 'Take a week, think about it, think hard and talk to me again.'

What were we doing that did not interest Baccot? Beneath the Lycée Blaise-Pascal was a network of long interconnected cellars like catacombs. My only contact with the outside world, with the Party, was a woman, whom I knew only as Aglaé. She had smuggled three revolvers and some ammunition into the school and entrusted them to my care. A few friends, those I was closest to, and I would sneak soundlessly out of the dormitory at night – thanks to my father I was adept at such things – go down to the cellars and practise shooting at improvised targets. No one ever heard the deafening explosions that echoed in the depths, nobody found out what we were doing – very few people even knew that the cellars existed. But there were times, on days of red alert or when I had been warned by Aglaé, that I would come to class with the revolver in the pocket of the grey school smock that was the standard uniform for boarders. It is difficult to describe this period, and few have done so well. Among the day pupils, there were a number of *Vichystes*, boys with connections to the *Milice*, some who were even in the *Milice*. They knew who we were; we knew who they were; you have to imagine the schoolyard of Blaise-Pascal at break time, the factions watching each other, weighing each other up, scrutinizing each other and turning away. The kids from families of collaborators or *miliciens* were the same age as we were. At the time, Clermont-Ferrand had been occupied for a year (November 1942, the date of the Anglo-American landings in North Africa) by German troops, the *Wehrmacht* and the Gestapo, ruthlessly supported by Darnand's *Milice*, but the Communist Party action groups – the ones Baccot wanted to join – were making life difficult for them: intimidation, suspicion, fear stalked both camps. We had managed to get two or even three copies of every key in the school, most importantly the key to the double gate in the central quad, the gate that led directly into town, enabling us to evade the caretakers and supervisors. Aglaé supplied me with pamphlets, calls to resistance, denunciations of Nazi crimes, advice, information on how the war was progressing, poems by Aragon and Éluard, texts by Vercors published by Les Éditions de Minuit. We had divided Clermont-Ferrand into sectors. On weekends and Thursdays too we sneaked out of the lycée in groups of five to head for whichever sector we had been assigned: we worked calmly and quickly, slipping the tracts through letterboxes or under doors. In every group, two members acted as lookouts and we repeated these operations, careful to vary both times and places since distributing pamphlets almost immediately alerted the attention of the police and of the *Milice*. It was almost impossible to work by night – we did so only in extreme cases – since there was usually a curfew, and even when there was not, the town was swarming with German patrols.

What astonishes me, what seems incomprehensible to me even now is that, in 1943, in this one small *hypokhâgne* class, there were three Jews: my very dear friend André Wormser, the son of Georges Wormser, former *directeur de cabinet* to Georges Clemenceau (he stayed for only two months), a girl called Hélène Hoffnung and me, all three of us enrolled under our real names and without the obligatory and ignominious stamp – JEW – in red letters on our identity cards, and all, therefore, completely illegal. Since the summer of 1941, French Jews had been compelled to register so I possessed an identity card stamped this way. I still look for it sometimes – I mislaid it, probably during a period of change in my life – but I'm sure that a girlfriend kept it and it will turn up when the time is right. I remember my adolescent face – I was about to write 'my innocent face' – struck through diagonally with that stamped curse from the dawn of time. Back then, we did not know whether it was better to obey the new laws or to ignore them. For a brief period, my father had favoured obedience, but he soon became convinced that we should fear the worst and this branding of himself and his family seemed to him, to all of us, intolerable. We had identity cards printed in our own names, but without this vile stamp. We had sought refuge in Brioude, a sub-prefecture of the Haute-Loire where we had previously lived from 1934 to 1938 after my parents separated. My father had loved the area from when he had first gone there, for the treatment of his lungs, at the end of World War I: having volunteered in 1917 at the age of seventeen – his father had been fighting on the front line since 1914 – he had been the victim of a mustard gas attack at the Somme. Now, separated from my mother, and with a new wife, he chose to make a new life for himself in Brioude, taking with him his three children: my sister Évelyne, my brother Jacques and me, the eldest at nine. Yet in 1938 we returned for a time to Paris when I started secondary school at the Lycée Condorcet (the *petit lycée*). I had time to be profoundly shaken and terrorized by the force and the virulence of the anti-Semitism at this Parisian lycée. Paradoxically, the war, which was to expose me to far greater dangers, freed me of such fears: we left Paris for Brioude once more when war was declared in October 1939.

Since my father was almost forty, had three children and was a veteran of the 1914–18 war, he was not called up for active service, but enlisted as an '*affecté spécial*' working on projects related to the national defence. He was allowed to choose the region where he would work and opted for Brioude. For me, it was like a return to happier times, but our status had changed considerably: my father had been forced to give up his position, and what few possessions he had. Until the crushing defeat of the French army in May 1940, he drove coal trucks, coming home every night as black as a chimney sweep. Improbably, I found myself back at the Collège Lafayette that I had attended from 1934 to 1938, even though my father, when he came to collect me from my grandparents' house in Normandy where I had spent the last holidays before the war, had told me that I would have to give up school and go out to earn a living, just as he had been forced to do twenty years earlier. It was dark, I remember the starlit sky above my head, I was watching for German planes when he told me that he had decided to find me a position at the Post and Telegraphs. I bridled at this, the last thing in the world I wanted to be was a postman. My categorical refusal, together with the disgust of the headmaster of the Collège Lafayette, who was happy to have me back, won my father round and I was allowed, for a time at least, to continue my studies. Obviously, we were well known in this little town, and known to be Jews, though the people of Brioude did not seem to attach any special importance to the label. My father had many friends who refused to turn their backs on us with the advent of the Vichy regime's so-called '*État Français*' and the sinister quaverings of Maréchal Pétain. The defeat, and the division of France into the Occupied Zone and the area known as the 'Free Zone', saw a number of Jewish refugees arrive in Brioude, almost all foreigners, who had no legal protection. For me, as for Aragon in his poem 'L'Affiche rouge', their names were difficult to pronounce, more difficult even than my own. More often than not, when asked my last name, I spelled it out rather than saying it, and did so as quickly as possible, L-A-N-Z-M-A-N-N. I still do so today when I realize that my fame is not universal and has not reached the person I am speaking to, usually by telephone. I was amazed by the number of children in every family, by the extraordinary capacity for work and the talent of their parents, whether tailors, furriers, cobblers, by the ease with which they adapted to the most difficult conditions and by the self-evident affection they bore for each other. One gifted Jewish boy of Polish extraction was my classmate and soon became my friend. He was so brilliant, so far ahead of the class in every subject, and unaffectedly arrogant, knowing himself to be superior – how could he be otherwise? – that he aroused naked envy among the sons of Auvergne farmers and shopkeepers who made up most of the pupils at the school. Once I found him tied to one of the plane trees in the schoolyard, the other boys circling him in a vicious war dance, thumping him and uttering savage incoherent cries, which he met with his permanent smile of defiance and superiority. The boys at the Collège Lafayette were neither hateful nor anti-Semitic as those at the Lycée Condorcet had been. This was something different: Freiman was being made to pay for his brilliance. I rushed over, hurling abuse at his tormentors, who respected me as I had been at the school a long time. I managed to free him without throwing a single punch.

One day in the summer of 1942, Freiman, his family and most of the foreign Jewish refugees in Brioude were rounded up in dawn raids by the French police. Suddenly, they were no longer there; it was an extraordinary shock, an abrupt, incomprehensible absence, one that was felt throughout the little town, of which they had very much become a part, and which they had enlivened by their presence. My father, although I was unaware of it, was already a member of the Resistance, and he had had false papers made for us that we might need if we had to travel or had to show our papers in a sudden raid, as, month by month, the distinction between foreign Jew and French Jew was becoming increasingly slender. I remember I was Claude Bassier, born in Langeac, or sometimes Claude Chazelle from Brassac-les-Mines; the details of our false identities, including the dates and places of birth, could be verified in the local registry offices: employees and secretaries at the town halls had agreed, at great risk to themselves, to authenticate the false papers. Today, they would be called 'Righteous Gentiles', but they weren't thinking about such things: I never knew their names, they didn't care about posterity, they did what they did out of solidarity, modestly, in the name of simple humanity.

Why, at the beginning of the 1943 school year, after I had passed the *baccalauréat*, did my father enrol me as a boarder at Blaise-Pascal in Clermont-Ferrand under my real name? He had agreed to let me carry on with my studies – a career as a postman was not for me – but he felt that a university would be too dangerous, while a boarding school would afford me the best possible protection. Just as I did not know he was already a member of the MUR (*Mouvements unis de la Résistance*) when he sent me to the lycée, he certainly did not know that I had already been a member of the *Jeunesses communistes* for four months. It was a chance recruitment, our family was broadly left-wing but I had not read Marx or Engels or Lenin. In practice, being at a boarding school under a name other than my own would have been difficult, perhaps impossible and fraught with greater dangers. What is certain is that the headmaster of Blaise-Pascal, the deputy head, the chief supervisor and some of the teachers all knew about Wormser, Hélène Hoffnung and me. The very fact that they had allowed us to enrol was in itself a guarantee of our safety. Jean Perus, our head teacher, taught us literature, and after the war I found out that he too had been a member of the *Parti communiste* and had been actively involved in the Resistance, but there was never a word or a wink of complicity between us. He was a wonderful teacher and I have never forgotten the scornful curl of his lips when he would refute some interpretation of ours with a single sentence. He also forever cured me of *comparatisme* on the day when, asked to analyse a passage of Rabelais, I stupidly made a reference to Bergson, whom I had barely read. The scorn in his famous scowl turned to contempt: '*Mon petit*, Rabelais didn't know Bergson.'

One of the missions the Party had conferred on '*mon petit*' was very dangerous: collecting cases of revolvers and grenades from Clermont-Ferrand station. This I did with Hélène Hoffnung, whom I had recruited myself and who, like me, was a member of the hard core of the *Jeunesses communistes*. Hélène was well aware of the risks involved; she was also inventive, daring and possessed of extraordinary *sang-froid*. To fool the *Milice* sent out to hunt for supposedly Jewish faces in the streets of the city, Hélène, at my request, did her best to hide as much as possible her stubbornly Semitic features. I asked her to soften the proud Hebraic profile of her nose with a fringe of red curls and to wear lipstick that was neither too prim nor too flashy. We would set off together at dusk for the station, in a tender or a passionate embrace, like two happy students in love, each carrying a little suitcase. I was scared to death. At the station, we went to the agreed platform and stood at an appointed spot, looking out for the train. Our suitcases, set down at our feet, were exchanged for others of the same size and colour, though much heavier, with the speed and skill of a magician. Everything happened without a word and so quickly that I cannot remember the face of any of the Party couriers who delivered the weapons. However, at the same station Hélène and I witnessed a number of lightning swoops by men wearing the long gabardine coats and soft caps of the Gestapo: barely had their prey stepped from the train when those waiting for them suddenly drew pistols and they were seized, handcuffed and dragged off by waiting officers. It was a terrifying sight: the poor wretches would immediately realize that they had fallen into a trap, they paled and one could already see in their sallow faces the unrelenting torture they knew they would have to endure. 'Gestapo' (the *Geheime Staatspolizei*: 'Secret State Police') was then and will forever remain a synonym for terror, for good reason. In the interrogation rooms of the Gestapo, there was no Corporal Lynndie England taking photographs to send home to family and friends, no war trophies, no staged photographs of humiliated prisoners forced into pornographic or scatological positions for the camera. Abu Ghraib Prison was, certainly, both grotesque and vile, but physical torture was not practised there: no fingernails ripped out, eyes gouged out, bones broken, no escalating panoply of lethal violence intended permanently to break its victims if they did not die under torture. The Gestapo scorned images, it worked in secret – with the real, not the virtual. At the train station, Hélène would gaze at me lovingly, impassive, apparently unconcerned by the possibility of arrest that terrified me, she hugged me, kissed me full on the mouth as though we had just been reunited. We then set off with our heavy suitcases, enraptured with each other, walking straight past the uniformed and plain-clothes officials who infested the station to begin our slow journey back through the town, to the meeting point where the suitcases disappeared with the same magical sleight-of-hand as they had appeared. Every passing patrol, every suspicious movement was a cue for a kiss – more or less deep depending on the degree of danger. Since *'Rouge Baiser'* – kiss-proof lipstick – was a rare commodity in those far-off days, we always arrived back at the lycée, our mission accomplished, smeared with the signs of flagrant passion, although there was never anything sexual between us: we were two trained militants in the *Parti communiste français*, the Party that would later christen itself 'the Party of the 75,000 Martyrs'.

I had felt sure that the week I had insisted Baccot take to consider his options would not change his mind, and I was right. I told Aglaé of his request, he quickly left Blaise-Pascal and we heard nothing more until his suicide four months later. For four months Baccot, a member of a PCF action group, had gunned down Germans and *Milice* on the streets of Clermont-Ferrand. The arms parachuted in by the Allies were only for the Gaullist Resistance, so there was only one way for the Party to procure guns: from the enemy. Every German killed meant a revolver, a pistol, a machine gun gained. Baccot, in this brief period, showed extraordinary courage, daring, patience, cunning and determination. Finally spotted, identified and hunted down, he was cornered on the place de Jaude, the main square in Clermont-Ferrand: seeing himself surrounded, he took refuge in a *vespasienne* – one of the old spiral shell urinals with iron panels that give the user privacy from passers-by – and there in the middle of the urinal, he blew his brains out so as not be taken alive. There is a brief mention of Baccot's death in Marcel Ophüls' *Le Chagrin et la pitié* [*The Sorrow and the Pity*]. In hurried interviews, two retired school monitors who knew nothing about the Resistance movement at Blaise-Pascal, or more generally in Clermont-Ferrand, retained a vague memory of Baccot's fate. I have spoken about it many times to my friend Ophüls, although he is hardly to blame, since, though he is the director of the film, he did not conduct the preparatory investigation, but to present the town of Clermont-Ferrand, as the film does, as a symbol of collaboration is a sacrilege. Clermont, where Strasbourg University had moved its campus, was, on the contrary, one of the major centres of Resistance in the Auvergne and in France.

Baccot is unquestionably a hero and I have nothing but admiration for him. But I know that I could never have done what he did, putting a bullet through my brain if I had been captured, and that knowledge has burdened my whole life. What would I have done if Hélène Hoffnung and I had been asked to open those suitcases full of weapons? During the clandestine struggle, I undertook many objectively dangerous operations, but I reproach myself now for having done so without being fully aware of the consequences, because my actions were not accompanied by an acceptance of the ultimate price to be paid if we were caught: death. Would I have done what I did if I had fully evaluated the consequences of my actions? And even if it is plausible to suggest that recklessness is a form of bravery, to act without being inwardly prepared to make the supreme sacrifice is dilettantism, this is what I repeatedly tell myself today.

The question of courage and cowardice, you will have realized, is the scarlet thread that runs though this book, the thread that runs through my life. Sartre liked to quote a phrase by Michel Leiris, who, describing the suicide of officers who had failed in their missions, referred to 'military courage'. Among the conspirators in the 20 July assassination attempt on Hitler, there were those whose fellow officers, wishing to spare them the torture, trial and ignominious death on the scaffold, came into their offices and wordlessly handed them revolvers. They stepped outside and immediately there was a gunshot: German officers, loyal to an inviolable code of honour, killed themselves automatically, almost by reflex, without hesitating even for an instant, which is perhaps the best way to proceed. There is a magnificent scene in Jean-Jacques Annaud's film *Stalingrad* [*Enemy at the Gates*] in which a Soviet general whose troops retreated under fire when no order had been given to do so, is stripped of his command by a political commissar who then places a loaded pistol on the map table and withdraws. The shot rings out before he even has time to close the door. Such are the codes of '*courage militaire*' that I cannot evoke this scene without thinking of the final monologue in Sartre's *Les Séquestrés d'Altona* [*The Condemned of Altona*]: 'Everything will be dead, eyes, judges, time.' In Hegel's *The Phenomenology of Spirit*, the master becomes the master because he has put his life on the line, because he has taken the risk of losing it – the risk of the void – while the slave, attached to his body, his desires, his needs – to what Hegel calls the 'bodily situation', an appalling but literal translation – chooses submission over honour, favours the only thing worthy to his eyes: his skin, his life, even humiliated, even mutilated, *his* life. One of the unforgettable heroes of *Shoah*, Filip Müller, for three years a member of the 'special unit', the *Sonderkommando*, in Auschwitz, said to me after a gruelling day of filming, 'I wanted to live, live with every fibre of my being, one minute more, one day more, one month more.

You understand? To live!' How I understood! The other members of the special unit who shared this Calvary with Filip Müller, noble figures, gravediggers of their own people, at once heroes and martyrs, were, like him, simple, intelligent, good men. For the most part, despite the hell of the funeral pyres and the crematoria – that *'annus mundi'* in the words of the SS doctor Thilo – they never gave up their humanity. It is important to me to name them here: Yossele Warszawski from Warsaw who arrived from Paris; Lajb Panusz from Łomża; Ajzyk Kalniak, also from Łomża; Josef Dersinski from Hrodna; Lajb Langfus from Maków Mazowiecki; Jankiel Handelsman from Radom, who came from Paris; Kaminski, the *kapo;* Dov Paisikovich from Transylvania; Stanislaw Jankowski, known as Feinsilber from Warsaw, a veteran of the International Brigades, who also arrived from Paris; Zalman Gradowski and Zalman Lewental, the two chroniclers of the *Sonderkommando* who, night after night – because they believed none of them would survive – compelled themselves to keep the diary of this Gehenna, burying their notes in the clay beneath Crematoria II and III on the eve of the abortive *Sonderkommando* revolt of 7 October 1944, in which they lost their lives: manuscripts written in Yiddish in a firm, upright hand found foxed and mildewed – one in 1945, the other in 1962 – three-quarters of the pages are illegible and all the more harrowing for that fact. To the obscene questions: 'How could they? Why did they not kill themselves?' we must let them answer, and unconditionally respect that answer. To begin with, many of them did do so, many of them took their own lives, leaping into the blazing fire pits or begging to be killed at the first shock. What a shock it was! These are young men, eighteen, twenty, twenty-five, from Poland, from Hungary, from Greece, they arrive in Auschwitz after months or years of living in ghettos, of misery and humiliation, after a terrible journey (eleven days and eleven nights from Salonika to Auschwitz, nineteen from Rhodes or from Corfu by sea and land), they are dying of starvation, of thirst; barely have they stepped onto the ramp than they are 'selected'; torn from their families, they are shaved, tattooed, beaten senseless; with whips and snapping dogs they are driven through thin copses of silver birch in Birkenau to the stockade of Crematorium V or the Little Farm. And suddenly – but could one ever really be prepared for such a spectacle? – suddenly they see everything: the pits, the roar of the flames, the mass of bluish tangled bodies that spills out as the doors of the gas chambers swing open, twisted bodies they were forced to untangle, among which they recognize the flattened faces of their mothers, their little sisters, their brothers who arrived with them only a few short hours before. This was the first shock. The Jews of the sun-drenched shore of the Ionian Sea, the sweet Jews, the gentle Jews described by Albert Cohen, could not bear it: they threw themselves into the blaze, arms spread wide like divers. Two months later, these same men (by which I mean, those who did not jump) were going about their tedious task: armed with heavy birch rams, on a concrete slab they pounded femurs, tibias, the hard bones that the flames had not completely consumed; they did so singing all day long beneath the white skies of Auschwitz: '*Mamma, son tanto felice* . . .' ['Mamma, I'm so happy . . .'] But it is Zalman Lewental, the admirable Froissart of the *Sonderkommando*, who, in his upright handwriting, best answered the obscene question: 'The truth,' he wrote, 'is that you want to live, at any cost. You want to live because you are alive, because the whole world is alive. There is nothing but life . . .' No, my brothers, you were not the cadets of the Saumur Cavalry School in 1940 defending the bridges of the Loire, prepared to die in a Hegelian manner, for honour and the war of consciousnesses; no, you hated death and, in its kingdom, you have sanctified life absolutely.

The war of consciousnesses and the horror it has always inspired in me remind me once more of Goya, of one of the Black Paintings that hang in the Prado, in a room I dread entering every time, such is the terrible fascination this great painter's *Duelo a garrotazos* [*Duel with Clubs*] exerts on me. What is depicted is not a duel, but a fight to the death; you know at a glance there will be no quarter given, nor will the fight be stopped at first blood: it is set in a desolate, forsaken, rocky, lunar landscape at the beginning – or the end – of the world. There is nothing to win, nothing to conquer, just two human creatures fighting with clubs, two men, barely men, entirely men, buried up to their knees in a peat bog or perhaps quicksand. These immovable creatures, these men-trunks, these killer-trunks lash out at one another, gaining momentum from their legs trapped in the bog, a stupefying paralysis that only serves to redouble their murderous rage. Their extraordinary movement is limited to their arms: the gladiator on the left, his face already swollen, has his arm raised high while his opponent's arms are flung far back – in truth it is not a club he wields but a bludgeon, swollen at one end. The struggle is in their arms but also in their torsos, their backs, their waists, their heads. There is no fancy footwork here, no way to duck or sidestep, only twisting, thrusting and recoiling, extraordinary movements of the chest. But one would be wrong to think these legless men are trying to defend themselves; their chief concern is killing, and the resolve of each consciousness to secure the other's death is so primal that – and this is the excruciating lesson of the painting – there can be no master, no slave, no victor and no vanquished, but since neither values life over death, only two bloody, battered, twisted corpses lying dead beneath a great dark luminous sky of dread, the sky of Aragon or of Castile with its flashes of turquoise peeping through the dense black clouds. The greatness of Goya is to show his duellists bogged down in the mud, thereby making all pity, all entreaty, all forgiveness, all flight impossible. There is one man too many here. Before they are inexorably swallowed up by the quicksand, in a paroxysm of violence they settle the score of the outrage that is otherness. The painter thus presents us with the war between the consciousnesses at its most pure, the eternal inhuman dawn of all humanity. 'The century might have been a good one,' writes Sartre in the final monologue of *Les Séquestrés d'Altona*, 'had not man been watched from time immemorial by the flesh-eating enemy who had sworn to destroy him, by the hairless, baleful beast, by man.'

It was over *Duelo a garrotazos* that I had apagogically envisaged rolling the opening credits for my film *Tsahal*, about the Israeli army and the wars it was compelled to fight. In this film I tried to show – because this is my firm belief – that the young soldiers in this young army, the sons and grandsons of Filip Müller and his companions in catastrophe, are, deep down, the same men their fathers were. Despite the radical change and the vast conquest begun by the creation *ex nihilo* of a Jewish army, despite the training in bravery, the teaching of bravery, the constant struggle against the 'natural' of which I gave a thousand examples, in spite of what I referred to elsewhere as 'the reappropriation of violence by the Jews', Tsahal – the Hebrew abbreviation for IDF, or Israel Defence Forces – is not like other armies and in the Israeli soldiers' relationship to life, to death, one can hear the powerful, not so distant echo of the words of Zalman Lewental that I just quoted. These soldiers do not have violence in their blood and the privilege they accord to life, which makes their survival a founding principle, is at the root of the military tactics specific to this army and to no other. This choice of life over nothingness has not prevented Jewish soldiers, in each of the wars they have fought, from making great sacrifices; the supreme sacrifice when necessary. So many men, so many officers, for example, fell heroically during the terrible fighting in the Golan Heights in 1973 when the very survival of the nation was at stake, or in the fierce tank battle in the Sinai that became known as the Battle of the Chinese Farm, where Tsahal tanks, ancient British Centurion tanks dating from World War II and modernized by the Israelis, fired at point-blank range at brand new Soviet T-72s shipped by the USSR to Egypt. They do not have violence in their blood, they are willing to lay down their lives, but not risk them for the sake of honour, for the sake of appearances, to remain loyal to some noble deed, some tradition of caste. In an interview I gave when *Tsahal* was released, after a tear-gas grenade exploded during the first screening making the air in the cinema unbreathable for a week, I added to what I have just written, the better to illustrate it: 'The Israeli paratroopers are of a different breed to the French paratroopers who took part in Operation Turquoise [which had just taken place in Rwanda]. The proof being, they have their hair.' This is obvious in a number of powerful sequences in the film before and during the first parachute jump of the recruits. At the beginning of the film there is a long, slow travelling shot along a runway, panning across the soldiers waiting to board the pot-bellied C-130 Hercules planes that will take them up into the heavens, and from which they will shortly have to leap, one after the other, into the void. It is dawn, the sun has barely risen, most of them are asleep, half-dead from exhaustion or from fear. Fear, exhaustion, it's the same thing: fear is exhausting, exhaustion is a sign of fear. Besides, the armed adolescents of Israel are constantly exhausted. The harshness of the obligatory three-year military service saps their lifeblood: when they hitchhike to and from their bases, barely do they get into a car before they nod off in the passenger seat or in the back seat, falling into a deep sleep. The extraordinary thing is that, with unfailing sureness, they invariably wake up several hundred metres before the crossroads where they had asked to be dropped off. Now, lined up along the runway, sitting, lying down, leaning against each other or sprawled head to tail in poignant positions of innocence, of youth, of friendship, the parachutists of the opening sequence – boy and girls, because it is the girls who will have to jump first – still have their hair and this changes everything: in their faces seriousness vies with tenderness, humanity with asceticism, anxiety with confidence. And we hear the wonderful, warm voice of David Grossman in a voiceover as the camera pans in sure, rhythmic sweeps across the faces of the soldiers who will jump that morning. Grossman, whose twenty-eight-year-old son Uri, I learn as I write these lines, was killed in Lebanon on the last day of the war against Hezbollah. I met Uri – a blond, serious, cheerful boy of about ten – during the shooting of *Tsahal* when I was interviewing his father, not knowing at that time that I would use a part of this interview over the footage of the parachutists' first jump. 'We are born old,' David said to me, 'we are born with our history on our backs. We have a huge, troubled past. We have an intense, a harsh present. It requires a renunciation, a commitment to invest in the difficult challenge that is Israel today. But if we envisage the future, it is difficult to find an Israeli who speaks freely of Israel in, say, 2025, about the harvest of 2025. Because we feel that perhaps we do not have so much future. And when I say "Israel in 2025" I feel the icy blade of memory, as though I were violating some taboo. As though the proscription against thinking so far ahead were written in my genes. I think, to tell the truth, that what we feel is fear. The fear of annihilation . . .'

By contrast, the globalized, professionalized, mercenarized army rabble crops its hair as closely as possible, presents itself as a skinhead as a sign of strength and virility, of death to fear and to emotion, to make themselves terrifying. And it is terrifying, first and foremost by its ugliness, the desperate uniformity of chins, the backs of heads. Each appears to be a clone of the others, and the shaven head is perhaps the common denominator of the international police dispatched by states to the four corners of the earth in the name of a humanitarian, peaceful new order that is christened 'le devoir d'ingérence' [the duty to interfere]. Hair is considered to be a feminine attribute and, as such, is curiously left to conscript armies, which are quickly disappearing from the face of the earth. Tsahal is one of the last. After my 1994 interview was published, I received an indignant letter from a French general in command of a division of paratroopers who threatened a lawsuit if I did not make a public apology. I was informed, through various channels, that paras from I don't know which regiment were coming after me to prove just how efficient their buzz-cuts were. I replied that I had in no way intended to hurt or demoralize the general's regiment but that the issue of haircuts seemed to me an important one; that it was possible to exhibit great courage while preserving the singularity of the living human face, that is to say with hair uncut, rather than the repetitive masks of American marines, of Russian *Spetsnaz* or the French Foreign Legion (they are impossible to tell apart), which gloomily prefigure the rows of skulls with vacant sockets one finds in their thousands in the crypts of Italian monasteries. In short, I was pleading in favour of life over death and I suggested the general read one of the finest books about war ever written, Richard Hillary's *The Last Enemy* (titled *Falling Through Space* in the USA), which recounts how the Battle of Britain was won by the Spitfire pilots of the RAF, those young men of twenty, fresh from Oxford or Cambridge, having been to Shrewsbury School or Eton, who forever went down in history as the 'long-haired boys'. Between July and October 1940, 415 of these tousled boys lost their lives fighting the Luftwaffe's Messerschmitts and saved Britain: 'Never in the field of human conflict was so much owed by so many to so few,' Winston Churchill declared on 20 August in a speech to the House of Commons, expressing, in the grand rhetorical style he would use in his memoir, *The Second World War*, the debt owed to them by the British people. Churchill, like de Gaulle, is one of the great memoirists of the twentieth century. The general, thanks to me, read *The Last Enemy*, and I made an apology without retracting what I had said; we agreed a ceasefire that has been strictly observed.

Chapter 3

R ichard Hillary flew his first Spitfire in July 1940. I was not yet fifteen. Now, when I reread *The Last Enemy*, I realize that we were contemporaries. Superficially, this is not true since when I joined the Resistance, he had just died, but in essence it is true. Hillary, a crack pilot in the RAF, was shot down by a Messerschmitt Bf109 during a dogfight, having himself shot down five enemy planes. He was fished out of the North Sea with severe burns to his body, particularly to his face and hands, and went on to endure three months of hellish surgery in an attempt to repair the damage so that he might return to combat duty. He attended a number of conferences in the United States, and had time to write his brief masterpiece before returning to active service, working in the Operational Training Unit. The Battle of Britain, strictly speaking, had been fought and won, and the RAF had begun raids deep into German airspace. Hillary's hands, in any case, no longer had the mobility and the dexterity necessary to fly a fighter plane. Truth be told, they also could not fully control a heavy bomber. During a night training flight on 8 January 1943, he crashed while at the controls of the Bristol Blenheim, taking with him his radio-operator Wilfred Fison. I have read *The Last Enemy* so often – I know that few people today are familiar with the book – that I feel myself to be both its guardian and its witness, and his memory, intact in me, permits me to proclaim myself the contemporary of Richard

Hillary, the long-haired boy. The story he tells of his first encounter, one misty morning at a Gloucestershire airforce base, with a row of Spitfires that had just come off the assembly lines, the state-of-the-art of British aeronautical technology, machines as yet untried, jealously guarded for the Battle of Britain, which Churchill knew would be inevitable and decisive, these magnificent machines that pilots all over the Commonwealth dreamed of are the source of the passion for aeroplanes that haunts me to this day:

> The Spitfires stood in two lines outside 'A' Flight Pilots' room. The dull grey-brown of their camouflage could not conceal the clear-cut beauty, the wicked simplicity of their lines. I hooked up my parachute and climbed awkwardly into the low cockpit. I noticed how small my field of vision was. Kilmartin swung himself onto a wing and started to run through the instruments. I was conscious of his voice but heard nothing of what he said. I was to fly a Spitfire. It was what I had most wanted through all the long dreary months of training. If I could fly a Spitfire, it would be worth it. Well, I was about to achieve my ambition and felt nothing. I was numb, neither exhilarated nor scared. I noticed the white enamel undercarriage handle, 'Like a lavatory plug,' I thought. [. . .]
>
> Kilmartin had said, 'See if you can make her talk.' That meant the whole bag of tricks and I wanted ample room for mistakes and possible blacking-out. With one or two very sharp movements on the stick, I blacked myself out for a few seconds, but the machine was sweeter to handle than any other I had flown. I put it through every manoeuvre that I knew of and it responded beautifully. I ended with two flick rolls and turned back for home. I was filled with a sudden exhilarating confidence. I could fly a Spitfire; in any position I was its master. It remained to be seen whether I could fight in one.

Clearly, the past is not my strong suit. Rereading what I have just written, other images, deeply buried, almost forgotten recollections, uncovered by the trepan of memory, flood back with all their original power, so much so that I feel as though I am confusing the strata of my existence, as if they were on display before me. Sartre, in the preface to his biography of Flaubert, *L'Idiot de la famille* [*The Family Idiot*], wrote: 'We enter into death as into a mill.' So perhaps I am dead, since the chronology of my life seems to have completely collapsed; by a thousand paths I venture into its circles and spirals.

One day during the 'phony war', in the spring of 1940, before the German attack of 10 May, a French fighter plane – there were some, and very good ones – overflies the rooftop of our house in Brioude with a thunderous roar, the sound reaching us when the plane is already far off. But it comes back as the pilot makes several swooping passes at the same low altitude, dipping its wings a few hundred metres further on above a neighbouring house. My father explains that the lieutenant at the controls is the son of a woman we know and that this is his way of saying hello to his mother. The plane, he tells me, is a Morane 406, one of the finest French fighter planes. I had met the pilot, and although I've forgotten his name now, I remember being surprised by how tall he was. Much later, I would learn that fighter pilots are rarely tall for obvious reasons. I remember I was stunned by the extraordinary speed of the Morane, by the roar, by the pilot's daring. I swore to myself that I too would be a pilot, though at that time Spitfires had not appeared over French skies and I knew nothing of Richard Hillary.

A general alert over Clermont-Ferrand; sirens wail announcing an Allied air raid. In the dead of night, in the dormitories on the top floor of the Lycée Blaise-Pascal – it is February or March 1944 – all the boarders rush to the windows as squadrons of British and American bombers appear, great black shadows in serried formations, flying almost level with the rooftops of the school, defying the German flak, lighting up heaven and earth, creating broad daylight over their target: the Michelin factories, which they carefully mark out with multicoloured flares so as not to hit civilian houses. The thunderous noise of the bombing, which seems incredibly close, suddenly drowns out our cheering. Caught between the reddish glow of the burning factories beyond Montferrand and the implacable, never-ending stream of planes thirty metres above our heads, we don't know where to look – Blenheims, B-17s or B-29s laden with bombs. No fear, just pure exhilaration, the herald of great things. We did not imagine that, having spent a sleepless night watching, we would be summoned at dawn to clear away the smouldering debris, an exhausting task for which we are rewarded, at noon, by a visit from Maréchal Pétain. In a vengeful speech he denounced Anglo-American barbarism, even though we ourselves had witnessed the great risks taken by the crews to ensure they dropped their bombs only on their intended target.

Did I know then that, barely five years later, at the American military airbase in Frankfurt, I would board a similar 'flying fortress' – the nickname given to the B-17 – one of the thousands of planes used to airlift supplies to the former German capital, in defiance of the blockade imposed by the Soviets in June 1948? Having spent a year in Tübingen, I had just been appointed as a teaching assistant at the Freie Universität Berlin – the newly created university in West Berlin, since the old Humboldt university was in the Russian sector and under Soviet control. I left for Berlin one icy November morning. It was the first time I had ever taken a plane and my excitement at this harsh baptism of air merged with that of my destination: I would be flying to the East. Aboard the B-17 Flying Fortress, we sat like parachutists, in lines that ran the length of the body of the plane, through the bomb-bay. I felt very moved. Even today, the reasons and the circumstances for my two-year stay in Germany, so soon after the war, remain mysterious to me. I will talk about them later, but I cannot elucidate them entirely. The B-17 touched down at Tempelhof, the airport where Hitler landed on his return from Munich, having eliminated, in Bad Wiessee, Ernst Röhm's homosexual stormtroopers who had been instrumental in bringing him to power – something later depicted in a magnificent scene from Visconti's *The Damned*. Tempelhof is a dangerous airport, situated as it is in the heart of Berlin, surrounded by tall buildings. I peered through one of the few windows – military aircraft rarely have windows – and flying over Berlin was like flying over a world in ruins, of stumps and crumbling walls. My intense excitement was mixed with dread: to me, Berlin was the great East, and I had always been fearful of the East. I felt fine when heading West. It was stupid, because I have many fond memories of the East and besides, the earth is round, even if it took me some time to persuade myself of this. But at the same time, something in me obscurely sensed that to go east was to transgress; to confront the anguish of those great theatres of death, to follow in the footsteps of the millions who had never returned. The protocol resulting from the Wannsee Conference of 20 January 1942, a meeting of high-ranking bureaucrats of the Nazi regime intent on extending throughout Europe the Final Solution that was already being carried out in the East, clearly stipulated that Europe was to be combed from West to East: '*Vom Westen nach Osten durchgekämmt*'. At the time I had not heard of Wannsee or the protocol, but my conscience could not but intuit something it would take me years to learn, to discover, to expose: there was some reason for my sense of dread. I lived in the northern part of Berlin where, shortly after my arrival, the Americans opened up a new airfield in the middle of the countryside, called Tegel, which was more accessible and less dangerous than Tempelhof for the planes taking part in the airlift, which, night and day, took off and landed every 45 seconds. In my first weeks there, rather than sleeping, I spent my nights at the end of the runway, in the biting Prussian cold and snow, waiting for the powerful headlights of the planes to suddenly pierce the darkness, then I would lie flat on the ground as the plane, landing gear now down and locked, all but grazed my scalp as it touched down. Nowadays, Tegel is the international airport of Berlin; the city grew up around it.

When peace returned, my father went on living in Brioude. He remained there for more than a decade and I spent a two-month holiday with him there in the summer of 1945. On a grassy airstrip with no asphalt runway, instructors were giving flying lessons using single engine planes and gliders. I chose the glider because, of the club's two Stampe biplanes – whose reputation for aerobatics and stunt flying made them the highlight of any air show – one was out of service and the other being serviced when I enrolled. In three weeks in Brioude, I earned my first three gliding certificates. The training glider was barely a plane at all, it was called 'the Beam'. And it was little more than a wooden beam with rubber castors, one at the front, one at the back and two more, close together in the middle, beneath the pilot's seat. There was no cockpit, the student had to sit out in the open air on a makeshift seat with the joystick between his legs, a rudder bar with two pedals at his feet and, in front, the only controls, an altimeter and an air bubble in a globe to indicate the glider's position relative to the horizontal – a turn-and-slip indicator; behind, a pair of wings and, of course, the two tail fins. Training to be a glider pilot was a very particular discipline, one that I suspect has changed little to this day: you had to arrive on the airfield early in the morning and spend the whole day there, watch, ask as few questions as possible and, especially, keep all the planes maintained and ready to fly. You never knew when or if you might fly. I forgot to mention that the training gliders had two seats, the instructor was seated behind the student with a second set of controls. 'The Beam' was not – as gliders are today – towed aloft by a plane, but was pulled along by a metal cable from a windlass at the far end of the runway, several hundred metres from the glider: the cable of the windlass was attached by a snap hook to the nose of the glider. The instructor and the windlass operator communicated using hand signals: suddenly, the windlass would be taking in the cable, coiling it around a drum at increasing speed. To get the glider aloft, you pulled the joystick gently towards yourself and you stayed at about one metre from the ground until the cable had reached sufficient speed to make it possible to hoist this primitive machine into the air at a 45° angle. As it came to the point directly above the windlass – by which time it was important to have reached an altitude of 150 metres – a lever was pulled, abruptly releasing the cable, which fell back to the ground, whipping the air like a steel snake. Even with this heavy contraption that was difficult to manoeuvre and to steer, the feeling of freedom, of liberation at that moment was extraordinary, further heightened by the musical whistling of the air on the underside of the wing. But there was no time to dream, not even for a second: the glider had to be flown, otherwise it would drop like a stone and crash into the ground. Unlike planes equipped with an engine, a glider flies with its nose tilted towards the ground even when climbing, since it is speed alone that allows it to remain *airborne*, as the Americans say. But this was a training beam, there was no way to climb, it was simply a matter of descending while executing a number of figures; the student's ability to perfectly execute these figures determined his success. This was how one earned one's certificate. Moreover, Brioude airfield was not ideal for flying a glider: ascents were rare and unpredictable, you had to 'scratch' and 'scratch' hard to gain a few metres in altitude. One morning, after three weeks of theory lessons and assisted flights, the instructor suddenly said, without warning, 'It's all yours.' This meant I was to be let loose in the glider on my own, with the open air as my only cockpit and no parachute since I would not reach an altitude where it would have time to open. I was anxious to perform well, but confident and proud. I was not afraid, I've never been afraid of things. Strapped into my seat, I was completely focused, soundlessly repeating to myself the lessons and the figures I had learned. I think I was given a helmet. The first exercise was to fly in a straight line, losing as little altitude as possible after passing over the windlass and unhitching the steel serpent, then banking 180° and lining up again with the runway and landing in the opposite direction to the one I had taken off in. All of the manoeuvres were perfect; I felt so little fear that, as I banked, I took my eye off the air bubble indicating the horizon and banked the heavy, makeshift glider too much, almost to the vertical, until it all but stalled. I quickly saw what I had done and corrected my mistake, though it had not escaped the keen eye of the instructor, and I completed my landing with a perfect flare-out. The instructor did not mark me down, considering that my daring might – in this profession at certain times – be considered an asset. There and then, he awarded me my first certificate. The second figure was more complicated: I had to describe a perfect figure of eight, which meant landing facing the same direction as one had taken off. As the makeshift beam lost altitude quickly, it was impossible to complete a figure of eight without reaching a much greater altitude before releasing the cable, which meant the windlass had to reel the cable in much more quickly. I made no mistakes this time; I was exultant. I was immediately awarded my second certificate, and volunteered to try for the third. For this, I had to abandon 'the Beam' and begin three days of training on a potbellied C-800, a real glider, built for speed and capable of attaining much greater altitudes. The third test was all about attaining altitude; I passed with flying colours, leaving Brioude with my three certificates and the commendation of the jury in my pocket.

I promised myself I would carry on flying, but I didn't. My life was taken up by more pressing matters, by a relationship with time and with others diametrically opposed to the discipline and the settled way of life implicit in a passion for gliding, a passion for solitude. I would have needed a whole other life. Modern gliders are honed, streamlined, with enormous wingspans, designed to climb high and fly fast. I flew in one a couple of years ago, taking off from an airfield on the banks of the Durance. I was in the back seat, obviously, the passenger seat; I was impressed, but I felt none of the excitement I had felt in 'the Beam' that first time. The thing that in my adventurous existence has come closest to that thrill was a recent attempt at paraskiing on a twin-control hang-glider: gliding across a valley at 2,000 metres towards the sheer mountain face opposite, waiting to catch a rising air current. This is the principle of gliding: you turn in circles, nose down, careful to stay within the often narrow rising thermal, twisting and turning within it like a motorcyclist all but grazing imaginary asphalt, dangerously ascending the rockface. Doing this, I managed to reach 4,000 metres. The instructor, won over by my fearlessness and my head for heights, assured me that it would take me about three weeks to complete my paragliding licence and fly solo. Unfortunately, I did not have the time; once again, I would have needed another life.

This parenthesis, unplanned at this point in my narrative, is driven only by my concern for truth: contrary to what I have written, my passion for flying was not prompted by Spitfires or by Richard Hillary. I cannot close this without a leap across time and space, from Brioude to Israel at the time when I was shooting *Tsahal*, which saw the apogee of my career as a pilot. As I was directing a film about the Jewish army, obviously I wanted to know as much as possible about the subject, to familiarize myself with all its branches – the artillery, the infantry, the paratroops, the border guards, the tank divisions, the navy and, of course, the airforce – to experience something as close as possible to the actual conditions of battle that I had already experienced during the 'war of attrition' between Egypt and Israel in 1968 and 1969 when, filming a report on the Suez Canal in the bunkers on the Bar-Lev line, I experienced first-hand heavy bombing by the Egyptian artillery. At the time I had also, in the course of long night patrols in the Jordan Valley, come under fire from Palestinians attempting to lead raids on Israel from Jordan, 'skirmishes' that were often very murderous. Israel's losses during that strange war were such that, every morning, the photographs of those killed the previous day appeared in all the newspapers, often numbering a dozen or even twenty.

After Yitzhak Rabin, the Minister of Defence in 1987, had seen *Shoah*, he asked me if I might consider making a film about the War of Independence. I gave the matter some thought and, after a few days, I said 'no'. There are two possible accounts of that war: the Israeli and the Arab. What is at issue here is not truth, it is the fact that neither account can disregard the other and it is impossible to explore the motives of both camps simultaneously, at least not without making a very bad film, something a number of people have since done on the subject. I did, however, suggest to Rabin a film about the idea I have already mentioned, the reappropriation of force and violence by Israeli Jews. He accepted, saying, 'We don't have a single shekel to offer you, but I shall put the army at your disposal, we will hide nothing from you, you will be privy to all its secrets.' And it is true that I was shown much more than I chose to show. I knew all about the drones, for example, the unmanned planes, long before the First Gulf War. The American drones were, first and foremost, a magnificent Israeli invention. I saw missiles being made, rockets and sophisticated weapons about which I can still say nothing. But I also shared the daily life of tank troops, participated in manoeuvres, drove a Merkava, sat in the gunner's place firing from a stationary position but also from a tank moving at top speed, which is considerably more difficult. I took part in combined manoeuvres in the desert lasting forty-eight hours that involved infantry, paratroopers, tank divisions, the artillery, Cobra and Apache helicopters and bombers. Advancing, kilometre by kilometre, with the front-line foot-soldiers through the roar of machine guns and submachine guns firing live rounds while shells from a mobile artillery division explode 200 metres ahead of the shock troops to 'prepare and clean' the ground before them is a physical ordeal that is both exhausting and impressive. These exercises are designed to be so realistic that accidents, sometimes terrible accidents, are not uncommon. Everyone, from general down to private, is aware of this and it adds to the tension, to the exhaustion that ravages their faces, furrowed with sweat and sand within hours of manoeuvres beginning. Out of foolish pride, wanting to play the young man, I refused to protect my ears as I was advised, even ordered, to do. I am paying for it still.

Meeting up at Sde Dov, the domestic airport of Tel Aviv, at two o'clock in the morning with Uri Saguy, head of Aman (the Israeli Directorate of Military Intelligence), or with Amram Mitzna, commander-in-chief of Central Command, and later leader of the Labour Party, or with Matan Vilnai, Yossi Ben Hanan, or Talik, boarding a small aircraft capable of landing anywhere at a moment's notice with one or more of them in the dead of night; being the only person awake apart from the young pilot flying on instruments in the pure, profound darkness of the Sinai or the Negev, while Israel's generals, knowing what awaited them, snatched every possible minute of sleep, was an experience I found profoundly moving, as though I were there to watch over them, as though the precious sleep of these warriors, all devoid of airs and all younger than me, only depended on my vigilance. Night on the peninsula barely has time to pale before the harsh sun appears brutally in the east over the mountains of Moab, seeming to begin its course at great speed: I could literally see it scale the heavens as the little plane begins the final part of its descent in the suddenly audible din of gunfire. The manoeuvres – I was about to write 'the battle' – had already begun.

Having found these flights from Sde Dov so moving, what can I say about my first flight in a Phantom from Tel Nof airbase or, many years later, my first flight in an F-16 from Ramat David airbase in northern Israel? The sky that morning was lowering and the air-traffic controller was late in clearing my pilot, Eitan Ben Eliyahu – at the time second-in-command of the Israeli airforce (he would become commander-in-chief the following year) – to release the fearsome power of the plane's Pratt & Whitney turbofan engine. We spent a long time waiting at the end of the runway, but Eitan made up for it, taking off in a blaze like a torpedo, performing two flick rolls as we climbed. I got to know most of the airbases in Israel, questioned a hundred pilots; I remember a devout, taciturn Ashkenazi, at least twice as old as his colleagues, from whom I found it difficult to extract a word but who was, I knew from his colleagues, a tiger of aerial combat who had single-handedly brought down six Syrian MiG fighters in forty-eight hours in 1982. I could not imagine making the film without flying myself, without experiencing the 'black veil' – the loss of consciousness Richard Hillary describes – something all fighter pilots are familiar with despite even the most modern G-suits. The airforce authorities understood, and agreed to my request on condition that I successfully passed a physical. I was sixty-seven years old. The examination took a whole day and was intensely serious and meticulous, every one of my organs was examined scrupulously and, after my heart, my kidneys or my brain had been scanned, I was dispatched with a friendly pat on the back and the assurance that, barring accidents, I would live to be 120. This was just as well since the last call of the day was with the airforce dentist, who did no fillings and no extractions, but who, without a word, X-rayed my jaws from every possible angle. Not understanding his purpose I began to worry and finally I asked him why he was taking all these cinematic high-angle and low-angle shots. He replied impassively, 'The planes you will be flying are dangerous. They have been known to explode. And should your plane overshoot the border and stray a few kilometres into enemy airspace – which is easily done here – it could be shot down by a surface-to-air missile: your teeth will be all that is left of you and these X-rays will be the only means of identifying you.' Of course, I was required to sign a waiver absolving the state, the government and the army of all responsibility. I did so with a light heart.

I arrived on a sunny morning at Tel Nof, the central and one of the most important airbases in Israel, having passed a number of stringent checkpoints. There I was met by Relik Shafir, the thirty-three-year-old commander of the Phantom squadrons. He led me into the vast, comfortable pilots' lounge with its deep leather armchairs and began to tell me how hard the 1973 Yom Kippur War had been on the Phantom crews. Relik was much too young to have taken part, but these sudden, heavy losses and the confusion of the first days had left indelible traces and were part of the history of the

Tel Nof squadron. Accustomed, since the Six Day War in 1967, to being masters of the air, six years later the Israeli fighter jets found themselves being shot down as soon as they came close to Suez by the terrible SA-6 missiles, the latest Soviet technology, exported in quantities to Egypt and often operated by specialists from the USSR. The pain of the Yom Kippur War was still raw at Tel Nof: half of the planes had exploded in mid-air, their pilots and navigators had never returned. Improvised counter-measures had to be hurriedly devised, pilots had to learn to bank hard in the seconds before a missile hit, a manoeuvre that threw it off course, rendering it useless and making it possible for its intended target to shoot it down. The fighter pilots devised many other tricks and ruses to fool the SA-6s and in the latter half of the war, more often than not, the missiles were neutralized. Relik was tall, taller than most of the pilots, his face was at once grave and mischievous. He had taken part in the raid on Osirak, the Iraqi nuclear reactor, which had involved a long return flight over enemy territory. 'According to our estimates,' he said, 'it was likely that one or two of the eight planes would be shot down. I was flying one of the last two planes in the formation so there was a very real chance I would be killed . . .' I forgot to mention that he had seen *Shoah* and seemed to know it by heart. He went on, 'As we took off, we all felt the gravity of the moment, we knew that the fate of the state of Israel lay in our hands. And suddenly I knew who I was flying for. I bear my grandfather's first name and my daughter bears my father's sister's name. Both died in the Shoah. They were deported from Vilnius and were killed, probably in the Ponary massacre. Suddenly I knew that I was flying for them. I needed that. It helped me to know, as I boarded the plane, that even if my destiny should end in the saddest way, my death, inscribed in the lineage of those defenceless innocents, would be an accomplishment.'

I was disappointed when Relik explained that he was not to be my pilot and introduced me to Gad – I only ever knew his first name – a short, gentle-looking man, yet hard and muscled, who, like many

Israeli pilots, had been born and raised in a kibbutz. To tell the truth, my heart was in my boots. As Gad led me to what I would not call a changing room, I tried to win him round, telling him that I preferred to fly straight with no stunts. He replied that we would see, that he would make decisions based on my reactions, though he was clearly and understandably annoyed that I was asking him to turn a Phantom into a transport plane. In the 'dressing room', Rimbaud's lines from 'Les Chercheuses de poux' ['The Lice Hunters'] came to mind: 'There come to his bedside two tall charming sisters / their frail fingers tipped with silvery nails', as three ravishing young women busied themselves about me, attempting to undress me completely, leaving me in my underpants – though on reflection and given the amount of time that has passed, I am not even sure. The ceremonial dubbing of the modern knight could then begin: I was given underclothes expressly designed to absorb sweat, flying boots, a helmet, glasses and, most importantly, the G-suit that prevents blood draining away from the brain when the plane banks sharply, pulls out of a nose-dive or performs, when in fighting mode, any of a thousand impossible manoeuvres. In such circumstances the suit automatically applies pressure to the calves, the thighs and the abdomen, to prevent blood draining away from the brain. But in spite of this lifesaving invention, blackouts have not been eliminated: even very experienced pilots blackout at 10g when acceleration is such that their weight is ten times normal.

Gad and I were escorted to the plane by the young dressers, one of whom carried my helmet. The Phantom is a monster, one of the fastest aeroplanes in the world, boasting two General Electric J79-GE-15 axial-flow turbojets that look like half-open shark's jaws and can reach speeds of 2,500 kilometres per hour and altitudes of 19,000 metres. It is famously solidly built and fit for all types of combat missions. I climbed the ladder and slipped into the navigator's seat just behind the pilot; other uniformed young women strapped me in, placed a white skullcap designed to absorb perspiration on my head and my helmet over it. Gad checked that everything was in order, explained how the ejector seat functioned, informing me of what I should do in the event of danger or if he so ordered. 'You're sitting on an actual bomb there, so whatever you do, don't touch that lever.' He showed me how to turn on the microphone and headset that allowed us to communicate at all times, then finally handed me a paper bag: 'If you need to throw up, go ahead, don't feel embarrassed or afraid, we've all done it, just throw up into this bag.' He settled himself in the pilot's seat, strapped himself in, turned on the engines, exchanged a few words with the control tower, gave the thumbs up to let them know we were ready and that they could take away the chocks. We taxied to the far end of the runway to join the tailback of a hundred other Phantoms manned by young pilots, all waiting to take off. It was like rush hour at Chicago O'Hare, Dulles in Washington, McCarran in Las Vegas, JFK in New York or Charles de Gaulle in Paris combined. The navigators sitting at the rear of the other cockpits must have wondered as to the identity of this strange colleague in the pristine white helmet staring at them intently, tenderly. This colleague was in actuality preoccupied with the imminent takeoff, intensely aware of the great favour Tsahal had accorded him.

Gad took off quickly, gaining altitude, and then, over Jerusalem, dropping to fly as low as he was permitted over the city, and at first I felt a little like the peasant in Malraux's *Sierra de Teruel* [*Days of Hope*] who, from the air, does not recognize the lands he has worked all his life. But I quickly got my bearings, soon knowing where I was. Gad then headed straight for the Red Sea and, as we flew over Aravah, he clearly decided that the good times were over: now was the moment to test my mettle. In a series of quick, abrupt manoeuvres and sudden rolls, he brought me almost to the point of blackout – which I found an oddly pleasant sensation. We headed back for Tel Nof having flown one and a half times the length of Israel, and he informed me that I had experienced a force of 4g – not bad for my first flight in the monster. Besides I had not vomited, or even felt nauseous.

The Phantom taxied back to its hangar; above me, the cockpit was slid open and immediately the ground crew, all smiles, unstrapped me and helped me up and out of the plane. I stood on the top rung of the ladder, my return to earth was greeted by rapturous applause from a crowd of 200 people, by flashbulbs and cameras and – especially – by having Israeli champagne sprayed right in my face, which I welcomed, arms flung wide, like Schumacher winning a Grand Prix.

Tel Nof and my flight on the Phantom was a challenge that I had set myself. My flight from Ramat David aboard the F-16 was an entirely different matter: it was part of the shoot of *Tsahal* and it required two fighter jets, one filming the other while, strapped into an F-16 two-seater, and talking into a tape recorder, I attempted to comment on events as they occurred and the various phases of the flight. Eytan Ben Eliyahu, second-in-command of the airforce, who had been assigned as my pilot, was audacious. The son of an Iraqi Jewish father and Serbian Jewish mother, he was a flying ace of rare freedom and had performed the greatest exploits for the Israeli airforce. The F-16 is as terrifying as the Phantom, more terrifying maybe, but in a different way. In a sense, the F-16 is like 'the Beam' in Brioude: the canopy is so transparent and perched so close to the nose of the plane that, even at 10,000 metres, it feels like being aloft with no protection. To go into battle in an F-16 and in a Phantom are very different things: the F-16, in its fighter bomber version, has no need to see its target: the on-board computers that the pilot is trained to master can pinpoint a target at a range of fifty kilometres, a target the pilot could not possibly see even with his huge, transparent canopy. The basic F-16 fighter beats all its rivals by the stunning virtuosity of its design and the wide variety of manoeuvres it permits the élite pilots who handle – and manhandle – it as they see fit, secure in the knowledge that this marvel of the air will always obey their commands. The women who acted as 'dressers' at Ramat David were somewhat less charming than those at Tel Nof, but the procedure was the same, though Eytan was very different from Gad. As I was being strapped in, he turned and asked, 'Are you sure you want to do this? You can always say no, there's no shame.' I liked his tanned face with his hook nose; and I said, 'Let's do it,' though his words had served to heighten my fears. He began, as I described earlier, with a double flick roll, so that even as we took off, I was completely disoriented. I stayed calm as earth and sky whipped past violently. For a moment, Eytan consented to fly in a civil fashion, then suddenly his voice came over the headset: 'Take the stick and push it all the way forward and to the right,' he said in perfect, guttural English. I obeyed, if a little too timidly, and the F-16 banked into a half-roll, an unforgivable mistake, indicating a lack of decisiveness and daring. Eytan completed the failed roll and ordered me, in a brusque, military tone, to try again. This time I succeeded – with no training, no certificate – in getting the F-16 to perform a flick roll to the satisfaction of the second-in-command of the airforce. We were escorted by another F-16, piloted – I say this because it's true – by a tall lanky Jew from the Cape in South Africa, who had taken on board my cameraman. His heart in his mouth, he could barely operate the camera. At this point – you can see the footage in *Tsahal* – Eytan Ben Eliyahu decided to administer the supreme punishment, banking hard, plummeting in a vertiginous nose-dive and pulling out only at the very last minute. Proud of me, of my stoicism, my imperturbable stomach, he rewarded me by flying over the Lebanon as far as Beirut in a few short minutes, something he clearly should not have done. Flying back along the coast, we overflew – in a thunderous roar, I hope – the headquarters of UNIFIL (the United Nations Interim Force in Lebanon), I think we may even have dipped our wings. Although the French find such flyovers 'intolerable', they will continue for as long as the threat continues. Back at Ramat David, I was not welcomed with another champagne shower because I had already 'crossed the line', but I received something much more important to me: the congratulations and the praise of some of the greatest pilots in the country. I had been subjected to 7g, the equivalent of weighing 600 kilos – seven times my actual weight – suffering only a brief blackout, without whining or complaining, without screaming or throwing up. They considered this phenomenal. So did I.

Chapter 4

June 1940 was a month of implacable beauty: each day more dazzling, more glorious than the last. We were living on the outskirts of the little town of Brioude in the Auvergne, beyond the train station where, since the beginning of the war, my father loaded coal, on a secondary road, in a two-storey house with a backyard and a long sloping garden. The relentless flow of refugees heading south took the main road through this sub-prefecture of the Haute-Loire, and only the most astute, in search of petrol – an extremely precious commodity at the time – arrived at our doorstep because nearby stood a huge tank bearing the name of its owner – Desmarest, who later became chairman of Total – only casually and poorly protected by guards from the defeated army. The guards could sometimes be bribed and the drivers headed off with a full tank and several jerry cans as well.

Whenever he could, my father listened to the news on the wireless. I remember hearing two of Hitler's speeches with him, during the Munich Crisis of 1938 – although we still lived in Paris then, at the time we were spending our holidays in Saint-Chély-d'Apcher, in the Lozère, with Marcel Galtier, a secular republican headmaster whom I adored because he taught me everything, and first and foremost to fly-fish in the narrow, serpentine trout rivers of the Aubrac plateau. And so Galtier, my father and I listened to the threats and ravings of the Führer and my father said in a low voice, almost to himself, 'This is war.' He felt no 'sense of cowardly relief' after the sham treaty of Munich; on the contrary, it confirmed his opinion that war was inevitable. The seventeenth of June 1940 was another beautiful day: we were lunching in the courtyard when we heard the solemn announcement that Maréchal Pétain was to make a speech and, immediately afterwards, for the first time, we heard the quavering voice of the 'Saviour of Verdun' in full pomp and ceremony: 'I make the gift of my person to France . . . It makes me sick at heart to have to tell you that, today, we must stop fighting. I have this night approached the enemy . . .' and, a little later that same day: 'the pursuit of pleasure has prevailed over the spirit of sacrifice. People have asked too much and given too little. We have sought to spare our efforts: today we must face misfortune . . .' I don't know now whether I fully grasped the implications of this breast-beating, I went on playing with my dog, a three-month-old puppy that ran pell-mell after every stone I threw for him. He was a Great Dane, white with black patches, and was to grow up to be as huge and fierce as the dogs that had terrified me and my brother and sister when, living in Vaucresson before our parents separated, we used to take the steep path that led from our house to the school, past a large estate guarded day and night by monsters separated from us only by openwork railings along which they ran, their fierce barking accompanying our every step. My dog, Draggy, was a pedigree. My father, who loved dogs, had given him to me before the German attack in a rare moment of optimism, as he tried to forget what he never ceased to believe to be true, that the worst was inevitable.

Pétain's speeches brought him back to reality, to what was important: that evening he took me aside and said, 'You can't keep Draggy any more.' I pestered, I protested, I begged, I ranted and raved but he stood firm. He pointed to the grey wall and said, 'From now on we have to be as grey as that wall, we need to disappear, not draw attention to ourselves. In a few months, your dog will draw attention to us all.' He was right, I knew it, but I begged him to wait for a while. But the very next day he gave Draggy to a vet, a stout man with a brutish, ruddy face, asking him to find the dog a new master and also to give him his vaccinations, since it was time. But the man drank too much and made a mistake: instead of a vaccination, he gave my dog a lethal injection. My father heard the news at the same moment as I did; I saw the pain in his eyes and could not bring myself to reproach him. Thinking about it now, maybe he had in fact condemned Draggy to death himself, asked the vet to put him to sleep; I'll never know. It would have been difficult to find enough fresh meat to feed a hungry adult dog and it would have been expensive. Was this something he had considered?

Money was tight at home: my father's enforced work did not bring enough for us to live on. Over the summer, we learned that recruiters were looking for labourers to help with the grape harvest on the vast vineyards in the south of France – in Le Gard, L'Hérault, Le Roussillon; around Nîmes, Montpellier and Narbonne. This was a well-established custom: every autumn the major wine growers, whose estates numbered hundreds, sometimes thousands, of hectares, recruited seasonal workers from the Massif Central who were employed either as 'cutters' or as 'porters'. It was called – it still is, I think – a *colle* of grape-pickers, the word may be a contraction of *collecte*. There was a minimum age; they would not take anyone under sixteen. My brother and I – he was thirteen and a half, I was not yet fifteen – were big for our ages so we lied shamelessly and even succeeded in getting taken on as porters, hauling baskets of grapes, since that was better paid. The ruse was only possible because of the chaos and general disarray that followed France's defeat and the consequent lack of manpower: French men were on the run or prisoners of war in their thousands. We boarded a train jammed with boys from the Auvergne singing at the top of their lungs as though heading to war and, via Langeac, Langogne and Alès, made it through the Cévennes overnight to the flat countryside of the Pays du Gard. The boundless estate we were to work on, located in the commune of Junas-Aujargues, was the property of an aristocrat in big boots, a marquis if memory serves, who looked us up and down like cattle. Our dormitory was a huge but overcrowded barn where we were told to dump our rucksacks only to be immediately thrown in at the deep end without being given a moment's rest, beneath the watchful and superior stares of the foremen. There were the 'cutters' who, with a flourish of their *gouets* – their billhooks – would cut through the stem of each heavy bunch of grapes, which then fell into their baskets. Once the baskets were full, they were tipped into the *bacholes* – large panniers made of zinc or wicker – which were strapped to the backs of the porters. Jacques and I, exhausted from the journey, disoriented by our surroundings, drunk on sunshine and on the plump, delicious grapes we simply could not resist gorging on as they were loaded (as a result of which, that first night, we suffered a bout of 'the fabulous shits', to quote a phrase from *Notre-Dame-des-Fleurs*), collapsed in full view of everyone, after a vain and heroic struggle to stay upright under the weight of our panniers – which were only two-thirds full. Meanwhile all around us the other porters hurried, carrying their fifty-kilo panniers of grapes like experienced professionals. This was a disaster: we were forced to confess our ages and the marquis, who was overseeing the work, wanted to turn us away immediately but our genuine tears and explanations of how much we wanted to help our father persuaded one of the foremen to take pity on us, and he agreed to make us cutters, a task more suited to our strength and age.

We slept on beds of straw. My brother was on my left and on my right was Jacky, a sailor and a very handsome lad, much older than the rest of us who had travelled a lot in the navy before the war. He had taken Jacques and me under his wing. One night, by the light of the low moon framed in the wide-open doorway of the barn, Jacky started to masturbate and encouraged me to join him. I refused, in spite of my fondness for him, but mostly because his penis, stubby and thick and dark, so fascinated me that I could not allow myself to be distracted by anything else: it was the first time I had seen anyone masturbate.

There was another first, three weeks later at the end of the harvest: our first wages, the first money earned by the sweat of our backs. I felt a pride so new to me that the idea of spending even one franc seemed sacrilegious. I had to bring the entire sum home and give it to our father. At the station in Nîmes, waiting for the train to Brioude, I refused to give in to my brother's pleadings, even though, like him, I was dying of thirst. We were, when I think back, strange children, 'meek, obedient and pure' – as Sartre describes Genet somewhere – despite, or perhaps because of, the extraordinary obstacles we had been confronted with from an early age. The solemn, almost ceremonial handing over of our money to Papa was my reward for everything.

Shortly after we got home, Papa sublet two rooms to a Monsieur Legendre, a manager in some business that had been forced to relocate to Brioude, and his secretary, Mademoiselle Bordelet. Monsieur Legendre, fifty years old with a big, grey, handlebar moustache that was waxed, combed and brushed, a true Frenchman confident of his authority and his rights, took the room on the first floor above the dining room. The secretary's room was across the landing beyond the stairwell. My brother and I, who slept on the floor above, quickly guessed the nature of the frequent comings and goings between Mademoiselle Bordelet's room and Monsieur Legendre's. There was little to do, there were few distractions and no nightlife in Vichy France; our lodgers came home as soon as they finished work and did not go out again. Mademoiselle Bordelet prepared their meals in her employer's room, which had a gas ring and a coal-fired stove. We had our dinner later, we meaning Jacques, Évelyne and me, my father and his companion Hélène, a beautiful buxom Norman girl from Caen, not Jewish at all. Here too there was another first: the springs of Monsieur Legendre's bed began to squeak as the five of us sat down to dinner, the squeaking grew louder and faster, the rhythm attained cruising speed and then, in a frantic, thunderous sprint, culminated in a contented coughing-fit. The whole thing was all over in three minutes. Jacques, Évelyne and I glanced at each other, though we did not dare meet Papa's smile, and Hélène remarked, 'They could at least wait, it's not so late.' There followed other sounds – a patter of dainty footsteps, the clang of a saucepan, a tap running, the toilet flushing . . .

The whole thing started up again the following week, when my brother and I were alone in the house. Jacques leapt up as soon as we heard the inaugural squeak of Monsieur Legendre's bed and raced up the stairs. I followed my little brother, hypocritically forcing myself to move with slightly more dignity. It didn't last: Monsieur Legendre's pounding had reached its peak, although it could not drown out the counterpoint – much more overwhelming to us – of Mademoiselle Bordelet's moans. It was the first time either of us had heard a woman in ecstasy. Jacques, his eye pressed to the keyhole, was masturbating furiously, bestially. I tried to push him away and take his place, but his eye and his feet were fixed to the spot. Almost immediately we heard the last sprint and the final coughing fit and I realized, in that precise moment, that Mademoiselle Bordelet was tearing herself away from the bed and my brother could *see*. And what he could see was so new, so impressive, so riveting, that his hand stopped for a moment in amazement. He could not keep to himself such a secret, such a treasure, and he signalled that it was my turn to peer through the keyhole. In spite of the narrowness of the keyhole, the laws of optics meant that his field of vision was wide. The earthenware stove on which the secretary was heating food and the saucepan of water we had just heard clatter was in the centre of the frame, and I suddenly saw the extraordinary sight my brother had wanted to share with me: *she* was coming back. I saw her, naked, first one buttock as she set the saucepan on the stove, then her entire arse, *callipygian* I would describe it as now, perfectly curved. Then, as she leaned over the stove, I saw her in profile, saw her breast, the left breast because of the way the furniture was placed and the keyhole framed the scene, a firm, pert breast. Her movements were quick, precise, organized, methodical: the water in the saucepan was at precisely the right temperature, and as soon as she left Monsieur Legendre's embrace, she picked it up, rushed to the bidet in the bathroom, where – with no regret, no emotion – she washed away the humours and secretions of the cougher: contraception being unheard of *in illo tempore*. I have only the vaguest memory of Mademoiselle Bordelet's face, but the glimpses of her body are indelibly inscribed into my veins, onto my memory. Whenever we could, my brother and I took up our post outside the door, careful not to be caught by our parents or by Mademoiselle Bordelet herself: she sometimes unexpectedly went back to her room to sleep or to get some file she had forgotten. When she did, we just had time to launch ourselves up the spiral staircase leading to the floor above. She dashed across the landing, looking straight ahead, barely covered by a short, see-through nightdress that drove me insane. I am sure she knew that we were standing guard outside their door while she was being mounted. She knew, she must have known, and these flits to her room were as much to stir up her own desire as to kindle ours. Did I ever masturbate on that landing? Honestly, I must have done but I was not, from that age onwards, keen on masturbation. I did, on the other hand, imagine every possible violation of the mature Mademoiselle, devising meticulous plans – with and without my brother's participation. And I confess that I almost acted on them, almost crept into her room while she was sleeping. But there were too many people living in the house; this alone prevented my criminal plan. Had I gone through with it, I firmly believe that she would have joyfully taken my virginity; I certainly could not even have imagined I would have been charged with rape. But all these things took place in a very different time. I've just remembered her first name: she was called Denise. Life in France having resumed its normal routine, Monsieur Legendre and Denise were called back to head office in the spring of 1941, leaving Brioude and our house. Serious things could now begin.

The first anti-Semitic law passed by the Vichy regime in 1940, the even more draconian measures of June 1941 together with the rising tide of anti-Jewish propaganda and abuse on the radio fuelled my father's fatalism, gave it something on which to feed and grow. Though he knew nothing about the deportations that would come later, nor, obviously, about the Final Solution, he was undoubtedly aware of the arrests of foreign Jews in the south of France that began after the *Statut des Juifs* was passed in October, and the major roundups of Jews in the Occupied Zone in May, August and December 1941; he was filled with a terrible foreboding. Saving his three children, I learned only much later, was his chief concern. He spent several nights alone, digging a deep underground shelter in the garden where we might hide if there were a raid. The opening to this 'cave', some fifty metres behind the house, was hidden by branches. One day – or rather one night – our training began. My brother and I shared a bedroom; Évelyne was next door. I forgot to mention that my father had taken an oil can and, with fanatical care, had oiled every door, hinge and lock on every floor so that we could move about the preternaturally quiet house soundlessly; he had even found a way – having always been good with his hands – of silencing the creaking floorboards and the stairs. Now that Monsieur Legendre had left, he did not have to worry about squeaking bedsprings. When bedtime came and we put on our pyjamas, he taught us how to lay out our clothes in precisely the order we would need them to quickly get dressed again. He explained everything, so we knew that the doorbell would ring while we were fast asleep and we would have to make a dash for it as though the Gestapo really were breaking down the door. 'I'll be timing you,' he said. We didn't think of it as a game for very long. The bell was operated by pulling a chain and it pealed loud and clear. Suddenly, this unforgettable, imperious tolling, the clapper striking repeatedly against the bell, indicated that this was not someone politely waiting to be let in, but announced instead a brutal intrusion. We woke with a start and one of us went to rouse our little sister, still fast asleep; we quickly dressed in the dark, our actions becoming almost automatic as the training progressed, silently scrambling down two flights of stairs in pitch darkness, opening the door to the courtyard as though by magic and racing to the end of the garden where we pushed aside the branches and replaced them behind us, and sheltered in the cave where we waited, breathless. We waited, we watched for him, he might be fast or slow, it depended. He pretended to search for us, and never failed to find us. Through the branches we would see his SS jackboots, and heard his anguished Jewish father's voice: 'You moved, you made a noise.' 'No, Papa, that was a branch cracking.' 'You were talking, I heard you, they would have found you.' This would go on until finally he told us we could come out. He was not play-acting. He *was* the SS and their dogs. The training sessions were random, we were woken with a start at different times of night, but it paid off: we broke world speed records, each time beating our previous performance. In the last timed trial, he calculated that from leaping out of bed and creeping into the cave, it took a breathless one minute and twenty-nine seconds.

Neither the Gestapo nor the *Milice* ever rang our bell. It is true that my father, who had joined the Resistance early on – something I was unaware of – had taken other precautions after the massive roundup of Jews in the summer of 1942. With a number of carefully hand-picked Jewish volunteers – including me – he organized nightly bicycle patrols across Brioude, keeping watch on the approach roads from Clermont-Ferrand and Le Puy-en-Velay. From November, units of the *Wehrmacht* and of the German police had been permanently stationed in our sub-prefecture with their own *Kommandantur* and all related services. An unmistakeable sign that a roundup was imminent was the presence of the trucks, grey-green – 'the colour of the Germans', as Michael Podchlebnik, a survivor of Chełmno, says in *Shoah*. Sadly, he is dead now – men such as he should never die. A group of several such vehicles indicated that registered Jews were to be taken from their homes and rounded up at dawn. We, too,

knew their addresses and the patrols would set off to warn anyone
we thought might be in danger, who might need to hide or flee. We
know that on two occasions, thanks to our efforts, those who arrived
to round them up came away empty-handed.

Every time I think about Monny de Boully and of his appearance so
early one morning, not at the front door, but at the back, as though
he had materialized out of the garden, the lines from Edgar Allan
Poe's 'The Raven' immediately come to mind. Except for the time (it
happened not at midnight, but at daybreak), they perfectly describe
what I felt:

Once upon a midnight dreary, while I pondered weak and weary,
Over many a quaint and curious volume of forgotten lore,
While I nodded, nearly napping, *suddenly there came a tapping,*
As of some one gently rapping, rapping at my chamber door.
''Tis some visitor,' I muttered, 'tapping at my chamber door –
Only this, and nothing more.'

Or in Baudelaire's translation:

Une fois, sur le minuit lugubre, pendant que je méditais, faible
et fatigué,
Sur maint précieux et curieux volume d'une doctrine oubliée,
Pendant que je donnais de la tête, presque assoupi, *soudain il se*
fit un tapotement,
Comme de quelqu'un frappant doucement, frappant à la porte de ma
chambre.
'C'est quelque visiteur,' murmurai-je, 'qui frappe à la porte de ma
chambre;
Ce n'est que cela et rien de plus.'

It was at dawn in the spring of 1942. The 'little perceptions' instilled
in me by my father's training for the terrible bell must still have had

me on alert. How could one ever wake unless one was already alert? (This I learned later at Tübingen from the work of Gottfried Wilhelm Leibniz, the subject of my postgraduate degree in philosophy.) And Monny, with his gentle tapping, fell somewhat short of the rapping of Poe's Raven. He tapped at the back door with such incongruous quietness that I was obliged to get out of bed and pad barefoot down the soundless stairs, as though I were the one about to burst in on someone, catch him unawares, to press my ear to the door, fathoming the source of this incessant pattering, so unlike the brutal pounding I had been primed to anticipate and, finally, to open the door. There before me stood a stranger carrying a small suitcase, a man of about forty, tall, with a high forehead and eyes that shone with kindness and intelligence, though his face was a mask of fear. 'You are Claude,' he murmured, it was not even a question, and he brought his finger to his lips and whispered, 'Shhh . . . I'm Monsieur Sylvestre.' I'd never heard of a Monsieur Sylvestre – Amédée Sylvestre, according to the identity card he insisted on showing several times to my father, who was also awake by now. His papers were false. He had arrived in Brioude on the morning train, having suffered the rigorous, fanatical checks of the Germans as he crossed the border between occupied France and the so-called 'Free Zone', the French state of Vichy. It was an act of great courage, one that could have cost him his life. Terror and pride vied with one another in his face, terror at the risks he had so recently run and pride at having come through. Only love – the mad passion he bore my mother – could have given him the strength to face such dangers head on, especially as they had both only recently escaped the clutches of the Gestapo. While going to visit their friend the poet Max Jacob, in Saint-Benoît-sur-Loire, they had been arrested on the platform at Orléans station by the *Milice* picking people out by their facial features. They were not mistaken: my mother was obviously, strikingly Jewish. As Marthe Robert wrote to me, when my mother died in 1995: 'My dear Claude, I read about Paulette's death in *Le Monde* today. As you know, I knew her well. There was a time when

I went to visit her regularly, and I enjoyed her company. I particularly admired her beauty, she seemed to me to embody all the nobility of the ancient daughters of Israel.' Rereading Marthe's words, I cannot but be reminded of the congratulations of Monsieur Lebègue, a professor at the Sorbonne, before whom I had to give a commentary on a Renaissance play, Garnier's *Les Juives* [*The Jewesses*] for my *licence ès lettres* in classical literature: 'That ancient woman, who walks in front, is some great Lady. I see that all respect her . . .'

In Orléans, the *Milice* marched my mother and her lover, the poet Monny de Boully, to the Gestapo headquarters where they were grilled for a whole day. At the time of their arrest, Monny's papers identified him as Claude Pascal (Amédée Sylvestre, his most recent identity, was only a few days old, which is why he kept repeating the name, to remember it, to convince himself). My mother, whose thoughtlessness was equalled only by her comprehensive ignorance of Jewish surnames, gave her name as Aïcha Bensoussan. While Aïcha might sound Arabic, anyone named Bensoussan was certainly Jewish. She had, however, a perfectly good excuse for not knowing: the Bensoussans, numerous though they were, were all still on the far side of the Mediterranean, the Algerian War not yet having taken place, and in Paris the name simply sounded exotic, which was what she wanted, believing that its very outlandishness would protect her. Confronted by her German interrogators, Monny told me, my mother was obdurate, she faced them down, never even for a moment flustered, haughtily denying that she belonged to the Chosen People, pointing to a photograph of Göring on the desk in the interrogation room and declaring, 'Look, your own Field Marshal looks more Jewish than I do!' The previous autumn she had dragged Monny to the Paris Opéra where almost all the seats, from the stalls to the gods, were occupied by Nazi officers in full uniform. Since Monny was fluent in German he overheard the incredulous remarks as, row after row, people turned to stare at my mother: '*Guck mal, es gibt eine Jüdin dort!*' '*Ach! Quatsch, das ist ganz unmöglich. Dummheit! Sie ist wahrscheinlich eine Tscherkessin.'* ['Look, over there, there's a Jewess!' 'Rubbish, that's completely impossible. Don't be ridiculous, she's definitely a Circassian.'] The way she doggedly fought her corner with the Gestapo in Orléans rattled some of her interrogators. Monny, who was waiting his turn, could tell as much from their remarks. Because he too staunchly denied being Jewish, they called for the ultimate test. When he said he was uncircumcised, the *Obersturmführer* leading the interrogation ordered, *'Rufen sie die Ärtze an!'* ['Call in the doctors!'] Out of the corner of his eye, Monny noticed two henchmen slipping on white coats and heard them say to each other, *'Kennst du etwas in Schwänzen?' 'Ein bisschen.'* ['Do you know much about cocks?' 'A little bit.'] All this Monny told us on his first evening in Brioude. His gift for storytelling came from another world, the surrealistic genie that lived inside him and popped out when he began to tell a story, his mastery of ten languages, the impressive richness of his French – something that only foreigners manage – had us veering from panic to laughter, from joy to agony. Years later, when peace had returned, he regaled my friends so often with his story of the medical examination that I have to repeat it here. It goes without saying that, being a Jew from Belgrade – the son of rich bankers, by now stripped of everything they possessed and murdered, although he did not know this yet, that dark day in Orléans – he was of course circumcised. 'But I was so scared,' he used to say, 'that there was pretty much nothing to see, nothing to show them,' and, slipping his left little finger between the index and middle finger of his right hand, he mimicked the examination, one of the doctors sneaking a quick look and pronouncing the sententious conclusion, the life or death verdict: *'Alles ist in Ordnung. Der Herr ist nicht beschnitten.'* ['Everything is fine. The gentleman isn't circumcised.']

This triumphant proof was not, however, deemed conclusive, there remained serious doubts, and Monny and my mother were placed under guard and would undoubtedly have been reinterrogated later that night or the following morning if a wondrous fairy, a *deus ex machina* in the person of Jean Rousselot, the Orléans commissioner of police, had not intervened. He himself was a poet and not only knew Max Jacob, but also Monny and Paulette. He personally vouched for them with the head of the Gestapo, negotiating their release with fearlessness and authority. He personally escorted them to the station and put them on a train to Paris, saying, 'You can't stay here a moment longer. Half an hour from now they'll work it out and they'll hunt you down and this time they won't let you go. Get out of Orléans and when you arrive in Paris, don't go to the address on your papers.' Though their papers were false, the home address on them was real. That night, Monny and Paulette, who had lived in Paris with no ration cards under assumed names all through the Occupation, endlessly forced to move house, returned to their peripatetic Parisian life. It truly was a brotherhood of poets. Rousselot, a talented, handsome ladies' man, eventually left the police to devote himself entirely to poetry, which I reproached him for when I first met him. I didn't mean to imply he was a bad poet, simply that the police needed men of his calibre in the ranks. Because he truly was, as Ashkenazi Jews say when they want to distil the greatest virtues of a man into a single word, a *mensh*.

For my mother, Orléans had been a qualitative leap: her courage and her vitality were undiminished, as were her ability to face the worst without ever contemplating surrender, her confidence that she could argue her case, put forward her reasons, uncompromising about reason itself, but she no longer had her carefree spirit. She realized that optimism or an ill-judged decision would be met with the immediate sanction of death. Monny's sudden appearance in Brioude, the risks he had run, attested to this newfound awareness. She had consulted a clairvoyant, a misfortune-teller, who had told her she would not see her three children again, and my mother could not rest until Monny – about whom we knew nothing – came to see us: he was her eyes, her hands, her ears, her heart, her flesh, her spirit; he was she. Never had such a union existed. If Monny succeeded, then the clairvoyant was a blind, money-grubbing pedlar of lies: it would have been easy, meeting my mother in 1942 in some gypsy caravan, to get her to talk, intuit her deep-seated anxieties and, with sinister predictions, drive her into a paroxysm of fear. Is it permissible to have a complicated private life when the great course of history has itself become complicated and crazy? It was this meeting between History and *her* history, *our* history, that had sent my mother into a spin and Monny to us as her cathartic messenger.

I was nine years old when, coming home from school with my brother and sister, I found our house in Vaucresson deserted, and a brief note from my mother on the kitchen table in which she assured her 'darling children' that she had no choice but to leave, but that she loved us and would see us soon. My first reaction was one of relief rather than sadness: my parents' arguments had grown so frequent and so violent over the years that I lived in fear that the worst would happen, murder perhaps or suicide, I didn't know. That was in 1934. At the time, those women who, appalled by the conditions imposed on them by marriage, dared to throw caution and security to the wind, to leave their husbands and their children were extremely rare; one had to be made of steel to brave the stigmatism and the daily heroism to which they were condemning themselves. My mother left without a penny and, for a year, worked in a factory where she crimped sardine tins. She lived, until she met Monny, in a furnished room in the 18th *arrondissement* on the rue Myrha, facing the Goutte d'Or district.

By the time Monny tapped on the back door of our house in Brioude, we had been living without our mother for eight years; we had not seen her for more than three – what few scant letters had been exchanged since contained nothing of any significance. She had faded from my memory, had become distant, I no longer missed her and if, from time to time, I did think about her it was not her caresses or her gentle words that I remembered but, on the contrary, everything in her temperament that belied the ordinary representations of maternal love, everything in her or about her that had embarrassed or shamed the conformist little boy I was: the terrible stammer she could never master, the big nose it would take me some considerable time to think of as that of 'one of the ancient daughters of Israel', seeing it first and foremost as characteristically, spectacularly Jewish, the fits of rage when her beautiful eyes rolled, and which alone made it possible for her to control her stammering – anger released her tongue – her utter lack of mercy: how she would pinch me until she almost drew blood to force me to open my mouth so she could feed me huge spoonfuls of cod liver oil, a very 'fashion-able' elixir, which I immediately threw up, or *panade* – a disgusting bread soup that was also very popular at the time, and which I also immediately threw up.

Suddenly, in the middle of the war, when danger was at its height, this mother of shame and fear presented herself to me in a new light, by way of the love this extraordinary magician bore her. She seemed like a mysterious stranger beside me, and in the nine years during which she had struggled with maternity, I had utterly failed to notice or to perceive her richness, had failed to understand who she truly was. Unlike me, my father and Monny shared the same knowledge: one loved Paulette, one had loved her, still loved her perhaps, had never truly stopped loving her. Monny dazzled us in the week he spent in Brioude lodging in Monsieur Legendre's room. My father was as charmed by him as I was. He realized that Monny opened up to my mother an entire universe, one that fulfilled a vital need and which he had not had the means to offer her. A remarkable brotherly relationship, born perhaps out of circumstance (my brother Jacques had recently gone to work as a labourer on a local farm), developed between the three of us: Monny not only told us about the Gestapo, but of the days and nights my mother spent hiding in a wardrobe, the forced departures, the escapes, the mutual support, the heroes, the betrayals. In this sleepy yet unsettled sub-prefecture, Monny was Paris personified: the big city, culture, poetry and thought.

Monny wrote to Paulette every night, becoming increasingly worried as the moment approached for his departure, as he would have to face the same dangers as on his journey to get here. Sitting at my father's desk, in his beautiful handwriting, that of a poet and a foreigner, he wrote cards and letters that he invariably concluded with this pledge of love: 'Yours, Paulette, yours alone for all eternity'. And after each of them he would ask me, 'Do you want to add a few words for your mother?' The only thing I could add were platitudes or professions of a filial attachment that would prove genuine only in time. For a whole week, my timid, adolescent pen hesitated to inscribe these feeble or untruthful thoughts beneath his 'Yours, Paulette, yours alone for all eternity'. But I had no hesitation in having his immortal challenge carved on the headstone that stands over my mother's grave in Montparnasse cemetery. They are buried side by side, next to my sister who committed suicide at the age of thirty-six on 18 November 1966. Two years later, Monny was struck down by a heart attack while crossing the Champs-Élysées on my mother's arm. On the same stone, one can also read four lines from one of his poems, a heartrending poem of inconceivable death and nothingness, of the inconceivable thought:

Past, present, future, where have you gone
Here is nowhere
Throw the harpoon on high,
On high among the monotonous stars.

Chapter 5

This journey will have marked my whole life. The fear, the shame and the remorse were so intense that its central event is graven in me with the clarity, the violence of a primal scene, sweeping everything away – what came before and what came after – blurring or erasing the circumstances of my departure. However much, now I come to recount it, I furiously spin the spinning top of memory, I still do not know who decided, how it was decided, that I should go to Paris under a false identity: despite everything Monny had told her, my mother's superstitious fears had flared up rather than died away. The pressure put on my father to consent to such a risk must have been very great. At Vierzon, I passed the demarcation line. My name now was Claude Bassier, my papers were perfect and I knew what I was to say if interrogated: I was going to visit my paternal grandparents (the school holidays had begun) in Normandy. I remember the long wait through the night at the station in Vierzon, the glare of spotlights on the platforms and the trains, I remember the dogs, the thud of boots, the brutal way the compartment doors were flung open, the meticulous inspection of my papers by uniformed Germans and French policemen, the interrogation conducted by the former. My reply to the question that indeed they asked satisfied them.

I arrived in Paris in the early morning, expecting Monny to be waiting for me at the station. There was no one; I waited for a long time. But this eventuality, as was routine in the clandestine life we lived back then, had been anticipated: I had been given an address to which I could go if no one came to meet me. Despite my hazy memory of the journey, so much of which I only half remember, I still clearly remember the address: 97 rue Compans, in the 19th *arrondissement*, a long, broad, quiet, rather steep street. I also remember the name of the Swedish man who owned the refuge. He had graciously lent it to Monny and my mother, though he was fully aware that they were Jewish, that they were perpetual fugitives: Hans Eckegaard. I rang the bell at number 97 and was immediately kidnapped: the concierge of the building had been warned I would be coming and, without even stopping to check that I was indeed the person he was waiting for, he clapped his hand over my mouth and dragged me to the top floor, to a large bright room whose huge picture-windows overlooked three cardinal points in Paris, since the rue Compans ends at the Buttes-Chaumont. Allowing me no time to admire the beauty of Paris, the concierge breathlessly explained that, relying on a tip-off, plain-clothes Germans had arrived the night before to arrest Paulette, who had been alone in the apartment at the time, but they had offered to let her buy her freedom: in return for a considerable sum of money – money she did not have – they agreed to defer her arrest. This odious sport was increasingly popular at the time, the 'sportsmen' being either corrupt Gestapo officers working with the *Commissariat aux questions juives* or scum from the French Gestapo, the famous 'rue Lauriston torturers'. I wouldn't swear that ordinary Parisian policemen did not also participate in this vile game. The concierge was very friendly with Monny and my mother who had told him about the incident. She had kept her cool with the two Germans, had grimly bargained for a lower sum – although she did not have a penny to her name – which she promised to raise if they gave her three days' grace. They agreed but insisted the meeting take place in two days' time, not at the rue Compans but in a café, and she had sworn she would come. Throughout the conversation, my mother had been desperately afraid that Monny would reappear prematurely, which would have called a halt to the bargaining. What little money they had, he earned working as a dealer in old books. Leading booksellers, impressed by his great cultivation, his knowledge of books and his talents as a salesman, entrusted him with precious – sometimes priceless – books, which he sold on to other booksellers, claiming to have discovered them in a private collection. But the privileged stops on his rounds selling incunabula were always the same: Thomas Scheler, rue de Tournon, who sheltered them more than once; Eugène Rossignol, rue Bonaparte; Blaizot; Bérès; and I've forgotten some. Monny, the son of a banker from Belgrade, is considered these days to be the Serbian Rimbaud. He had been summoned to Paris by André Breton and Louis Aragon who, having read the poems he had written as a young man, were keen that he should join the French surrealist movement. He had been praised to the skies, been excommunicated, come back into favour, he had been a member of every faction, every group. He cared little: every month a cheque arrived promptly from his father's bank. This extraordinary freedom came to an abrupt end with the war, a few short months after he and my mother first met on one of the red banquettes in La Coupole in Montparnasse and fell head over heels in love. This mad passion had given him the courage and the imagination to launch himself on a new career, making it possible for them to survive clandestinely in Paris for the five years of the Occupation. It was the first time he had ever had to work for a living.

Hardly had the blackmailers left than Paulette, fearing they might come back, and desperate to protect Monny, grabbed their bag – which always stood packed and ready in case they had to disappear – and got out of the apartment as quickly as she could, asking the concierge to warn Monny the moment he returned and to explain things to me if I showed up on my own the following morning. She hid with her elder sister, Sophie, in their mother's family home in Clichy. Sophie, too, spent the war years in Paris but did not suffer the same worries because she was married to Antonio (known as Toni) Gaggio, a pure-blooded Venetian. Sophie was a great beauty with dark eyes, she had no stammer, no Jewish nose and it brings tears to my eyes whenever, looking through the photos in the Auschwitz Album, taken by the Nazis on the *Judenrampe* as convoys of Hungarian Jews disembarked, most of them destined for the gas chambers, I come upon an uncanny photograph of my aunt's double, waiting for the selection process to begin. She *is* Sophie, her beautiful face stamped with suspicion and anguish; she knows she is going to die and she cannot, does not want to believe it.

There is no possible comparison to be made between Monny and Toni, except for one thing: Toni loved Sophie as much as Monny loved Paulette. He proved it when, after years of ceaselessly, fruitlessly courting her, he had himself circumcised at the age of thirty-five to please my grandfather, Yankel Grobermann, a Jew of strict observance – 'affectations', as my intractable mother translated – and a former horse-breeder or groom, I don't remember which, 1.94 metres tall, born in Kishinev, the city of the pogroms, in Bessarabia, who would have considered allowing his eldest daughter to marry an uncircumcised man the worst sacrilege. The trauma of his belated entry into the Covenant was such that my uncle by marriage spent the rest of his life playing cards – *belote* mostly – in the bistros of Clichy, where he became a celebrated champion.

The concierge at number 97 did not leave me in that lovely, bright room but led me, from terrace to terrace, rooftop to rooftop, to a building far from the rue Compans. He opened the door to a maid's room in the attic furnished only with a bed and told me to wait there until he received further instructions. Exhausted and bewildered, I fell asleep, waking later that evening with nothing familiar in sight that might dispel my confusion. A stranger finally came to pick me up and took me, by ways and means of which I have absolutely no memory, to my mother, in an apartment outside the city at an address I have long since forgotten too. I remember only an excess of gilded softness. Everyone was there: Sophie and her daughters, my cousins Micheline and Jacqueline with their long Venetian-blonde hair, beautiful, shapely, attractive; Toni, whom I think I met for the first time that night; Monny, my fixed star, his face again a mask of fear; and my mother to whose powerful embrace and kisses stronger than death I had to submit before I even had a chance to look at her. She hadn't changed, though her big lips as she kissed me publicly, voraciously, made her nose seem smaller. I barely noticed her stammer, so completely was it tempered by the circumstances – the cool-headedness she had shown, the blackmail, the appointment she was to keep with the Germans the next day, the necessity of once again having to find a new refuge.

The most pressing issue was to decide whether my mother should keep her German appointment at the scheduled place and time. She was in favour; everyone else was against the idea, she was alone in wanting to go. Furthermore she wanted to bring money – a derisory sum compared to what had been agreed – but she believed her perse-cutor would take the money as a gesture of goodwill, and besides, in accepting it, he would compromise himself. Monny, Toni and I pointed out the madness of this plan: the officer might get angry and arrest her there and then. Why throw herself into the lion's jaws again, now that the cover of the house on the rue Compans had been blown and they would have to look for somewhere else in any case? I cannot now remember the name or address where the meeting was to take place. It was a large café that Paulette knew; spacious, with lots of tables. But there could be no question of her going alone: Monny and I would go in first and sit at a table like father and son, so we could check out the café, look for any warning signs that this might be a trap. My mother made her entrance; exquisitely made-up, feminine, seductively radiant at the age of thirty-nine. She glanced around, taking in the whole room, careful not to linger when she saw us, then headed straight for a table some distance away, a table we had paid no attention to, where *he* was waiting for her. We could not bear to look. Everything happened quickly. He was the first to leave. My mother had asked for another forty-eight hours so that she could bring some more money – it would take her two weeks to get hold of the whole sum, she explained, offering to pay him in instalments, every two days, in the same café. She never went back.

The following day my mother decided that I was dressed like a peasant, my wooden-soled shoes were provincial and her elder son should wear something a little more elegant, more Parisian – even if the new shoes would inevitably have wooden soles. We went to Chaussures André, a famous Jewish emporium – now Aryanized – on the boulevard des Capucines, with an extensive clientele, countless shop assistants and a vast selection of shoes. This, as it turned out, proved to be the source of the problem. Because to choose is to kill. My mother was incapable of choosing, she wanted everything. I'm like her. The title of my dissertation for my philosophy degree was *Possibles and Incompossibles in the Philosophy of Leibniz*, 'incompossible' referring to the fact that there are things that cannot coexist. To choose one is to preclude the existence of the other. Any choice is a murder, and leaders, apparently, can be defined by their capacity to murder, we call them 'decision-makers' and we pay them handsomely for it. It is no accident that *Shoah* runs to nine and a half hours. The shop assistants addressed themselves to me, but it was my mother who answered – to her, I was still the little boy she had not seen for almost four years. As she spoke, her stammer became worse and worse, taking longer and longer since she was absolutely determined to finish every sentence – she could not bear to be second-guessed before she finished, still less for someone to have the nerve to complete a sentence for her: she had to enunciate every last syllable even if one had already understood. Shoes and boxes piled up around the stool where I sat, trying them on; none of them seemed right to her and if, by chance, she narrowed the choice down to two pairs, the torment of choosing, of hesitating between the two, only made her stammer worse, her voice louder.

Distraught and exhausted, the salesgirl moved her stepladder from shelf to shelf, took down yet another box, yet another pair of shoes only for my mother to reject them. I tried on pair after pair, even I was exhausted simply from trying them on. There were pairs I had liked that my mother had dismissed, and I was so desperate for the whole thing to be over that I went into raptures over each new pair. Time passed, trickling by more and more slowly. The colleagues of the girl serving us had finished work; they watched, they stared at us, as did other customers; Paulette did not even notice. I felt panic well up; I could see, could hear what these people could see and hear, the terrible stammer, the enormous Jewish nose of my mother, who remained utterly oblivious to the situation, to the danger she was putting us both in. The head of the department came over, visibly hostile, looked my mother up and down and said, 'Is something the matter, madame?' From the bottom of the pile, I dug out my peasant boots, slipped them on and, unable to contain my rising panic, I rushed out, weaving between the displays, until I came to an exit and I ran. So terrified was I that my mother would catch up with me and I would have to walk with her, travel on the métro with her, listening to her furious diatribe, that I did not stop running until I was some distance from the shop.

There was in France, in the history of torture, one medieval method known as 'the Boot', which was designed to crush the legs of the person from whom one wanted to force a confession: for the 'ordinary question', four wedges were hammered between narrow pieces of board, securely lashed around the calves, creating unbearable pressure on the bone; for the 'extraordinary question', eight wedges were driven in. For a long time, whenever I described this unbearable incident at Chaussures André, I would refer to it as 'the day of the Boot'. It is no laughing matter: I could not stop myself from deserting my mother, leaving her alone in what was an exceedingly dangerous situation, because she was putting me in danger. I was afraid of her, I was ashamed of her; that afternoon I behaved like a dyed-in-the-wool anti-Semite of the worst kind: a Jewish anti-Semite. There is no room for argument, I have no excuses and retelling that scene in the shoe shop as though I were trying to explain or to justify my cowardice, to excuse my abandonment with a concatenation of reasons, can no more wash away the horror of what I did than all the perfumes of Arabia could sweeten the bloody hands of Lady Macbeth.

Earlier I wrote that in 1938 – the period we spent in Paris with my father and his beautiful new companion Hélène, between the two periods we lived in Brioude – I had become aware of the power, the viciousness of the anti-Semitism at the Lycée Condorcet. But I also became aware of the fear and the cowardice in myself. Hiding behind a pillar in the school playground I watched – petrified, making no attempt to intervene, terrified that I might be discovered – as my classmates all but lynched a lanky, red-haired Jew named Lévy who had all the features of pre-war anti-Semitic caricatures. They were twenty against one and they beat him until he bled. Lévy simply tried to dodge the blows, making no attempt to defend himself, and the prefects turned a blind eye; it became a sort of ritual: once a week, they would 'get' the Jew. Fear pervaded the school. I remember in class, while the teacher was discussing Shylock's 'pound of flesh' in *The Merchant of Venice*, one of my classmates turned to me and hissed, between clenched teeth, 'You're another little Jew, aren't you?' Instead of leaping to my feet and punching him, I protested, denied it, brushing aside the insult as though answering a question of fact politely put to me; 'No, I'm not a Jew.'

None of this is news, it is an old, old story, one that is written in our genes, one difficult to understand today when circumstances have changed so much. In Groutel, a primitive hamlet of about ten farms between Le Mans and Alençon, where my paternal grandparents had retired, my grandmother, Anna, born in Riga and utterly unable to read or write French, asked my father, as soon as I graduated to the *sixième*, to get me to write to her in Latin – a language she could no more read than she could French. I was, as I have said, a docile child and I did as I was told, and sent Anna *née* Ratut missives in dog-Latin. What did she do with them? She tramped the six kilometres of dusty or waterlogged dirt track that ran from Groutel to Champfleur, the nearest parish, and asked, in the inimitable pidgin French she spoke when not speaking Yiddish, to see Monsieur le Curé. Then, blushing with pride, she would brandish my latest screed: 'Look, Father, my grandson, he can write in Latin.' My dog-Latin, in some way I do not understand, reinforced Anna's *'vieille-France'* status, brilliantly emphasizing that the enzymes of integration were at work, ringing my formidable grandmother's head with a halo of conformity.

But from Anna, I must return to Paulette: the tribunal that awaited me when, penniless and having nowhere to go, I reappeared that evening dragging the heels of my ugly, tattered boots, showed absolutely no mercy. Nor did I seek any; I admitted everything. My mother did not stammer once and her perfect diction, which, more than anything, attested to her anguish, had me sobbing, hiccupping and sniffling. The question of filial love, which was to haunt both of us all our lives, was openly, explicitly at issue that night and it could not be resolved with words or with pretence. She knew this, I knew this, it was abandonment for abandonment, the inexhaustible subject of our later conversations, arguments, promises and attempts to make peace. Monny proved a tactful and sensitive diplomat, and it was thanks to him that I did not leave Paris mortified with shame to return at once to the Auvergne. But the man who truly cured me, who delivered me from shame by helping me to understand what had happened to me, describing in perfect detail what I had felt on 'the day of the Boot', was Jean-Paul Sartre. When, four years later, after the war, I read his *Réflexions sur la question juive [Anti-Semite and Jew]*, I first devoured the chapter 'The Portrait of the Anti-Semite', and with every line I felt alive again or, to be more precise, I felt I had been given permission to *live*. Later, I came to the description of what Sartre calls the 'Jewish inauthenticity' and in it I suddenly found a portrait of myself, perfectly depicted: I was all the more moved because if Sartre, the greatest French writer, understood us as no one else had ever done, he never condemned: 'When there is another Jew with him he feels himself endangered *by this other* [. . .] He is so afraid of the discoveries that the Christians are going to make that he hastens to give them warning, he becomes himself an anti-Semite by impatience and for the sake of others and he who a moment before could not even see the ethnic characteristics of his son or his nephew now looks at his coreligionist with the eyes of an anti-Semite. Each Jewish trait he detects is like a dagger thrust, for it seems to him that he finds it in himself but out of reach, objective, incurable, a given [. . .]'

Paulette stammered because – just as later, in the Polish ghettos during the Nazi 'actions', newborn babies were muffled up and concealed in secret hiding places known as *malines* so their cries would not lead to the discovery of whole families – just so had my mother had a pillow pressed over her face so she could be secretly stowed away in Odessa, where she was born, on to a ship bound for Marseille. This was in 1903; she was three months old. After the terrible pogrom of Kishinev, Yankel, my gargantuan grandfather, like so many other Jews, had decided to leave for the West. This would also mean he avoided having to spend seven years in the Tsarist army, serving as cannon-fodder in the far-flung limits of the empire during the Russo-Japanese War. This, aside from the pogroms, was what awaited the Jews. They arrived penniless in Paris after a breathless, tortuous journey to find scant help from a relative who had arrived there some years earlier. They lived in terrible poverty on the barrière de Clichy then known as *la zone*. 'They' meaning Yankel, a diligent, tireless worker, an observant Jew, contemptuous of women, who ignored his two daughters Paulette and Sophie and worshipped his two sons, particularly the elder, Robert, known as Bobby; then there was Perl or Perla, my grandmother of whom I have only a vague memory from when I was a small child, a memory of great dark eyes set in a pale face at the end of a corridor, or paler still, lying down, her heavy hand stroking my hair, in a bed with white sheets, possibly her deathbed, though she was still alive. I maintain that I remember Yankel and his funeral, but my mother tells me that this is impossible because I was too young, that it was because my father, doubly loved by Yankel for being both male and Jewish, talked to me so often about him that I imagined that I knew him. In the photographs I have of him he has broad, square shoulders and a neck as short as my own with a head that seems to sink into his chest. My father told me that, one summer afternoon after a picnic, the two of them were standing side by side, relieving themselves, when suddenly my grandfather started to piss blood; he died in excruciating pain of cancer of the bladder.

Every day Yankel and his elder son left Clichy dragging a hand cart behind them, heading for the auction rooms on the rue Drouot. There, they bought cheap, clapped-out folding metal beds, spending their nights patching up and repairing them so that by morning they were presentable and serviceable once more. Working like a galley-slave and hoarding every penny – apparently he refused to pay for his daughters' sanitary napkins when they first got their periods – he was the living embodiment of what Karl Marx calls the primitive accumulation of capital. Soon, the hand-cart was replaced by a horse-drawn carriage, they diversified in what they bought and sold and no longer lived from day to day, they needed warehouse space, and so on. Yankel Grobermann became a respected name in the singular world of the salvage trade at the auction rooms. But a qualitative leap occurred during World War I, at the end of 1916 or the beginning of 1917: an American dealer arrived in Paris looking for a supplier who could deliver living- and dining-room furniture in bulk – armchairs, sideboards, overmantels, four-poster beds and I don't know what else, authentic furniture for the first film studios in the United States, which by then were blossoming like spring flowers. Unlike my paternal grandfather Itzhak Lanzmann, who became a French citizen in 1913 at the age of thirty-nine and was called up in

1914 to serve in the infantry with young men of twenty, 'the class of 1914', the very same day a brick was thrown through the window of his furniture shop at 70 rue Lamarck in the 18th *arrondissement* because his name sounded German; Yankel had not been in France long enough to claim French citizenship. This was his good fortune: he was not called up and, after he met the American, he began to clean out the châteaux of France, buying up antique furniture of any style, any period, from aristocrats who to their amazement found themselves being paid in cold hard cash by this tall, lanky, broad-shouldered man with an unrecognizable accent. The patrimony of France languished for weeks or months in the Grobermann warehouses at Clichy before it was shipped by the carriage-load, the train-load, the boat-load to the New World. My mother told me that, in the 1920s, when watching Chaplin or Buster Keaton films with Yankel, she would sometimes get a shock and shout, right there in the cinema, 'Look, Papa, it's the red sitting room!'

My mother's real name was not Paulette, but Pauline, and I have never understood why she was never called Pauline. So, Pauline and her sister Sophie were both brilliant students. Pauline was gifted in maths and the sciences, although she also had a strong affinity with words and books. But Yankel paid no heed to his daughters' talents and refused to sign their school reports. For the girls this was simply the way it was and each routinely signed their father's name on the other's report. During the war, catastrophe struck. At sixteen, Bobby, the eldest boy, looked ten years older than his age, heavy-set like his father with a rugged face and a powerful masculinity that appealed to women. He was murdered by a Breton woman who was pregnant by him; she put a bullet in his head as he lay sleeping. She was thirty-five years old. She was arrested, imprisoned and received a long sentence, giving birth in prison. Yankel was devastated by the murder of his son, and everyone in the family refused to see the child who was the fruit of the crime. Everyone except Pauline: she saw him, took care of him, claiming that he had already paid a terrible price, and I remember when I was about twelve spending an afternoon with him and my mother in Luna Park. He seemed gentle, too gentle. He was my cousin, but we had nothing in common. I've forgotten his first name and I never knew his surname; I never saw him again. Later my mother told me that he had been killed during World War II.

Unlike Yankel, my paternal grandfather, Itzhak was not very tall. I knew him for a long time and loved him as long as I knew him. He was the spitting image of Charlie Chaplin, and when we were children he would make us laugh with mimicry and making faces undoubtedly copied from his illustrious model. I laughed uncontrollably; the only way I could stifle my hilarity was to bury my face in my grandfather's hair, which smelt of freshly baked bread; it impregnates my nostrils still. Like many pre-war Jewish merchants, my grandfather had changed Itzhak, his 'barbarous' first name, to the more 'refined' Léon, which became a surname. At the auction rooms on the rue Drouot, his business contacts addressed him as Monsieur Léon. Similarly, André, he of the shoe shop, I'm convinced, originally must have been called Moishe or Itzhak or even Yankel, why not? My grandmother Anna, for whom I wrote crude Latin, was known as Madame Léon. Léon, then, had been born in 1874 in Vileyka – a *shtetl* of shifting and uncertain orthography – on the outskirts of Minsk in Belarus. Typical Jewish hotchpotch: his father, my great-grandfather – though I'm not even sure of these details – ran a kosher butcher's shop, had thirteen children, experienced appalling poverty and anti-Semitism and the call of the West, to which Itzhak succumbed at the age of thirteen, leaving his family and his village accompanied only by one older brother. A stopover turned into several years in Berlin, where he learned the tailor's craft. I do not know the fate, nor even the first name, of his brother, who was, after all, my great-uncle. From snatches of information overheard, I know that Itzhak left Germany for France, although he thought he was merely passing through, his final destination being the United States. For better or worse, in Paris he met Anna, someone else who was also 'passing through'. Here is another Jewish hotchpotch: Anna was born in Riga and later her father, my paternal great-grandfather, a Rabbi according to Anna, took his wife and children to live in Amsterdam. In the house in Groutel, above my grandparents' bed, where a crucifix usually hangs in Norman houses, was an impressive photograph of the rabbi: a long face soothed by ascetism, a flowing black beard. To the eyes of the little French boy I was, my great-grandfather seemed like a sentinel to some strange and distant world, a world I could reach only through transgression, whenever I had the privilege – which was rarely – of being admitted to this holy of holies. When Anna met Itzhak, who was not yet Monsieur Léon, she too was bound for Ellis Island and the United States. They fell in love, fell in love with Paris and decided to stay there, worked at several jobs, briefly ran a restaurant. But it was on the rue Drouot, at the auction rooms, that they finally found their safe harbour. By dint of hard work, of listening, attentiveness and practice, they became experts and connoisseurs of antique furniture, carving out a niche for themselves in the world of Jewish antique dealers – who were then numerous in that area of Paris. As a small child, when she took me to the rue Drouot, I could gauge the respect the merchants accorded my grandmother. It sometimes happened that dealers colluded, agreeing not to bid on a particular lot to avoid driving up the price, thereby allowing one of them to buy the piece for considerably less than its true value – real or imagined, since an auction, like a game of poker, depends upon bluffing, and on illusion. Once the auction was over, the poker-faced bluffing recommenced in the back room or the cellar of one of the neighbouring bistros, so that the 'real' value of the piece could be determined. The conspirators gathered around a large oval table and the auction began once more, bidding beginning at the price paid by whoever had bought the lot. This was the 'revision' and it was a furtive practice, although tolerated, so it was said. Nowadays, revision is strictly forbidden – it is considered to be an inverted insider trading. Hidden behind Anna's long black skirts, I watched, turning from the visible tension on the faces of the bidders, to my grandmother's expressionless calm; her perfect poker-face. The undersold object – a piece of furniture, a painting, a rug or a piece of jewellery – went to the highest bidder, but the winner then had to pay, according to a complicated system, all those who had risked a bid on the lot before him, immediately, and in hard cash. More often than not, Anna walked away with crisp crackling banknotes in her purse. Perhaps the Lanzmanns and the Grobermanns attended the same 'revisions' – they were, after all, destined to meet, to become allies. But the war postponed the fated meeting: from August 1914 until November 1918 Itzhak Lanzmann fought as a front-line infantryman, he fought at the Marne, at Verdun, on the Somme, he was wounded three times, was awarded a Médaille militaire and the Croix de Guerre *avec palme*. On the rare occasions that he came home on leave or to convalesce when discharged from hospital, he refused to sleep on a soft mattress, insisting on sleeping on the bare floor, so accustomed was he to the hardship of the trenches. Anna, left alone with their two sons, Armand, my father, and his younger brother Michel, endured the war bravely and angrily, keeping shop, educating her sons as best she could in this country that was unreadable, indecipherable to her, a country where she understood neither the character, nor the codes, nor the language. My father had such difficulty accepting this '*étrangeté de vivre*' ['strangeness of living'], to quote Saint-John Perse, this difficulty of being French in France, that he enlisted at the age of seventeen. I have already explained how his lungs were damaged by mustard gas and how this bound us for so long to the Auvergne. I don't know which distracted, xenophobic pencil-pusher of a registrar changed the first 'n' in Lanzmann to a 'u' when his brother was born, but Michel, my uncle, was registered as Lauzmann, married a moustachioed Aryan and so loathed his elder brother that he never reinstated his true name. I have a cousin, an anorexic girl, later a regional prefect's wife, a perfectly charming woman, with whom I once discussed this war of names.

My father and mother were married without ever having met. A *shadchen* – a matchmaker or a go-between, possibly a woman – arranged the whole thing. This Jewish Frosine matched, assessed the assets, decided on the size of the dowry. The Grobermanns were considerably richer than the Lanzmanns: Yrankel gave each of his daughters 200,000 gold francs – apparently a lot of money – and my father found himself running a vast shop selling 'reproduction antiques' just opposite the auction rooms on the corner of the rue Drouot and the rue Rossini. The shop is still there and the building itself has not changed, but these days it houses an auctioneer's office. Armand and Pauline met twice before the wedding and did not dislike each other. My father was a handsome man, he remained slim his whole life, enjoyed sex, liked women as much as they liked him and was so profligate that after a few years the shop passed to his younger brother Lauzmann, notorious among the Lanzmanns for being a miser, a salesman with no charisma, and a man I barely knew, so estranged were the two brothers.

To her dying day, my mother threatened to reveal the dark and terrible secret that would make me understand what a monster my father had been, the reason she clung so fiercely to her resolute hatred of him. It was a threat she made good on shortly before she passed away, as though conferring on me one last sacrament, but, from conjecture, cross-checks, intuition, comparisons, I thought I had already worked out my father's heinous crime. I was not wrong: not content with having taken her virginity, on their wedding night my barbaric sire attempted to sodomize Pauline. I don't approve of his actions. Though, as I have said, she considered religion to be little more than 'playacting', my mother was still very much a Jew of the Torah, an extremely prudish woman despite her loose language, and she hated everything to do with carnal relations, which she deemed to be against nature. Among our people, there are still many women of her view: when it is not in the missionary position or in some languorous side position, but bestially, or with the woman on all fours in the position known as *du duc d'Aumale*, such women refuse this 'animal coupling', crushed as they are by both the Law and the Superego, arching their whole bodies, twisting them so forcefully (I am thinking of Mademoiselle Bordelet) that every curve, every orifice disappears and the aggressor might as well not have bothered.

Before Vaucresson, we lived in a third-floor apartment on the place des Batignolles in the 17th *arrondissement* of Paris, a place I associate with cheerless memories. A world full of sound and fury that somehow filtered through to me, with names that surface like unforgotten markers: Aristide Briand, the Treaty of Rapallo, the Stavisky Affair, the election of Albert Lebrun, the Croix-de-Feu, the Ligues, a bandana-wearing murderer who hid in doorways at night and stabbed his victims to death, the war between my mother and my father that drove both of them mad. Separately, she with Monny and he with the beautiful Hélène, they experienced passionate, peaceable relationships. But together, excepting a few surprising moments of calm, it was constantly stormy, a succession of escalating confrontations and provocations, my father trying desperately to impose his authority over this indomitable creature, trying to terrify a woman who was afraid of nothing, who would strut around proudly until she died.

I am six years old, maybe seven, Jacques, Évelyne and I are sleeping in the same room (Évelyne is still a baby, she is two years old at most), I am awake, I know my father is waiting for my mother in the entrance hall, soundlessly I open the door and, my heart pounding, I watch my father as he watches for her: apart from the lack of a bandana, he looks like the man who hides in doorways, his hand closes around the handle of a long butcher's knife and I wait for the inevitable, incapable of revealing my presence. The key turns in the lock, the door opens, it is her, with her long black hair, she is not coming back from seeing a lover, she has not been cheating on him, she needed to get out, she couldn't stand it any more, the prison of marriage and motherhood were suffocating her. She finds him, knife raised as though to strike her down, she laughs, she stammers and her stubborn stammering infuriates my father even more: 'Y . . . Y . . . You wouldn't d . . . d . . . dare . . . G . . . g . . . go ahead,' she taunts him. 'You're nothing but a coward.' He does not bring down the knife but plunges his other hand into his pocket, takes out a gun and fires, not at my mother, but randomly at the dining-room walls. Muted, abrupt explosions, it is a small bore pistol, a 6.35, but the bullets are genuine, the walls are really riddled, it will take days to plaster over the holes. Having chosen the path of jealousy and violence, Armand was forced either to kill or to put on an act. Paulette never missed an opportunity to call him 'the actor'.

Another day – I think it is still daylight – he is waiting for her in the lobby of the building and, peering over the banister on the landing, I watch, petrified, her ascent to Calvary. She comes in, sees him, tries to run, but he catches her, grabs her long black hair and drags her, step by step, up to our floor with her struggling and refusing to be dragged every inch of the way.

Another night: the screams and moans from their bedroom are so piercing I am convinced one of them is about to die. I rush into their room, I think I can see daggers under one of the pillows, I throw the window wide open and in my most calm, most adult voice, I warn them, 'If you don't stop right now, I'm calling for help.' The bedroom overlooked the place des Batignolles.

Very early, from the age of six or seven, I felt responsible for everyone, for my parents, my brother, my sister. Sometimes, later, when I was left for the evening to babysit my brother and sister, who played around and made fun of me, I would find myself turning on the gas burners fifteen times to make sure I had turned them off properly, then later in bed, as I was nodding off, I would feel I needed to get up and turn them on and off again. Or go into the living room to check under the armchairs and the sofa and behind the curtains to make sure there was no bandana-wearing murderer lurking there.

We left Paris for Vaucresson and a new life with a garden and a huge shaggy, impossibly white mountain dog, so powerful, affectionate and good-natured that he even allowed my father to put a bridle on him so that he could pull us around in a cart that my father had made. Because of Flaherty and his famous film, our dog was called Nanook. Vaucresson to me is Nanook; it is the terrifying Great Danes I mentioned earlier; it is my father coming home late one night, covered in dust, bleeding, caught and beaten by police in the riots of 6 February 1934; it is my mother's letter lying on the kitchen table one day when we came home from school, marking the end of this brief new life.

Jacques and I spent almost a year without father or mother, living in a boarding house run by a widow in Le Perche, just outside Nogent-le-Rotrou, with Évelyne lodging nearby on a farm. Every day we walked down a long hill to the primary school in Mâle where we were taught by Monsieur Étournay, our father showing up irregularly, in an American car, my mother not knowing where we were, all ties having been severed. One day Armand turned up in yet another new car accompanied by a beautiful woman: Hélène. They took us to a restaurant and, on the way, Hélène turned to us, huddled together on the back seat, and said, 'Would you like me to be your *Manou*?' 'Yes,' we chorused. The separation from Monsieur Étournay was heartwrenching. Pointing to me, he said reproachfully to my father, 'You're taking away my best pupil.' Cycling up the steep hills of Perche in search of the places of my childhood some years ago, I ran into him. Though over ninety, he was still as tall, as ramrod straight as ever. 'I've followed your career in the newspapers and on television,' he told me. He also 'followed' my brother Jacques. Only recently I heard that he had died. Driving out of Mâle on the Paris road, we collected Évelyne from the farm and so began our first migration to Brioude and the Auvergne. Hélène, out of love, was prepared to take on three children who were not hers.

Inevitably, our relationship with our mother resumed. We took the train to visit her once or twice a year, though never for more than a day, and each time she was waiting for us at the Gare de Lyon. Her friends, whom she had met through Toni, the 'Circumcised of Venice', were Italian anti-Fascists living in exile after Mussolini's rise to power. I remember one of them, a man named Giulio who came with her to the station, her lover probably, an anarchist as aloof as Lacenaire in *Les Enfants du paradis*. Barely had we clambered down from the carriage when he asked me in a thick accent, 'What do you want to be when you grow up?' Taken aback and having no idea what my future would be, I gave the most conformist answer: 'A teacher.' 'Silly fool,' Giulio muttered to himself through teeth clenched in scorn. The celebration in my mother's twelve-square-metre cheap furnished room on the rue Myrha consisted of horsemeat – cheaper than beef – chopped and served raw seasoned with salt and pepper. It was absolutely delicious; to this day I eat it often. Raw horsemeat followed by blackcurrant sorbet on a café terrace on the boulevard Barbès, a trip to the cinema, this was how our visits usually played out, not forgetting the excitement my brother and I felt when, behind a screen, my mother raised her arms to perfume her underarms or undress, without a hint of embarrassment or prudishness, oblivious to the fact that the mirrored wardrobe door reflected her naked body back to her sons.

After leaving our mother we would go to Groutel and our paternal grandparents: Monsieur Léon whose hair smelt of freshly baked bread, and Anna, whose childhood in Amsterdam and her time in charge while her husband had been away at war had turned her into a tyrant obsessed with cleanliness. Day and night she scrubbed and polished two houses: the big house, in which we rarely set foot, and the old house, where they lived, whose polished brasses and Delft porcelain evoked a Dutch interior. And in fact, with her snub nose and despite her Yiddish accent, she looked more like a peasant woman from the polders than an East European Jew. Her tirades, when we came home filthy or muddy or with dirty fingernails, terrified us but we always ended up helpless with laughter, egged on by winks of complicity from our grandfather. Seeing this would make her even angrier, and one day, determined to prove to her son Armand that his offspring had filth in their veins, she cut our dirty fingernails, put the parings in an envelope and sent them to him. Anna and Itzhak had retired to Groutel early, they never went to Paris and, aside from a small private income in the form of 'coupons' – that was their word – they were completely self-sufficient. The potatoes, beans, lettuces, tomatoes, seasonal fruits – all the produce of their extensive kitchen garden – my grandfather tended entirely by himself, digging, planting, hoeing, weeding, picking. He was a true, a seasoned, farmer and this earned him the respect of the overweight Norman farmers – with their fat paunches and bloated lands – the Labrasseurs, the Roustaings, the Clouets, who knew that Grandfather was a veteran of the Marne and of Verdun and unquestioningly accepted the fable of the Lanzmann family's Alsatian origins. Besides his garden, Itzhak had a poultry yard of the sort that no longer exists, with laying hens, their eggs taken from the nest and swallowed immediately, fighting cocks that crowed at daybreak, ducks and ducklings, some fifty hutches with rabbits, snow-white and grey, whose back paws Grandfather tied together before stunning them with a karate chop to the back of the neck, then severing the carotid artery. He would gut them, plunging his hands into the steaming, still palpitating entrails, skinning them and drying the pelts on wooden braces. I would not have missed seeing him executing rabbits, wringing the necks of chickens, beheading ducks with an axe on a block of wood, for anything in the world. There was only one exception to this self-sufficiency: a weekly trip in the black Mathis car to the market at Alençon to buy seeds, tools, sometimes a little red meat and always some cooked ham for which Anna, in her cloche hat, doggedly haggled in her hilarious Franco-Yiddish, arguing that it was 'for a *pension*', to get the best possible price. I should say ham of that quality no longer exists: the flavour was exquisite, my grandmother kept it in a meat-safe of fine wire mesh, which she hung from the ceiling of the cool cellar next to the 'old house'. Nowadays, a fridge keeps the best ham fresh for only a couple of days but the slices my grandmother bought stayed fresh for a whole week.

Having left Vileyka, my grandfather, perhaps motivated by some extraordinary prescience, had cut all ties with the Jewish world and with his old friends. With the exception of a man named Joseph Katz, a comrade-in-arms during the war who was also from Belarus, and whose face and accent I adored, who visited him in Groutel once or twice, my grandfather saw no one from Paris after he moved, other than his children and grandchildren. When he and Anna wanted to keep something from us, they spoke in some unintelligible language, harsh and guttural with rare soft sounds, a language of secrecy and perhaps shame. This was Yiddish. Of the enormous families they came from, families of twelve and thirteen children, we never met a single member, except once, in Paris, when a red-haired Englishman, a professional boxer, was introduced to us as cousin Harry. Many of these relatives must have died in the Shoah, but not all. Assimilation is another form of annihilation, a triumph of forgetting. One of my real sorrows is losing a letter, sent to me in Israel while I was shooting *Shoah*, in which a recent emigrant, born in Australia, sent me proof that we were from the same family, that her grandfather and mine had had the same surname and were born in the same *shtetl*. Her letter was lost in the chaos of shooting the film, I never found it again, nor could I remember my relative's name. If one day she should read these lines I implore her to contact me.

That Itzhak Lanzmann had severed all ties with the past to become a French farmer at least five years before the war may perhaps explain why he and my grandmother managed to survive under Nazi rule for five years, without changing their surname, and in the heart of the Occupied Zone. Groutel, as I have said, numbered only a handful of farms and, in spite of investigations and incursions by the police and the Germans, the other farmers kept silent and thus saved their 'Alsatian' neighbours. They too would be considered 'Righteous Gentiles' nowadays, but they cared little about that. The memory of the gargantuan Madame Lebrasseur, who mixed a few drops of calvados into the bottles she prepared for her newborn baby because 'it's good for your health', is indelibly engraved on my memory. I like the Normans.

Chapter 6

I am incapable of saying now whether it was my father or I who first opened up to the other. He was walking me back to the train station at Brioude one Sunday afternoon, as I was returning to the Lycée Blaise-Pascal, having spent two days at home. It must have been February 1944. As we walked, each of us learned what the other had been doing. He told me, in strict confidence, that he was head of the MUR for the Haute-Loire, dealing, I think he said, with the parachute drops of weapons, or going out in the dead of night to improvised landing strips in fields to meet small British Lysander planes bringing agents or important people from England or Algeria and spiriting others away. MUR meant de Gaulle, Jean Moulin – by now already dead – all the power of the Allied forces four or five months from D-Day; it meant marshalling Resistance fighters to go up to the *maquis*, a genuinely free zone as large as Vercors in the high plains of La Margeride, from which convoys of German reinforcements travelling north to the landing sites could be attacked. A trick of memory: though I will not change the first sentence of this chapter, as I write these lines, I realize that my father was the first to speak. When he finished it was my turn, and I told him everything: the *Jeunesses communistes*, the FUJP, Aglaé, training in the basement of the school, distributing tracts, switching the suitcases, the possibility of having to fight with the FTP (the *Francs-tireurs et partisans* – the Communist *maquis*), the nagging problem of the lack of weapons. As I spoke, Papa paled and, by the time we walked into the train station, his face was ashen.

He had just enough time to say, 'Be very careful, please. Come back soon. We need to talk about this.'

At this point, I should say that by February 1944 the FUJP no longer existed, having been disbanded some weeks earlier in the schoolyard of the Lycée Blaise-Pascal and in the dormitories of our various feeder schools for the Grandes écoles. The bearer of the bad news – or of the truth, since, in accordance with Party instructions, I had concealed the fact – was another Jew whom I knew from Brioude where his family had taken refuge for a while. Marcovici, whose first name was also Claude, appeared one day during the midday break and went from group to group, holding a private conversation with each. Well dressed, self-assured and flashing wads of bills, he introduced himself as an agent of the AS (*Armée secrète*), the armed wing of the MUR dedicated to shock tactics. But his main aim was to explain that the FUJP had been infiltrated by the Communist Party, something that horrified many of the people we had recruited. You have to imagine another group of young men, myself and the forty young Communists who would remain loyal to me, running from group to group trying to retain our troops, taking issue with Marcovici, his methods, his attempt at poaching, which I found odious, raising the tone of the discussion, maintaining, proving to them that fundamentally I had not lied, that the Communists were the heart and soul of the French Resistance and that their efforts were worth just as much as the hired guns of the AS whose right-wing credentials were well known. What of the sacrifices and the heroism of the Red Army, we asked, what of Stalingrad a year earlier, which we knew was the turning point of the war, the watershed? All this went on with both groups trying to hide from the Vichy supporters, the sons of members of the *Milice*, themselves future members of the *Milice*, who were watching, sensing that something major, something unheard-of was taking place. In Venice, in the Scuola di San Giorgio degli Schiavoni, every time I see Carpaccio's painting – one of eight – depicting the companions of St Jerome desperately fleeing, cassocks flying, at the appearance of a lion in their peaceful cloisters, I cannot help but remember – how strange it is! – those two days of breathless, frantic running, the pleas, to prevent everyone deserting us. And yet, with only two exceptions, that is what they did. Our numbers slashed, we closed ranks, leaving only the hard-liners, which I believed was for the best.

Two weeks later I was back in Brioude, where my father immediately announced that he had a serious offer he wanted to make to me. He had taken it upon himself to speak to his peers and to his superior officers and he proposed, in their name and in his own, that when the time came to rally all Resistance fighters to go up to the *maquis*, the forty members of my group at Blaise-Pascal should be integrated into the forces of the MUR and fight the Germans with them. We would retain our identity as *Jeunesses communistes*, retain our freedom of speech and even keep the right to make our own propaganda on condition that we were prepared to accept overall discipline and obey, like everyone else, the orders issued to us. He explained that it had been very difficult for him to secure this agreement, which I could well believe. He was clearly doing this to protect me, preferring to watch out for me himself, to be at my side when danger came.

Back in Clermont, I reported all this to Aglaé. She listened gravely, questioned me about my father and took notes. The very next day she relayed to me the orders of the Party – not just the orders, but congratulations of senior officials from the *Parti communiste français*. What I had achieved, thanks to my father, was unprecedented and moreover of the greatest importance, they said, and we should absolutely accept, I had the blessing of the whole Party. As she told me this, Aglaé flushed with pleasure, as though she were conferring a knighthood on me. Incredulous and happy, I shared the news with my comrades and sent a message to Brioude to say that the proposal was accepted, that an unwritten but formal contract had been agreed and we were ready to mobilize as soon as the order came.

There was the massive bombing of the Michelin factory in Clermont-Ferrand; tensions in the city and at school mounted.

Rumours, warnings, advice came to me in a constant stream from the Party: I had to be careful, the Gestapo might arrest me at any moment. They knew who I was and what I was doing. Separately, both the Party and my father decided that we should leave the school as quickly as possible. We did so in small groups, early one Sunday morning, taking the *défense passive* helmets issued by the Vichy authorities for our protection during bombing raids. At the station, we hung around, pretending not to know each other as we waited for the first train south, then climbed aboard different carriages. Aglaé was there accompanied by three comrades from the PCF, adults, men with influence, whom she introduced to me by their pseudonyms as high-ranking comrades, and I noticed others whom I didn't know on the platform, clearly on the alert, responsible for guarding them. I was told they had insisted on coming to convey the Party's solemn appreciation. One of them, apparently the most senior of the three, said, 'We must rejoice, comrade, in what you have achieved. Your initiative and your loyalty to the Party will be rewarded.' I would hear the phrase 'we must rejoice' again, many years later, as a constant refrain from Raymond Guyot, a member of the *Bureau politique* of the PCF and brother-in-law of Artur London, former Czech Deputy Minister for Foreign Affairs, one of the few accused to survive the Slánský Trial, and the author of an admirable book about it, *L'Aveu* [*The Confession*]. Even when things were at their worst, Raymond Guyot invariably began whatever he had to say with 'we must rejoice'. I did rejoice then: it felt almost like being awarded the Order of Lenin there on the platform of Clermont-Ferrand station.

I found out later that half an hour after the train moved off, the Gestapo burst into the Lycée Blaise-Pascal in order to arrest me. They searched everywhere, the classrooms, the study halls, the dormitories, but they did not realize – and nor did the school officials who helped with their search, as it was a Sunday – that I had not left alone. Drastic precautions had also been taken in Brioude when we arrived at the station there. My father was waiting for us, in boots but no uniform, yet he already had a military bearing. We hardly spoke. Still moving in small groups, we walked to the wood-gas trucks, which headed via secondary roads towards the main Brioude–Saint-Flour thoroughfare before turning right for Saint-Beauzire, then down into a little valley to the small, tightly packed houses of the village of Saint-Laurent-Chabreuges, which lay sheltered and crushed by the soaring medieval castle, unspoiled, magical, haunted, with its big towers, its squat keep, its crenellations, its huge moat surrounded by deep forests and lush grasslands.

The lord of the manor, Vicomte Aymery de Pontgibaud, welcomed us with a blustering speech, explaining that our lives up until now had all been fun and games but that from today, as we would discover, things were about to change. We had come to train for war, real war. Vicomte Aymery de Pontgibaud had an ascetic gauntness, with hollow cheeks and deep eye sockets, blazing with a French flame. He was killed on the Rhine some months later. We were billeted in the state rooms, not the attic rooms, in four-poster beds fashioned for marquises and vicomtesses. The Château de Chabreuges had been put at the disposal of the Resistance. But we did not exactly live like kings: Aymery would appear at all hours of the night, a candlestick in his left hand, a revolver in his right, invariably followed by the white goat that trailed everywhere after him. 'On your feet, you bastards!' he would yell, brandishing his gun, going from room to room, waking everyone with a start. At which point we would be treated to hellish gymnastics in the damp forest, forced to march, to run, crawl, jump or trek for hours, wading through the turbulent Alagnon with its deep pools and unsuspected rapids. We ate little and we too became an ascetic troop but we never mutinied or complained, for our leader shared our plight.

The long-awaited day arrived: trucks drove across the drawbridge, offering the astonishing, unforgettable sight of containers filled with weapons parachuted in from England. We opened them with great respect: Sten guns, imposing Bren guns with their curved box-magazines, grenades with their pins and their safety-catches that, when armed, would explode in bursts of shards, the Colt automatic pistols, and Gammon Bombs in the shape of huge black pears designed for blowing up bridges or armoured vehicles. All these were carefully laid out on tarpaulins. But I'm forgetting the most important thing: grease. All of these implements of death gleamed with a thick protective coating of gold or green grease, proof that they were brand new, a coating that had to be cleaned off before they could be used. Our group was allocated only a small part of this arsenal, the remainder was stored away in caches in the castle until the – imminent, we were told – general mobilization heading for La Margeride, where they would be distributed to other units.

The morning after this historic day, one of my men, who had been posted on sentry duty at the castle gate, which opened on to the rarely used secondary road to Saint-Beauzire, came rushing up, panting for breath, to say there were two men asking for me at the gate, which he had left locked. He seemed worried, so I went up to the far end of the castle grounds along the path leading to the gate and caught a glimpse of the messengers before going to meet them, I on one side of the iron gate, they on the other, and we talked. Or rather, they talked. They were thick-set men, two blocks of stone with the characteristic faces of Communists, insensible to doubt, hardened by conviction: 'Comrade, we have come to give you orders from the Party, we know the shipment of weapons has arrived. You are to grab as many as you can, load them onto trucks, and you and your group are to go to the FTP *maquis* of Commandant Raffy at La Chaise-Dieu. You must act tonight or tomorrow at the latest, as soon as you possibly can; the weapons will not be here for long.' I listened, petrified, unable to believe what I was hearing: this was a clear breach of an agreement, a contract, a pact. I tried to argue, 'That's not what I was told at Clermont-Ferrand, when the Party approved my actions and congratulated me. There was never any question of breaking my undertaking with my father.' 'The situation has changed, comrade, the struggle has entered a new phase. The Party knows what it is doing and you must obey the Party's orders.' This, I pointed out, would be difficult if not impossible to carry out, the vicomte and his men were always around, the weapons had already been stowed somewhere in the castle cellars, I knew not where. Although my men had been trained in physical endurance, they had had no military training, they didn't know how to use a gun and there was no way we could get our hands on the weapons and leave the castle grounds without a fight; there would be losses. I added that it seemed to me extraordinarily risky to try to make the journey from Chabreuges to La Chaise-Dieu in trucks loaded with weapons, across sixty kilometres of difficult mountain roads, with German contingents stationed in Brioude and in many of the other small villages we would have to drive through. They replied that the Party would put guides at our disposal to lead us to the *maquis* of Raffy, the hero of the *Francs-tireurs et partisans*. My only thought was to buy time. To persuade the men to leave, I told them I would have to think about it and that I would do what I could. There was something obdurate, something threatening in their eyes, in their stillness. They went away.

I had not the least intention of complying with their orders. I was sickened by the thought of betraying my father, the very idea of putting him in such a position horrified me. I didn't waver for a second: I told him that very day so that every possible measure could be taken to safeguard the weapons. He informed the vicomte, and for a time the castle became a fortress. I also decided to inform the Blaise-Pascal *Jeunesses communistes*, and I told them, 'I believe that what the Party is asking me to do is an abuse of power, an act of treachery. It would not only mean tearing up the agreement made with the MUR as an organization, it would also mean deceiving my own father and placing him in serious danger. I have no intention of complying with the order and will keep to my part of the original agreement. Any of you who wish to can leave, but you do so at your own risk, on foot and with no weapons.' They discussed the matter for a long time, but I withdrew and took no part in the conversation. In the end, half of them left, some heading for La Chaise-Dieu, others returning to Clermont-Ferrand; the remainder stood by me. My father was even more astonished than I was by the cold cynicism of the Party. Like Albert Camus, who condemned the blind terrorism of which his mother might have been a victim during the war in Algeria, saying, 'I believe in justice, but I will defend my mother before justice', I too instinctively chose my loyalty to my father over my loyalty to the Party, which refused to keep its word. Some days later, I was informed that the PCF had pronounced my death sentence and the Michelin factory killers had been charged with carrying out the order. This was a threat I could not but take very seriously and the risk grew greater with every day that passed before moving up to the *maquis*. For me, the *maquis* would not simply be a place from which to launch attacks on the Germans, it would be a refuge from my executioners. Thus, with mounting impatience, I waited for the signal to depart.

I was already familiar with La Margeride, a vast massif rising to 1,500 metres on the borders of the departments of Haute-Loire, Cantal and Lozère, all three conducive to raids and ambushes and extending westward into the lush desert of Aubrac. I knew the area because the previous autumn – less than a year earlier – I had been appointed 'threshing supervisor' for the Saugues region, by the Ministry or the prefecture, I don't remember which. I had passed my philosophy *baccalauréat* at Puy-en-Verlay in June. Propaganda for the STO (the Compulsory Work Service in Germany) was in full spate and being appointed threshing supervisor – a post offered only to those who passed their *baccalauréat* with distinction – meant that a call-up from the STO could be deferred. In fact, one of the reasons my father had sent me to board at Blaise-Pascal was to keep me out of the STO. One of my closest friends from school, Armand Monnier (whose father was a steam-engine driver at Langeac depot and the spitting image of Julien Carette in Renoir's *La Bête humaine*), had also been appointed threshing supervisor in the neighbouring village.

Officially, we were agents of the regime and it was our responsibility to ensure that farmers did not divert grain that had been requisitioned by the Germans. The threshing machine was set up for several days in each village and farmers brought their sheaves of grain. We had been given special ledgers and were supposed to monitor the whole process, noting how many sheaves each farmer brought and how much grain he was entitled to take away. We did not exactly get a warm welcome from the farmers at first. The mayor of each village would arrange for us a room or a garret where we could sleep and saw to it that we were fed. However, Monnier and I immediately put at their ease the people under our control: 'It's up to you – you give us whatever figures you want us to write down, we have no intention of checking anything.' After that, everything went smoothly. Monnier and I feasted, we roamed the hills under cloudless skies, basked in the sun, learned poetry by heart, recited it, noodled or tickled for fish in the deep pools of the teeming rivers of the Auvergne. It was for me a glorious end-of-holiday. I was already enrolled in the *Jeunesses communistes*, Clermont-Ferrand was ahead of me, and meanwhile the grateful farmers loaded provisions on us: exquisite *saucissons*, sausages, tripe, ham, butter, eggs, and more. We made the long journey down from Saugues to Langeac, Langeac to Brioude on our bicycles, freewheeling as fast as we could, knapsacks stuffed with infinitely precious goods, roaring *La Légende des siècles* [*The Legend of the Ages*] or 'Le Bateau ivre' ['The Drunken Boat'] at the tops of our lungs. I was by now a past-master at breaking the rules: early in 1941, the Minister for Education of the Vichy government had come up with the splendid idea of requiring pupils in every school and lycée to write an essay in praise of the Maréchal. The Collège Lafayette was no exception. Unaware of the risk I was running, I sat, arms folded, for the whole period allocated for the essay, then ostentatiously handed in a blank sheet. The headmaster was a good man; he summoned me the following day, along with my father. 'I am compelled to take disciplinary action against you,' he said. 'You must now leave the school, but I'll find some way of having you readmitted. Don't say a word about this, it must be just between ourselves.' He was as good as his word, and within a month I was back at my desk.

The mass mobilization of 6,000 men into the Margeride highlands – to posts on Mont Mouchet, Venteuges, Chamblard, La Truyère, Le Plomb du Cantal – began around 15 May 1944, right under the noses of the Germans and the *Milice* who were on red alert, and was no simple matter. We had left the château and were scattered in various billets to wait, which made it easier for us to muster and load into trucks. We were dispersed among the huts in the vineyards overlooking the Brioude–Vieille-Brioude road; the trucks were supposed to pick us up at nightfall and take us towards the foothills of the massif via Vieille-Brioude, Saint-Ilpize and Lavoûte-Chilhac, following the twists and the hairpin bends of the Allier Valley. I was waiting with my group when I received the order to go back to my father's house in town, to help move some equipment. There I found my father, ready to set off and very busy, finishing loading a huge bicycle-trailer crammed with munitions and grenades covered by clothes and other innocuous-looking objects, which was to be taken to the hut from where I had just come. A man of about thirty called Bagelman was there, I'd seen him before, he was obviously Jewish, the personification of gentleness and non-violence, sheer terror etched on his face. I don't know what prompted my father to make such a foolish decision, whether it was Bagelman's age or his determination to protect me at all costs, but whatever the reason it was to Bagelman, not to me, that he entrusted the loaded revolver that was meant to keep us safe or to help us escape if anything were to happen. We would have to double back all the way through Brioude, which was spread across several kilometres, making it extremely dangerous. Bagelman slipped the revolver, like a wallet, into the inside pocket of his jacket. We set off; I feared the worst.

Everything went without a hitch until we were about a hundred metres from the edge of town, when suddenly a sort of gnome wearing a hat appeared, very agitated, leaping around us as though surrounded on all sides by enemies. '*Milice!*' he shouted. 'Hands up!' He pulled an automatic pistol from the holster on his hip and screamed, 'Where are you going? What have you got there?' and started pulling at the tarpaulin on the trailer and rummaging around, all the while waving his gun in the air. Now was the moment to kill him, the only moment; to kill him on the spot was the only way out. If we did not, we were doomed. Bagelman was literally green with fright, paralysed, incapable of taking action. I cursed my father for giving him the gun. Twice I kicked him in the shins and whispered, 'Do it! Do it!' But he stubbornly kept his hands in the air; I had lowered mine, ready to run when the *milicien* discovered the grenades. He hurled himself at me, jabbed his gun into my belly, shouting, 'Get your hands up!' as he frisked Bagelman with his free hand, taking the revolver. We could already see the plane trees on the Vielle-Brioude road, but he forced us to turn round and go back, the two of us in front pushing the trailer, him in the rear threatening us with his pistol and the revolver. He was yelling, trying to alert the other *miliciens* whom he knew must be close by: it was a good arrest, he was proud of himself, he wanted to show off. My father – this was my last hope, and it came true – suddenly appeared on a bicycle around the corner of the last street and, realizing immediately what was happening, dropped the bicycle, drew the Colt .45 he loved so much – and which I still have – and began to fire. Everything happened quickly. The stupefied *milicien* ducked behind a plane tree and fired back, missing my father and missing Bagelman, who ran off into the vineyards shitting his pants. I dodged from behind one plane tree to the next, trying to get to my father. The firing continued until the *milicien*, discouraged, retreated. By this time it was dark and we managed to recover the trailer and its contents. Had my father not arrived we would either have been executed on the spot, tortured and then killed, or deported to a concentration camp. In fact, the centre of Brioude was burned to the ground by the Nazis only a few weeks later, and many of those captured were lined up and shot, while others were sent to the camps. I saw Bagelman once after the war. He had dropped the 'man' from his name and was calling himself Bagel, but this did not expunge his criminal lack of courage, his inability to act and save our lives, the responsibility with which he had been formally entrusted. He tried to strike up a conversation; I couldn't bring myself to utter a single word. I have never been able to forgive him.

At dawn on 6 June 1944, I was at Venteuges – or maybe Chamblard, I don't remember – in a trench where I had spent the night manning a Bren gun. We were waiting for the Germans, who in recent days had launched a number of attacks using tanks, artillery and even air cover, sustaining heavy losses in spite of their overwhelming superiority in weaponry, manpower and experience. My brother Jacques, who had joined us, was in a trench in the second line. Towards five o'clock, Papa came over to me, clearly in high spirits and said, 'The Allies are landing in Normandy right now.' After the Normandy landings, all German troops in southern France received orders to begin marching to Normandy by any means necessary – which meant making a breach through the 'liberated territory' of La Margeride. On 10 June, they launched a three-pronged attack from the west, north and east and, after savage fighting, were forced to retreat. The following day, they attacked again, this time with considerable reinforcements, and my company was told to fall back before we could fight. The journey back to Saint-Beauzire, the designated rallying point, through Monistrol-d'Allier, mostly on foot with a few short kilometres by train, was an odyssey. There was further battle on 20 June in the enclave of La Truyère, but the battle at La Margeride was over, the consequences less tragic than at Vercors, though, as there, villages had been destroyed, villagers shot in reprisals at Ruynes-en-Margeride, at Clavières, at Pinols, at Auvers, hostages killed in cold blood like those on the Soubizergues bridge, just outside Saint-Flour. In the retreat, it was every man for himself. I remember two skinny Corsican boys, the Leandri brothers, who were scared of nothing and had impressed me with the flick-knives they had brought from their *Île de Beauté*. The companies that had fought at La Margeride had fractured into twenty or so autonomous guerrilla units, forced to be self-sufficient through the rest of June and all of July, raiding *bureaux de tabac*, threatening farmers at gunpoint and forcing them to hand over food in exchange for receipts that were of no value whatsoever now. From our base at Saint-Beauzire we laid crude ambushes for SS units, which, being attacked on all sides, turned in circles around the treacherous roads of the Auvergne. It's true that we did not have the luxury of thinking out and planning these traps as we should have because we had very little advance warning of the enemy's arrival – in fact, they sometimes appeared unexpectedly. We worked in small, informal elective groups with no real leader. Some of the ambushes went against the nature of true guerrilla actions: harry the enemy, then withdraw before they have time to react – the Germans, professional soldiers, were incredibly swift, after their initial losses taking up positions from which they could spray us with machine-gun fire and mortars – and always protect the rear, or fall back. I remember a hastily organized ambush on a level stretch of the Limagne plain: we lay, barely camouflaged, in the ditches along Route Nationale 102, without so much as a hillock behind which we might shelter, armed only with submachine guns and grenades, waiting for a convoy that appeared prepared for all eventualities, with outriders up front, a calculated distance between the vehicles. At the last minute, our sense of our weakness and amateurishness prevailed; lying flat against the ground, praying we would not be spotted, we watched the long German convoy drive slowly past. On the way back, some of the group vented their anger by throwing grenades into the rivers as we walked: only fish died that day.

After the La Margeride units had scattered, my father was called away, so he was no longer with us. One fine day my brother disappeared, and we would not see him again until much later, after he had survived incredible life-threatening experiences that he has related in a number of his books. In mid-July, I and a handful of survivors from Blaise-Pascal decided to go up into the hills of Cantal, between Aurrilac and Saint-Flour, to meet up with those whom Marcovici had poached. This *maquis* was run by the *Armée secrète*, but that didn't matter, there had been many favourable reports about their organizational skills and their command. After three days' uninterrupted march, we eventually found them high up in the mountains. The reunion, for both sides, was warm and friendly. We all lived together in *burons* – stone shepherds' huts – high in the mountains equipped with racks for maturing rounds of Cantal. We gorged ourselves on this delicious cheese, which, together with steaks from freshly killed dairy cows, was the only food we had: over time this diet led to spectacular outbreaks of boils that were incurable until the Americans arrived bringing penicillin. Later, I almost died of an anthrax infection inside my nostrils, my face was completely deformed, bloated to twice its usual size. I was only saved when it was decided to inject massive doses of antibiotics directly into my nose.

Finally, the day came when we pulled off a genuine, textbook, meticulously planned ambush. It is the one I remember best: I have, as you will see, good reasons never to have forgotten it. As soon as dusk fell, we trekked down the slopes of the mountain to take up positions overlooking the winding curves of the Aurillac–Saint-Flour road. A major *Wehrmacht* convoy some two kilometres long, comprising several thousand men, was due to leave Aurillac at dawn and make its way through the Lioran tunnel. We would be waiting for them by the entrance, at a spot known as Pas de Compaing, perfectly chosen since at that point the rising road – almost a gorge – would considerably slow the vehicles. Several carefully spaced positions were set up from which we could fire on the German trucks either from in front or from behind. I have forgotten how many posts there were, but I remember that mine was the last. There were two of us manning a Bren gun; my companion, someone I had never met before moving up to the *burons*, was a man of about thirty-five who wore a beret and

106

never said a word. He had had experience under fire, having served in 1939–40, and he was to man the Bren gun, my job that day being to feed it, ejecting the empty magazine and quickly screwing in a full one so that he could continue to fire almost uninterruptedly. The ambush was perfect, methodically thought out; we would inflict losses on the enemy. Throughout the night, infantrymen moved from one post to the next issuing orders: we were not to shoot until the first position opened fire; until then we were to allow the German trucks to drive past unmolested, even if it felt as though we were letting them get away. These orders were scrupulously observed and everything played out as envisaged. Unfortunately, the span of the ambush positions was much shorter than that of the German convoy!

What a thrill! We heard them long before we saw them. The first truck slowly came into view around a bend like an apparition and we had time to study it: the tarpaulin was down, there were four benches with soldiers in helmets sitting facing each other, the butts of their rifles on the floor held between their knees. Then came the second truck, the third, and another; all the while my companion, eye glued to the backsight adjuster, tracked the convoy with the barrel of the Bren gun; his excitement as each new vehicle appeared was so intense that I thought he might disobey orders and begin firing. In front of me, I had a haversack stuffed with magazine cartridges. Then, all of a sudden, from up ahead came the loud, deep roar of a Gammon grenade exploding over the first truck, stopping it dead, followed by similar explosions and by furious, deafening bursts of fire from the battery of machine guns at the various posts. My marksman, until now so calm, so taciturn, suddenly revealed himself to be a very different man: firing relentlessly as I fed the gun as quickly as he fired, he screamed, 'Take that, you fucker! That's for Papa! And that's for Papa!' His father, I later learned, had been killed in 1914: this was his vengeance. Many of the Germans were lying dead in the trucks or on the road, while others, with a calm that attested to unfailing courage and training, had hurtled down the ravine and were already climbing up the other side, from where they began to return fire with unerring accuracy. They were not alone: the whole back section of the convoy, which had not been involved in the ambush, sprang into action, scaling the slopes of the mountain and setting up machine guns and mortars.

The order to fall back, as always in such circumstances, came too late and my marksman, who thought he was there for eternity, was too keyed up to pull back even after the order was screamed at us. Carrying our weapons, we breathlessly climbed the steep hillside as bullets whistled and mortars exploded all around us, some of our numbers falling as they ran. We reached the first ridge, about one hundred metres above the road, and set up our machine gun again. But two bodies lay below us on the slope. One of those in the shelter of the ridge above – his name was Schuster – shouted, 'That's Rouchon!' and rushed down to help him. He too was mown down after only a few metres. A third man, Lheritier, leapt to his feet, only to be shot where he stood. The whole hillside was a lethal hornet's nest. I should have gone myself, I hesitated for a second, for a second too long. I was fond of Rouchon, he had been in my philosophy class at Blaise-Pascal, a boarder like me, we had shared a prep room. His mother always sent him brioches and clafoutis from Riom, which he kept in his locker and shared with us. He was heavy-set and a little chubby, with the smile of a cherub; we called him Gaz, because the cakes his mother sent were too rich for him and gave him wind. I should have tried to help him. There was no way I could have succeeded and come out alive, but I should have tried, I should have rushed to him without thinking, like Schuster and Lheritier. I have blamed myself my whole life for not doing so. Was it cowardice? Perhaps. But it was not of the same scale or the same kind as that of Bagelman. I would have killed the *milicien* – of that I am certain.

The German gunfire continued to swell, heavy artillery and long-range guns joined the fray and other machine-gun posts began to sweep the hillside behind the ridge where we had taken shelter.

We had to change tactics, switching from a guerrilla ambush to a pitched battle for which we were neither prepared nor armed. The retreat was a mad and dangerous escapade that lasted the whole day and night, as we tore up and down steep slopes, constantly afraid of being followed or even surrounded by the Germans. We were forced to leave our dead on the battlefield, but we took turns carrying the wounded on makeshift stretchers. I remember one stop in the middle of the night, deep in the valley, near a cool river. We were hungry and had nothing to eat save for a little Cantal and we slaked our thirst – made all the more keen by the cheese – by plunging our faces into the small waterfall to drink. One of the wounded – his name was Faubert – asked for something to drink and the medical student with the company agreed that we could give him water. Then Faubert, who had been shot in the stomach, said, 'I thought you weren't allowed to drink if you got a bullet in the stomach.' The medical student shrugged his shoulders and said, 'Of course you can, it's fine.' At that moment Faubert realized that he was doomed. He died that night. At first light we came within sight of Salers, completely shattered, having walked for twenty-four hours and covered sixty kilometres of mountainous terrain. You only have to look at a map to imagine the extreme difficulties we faced. We collapsed almost where we stood in deserted stables with no hay or straw, without even thinking about eating or drinking, and slept until evening. Exhaustion won out over everything.

I don't know how, a week later, on 14 August 1944 (the first ambush took place on 7 August) we found ourselves in the same place, but on the opposite slope, waiting for another German convoy that was also coming from Aurillac. We were probably driven there in trucks taking tortuous routes on secondary roads. But the situation was radically different: the Germans had learned their lesson from our previous ambush. Before allowing the vehicles to move forward, they now meticulously cleared the slopes to the left and the right of the road, attacking before they were attacked, making it impossible for us to do so, deploying small, battle-hardened units equipped with heavy machine guns, mortars and even tractor-drawn heavy artillery in the hills. On our side, things had changed too: the man who had until then been in command of our group, a man respected and loved by his men, had been dismissed from his post ('transferred', we were told, although in fact it was a punishment inflicted on him for some obscure reason) and replaced by someone whom none of us knew, imposed on us from on high, even though the very existence and the fighting conditions of the *maquisards* demanded a spirit of brotherhood between leaders and combatants. We quickly realized that an ambush like the one of 7 August would be impossible. It was a glorious summer day when we received orders to set up a post on a hill overlooking the village of Saint-Jacques-des-Blats, about five kilometres from the western entrance to the tunnel from where, with the naked eye, we could see the Germans calmly watching us through binoculars, unpacking their weaponry, sending out detachments along the hillside in what looked very like a flanking manoeuvre. The enemy seemed to have, and to be taking, all the time in the world. Our new leader was a tall guy with a crew-cut; he stood with rocklike stillness, clearly determined to impress us with his impassivity. What little we knew about him did not make us well disposed towards him: he came from a movement called *Jeunesse et Montagne*, founded after the defeat in 1940 by a regiment of *Chasseurs alpins* – the élite French mountain infantry – and a handful of aviators, its aim to revitalize the country through a combination of pure mountain air, farming and physical labour. Headquartered and with an entire bureaucracy in Vichy, very similar to Maréchal Petain's *Chantiers de la jeunesse française*, its motto was '*Faire face*', which meant endure with a steadfast soul, submit to fate without in any way involving the spirit of resistance. They didn't join forces with the *maquisards* until very late, infiltrating our ranks by virtue of their past and their military training. What I had been expecting since the beginning finally occurred: the Germans, tired of being taken as harmless tourists, began shelling us with mortars of incredible precision along with bursts of machine-gun fire that seemed to come from all points of the compass. They were clearly determined to flush us out and it was futile for us to remain as we had neither the means to meet them head on, nor to attack them. Our comrade from *Jeunesse et Montagne*, however, did not see things our way. He 'faced' head on the machine-gun fire and mortar attack; his large frame did not tremble and the bullets saluted his stoic endurance by avoiding him while the fear of dying stupidly, pointlessly, began to spread through the veterans of the Resistance, of whom I was one. Twenty metres from the rocky outcrop where our leader hoped to earn his stripes, admiration and a career, was a section of rock that could shelter us from the hellish machine-gun fire. Without a word, we all took cover. *Jeunesse et Montagne* had no choice but to join us, barking 'desertion of duty in the face of the enemy' and other nonsense, but he was forced to lead us on a long retreat over hills and through forests beneath bombs dropped from a determined and effective German plane that wounded several of our men, until we reached a safe haven; never had sky and nature, the murmur of mountain streams, seemed as precious to me as at that moment.

By the end of August 1944 all of the Auvergne had been liberated. My father entered Brioude at the head of two columns of *maquisards*. Even now I cannot look at the photo of him taken that day without being moved: he was forty-four years old. As I have said, before they retreated, the Germans burned all the buildings around the small town's main square, shot a number of prisoners and took others with them to be deported to a concentration camp. Not all of them returned.

The purge was brutal, equal to everything that had been suffered during the four years of the Occupation: special tribunals, courts-martial hastily convened in the fields followed by swift summary execution. Onlookers jostled, eager to see the executions. I was present at one of them where the condemned man was a young bourgeois of no more than twenty-five, who had signed up with the *Milice* following an extreme right-wing family tradition; he pleaded, he begged, he did not want to die. The executioner – I've forgotten his name, but his feverish eyes, his hollow cheeks, his scrawny frame and the formidable swiftness of his movements are still imprinted on my memory – grabbed him suddenly by the earlobe, dragged him quickly for some twenty metres, stepped back to look at him and shot him down in a vertical spray of machine-gun fire that stitched him with blood from groin to face. The feverish executioner had a great reputation, he was often called upon, sometimes travelling considerable distances.

The *maquisards* of the Auvergne were soon integrated into the *Forces françaises de l'intérieur*, under the command of Général de Lattre de Tassigny. My brother reappeared, having escaped a German firing squad in Provence – he has told his story. By train or on foot, we were sent north-eastward and stationed in a tiny village on the borders of Burgundy that bears the pretty name of Perrigny-sur-l'Ognon. It was at Perrigny that I encountered my first US military truck, driven by a huge, smiling black man who had me climb aboard, offering me a pack of opium-laced Camel cigarettes as he drove like a madman through the lashing rain of a September night. I don't remember whether I had smoked before, but it was the first time I had tried American cigarettes and I chain-smoked uncontrollably. I indicated to the driver that he should drop me at the next village, then sought shelter in the only café that was still open. I drank wine, then went out into the now pouring rain; I didn't feel anything. A Military Police patrol found me the next morning lying half-drowned in an overflowing gutter. The Americans dazzled us with the beauty and variety of their weaponry, by the endless parade of tanks, the number and the rich palette of their vehicles as they drove towards Belfort and the front line. We went too, though we were third-tier soldiers, since the Free French of the First Army were much better equipped and the assimilation of the ex-*maquisards* was far from perfect.

At Belfort, we were told that we would only be truly integrated if we signed up for the duration of the war, including the war with Japan. This was in November and we were given two weeks to decide. In the meantime, we were entitled to a furlough. Jacques and I leapt at the chance and teamed up with some twenty others who had decided to go up to Paris. We were carrying Soviet rifles stamped with the hammer and sickle, taken from Ukrainian mercenaries in the Vlasov army who had gone over to the enemy side – that is, to the Germans – with bag and baggage, in so doing providing the enemy with the largest contingent of guards for the death camps in Poland. We reached Paris, packed tightly together on the platform of an open truck, shivering beneath our greatcoats; one of the group managed, while cleaning his revolver, to put a bullet in his thigh. Paris, at last. By now, my mother and Monny were living in a little flat near the École militaire. My brother and I showed up unannounced, Paulette-Pauline opened the door and almost keeled over from shock before dissolving into floods of tears. I knew that, for us, the war was over.

Chapter 7

For Jacques and me, this two-week furlough in Paris before returning to our unit to announce that, no, we would definitely not be signing up until the end of the war was like discovering a new world. Every minute brought with it fun, festivity or some surprise. Paris had been liberated for barely three months and adjusting to this new-found liberty did not come easily. My mother paled at the sound of a police car siren and it was difficult for me to understand that it was going to take her some time to adjust to all these 'returns': of her sons become men, of peace, the advent of a new life both private and public, where everything would have to be reinvented from the *tabula rasa* of the Occupation. Paulette's first pronouncement was that she could not bear to see us in our badly cut military greatcoats: we needed new clothes. The day after we arrived, Monny was given the task of taking us to Paquito San Miguel, a celebrated tailor on the place Saint-Augustin to whom he had sold some rare first editions the previous year. My mother did not think it excessive that her sons, not yet twenty, should have tailor-made suits, expensive despite the special price offered by Paquito, a charming, vivacious Spaniard, who was clearly dazzled by Monny and of whom he seemed to be fond. Thus Paulette took it upon herself to demob us: how could we go back to war after we had seen ourselves, dressed to the nines like Spanish *infantes*, reflected in the vast mirrors of Paquito's showrooms?

Yet back we went, in our old greatcoats, if only to inform the authorities that we were becoming civilians, that our mother could not bear the idea of being separated from us again and had insisted that I go back to my studies. The Battle of Belfort was about to start, but I was impatient to be done with it all. Paris was calling.

I discovered everything all at once: Monny's extraordinary eloquence, his brio, his verve, the surrealistic genius that animated his language and his relationships with people, his generosity towards us, boundless as the love he bore my mother. He might have considered our presence in that little two-room apartment on the rue Alexandre-Cabanel, crammed with books, paintings and precious things, to be the insufferable incursion of a past in which he had no part, forcing him to take on a heavy burden, a responsibility others would have rejected, evaded or begrudgingly accepted. Monny did none of these things, the thought never occurred to him, Paulette's children were his now, and he would do anything for us. In addition to love, intelligence was what cemented this miraculous harmony, freedom too, and the understanding that beyond these cardinal virtues there would be no taboos either of behaviour or in what was said.

Paulette had not yet adjusted and was determined to examine her offspring closely, oblivious to our prudishness as young men, hurling herself into a diffident and desperate search of lost time: all those years in which she had not been able to bathe her children, as mothers do, had to be made good. I can still see us that first week in Paris, Monny, Jacques and me, naked as the day we were born, lined up outside the bathroom as though for a recruiting board. We entered in turn: she officiated, washing and soaping us from head to foot, grooming us, currying us and rubbing us down, inspecting us from every angle, her lip curled at the sight of a stooped shoulder, one testicle higher than the other. 'You get that from *le père* Lanzmann,' she grumbled. '*Le père* Lanzmann' clearly being her unforgivable sodomite of a husband. But our relationship could be as stormy as it was miraculous. Our mother took it upon herself to drag us to a fashionable hair salon, insisting on being present while we had our hair cut, imposing her increasingly stuttering views on the hairdresser, treating us like ten-year-olds to the astonishment of the other clients, mercilessly crushing our vanity, the image we had of ourselves, the one we wanted to project. I was reliving the dark hours we had spent together in Chaussures André but Jacques was the first to crack, grabbing a pair of scissors, brandishing it, gesturing as though to stab her in the back. He stopped himself, but she sensed the blade and started rolling her mad eyes. I seized the weapon from him, made a throat-cutting gesture and shouted to my brother, 'Come on!' and we made a run for it, just as I had the day we had gone shopping for boots. Once again, it took time, and Monny's infinite tact, before we were reconciled.

In January 1945, I was enrolled as a boarder at the Lycée Louis-le-Grand, in *Lettres supérieures*. To be admitted in the middle of the school year, having missed a whole term, was an achievement: Monny had interceded on my behalf with his friend Ferdinand Alquié, who had taken part with him in the great battles of surrealism and who now held the chair of philosophy teaching *khâgne* students, those preparing for the École normale supérieure. He had argued that I had just left the Resistance, the *maquis*, the war and that at Blaise-Pascal I had been an *hypokhâgne* student whose school year, though not completed, was more than equivalent to a single term at Louis-le-Grand. At the lycée, there were two classes of *Lettres supérieures* and two of *Première supérieur*, known as K1 and K2. The study and work rooms were shared by all the boarders for both classes. The night I arrived a spontaneous meeting was held to protest against the trial of Robert Brasillach, which was due to start any day now. To my astonishment, the majority of the senior pupils at Louis-le-Grand, followed, sheep-like, by most of the juniors, proposed naming one of our study halls after Brasillach – the K1 hall, which, as it happened, was mine. The fact that Brasillach, a former pupil of Louis-le-Grand, had sat at the very desks where we now sat, completely eclipsed the appalling calls to murder Jews uttered by this collaborationist writer in *Je suis partout* and various rags in thrall to the Nazis. This, it seemed, counted for nothing, it didn't matter, and I immediately realized with a disgust that I have perhaps never entirely lost, that the great ship France had continued on its way, insensible to the catastrophe of others, the destruction of millions of lives, of a whole world.

That was my first day, I knew no one, I was anxious, intimidated, I could not understand this praise heaped on Brasillach, absolving him of the worst, and I did not dare disagree with this crowd of bourgeois boys whose every pore, every look, every breath oozed authority. The war had passed them by; they had suffered little because of it. France had continued to 'function' and they with it. This was what mattered. Then, suddenly, a voice arose: laconic yet lyrical, its Midi accent modulated by a precision of speech and an expressiveness of gesture determined to persuade – gestures of prayer, in fact – imposing silence, demanding to be heard and in so doing, setting mine free. The voice was that of Jean Cau: I can see him still, lean as a wolf in his black student's dress, his high cheekbones, his sunken cheeks, his wolf-like nostrils, his jug ears. Together we began not to argue or debate, but to defy and insult and very quickly to lash out, throwing anything that came to hand. Several boys were injured, and a stinking, blood-spattered giant, who shall remain nameless, punched me full in the face. Alerted by the ruckus, the *surveillant général*, a short man by the name of Louvet whose life we would later make difficult, flung open the door. We told him that this *khâgne* was a pack of traitors and that if the study hall was renamed 'Brasillach', we would lodge a complaint and have the ringleaders hauled into court.

Brasillach's trial took place on 19 January. As expected, he was condemned to death and, in spite of pleas by celebrated intellectuals, executed by firing squad on 6 February at the Fort de Montrouge. No room at Louis-le-Grand ever bore his name. But, on the subject of his death, de Gaulle wrote something magnificent, something I did not know when I was drafting the first chapter of this book; something that I dare to say – without, I hope, being too shocking – deeply binds the General and me. To a reporter who had criticized him for not granting Brasillach a pardon, Général de Gaulle movingly confided:

Robert Brasillach was, indeed, the only writer guilty of treason, of those who did not actively serve the enemy, for whom I deviated from the principles I had set down for myself: I did not commute his sentence. If he was executed on that chill, sad, misty morning of 6 February 1945, in spite of pleas from the worthiest of his contemporaries, it is that I considered I owed *him* to France. It cannot be explained. In literature too talent confers responsibility and I felt obliged to reject this appeal, perhaps, after all, because it appeared to me that Brasillach had completely lost his way [. . .] *If I remember that particular morning so well, on the last night of every man I could pardon, I did not sleep. In my own way, I had to go with him.* [my italics]

And so the General did not sleep any more than I did on the night before a capital execution, and so, when I wrote earlier: 'Mauriac understood that one did not wake de Gaulle and that, besides, it would have made no difference', only the second part of that sentence was true: there would have been no need to wake de Gaulle since he was not asleep. If one tallied – and it would be possible – the number of pardons he refused to grant, one could calculate the minimum number of his sleepless nights.

It is hardly surprising that Jean Cau became my closest friend. Although he was in K2 and I was in K1, we were inseparable: we slept in the same dormitory, our beds next to each other. The son of a railwayman from Carcassonne and a mother who worked as a cleaner, Cau knew no one in Paris, and since all of the boarders needed a 'guardian' in order to be granted weekend leave on Saturday and Sunday – we had to be back by seven o'clock on Sunday – my mother naturally became his guardian. She had furnished a *chambre de bonne* for me on the sixth floor of her building on the rue Alexandre-Cabanel, and since Cau did not have a penny to his name, I offered him my meagre hospitality: one of us slept in the bed, the other on the floor on a mattress provided for the purpose, alternating each weekend. Paulette took to Cau right away and he returned the favour with a radical act of naming, having a habit of giving nicknames to everyone. My mother became 'the Mother', a generic creature, Alma Mater, not simply mine but that of all of my friends, the boys from the provinces who came to study at Louis-le-Grand in September 1946, whom she loved like sons, differently and perhaps even more than she did her real sons since, as we have seen, her relationship with us was less than indulgent. Following Cau's example, they all called her 'the Mother', never feeling threatened by her, never suffering from her Jewish nose or her stammer, sensitive instead to her extraordinary curiosity for life, for their past, their loves, the way she drew all of them out, teasing them to confide in her with astonishing fervour. She fascinated them by her keen intelligence, flushing out compromise, pretence and self-deception; by her culture, deepened every night as she read until dawn, the book propped between Monny's shoulder blades, which served as a book-rest; her humour, her vitality. As often as not she greeted them wearing a dressing gown, moving about the apartment with the agility and speed of a tiger. Never, in Carcassonne, in Luçon, in Mâcon, in their home towns, had René Guyonnet or Maurice Bouvet, whose father had been shot by the *Milice* in front of him, had the opportunity of meeting a 'mother' of such calibre. Every one of them remained faithful to her; their relationships with her proved indestructible long after their ties to me had weakened.

In the study halls every boarder had a locker. Cau's locker soon became a veritable grocery store, with set opening and closing times, operated under the noses of the *surveillants*. Paris was then swarming with American GIs on leave, selling cartons of cigarettes, chocolate, sweets, chewing gum, tinned food, shirts, trousers, jackets and every conceivable uniform. There were particular trading posts; you simply had to know where they were. Cau knew them and the future writer proved to have a real talent as a black marketeer, selling what he bought from the Americans to boarders and day pupils at the lycée, and not just to *khâgneux* but to the *taupins* – the maths students – at prices that made it possible for him to quickly amass a small fortune. He operated with a grim determination, indifferent to what the *talas* (*talas*, in the codified language of the *khâgneux*, meant '*ceux qui vonT-À-LA messe*', 'those who went to mass') thought of him, and he was such a brilliant student and his essays so exceptional that their admiration soon equalled the contempt they felt for his work as a black marketeer. It quickly became clear to me that my best friend did not give a damn whether he passed the entrance exam to get in to the École normale supérieur. He had only two, non-conflicting interests in life: literature and women. This brought us even closer. He wanted to be a writer and, as I will show later, never has a vocation been so determined, proclaimed and so soon realized. We spent every Saturday night in a battle worthy of Corneille between our duties and our desires, between our passion for language and the pursuit of women, something which, in itself, required language of a very different order, the more so as our words had to compensate for our lack of money, our inability to buy a girl dinner or, very often, even a drink. Cau was an indefatigable talker, he had a fine knowledge of the classics and liked to declaim pieces by Valéry or Péguy. I remember one night just before dawn, on the Champs-Élysées near the place de la Concorde, both of us having already walked at least twenty-five kilometres, when he began reciting Péguy in a lyrical voice that delighted in itself, and which was directed at himself rather than at me:

Mother, here lie your sons who fought so hard
Happy those who died for the carnal earth
But only if it be for a just war . . .

He was a dyed-in-the-wool male chauvinist, his favourite writer that first winter we spent hunting was Montherlant, the Montherlant of *Les Jeunes filles* [*Young Women*], *Le Démon du bien* [*The Demon of Good*], *Pitié pour les femmes* [*Pity the Women*], *La Reine morte* [*The Dead Queen*], 'Portugal splayed like a naked woman upon the flank of Spain'. The whole summer that followed our first year at Louis-le-Grand, while I was on holiday in Brioude learning to fly on 'the Beam', I received long, fervent letters from Cau in which he did his utmost to inculcate in me his righteous passion for Henry de Montherlant. So I read Montherlant, I liked some of his books, but I was much less systematic than my friend who invariably went his own way and whose mind was all but impossible to change. Sadly, I lost those letters. Later, I met Montherlant shortly before his suicide, standing upright in his low-ceilinged apartment on the quai Voltaire, hieratic, inwardly watchful, masked by solitude and the prideful knowledge of his forthcoming death, which saddened me when it was announced. But I realize that these last sentences could have applied just as well to Cau himself when, some fifteen years ago, he discovered he had an incurable, terminal disease. He barricaded himself behind the same pride, refused to be seen as diminished, fearing above all else the pity that his illness might evoke. He and Montherlant both dealt with death. Cau and I were on bad terms for a long time, or rather life put us on bad terms, but I remember, while on a plane between Paris and New York, reading his magnificent portrait of Sartre – precise, intelligent, affectionate and hilarious – in his book *Croquis de mémoire* [*Sketches From Memory*], and the first thing I did when I reached my hotel room in Manhattan was to call him to convey my admiration, to tell him my friendship held fast, and that I embraced him. He was, I think, as moved as I was. We met up as soon as I returned to Paris. Our quarrel was over.

But I have gone too fast. Why? I will return to our twenties. The Champs-Élysées was our favourite hunting ground; tirelessly, we walked up and down the 'most beautiful avenue in the world', a well-deserved appelation, as much for its subtle opulence, the style and sophistication of the shops that lined the avenue, as for our reasons for hanging out there. Whenever we went there we were amazed – as though each time were the first – by the majestic sweep connecting the place de la Concorde with the Arc de Triomphe. Nowadays, you can no longer 'see' the Champs-Élysées, blighted as it is by fast-food restaurants, ugly shops and overcrowded pavements that make strolling impossible, the ceaseless roar of the traffic. Back then, there were girls who sauntered down the Champs-Élysées, girls who loitered, alone or in pairs, they were in no hurry, they had time, we could spot them, weigh them up, follow them or walk past, accost them. We had devised a highly democratic system, perfected over the course of our adventures. The principal rule was that we took turns; regardless of the charms or the appeal of the prey we lusted after, only he whose turn it was to take a chance had the right to do so, even if the other's previous attempt had ended in failure. If, for example, it was Cau's turn, I would hang back, following from a respectful distance, yet close enough to read and interpret the signs he made according to a mutually agreed, strictly observed code: scratching his right ear meant 'For pity's sake, keep following us, this is never going to work out'; a hand on his thigh meant 'I'm not sure! Don't leave!'; a clenched fist: 'There's hope, but don't go yet . . .'; left hand raised, fingers splayed: 'Success! I've nailed her! Get on with your life!' This last scenario was rare, but the proportion of conquests, both for him and for me, all things considered, was not insignificant. As I said, we had no money, or so little that we had to compensate with words, words so stunning they would literally stun the object of our desire. Cau and I were past-masters of the art, and yet how often – discovering some hint of stupidity or nullifying vulgarity in a girl we had all but conquered – how often did we abandon her, hoping that the other was still somewhere nearby so we might carry on the wild, interminable conversation that was the warp and weft of our youth?

Just as a lioness teaches her cubs to hunt, so Monny taught my brother and me – Cau sometimes joined the hunting party – the tricks of seduction, the thousand ruses and stratagems all based on the element of surprise created by his dazzling mastery of language and his genuinely surrealistic ability to shock. Sometimes, after dinner on a summer evening, he said to Paulette as she meandered through the apartment, 'I'm taking them out: they need educating.' She gave us her blessing, enfolding us in her beaming smile, and we stamped with joy since Monny, as we well knew, was imaginative and entirely devoid of what people mistakenly call human respect, in other words conformity. So we strolled along the peaceful avenues around the École militaire under street lamps that cast our shadows on the pavement. A tall, beautiful woman of about thirty with a stern face followed by her female companion was about to pass us when suddenly Monny's sepulchral tones stopped her in her tracks, irresistibly so: 'Oh, madame, do not step on my shadow, it is in pain!' Without allowing her to go on her way or regain her composure, Monny took her hand, kissed it ceremoniously and, gesturing to me, said, 'May I introduce my stepson Claude, a brilliant boy, a boarder at the Lycée Louis-le-Grand, who has just come back from the war.' (It was just Monny and me that particular night.) The lady was completely disarmed by this unusual situation: seduction is not generally a family activity. Monny did the talking, I said nothing; he sang my praises, making me an object of desire. We learned that the beautiful woman's name was Élise and that she owned a hairdressing salon with twenty staff in the 16th *arrondissement*. Monny suggested – as he invariably did, he was never unfaithful to my mother – that she come back and have a drink at our place on the rue Alexandre-Cabanel as Paulette would be delighted to meet her. And so it was: Élise, her head in a spin, at once flattered and interrogated by my mother, fell in love with the family as a whole and could not resist the praise heaped on me. She became my mistress the following Saturday: we would meet either in my *chambre de bonne*, which, being terribly bourgeois, excited her immensely, or in a boudoir of the vast apartment on the rue de Longchamp she shared with a husband she no longer loved, whom she despised, in fact, as is often the case when a woman decides to take a lover. The ritual differed according to which room we were in. The *chambre de bonne* did not lend itself to languor, to foreplay; it barely lent itself to talk. The boudoir, on the other hand, was a small but exquisitely appointed room, the walls were hung with drapes, there were comfortable armchairs, deep sofas, a mahogany door that opened on to a bar generously stocked with hard liquor. Since I was studying philosophy, my beautiful *patronne* insisted that I give her lessons. It was imperative, when we met at the rue de Longchamp, to begin with elevated conversation, objections and, on my part, responses designed to win her over. From these lofty heights, Élise elevated herself further, sipping glass after glass of *vieil armagnac* until finally she bowed her blonde head and her pronounced jaw towards my erect penis, nibbling along the length of it through my trousers in an agonizingly pleasurable torment while I – such was our ritual – continued to philosophize. I was not allowed to stop until she suddenly decided to ravish me, opening my trousers and freeing my penis, not bothering to undress herself, her skirt like a corolla concealing the wrongdoing. As she straddled me, she repeated with mounting passion, 'You're so handsome, Claude, so handsome, oh Claude, you're so handsome.' I was unaware that I had been gifted with such great beauty and only much later, in my *chambre de bonne*, did I realize what 'you're so handsome' meant. One morning, after a rough night, just this once I failed to rise to the occasion, and Élise's face, contorted with anger, became hateful as she spat, 'Oh Claude, you're not handsome any more.' So beauty was tumescence and detumescence was non-beauty; such is idealism. I was probably in the same state as Monny when he was being inspected by the Gestapo's fake doctors. I told the story that night over dinner, and for years 'you're so handsome' and 'you're not handsome any more' were common family catchphrases.

To tell the truth, although, as I said earlier, Cau and I were past-masters in the art of using words to seduce, I hate, loathe in fact, with every fibre of my being, the billing and cooing of courtship, a waste of time, conventional clichés, nothing but air. The older I got, the less I went along with it, and these days I head straight, as Husserl might say, for 'the thing itself', *die Sache selbst*, which, as it happens, suits me. This repugnance probably explains my taste for womanly women and my lack of interest in virgins. I don't like to seduce. I understood the reasons for this in October 1943, fifteen months before I met Cau. In the boarders' study hall of the Lycée Blaise-Pascal in Clermont-Ferrand, a student a little older than me, with a high forehead and piercing blue, slightly bulging eyes, hair that was already white, a slight figure and a gentle voice, who moved in a silent glissade rather than a stride, came up to me and presented me with a heavy tome as an offering, telling me, 'You *must* read this.' It was Sartre's *L'Être et le néant* [*Being and Nothingness*], which had just been published. My fellow student's name was Granger – Gilles-Gaston Granger – who, as we know, grew up to be a celebrated epistemological philosopher. Only one other person – later, in our *khâgne* at the Lycée Louis-le-Grand – gave me that same feeling that I was dealing with a born philosopher, and he too was called Gilles: Gilles Deleuze. Filled with fear and trembling, I plunged into *L'Être et le néant*, losing courage as I read the thirty-page introduction, crushed by the pre-reflexive *cogito*, the being of *percipi* and of *percipere*. I would have been put off philosophy for life were it not that the book suddenly became fantastically concrete, luminous, illuminating, in particular the chapter on *mauvais foi* [bad faith].This would later serve me in one of my classes at the University of Berlin, which, as it happens, was about seduction and in which I linked Sartre and Stendhal, *L'Être et le néant* and *Le Rouge et le noir* [*The Red and the Black*]. Sartre spends a whole page on the billing and cooing between a woman who goes on a first date with the man who is courting her. She is profoundly aware that the goal is fornication; Sartre writes, 'but the desire, cruel and naked, would humiliate and horrify her'. Her suitor must show her admiration and respect, must address himself to her *personality*, to her whole freedom, yet at the same time make her feel the passion that her sexual body inspires. She does not want one without the other, admiration and respect must signify desire; sexual desire is acceptable only if it is dressed up in a spirituality that transcends the bonds of earth. 'Now suppose he takes her hand,' Sartre goes on.

> This act of her companion risks changing the situation by calling for an immediate decision. To leave the hand there is to consent in herself to flirt. To take it away is to break that troubled and unstable harmony which gives the hour its charm. The aim is to postpone the moment of decision as long as possible. We know what happens next: the young woman leaves her hand there, but *she does not notice* that she is leaving it [. . .] because it happens that she is, at this moment, all intellect. She draws her companion up to the most lofty regions of sentimental speculation [. . .] And during this time the divorce of the body from the soul is accomplished; the hand rests inert between the warm hands of her companion – neither consenting nor resisting – a thing.

Death to idealism. Even if *L'Être et le néant* is a work of *hard* philosophy, Sartre's example is *soft*, or, to use a phrase of Engels, 'a kindergarten example' when compared to the extreme euphemisms of my nibbling Élise: in Sartre's example, the couple are merely holding hands, in the preliminaries of foreplay. With Élise we were at 'the thing itself', *in medias res*, at the heart of the action, the idealistic poetic licence ('handsome') being the condition itself, a licence to unbridled licentiousness. Bad faith, as we can see, knows neither limits nor boundaries.

Like Cau, Ferdinand Alquié, our philosophy teacher in K1, was from Carcassonne. Like Cau, he had done his best to lose his Languedoc accent, but unlike my friend, who had almost succeeded in doing so, Alquié still retained his accent, inventing a unique combination of word and action: he articulated each word, each syllable, deconstructing his sentences the better to be understood, all the while connecting these delicious, random Occitan pebbles through an extraordinary ballet of hands and arms, combining the graceful arcs of a Sevillian *bailadora* with the angular elbow movements of princely dancers from South-east Asia. To the end of my days I will remember the way in which, during one of his lessons on sexual perversion, opening and closing his incredibly expressive fingers, he married the gesture of strangling a pigeon with the word *jouir* [to have an orgasm], which he rolled around his tongue, drawing out the sound. He was talking to us about a woman (I don't remember whether he was quoting Krafft-Ebing, Freud or André Breton) who could only reach orgasm by strangling a dove. I adored him, we all adored him. He had majored in philosophy in 1931 and was a short, very thin, always elegant man with heavy-lidded, shadowy eyes, and we all knew how fortunate we were, at twenty, to have such a teacher: an impeccable historian of philosophy, a philosopher in his own right, contemptuous of fads, gossip and intrigue; one who, in teaching us seriously without taking himself seriously, taught us to think for ourselves and not to bow to pressure. I liked his wife too, a beautiful, buxom blonde woman from Normandy, taller than he was and full of life. From time to time I liked to imagine him engulfed, like the turtle dove, in the pale, strong, beautiful arms of Denise.

In his youth, when a student, Ferdinand had frequented prostitutes, and liked them, because he was working hard and had no time to court women. He assured us that with each of these women, he had known a sincere form of tenderness, of love, in which both parties retained their freedom and respected the other's. The very opposite of what is said nowadays about sexual slavery. *O tempora, o mores!* In our literature classes or *Première supérieure* classes, our teacher extolled what he called 'abstract love', love abstracted from conjugal hell;

duty, demands, convention and boredom. It was normal that a well-brought-up boy should want to experience the delightful promises of such a tutor. I talked about this with Monny who, in spite of his surrealist austerity, was not shocked.

The result was that, on one of my father's visits to Paris, after dinner at the rue Alexandre-Cabanel – my mother, for once, having graciously agreed to receive the sodomite – I found myself, with my father and my 'stepfather', in the magnificent lobby of one of the most opulent brothels in Paris, Le Sphinx, on the boulevard Edgar-Quinet in the 16th *arrondissement*. The cashier at the establishment – possibly also the *sous-maîtresse* – was the sister of O'dett, one of the most famous pre-war comic singers, who had all of Paris in stitches with his imitations of Hitler, and whom we had known in the Auvergne where he had been forced to flee during the German Occupation. The courtesans of the Sphinx, who moved about between the tables from customer to customer – many of whom had come simply to look – were all, to my eyes, bewitchingly beautiful and O'dett's sister assigned me to a sculptural dark-haired girl who, under the tender gaze of my fathers, both still in the prime of life, led me up the stairs. I was gone for some time, thanks to the praise showered on me by the *sous-maîtresse*. The ensuing dialogue I owe to Monny who, for years, told the story over and over. Since he and my father thought it odd I had been gone such a long time, they asked O'dett's sister in unison, 'What the hell is he up to?' 'Leave him, leave him, *il est heurrrreux*,' she said, rolling her Rs.

Cau went crazy when I told him the story and he was determined to find out for himself what a luxury brothel was like. I pointed out that it was very expensive (my fathers, who had paid for me, had been given a special price) and that neither he nor I had a *sou* to our name. I don't care, he said. We decided not to go to the Sphinx, which was old-fashioned, but to the One-Two-Two or the Chabanais, rival brothels of similar standing. In the end we settled on the One-Two-Two, at 122 rue de Provence, a windowless seven-storey building near the

Galeries Lafayette. I'll pass over the ritual of our entrance: the door was opened just a crack and we were led into a small alcove like a confessional where, hearts hammering, we waited. Unlike the Sphinx, the One-Two-Two had no bar where clients could wait and meet; adopting all the precautions of a psychoanalyst's consulting rooms, secrecy was paramount. For this reason, the great and the good of this world, or, rather, 'the world of yesterday' to borrow the title of Stefan Zweig's devastating book, preferred the One-Two-Two over the Sphinx, knowing that anonymity was guaranteed. After the confessional box, the lift led to the *salon de choix* towards which we were ushered by a small woman dressed in a short black skirt. Fabienne Jamet, the proprietor – not of the 'bawdy house' but of the 'bawdy building' (her husband Marcel had added four floors in the early 1930s) – described the last part of the ritual thus:

Having escorted the client to the main hall, the woman in black disappeared. What man has not fantasized about thirty nubile young girls offered for his pleasure? Well here, suddenly, his fantasy became reality. Imagine a vast circular room, the floor covered with a carpet designed to look like moss, with tall colonnades supporting a canopy in the style of a Greek temple. Between each pair of pillars was a pedestal illuminated by a spotlight, and upon each pedestal, a woman, who might be slim or voluptuous, tall, bejewelled, in evening dress, frozen like a statue, shoulders bare, sometimes with one breast completely exposed. Other young women were seated on the moss, skirts gracefully spread like the petals of a flower. Fabrics in reds, pinks, blues, yellows. Lights. Pale flesh. Bare arms. Radiant make-up. Long legs swathed in silk glimpsed through a slit skirt. Pert breasts. A spectacular *déjeuner sur l'herbe*. The man's palms would begin to sweat, he would grow excited. From behind him, a woman's voice would whisper, 'Has Monsieur made his choice?' A wave of overwhelming desire surged through him. All of them. And then reason prevails. For that he would require the might of Hercules himself. Alas, he is merely a man . . .

'Have the *messieurs* made their choice?' the woman in black whispered to us. We had already twice passed slowly along the line of women-objects who, on our first tour, had gazed at us, smiling, gesturing, enticing, changing their poses, but were now staring at us fixedly with a rebellious glare and an air of freedom. They seemed to harden beneath our silent inspection. Cau's face, a mask of severity, eyes down, his sidelong glances, playing the flesh trader, examining only legs, stomachs, breasts, arses, never venturing above their necks to their faces; my expression, unlike his, was clearly panicked, because I could see only their eyes, I had forgotten the flesh. We made two more passes and finally Cau had the nerve to say listlessly, 'No, I'm afraid it won't do.' Thirty hand-picked beauties whom crowned heads, ambassadors and iron-masters fought to be with, reserved months in advance, were being insulted in their very being by a couple of twenty-year-old jerks. We left with our tails between our legs to a rising crescendo of boos and insults: 'Little fuckers, fairies, queers, losers, cheapskates, pussies, voyeurs, filthy little oglers!' Our problem was not a lack of Herculean strength, but they were right: to pretend to be disgusted, not to make a choice in the *salon de choix* was an unspeakably boorish act, a crime that makes me blush to this day.

Had we waited a week or two, this humiliating escapade might have been avoided: Marthe Richard, a former prostitute from Nancy, a man-eater, the widow of several rich men, aviatrix, compulsive liar, spy, member of the Resistance and friend to the Germans, supported by the serried ranks of the Catholic party, the *Mouvement républicain populaire*, which was very influential at the time, managed to convince the municipality of Paris to close the brothels. The Sphinx, the Chabanais and the One-Two-Two disappeared forever, as did the ordinary knocking shops, whose proprietors immediately rushed to open whole streets of cheap hotels. By this act, Marthe Richard earned herself the nickname '*Veuve qui clôt*', 'the widow who closes' – a pun on *Veuve Clicquot*, coined by Antoine Blondin, a talented somewhat right-wing writer. Prostitution, however, continued to thrive, tirelessly finding new guises, to become the terrible slavery of globalized prostitution. I've just remembered an issue of *Les Temps modernes* from December 1947 that had an article entitled 'A Prostitute's Life'. The prostitute told how she had moved from a brothel for German soldiers billeted in France to a brothel serving American GIs. Germans and Americans alike beat a path to her door, under the watchful eye (so that order could be maintained) of their Military Police: she never left her bed, she explained, never closed her legs, kept them spread for days on end to save time. I remember a conversation with Deleuze, in his mother's apartment on the rue Daubigny. His perceptiveness shone forth in everything he said. He knew how to take a formula entombed in marble and make sense of the whole world: 'Where there is trade in things,' he told me, 'there is trade in humans.'

Deleuze's formulations did not bring a conversation to an end but, on the contrary, opened it up, always revealing and illuminating a whole horizon of concepts. When we were twenty it was an immense joy, a godsend we were entirely aware of. But to watch Deleuze write was, to me, a source of infinite wonder: his handwriting was large and cursive and he seemed to press his pen onto the paper with all his strength; he wrote with no margins, no space between the lines, often at great speed as though obedient to some imperious dictation that would countenance neither break nor pause. To watch his fingers, with their abnormally long, sharp nails that all but hid his pen as they raced along, was an extraordinary spectacle that, to my eyes, testified to his genius.

Chapter 8

In those first post-war months, I was also present at long writing sessions of a very different kind: I watched Paul Éluard write, in that beautiful script as blue as his eyes, Aragon, Cocteau, Francis Ponge and others. These were the most famous. The great poets needed money, as did Monny. Since he had spent the war years buying and selling rare books, he knew not only the bibliophiles and the booksellers of Paris I mentioned earlier, but also dealers in autographs, letters and manuscripts. So he set up a business dealing in manuscripts, specifically of poems, either complete, if the poem was short, or in individual pages. All this with the consent – or rather the complicity – of the poets themselves, to whom he handed over the proceeds of the sale, less a commission. And so, ten times in a single morning I watched Paul Éluard write out the same page – 'I write your name, liberty . . .' – each with different crossings-out and deletions. This took considerable time, it required thought, it could not be done in a slipshod way. Obviously, Monny did not sell all ten copies to the same dealer. It was a con, I suppose, but a perfectly moral once, since everyone involved profited: Monny, Éluard, the dealer – and the collector, thrilled to own an original Éluard. Because it truly was an original, the 'real' original having long since disappeared, either through carelessness, or because Éluard – and the others – had no idea that it might one day have value as a piece of art. It was Monny who, literally, added value, or created it if it did not yet exist. Each poet had an individual style: Éluard was meticulous, serene; Aragon, hurried, not daring to look in the face those who witnessed what his superego considered to be a suspect act.

After the session of 'I write your name, liberty . . .', Nusch, Éluard's wife, had joined him, and my mother served an impromptu lunch in their room filled with overflowing bookshelves, littered with the graffiti of the poets, originals rejected by Monny as 'not sufficiently authentic' (the other room was the bedroom). Nusch had beautifully chiselled lips, her blood-red lipstick emphasized her voracity, her long black hair highlighted her bone structure, her whole body, the way that she moved, exuded a fiery sensuality. Éluard, who was tall and somewhat ungainly with astonished watery-blue eyes, was clearly in thrall to her. At some point the conversation turned to Jesus, and Nusch, who had been silent, seemed to wake suddenly from a long sleep, realizing what was being discussed and passionately interjected, 'Ah, yes, Jesus de Saint-Nazaire!' One day Monny sent me round to Éluard's house with an envelope containing a thick wad of banknotes. Éluard invited me into the kitchen, which overlooked the street; I heard moans from the adjoining room, the door to which was ajar. In the bevelled mirror, I glimpsed the red pompom of a marine's beret. Éluard seemed to have quickly thrown on pyjamas before opening the door to me.

For Paulette, who adored anything to do with culture, these years were among the happiest she had known. Every Saturday she held a real *salon littéraire*, which I was instructed to attend although it clashed with the hunting escapades Cau and I carefully planned during our ascetic weeks at boarding school. One evening the guest of honour was Jean Cocteau, who began speaking and went on in his mesmerizing fashion, without cease. After he left, my mother berated me for not saying a word, which was understandable given that I was a proud, intimidated philosophy student who had reluctantly sacrificed his night out on the town to be there. I had listened, that was all, and in any case Cocteau had left no openings for anyone else to speak. To pit my wits against him, as she probably hoped, would have been ridiculous. Monny could do so, he was more than equal to the enchanter when he decided to spar with him. But Paulette was not content simply to reproach me; she suddenly exploded, 'His feet! Did you see his feet? Jean's tiny feet, did you notice them?' she said through teeth gritted with rage and regret. I realized that she had been comparing them to mine, which must have seemed lumpen and oafish, whereas Cocteau's feet – every toe and even the arch – seemed to her to be shaped by the keenest intelligence.

I was very fond of the author of Les Parti pris des choses [The Voice of Things], another of Monny's forgers. Francis Ponge, that extraordinary poet, was a man of few words; more often than not he dressed in English tweeds, with a ruddy complexion, forehead, cheeks and neck. He was a big man, with not an ounce of fat on him, and the way he held himself indicated formidable reserves of energy. He used to arrive with his wife, a tall, blonde, anaemic-looking woman who constantly played the martyr, eyes rolled heavenward in mute supplication. The Ponges were comfortable with Monny and Paulette, who were good at winning people's trust and had a gift for inciting the most intimate confidences, and this is how we came to learn of the illness the Ponges suffered from. We learned it from husband and wife simultaneously, they suffered together, talked about it together and took little trouble to hide it. Francis Ponge suffered from priapism, he was in an almost constant state of arousal; his permanently flushed complexion he owed to his dilated blood vessels, as though he were constantly being drip-fed Viagra or Cialis, drugs that did not exist at the time. Ponge loved his wife and was never unfaithful to her. The doctors could do nothing and were powerless to help.

Cau was convinced that if a young man from the provinces wanted to succeed in literature, he had to become the secretary of a famous writer. For him, it was an obligatory apprenticeship, in the mould of Balzac, a rite of passage and one he talked to me about for weeks, trying to pluck up the courage to act. One afternoon in study hall, he began writing dozens of letters, addressed to Sartre, to Malraux, to Camus, to Gide, to Mauriac, to Paulhan, to Julien Benda whom he admired because of *La Trahison des clercs* [*The Betrayal of the Scholars*], to Montherlant, to Aragon, and others whom I've forgotten; letters that were almost identical in form and content, varying only in what he knew about the addressee. He showed them to me; I thought they were excellent and gave them my seal of approval, although not, I confess, without a pang of jealousy because, after all, the idea of earning my living from such an exceptional profession also appealed to me. This was in 1946, and we were now in *khâgne*, our second year of preparation for the École normale supérieure, and though we enjoyed Alquié's lessons – on one occasion I got the top mark for my philosophy dissertation, and, coming ahead of Deleuze and other big names such as Le Goff, who would later be a leading light in medieval history, I felt pretty proud of myself; I should add that it happened only once and I felt that Deleuze had been the victim of a terrible injustice – although, as I say, we enjoyed Alquié's classes, I could not see either Cau or myself, after the long parenthesis of war and adventure, embarking on an academic career, in spite of the many admirable historians of philosophy and philosophers under whom I was later to study, including Martial Guéroult, Jean Hyppolite, Jean Laporte, Georges Canguilhem and Gaston Bachelard.

Cau received only one reply to all the letters he sent; it came from Sartre, who offered to meet him on whatever day suited him between two and three o'clock at the Café de Flore. Cau must surely have written his own account of this fateful encounter, but I remember what he told me at the time: Sartre's candour, in stark contrast to all the glory heaped on him, which no one today can imagine, his brotherly manner and his utter lack of self-importance made a great impact on Cau. At that meeting, there and then, Sartre dug out at least a hundred crumpled letters from the pockets of his trousers and jacket, which he handed to my friend saying, 'See what you can do with these.' Thus I can affirm that the first session of Sartre's secretarial work took place in the study hall of the Lycée Louis-le-Grand. Neither Sartre nor Cau had the faintest idea of the nature or the scope of the role of secretary. Nonetheless, Cau consequently devised both the method and its object, gradually compelling Sartre to organize the contents of his pockets, then his finances (with mindless generosity Sartre regularly doled out money that he had only just earned to anyone who asked) and, finally, his schedule, thereby freeing up for Sartre the vast swathes of time he desperately needed to do his work. It quickly became clear that Cau would need a real office in the little flat Sartre shared with his mother, Madame Mancy, on the fourth floor of 42 rue Bonaparte, with its windows overlooking the place Saint-Germain-des-Prés and the junction that today bears his name and that of Simone de Beauvoir. Sometime in 1946, Cau gave up the preparatory course for the École normale supérieure, took a room in a hotel on the rue des Écoles and, now secretary to a great writer, set about becoming a writer himself.

After his departure, I too left the boarding school, although I continued my studies, and I moved full-time into the sixth floor *chambre de bonne* on the rue Alexandre-Cabanel. My friendship with Cau did not change, in fact we probably spent more time together than we had before, but now Deleuze and I were forging a close friendship based, for my part, on an enormous admiration for him, and for his, on my ability to listen, to be astonished, to demonstrate a keen understanding and a properly philosophical enthusiasm. A year and a half my senior, he thought of our relationship as that of master and disciple: we talked for hours in his apartment on the rue Daubigny, he recommended books to me and, for a while, he even set up a little group consisting of Tournier, Butor, Robert Genton and Bamberger to which, with a complete lack of miserliness, he gave brilliant presentations on a thousand different subjects to prepare us for our examination.

I forgot to mention that, the previous year, when I was in *hypokhâgne*, having discovered that there was a cell of Communist students at Louis-le-Grand, I introduced myself to the secretary. He was a handsome young man with an open, intelligent face and very black hair. At first he thought I had come for information, or to enrol, since the reputation of the *Parti communiste – Le Parti des 75,000 fusillés*, as *L'Humanité* repeated daily – was so great at the time. I set him straight on this point and, utterly deadpan, declared, 'I am here, comrade, to insist that the death sentence imposed on me by the Party be carried out. It has been more than a year now, and the waiting is unbearable.' The handsome secretary, who was studying history and politics, immediately realized he was dealing with an angry young man, with someone who in reality had no wish to die but who wanted a serious and scandalous miscarriage of justice to be righted. I explained the situation in detail and he listened attentively; he knew Aglaé and revealed to me her real name, Annie Blanchard – she would later become a professor at the University of Bordeaux. 'Stupid bastards,' he said, none too surprised, when I had finished, 'don't worry about it, I'll sort it all out today,' and he offered to retrieve my Party membership card. 'We'll see about that later,' I said, 'there's no hurry.' The following day he summoned me in order to offer a solemn apology on behalf of the *Parti communiste* – which he would himself leave shortly afterwards. His name was Jean Poperen, he became famous in the *Parti socialiste*, becoming, during Mitterrand's presidency, an influential member of the old guard. He was also a wonderful man whom I would see many times.

That final year of *khâgne*, as a day pupil, was not simply one of studies, but also of youthful indiscretions and mad escapades. I suppose that my childhood, the responsibility of being the eldest, had weighed too heavily on me; the war years also had been heavy, the fear, the perilous balance between life and death. The new freedom opening up before me required, like proofs of its existence, gratuitous acts. I was reading Gide and Sartre, and to commit such acts seemed to me an innermost obligation that would truly sanction my passage into manhood. Was I cured of the war? I embarked on these transgressions like an act of bravery: I would have felt ashamed to seem a coward by not doing them.

After a vicious argument, my mother cut off my allowance and I resolved to be no longer dependent on her. Within a few days my financial situation became intolerable: I wasn't a boarder any more and I found I was incapable of providing for even the basic necessities, such as food. Cau and I spent hours going over the most lunatic ways of finding me some money, foolishly persuading ourselves that we had to take it from its source: from the rich. With my last sous, I rented a priest's outfit – the soutane, alb, hat, dog-collar – I bought a missal and stored everything overnight in Cau's room on the rue des Écoles, although he clearly thought I wouldn't dare go through with the plan. I spent the whole evening poring over maps of the smartest neighbourhoods in Paris and decided to begin my quest – for I intended to collect money – on the rue de l'Alboni, a very short street in the 16th *arrondissement*, whose buildings are all on the odd-numbered side and which, most important for my purposes, was close to Passy station and the pont Bir-Hakeim, on the Nation-Étoile métro line that served my mother's house. The following morning, Cau ceremonially dressed me, in much the same way as, years later, those young Israeli airforce dressers would strap me into my G-suit. This would transform me into a fighter pilot. As Cau and I looked in the wardrobe mirror, the priest's robes transformed me into a parish priest. No one could doubt I was a young cleric, serious, gentle, fervent, with my missal under my arm and a large exercise book I'd bought at the last minute, in which to inscribe the names of benefactors who donated small change, maybe a large banknote, to the Institute for the Deaf and Dumb of the rue Saint-Jacques, which I would pretend to represent. It was too late now to turn back.

At the very first building, 1 rue de l'Alboni, I was prevented from going even as far as the lift by the concierge: 'Where are you going,

Father?' 'I'm making a collection, Madame, for the deaf and dumb . . .'
I did not even have time to finish the sentence, before the virago
virtually roared, 'There's no collecting in this building!'

I didn't have to be told twice. I fled the building and the street.
I had chosen the wrong time of day, I realized, the time when
concierges prowled the stairwells, cleaning and dusting, delivering
the post. I strode unctuously down the boulevard Delessert, before
suddenly becoming aware that, with every step, my suede shoes
were visible beneath my cassock. I returned to the rue de l'Alboni an
hour later and decided to start again, but at the far end. This time,
no one barred my way, and I took the lift to the sixth floor, where I
rang the only doorbell, and a door was opened to this young priest
by a marvellous apparition, a beautiful, smiling woman. She listened
attentively to my request and said, 'Wait here a moment, Father,' and
came back with a sizeable donation. I took my exercise book, asked
if I could note down her name 'to include you in our list of benefactors'. She declined. 'We'll pray for you,' I said as I left. I took the
stairs to the floor below, quickly calculating that at this rate I would
soon make a fortune. Castles in the air and all that . . . An imposing
matron appeared in the doorway of the fifth-floor apartment and
said, 'I'm sorry, Father, we do good works and we donate directly
to the archdiocese. People do not make collections around here.'
Keeping my composure, I calmly replied, 'Madame, the Deaf and
Dumb Institute of the rue Saint-Jacques is entirely independent of
the archdiocese; we receive no funding from them.' 'Just a moment,
Father,' she said, and disappeared into the depths of an immense
apartment, leaving me standing in the open doorway. Should I wait
or should I run? That was the question. The minutes ticked by slowly,
each one longer than the last, and I thought I could hear a breathless telephone conversation somewhere down a corridor. The priest
stopped weighing the pros and cons, hiked up his cassock, took the
stairs two at a time, rushed past the concierge's lodge, strode swiftly
up the rue de l'Alboni to Passy station and vanished. Four stops

later, he was catching his breath in his *chambre de bonne* wondering whether to try again or give up.

I decided I couldn't leave it at that: the experiment had been far from conclusive and I chose to try again. I didn't go far. I easily gained access to a building on the avenue de Suffren, where the first door was opened by two Spanish maids who, at the sight of me, immediately took out their purses and gave me some change; the second door was opened by a small, plump, charming woman who invited me in and had me sit in a large living room, never doubting for a moment that I was a man of the cloth. She asked me about the Institute I was collecting for and about my vocation as a priest. She seemed to know a lot about the subject. Suddenly, she said, 'Won't you please stay to lunch, Father? My brother, who is a canon at St Francis-Xavier, will be here any moment now.' I responded as quick as lightning, said I would be delighted, then got up, saying, 'Excuse me a moment, I've forgotten something,' and dashed into the hall, not bothering to close the door as I took the stairs four at a time.

I recounted my exploits to Cau that afternoon and we were forced to face the fact that my dreams of riches had actually cost me money: my charity collection had not even made enough to pay for the rental of the soutane; it was imperative I make up with Paulette. Cau offered to act as a go-between, to tell my mother I had a wonderful surprise, something she would never guess. He walked in front of me down the rue Alexandre-Cabanel and helped me put on the priest's garb in the stairwell of the building so that the Spanish concierge did not see. Then he went to the door and rang the bell. My mother, who was on her own that day, let him in. A few moments later, I rang the bell. I was not expecting what came next: she opened the door, stared at me without saying a word, then slapped me twice, resoundingly across the face and, without stammering, screamed, 'A priest? In my house? Never!' Rather than calming me, my mother's slaps spurred me on, I had to up the ante, I had to go all the way – that was how I was. I put on the cassock again the next morning and went to class at the Lycée Louis-le-Grand when the boarders were studying, when the future élite of France were diligently working. My fellow students' astonishment at this strange irruption was marked by a silence that lasted several minutes, broken by clapping and booing from the group, which immediately split into opposing factions. I had all but managed to incite civil war in the class when I took a bottle of champagne from under my cassock – to celebrate my conversion, I announced.

After another day of fabulous poverty, and hours of deliberation with Sartre's newly appointed secretary in his hotel room, we decided that I should go to Deauville, stand in the doorway of one of the casinos and solicit donations from lucky gamblers. I'd never been to Deauville, had never seen a casino, which I considered a place of utter wickedness since in such places people gambled money, 'the economic sanction of work', as Deleuze used to call it, one of the many revelatory phrases I mentioned earlier. In fact, money and life are one and the same thing: a financial wound can be fatal, a gambling debt is a debt of honour, and there are those who chose death before dishonour. I was mad, I was starving and I had no experience of the world: I assumed the rich were naturally generous, I hadn't yet read Albert Cohen or the bitter, hilarious account of the transformation of *Les Valeureux* [*The Valiant*], those fictional Cephalonian cousins to Solal, Under-Secretary General of the League of Nations, after he gave them a big cheque drawn on a Swiss bank account. The Valiant – Mangeclous, Saltiel, Mattathias, Salomon and Michaël – who had been the embodiment of Ionian innocence, credulity, imagination, fantasy, goodness and impulsiveness, suddenly became melancholy hawks, constantly on the alert, the moment they pocketed the cheque (they pronounce it Czech), having lost all joy, all gaiety, seeking out the most sordid dives in which to eat. 'They were,' writes Cohen, 'struck down with the disease of the rich; they thought themselves poor.' In Deauville, the gentleman, beaming from his winnings at the tables, to whom I addressed a modest, well-turned plea for a contribution – it was two in the morning, I was thirsty and famished, having hitchhiked from Paris to Deauville – walked straight past without even looking at me, but he muttered, '*Je suis navré, cher ami.*' It was the first time I had heard the word *navré*, 'heartbroken', spoken by anyone and it sounded very different from '*Mais, vrai, j'ai trop pleuré! Les Aubes sont navrantes*' ['True, I have wept too much! Dawns are heartbreaking'] in Rimbaud's 'Le Bateau ivre'. This was my only attempt at begging. I went and lay down under the arches that ran along the boardwalk next to the beach, shivering, curled up in a ball until the dawn, which was, truly, heartbreaking.

This year of ever more insane challenges and dares I set myself reached its height with the theft of philosophical works from PUF – the Presses Universitaires de France – on the place de la Sorbonne. Stealing books was both a fad and almost a moral obligation to which a number of us felt pledged. Not to steal books was considered cowardice; thieves boasted of their exploits to their fellow thieves – not all the *khâgne* students stole – recounting the events leading up to the crime in great detail. The rivalry between thieves was ruthless. It's important to know that the thieves were, first and foremost, passionate readers. It is impossible to explain to young people today how we pounced on the first two volumes of Sartre's *Les Chemins de la liberté* [*The Roads to Freedom*] – *L'Âge de raison* [*The Age of Reason*] and *Le Sursi* [*The Reprieve*] – the instant they were published in late 1945. Contrary to the clichés of anti-Sartrian *doxa*, the volumes of *Les Chemins de la liberté* were not literary exemplifications of his philosphical theses, but genuine novels, with a wealth of ambiguous, contradictory and fantastically *alive* characters in the grips of the indomitable *conatus* of liberty; its immortal youth, its fragility, and perennial return of anguish that it constantly stirs up. To us, at the age of twenty, *Les Chemins de la liberté* was a 'literary injunction' that clamoured to be *imitated* – in the same way that St François de Sales spoke about *The Imitation of Christ*, the height of devotion. *Les Chemins de la liberté* required an action, our action. Boris, in *L'Âge de raison*, stole books from the Librairie Garbure 'on the corner of the rue de Vaugirard and the boulevard Saint-Michel' – in other words, the place de la Sorbonne, the precise location of PUF, the sole theatre of my exploits. I was taking over from Boris, I was the hero of my own Sartrian novel, as Cau and others, whose names I won't mention, were heroes in the same mould. Sartre meticulously describes the hesitations, the tactics, the mounting tension, the countdowns Boris imposes on himself before the dazzling act of appropriation; just as Malraux, in the three opening pages of *La Condition humaine* [*Man's Fate*], closely watches and details, in a suffocating tension of imminence, the inner resistance that Ch'en must overcome in order to strike through the mosquito net and stab the man he has a mission to kill.

I only ever stole philosophy books. In my *chambre de bonne* on the rue Alexandre-Cabanel I amassed quite a library of abstruse works, many of them in several volumes, such as Hegel's *The Phenomenology of Spirit* translated by Jean Hyppolite, the two volumes of *L'Évolution et la structure de la doctrine de la science chez Fichte* [*The Evolution and Structure of the 'Doctrine of Science' in Fichte*] by Martial Guéroult, or, in a different genre, *L'Action* [*Essay on a Critique of Life and a Science of Practice*] by Maurice Blondel, or again, since I was eclectic, *Le Moi, le monde et Dieu* [*The Ego, the World and God*] by Lachièze-Rey. The latter had studied under Jean Laporte, the thesis adviser on my *études supérieures* philosophy thesis, to whom he had sent his book, and who thanked him with the words, '*Mon cher ami*, I acknowledge without delay receipt of *Le Moi, le monde et Dieu*. And yet I cannot help but wonder, not without a certain trepidation, what the subject for your next book will be.' Laporte still laughed about it when he told me the story. I have to confess that I was a talented thief: good at keeping my head, skilled at reconnoitring a place, familiar with every nook and cranny on the ground and first floors of PUF, effortlessly able to identify the numerous security guards the management had specifically hired to neutralize my peers because of the thriving thievery from the shop. But I was also decisive, capable of acting very quickly, slipping the book I wanted into my briefcase or between the pages of a newspaper with the skill of a Neapolitan conjurer. I began to think I was invincible; I was convinced I had earned the title of best thief at Louis-le-Grand.

It was Hegel – Georg Wilhelm Friedrich – who brought about my ruin. Whereas Ferdinand Alquié had taught us philosophy in K1, Jean Hyppolite was his opposite number in K2. He and Sartre had studied together at the École normale supérieure and he had not only translated Hegel, but was considered an eminent authority on the subject; we had all been waiting with bated breath for the release of his long deferred magnum opus: *The Genesis and Structure of Hegel's Phenomenology of Spirit.* Finally, his publisher, Aubier, announced the publication date. I rushed to the bookshop and froze, seized by reverential dread at its beauty, its heft and thickness; skim-reading from the first page on, it seemed to be the only book that might make accessible the fundamental thinking of the great German philosopher. I needed this book; to me it represented the ultimate challenge after which, I was certain, I would give up stealing, since nothing could ever match it. It was my Holy Grail. I later realized that the quest was more important than the reading, the possession more important than the content. If reading had been paramount, I could have spent many quiet, studious hours in the library. But Georg Wilhelm Friedrich Hegel and Jean Hyppolite had thrown down the gauntlet. The trouble was that I spent days, weeks probably, picking up that gauntlet; having spent hours browsing the shelves of PUF, solemnly leafing through other books to throw any security guards off the scent, a powerful, uncontrollable force stayed my hand the moment I tried to act. I was scared; I couldn't bring myself to do it. I endlessly procrastinated and my feints and my faint-heartedness, rather than making me invisible, only called attention to me. Unable to bear it any longer, unable to stand my own cowardice yet incapable of giving up, I went about the theft in the most foolish way possible. One afternoon I strode into the PUF bookshop, headed straight upstairs to the philosophy section, knowing exactly where to find *The Genesis and Structure of Hegel's Phenomenology of Spirit*, picked up a copy without encountering any opposition, slipped it into my briefcase, went back downstairs, walked straight past the cash desk and opened the door on to the place de la Sorbonne; only when I stepped out into the fresh air did I dare to breathe, believing for a moment that I was free and triumphant. But I had not taken three steps before a hand was brutally shoved into the right pocket of my jacket, gripping my hip and stopping me in my tracks. I turned to face my aggressor, a short man of about forty, wearing a trilby hat. 'Young man,' he whispered to me, 'have you by any chance forgotten to pay for a book?' He held me hard, I didn't have a penny and since I was incapable of pretending, of making up a lie, I had no choice but to tell him the truth. 'No, I didn't forget. I don't have any money, I stole it, but here it is, here's your book, have it back, I don't care,' I said, taking it out of my briefcase and insolently proffering it to him as he tightened his grip. 'If you think that's how it's going to work out, young man, you're mistaken. Hold out your arms,' he ordered, suddenly brandishing a pair of handcuffs and cuffing one of my wrists with astonishing dexterity. 'No, please, not handcuffs, not here, everyone knows me, I won't try to make a run for it.' He looked me up and down. 'OK,' he said, 'I can see you're not a lout,' and removed the handcuffs, grabbing me by the arm and, sticking very close, walking me across the place de la Sorbonne and down the rue de la Sorbonne towards the rue des Écoles. From a distance his hug might have seemed paternal, but no father ever hugged his child as fiercely. He knew where we were headed, I did not. As we walked, he took it upon himself, in his soft voice, to tell me what a loser I was and to lecture me about stealing from bookshops, smugly explaining all the tricks I already knew, all the ruses I had put into practice perfectly on every previous occasion before I had suddenly become paralysed with fear, frozen to the spot, before the baleful refulgence of the Hegelian grail. Then, out of the blue, he announced, 'After we've been to the police station, we're going to your house, I need to check that you don't have any other stolen books.' I stopped dead, like a mule refusing to go any further, as I remembered that Alquié and his blonde wife were to have dinner at our place that evening. I said, 'You saw how useless I am. You caught me on my first attempt, I haven't stolen anything else.' 'I believe you, but we'll just check anyway.' At that, I staked everything I had: 'Let's go now then. If we go later my mother will be there and if she finds out I've been stealing, it'll kill her. She went through a lot during the war.' He held me firmly, forcing me onward, towards the rue Saint-Jacques and the boulevard Saint-Germain. 'No,' he insisted, 'we'll go afterwards.' 'We have to go now,' I said. 'Look, I'll be honest with you, I stole two other books – well, one book. But it's in two volumes, *L'Action* by Blondel, so it's like I only stole one.'

By this time we had reached the police station on the rue Dante, he flung the door open, shoved me roughly inside and the gentle voice of Dr Jekyll became the savage howl of Mr Hyde as, in front of his police colleagues, he brutally twisted my arm behind my back and tossed the copy of *Genesis and Structure* on to the desk, roaring, 'Look at him, another thieving bastard, I caught him in the act.' A tall cop came over and stood in front of me, ostentatiously rolled a gob of spit in his mouth, then spat in my face and gave me a hard slap that left me dazed.

I waited for what seemed to me an eternity, sitting on a bench until a detective could be found to interrogate me. Mr Hyde, who was a private detective employed by PUF, seemed calmer now and all the cops who had been there when I first arrived had now disappeared. One of them had picked up *Genesis and Structure* and tried to read the first page – completely incomprehensible to a layman – then turned to page two, page three, increasingly nervously leafing through the whole book before setting it back down with a sneer. Standing in front of me, he too slapped me across the face with the sacrificial commentary, 'You see, you bastard, I'd rather go through my whole life without reading rather than steal a book.' The time finally came for my interrogation, something that was quickly dispatched as daylight was failing now and everyone was in a hurry to have the matter settled. I repeated my confession and the officer said to me, 'Tomorrow, you'll bring back the other books you stole and thank PUF. They won't take the matter any further. You're very lucky.' I couldn't believe it. I signed my statement, Mr Hyde tucked *Genesis and Structure* under one arm, put the other through mine and we walked back from the police station towards the place de la Sorbonne, and Dr Jekyll resurfaced, all charm, all smiles. I said, 'Let's go to my place quickly, my mother might not be back yet.' 'No, no, that's OK, I trust you. Bring back the two volumes of *L'Action* tomorrow morning.' But his series of transformations was not yet finished: barely had we stepped into the bookshop – which was crowded, given the hour – than Mr Hyde re-emerged, grabbing me by the scruff of the neck and, thundering for all the staff and customers to hear, 'I nabbed another one!' He jumped around waving his arms, a little like the *milicien* in Brioude, then marched me roughly up the stairs, barking at the astonished philosophers, and pushed me into a tiny office occupied by the manager and a very curvaceous secretary. She stared contemptuously at my face, still flecked with spit and red from being slapped. The manager immediately checked the price of the book and shrugged his shoulders in a weary, fatalistic fashion. I stammered that I had also stolen the Blondel, promising that I would bring it back the following morning. 'Thank the manager,' Jekyll-Hyde commanded. This I did.

Washed in purifying waters, forever cured, I spent a very joyous, friendly, philosophical evening with Alquié, his wife, Monny and my mother. I was careful to humble myself again when I returned the two volumes of *L'Action*, and put the whole sordid story completely out of my mind, not knowing that it would rear its ugly head some months later. One afternoon, when I got home from the lycée, my

147

mother greeted me with the words, 'Have you been hiding something from me?' I said, 'No,' then under her hard inquisitorial glare, added, '*Maman*, I hide so many things from you that it's like I tell you everything.' 'What about this?' she retorted, brandishing a piece of paper that I was flabbergasted to see was a summons ordering me to appear before a magistrate's court for 'Theft, to the detriment of the bookshop owned by Presses Universitaires de France'. Despite the assurances I had been given, the bookshop had pressed charges. I told my mother exactly what had happened, begging her to say nothing to Monny. She replied that this was serious, that she could not keep it from him, and that the first thing we had to do was engage a lawyer. I said I didn't want a lawyer, that I was quite capable of defending myself, that stealing philosophy books wasn't the same as mugging an old lady for her handbag, or being involved in a stick-up. Monny, whom she told as soon as he got home, agreed with her and accused me of being reckless.

We lived at number 11, and there was a lawyer living next door at 11 *bis*. It was late, but Monny immediately took me over to see him. The lawyer showed us in and Monny explained that I was in the throes of an unwholesome passion for philosophy, citing my tutor and his friend Ferdinand Alquié, and Jean Hyppolite, the author of the stolen work, who lived – I knew this because he had invited me to his home – fifty metres away, at 7 rue Alexandre-Cabanel. The lawyer, whose name I have forgotten, suggested that statements from the two philosophers would be very useful at the trial. A guilty verdict would *ipso facto* lead to a criminal record, meaning I would be ineligible to matriculate at the École normale supérieure. So I asked for a meeting, to which Hyppolite happily agreed and, I have to say, I never imagined that such complicity could exist between victim and thief. His first words were, 'So, you like my book so much you're prepared to steal it?' 'It's worth stealing,' I said, 'it's even worth buying, which is what I had to do in order to read it.' And I proved to the author that I really had read his book. Jean Hyppolite was ecstatic, exuding transcendental joy from every pore, puffed up with pride. Never before had anyone so flattered him: for a *khâgne* student to steal *Genesis and Structure* was the ultimate accolade, the equivalent of being a bestseller. Feeling obliged to take me to task, he adopted a half-heartedly stern tone throughout our conversation, but pleasure got the better of him at every turn. This great Hegelian scholar was a charming man with a lisp who, in his youth, in verbal sparring-matches with Sartre, invariably remarked, 'If you want to split hairs, let's split hairs,' which Sartre imitated to perfection. Hyppolite agreed to write a long letter of mitigation, testifying to my gift for philosophy, a letter so beautiful that, on its own, it would have been enough to have me acquitted. That a victim should attest to the intellectual brilliance of the thief who stole from him is rare in the annals of jurisprudence.

With Alquié, things were very different. He judged me harshly and I did not dare think he might have been moved by base motives, envy or jealousy, since his books, in limpid French, were neither large nor daunting enough to merit being stolen. He kept me in his office for several hours, starting out drily with Kant's categorical imperative, asking whether, in my misdemeanour, there was some maxim that could become a universal law. He treated me to a private lesson in moral philosophy. Yet Alquié was genuinely fond of me, and he too sent a letter to the court that spoke so highly of me that, to the end of my days and in my darkest hours, it would have provided inexhaustible fuel for my ego, had I kept it.

The trial was very disappointing. My case was the first to be called, my lawyer approached the bench with some papers – probably the letters, which had already been added to the case file. I heard, '*Monsieur le président*, if I might . . .' and the magistrate, already swayed, interrupted, leaned down to the clerk of the court and immediately pronounced his verdict, which to me was an inaudible mumble. The next case was called. The whole affair had taken less than three minutes. My lawyer, who had a sharp ear, informed me that I had

been sentenced to pay a fine of 4,800 francs, suspended. The philosophical conspiracy had been successful; I would not have a criminal
record, I was eligible to sit my entrance exams. This, as it turned out,
proved of no particular use: my life was to play out otherwise.

Chapter 9

wo events that were to prove critical in shaping my life occurred in the tumultuous year of 1946: my sister Évelyne's arrival in Paris and my meeting with Judith Magre. A noble soul, if fortunate enough to encounter Monny and Paulette, could not but immediately be captivated by their charm. In this case, the infatuation between them and Judith was mutual. They met by chance at the Café de Flore and were so smitten with each other that after several hours' conversation Judith was invited to the rue Alexandre-Cabanel for dinner. I happened to be there, I was introduced and, as usual, showered with praise by Monny and Paulette. I, meanwhile, was immediately taken with this nervous sylph-like girl of twenty, by her firm, slender body, her deep voice rich with every possible inflection, her face with its high cheekbones, her blazing eyes, her sensual red lips, her strong nose. At the time, her name was neither Judith nor Magre: obedient to some imperious inner voice, she had fled without a penny to her name from a family of industrialists in the provinces and enrolled at the Cours Simon, where she trained to become the towering actress we all now know. In the lift on the way down from my mother's apartment to the ground floor, we fell into each other's arms, never for a moment breaking our wordless, passionate embrace, which we continued in the service lift, the only way to get to my *chambre de bonne* on the sixth floor. We still had not said a word to each other; everything went without saying. For six months we lived out a torrid passion, we spent the whole night making love before my entrance exam for the École normale supérieure and, obviously, I failed. Judith then left to go on tour and I never heard from her. I suffered like an animal. She vanished from my life for fifteen years. In the early 1960s, we bumped into each other on the rue des Saints-Pères, I married her in 1963, she was my first wife. I might come back to that, perhaps.

Évelyne, who was still living in Brioude with my father, came to Paris for a few days' holiday that year. Through me she met Deleuze, and the moment they set eyes on one another I had the feeling of being a helpless witness to something inevitable. She was sixteen, with the body of a pin-up, huge cobalt-blue eyes and a beautiful Semitic nose. I hadn't seen my sister for months and in that time the gawky, angular adolescent had blossomed into an attractive young woman, brimming with intelligence, vivacity and humour. From his first words, she fell in love with Deleuze, fell in love with philosophy, the irony and philosophical humour that, in him, went hand in hand with the great thrusts by which he illumi- nated the world, sweeping away stupidity, transforming anyone who listened to him into an accomplice, a witness, a disciple, a producer of thought, inspiring others through his extraordinary sagacity, his capacity for astonishment before things that seemed self-evident. At sixteen, Évelyne threw herself into this love affair, heedlessly, recklessly, dazzled by the concepts, and she began to speak, to reason, to mock like Deleuze himself. She was in thrall to him as so many others, men and women, would be throughout the philosopher's life. In Vincennes and elsewhere I have known people who, without realizing it, imitated the tone and rhythm and the modulations of Deleuze's voice. My sister was more smitten than most because she was very young: she did not lie, she knew nothing of compromise, she was prey to the demon of the absolute. During the war, in order to protect her, Hélène *la Normande* had persuaded my father to allow Évelyne to convert to Catholicism and be baptized. She had made her first communion in the basilica at Brioude, a jewel of Romanesque architecture, and I still remember her solemnity, her earnestness as she received the host beneath her white veil. She devoted herself entirely to Christianity, she was St Blandina in the lions' den, with all her soul she loved the Abbé Goergé, her spiritual adviser, and was determined to become a missionary in distant lands. Évelyne extended her stay in Paris – or came back soon afterwards, I don't remember. In any case, she and Deleuze were soon inseparable; Paulette welcomed him with an excessive fondness that cut her short at the first syllable of his first name: 'Gi-gi-gi'. Like her daughter, she was thrilled by Gilles' manifest genius. Then one day, as he and I crossed the pont de Bir-Hakeim beneath a gloomy sky, he asked if I would be prepared to do him a great and difficult favour. Worried, not daring to believe that he would ask the impossible of me, I said, 'Yes, of course,' only to refuse when he told me what it was: he wanted to break up with my sister and he wanted me to tell her. It was a terrible shock. I feared and anticipated the worst for Évelyne; but I was also hurt and dumbfounded by the cowardice of my friend, who was both using me and making a fool of me. At that moment, on the bridge, leaning on the railing next to him, looking down on the Seine, with the roar of the traffic from the passing métros overhead, something in my bond with Deleuze was irreparably broken. What I most feared came to pass. My little sister headed back to Normandy not knowing anything and I told my mother, Monny and my father, preparing them for any eventuality, asking them to look out for her and not to leave her alone. She was in Brioude when she received Deleuze's letter, awkward as such letters invariably are, but this one more so than others, as intelligence attempted to struggle against violence with unequal weapons. I read the letter many years later, feeling very ill at ease, after Évelyne showed it to Sartre. She wanted to die; she could not be left alone for an instant.

It was Serge Rezvani who brought her back to herself. We had met through my brother: these future writers had chosen painting, they wanted to be artists, and painters they became. Together with Dmitrienko the Russian and the Welshman Raymond Mason, they founded a group called *Jouir*, or, as it was known, the Boulogne School, since the four of them lived a Spartan, industrious, creative life in a tumbledown folly on the banks of the Seine. These talented young painters and sculptors were quickly recognized when the Galerie Maeght exhibited works by all four of them, in November 1947, for a show entitled *Les Mains éblouies* ['The Dazzled Hands']. The apartment on the rue Alexandre-Cabanel, Paulette and Monny, inevitably became, for Serge, a haven and his only home. With the family's consent – more than that, its blessing – he took Évelyne to the south of France to the still-unspoiled coast of Les Maures in the Var, where they spent several months sleeping under the stars and fishing for their food. By the time they returned to Paris, Serge and Évelyne had decided to get married. The wedding took place in Brioude. Serge assures me I was there but I have no memory of it.

With his painter's eye, Serge was an astute and admiring judge of the beauty and expressivity of the face, and perfect body, of his wife. He persuaded Évelyne to become an actress. In the difficult act of remembering I have set myself today, forty years after her suicide, I find an old photograph of Évelyne, undoubtedly taken by Serge, completely naked, sitting in the noonday sun on a rock by the sea. She is seen in profile, one arm clasping her left knee, her face is hidden, as she stares into the distance, veiled by a curtain of golden hair. A naked woman in profile: the body must be stamped with something of the divine to hold such a pose and for every part of it to remain exemplary – the posture of the feet, the tenderly muscular calves, the long thighs, the buttocks hard as the rock on which she sits, the flat stomach, the narrow waist, the high, firm, plump breasts, a woman's breasts not a girl's, the perfect curve of the back, the shoulders, the slender arms. How old was she? Seventeen, eighteen perhaps? As I look at her, two lines from Gombrowicz's *Operetta*, a play in which Judith appeared at the Théâtre National de Chaillot, ring out:

O nudity forever young, hail!
Hail, O youth forever nude!

Évelyne was entranced by the idea of being an actress, she seemed happy and she enrolled in turn at the Cours Simon. I don't know whether she knew Judith at the time or whether they met later. René Simon, the founder of the drama school, had a powerful influence on his students, both male and female. He decided that my sister, with her flawless body, should have a career in films, but that her Jewish intellectual nose was an insurmountable obstacle. It was overcome. Against her husband's advice, Évelyne could not rest until she had plastic surgery, a victim of the ontological problem my mother's nose imposed on all her progeny. Having a nose job was a new and exciting fashion in those days, a liberating adventure according to its pioneers, who undoubtedly associated it, in a roundabout though understandable way, with the liberation of France and the liberation of women, for which Simone de Beauvoir's *Le Deuxième sexe* [*The Second Sex*] was the first act. The leading plastic surgeon of the day was so popular that he gave his name to the procedure: people referred to 'the Claoué nose', which was not, however, always a success. Juliette Greco had a Claoué nose. Évelyne Rey – this was the stage name my sister had decided on – had one too, and very beautiful it was. I only saw it later since, for much of the time during her years with Serge, I was in the Auvergne, in Tübingen and later in Berlin.

During one of my trips to Paris, I arranged to met her and Serge at the Royal, a lively café in Saint-Germain-des-Prés – a real bistro with a huge, curved bar, tall bar stools upholstered in red and an enormous back room – just opposite Les Deux Magots, on the corner of the rue de Rennes and the boulevard Saint-Germain. No one at the time could have imagined that the Royal would one day vanish to be replaced by the Drugstore Saint-Germain, which in turn would come to seem as though it had always existed, and would always exist. But the Drugstore too is dead; it died both a natural death and by a terrorist's bomb. It was replaced by a boutique belonging to the king of Italian fashion, with a chic, expensive restaurant on the first floor. The persistence and the disfigurement of places are the rhythm and measure of our lives. I have seen as much in other, desperate circumstances during the filming of *Shoah*, when I encountered the landscape of extermination in Poland. This battle, this contrast between continuity and destruction, was for me an overwhelming shock, a veritable explosion, the source of everything. Of course Saint-Germain-des-Prés and the Quartier Latin are not killing fields: that the Royal, the bookshop Le Divan on the corner of the rue Bonaparte at the far end of the square, even the PUF bookshop on the boulevard Saint-Michel, the theatre of my petty thefts, have, with so many others, succumbed to the fluidity of fashion is simply sad. More than sad, perhaps: we may be alive, but we no longer recognize the places of our lives; we are no longer contemporaries in our own present. Few now share with me the knowledge that the Royal existed and I still think, with absolute admiration and scepticism, of the plaque on the wall at 1 quai aux Fleurs, where Vladimir Jankélévitch lived, as I did for a while. On it one can read this *pensée* by the philosopher, a passage from one of his books, which so moved me that I immediately learned it by heart and often repeat it to myself at night or when I happen to pass the quai aux Fleurs: 'He who has been cannot henceforth not have been. Henceforth, the mysterious and obscure fact of having lived is his *viaticum* for eternity.'

So, barely had I met Rezvani and my sister at the Royal than Deleuze appeared in my field of vision, or, rather, the field of vision of all three of us. In a second we saw each other, four glances exchanged in an instant: me seeing Évelyne as she saw Deleuze,

Deleuze seeing Évelyne, Serge seeing the two of them seeing each other, a fateful, shimmering *mise en abyme*. I knew, we all knew in that instant, that Évelyne would inevitably go back to Deleuze. In Howard Hawks's splendid film noir, *Scarface*, two arms reach out, two lighters simultaneously blaze, each offering a flame to the cigarette that the *femme fatale* has just brought to her lips. There are three of them: the woman, the old mobster whose mistress she is, and the young wolf who covets both his boss's woman and his empire. It is she who must decide: she hesitates between the two flames. The suspense is agonizing, not a word is exchanged, not a second too long, she chooses, as one kills, the young man. We know that her choice is a death sentence and that the same hand that holds the chosen lighter will gun down the man whose flame was spurned. Pure cinema.

Deleuze still lived with his mother on the rue Daubigny, but he set Évelyne up in an apartment in a nearby, equally bleak street in the 17th *arrondissement*, which, for her, was far from everything, first and foremost those places that an aspiring actress was professionally obliged to frequent. I visited her one day in the furnished one-bedroom apartment he had rented and found her miserable, almost exiled. I felt as though he were hiding her away, forcing her to live a clandestine existence, sneaking around furtively to visit her when it suited him as a man might visit a brothel. How long this second affair – incarceration would be more accurate – continued, I don't know, nor can I relate what my sister later confided to me about her lover's behaviour, the means and the ruses he felt the need to employ when he decided to end it with her, since his philosophical '*desirante*' subversiveness demanded, if it were both to thrive and have free rein, a bourgeois respectability that Évelyne could never offer him. Their break-up also ended our friendship; except in passing, I never saw Deleuze again. My admiration for him remained intact and indeed grew with time, but my affection for him was gone. The violence of his own suicide rekindled it.

In her heart of hearts, Évelyne was deeply, permanently wounded, but the theatre, rather than the cinema, saved her; here she truly learned to act, learned the profession the hard way, working with the repertory company Centre Dramatique de l'Ouest, touring towns in Brittany and Normandy. I came across a letter she wrote to Paulette and Monny in which she lists the places and dates, day by day, almost without break or rest, the Cinéma Familial in Lannion, the Théâtre Comœdia in Brest, village halls in Loudéac and Vitré, the NEF hall in Vannes, the concert hall in Le Mans, the Beaux-Arts in Cherbourg, theatres in Quimper, Pontivy, Mayenne, Saint-Lô, Coutances. It was Molière's *Illustre Théâtre*, going from town to town come rain, snow or heatwave, but, as she wrote, no matter what the weather, theatres are invariably freezing cold, dressing rooms filthy and often stinking. It doesn't matter, she went on, 'I adore this life, it would break my heart to leave it.' When she came back to Paris, she continued to act, both in the theatre and on television. I saw her perform – perfect, poignant, understated – in *The Three Sisters*, in Colette Audry's *Soledad*, Audiberti's *Le Ouallou* [*The Slammer*], Arthur Adamov's *Ping-Pong*. In 1953, she gave a magisterial performance as the child-killer Estelle in Sartre's *Huis clos* [*No Exit*] at the Comédie Caumartin with Christiane Lénier and François Chaumette, a role she performed on many more occasions with different actors in different theatres in the years that followed, even in a television production with Judith playing Inès and Michel Auclair as Garcin, directed by Michel Mitrani.

I mention all this not because I want to dwell on my sister's career – the usual career path of a young, gifted actress – but simply to tell the truth. Where, if not in this book, will it be told? Since her suicide, on 18 November 1966, the official version would have it that she only ever acted in plays that Sartre had written expressly for her. Ambiguous phrases – for example, in the Pléiade edition of Sartre's works for theatre – imply that Sartre insisted she be cast as Estelle at the Comédie Caumartin. I can attest that this is not true, that Sartre did not then know my sister. He had never seen her act, until one morning I – who by then had been living with Simone de Beauvoir for a year – got a call from him, and I quote him here verbatim: 'Apparently, your sister is very good in *Huis clos*, I'd like to go and see it. Set it up with Castor [Simone de Beauvoir], and we'll take her to dinner afterwards.' In relaying Sartre's imperious command to Castor, my only comment was to quote Comte Mosca in *La Chartreuse de Parme* [*The Charterhouse of Parma*] when he learns Sanseverina is about to meet Fabrice: 'If once the word "love" is spoken between them, I am lost.' It was inevitable that Sartre and Évelyne would have an affair, everything pointed to it: Sartre's taste for seduction, my sister's fondness for philosophy – it would take a thinker of Sartre's stature to heal the wounds opened by Deleuze; and also the symmetry of a brother in a relationship with de Beauvoir and a sister with Sartre. The consequences for Évelyne frightened Castor and me, I would go so far as to say that I was terrified, knowing Évelyne to be entranced with the absolute, incapable of not giving herself utterly. I considered the risks that such an affair would entail, to say nothing of the complications she would bring to Sartre's tortuous love life, given that he never broke up with anyone, holding on to his mistresses long after passion and sex had ceased to be part of the relationship. Castor and I did everything in our power to postpone the encounter between them, but he was determined to see this Estelle; he would not give up, he became impatient, we had to do it.

If I feel it necessary to highlight my fears and reservations here, it is because the contrary has been alleged in a number of books and so-called biographies, eager to pounce on the great paradox of the Lanzmann family, incestuous careerists, prepared to do anything to climb the greasy pole. According to them I delivered my sister up to Sartre just as I had to Deleuze before him. At the root of this notion are two books by Serge Rezvani, *Les Années-lumières* [*Light-Years*], published in 1967, a few months after Évelyne's death, and

Le Testament amoureux [*The Lovers' Testament*], published in 1981. His reasons for the resentment that caused him to malign our whole family and plunge my mother into a long depression are only too obvious and I don't intend to dwell on them. I sued both the publisher and the author of *Le Testament amoureux* and won, resulting in the removal of most of the passages I had asked to be suppressed. It was republished with 'blank pages'. In September 2003, twenty-two years later, I received a letter from Serge, from which I here reproduce certain passages:

> Claude, suddenly and without truly understanding my reasons, I feel the need to write to you. Many years have passed. More than twenty years since *Le Testament amoureux* was published and many decades since our first meeting, our friendship, our family ties: Évelyne with all the pain she represents for me, for you, for Jacques, for Paulette . . . Since then, I have suffered other losses in my personal life . . . So many losses that it 'woke me up', so to speak . . . This is probably why I felt the sudden need this morning to make my peace with you because I have realized – after all these years – how much I hurt you. I truly beg you to forgive me. Perhaps you will find it impossible to overcome your bitterness. If so, peace! At least I will have made this gesture . . . I want to embrace you, in spite of everything, a repentant brother . . .

I was grateful to Serge for sending me this completely unexpected letter, and I wrote back, but so far we have not seen each other again. The copies of his book that were sold before the lawsuit could obviously not be recalled and the poison continues to work in weak minds. *Tête-à-Tête*, the umpteenth American biography of the Sartre–de Beauvoir partnership, was made up entirely of petty spite and sordid rumours intended for an ignorant public, relying heavily on that first version of *Le Testament amoureux*; sadly, it succeeded in finding a French publisher willing to translate and publish it. I didn't even need to go to court, the publisher quickly realized his mistake, stopped distributing the book and reprinted it, having removed the most unbearably vile and stupid passages. I had written to the publisher, quoting Hegel: 'No man is a hero to his valet. This is not because the hero is no hero, but because the valet is a valet.' Three months after my brother Jacques' death in 2006, I received another letter from Serge.

My dear Claude, I only belatedly heard about Jacquot's death! It saddened me deeply. We were bound, and will always be bound by so many youthful memories. This has been compounded today by another great sadness – Hazel Rowley's book . . . I refused to speak to her about Évelyne, about you, about our shared memories. You know how sorry I am about *Le Testament amoureux*! . . . I did not wish to let this sorrowful event pass without conveying my deep, unchanging affection for you. *Je t'embrasse en frère.*

Évelyne Rey, with the author of the famous play in the audience, was dazzling that night at the Comédie Caumartin. Castor sat in the middle, Sartre on her left, me on her right. I was divided, at war with myself, intensely proud of my sister's performance but terrorized, because in every one of her lines, her gestures, her movements, the properly Sartrian 'bad faith' of the mother who has killed her child, trying to come to some compromise with the truth, only served to make the unavoidable inevitable. With every line she made it more and more obvious, and each time I squeezed de Beauvoir's knee, my way of saying, 'Oh no, this is a disaster!' She clearly understood perfectly because at other moments she squeezed mine, to say, 'We are lost', as though we both formed a single Comte Mosca. Supper in a restaurant near the theatre was candlelit and perfect in every way. My sister was radiant, so beautiful she took your breath away, and Sartre played the didactic lady-killer, explaining in his metallic, authoritative voice that she was the finest Estelle he had ever seen, towering over Gaby Sylvia, who had created the role. Sartre had everything it took to seduce Évelyne, complimenting her, his reasons articulate, cogent and neatly strung together. Watching this formidable thinking machine at work, the well-oiled gears and pistons revving until it was at full throttle, left you stunned with admiration, all the more so if the goal of his implacable, passionate logic was to flatter you. Sartre's enemies mocked him for his ugliness, his squint, caricatured him as a toad, a gnome, some sordid, baleful creature. I found him handsome in a way, powerfully charming, I liked the extraordinary energy of his approach, his physical courage and, above all, that voice of tempered steel, the quintessence of irrefutable intelligence. Consequently, I was not surprised to see my predictions come true, to see my sister begin to fall in love with him. He loved her madly. I saw it when we travelled together, he, Castor and I, stamping impatiently, like a child, waiting for her to phone, throwing a tantrum when she was late, cursing and insulting her when she didn't call. At such times, I was the one he gave dirty looks to, a justified primitivism since Évelyne and I were of the same blood. He was utterly incapable of sublimating his jealousy: it was so natural to him that he did not even try to disguise it. When jealousy pricked him, he lapsed into a vile mood and his sad passion transformed his steely sovereign voice into that of a sadistic grand inquisitor. If the answers were satisfactory, he returned composed, showering praise on the very person who had him harbouring such serious suspicions. He spent hours on the phone with her, talking to her about the plays she was in, judging the playwrights, questioning her about the actors, meticulously dissecting the production. Yet still he wrote her long letters the following day in which he picked up and further developed his arguments. These missives were, first and foremost, letters of love and literature, inextricably intertwined. I can see him still, sitting beneath the arbour in the garden of the hotel in Albi, writing without let-up for two whole afternoons, including an unforgettable description of the red-brick town of Albi and its cathedral, which he read to Castor and me in the evening. We were first to hear both his declarations of love to my sister and his thoughts about Albi. For us, this went without saying, as it did for her. Whatever happened to that letter from Albi? Who took it, kept it or sold it after Évelyne's death? I'll never know.

Like Deleuze, Sartre set my sister up in an apartment at 26 rue Jacob, a stone's throw from his place, in an elegant *hôtel particulier*; a large first-floor apartment with windows overlooking the main courtyard, unlike the apartments at the rear, which faced a gloomy garden with staggered rows of tall, slender trees. Afterwards there was a scandal concerning this apartment: one of the later tenants, Alain Juppé, then Prime Minister, was accused of paying rent well below the market value. It turned out that the *hôtel particulier* belonged to the City of Paris, and tenancies were granted by the Hôtel de Ville. I wonder what connection Sartre had with the Hôtel de Ville and I tell myself, happily, that the rent he paid was not exorbitant. However, this 180-square-metre love-nest was warm and welcoming: my sister had a wonderful sense of hospitality, and it was a pleasure to spend time there, to dine with her and with Sartre in the vast main room, which was also the bedroom, or in the kitchen, which was a cosy and inviting room with state-of-the-art fittings. The difference between this and her arrangement with Deleuze was not only that Saint-Germain-des-Prés, especially back then, was much more appealing than the dreary plains and arteries of the 17th *arrondissement*, but that Sartre, though he continued to work 300 metres away in his tiny apartment at 42 rue Bonaparte, to all intents and purposes lived with Évelyne, at least in the beginning, in the first flush of passion. And although she admired him unreservedly, she was never in thrall to him as she had been with Deleuze. Sartre's infantile fits of jealousy did not change the fact that, as a philosophical advocate of freedom, he had insisted from the first that this be the basis for their relationship, allowing my sister to develop and to maintain a certain intimate and sarcastic distance from him, making it possible for her to deal with and to protect herself from what was imposed on her. Michelle Vian being Sartre's *maîtresse en titre* meant that absolute secrecy about the newcomer was enforced, notwithstanding the flames of passion burning in the heart of the sultan of the rue Bonaparte. Évelyne would never be centre stage, or be granted the status of favourite; she would have to content herself with being his darling yet in the shadows, with the understanding that their relationship was a jealously guarded secret, shared only with the inner circle – such as Castor and me. And so their liaison was crowned with an exquisite, a precious quality that would have been impossible under the harsh spotlight of a public affair.

What remains most vivid to me when I think of those early years in the rue Jacob is how joyous their relationship was. With Sartre, as with Castor, the only inexhaustible subject of conversation was the world. The world was what we had read in the newspapers, in books, it included politics, people we knew, people we had met, friends, enemies, endless gossip, catty, witty, partisan, and not remotely *'enculturé'* to use one of Sartre's words, an endless backbiting that we resumed after work. It was something at which Évelyne excelled, given her caustic wit, her keen eye and her hilarious turns of phrase. People were struck by her combination of beauty and intelligence; she had many friends, both men and women. Sartre paid for the apartment and gave her money – as he did to his other mistresses – when she wasn't working. *'Voilà le sou'* was the invariable note that accompanied a cheque. My sister was happy for several years; she had her acting, she had Sartre, to whom she was faithful until she finally decided to leave him because she could no longer bear the enforced secrecy. In the beginning it had been easy, but as time went on it had become intolerable. Sartre's holidays were exclusively reserved for Castor and Michelle Vian, and when she realized that this would never change, Évelyne resolved to give him up, after two years or perhaps three, I'm not sure. But both valued the special relationship they had; Évelyne stayed on in the apartment on the rue Jacob and Sartre visited several times a week, advising her in everything, he was her closest confidant and the one to whom she most often turned. The term 'break-up' in the ordinary sense is inadequate: it was both a change and something permanent. My sister, who was the epitome of loyalty and discretion, never broke the promise she had made to Sartre; Michelle Vian never learned about their relationship from her. Obviously, quite a lot of people were aware of the relationship and yet it remained a secret until her suicide, one she did nothing to betray. In her *Memoirs*, Simone de Beauvoir kept the code of *omertà*, passing over the relationship between Sartre and Évelyne in silence, something that I know caused her considerable pain since, in so doing, an important period in her life was obliterated. Quite recently, I was told that Michelle Vian did not learn of the relationship until after Sartre's death: there are none so blind as those who will not see!

Évelyne's tact was also evident in the fact that, although she was surrounded by handsome men – actors, directors and intellectuals – Sartre's successor was neither taller nor more handsome, and he was certainly not rich. It was Robert Dupuy, whom she referred to by the nickname 'Roro', a big-hearted lawyer of keen intelligence; Sartre, who was invited to dinner with them on several occasions, was very fond of him. To tell the truth, I think that my sister felt more at ease, reassured by ugly men. Love, for her, was something other than the dual mirage of alluring images; love was first and foremost of the soul, since Évelyne found it difficult to accept her beauty, so evident to others but so problematic to her: she never felt that she was beautiful, never considered herself inherently beautiful, so it was a constant source of uncertainty, of anxious self-doubt that could never be assuaged. A beautiful woman is merely an ugly woman in disguise, Sartre wrote somewhere, and it was not for nothing that Évelyne delighted in the fierce materialism of Albert Cohen's *Belle du seigneur* [*Her Lover*]. Before the handsome Solal seduces the exquisite Ariane by explaining to her in stunning detail the theorems, lemmas and scholia on which his loathing of seduction is based, he begins by making himself loathsome to her – *horribile visu* – by covering up his front teeth with black tape, leaving only the two gleaming canines to make himself look like a toothless old man. 'A pair of canine teeth, he later mocked her after she had surrendered to him body and soul, that is what your love is worth.'

This whole period of Évelyne's life, before and after Sartre, coincides with the Algerian War. Like the rest of us, she was in favour of independence and a passionate campaigner. She attended every demonstration and was beaten by police on several occasions. Sometimes we were arrested together and would spend the night in a cell in Saint-Sulpice police station stichomythically reciting to one another couplets from the great tragedies or alternating stanzas from Hugo's *La Légende des siècles* with such brio that, towards four o'clock in the morning, just as in his 'Booz endormi' ['Boaz Asleep'], '*une immense bonté tombait du firmament*' ['a great goodness tumbled from the firmament'], causing the weary, human eyes of our guards to mist over. Algerians wanted by the police were given refuge at Evelyne's apartment on the rue Jacob while she was rehearsing *Les Séquestrés d'Altona*, Sartre's magnificent play about man's hatred of man, which transposes the denunciation of the crimes and tortures we were committing on the far side of the Mediterranean to post-war Germany.

The première took place in September 1959 at the Théâtre de la Renaissance and Johanna, Évelyne's role, was written specifically for her. As we know, all of Sartre's plays were written for women and, as Cau puts it so beautifully in *Croquis de mémoire*: 'rather than give them flowers, he offered plays'. But *Les Séquestrés d'Altona* was the only dramatic piece he wrote for Évelyne, though by then their love affair had been over for several years. It was a wonderful gift: Johanna is a great female role, an actress forced to abandon her profession after she marries, fascinated by the half-feigned madness of her brother-in-law Franz, who has imprisoned himself in his room; though she is in love with him, she is also the embodiment of lucidity and strength, cardinal virtues that lead her not to live out her love for a torturer. There were problems with *Les Séquestrés d'Altona* from the moment rehearsals began. Sartre was forced to cut the play, which was much too long, then cut it further, and as misunderstandings between him and the director François Darbon multiplied, he had to take over part of the responsibility for the *mise en scène*. All this contributed to an atmosphere of mounting tension and as a whole the play was not understood. Poirot-Delpech, the papal critic at *Le Monde*, stupidly referred to it as an 'illustrated philosophical thesis'. With the exception of Serge Reggiani, who was on stage for three hours, he 'forgave' the other actors, including my sister, for not breathing life into such a 'glacial and disembodied' work. Sartre had not written for the theatre for four years, and was being made to pay for his political stance in a pre-civil war atmosphere. (The play was performed again six years later, in 1965, with the same cast, directed by François Périer.)

In 1960, the year that followed the first production, politics seriously impinged on my sister's career and her life: together with the rest of us, and against my advice, since I foresaw the consequences, she signed the Manifesto of the 121, calling on conscripts to refuse to serve in Algeria. Reprisals were swift. At the time, she had been doing a lot of work for television – state-owned television – and she was immediately penalized, all her contracts cancelled, closing those doors to her for several years. She was thirty years old. Signing the Manifesto was a serious act: Jean Pouillon was a member of the editorial committee of *Les Temps modernes*, but as he was also a civil servant and secretary of the parliamentary debates at the Assemblée Nationale, he was immediately suspended. Simone Signoret, whom I tried to persuade to sign the Manifesto because she was a figurehead, and a friend of mine, immediately understood the dangers she would be running were she to sign. She told me of a conversation between Jean Gabin, various technicians and some minor actors on the set of a film they were making when war was declared in 1939. Everyone was upset, some of them were crying, but Gabin barked, 'I don't know what you're all snivelling about, you don't have much to lose. As for me . . .' In relating the story, she was trying to tell me that intellectuals, those who earned their living by the pen, depended only on themselves, while she would be blacklisted by television, where she appeared regularly, and by the theatre and the cinema. It took me three days to persuade her: it can truly be said that when she signed the Manifesto she was fully aware of what she was doing, which makes it all the more to her credit. Évelyne, I believed, did so unthinkingly.

History picked up speed. In July 1961, Sartre's apartment at 42 rue Bonaparte was blown up for the first time by the OAS (the *Organisation armée secrète*, a militant group determined that Algeria would remain French and resolved to spread panic in France). Sartre and de Beauvoir exiled themselves to a dismal three-room apartment where, when I went to visit, I practised the various ruses for shaking off a tail that I had learned during my time in the Resistance. The evenings we spent together there were wonderful. They were in fine form and neither of them were inclined to panic. As long as he could write, Sartre was unruffled. Évelyne had to leave the beautiful future apartment of Alain Juppé, which had become too expensive for Sartre as he was on the run; since she was unemployed, she moved to quarters in the same building on the second floor at the rear, which, though very nice, were a third the size and overlooked a melancholy quincunx of trees. She was now the lover of Norbert Bensaïd, an eminent doctor and psychoanalyst, who, despite his numerous promises, ultimately never left his wife. I have read his letters, which were awkward, embarrassed, evasive and ultimately boring, as might be the letters of any man in such a cowardly position. She had other lovers, more than she should have had, perhaps, and every time I was told about one, I would recite two lines from Musset's 'Rolla': 'It is as though, on each new love, you see, / The sun arise from night's eternity'. When the Algerians were released from French prisons, both before and after the signing of the Évian Accords, for some of them the rue Jacob was a stopover and a haven. Ahmed Taleb Ibrahimi, who went on to become the Minister for Foreign Affairs in the first Algerian government and later the Minister for Education, a supporter of extreme Arabization, of strict Islamic teaching and of polygamy, was Évelyne's lover for the few days he spent there. I met him, a thin man with a neatly trimmed beard and the fine features of an intellectual consumed from within. He was careful not to say what he truly thought. I helped him, I liked him and I think he liked me, but I never heard from him again: a number of messages from me went unanswered. In the photos of the period my sister is still beautiful but she seems distraught, you can read the terror on her face.

In September 1965, on the opening night of the revival of Les Séquestrés d'Altona at the Théâtre de l'Athénée, I was backstage in Évelyne's dressing room with Sartre and Simone de Beauvoir some minutes before she went on stage. The theatre was full, we could clearly hear the audience's impatient stamping, since the performance was late starting. Évelyne, who was in the first scene, did not want to go on. Dressed in Johanna's luxurious white dress, her hair in a German braid, she trembled from head to foot before suddenly bursting into convulsive sobs, followed by a heartbreaking wail that drowned out the noise of the audience. The three of us surrounded her, kissing her in turn and talking to her, trying to convince her that everything would be fine, that she was, that she would be, wonderful. To me, it seemed clear that disaster was inevitable: for her, for Sartre, for the play, for the theatre. An announcement was made that there was a technical hitch, then, suddenly, inexplicably, she pulled herself together, dried her eyes, redid her make-up and went on stage. She acted very well: her voice was brittle, almost emotionless; I had never seen her as good in this play. Sartre must have resented her for it; I can understand him.

I found a letter from her addressed to our mother, from when she was studying at the Centre Dramatique de l'Ouest. In it she announces that they would be performing in Paris and writes: 'You'll all be there, you, Monny, Claude and Jacques, I'll be sick with fear. It's such a shame, I get completely paralysed by stage-fright. I always give my best performances in little godforsaken villages where I don't have to be afraid that friends or family will be watching.' At the Théâtre de l'Athénée, all of Paris was watching, the stakes were high and stage-fright, rather than spurring her on as it does most actors – as it did Judith – made her even more afraid of the public and the judgement of others. Her terrifying outburst was evidence of an existential failure, the consequences of which she could not fail to draw. As soon as the play was over, she fell ill. It had been expected that she would go on a long European tour with the play in January 1966; instead she was urgently admitted to the Clinique Claude Bernard where she was diagnosed with purulent pleurisy of the right lung. She was in hospital from 17 January until 5 March 1966, suffering day and night, after which she endured ongoing complications requiring injections in the following months before being readmitted to the clinic in early August. Whenever I went to see her at the hospital, I invariably ran into Claude Roy, either in the corridors or in her room. He visited her daily, sometimes several times a day. He claimed to be hopelessly in love with her, he told her as much, convinced her of it, persuaded her with an avalanche of cards, love letters, poems, telegrams, *pneumatiques,* etc. Leaving her room, he stopped off at the matron's office, scribbled out a madrigal on Assistance Publique notepaper and asked for it to be taken to Évelyne immediately. I have all of Claude's letters, he was a born writer, poetry welled up in him, it was his innate language, he was incredibly gifted, unbelievably talented, inventive, a real box of tricks, an astounding magician. Rereading his letters years later, I am still in awe of his gifts, and I wonder how a woman who was so physically weak and fighting for her life – since Évelyne was allergic to the only antibiotic that might have been effective, forcing her doctors to find alternative ways to treat her – could resist such a bombardment of love, especially if she was as enamoured of the words as of their sender, of the sudden changes of subject, strange associations, the linguistic games of this poet who proclaimed her to be his muse, his inspiration, the fount of this spectacular creativity that so astonished her? They had known each other for a long time, but it was only when he saw her lying in a hospital bed that his curious passion revealed itself. In the months that followed, they talked about living together, but Évelyne could not think so far ahead. She was convinced that, after her recovery, they would spend the summer together by the sea as he had so often promised; this was all that mattered to her. As the holidays approached, the decision became pressing. Claude's wife, the actress Loleh Bellon, gave him an ultimatum: 'It's her or me.' He was deeply attached to Loleh: she was his bedrock, beside which his amorous poetic effusions to my sister mattered little. Claude, ineffably civilized, broke up with Évelyne with barbaric brutality. I have two of his letters here in front of me, one undated, tender still, but with a tenderness that sounds hollow, where he begins to distance himself, telling her that he will not be able to see her over the next few days, writing: 'You were very wise not to take the cyanide capsule or throw yourself on the electric fence, because you are destined to do fascinating and beautiful things with your life . . .' Clearly, he knew that she had already seriously contemplated suicide, but this did not stop him from sending his last letter to her, dated 27 July 1966, just before he headed off into the sun with his lawfully wedded wife, disappearing entirely. It is clear from reading it that Évelyne had said to him, 'I curse you': he defends himself piteously against this curse. She had counted on her holiday with Claude as the beginning of a new life for her, something that would open up new horizons. She had turned thirty-six on 9 July. I had never seen her as desperate, as gaunt, as distraught as she was after this break-up; the broken promise, the withdrawal of love, which she had entirely failed to anticipate.

She would not even hear talk of returning to the theatre, but thought – we all thought – that she would be able to make films and, in the short term, documentary features for television. She was curious about everything and her nature was such that people found it easy to trust her, she could get them to talk, to open up their deepest selves. Éliane Victor, who at the time presented the celebrated television programme *Les Femmes . . . aussi*, and who was very fond of Évelyne, asked her to produce a piece about women in Tunisia. She travelled there in August, and again in September, researching locations. The filming itself took place in October and she started to edit as soon as she got back. She became very close to Bahia, one of the Tunisian women she had chosen as the heroine of her film, and had been adopted by the whole family. She felt as though she had discovered something essential, something that would not prove fleeting.

On the afternoon of 18 November 1966, Pierre Lazareff, the managing editor of *France-Soir*, *Elle* and the various magazines and newspapers of what was, back then, the most important press group in France – at the time I was writing a long feature each month for *Elle*, which was run by his wife Hélène, and I worked one afternoon and one evening a week as part of the famous team of rewriters at *France Dimanche* – called me in person from his second-floor office on the rue Réaumur: 'Claude, you must come and see me, it's urgent.' From his tone it was clear that he was upset, because he was a good man. He told me, 'Go to the rue Jacob straight away, a terrible thing has happened.' It was Norbert Bensaïd who opened the door to me, clearly distraught: he had found my sister's body an hour earlier. I rushed to her bed, she was lying on her side, her face was beautiful, gentle, peaceful. I pulled back the sheets, her body was burning up, it was impossible to think that the breath of life had left her forever. Incredulous, I asked Norbert if there was anything we could do, anything that might bring her round. He told me she had been dead for several hours; if her body was still warm it was because the apartment was overheated. She had not only taken barbiturates, she had taken a poison for which there was no antidote. She had made absolutely sure that there was no chance that she might be saved, calling her cleaning lady and instructing her not to come at the usual hour and telling Norbert, who had been very worried and rang her almost every day, that she would not be in Paris. She had arranged things so that by the time she was discovered, she would be dead.

She had left three letters, laid out carefully, each envelope with a name and address written in pencil, one for Sartre, one for her friend Dolores Ruspoli, one for me. The letters were brief, but it must have been to Dolores that she wrote the last letter, because mid-way through a sentence her handwriting suddenly trails off and plunges from the horizontal to the vertical, a sign that the poison had done its work and she no longer had the strength to continue. She had probably done the fatal deed in the middle of the night, towards four o'clock. She was clear-headed when she did so, there is no pathos in the letters, she briefly put her affairs in order, knowing that she was dying. To me: 'My dear Claudie, I implore you, the script for the whole programme is here, I want you to ask Éliane to look at the edit of the film carefully, to ensure all the important narration is in there; I would be grateful if you could go, that way at least I will have done one good thing. Claude, my brother, my darling little brother, I love you. É.' To Dolores: 'My Dodo, don't let them knock me about too much. I'm not getting any better in myself, even though on the outside, everything is going really well. At least I managed that. I love you. I want you to have the apartment. Robert will talk to you about it.' I don't remember whether I read these letters as soon as I saw her there on the bed or whether I did so later. I don't have her letter to Sartre, but I remember that it was affectionate. As every day at this time, Castor and Sartre were working together in his new little apartment at 222 boulevard Raspail. Norbert and I held each other and sobbed. It was utterly unbearable.

Norbert left, I stayed with her, there could be no question of leaving her alone and, as I sat with her, with my dead sister, I felt a sharp pang of remorse, one that has never left me: if she had phoned me before she took the poison, I would have been here in a flash and maybe I could have prevented it. But she did not call, she knew that Judith, who was living with me, didn't like her; she wouldn't have dared, she hadn't dared. I told myself that I had to let everyone know, my brother, Paulette, Monny, my father, Castor, Sartre, but for a long time I simply sat there, saddened at the thought of being the bearer of such tragic news, knowing the suffering it would cause. I called Castor, who burst into tears. I said, 'You have to come,' and I heard her speak to Sartre. She said, 'I'll come. Sartre doesn't want to.' I insisted, 'It's unthinkable that he wouldn't come, he has no right not to.' He came. My brother's first words when he arrived – he was a media star at the time and very busy – shocked me. He took me by the shoulders and said, 'Claudie, swear to me that you'll never do such a thing!' All of Paris came, all Saint-Germain-des-Prés, all the actors she had worked with, all those who loved her, all her lovers, past and present, with the exception of Deleuze and Rezvani, came; they came by day and by night in an unending convivial wake. Sartre and Castor spent several hours there every evening, sipping their Chivas, Évelyne's countless friends were happy to see them, to speak to them simply, everyone recalling memories of Évelyne when she was alive. From time to time, one or other of them would leave the group and go and sit on Évelyne's bed, stroking her hair, kissing her cold forehead. I had unwillingly become a kind of *chef du protocol*, the master of ceremonies, because many of those who came would never have met each other in the normal course of events, or their encounters would have been explosive.

Paulette, shattered as much by the way in which her daughter had died as by the death itself, unleashed her gifts as a detective, her talents as an investigator, doggedly tenacious, publicly demanding explanations. She blamed me, she blamed Sartre, I had to come up with stratagems to keep her away, to prevent her from confronting him. But every suicide requires a guilty party, a scapegoat. The most obvious was Claude Roy: I had found his letters in the apartment. I couldn't bear the thought that he might come to the funeral, none of us could. Sartre sent him a harsh letter, I've forgotten exactly what he said, but he told him he would not be welcome. Claude did not come, but I do remember the first words of his reply to Sartre: 'Sartre, your grief must have been dreadful, your letter was.' We agreed that he knew how to write.

We kept Évelyne at home for far too long, almost ten days, and the sweetish scent of her corpse pervaded the room. Since the funeral could not take place at the weekend, it was deferred to the beginning of the following week and the undertakers had to armour her body with plates of ice. When the coffin was brought out to be taken to Montparnasse cemetery, the tall-treed garden and the main courtyard of number 26, and the whole of the rue Jacob itself, was thronged with a silent, grieving, contemplative crowd. For everyone who followed the hearse, the death of Évelyne Rey was shattering.

As the years went by, I found it increasingly unfair that Claude Roy had been made the scapegoat of her suicide. If there is blame to be apportioned, it should be shared, and there are many of us who must shoulder some responsibility. It is not a game I wish to play. I met Claude at the Festival d'Avignon once, I told him I was sorry, offered to make peace and we did so.

Bahia, ou ces femmes de Tunisie [*Bahia, or the Women of Tunisia*], the television programme Évelyne was rightly proud of, was broadcast almost two years after her suicide, on 3 January 1968; it was fifty minutes long and was universally praised for its great intelligence and humanity. Robert Morris held the camera. My sister, beautiful, young, slim, her hair in braids, is on screen with sweet-faced Bahia for almost the whole film. And today, as I write these lines, more than forty years after the film was shot, I received – to my surprise – a diary from Jelila Hafsia, a Tunisian intellectual I don't know, entitled *Instants de vie – chronique familière* [*Moments in Life – a Family Chronicle*], whose first entry is dated 1 June 1964. She explains to me that she worked as an interpreter for Évelyne in her conversations with Bahia and recommends that I read some of the relevant passages. I shall quote one or two:

Monday, 21 November 1966. I got a phone call from Moncef telling me that Évelyne Rey is dead. It's awful. I can hardly believe it. I had a letter from her three days ago. She wanted to spend a few days with us in the south. So young, so beautiful, so generous . . . The days we spent together, she and I . . . Why this suicide? She left Tunisia a fortnight ago in good spirits, happy to be alive . . . Her fears had receded . . . She was so happy with the film. I buy *Le Monde*. Read it with a terrible sense of sadness: 'Death of the actress Évelyne Rey. The actress took her own life on Thursday night by swallowing the contents of a tube of barbiturates.' The whole world seems meaningless to me.

Wednesday, 23 November 1966. Last night, I had a sudden desire to see Évelyne, and I felt sad, terribly sad. I couldn't sleep. Her youth, her beauty, her kindness. Why? Making the film had been really important to her – her encounters with Bahia . . . How do I tell Bahia?

Friday, 25 November 1966. I went to Mellassine in Tunis to see Bahia. I had to talk to her, to tell her that Évelyne won't be coming back . . . Bahia collapsed . . .

My sister's suicide devastated me; I thought I would always live in the shadow of her death, that it would be the only way of remaining loyal to her. A friend of Sartre's, Claude Day, whom I did not really know but in whom I confided and who had also suffered great misfortune, told me, 'You're wrong, you will forget, life always prevails.' She was right. And wrong. I have forgotten nothing. I have lived. But November is still worthless to me, it is the month of Évelyne's death, it is also the month of my birth.

Chapter 10

Voglio morire, voglio morire' ['I want to die, I want to die'], at almost
regular intervals the cry broke the silence of the sweltering
night in the Florence train station. Swaggering, Mussolini-style
architecture, with Carrara marble platforms, but empty of trains,
except for a prison wagon full of common-law criminals waiting for
an improbable locomotive, the serried convicts suffering the agonies
of ignorance, of helplessness, of thirst, of overcrowding. Even we, as
we lay on the cool marble, exhausted from having paced the platforms
for hours looking for any train heading south, only to find that no
one – in the chaos of the Italian railways in that summer of 1946 –
could tell us when or if there would be a train, whether it would be a
passenger train or a freight train like those used in the deportations;
even we felt close to the howling man and his desperate pleas. There
were five of us, all *khâgne* students. Cau, who had just taken up his
position as secretary to Sartre, had assumed the role of leader because
Sartre had entrusted him with a message to take to his publisher in
Milan, asking him to give us the lire we needed for our journey
since, the currency exchange regulations being both complicated
and erratic, it was almost impossible to get lire in France. We had all
handed over what money we had to Cau, and he had set himself up
as paymaster-general. This was our first trip abroad. I was intensely
excited, the connecting of names with places, the names of stations

fleetingly glimpsed in the darkness – Brig, Simplon, Domodossola, Stresa – all attested to the truth of the world, merging language and reality, poignantly revealing the truth. Thinking back now it seems as though our youth and the youth of the world were melded there, and it is certainly true that any first time has a distinct flavour. And yet even now, I may experience something as intensely as I did when I was twenty; on reflection, I think it has nothing to do with youth or with age. Not long ago, driving from Río Gallegos in Tierra del Fuego across the vast plains of Argentine Patagonia, alone behind the wheel of a rental car, heading for the Chilean border and the magnificent Perito Moreno glacier, I kept repeating over and over, with the same joy I felt on that first train trip to Milan, 'I'm in Patagonia, I'm in Patagonia.' Yet it wasn't *real*, though I might have seen a few small herds of white llamas, Patagonia was not truly incarnate in me. It suddenly became so at dusk, on the last stretch of unpaved road after the little town of El Calafate, in the sweeping of my headlights, when a long-legged hare leaped like an arrow and hopped across the road in front of me. I had just seen a Patagonian hare, a magical animal. Now all of Patagonia suddenly pierced my heart with the sure knowledge of our mutual presence. I am neither indifferent to, nor weary of, this world; had I a hundred lives, I know I would not tire of it.

Milan, which over many years and numerous visits I came to think of as a heavy Lombard city, charmless and rather ugly, Milan dazzled me when we arrived there one morning. It was the first coloured city I had ever seen: the reds, the yellows, the ochres of its walls, its roofs, thrilled me with their newness. We stayed just long enough for our leader to get our money, because the itinerary of this rite-of-passage had been decided by him and voted on by everyone else: Venice, Florence and Naples, skipping Rome and the rest of Italy. But I know by heart the first lines of very many books, and as I wandered alone around the Duomo, I endlessly repeated once again, so that Milan and I could be one, the opening lines of *La Chartreuse de Parme*: 'On 15 May 1796, General Bonaparte made his entry into Milan at the head of a youthful army which had just crossed the bridge at Lodi, and announced to the world that after so many centuries, Caesar and Alexander had a successor.'

On to Venice, with no time to lose. Our paymaster-general, dazzled by the thickness of the wad of lire he had just received and by the then spectacular size of Italian banknotes, kept our money in his overstuffed back pocket, feeling invulnerable. I warned him, 'Be careful, we should divide it up.' 'We'll divide it up this evening,' he said, periodically slapping his pocket to ensure the loot was still there, and inadvertently, every time he did so, signalling its existence to exceptionally brilliant and well-trained pickpockets. It happened on our very first day, on a *vaporetto* on the Grand Canal: the paymaster's pocket was neatly sliced with a razor and emptied without him noticing a thing. The trip was over before it had even begun and the magnitude of the catastrophe was such that it precluded any anger or reproach. Between the five of us, we managed to rustle up enough money to last a day. Cau wanted to ring Sartre for help but didn't know where he was. I remembered that Toni Gaggio, my aunt Sophie's husband – the circumcised Venetian *belote* champion of Clichy – had mentioned before we left that a close relative owned a glassworks on Murano. My mother, ever prudent and fretful, had insisted that I take the address. I called, using my best Italo-Latin; the voice on the other end was at first curt and peremptory, but the name Toni Gaggio was like an Open Sesame and he agreed to meet with us the following day. I have racked my brains but I cannot remember the name of this captain of industry. His factory was massive, with glass-blowers describing convoluted arabesques of liquid glass in the air. The five of us were led upstairs to an immense office with windows overlooking the lagoon on all sides, where Il Duce was waiting for us. He was considerably shorter than Mussolini, but like him drew himself up to his full height and had the same way of clenching his jaw, throwing his head back, flaring his nostrils – in other words, posing as though for a round of applause exactly like the dictator addressing the Fascist hordes from the balcony of Rome's Palazzo di Venezia. Fifteen months earlier, Benito Mussolini, together with his mistress Clara Petacci, had been executed by Communist partisans, their corpses strung up by the feet in a Milan street, but here he was, resurrected, in the office of Toni's relative, who displayed photos of himself being decorated by Il Duce, of leading marches of Blackshirts next to the Leader; moving snapshots of him taking part, as a young man, in the 1922 March on Rome. He was a true Fascist, proud of the fact, and whatever *Paisà* or *Rome, Open City* might suggest, Mussolini's influence in Venice, in Tuscany, the Abruzzi, Romagna and Campania was and remains much greater than the later history of the Italian Left and Communism has been prepared to admit. Cau was very uncomfortable, glancing around nervously, while our other companions, Maurice Bouvet, René Guyonnet and René Bray, said nothing. I was the only one to speak and, since this Fascist caricature strangely inspired in me a sort of sympathy, I found it all the easier. I told him everything, promising to repay him as soon as we got back to France; he asked me how much had been stolen and didn't skimp, barking an order, summoning a foreman, instructing him to give us a tour of the factory before calling me back into his office and handing me, with panache, the exact amount that had been stolen from Cau. It was a family affair between him, Gaggio and me.

I have intentionally referred to the deep, abiding influence of Mussolini. A year ago, I wanted to visit once more the Paestum temples south of Salerno in the heart of Campania, to see again the sublime fresco of the Diver. These are the most perfect of the peripteral Doric temples, and I have always loved to dive – I still do on occasion. I had dinner in the evening near the edge of the temple complex, in a restaurant where I knew I could get some incomparable *mozzarella di bufala*, one of the joys of the Paestum region. On previous visits I had not noticed that this particular restaurant backed on to a large patrician house, which – having gone to wash my hands – I wandered into almost by accident, only to experience, sixty years later, the same stupefied astonishment I had felt in Venice in our benefactor's office: I allowed myself to be led from room to room, floor to floor, past photographs of the current proprietors in the company of Mussolini, with his son-in-law Galeazzo Ciano, both wearing black shirts, arms outstretched in a hearty Fascist salute. Nothing was hidden, there was no shame, no crime, this was the history of Italy and for me it was like an exhumation.

In Venice we divided up the money, but the Italian thieves proved more cunning, surprising and inventive than my sensible friends. Each of them in turn was fleeced again; I was the only one whose vigilance never failed me. The phenomenon reached its apogee in Naples on the eve of our return to France. The five of us were sharing one room in a dubious *pensione*. We had just enough to pay for our train tickets and our fear of being robbed had grown exponentially, superstitiously, to become a mortal terror. Since by this time we could barely stand the sight of each other, it had been decided that on our last day in Naples we would each do our own thing, but the money for the tickets was to be put in an impregnable strong-box and left in the room. When we returned that evening, Guyonnet, the future managing editor of *L'Express*, was missing. Someone decided to check: the money was also missing. Guyonnet arrived back late, looking business-like, wearing the sunglasses he wore day and night to render him anonymous, carrying a large parcel tied up with string that he set down carefully like a treasure on the table. 'What do you think of this?' he asked, opening it up. Aside from the mood of mystery, and the impassive poker-face he preserved in all circumstances, Guyonnet, who was from Luçon in the Vendée, had another abiding passion: the American language. He had already translated one of the first 'Série Noire' published by Gallimard. Now, on his last tour of the port of Naples, he had been approached by an 'American marine' who offered to sell him pure cashmere, worth its weight in gold, a deal that had to be concluded immediately because his ship was about to put out to sea. Feverish with excitement, Guyonnet had rushed back to the *pensione* and took it upon himself to seize all the money for the journey home to finance the deal of the century. 'What do you think of this?' The cashmere was nothing but paper, which, the moment it was touched, disintegrated into scraps, strips, confetti, into air! That evening I hated my dear friend as much as I hated Bagelman who couldn't bring himself to shoot the *milicien*. The following morning we went to the French consul in Naples to beg him to arrange for us to be repatriated. Understandably, he bemoaned the stupidity of his compatriots. Only Sartre's name stirred him into action. During the forty-hour journey from Naples to Nice, Guyonnet was completely ostracized. Forty hours standing on a train, with no possibility of sitting down: by the time I got to Nice my ankles had swollen to four times their size; it was three days before I could walk again.

After the summer, I enrolled in the Sorbonne, effortlessly studied for a number of *certificats de licence*, attended the philosophy lectures of Jean Wahl, Martial Guéroult, who for me represented an ideal of humanity, Gaston Bachelard with his wonderful, thick Burgundian accent, Georges Canguilhem and Jean Laporte, who agreed to supervise my postgraduate diploma. As I have already mentioned, I chose to focus on Leibniz and monadology, more specifically, on 'possibles and incompossibles' in the philosophy of that extraordinary mind that, even now, continually illuminates my thoughts and surprises me by its modernity. Michel Tournier persuaded me to join him in Germany, at the University of Tübingen in the French Occupied Zone. With orders from the military government, French students could get a sort of grant in the form of sixty meals per month at the Maison de France, a comfortable property from which you could look down on the Neckar Valley and young, muscular German boys rowing, just like the students at Oxford and Cambridge. The grant also entitled you to a room with a local family. Tournier, who had arrived there several months before me, met me at the station and, although he was living near the castle, informed me that the room allocated to me was on Hegelstraße, a road running parallel to the railway, from which I could hear the trains twenty-four hours a day. The landlord of this less-than-prestigious address was a short, chubby, rather jolly man from Schwaben. His name was Riese, which means 'giant'. His wife was a German matron with a soft voice who was prepared to do anything for me. In addition to my room/office, I had use of the living room. And so I spent several hours a day reading Leibniz on Hegel's street, convincing myself of the profound truth of monadology, each monad being an entire world in itself, but hermetic, with no door, no window (I'd say to Tournier, who was working on Plato, 'I will never know what your life is like, mine will forever be alien to you'), if a little more sceptical about the great detour into Leibniz's 'system of pre-established harmony' that was needed to make it all work. I was charmed by his letters to Queen Christina of Sweden: 'I come once more to speak to you, Madame, of my beloved unities . . .' 'Why is there something rather than nothing?', a way of dealing with the radical nature of contingency, his theory of 'little perceptions' prefiguring Freud and the subconscious, his principle of 'the identity of indiscernibles' kept me busy for the winter of 1947. Deleuze, who would later write about Leibniz – the possible and the incompossible were a major preoccupation for him – twice came to visit Tournier and me: for him, as for us, Germany was still philosophy's mother country and we could not imagine its overthrow, as was hoped for by Vladimir Jankélévitch, for example. But it was with the future author of *Vendredi ou les limbes du Pacifique* [*Friday, or the Other Island*], *Le Roi des aulnes* [*The Erl-King* or *The Ogre*] and *Météores* [*Gemini*] that I spent most of my free time. Tournier was from a family of German scholars, spoke the language fluently and, as a child, had spent time in Hitler's Germany. He rode and encouraged me to go with him. There was a military riding school in Tübingen run by a Colonel Whitechurch. I joined up, and, under the tutelage of a former *Wehrmacht* instructor continually barking insults and orders, I learned to perform riding figures, to ride bareback, to dismount a horse at full gallop, to run in the sawdust alongside the animal and get back into the saddle. I was pretty good and with every lesson I improved. Happiness for me was heading off with the school for long rides through the forest; riding a tall mare called Ténébreuse who would sometimes take off through the trees at a wild, terrifying gallop and, so as not to shatter a knee against a tree trunk, I had to saw at the reins with all my strength and force her to stop, steaming, rearing and trembling. On Ténébreuse, I also learned to show-jump.

Tournier had a jovial, hail-fellow-well-met, barrack-room buddy side; he was succinct and clear-thinking, but would suddenly, without warning, become absent, swallowed up by who knew what abyss. This was a different Tournier, one prey to bouts of bleak isolation that could last for hours or days, though it was probably in this crucible that the malign reversals of the dark, dizzying masterpieces he would one day write were forged. In Tübingen he was friends with Thomas Harlan, the son of Veit Harlan, the director of *Jud Süss* [*Jew Süss*], the anti-Semitic film commissioned by Goebbels and adapted – so perversely as to utterly turn it on its head – from the wonderful novel by Lion Feuchtwanger, a hymn to the Jews of medieval Germany that is impossible to read without tears. I fancied a French secretary attached to the military government, or rather to the Security Services, who consented to come to my room on the Hegelstraße once or twice, teasing me with her long beautiful legs, her high heels. But the moment I tried to press what I assumed was my advantage, she stopped me dead: 'I could never make love with a Jew,' she declared abruptly. I asked why. It was simple: the Jews had ruined her family and, her eyes blazing vengefully, she began to recount an outrageous story worthy of the *Rassenschande* [race-shame], the charge Nazis levelled against those who sullied the purity of the race by fraternizing with Jews. This Jew threw her out and she left, petulant. The following day I received a threatening visit from her boss, the red-faced alcoholic chief of the Security Services, who was clearly also her lover and who had brought a henchman with him. He advised me to cease my obscene harassment immediately and to 'watch my step' because I could 'very easily be deported'. The faces of these good Frenchmen were deformed by poisonous anti-Semitism. My relationships with German students were, thankfully, more compatible and less frustrating.

Wendi von Neurath, whom I met through Tournier, invited me to spend the weekend at her family home near Stuttgart, about a hundred kilometres from Tübingen. She was an attractive girl, of medium height, a little plump, with every pore exuding goodwill and morality in action. Her uncle, Konstantin von Neurath, a career diplomat from a long line of aristocrats, had been an ambassador, then Minister of Foreign Affairs in both the von Papen government that cleared Hitler's path to power and in Hitler's government until 1938, and later *Reichsprotektor* of the Protectorate of Bohemia and Moravia until relieved of his duties in 1941 for being too lenient – he was succeeded by none other than Reinhard Heydrich before he was assassinated by Czech partisans. Von Neurath was subsequently named ambassador to Ankara, and was among the accused at the Nuremberg trials. He was sentenced to fifteen years in prison, but served only eight. He was released in 1954, seven years after my visit to the ancestral family home. Wendi's mother was Konstantin's sister and their place was very different from what in France we call a *grande propriété*: it was what the Germans call a *Gut*, literally a 'good', sprawling over thousands of hectares where the feudal system still more or less prevailed: here were hundreds of peasant farmers who, before my incredulous eyes, knelt before Baroness von Neurath, a tall, lean woman whose certainties and habits seemed invincible against the hustle and bustle of History. I told myself that, far from what people claimed, the deep-rooted fabric of the German fatherland had not all been destroyed. It lived on in Tübingen, in hundreds of small towns in Swabia, in countless villages. Decades later, as I toiled back and forth across Germany, researching and filming *Shoah*, I arrived in the beautiful little medieval town of Günzburg, so picture-perfect that it was almost a caricature: birthplace of Dr Josef Mengele,

Auschwitz's 'angel of death', and the site of the Mengele factories. In the many kilometres of fields and meadows around Günzburg, the side-panels and roofs of tractors and combine-harvesters still proudly bore the name MENGELE, repeated *ad nauseam*.

The von Neurath *Gut* was near Vaihingen. I arrived one Saturday evening and spent a restive night beneath a thick eiderdown in a virginal white bedroom, but it is Sunday lunch the following day that is forever etched on my memory. At least fifteen *Wehrmacht* generals and general officers were seated around the long, solid wood table, reserved, almost silent, most of them in uniform. They were connected to the family by caste or by blood, and had been released from jail or from prisoner-of-war camps. The baroness, as a mark of honour, seated me on her right, and I began talking about my travels in Italy. One of the high-ranking guests suddenly awakened from his deep dogmatic sleep and in a booming voice eructated, '*Ich hass die Italiener*' ['I hate the Italians'], clearly he held them entirely responsible for the invincible army's defeat, then he slumped back in silence. That afternoon, Wendi took me on a tour of the estate and at a certain point, though there was no boundary, no marker, no sign, I suddenly found myself at the heart of a concentration camp, with wooden bunk beds, rows of latrines, a gallows, whips, tattered clothing, wooden clogs, everything a chaotic mess, yet entirely distinct. This was the Stuttgart-Vaihingen concentration camp, the first I ever saw. It is familiar to historians these days and it had not lagged behind other, more famous camps in the harshness and cruelty of its treatment of prisoners. Wendi was crying; the camp was a part of the von Neurath *Gut* and the family could not have been unaware of what was happening here.

Much later, I learned that Wendi, like a number of young Germans who wanted to expiate the sins of their fathers, joined an organization called *Aktion Sühnezeichen*: she went to Israel (the state was founded the following year) and began to work with Jewish survivors. Some Germans went much further in their attempts at reparation:

in Israel I met Dieter von Schwarze, the son of another aristocratic family, an uncompromising man who felt that helping survivors was not enough. He had to become a Jew: he and his wife set about converting to the most strictly Orthodox Judaism, passing the all-but-impossible tests imposed on those determined to convert – in order to discourage them, since Judaism, as we know, does not proselytize. Dieter and his wife stood firm, they succeeded in converting, learned Hebrew, settled in Jerusalem; they chose a Hebrew surname, he grew a beard and she wore a *sheitel*, the wig Orthodox Jewish married women wear to inhibit desire. Two of their sons became brilliant officers in the Tsahal. Dieter and his wife later returned to live in Germany under their original name; their children have founded a line in Israel.

I saw Wendi before leaving Tübingen for Berlin; she lent me 100 marks – 100 Deutschmarks after the *Währungsreform*, the currency reform intended by the Americans and Adenauer to make the mark a strong currency once more – and although I promised to pay her back, I never did: the paths of my life have been such that I lost track of her, and later I forgot. In 1986, in Washington shortly after the release of *Shoah*, I discovered that she was the wife of the German ambassador. Her birthright and her destiny had caught up with her; she had heard of *Shoah*, which had been screened at the Berlin Film Festival that year, but seemed not to care a damn about it. We arranged to meet at the ambassador's residence, and she seemed to me now to be entirely suited to her role, speaking passionately but superficially about daily life as an ambassador's wife. She would have liked to have had dinner with me, but her diary was full and her husband was about to show up at any moment to take her to some reception or other. I told her I remembered my debt to her and that I wanted to honour it as I had always intended. She nodded gravely, approvingly, but did not suggest waiving the debt. 'I'll pay you back in dollars,' I said, 'I'll have to adjust the figure after so many years.' The ambassador's arrival – he too was an aristocrat from one of the noblest families, a wounded veteran of the Battle of Kursk, his steel-blue eyes set in a ravaged face, as tall and slim as Wendi's mother – brought our meeting to a close. I still have not repaid her.

When the director of the Maison de France in Tübingen, who reported both to the military government and to the French Ministry for Foreign Affairs, informed me at the end of the year that there was a vacant position for a lecturer at the newly created University of Berlin, I applied and was accepted: I would be lecturing in philosophy and literature, but I would also be responsible for the Centre Culturel Français, which had been founded a year earlier and was not, I was told, satisfactory. I had never taught before; Berlin to me meant the Cold War at its hottest, the Berlin Blockade; my nature, in spite of my legitimate worries and fears, insisted that I could not refuse; I landed at Tempelhof in late November; I was not yet twenty-three. This dual role, or rather the two hats I was expected to wear, afforded me greater freedom than if I had only one, but, as I quickly realized, it also increased the constraints on me. In that immense, formless Berlin, I could not live where I pleased; although there were areas still devastated from the bombing, some middle-class and aristocratic residential areas such as Grünewald, Dahlem, Zehlendorf, Wannsee and Fronhau were as unscathed as Günzburg or Tübingen. The Freie Universität Berlin was in Dahlem, in the American sector of the city, but I was permitted to live only in Frohnau, in the French sector, in the far north of the capital, thirty kilometres from the university and thirty-five from the Centre Culturel, at the far end of the Kurfürstendamm. I was expected to present myself together with the papers given to me by the military administration on whom I would depend for the best part of my material existence, as well as to the French Embassy because, without wishing to be, I was registered among the Foreign Affairs personnel, and finally attached to the German administration at the university, which would pay my salary after deducting the *Kirchensteuer* – the church tax levied on all Berliners – a group to which I now belonged, of which I was rather proud. Général Ganeval was commander-in-chief; he would later be military attaché to René Coty, the President of the Republic, the same '*bon Monsieur Coty*' who caved in to the police lobby and allowed Jacques Fesch, who had become a saint while on death row, to go to the guillotine. But there were also French diplomats, aristocrats again for the most part, such as François Seydoux de Clausonne and a certain Marquis de Noblet d'Anglures who dealt with cultural affairs: a charming man with fine features who held audiences with me in his bedroom while he was getting dressed, like a *levée* with Louis XIV. He wore a nightcap, and from time to time, impassive and emotionless, he would let out a resounding, malodorous fart. He was a marquis, I was very young for a lecturer and to him I was nothing more than a pleb, and a Jew to boot; this was his way of letting me know what he thought.

I was assigned a large, opulent villa in Frohnau whose owners – such is the law of the victor – were compelled to occupy the mezzanine floor and the cellar. But even so, the house was too big for one person, and I was allocated a housemate, a French journalist of Romanian origin, also Jewish, Benno Sternberg, a small, skinny, short-sighted man, curious about everything, much older than me and with a rich and varied experience of politics, a real Trotskyite; in fact, he had personally known Lev Davidovitch Bronstein, whom he worshipped. Benno and I quickly became firm friends, our friendship would last until his untimely death. He had been a member of every faction and Fraktion of Trotskyism and was a Fraktionist at heart, preferring schism to compromise, never afraid to be alone in his opinion. I think of him every time I reread *Nekrassov*, Sartre's brilliantly comic play. On the night of its première at the Théâtre Antoine, Jean le Poulain, a wonderful, slightly portly actor, played the role of a Trotskyite who learns that someone else wants to join his Fraktion. Distractedly, incredulously, le Poulain exclaims, 'What, my party would have two members!' Benno occupied one floor of the huge house and I the other, but we threw joint parties and receptions.

The Freie Universität at the time was a den of Nazis, the denazification that was the order of the day everywhere being nothing more than a joke. I wasn't immediately aware of this state of affairs, but after a few weeks I became convinced of it, and in the year that I spent in Berlin I continued to come across ever-more flagrant proofs. My every movement was closely watched by a Fräulein Doktor Margass, the *Rektor's* spy, an ugly, fat woman whose face occasionally appeared at the round dormer window that opened on to my crowded lecture hall. I quickly discovered that I liked teaching and my students repaid my efforts by their assiduous attendance. I lectured in French according to the combinative method that I invented – as mentioned earlier – in which I wove *Le Rouge et le noir* and *L'Être et le néant* into a single coil. The girls were in the front rows, the boys at the back, seated or standing, because there wasn't enough room for everyone. The girls were of normal student age, but the boys were all older than I was, most of them just back from prisoner-of-war camps. I remember that when I quoted Sartre's 'the hand rests inert between the warm hands of her companion – neither consenting nor resisting – a thing', carried away by my zeal and a demonstrative enthusiasm, I grabbed the hand of the nearest girl – who was also one of the prettiest, something that did not escape the eagle eye of the vile Margass, who had opened the skylight at that moment.

One day – I had been teaching for several months by then – a student delegation asked to see me. They knew that I was Jewish. It was not openly discussed, but I had made no secret of the fact. They liked me, we had an excellent rapport, one based on freedom. I was almost certainly the only one of my kind at the university. To my surprise, they asked me if I would agree to hold a seminar with them and for them on the subject of anti-Semitism. I was surprised, moved. I didn't feel qualified, but I accepted and we began to work, proceeding by a Socratic, maieutic method – which is something I'm rather good at. It was very rewarding; their questions helped me immensely and I in turn helped them. It was not an *ex cathedra* exposé but an ongoing, egalitarian exchange between individuals of the same age. I talked to them about what had happened to me, to my family, about the war, the Resistance, the Shoah – or at least what I knew of it then, which was not much, truth be told, numbers and abstract ideas – but I talked to them in particular about Sartre's *Réflexions sur la question juive*. Mostly I talked to them about this book, at first about the 'portrait of the anti-Semite', which was visibly illuminating for them; I read them whole passages from it. Yes, *Réflexions sur la question juive* was the cornerstone of that seminar. I've often mentioned, and mention here again, the crucial role this book played in my life. I was identical to the Jew described in it, raised outside any religion, any tradition, any culture that might be called Jewish; of any obvious inheritance, properly speaking. This seminar on anti-Semitism inextricably led to my first trip, three years later, in 1952, to Israel: I knew I needed to go beyond Sartre's book, that there were many other things to discover, to think about – I later talked to Sartre himself about it, and he approved. The seminar was held once a week and it gripped us all, myself and the students.

So that I could get around, the French military government had allocated to me a car, a Volkswagen Beetle, the 'car of the people' that Hitler had made part of his political agenda in 1934. I did not have it entirely to myself since I had also been designated a driver, a man who unashamedly wore a Hitler moustache and always stood to attention before me. When he opened the door, he would doff his cap, click his heels in military fashion and roar, '*Zu Befehl, Herr Lanzmann.*' He had been a chauffeur to some general on the Eastern Front and he now spied for both the French military government and for the university. Sometimes, after class, it happened that – Berlin being so vast – I offered one of the boys or girls in my class a lift, or even piled several students into the Beetle, something that did not please the driver, who liked to think of himself as a chauffeur, not a taxi driver. He reported everything. For my part, I had only one desire, to drive the car myself, so I was constantly at odds with the designated driver. Ultimately, I won my case and he had to give me the keys; it was a joy to be alone, at the wheel of the people's Beetle driving through the ruins of Berlin. The chauffeur never forgave me.

One fine morning he arrived with a smile, bearing an official notice from Général Ganeval, whom I mentioned earlier, summoning me. The general was a man of great poise, about fifty, with white hair. I had not met him at the time. He received me in his lavishly appointed office, and his first words were: 'Young man, I hear you've been dabbling in politics.' I was completely taken aback. 'Politics, *mon général?*' 'You are conducting a seminar with German students on anti-Semitism, are you not?' 'Yes, sir, I am, only because they asked and – after everything that's happened – I don't see how a seminar on anti-Semitism at Berlin University can be seen as political, or why I would be wrong to hold one.' He curtly replied, 'It *is* political, and you have no right to engage in politics. Berlin is a sensitive city, a melting pot of five nationalities: Russians, English, Americans, French and Germans.' I protested strongly, told him I did not understand, that I did not know how I could explain such an act of censorship to my students. He was disdainful, almost hostile, reiterating his veto and refusing any further discussion. I left, confused and appalled, without a word. Then I decided to write to him, repeating that I considered his position indefensible and that I could not remain silent on the matter. My letter clearly had the desired effect, and he summoned me again, this time greeting me rather affably, 'Young man, as Barrès puts it, "I feel for anyone who is not a rebel at twenty",' – I found this reference to Barrès perverse. Nonetheless the general reissued a formal military order for me to terminate the seminar. But Barrès' disciple did not surrender, he carried on in secret, with the agreement of his students, holding the seminar off-campus. Once again, my insubordination was quickly reported and I was summoned to see the marquis in his room early one Sunday morning: after an introductory fart, he told me, all smiles, that of course he understood, but that if I persisted in my course of action, I would lose my post.

With a heavy heart the students and I agreed to put an end to the seminar. One of them – Heinz Elfeld, I've never forgotten his name, a tall boy with bushy eyebrows over deep-set coal-black eyes, always silent, but never missing any of these seminars – came to tell me that he wanted to leave Germany, that he could not bear to go on living there. I questioned him and discovered that he had served with the *Waffen* SS (the paramilitary arm of the SS) on the Russian front. There was something decent and genuine in the way he spoke; I arranged for him to get a grant to study in Paris, which he did. Years later, on the boulevard Saint-Michel, I heard someone calling me: 'Monsieur! Monsieur!' It was Elfeld, completely transformed, happy and smiling as he told me he had fallen in love with a young Jewish girl.

I loved, I still love, Berlin and I will never truly get to the bottom of the enigma that the ex-capital of the Reich, now the capital of a reunified Germany, represents for me. I can spend hours at the Paris Bar or the Café Einstein where I tirelessly observe those open, free, serious young German couples, so similar to those memories of my mind's eye. But I have been back to Berlin many times since 1948. A few years after the fall of the Wall, during a cruise on the River Spree, which runs through the city, I was struck by the architecture of the new Berlin: light, airy, imaginative, utterly at odds with the original ruins I had seen, or even of the first reconstruction, which I witnessed, as though history has decreed that this metropolis should be in a state of perpetual renewal. Earlier, in 1989, I had discovered the Bauhaus-Archiv by the Landwehrkanal, where the body of Rosa Luxemburg had been dumped after she was murdered (my friend Marc Sagnol, a dedicated ferreter-out of evidence of the Jewish presence in Germany, in Eastern Europe, in Russia, the Ukraine and Moldavia, was the first person to show me where her floating corpse had been found; I go there now every time I visit Berlin, without quite knowing why, it is like self-imposed duty I cannot shirk); I also discovered undeveloped areas, huge abandoned spaces that flanked both sides of the Wall in the heart of the city. During the interminable years of the Cold War, I had visited East Berlin with an official permit on many occasions, but had never seen these places because, since they abutted the Wall, it was forbidden. But, as I now realized, these barren wastelands were precisely where Nazi institutions had been. Had I seen them before making *Shoah*, I would probably not have been able to read them, to decipher them. Because of *Shoah*, my vision had become acute, sensitive. The name Prinz-Albrecht-Straße spoke to me; here and in the vicinity had stood the edifices of the Nazi terror: the *Reichssicherheitshauptamt* (Reich Security Head Office), the *Auswärtiges Amt* (Foreign Office), the Gestapo, the heart of Hitler's totalitarian system. Beneath one of these waste grounds, down a few steps, one could access a small subterranean exhibition, not very substantial, in just a few rooms, of photographs – some already known, others not – with powerful, sobering captions. The site was called the 'Topography of Terror'. I wondered which Germans had had the idea for this place and, although I did not know them, I felt a certain affinity with them. The past comes alive in this handful of open rooms in a no-man's land to which no one has laid claim, where everything seemed possible. At that moment I realized that Berlin was a city without equal, because it was possible to read the entire past of our time in this urban landscape as clearly as in the strata of an archaeological dig – Imperial Berlin, the Berlin of Kaiser Wilhelm, Nazi Berlin, Allied Berlin, Red (Communist) Berlin – all coexisting, coalescing, merging into a unique site of twentieth-century history. For me, it was like a miracle of memory, a fragile miracle that had to be preserved at all costs. It occurred to me that if the architects and urban planners of the new Berlin wanted to shoulder their responsibility to history, they should leave this place untouched, preserve this empty space in the middle of the city, this hole that I personally referred to as the *trou de mémoire* [lapse of memory]. I remember raising the subject once at a colloquium, though with no hope at all: property developers invariably have the last word, and they, like nature, abhor a vacuum. Indeed, the 'hole' I dreamed of no longer exists, it is now the new Potsdamer Platz, with its futuristic, often wonderful architecture.

Truly, I loved Berlin from that first year, overcoming my fear of the East. The collapse of the Third Reich, the surrender, had instilled in the people of Berlin a sort of wild, unbridled freedom fused with extraordinary courage and discipline. Day and night, groups of women known as *Trümmerfrauen*, 'rubble women', cleared away bricks from ruined buildings, piling them into tall pyramids at crossroads. The buildings on the Kurfürstendamm at first appeared to be unscathed, but it was like a film set; more often than not, behind the façades, there was nothing other than struts holding them up, but sometimes, on certain floors, there would be entire apartments left almost untouched or already reconstructed. I remember the apartment of a Greek consul, more German than Prussian, called Papaianou, who used to invite me to lavish parties attended by overbearing surgeons, lawyers and *nouveau riche* property developers who congregated and held forth in dark corners and restrooms, while their elegant wives pressed their insatiable red lips to mine, deftly palming their telephone numbers scribbled quickly on a ticket. This was how I met the Countess von B, a haughty beauty who turned out to be a whore – she asked me for money the first time we found ourselves in bed together. The count, her husband, had a hangdog expression and it was difficult to say whether he had knowingly married a prostitute or whether she had become one after the collapse of Germany and the destruction of the von B factories, which had since been rebuilt: industry always rises from the dead.

In certain snow-covered streets in West Berlin, one might see men – in ill-assorted clothes, caps and boots – speaking various languages, but often Yiddish, as these were DPs, displaced persons, men who had been freed from the concentration camps in 1945. There were many Jews among them; they had been waiting here for three years now, to go to America, Australia, Israel. In fact, they were quite content in Berlin because they were untouchable. After what they had been through, they were above the law, and besides, no one seemed quite sure what the law was. They trafficked in everything: cartons of American cigarettes, raw materials, shares, including Japanese industrial shares, which were at an all-time low, but which they knew would rise again. A number of them became extremely rich: Yossele Rosensaft, known as 'the king of Belsen' for surviving all the tortures inflicted on him in the Nazi camps before being liberated from Bergen-Belsen by the Allies, this steely little man of extraordinary intelligence built his fortune this way. I visited him in his New York apartment on 71st and Madison when I was preparing to make *Shoah*. He showed me his most unusual collection of French Impressionist paintings. We had been in Berlin at the same time, we discovered. (He later died of a massive heart attack in the lobby of Claridge's hotel in London.) DPs were not unique to Berlin, they could be found in all the big German cities: Frankfurt, Hamburg, Munich. Some, curiously, rebuilt their lives in Germany where they were to form the kernel of the future Jewish community. The first person to dare to break the German post-war taboo forbidding attacks on Jews was Fassbinder, in a play entitled *Der Müll, die Stadt und der Tod* [*Garbage, the City and Death*], in which he shamefully attacked the Jewish property developers in Frankfurt, many of whom were former DPs. While they spent fortunes buying up worthless land in order to build the Frankfurt of the future, Fassbinder made the hero of his story an ammoral man with no faith and no name, presented as '*der reiche Jude*' – 'the rich Jew' – a man whose greed was consubstantial with his nature. It was made into a film in 1977 by the Swiss director Daniel Schmid under the title *Shadow of Angels*.[1]

---

[1] Deleuze, who was called on to defend and support this repugnant film, wrote that, although he had kept his 'eyes wide open', he could not see the shadow of a shadow of anti-Semitism in *Shadow of Angels*. I replied in the pages of *Le Monde* – I was working on *Shoah* at the time – with a page-long article entitled 'Night and Fog'.

After the summer holidays of 1949, I returned to Berlin and my students for a second year of teaching. The cancellation of the seminar had encouraged them to launch an investigation into the existence of a Nazi bureaucracy within the university administration. For my part, I could not bear the contradiction between official Allied propaganda about the necessity of denazification and the ban imposed on me by the French military government. So I decided to tell the truth about the Freie Universität. I wrote a long, well-documented article that I naturally submitted to *Der Kurier*, the daily newspaper in the French sector, whose articles had to be vetted by the French censor. Général Ganeval was immediately informed. Publication was out of the question, it was rejected outright and attempts were made to intimidate me. It met with the same fate with the British, who were manipulated by their French counterparts. A scandal was to be avoided at all costs. The Americans wanted to publish the article because the university was in their sector and directly concerned them, but in the end they too lacked the courage of their convictions. There remained one last possibility – the press in East Berlin, in the Soviet sector, which, since the previous October, was also capital of the newly created German Democratic Republic. It was still possible to move freely between West and East – the Wall had not yet been built – you had only to take the S-Bahn, which ran overground for the most part, to get to East Berlin, getting off at Friedrichstraße. This ability to move about freely was very important to the Russians and the German Communists: the Soviet bloc was at the height of its powers, World Festivals of Youth and Students were organized in East Berlin, and they wanted to bring together as many people as possible. Like it or not, there was something powerful and fraternal in those vast Red communions.

The *Berliner Zeitung*, the main newspaper in East Berlin, which still exists, immediately accepted my article, publishing it in two instalments, with a double-page spread on each occasion. But the *Berliner Zeitung* had also discovered that Edwin Redslob, the *Rektor* of the Freie Universität, had written courtly sonnets dedicated to Emmy Goering, the *Reichsmarschall*'s wife, the former actress Emmy Sonnemann, praising her graceful elbows as she served tea to Nazi dignitaries. So here, then, was my vitriolic article about the Freie Universität and the censored seminar, with, in a box in the centre of the page, in bold type, the *Rektor*'s poems to the wife of the *Reichsmarschall* recently condemned to death at Nuremberg, who had preferred cyanide to the gallows. I knew nothing about this before publication. What a scandal! A double scandal. The *Rektor* was later dismissed along with a number of others. Général Ganeval's reputation did not emerge unscathed, and I was told that he seriously considered having me placed under close arrest. I had expected that, however, and had left my apartment for several days. In fact, I was no longer living in Frohnau, but in Zehlendorf, in an apartment not far from the university that I paid for out of my own pocket. I was therefore entirely free of the French military administration. Apparently, I remained on a sort of blacklist at the Quai d'Orsay for several years. *Je ne regrette rien.*

When I returned to France, the issue of earning a living was pressing. From Cau, I found out that Suzanne Blum, a celebrated lawyer, had decided to learn philosophy. She lived on the rue de Varenne in what I considered to be a lavish apartment. Her brother, André Blumel, had been secretary to Léon Blum and they had remained close. Suzanne Blum had spent the war years in England and the United States with Pierre Lazareff and the founders of *France-Soir* and the other newspapers in the group. Suzanne was a tall, intelligent, attentive woman and three times a week I taught her what I knew, it was truly *philosophie dans le boudoir*, since her boudoir was my classroom. She learned fast, was very fond of me, and claimed that she would help me find a career. She even seriously considered marrying me off to a Rothschild – I never knew which one – which would surely have had beneficial consequences for my later life. She recommended me highly to Pierre Lazareff and Charles Gombault and I was quickly engaged as a ghost writer, or, as they were called, a 'rewriter', for the popular high-circulation papers of the Lazareff group. This anonymous work was entertaining and offered me extraordinary freedom, I learned a great deal and the team, under the gentle but firm hand of Roger Grenier – a future star at Gallimard – included many aspiring writers who considered not pursuing a career and reserving time for themselves to be something beyond price. Grenier astonished me by his speed and his ability to rewrite without apparent effort: he sat in front of his typewriter and typed away for hours, completely unaffected by writer's block.

But I was still haunted by Germany and suggested to Lazareff that I might head off for the summer to the newly created German Democratic Republic and write a feature for *France-Soir*. I thought perhaps my contacts at the *Berliner Zeitung* might prove useful. He agreed and I flew back to Berlin in a French military plane; we were caught in a storm and the plane pitched and shook for the duration of the flight while the other passengers, a group of senators, rushed to the toilet to throw up, the stench of vomit only serving to make their nausea worse; they murmured to each other, 'Try to rest, *cher ami*, try to rest.' To enter the GDR, I required a visa from the Soviet authorities. I went to the Russian headquarters in Berlin-Pankow and explained what I was planning. The duty-officer asked which newspaper I would be writing for. At the time I didn't have a press pass or any form of accreditation; I told him I was a freelance and, as proof of my good faith, showed him my articles on the Freie Universität in the *Berliner Zeitung*. It was no good, the only newspaper that would have militated in my favour was *L'Humanité*. I didn't mention *France-Soir*, but I dared to mention *Le Monde*. He replied that it was a capitalist newspaper in which I would never be allowed to publish the truth about the GDR. The Cold War was a serious business, the Korean War was about to erupt and, in France, the demonstrations organized by the *Parti communiste* generally ended in violent confrontations with the so-called 'forces of law and order'. So instead I took advantage of the famous Leipziger Messe – the Leipzig Trade Fair – which anyone could attend, in order to secretly infiltrate the GDR. Thinking back now on the young man I was then, I realize it was sheer madness: I took a serious risk, the trip was an odyssey. Pastor Casalis, whom I had met while living in Frohnau during my first stay in Berlin, and who introduced me – to my astonishment and then delight – to Protestant energy and optimism, had given me the addresses of some of his East German colleagues who had formed a network called the *Bekennende Kirche*, the Confessional Church. 'They'll help you,' he told me as I prepared to launch myself into the unknown. This turned out not to be the case: every time I introduced myself to one of the Lutheran fathers he turned pale, then green, and unceremoniously gave me to understand that I was putting him in danger. Not one of them helped me. Without a visa, it was impossible to stay in a hotel. In Weimar, Dresden and Jena, I slept in public squares, under bushes in parks. I remember a terrifying night in Halle as the VOPO – the *Volkspolizei* – combed the streets of the city and I spent all the hours of darkness on the move. But I managed to take a boat down the Elbe from Dresden towards what is known as Saxon Switzerland.

By the time I made it back to Paris – in spite of these difficulties – I had seen and read rather a lot, and had spoken to many people, including friends I had made in East Berlin. I wrote a dozen articles, which I submitted to *France-Soir*. After much hesitation they rejected them: what I had written did not have sufficiently broad appeal and was considered too favourable to the Eastern bloc. So I sent the articles to *Le Monde*, where I knew absolutely no one. Four days later, the editor replied that he would be very happy to publish me because the tone of my articles was as fresh as the information they contained. They were quickly published, one a day, the first appearing on the front page under the headline 'Germany Behind the Iron Curtain'. Had I been caught, I might have spent years in prison. In spite of that, the articles were, I believe, objective and nuanced.

Cau told me that Sartre had read my articles and found them interesting. In fact, I saw the great man shortly afterwards at a dazzling conference on Kafka and introduced myself. He said, 'Oh, so you're Lanzmann,' and suggested I might like to join the editorial meetings of Les Temps modernes, held in a smoky room on the fourth floor of 42 rue Bonaparte that overlooked the church and the place Saint-Germain-des-Prés. So much has been said about these meetings that I will not dwell on them. Even now I am moved when I recall the unique trust Sartre had in young people who were completely, or virtually, unknown. He assigned subjects in his wonderful metallic voice, so warm that it convinced us all that, however difficult they appeared, we were equal to the task. Sartre was truly intelligence in action and at work, his generosity rooted in intelligence, his lively and intensely experienced sense of equality by miraculous contagion affected us all. We left these meetings enthused, our minds alert, enterprising, ready both for battle and for solitude. What he wrote about himself at the end of Les Mots [Words] – 'If I relegate impossible Salvation to the prop room, what remains? A whole man, composed of all men and as good as all of them and no better than any' – I understood the truth of this from our first meetings at Les Temps modernes, even if my sister made fun of him, saying, 'Maybe, but you think you're the first of the last.' Merleau-Ponty spoke rarely, holding back, a philosophical statue of the Commendatore, watching and listening, amused, surprised, sceptical as his comrade talked about the latest films he had seen and assigned to his willing volunteers the task of writing them up in short paragraphs or in even briefer, but often savage, notes. Whether cinematographic or literary, the team of critics at Les Temps modernes was constantly changing, there were no permanent positions: Cau, Jean Pouillon, Jacques-Laurent Bost, both former pupils of Sartre at the Lycée du Havre, Francis Jeanson, François Erval with his formidable Hungarian accent and his invaluable knowledge of publishers and their forthcoming titles – magazines at the time published entire chapters of major novels in *bonnes feuilles* [advance sheets] – Roger Stéphane, the flamboyant liberator of Paris who gossiped about everything, J. H. Roy who travelled all the way from Châtellerault by train to attend the meetings. Some I've missed, some I've forgotten.

And Simone de Beauvoir. We've finally come to her. From the first, I loved the veil of her voice, her blue eyes, the purity of her face and, more especially, of her nostrils. Something in the way I looked at her, in my attentiveness when she spoke or interrupted Sartre, referring to him as '*vous autre*', must have alerted her to my attraction for her. I sweated blood over the first article I wrote for *Les Temps modernes* in my *chambre de bonne* on the rue Alexandre-Cabanel; I worked on it determinedly for weeks. I had called it 'On the Press of Freedom', punning on a title by the young Marx, 'On the Freedom of the Press', published by the *Neue Rheinische Zeitung*. The article was an extended meditation on the nature of the press, inspired by my experience with the Lazareff group. I argued that the press – we didn't talk about the media back then – being in essence publicity (not in the sense of advertising, but in the sense of 'making public'), can only be publicity of the truth, that truth and publicity are consubstantial. The opposite of publicity is not falsehood, but silence, censorship. Why would anyone publish a falsehood? And this is why the press – it is the worst crime it can commit, an attempt on its very essence – can lie with impunity. Even if he knows that everything in it is false, a tyrant's subject reads the tyrant's press. Because it is written! I concluded with the dizzying possibilities of propaganda. My text was praised by Sartre and Simone de Beauvoir and appeared in *Les Temps modernes* in April 1952, but it was published under the name David Gruber, a pen-name I based on Grobermann, my mother's maiden name. After all, I was a rewriter at *France-Soir* and I was hoping to remain one. The magazine *Esprit* carried a flattering notice about the article. My second piece appeared in July of the same year, a shorter piece entitled 'There Had to Be Blood', an eye-witness account of the demonstration of 28 May. I remember it as though it were yesterday; I've never forgotten the name of the Algerian worker who was killed by the riot police on the boulevard Magenta: Hocine Belaïd. The Korean War had begun and the Communists had accused General Ridgway, the head of the American armed forces, of using bacterial weapons. Demonstrators were chanting *'Ridgway la peste'* ['Ridgway the plague'], as Baylot, the Prefect of Police, and Brune, the Minister of the Interior, dreamed up the 'homing-pigeon conspiracy' in order to be able to arrest Jacques Duclos – the great Communist orator, with a gravelly voice and a belly like a barrel, who was second-in-command of the *Parti communiste* – on trumped-up charges, accusing Duclos of subverting state security. While Sartre, thinking about the demonstration, got down to writing his irascible and theoretical political *roman-fleuve, Les Communistes et la paix [The Communists and Peace]*, which cannot be lightly dismissed as it so often is nowadays by those who have not read it, accusing it of recurrent Sartrian 'errors'. The book is, in fact, more theoretical than ideological, already pregnant with many of the ideas that would later appear in *Critique de la raison dialectique [Critique of Dialectical Reason]*. Together with Deleuze, we characterized the demonstration as *'fuite en public devant la police'* ['a public flight from the police']. Demonstrations at the time were extremely violent. There had been a march against *Le Figaro*, whose offices back then were at the Rond Point des Champs-Élysées. The marchers chanted, 'Figaro SS, Figaro Nazi'. Neither side favoured subtlety. I wasn't marching, but I was there as an observer when suddenly, on the pavement of the Champs-Élysées, I was swept up in a riot police charge: helmets on, batons high, the *gardes mobiles* were unhinged and didn't care whether their batons hit the right target. I was, according to the beautiful theory we elaborated, guilty of 'fleeing in public before the police'; I tried to blend into a cinema queue. Seeing the cops arrive, some woman – a born informer – started squealing, 'Here he is, He's here! He's right here!' My forehead was split open by a cosh and I was kicked in the stomach as I was dragged from the queue and bundled into a police van. The riot police had a field day: they slapped me, punched me, heaped abuse on me – their insults taking an anti-Semitic turn after they checked my papers – they spat in my face. I was called *'gueule de raie'* ['skate-face'] and *'lotte pourrie'* ['putrid monkfish']. Ever since that day I've been completely allergic to those fish, delicious, I'm told, but the very names are enough to make me nauseous. I was held in the police van overnight and released – or rather, chucked out – at dawn, in a terrible state. I stumbled around Paris for hours not knowing where to go, not wanting to go anywhere. I felt humiliated, exhausted, defeated.

Simone de Beauvoir has already described how our love affair began. She did it in her way, I will do it in mine; we don't remember the same things, which is normal. In July 1952, after my second article appeared in *Les Temps modernes*, I decided to leave for Israel, to spend some time there and write a feature, as I had done in East Germany. Strangely enough, during the creation of Israel, just when the War of Independence was at its height, Germany kept me busy; I was living in Tübingen and Cold War Berlin. My life was moving at a different pace to that of history and current events. It needed to wander, to take shortcuts that would later cohere and converge in other accomplishments. The morning after a party at the rue de la Bûcherie to celebrate the departure of Cau and Jacques-Laurent Bost for Brazil, I found the courage – or the gall – to phone Simone de Beauvoir and invite her to the cinema that evening. I myself was leaving the following day for Marseille where I would take a boat to Israel. 'Which film?' she asked bluntly, clearly ill-disposed to wasting her time. 'Any film,' I said, my way of saying that it was not the point of my invitation. She understood. We did not see a film, but spent the whole evening in her room lined with red drapes on the top floor of 11 rue de la Bûcherie, gazing at Notre-Dame, nocturnal and unreal. I don't remember now whether we ate; what happened afterwards has overshadowed all the rest. I took her in my arms, each of us as nervous and as frightened as the other. We lay wrapped together for a long time after we made love. She put her head on my chest and said: 'Oh, your heart, how it beats!', which overwhelmed me. Suddenly, hurriedly, as though she absolutely owed me a truth I had never asked for, she said, 'I must tell you, there have been five men in my life,' and she gave me their names. Then she added, again without my asking, that for a long time her relationship with Sartre had been neither romantic nor sexual. I was even more moved: this was not going to be a brief affair, she was establishing a different, infinitely more serious relationship between us. I was to be the sixth man, she had decided as much; pride and anxiety fought within me. The following morning, she left to join Sartre in Italy, at the wheel of an Aronde, her first car, which she was driving for the first time. I went to catch the train to Marseille.

Chapter 11

Perhaps I was playing at scaring myself, but the boarding of the Jews onto the SS *Kedmah* felt to me like a deportation to the death camps. Why the double line of riot police, armed, helmeted, ready for action, flanking us on either side, forcing us to mark time under the sweltering early August sun until we came to the gangway? The immigrants had reached Marseille after long journeys from Romania, Bulgaria, Morocco, Tunisia, Egypt, Iraq, Iran by the various daring paths that had been opened up since 1947 by the Jewish Agency for Israel and the men of Mossad to circumvent the British blockade. They were gripped by a single idea: leaving Europe, or their former homelands, to make a new life for themselves far away in Eretz Israel. Whole families peacefully waited their turn, anxious about their exile. I could not understand the need for this brutal deployment of police. And why – given that I had very little money – was I assigned a first-class cabin? I shared it with a rabbi, a chief rabbi from Marrakech if I remember rightly, who was going to Israel on a reconnaissance trip. In any case he was – to my shame – the first rabbi I had ever met. He was in the prime of life, and I was astonished by how tall and thin he was, by his silver beard, his eyes of a piercing blue that was not at all African, and the big hand-knitted and flawlessly white wool socks he wore day and night. He spoke only Arabic and Hebrew, both languages unintelligible to me, and the moment I entered the cabin he pointed a cruel accusing finger at me and asked, *'Yehudi?'* I realized that it was important for him to know my affiliation and I answered, using one of the few words of Hebrew I knew, *'ken'*, 'yes'. He looked at me, his sharp blue eyes like knives, trying to decide whether I was not only a liar but an impostor, refuting my *'ken'* with a furious *'lo'*, no, I was not Jewish, I couldn't be Jewish. Sartre's statement from *Réflexions sur la question juive,* 'it is the anti-Semite that creates the Jew', or indeed the book of my friend Robert Misrahi, *La Condition réflexive de l'homme juif* [*The Reflexive Condition of the Jewish Man*], which worked to generate a Jewish identity in a conceptual vacuum, were both dealt a serious blow even before the SS *Kedmah* had weighed anchor. After three days at sea, my chief rabbi – I've just remembered his name, though I can't be sure: Maklouf Abyssirar – knew the full measure of my heathenism. I had left our cabin one Friday afternoon shortly before the start of Shabbat – in fact, I then knew nothing whatever about that fundamental, ancestral rite, which had never been observed in my family – and I had left the light on. I spent the night on deck under the stars, which studded the deep, dark sky, chatting to some Israelis I had just met – to Dahlia Kaufmann, who captivated me by her seriousness and the story of her life as she told it to me; to Yigal Alon, a senior officer in the Palmach, an élite unit of the Israeli army at its inception and later Israeli Minister of Foreign Affairs, who was on his way back from a sabbatical year at Oxford and heading for Ginossar, his kibbutz on the western bank of the Sea of Galilee; and to Julius Ebenstein, the Mozartian born in Vienna, managing to escape just after the Anschluss, but retaining an enduring nostalgia for the city. I returned to the cabin at about four o'clock, just before dawn, and found the rabbi lying on his berth in his socks, his eyes wide open and the lights still on. The ancient tenets of our religion forbade him from turning off the lights and on the ship there were no *Shabbes goys* – Shabbat goys – like those who operate the lifts in Israeli hotels nowadays, as required by Jewish-American tourists. In that dawn, I was summarily excommunicated and cursed, both in Hebrew and in Arabic.

On the second day of sailing, our first morning at sea, a cleaning woman came into the cabin carrying a bucket and a scrubbing brush, knelt on the floor and began to clean it. It was too much for me, I couldn't bear for an Israeli woman – it was clear to me that that was what she was – to be my maid. I got up, explained to her in English that I would do it myself, took the bucket and the brush and attempted to finish what she had started. She stared at me in aston-ishment, obviously upset and understandably convinced I was mad. In the days that followed, she arranged to come in and clean while I was out. I could easily imagine Jewish cleaning women in France or anywhere else, but not in Israel. I knew very little about the country, but the image uppermost in my mind – one shared by most of the immigrants aboard the *Kedmah* to whom I spoke during the crossing – was the image of the desert. Israel had to be a desert, a virgin land to be conquered, where each man would be the first, and would begin the world anew with bare hands in a spirit of unprecedented brother-hood and equality. I could not conceive of Israel as an actual society of classes, of rulers and the ruled, of old hands and newcomers, with all the inertia and the weight of the real. I was wrong, of course, but I was also right. I realized this when Dahlia began to tell me her life story under a starry sky in the prow of the *Kedmah*, whose stem I could hear slicing through the water with the powerful, regular sigh of silk being torn. She was a German Jew and had been one of the famous group of Aliyah Youth that the Jewish Agency had managed to get out of Germany in 1938 shortly before *Kristallnacht*. Raised as Zionists, by the time they were adolescents they were enthusiastic, ardent pioneers, founding the Beit Ha'arava kibbutz on the shores of the Dead Sea, 400 metres below sea level, on the rugged, lunar, sweltering plain that stretches the length of the Jordan Rift Valley from Jericho to Qumran where the famous Dead Sea Scrolls were later found in a cave. She told me how they shuttled back and forth with buckets and wheelbarrows, drawing fresh water from the River Jordan to water the desert land they had been given, washing away the deep layer of salt that made it barren. The flowering of the first tomato plants, the intense red of the fruits, was celebrated as a great victory of farming over nature. She told me of the hard, rough, uncompromising life of the first kibbutzim who were entirely communitarian and egalitarian; the way it aged a body prematurely, the strictness of the laws imposed – the first woman to wear lipstick was regarded as a heroine by some and corrupt by others. In Beit Ha'arava, Dahlia had married Hoshea Kaufmann. The creation of the state, the War of Independence, the treaties – not peace treaties, but an armistice between Israel and its Arab enemies, under the terms of which Beit Ha'arava became part of Transjordan – were a tragedy to those who had founded it. They all lost not only their lands, but the sense of their own lives; the ties that bound them were broken. Having lost their kibbutz, they went their separate ways, couples drifted apart, Dahlia moved to another 'pioneer' kibbutz by the sea in the very north of Israel, on the Lebanese border, Gesher Haziv, which had recently been founded by Argentinian and Brazilian Jews, while Hoshea left to teach in the large, highly politicized Hashomer Hatza'ir kibbutz of Mishmar Ha'emek in the Jezreel Valley. I would later meet him through Dahlia; he seemed utterly disconsolate about everything. Another night on the ship, Julius Ebenstein took over from Dahlia: he talked to me about young Israelis – he had two children waiting for him at home in Tel Aviv – about their devotion, their selflessness, their limitless idealism. A bright sliver of crescent moon shone in the west as Julius pointed a finger as commanding as that of the chief rabbi towards the heavens: 'You can ask the impossible of them and they'll go for it.' He invited me to come and visit him when I was in Tel Aviv. At the time, little did I know how generous he would be to me.

The Israeli coast was approaching, and as we slipped into the beautiful harbour of Haifa, we could see the different strata of Jewish immigration rising in terraces up the slopes of Mt Carmel, could clearly see that the oldest settlements at the top of the mountain were the richest and that Israel, unquestionably a promised land, was not the virginal desert of our imagination. Dahlia wanted to guide my first steps in Haifa, to help me find a hotel or perhaps take me north to her kibbutz, where we could go for a midnight swim on my first eastern Mediterranean beach. She said, 'As a foreigner, you'll get through customs quickly; for Israelis coming home, going through customs is arduous, meticulous and fussy, they search every bag. You'll be finished long before me so why don't you wait for me at the Eden Café just outside the port? I'll come and find you.' She wasn't wrong, it was quick, I walked down the gangway with my suitcase, which was very heavy. At four o'clock, the afternoon heat was oppressive, so I decided to take one of the taxis waiting for passengers. I gave the driver the address: Eden Café. He drove precisely 350 metres, past the entrance to the port and stopped almost immediately on a white, deserted square, crushed by the sun, which made me think of the square in Argos in Sartre's play Les Mouches [The Flies]. He pointed to the Eden Café, its entrance hidden behind a curtain of beads like long rosaries. I asked the driver how much I owed him and was stunned by his response. I paid, resolving never again to take a taxi: with fares as high as this, I could not afford to.

Blinded by the harsh light, I parted the amber pendants of the curtain and suddenly found myself in darkness. I could no longer see anything and it took some time for my eyes to adjust. But I could hear, from the depths of the room, women's coarse voices, speaking in a language that sounded unfamiliar although I still understood snatches of this strange French, one that I had never heard before. I worked out that stockings were being fiercely bartered for lipstick. To my left, I made out a counter that served as a bar and a little man behind it. He asked me if I had just arrived on the Kedmah. I nodded and asked him in turn, 'Tell me, sir, the taxis in Israel are very expensive.' 'How much did he take you for?' Our exchange was conducted in English, but barely had I replied than the barman gave a booming laugh and in gruff Hebrew began to recount my misadventure to the silhouettes I now made out in the gloom. They all laughed until they cried, their echoing laughter rising rather than fading as though they were proud of how easily my gullibility had been abused. Then suddenly, a screaming figure appeared before me, so close he might have touched me: 'Death to the Jews! Death to the Jews! Death to the Jews!' I stood petrified and incredulous as he went on, 'Ha ha, you've been conned by the Jews. Death to the Jews! Death to the Jews!' No one in the Eden Café protested, the mocking laughter increased around me, I didn't know what to think and decided that these Jews must be remarkably open-minded, that the irreverent man was probably an Arab regular, a bit mad, but they put up with him as though he were part of the furniture. Then, timidly, in a small voice, I dared to ask, 'But . . . aren't you Jewish?' He roared, 'Of course I'm a Jew, I'm a Jew, but a Jew of the heart. I'd rather be called a "filthy Jew" in Casablanca or Marrakech than called a "filthy *Schwarze*" here.' Such was my introduction to Israel – unusual, I grant.

I had been brutally confronted by an issue that I would have time to explore at leisure throughout my stay. The women in the outrageous make-up haggling over stockings and lipsticks were Jewish prostitutes from the Maghreb and this doomsayer was their pimp. I saw him again during my few days in Haifa, and we got along well. I learned a lot from him. 'Les *Schwarzes*', meaning 'blacks', referred to the Sephardic Jews of recent *aliyahs*, part of the mass immigration Israel encouraged by any means necessary, lying unstintingly and making false promises about living standards. As Léon Rouach, curator of the Dimona Museum, would put it twenty years later in my film *Pourquoi Israël* [*Israel, Why*], 'Lying is bad, but the country itself was seriously under threat. To build it we had to fill it, and to fill it we had to lie!' And one should read into these words no naïveté, no cynicism, no resentment, but on the contrary the overwhelming candour of the men and women who complied, understanding and endorsing the liars' justifications through the very suffering inflicted on them.

From north to south, from east to west, from Galilee to Negev, the country was dotted with *ma'abarot,* vast tent 'cities' in which destitute immigrants waited for what was called their *klita,* their 'integration'. They were, in fact, refugee camps where these newcomers might have to stay for months or even years before jobs were found for them, or houses built. I visited a number of these *ma'abarot* with a thirty-year-old Ashkenazi bureaucrat employed by the Jewish Agency, who dealt with everything related to the *klita,* whom I met again years later as Israel's ambassador to the UN, and later still as president of a university. I didn't like his stupidly superior way of evaluating those in his charge. Of the Romanians, he said, 'They're good material'; Bulgarians, Iraqis and Iranians also occupied a higher echelon of his value system. Moroccan Jews he considered to be the dregs of the Chosen People. As we arrived at what seemed to me an immense *ma'abara* in Beit She'an Valley, with hundreds upon hundreds of family tents that he had to inspect, I noticed on the road near the entrance groups of unshaven men gaping and staring at us with a malevolent air. My guide said, 'You'll see, they're very unhappy because they've been assigned two Ashkenazi rabbis. It's war between them and the Jewish Agency.' The idlers clearly had keen ears and realized that I spoke French. They rushed over and surrounded us, questioning me, '*Monsieur, Monsieur, vous êtes froncé?*' I said, 'Yes.' 'Oh, *la Fronce, Monsieur, la Fronce.*' And they went on: 'Israel, Monsieur, Israel is worse than the Gestapo!' My guide, assessor of human material that he was, gave a forced laugh, but was not displeased to see his view of the lowest orders thus confirmed. I asked, 'You experienced the Gestapo?' 'No, Monsieur, but we know.' They complained about everything: Ashkenazi oppression, the heat, the paltry sums of money they had been given, and the work offered to them that was unworthy of their talents and their former positions. I knew that kibbutzim bemoaned a shortage of kibbutzniks, of volunteers, of manpower. 'Why don't you join a kibbutz?' I asked. 'Men like you are in demand.' 'Never!' they roared in concert. 'We could never do that. You need a brain like a mule to live that kind of life.' Then one of them, who appeared to be the leader, remonstrated, 'Only one man can save us, Monsieur, you don't see who?' I honestly didn't and answered, 'I very much doubt only one man can save you, you would need a great many. Most of all, you will save yourselves.' I also explained – it goes without saying that this all took place at the end of my trip – the enormous difficulties faced by this tiny newborn country, unwittingly becoming a quasi-official propagandist as I did so. They harped on with their riddle about the supreme saviour: 'Just one man, Monsieur, one man, honestly, you don't know who?' The cat got my tongue. 'Rothschild, Monsieur, only Rothschild can get us out of this place.' They were not from the rich Jewish élite of Arab countries, but came from poor communities living in the *mellahs*, the ghettos of Morocco, and were accustomed to receiving regular donations from wealthy Jews in other countries, of whom the Rothschilds, whose reputation as generous donors was well established, were the best-known. Nothing had prepared these men for what Israel required of them. When I asked what they had done in their former lives, again they replied in glorious concert, 'Driver.' Whether of taxis and trucks, I had no idea, but I had never imagined that the People of the Book had produced so many charioteers. They had, in fact, been shopkeepers, barbers or beggars. Twenty years later, during the filming of *Pourquoi Israël*, I had a similar experience with another immigrant, Russian this time. He too claimed to have driven heavy goods vehicles, in Kiev (the Ukraine was not yet independent). Just as the Moroccans had not been able to contemplate giving up their imaginary trucks for pickaxes, so he found it demeaning to have to work in a soya factory instead of rattling along the potholed roads of Bessarabia. For all of them, there was clearly something honourable about being a driver, devouring the immense spaces between here and elsewhere, ubiquitous and supreme.

The messianic call has always been so powerful that, ever since the destruction of the Second Temple, there have been continuous

waves of Jewish immigrants. The magnetic power of Zion did not
need to wait for political Zionism to exert its pull on mystics, those
disillusioned by life, errant adventurers and others exhausted by
persecution. It was not during this first visit, but on a later one,
in Rehavia, the peaceful German Jewish quarter of Jerusalem: in
its library, a magnificent haunt and an inestimable treasure, with
thousands of books amassed over a lifetime of study; serried ranks
of tall black spines of countless Talmudic volumes – it was here that
Gershom Scholem – a Berliner by birth, master of all cabbalistic
knowledge, an uncompromising Zionist, but open, friend of Walter
Benjamin and me – read me the letters that desperate eighteenth-
century immigrants in Tiberias, on the western shore of the Sea of
Galilee, sent to their families left behind in Poland, attempting to
describe the unbearable harshness of a life lived in this forbidding
climate – the stifling heat at 250 metres below sea level, the deadly
mosquitoes, the incurable malaria. Some wrote that they intended to
take their own lives and it is true that, even today, among the black-
ened headstones of the old cemetery of Tiberias, there is a peripheral
circle of graves of those who committed suicide; a compromise
between fraternal mercy and the Jewish prohibition against taking
one's life. In Berlin, in the vast cemetery of Weissensee, which I
visited while preparing to film *Shoah*, the graves of those who took
their own lives, because they were too old or too disheartened to
try to flee the Nazis, are similarly all on the edge of the Jewish plots
of this necropolis. Joachim Prinz, whom I met in the United States,
at the head of a thriving congregation in New Jersey, told me how
famous he had been among the rich Jewish bourgeoisie of Berlin. He
was renowned for his wonderful baritone voice and the lyrical beauty
of his funeral orations: people fought to have this Jewish Bossuet
officiate, and there were those who were ready to pre-empt the call
of God if it ensured that Prinz, and not some other rabbi, would give
their funeral oration. One day in 1936 Prinz received an affidavit
from America, allowing him and his family to leave Germany within

six months. In Berlin, when he announced this sad news, panic spread. Joachim, a good man, full of life and good humour, assured me that between making the announcement and the day his family emigrated, the number of Jewish suicides in the German capital rose significantly, and that in his last weeks he worked ceaselessly, sometimes spending entire mornings in the synagogue.

Before reaching Tel Aviv, a Jew amongst Jews, lost and with no reference points, I went to visit Dahlia in her kibbutz on the Lebanese border, to the far west of the demarcation line, facing the cliffs of Rosh Hanikra – Ras el-Naqura in Arabic – HQ of the UN Interim Force in Lebanon, which, as we know, does not take kindly to flyovers by Israeli fighter planes. Gesher Haziv was my first kibbutz and I was invited to share the frugal fare of its members: warm, generous South Americans, happy, like most of the kibbutzniks, to live like sentries watching over the changing borders of Israel, never truly defined, or recognized; an epic justification for the sacrifices to which they acquiesced. Dahlia explained to me that the whole state, town and country, was going through a terrible period called *Tzena*, which translates as 'austerity'. There was little to eat in Israel, people were dying of starvation, and I suffered greater exhaustion through lack of nourishment during my stay there than during the German Occupation in France. Dahlia led me to the sandy beach that ringed the olive groves of the kibbutz and I began to run, naked, my belly empty, towards the waters of the eastern Mediterranean, to dive in and, beneath the crescent moon, take an initiatory bathe. She ran beside me, shouting at me to stop and, when I did not obey, wrapped her arms around me, hugged me with her whole body, saying, 'The sea is very dangerous, it can be deadly, you can't swim here, we need to go further south.' We made love that night and at dawn we bathed much further away. Drownings were not uncommon all along the coast of Israel, from north to south, although nowadays, tourism has developed to such an extent that safety measures have been taken and most beaches are supervised.

This was not the case in 1952, nor twenty-five years later in 1977 when my life was saved by sheer miracle. A dark period for me, it was when I was filming *Shoah*, which amounts to the same thing. The film I had been working on for four years had already ground to a halt; I no longer had the funds to carry on and the Israelis, having seen *Pourquoi Israël*, which they considered to be the greatest film ever made about their country, had suggested I embark on a film about the Shoah. They had instigated and financed the initial research, but had recently informed me that, with no end in sight, they could no longer continue to support my work. One Sunday in spring, shortly after I was informed of this decision, Deborah, a Persian kitten belonging to my second wife Angelika, leapt like a black arrow from the window of our Paris apartment into the garden. I dashed down the stairs, missing a step. Fractured foot, pain, hospital emergency room, incompetent treatment, badly applied plaster cast, new plaster cast, crutches; it was twelve weeks before I was declared well again. The verdict was pronounced not in Paris but in Jerusalem, by a professor, a specialist who recommended swimming as the best means of getting back on my feet and building up my leg muscles. Why Jerusalem rather than Hôpital Cochin in Paris where the original plaster cast had been put on? Because that summer, Menachem Begin had won the Israeli election and become Prime Minister. Since it had been the defeated Israeli Labour Party that had refused to continue subsidizing my film, and while I was laid up in plaster, I decided to write to Begin, the conqueror, whom I didn't know, but something I remembered from my first trip to Jerusalem in 1952 told me that he would listen to me. One morning – just a few days after my night beneath the stars with Dahlia – I arrived at a little square in Jerusalem: perched on a barrel – like Sartre at Billancourt – his voice barely amplified by a second-rate megaphone, his face half-hidden by thick glasses, a man is haranguing a meagre crowd. 'That's Begin,' my guide tells me, translating his fiery words. With every breath and all his energy, Begin implores the Israeli government and each individual Israeli not to accept German 'reparations'. In doing so Israel would lose its soul and its *raison d'être*. A desperate yet magnificent speech, since he knows well that Israel has already said 'yes'; that Nahum Goldmann, the flamboyant president of the World Jewish Council, has arranged everything, planned everything with Chancellor Adenauer. But Begin's campaign was just beginning: some time later, he managed to organize a massive, memorable rally in front of the Knesset, bringing together tens of thousands of people. And yet, that first speech I have just referred to was so new to me, and Begin so impressive, that I devoted several sequences in *Pourquoi Israël* to this central issue of *Wiedergutmachung* – 'reparations'.

The newly elected Prime Minister quickly replied to my request and a meeting was arranged in his office in Jerusalem. It was also agreed that an Israeli doctor would remove my cast later that day. Begin did not disappoint me, everything went as I had expected, as I had hoped, earning him my undying gratitude. But the details and the methods of this new funding needed to be agreed with his advisers, notably with Eliyahu Ben-Elissar, a secretive man devoid of emotions, a former member of Mossad, Israel's first ambassador to Egypt and later ambassador to France, where he died suddenly of cardiac arrest. In return for the help that Israel was prepared to give me, I had to agree that the film would be completed within eighteen months and would run for no longer than two hours. This was so far from what I knew to be the truth that, in something of a state of shock, I promised and signed whatever was asked of me. The monies allocated made it possible for me to continue my research, though not to begin shooting; I was convinced it would take years to complete my work and that the film would be at least four times longer than envisaged. Truth be told, I felt that the help I was being offered would be the film's death knell and I said to myself, as I had done several times before, that there was no point in persevering, that it would be better to give up. I was the only person who foresaw what this work might be and I was sick and tired of trying to win over bureaucrats who knew nothing about cinema, or the Shoah, tired of having to try to communicate clearly ideas that were still opaque to me. *Shoah* had slowly begun to take shape, but I knew that such a film had to be an adventure that by its very nature would go way beyond any boundaries imposed on it.

I was at my lowest ebb. Angelika, who had come to Israel with me, persuaded me to rest, to give myself time to think and to learn how to use my foot again. We left for Caesarea and its magnificent and compact sand beach, flanked by a Roman aqueduct; the sea beckoned through its arches, shimmering and inviting, while here and there between them, signposts bearing a skull or crossed bones and brief explanations in Hebrew seemed to warn of some vague, incomprehensible danger. Despite what I had been told on my first night in Gesher Haziv, I ignored the signs. The weather was fabulous, the sea that day almost glassily calm, unusual in this part of the eastern Mediterranean where the beaches are famous as a surfer's paradise. I waded cautiously into the water, careful not to put too much weight on my bad foot; as soon as I could, I dived in and vigorously swam out towards the open sea. Striking out rather than following the shoreline has always been my practice, it would have been my motto had my birth gifted me with a coat of arms on which to emblazon it. I am a good swimmer, my breaststroke was strong and I told myself that the Israeli doctor had been right: with therapy like this, my musculature would soon be back to normal. Yet to swim away from the shore was foolish and dangerous. I must have swum out some fifty strokes; even twenty would have been too far. I tried to head back to land, the sun was at its height, the beach dazzling, clearly outlined; I swam, but the beach seemed no nearer. I swam harder, more determinedly, and suddenly realized that in fact the opposite was true: the beach was receding. At that moment, everything comes into sharp focus: Angelika's silhouette at the water's edge, watching me, already somewhat worried; the sun's glare blinding me intermittently; the swell and the waves obstructing my view of the beach; and above all, subsuming these still disparate signs into a single feeling: exhaustion. It overwhelms me. I can't go on. My foot hurts, I realize that I won't make it to the beach, I won't get back. I start to shout, I holler for help, I wave my arms so that Angelika, who seems small and very far away now, will notice me and I imagine her helplessly running back and forth on the deserted beach. I remember that there was not a living soul on the shore when I stepped into the water. Angelika is a bad swimmer, there's nothing she can do to help, she would need a boat. Tragedy erupts under a midday sun, I feebly try to go on swimming, I swallow salt water, it chokes me. Then suddenly a voice from somewhere close by on my right calls to me in English. Through a curtain of spray, I see a tall fair-haired man, alerted by Angelika. My joy is short-lived; it seems to me that he too is breathless and exhausted; he says, 'I am not a good swimmer but I will try to help you.' He swims behind me and shoves me hard in the back, trying to push me forwards. I know this is not the right way to go about it, which he soon realizes too, and also that he is tiring himself even more. He gives up almost immediately. 'I am very sorry,' he says, 'but I have to leave you, I have my wife and my little son on the beach, I am not even sure to succeed to return. Goodbye, forgive me.' He disappears as suddenly as he had appeared.

There is no beach, no sun, I am half-blinded by the salt, choking on the sea water, I have stopped struggling. I will die. Strangely, I feel calmer and I imagine death by asphyxiation not as an end, but as a transition, a horrible moment in time, a particularly horrible moment to go through, after which I will once again be able to breathe freely, deeply, inhale great lungfuls of pure air; a strait, a fissure, a needle's eye: on the far side, life will begin again. And so I wait for death, motionless, I no longer swim, I float on my back, allow myself to drift, I have not lost consciousness. Suddenly, a voice, another voice, with a perfect English accent, hails me from behind, 'What is your name?' I answer. Then, 'What is your first name?' . . . 'Claude, I will try to rescue you. Can you help me?' I answer, 'Yes, I think so.' 'Move your legs . . . move your arms . . . OK, you will help me with your legs.' I feel myself gripped firmly under the arms and dragged, not towards the shore, but out towards the open sea. In the commanding voice of a professional, he orders me to help, kicking my legs in a backstroke. Yossi – my saviour's first name – has us describe a long arc, out to sea then back inland much further along the shore where there are no treacherous currents, where I should have gone swimming had I been familiar with Caesarea. It takes him almost two hours to haul me back to land. Had I been unable to help him, he confided later, he would have knocked me out: it's easier to drag a dead weight than a panicked swimmer. A law student in Tel Aviv, born in a nearby *moshav* founded by Moroccan Jews, where he happened to be spending the weekend with his parents, Yossi Ben Shettrit was a qualified lifeguard and, aside from the fair-haired man, had been the only other person on Caesarea beach that day. The miracle is that Angelika managed to find him. The previous Sunday, at precisely the same spot, the British ambassador to Israel had drowned and Yossi, alerted too late, had only recovered his corpse. Six employees of the Dan Caesarea hotel had died there in the space of six months. As soon as we reached the beach, Yossi took me to an infirmary to make sure I had no water in my lungs. Everything was fine, even the fair-haired man – I hope he may forgive me for referring to him like this, I have never been able to recall his name – after a long detour, managed to find his way, exhausted, back to his wife and his young son.

I invited both of my rescuers to dinner the following evening and expressed a gratitude I did not really feel. To be alive did not have me jumping for joy. Looking back now on that strange episode, I tell myself that, having realized that the promises I had made to Ben-Elissar and to Israel were impossible to keep, I had deliberately flirted with death. This was 1977, *Shoah* would only be completed eight years later and I knew that, year after year, I would have to lie to all those who helped me: Israeli and French, governments and individuals, rich, not so rich, even poor. And lie to myself too, because

I needed hope if I were to go on: 'next year', I told myself, as they say while waiting for the Messiah, 'next year in Jerusalem', while at the same time being completely aware that what I was telling myself, and everyone, was entirely untrue. I would be intractable and would obey only my own dictates. *Shoah* was a never-ending relay race: those who supported me for a while later gave up and I had to persuade others to take up the torch, and still others to replace them, on it went to the very end – even after it was finished, as once the film was completed there was no money to pay for a first print. When asked how *Shoah* was made, I sometimes answer: 'If someone had said "the film has to be completed by such and such a date or your head will be cut off", I would have been decapitated,' despite, as I have mentioned, my particular dread of this form of capital punishment. To tell the truth, this is precisely what had happened in Ben-Elissar's office. Even though there had been no mention of the guillotine, at least that is how I had felt. Yet I yielded to nothing and to no one, I was guided by the exigencies of the film itself, these were the only demands I followed. I was the master of time and that is, perhaps, what I am most proud of. Reading them back, these last two sentences have a gentle, peaceful ring, but I alone had to carry the burden of anxiety, I alone know what the lies, the pledges and the false promises cost me. I was like the state of Israel with its immigrants. How many times during the gestation of the film did I realize, with incredulous terror, as though woken suddenly and called to account, that two years, four, five, seven, nine, ten years had already slipped by? In the end, as everyone knows, I betrayed no one: *Shoah* exists as it should exist. '*Ein Brera*' is another common Hebrew phrase – it means 'there is no alternative'.

The generosity and the warmth shown me by Julius Ebenstein and his wife when, in 1952, I showed up unannounced at the door of their apartment at 19 Mapu Street, Tel Aviv, were remarkable. They asked how long I planned to stay; I answered, 'One night.' I stayed for three months. They were renting a four-room apartment overlooking a small garden on the ground floor of a three-storey building built on piles, like most of those dating from the 1920s, and it was already considerably dilapidated thanks to the heat and cheap construction materials. Their children, Sivit and Gaby, who each had their own room, were made to share one and I was given the other. Whenever I left Tel Aviv to journey inland, they kept the room for me. With a trust I found staggering, they gave me keys to the house on my second day there, and I could come and go, day or night, knowing I would find the bed made up. The two children were touchingly beautiful, Julius was about forty and his wife, who was also Viennese, had the classic face of a Jewish intellectual, her glasses perched on a strong, straight nose. In the stories of their lives, they were the quintessence of Israel. Fleeing the Nazis, they had first worked in a kibbutz and adapted to the harsh work of community life, entirely forsaking private property. But in their heart of hearts, both of them still had an ineradicable nostalgia for the big city. Though Tel Aviv could not compare to Vienna, after a few years they left the kibbutz for Mapu Street. But the feeling was illusory, since what they really missed, despite their two marvellous little *sabras*, their native-born children, was Vienna. Julius, a composer by profession, was obsessed with the idea of founding a Mozarteum in Tel Aviv to connect him with his native Prater, thereby allowing him to make three or four trips a year to his former homeland. The Mozarteum was his obsession, he spent most of his time coming up with improbable plans to finance it, and decided that, since I knew Sartre and Simone de Beauvoir, I might be able to help. It was on Mapu Street that I received my first letters from Castor, which became longer and longer and arrived almost daily once she knew that they were reaching me. The Ebensteins, in all their contradictions and heartbreak, were my family, my compass in all the strangeness I had to contend with. Nostalgia for Europe is one of the main themes of *Pourquoi Israël*; it was the memory of Julius that guided me while I was filming and it is Gert Granach, the Spartacist singer who, from the opening scenes, through the inhalations and exhalations of his accordion, incarnates the overwhelming feeling of *Sehnsucht* of German-speaking Jews, his beautiful, sad, ironic voice evoking Karl Liebknecht and Rosa Luxemburg to whom I also pay tribute, as I mentioned, whenever I am in Berlin, standing for a moment in silence on the Landwehrkanal on the spot where her corpse was dumped. I also still associate Mapu Street, this haven of peace, of contemplation and hospitality, with rationing and ravening hunger, day and night, the worst I have ever known. The Ebensteins had little money and I had almost none, we did not know how to find the black market and to be honest I don't believe it existed: all of Israel was starving. I remember long, hopeless shopping trips, pleading just to be able to bring back a beef sausage, a rare and wonderful delicacy. I have just said that the *memory* of Julius guided me. Why the memory? Nostalgia, *Sehnsucht*, finally proved too strong: he left Israel and went back to Austria; his wife, refusing to admit defeat, visited him every three months before she finally packed her bags and moved back to Vienna; Gaby, their wonderful *sabra* son, became a *chef de rang* in a hotel in Carinthia. Only Sivit stayed behind: she is a psychoanalyst, extremely left-wing, and has a complex relationship with Israel. I was stunned when I heard that Julius had moved back to Vienna; somehow I felt betrayed, but I know all too well that human beings should never ask of themselves things that are too difficult. Many of my other friends in Israel missed *'l'Europe aux anciens parapets'* ['the Europe of the ancient parapets'], and *'la flache noire et froide'* ['the cold black pool'] in 'Le Bateau ivre' can be a cure for an excess of harsh sunlight, the merciless constancy of threats and violence.

The moment he saw me, Ben Gurion did not beat about the bush; he prodded my chest with a steely finger and said, 'So, what are you waiting for? When are you coming? We need men like you here.' The guide from the Jewish Agency who accompanied me almost everywhere and who had arranged this meeting with the mythic Prime Minister and his wife, the charming Paula, had probably advised him

I was 'good material'. Ben Gurion, like Begin, was impressive but the former had defeated the latter because he had not been afraid to fire on the *Altalena*, the ship that, just after independence was declared, had brought to Israel's shores not only fighters but also weapons for the Irgun. Ben Gurion would not tolerate any power that challenged his authority and resigned himself to the fact that Jews would kill other Jews, the founding act of a true state. As we have seen, Menachem Begin had to wait almost thirty years before, in turn, becoming Prime Minister, to the horror of the bourgeois Ashkenazi Jews of Jerusalem and Haifa who could already see the proles invading their living rooms. Ben Gurion had an obvious charisma that was difficult to resist, yet to his annoyance I stammered that I needed to see the country, to think about it; he would have preferred a passionate response. I do not know what would have happened if I had not been receiving Simone de Beauvoir's expansive love letters promising me a future and committing me, even if I did not write as often as she did. I felt at ease in Israel and this first trip might easily have lasted much longer.

In a sense, I am of old French stock, much older certainly than most French Jews. My father was born in Paris on 14 July 1900, my family has been in France since the late nineteenth century; I would go so far as to say that I feel so securely French that Israel has never been problematic for me as it has been for the more recently assimilated Jews who arrived in France between the wars or after World War II. They experienced the creation of Israel as something disturbingly personal rather than a gain for the Jewish people: the choice they had made to settle in France seemed fragile, revocable; the existence of another possibility challenged or even contradicted their difficult initial decision, throwing them back into a Jewish world from which they had emerged at times with great difficulty. Some fought in the War of Independence, returned to France and over the years became hardened into an anti-Zionism about which they never ceased to theorize. Israel mattered and was of concern to me for very different

reasons: I might be of old French stock through language, educa-
tion, culture, and so on, but these Jews from Lithuania, Bulgaria,
Germany or Czechoslovakia whom I knew neither from Adam nor
Eve reminded me of the contingent nature of my nationality. Like
them, I might have been born in Berlin, in Prague, in Vilnius; that
I had been born in Paris was merely a quirk of geography. Going to
Israel revealed to me that I was both innately French and yet also
coincidentally French, not at all 'of old stock'.

I remember two brothers who owned a hotel where I spent the
night in the holy city of Safed in Galilee, two tall, thin men with
blank faces, as silent as the shimmering stone of the steps on which
they sat for hours in the sun without saying a word. Safed, the city of
mystics celebrated in the kabbala, the city from which, it is written,
the Messiah will set out for Jerusalem and which, through the twenty
centuries of the Jewish diaspora, was never abandoned by its Jews,
whether kabbalists or grocers, kabbalists *and* grocers. Like Hebron, it
was one of the focal points in the 1929 Palestine riots, an organized
uprising during which many Jews were massacred. In 1948, when
independence was declared, the Arabs attacked again, certain they
would be victorious; the Jews of Safed took up arms and, with the help
of reinforcements from the Haganah, held the city for Israel. With
rapt attention I spent hours watching these two property-owning
brothers, who had clearly unhesitatingly defended their possessions
and were so firmly rooted in this land that language seemed to have
become useless to them. The distance between them and me was
infinite, I am not even sure that they were aware of my presence;
nothing that I might think mattered to them. These silent men were
truly Israeli 'of old stock', they carried their country, its ancient and
recent history, in their bones, their blood. Compared to them, I was
an elf, I carried no weight: neither Joan of Arc nor the Vase of Soissons
nor Bertrand du Guesclin flowed through my veins, and the symbols
of the glory of France that so enraptured de Gaulle as a child – 'night
falling over Notre-Dame, the majesty of evening at Versailles, the Arc

de Triomphe in the sun, flags of conquest waving in the vault of the Invalides' – these symbols did not anchor me, did not bind me. I was an insider and an outsider in France, an outsider and an insider in Israel, which from the first seemed both strange and familiar. If the flags of conquest waving in the vault of Les Invalides did not move me as they moved the future General, at least I was aware of them. But I knew nothing about Israel, about the language, the history, the rules, about the mores, the religion or the influence it exerted.

Nightfall in Israel I found particularly disturbing; twilight was very brief, night came suddenly, unannounced. Not knowing that all life ceased as though by magic even before the Shabbat began, one Friday I found myself trapped in Afula, a bleak little town in lower Galilee in the Jezreel Valley. I had intended to return to Tel Aviv that evening but it proved impossible: there were no buses until the following evening, no means of transport, not a café nor a restaurant was open, there was no one in the only hotel to welcome a lost traveller, the streets were deserted, there were no cars, no pedestrians; it was a ghost town, petrified as though after the eruption of some Vesuvius. I never want to relive that night in Afula, which remains in my memory as the epitome of hostility and terror, a nightmare so terrible that I wanted to flee the country. Even today, when I go to Israel, I dread the weekly return of the Shabbat and the uneasiness I feel every time, regardless of where I am. The entire life of Afula had taken shelter, strictly observant, it had converged, without a single exception, on the synagogues. If I wanted to see another human being, it was to a synagogue I had to go. And so I loitered like a fearful thief outside these places of worship, not daring to enter, not understanding what was said, what was read, what was happening; feeling rejected, brushed aside, excluded by those I stubbornly, desperately considered my own people because by chance or by geography I might have been in their place and they in mine. But they were real Jews, they had the knowledge, knew the prayers, the liturgy, some of them undoubtedly knew the Talmud. Whatever the case, that night, I understood the true might of religion, the power of strict observance. And still I had seen nothing yet.

In Jerusalem for Simchat Torah – the Rejoicing of the Torah – people in the synagogues and surrounding streets celebrated the end of the cycle of Torah readings, and the beginning of the new. This timeless celebration takes place once a year. In Mea Shearim, a neighbourhood of uncompromising, ultra-Orthodox Judaism, I could not tear my eyes from the astounding spectacle I was witnessing: on a hot October night, clothed in heavy caftans and *shtreimels* – fur hats – designed for the Polish weather, capable of dancing through the entire night with no rest, no break, with the endlessly renewed passion required by the sublime rapture of the event, their right arms clasping to their chests newborns long since lulled to sleep by their fathers' tireless gallopade, their left hands clutching the sacred scroll of the Torah whose public reading will begin again at dawn, ecstatic and bathed in sweat, the ultra-Orthodox Hasidim attest to the powerful mystic dimension of radical Judaism. That same power possessed by miraculous, venerated rabbis to whom Talmudic scholars flock like supplicants, determined to be taught only by such masters who in turn sat at the feet of another great master, who in turn ... Such is the sanctity of the tradition, the burning heart of Judaism. The day after Simchat Torah I was taken to the *yeshiva* of the most venerated of the masters of his generation, a descendant of one of the founding Lithuanian families – a very old man who had, by extraordinary chance, survived the Shoah. He presided at the head of a very long table, surrounded by men in black, the teachers of his congregation, and by students, all wearing their black broad-brimmed hats, arranged down each side of the table in diminishing order of age and importance. A plate was set before each guest and, as one moved down the table away from the master, so the commotion increased. Already, though I did not understand why, people were jostling, trying to get closer to the table, which was at least ten metres long. Then suddenly, everyone froze in a vast palpable, deferential silence, all conversation ceased and all eyes, shining with desire, converged on plates of herring being set before the master. He began to eat heartily, from time to time taking a herring to give to one of those standing nearby who would thank him effusively, expressing both his gratitude for the food and his devotion for the transubstantiation the master's touch brought to an ordinary Jewish meal. Meanwhile, at the other end of the table, the starving, fed all day on Talmudic studies, exhausted from a night of twisting and dancing, were pawing the ground impatiently. Then, with the almost diabolical nimbleness and precision of a knife-thrower or a javelin-thrower, the elderly rabbi grabbed a herring and tossed it onto this or that plate, rarely missing his target. The elect, flushed at having been chosen, immediately had to defend his herring from his neighbours' ravenous mouths. But the old master of the Talmud was also a master strategist: there would be enough for everyone; when he tired of throwing, his assistants took over with regrettably poorer aim, sparking greedy scuffles. To me, the scene was primal, initiatory, powerfully moving, not at all picturesque. These herring eaters, in the middle of the *Tzena*, this dauntless, uncompromising community, were my people, the Jewish people, stronger than a thousand dead and I would not disown them. I wished that Sartre, author of *Réflexions sur la question juive*, my friend, had been with me that evening. I would tell him what I had just seen.

In *Pourquoi Israël* there are two metaphysical leitmotifs running through the film that give it power and *vis comica*: one concerns normality and abnormality, the other – which is open-ended and offers no solution – concerns the question 'Who is a Jew?' Ben Gurion's celebrated words, 'Israel will be a normal country the day we have our own prostitutes, our gangsters, our police, our prisons,' were already a reality for me, as we have seen, the moment I arrived in Haifa and set foot in this promised land. And yet, Ben Gurion, that great architect of the state, fell a little short: he was unable to see Israel as I did, as other new arrivals did. For me, as I showed in a number of scenes in the film, it was this very normality that was abnormal and which created what I call the playful nature of the Jewish state. In one hilarious sequence in the film, a group of Jewish-American tourists visits a supermarket in Jerusalem that looks just like any other supermarket in the world. And that's precisely what they love about it, it is the banality that astonishes them: 'Jewish bread!' 'Jewish tuna! In pure oil!' 'It's amazing!' etc. They can't believe it: for as long as there are new, innocent eyes in the diaspora to look in wonderment – in an endless, dizzying dialectic of sameness and otherness, of within and without – on the existence of a Jewish state, a Jewish army, Jewish police, Jewish strikers or a sacred union between rich and poor, the country will still have – all the more so if it remains ringed by enemies – a long road to travel before reaching the non-paradoxical normality Ben Gurion set out as an ideal. It will not happen soon.

'"Who is a Jew?" The most important issue in Israel, the only issue worthy of consideration, is not poverty, education, the lack of money to buy fighter bombers or the defence of the country in general; it is to know who is Jewish. The former are technical problems, they can be solved, there is no doubt about that. While "Who is a Jew?" questions the very meaning of a Jewish nation.' This is what Zushy Posner says to me as we make our way through the orange groves heavy with ripe fruit in another scene from *Pourquoi Israël*. A Hasid and a Lubavitcher, Zushy's mission is to spread Judaism among the Jews. The Hasidim, weary of the harshness and intransigence of the Law, aim to promote spirituality and infectious Joy. They are always good-humoured, they smile and talk to strangers, immediately offer to give them *tefillin*, phylacteries, which they wind around their arms with the skill of a conjurer. They do not proselytize, they are not interested in converting gentiles. The issue for them, the only important issue from their point of view is, what is the use of a Jewish state if the population is made up of the ignorant or unbelievers? Posner immediately recognized that I was the perfect prey. And yet, in the thrust and fire of my questions, he immediately became caught up in tortuous questions of identity, even as the combination of his radical pessimism about human nature, his cheerfulness and his humour allowed him to extricate himself from anything with grace and intelligence. I ask him, 'So you think you could make a good Jew out of me?' He replies, 'You are a good Jew. Every Jew is a good Jew. But some could be better.' I tell him that what he is saying is terribly unjust: 'You're saying that you would prefer me, who knows nothing about Judaism, to a non-Jew who has worked hard, studied and overcome every obstacle the process of conversion puts in his path just because my mother is Jewish?' 'So, start studying,' he says, a cynical twinkle in his eye, indicating he knows I will do nothing of the sort.

Nor did I. *I could not* do it. It was not laziness, but primeval choice, an act of *non-thétique* consciousness that involved my entire existence. I would never have made *Pourquoi Israël* or *Tsahal* if I had chosen to live there, if I had learned Hebrew, if, in other words, I had 'started studying', if integration had been my goal. Just as I could never have devoted twelve years of my life to a work such as *Shoah* if I had been sent to the camps. These things are mysterious, or perhaps they are not. There can be no true creation without opacity, the creator does not have to be transparent to himself. One thing is certain, the role of the witness, which became mine on my first visit to Israel and has constantly grown and reconfirmed itself with time and with each film, required me to be both within and without, as though I had been assigned a precise position.

Pourquoi Israël premièred at the New York Film Festival on 7 October 1973. The morning before the screening I was shaving in the bathroom of my room at the Algonquin Hotel on West 44th Street when I heard a scream. It was Angelika, whom I would marry in Jerusalem a year later, watching a small television: Egyptian troops were crossing the Suez Canal, destroying the forts on the Bar-Lev line. As a result, my screening took place in singular and distressing circumstances.

During the press conference that followed, an American journalist, possibly Jewish, asked me, 'But sir, what is your homeland? Is it France? Is it Israel?' Brusquely and without taking time to think, I answered, and perhaps it sheds light on the mystery I have just outlined: 'Madame, my homeland is my film.'

Chapter 12

But I wasn't thinking about a film when, twenty years earlier, I boarded a boat in Haifa on a bleak November morning to head back to France. My mind was teeming with dark thoughts; I was sad to leave this country and I knew deep down, though I could not clearly formulate the thought, that I would not complete the project that had brought me here: a feature for *Le Monde* along the lines of the one I had written the previous year about the German Democratic Republic, published, you will remember, under the title 'Germany Behind the Iron Curtain'. For me, Israel had passed from the public to the private domain, the most intimate, truth be told: the questions this young nation prompted, forced me to confront, were personal and I felt it would be somehow obscene to expose them to the glare of publicity. Would I even have been capable of doing so? I am convinced that I would not; I was not equipped to answer them in the way I intended and the idea of producing supposedly objective and necessarily superficial articles about Israel seemed to me impossible and undignified.

Returning to Paris, to Simone de Beauvoir, whom I knew from her letters to be more and more in love, more determined, impatient and understanding, only served to increase my anxiety. I had spent one night with her and her boldness had now committed me more quickly and more deeply than I might have wished. One part of my life was coming to an end, and something else, mysterious and weighty, was beginning. I had the feeling of being carried headlong by fate; in short, I felt I no longer had complete mastery of my actions, my plans and, especially, of my own internal time.

The reality of nature would quickly put an end to these doubts, revealing them for what they truly were: a luxury, which carried little weight in the face of the frenzied elements. A storm broke in the dead of night some hours after we left Haifa. Until this year of 1952, no ship in living memory had had to ride out a Mediterranean storm as prolonged, as relentless and as ferocious as this one. We were pitched into troughs ten metres deep and it seemed impossible that this fragile skiff, its very structure groaning mournfully between cliffs of water, desperately, might scale another mountain only to be pitched down again towards the next wave. Aside from the crew, some of whom were quite ill, two people, only two, watched over this *bateau ivre* for four days and nights: the captain, Eliezer Hodorov, formerly of the Soviet merchant navy, and me. I would not have gone into the bowels of the ship for anything in the world, not even to escape the torrential spray sweeping the decks or the force 10 gale: the acrid stench of human vomit – people threw up in the cabins, in the gangways, the latrines were like cesspits – sapped the will. I refused to go down, it was as simple as that. The valiant Eliezer agreed to my request; I was tightly lashed to the poop deck facing the bow and, in order to hold out, I imagined myself slicing through the waves, as though I were the prow, the figurehead. At dinnertime, as the wind and the groaning of the Zim Israel Shipping Company steamer redoubled, Captain Eliezer and I sat facing each another, the only people in the first-class dining room, drinking Greek wine and – laid on for my benefit – a fine Bordeaux. The storm eased and finally cleared after four days. Damage to the ship, both inside and out, was considerable and everything had to be cleaned and disinfected. As sole master on board, Eliezer decided to call in at Naples, an unexpected stopover, where we spent forty-eight hours before heading back out to sea, which remained calm all the way to Marseille.

Castor's eyes, her arms, her mouth, her hands moving over my body as though to recognize it, the long, slightly tremulous embrace of our reunion, as we stood in the red room, on the top floor of the rue de la Bûcherie, calmed all my fears. Joy, in her, did not preclude seriousness; on the contrary, they melded into a rare attentiveness to the humanity of the other. Without my saying a word she understood the complex feelings that this strange return to a home that was not mine after such a journey aroused in me. I instinctively began to speak, to tell her my doubts, my hesitations; the love between us was not love at first sight, it had to be learned and take its time. But she had sensed all this, knew it just as I did. From the beginning, the rapport between us was both intellectual and carnal. Without even discussing it, we settled down together, into this single room, furnished before I arrived with a large round table, a bed, a bookcase and her school desk. I complied. It all went without saying. The only change to the room was the addition of another desk, identical to hers but which, unlike hers, did not face Notre-Dame but a window-less side wall. Although Castor's rigorous, inflexible discipline, second nature to a brilliant student and a professional writer, was completely unfamiliar to me, I tried to submit to it. I endeavoured to outsmart myself, sitting down to write at my brand new desk, in the way a man of little faith is advised to kneel in order that he might believe. It didn't work. I sat gazing, feeling cramped and restricted by a timetable that was not my own. I wasn't ready. Turning, I saw Castor's beautiful face, moving in its concentration, as I watched her pen race – what am I saying? – fly, hardly seeming to touch down, as she worked on a novel for which she had not yet found a title. I would soon find one for her: *Les Mandarins*. The rhythm of the ordinary days was unchanging: we spent the mornings together, she wrote and I did not always pretend to, she lunched with Sartre, or with me or with someone else – sometimes the three of us had lunch. She spent her afternoons in Sartre's office, where she had her own desk. One evening was reserved for Sartre, the next for me; the nights we spent together. But we also often had dinner together, sometimes the three of us, on occasion with the rare friends, such as Giacometti, of whom Sartre was particularly fond.

Castor arranged for us to lunch with Sartre the day after my return. We met at La Palette, a restaurant in Montparnasse he liked, where we could talk without people at neighbouring tables eavesdropping; sadly, the place no longer exists. This, obviously, was the first time I saw Sartre in my new role as Castor's lover: he gave his blessing to this union, this 'marriage', to use Castor's word, who in her love letters referred to me as her 'husband', and often signed them 'your wife'. Sartre knew everything about me that she did, she had read him all my letters, following the rule of radical transparency that she later urged on me despite my resistance. He beamed at her palpable happiness, was cheerful and genuinely friendly towards me. Both, with touching seriousness, questioned me about Israel, or rather they listened since I did all the talking, revealing a world completely unfamiliar to them, a world that my letters had only hinted at. I explained to Sartre how his *Réflexions sur la question juive* needed to be reviewed, revised, augmented, that Jews had not waited for anti-Semites in order to exist, that I had discovered a whole world out there, a religion, secular traditions, a people subject to history in its own way, in spite of pogroms, persecutions, the Holocaust. I told them I had given up the idea of writing articles for *Le Monde*, the pretext for my trip, since everything I had seen and experienced challenged me, raising personal questions that I did not dare to reveal publicly. Here, once again, I witnessed Sartre's intellectual good faith, his openness to other people, his ability to recognize his errors. He told me, 'You have discovered the singularity of Jewishness. You're right to give up writing articles about Israel. Write a book.' I was inspired by his words. This was the solution. In a book I could elaborate on the Jewish condition, about Israel, about myself, about Israel and myself, freely, without indecency. But it proved to be more difficult than I thought. I was raw, although I did not realize it. I would have to go far in my questioning, face realities that even now I find difficult to name; confess to things at the age of twenty-seven that I can barely relate, even today, in these pages. But I set to work, writing in the afternoons rather than the mornings, when I was alone in our room. I wrote about a hundred pages, now lost unfortunately. Sartre and Castor read them, judged them to be excellent and encouraged me to carry on. But I couldn't; I no longer wished to, I postponed writing, realizing that I needed to grow up, to grow older, if I were to resolve the questions that stirred in me differently. One cannot simply sit down to write and transform the material of one's life into a book; this is often the weakness of professional literary writers. I was a man slow to mature, I was not afraid of the passing of time. Something told me that my life would reach its full potential in its second half.

Twenty years later, the articles I did not write and the book that came to nothing were to become *Pourquoi Israël*, a film I made relatively quickly because I knew precisely what I wanted to say. True, I had gone back to Israel several times. The shock of my first visit had led to other discoveries that were crucial to me, such as the role of German Jews in the making of the country, other torments, such as the wars: the 1956 Sinai War, the Six Day War in 1967, the 'war of attrition' of 1968–9. My knowledge of Israel constantly increased, especially as I spent a lot of time working on a special, 1,000-page issue of *Les Temps modernes* devoted to the Arab–Israeli conflict in which Arabs agreed, for the first time, not to debate or discuss, but to appear alongside Israelis in the same publication. Many moments came together in *Pourquoi Israël* and contributed to its being made, but the final trigger, the last event and certainly the most crucial, was falling in love with Angelika Schrobsdorff in Jerusalem, so that making the film was the only way for me to see her again. I met Angelika seventeen years after I began to share my life with Simone de Beauvoir to whom, if you will forgive this herniated digression into my chronology, I now return.

We truly shared our lives. We lived together as a married couple for seven years, from 1952 to 1959. I am the only man with whom Simone de Beauvoir lived a quasi-marital existence. We even succeeded in living together for two years in one twenty-seven-square-metre room and were, she as much as I, when we thought or talked about it, justifiably proud of our relationship. I found it normal and reasonable that she went away, or spent a large part of her holidays with Sartre; he found it normal and reasonable that she did the same with me. I was sometimes sad, found that time dragged when she was away on long trips, to China or Cuba, for example, but I never felt the slightest pang of jealousy. Before going on a journey, she was immensely considerate, going so far as to draw up charts or tables listing every stopover, how long she would be in each place, the names of hotels, consulates and embassies where I could reach her in case of emergency. But these separations also meant salvoes of letters; some days I received machine-gun bursts of extraordinarily detailed letters, peppered with unfamiliar names that I found difficult to decipher. All three of us were easy to live with. She and Sartre – and this has long been my conviction too – believed that it was only possible truly to discuss things with those with whom one is already in agreement on the fundamentals. This was why they loathed polite small-talk and large, typically French formal dinners, preferring the intimacy of the *tête-à-tête*. Two people together, talking to each other, was to them – and to me, it is something I learned from them – the only way for individuals to understand one another, to get along, to move forward, to think. The formula for this relationship was '*Chacun sa réception*', 'each to his own'.

In the spring of 1953 or, rather, shortly before spring, the three of us went to Saint-Tropez ostensibly to take a break, which for Sartre meant working relentlessly, even more so than he did in Paris, because it was more peaceful. Saint-Tropez was delightful and deserted; we were staying at the Hôtel la Ponche. Sartre had his room; Castor and I ours. Only two restaurants on the harbour were open; they were next door to each other, their terraces separated by a thick canvas partition, which limited what one could see, but not what one could hear. Curious, I wondered how '*Chacun sa réception*' was going to work in practice given our extreme proximity. It went like this: on Monday, Castor had dinner with Sartre in one of the two restaurants, while I dined in the other – we were invariably the only diners in our respective restaurants. Castor had a voice that carried, she knew that I was just on the other side of the canvas and she had no secrets from me: I heard every word she said, nor did I miss any of Sartre's metallic pronouncements. I read – or tried to read. That night, when she and I retired to our room, she recounted in detail everything I had already heard. Then on Tuesday, it was Sartre's turn to be exiled and overhear every word we said, which Castor faithfully repeated to him the following day. Wednesday was more civilized: the three of us had dinner together, which spared us one account of the proceedings. Yes, the understanding between us was idyllic. Our afternoon drives to Les Maures or to L'Esterel – with Sartre, if we managed to tear him from his work – were, for me, who had travelled little in France at that time, an initiation into seeing, into the world. I was learning to look through their eyes and I can say that they shaped me; but it was not entirely one-sided, we had intense, closely argued discussions, and the admiration I felt for both of them did not make them any less egalitarian. They helped me to think; I gave them food for thought.

Conformism being utterly alien to them, neither of them saw any contradiction, any break with the unity of self – a self in which they firmly did not believe – in the fact that I was writing for *Les Temps modernes* (I wrote rather a lot for the periodical that year) while earning my living as a rewriter at *France Dimanche*. This scandalized certain fine souls of the patrician press, who were none the less calmly prepared, whenever sales dropped, to boost circulation with licentious ads including addresses and phone numbers. *France Dimanche* had another considerable advantage for me: I had long 'holidays'. The management knew about my relationship with Castor, and when I was due back at work, she and I would make up a sudden illness or an accident and she would dispatch a telegram from Estremadura or the Peloponnese explaining that my return had to be postponed. No one believed it, but they were indulgent, and flattered to receive these anxious messages from Simone de Beauvoir. One of my co-rewriters, Gérard Jarlot, who had published an anti-novel entitled *Un chat qui aboie* [*A Cat That Barks*] in Gallimard's *Collection Blanche*, was the lover of Marguerite Duras, but their adventures never took them further than Neauphle-le-Château and he was always back at work on time. Pierre Lazareff and his immediate colleagues were Jewish, but there were a number of dyed-in-the-wool anti-Semites on the editorial staff at *France Dimanche* who came out with coarse, unsubtle anti-Jewish jokes week after week for years after the war as though nothing had happened. One of them, who was closely related to a famous geographer and author of a set text in schools, who had lost an arm in some battle or other, brandished his empty sleeve proudly like a banner and did his best to hire former *miliciens* who had been convicted after the Liberation. The entire rewriting team threatened to resign en masse; I felt as though I were reliving the episode at Lycée Louis-le-Grand where the students had tried to have our study hall named after Brasillach. France was still infected to the marrow.

Castor's thirst for travel was unquenchable; she looked at the world with eyes that were never jaded, and revisiting places she knew with me – teaching me, in other words – allowed her to see them through fresh eyes, rekindling the feelings she had had the first time. She wrote extensively about our adventures and peregrinations in her *Memoirs*, never getting a date wrong, since she kept a log. As I have already said, we do not have the same memories and I leave chronological fidelity to her and recount here, randomly and chaotically, those things that, to me, are unforgettable. It is important to know that Sartre and Castor took their holidays according to the school timetable, like the teachers they had once been: two months in summer, Christmas, Easter, and so on.

Castor goes skiing for two weeks in December and January, when the weather is at its coldest, to Kleine Scheidegg, a windswept pass at the foot of the Jungfrau in the Bernese Oberland, 2,061 metres above sea level, with views of the terrible north face of the Eiger and the Mönch. She has skied before, I never have. It is –15°C, the pistes are frozen and iced over. We don't even consider hiring a skiing instructor, she knows how to snowplough down a slope, braking hard, never allowing herself to be carried away; she is so careful that if by chance she finds herself on a sheer slope, she looks as though she is going up rather than down. The same cannot be said for me, I get carried away on the black ice, hurtling downhill at top speed; neither able nor knowing how to turn, stopping myself by crashing head first into a pine tree, splitting my forehead in the process and bleeding profusely. Back then, people used long wooden skis – mine were 2.2 metres. The following day, we hired an instructor and I began to learn in earnest.

I can say that later I became an able, fearless skier, undaunted by sheer, even vertical slopes, capable of skiing anywhere. My fondest memories of that trip are of the nights and days – common in December and January – when it snowed without let-up and we were forced to stay indoors, in the modest rooms of the Kleine Scheidegg hotel. Lying side by side on the bed reading vast novels that seemed written for just such an occasion, such as Road to Calvary by Aleksei Tolstoy – the very talented offspring of an impoverished branch of the dynasty of the great Lev Nikolaievich – which I devoured with passion: it is an epic, thrilling account of the Russo-German war, the Bolshevik revolution, the pitiless struggle against the White Russians and their defeat. Or The Eyes of Reason, a sweeping, subtle tale by East German writer Stefan Heym about the influence on hearts and minds of the Communist putsch of 1948, the Prague Coup. Our long vacations were divided between utterly insane forced marches, systematically crisscrossing a country, a province or a city, and studious hours or days spent reading. Castor was an avid reader, and I spent many hours reading by her side, not only when it was snowing, but also in the blazing noon-day sun. I remember reading *Moby Dick* on the terrace of a hotel, on a rocky outcrop south of Paestum. On the day of our departure, I could not tear myself away from Melville's description of the Indian Ocean's 'endless swathes of blue upon the yellow sea'. Faced with what I believed to be a perfect metaphor, nothing seemed to matter; I wanted to go on reading, and we had a terrible scene.

Our first summer holidays were spectacular: in spite of the willingness on all our parts, adapting to this new life and its restrictive living arrangements had been difficult for me, and it was taking its toll on my body, which now struck back, inflicting on me a very painful bout of furunculosis – boils – the likes of which I had not suffered since the *maquis* in Cantal. The trip we had organized was complicated: first the Swiss mountains, so that I could recover my health and strength, then a brief stopover in Milan with Castor's sister Hélène de Beauvoir, who was married to a cultural attaché, Lionel de Roulet, whose every word dripped with some secondary, slightly pompous significance. Our adventure was to continue via Trieste, Croatia, along the Dalmatian coast to Dubrovnik, then back up via Sarajevo across the great Serbian plain, Ljubljana and Slovenia, crossing into Italy at Tarvisio, then back to Switzerland, and all of it depending on the weather and the time available. I was the one driving the Simca Aronde and as we left Paris on Route Nationale 6, my posture behind the wheel was decidedly lopsided, because a red patch on my left shoulder blade that I had decided to ignore had just erupted into a three-headed carbuncle and I was in terrible pain. The monstrous abscess exploded at about eleven o'clock that night, just as we were coming into Tournus, where we stopped. With boiling water, cotton wool and compresses, the delightful Castor spent a greater part of the night mopping up the pus that welled up as soon as pressure was applied. The pain became bearable and then eased; when I could finally look up into her pure face of a woman in love, filled with despair and tender compassion, it reminded me of Giotto's women in the Scrovegni Chapel frescoes in Padua.

The following day, as we headed towards Switzerland, I felt no pain and assumed that I was cured. Being ill did not figure in my plans and certainly not in Castor's: taking out the Swiss Army map that she could read like a high-ranking officer, she began to plot the following day's route: a hike that would take eight hours – and that only if we were in peak condition – from one mountain pass to the next in the *grand cirque* overlooking Grindelwald, facing the daunting sweep of peaks rising to more than 4,000 metres, among them the Mönch, the Eiger and the Jungfrau. Our goal was an isolated refuge in a magnificent landscape; we were both excited and set off at a fast clip wearing espadrilles, with no protective creams or potions for our lips or faces, no cover for our exposed heads. My three-headed carbuncle was nothing but a bizarre memory and I was astonished at my body's ability to heal itself, scorning my bad blood and the *staphylococcus aureus* still lying in wait: scorning it, that is, until a second boil erupted two-thirds of the way through our hike, on my knee, the worst possible place. The pain was excruciating, the boil swelled and expanded quickly and two heads appeared; we were miles from anywhere and had no medication, no first-aid kit. Nothing could be done, it was 'march or die'. Sunburn exacerbated the fever from the carbuncle, I moved painfully, limping as I walked; Castor, who was also red as a beetroot, sunburnt and sweating, shuffled like a sleepwalker, her eyes glazed. Dusk took us by surprise, we lost our way and did not finally make it to the shelter until midnight where, miraculously, we found a group of well-equipped Swiss climbers who took pity on us, scolded us, gave us soothing creams, fed me analgesics and gave Castor some food. I didn't eat, my temperature was almost 40°, and the vicious carbuncle, its maturation probably accelerated by our long hike, burst in a liberating geyser. When we reached Milan, a Lombard doctor prescribed a heavy dose of antibiotics as the only cure, but I suffered a relapse in Mostar, with a high fever, and I was treated in a hospital in Sarajevo. After that, the trip went smoothly. I was inured, cured, my initiation into the Sartre family was complete.

It is night, we are driving along a narrow, pitted road through dense, dark forest taking a short cut Castor spotted on the map as we were driving north in Yugoslavia. I am at the wheel. In the beam from the headlights, hares bound suddenly across the road. There seem to be hundreds of them. In an effort to avoid them, I slow the car each time, swerving dangerously. I kill only three – something of a feat. I stop the car. We get out and go back to look for victims; the Aronde is spattered with blood. In the rare villages we come upon, we give them to the first people we encounter. I like hares, I respect them, they are noble animals. I learned by heart the children's story by the Argentinian poet Silvina Ocampo, *La liebre dorada* [*The Golden Hare*], which I have used as an epigraph to this book. If there is any truth to metempsychosis and if I were given the choice, I would unhesitatingly choose to come back as a hare. In *Shoah*, there are two shots that are fleeting but crucial to me, though there is latency of a fraction of a second before we clearly see what the camera sees: a hare, its fur the colour of the earth, sitting by the barbed-wire fence at Birkenau extermination camp. Over this first image is a voiceover, it is Rudolf Vrba, one of the heroes of the film, an unrivalled hero since he managed to escape this accursed place filled with ashes. But the hare is cunning and, as Vrba speaks, we see the animal flatten his back, hunker down and crawl under the barbed wire. He too escapes. There is no killing in Auschwitz-Birkenau now, not even of animals; all forms of hunting are forbidden. No one keeps count of the hares, but there are a lot of them and I like to think that many of my people chose, as I would, to come back as hares.

Since then, a passion for high mountains has run in my veins. Something for which, all my life, I have given thanks to Castor. The following summer we started out again in Switzerland, but instead of the Bernese Oberland, the Jungfrau and the Eiger, we headed for the mountains of the Valais, Zermatt, the Mont Cervin (Matterhorn), Mont Rose, peaks with mythological names such as Pollux and Castor, white shrouded twins that rise to more than 4,000 metres. We stayed at the Hotel Mont Rose – or rather Monte Rosa since the soft snowy peaks of the enchanting and deadly massif are as much Italian as they are Swiss. The Hotel Monte Rosa, which was, unsurprisingly, pink, was a large, squat building in the centre of Zermatt, whose noble rooms had balconies dramatically overlooking the soaring, misshapen pyramid of the Matterhorn, a petrified blade of stone that looks as if it would eviscerate the heavens but deviates from its line, its upper third twisting, as in the final stage of *seppuku*, in an attempt to inflict a fatal wound. Stepping into the hotel behind Castor, I was entranced, amazed by the place's codified opulence that resembled an English gentleman's club: the intimate bars with sofas and benches upholstered in red, smoking-rooms, libraries. I quickly realized there was no reason to be amazed since it had been the fathers – the grandfathers and great-grandfathers – of the Battle of Britain pilots, those 'long-haired boys', who in the nineteenth century had invented mountaineering in the Alps and in the early twentieth century in the Himalayas.

One name remains forever linked to the dark, heroic legend of the conquest of Everest, that of George Mallory. He and his climbing partner, Andrew Irvine, were spotted for the last time at 12.50 p.m. on 8 June 1924, moving steadily towards the summit. No one knows whether they ever reached it. The frozen body of Mallory was discovered in 1999 at 8,290 metres on the north face of the highest mountain in the world. Mallory, the son of a clergyman, weary of constantly being asked, 'Why do you want to climb Mt Everest?', opted for the simplest, the truest, the greatest answer: 'Because it's there.' Everest would not be conquered until twenty-nine years after his death. Curiously, the conqueror's name was Hillary – not Richard, but Edmund. George Mallory's youngest brother, Trafford-Leigh

Mallory, fought with the RAF in both world wars, was a veteran pilot in the Battle of Britain in 1940, and in 1943, just before the Normandy landings, he was named commander-in-chief of the Allied Expeditionary Air Force. In August 1944, with Normandy liberated, he was appointed to what was to be the most strategic role, commander–in-chief of South East Asia Command (SEAC). Despite adverse weather conditions, he decided to set off without delay for the SEAC headquarters in Ceylon, taking his wife and the senior officers with him. They never reached Asia. Ironically, Trafford joined George in the eternal snows: caught up in a storm, his plane crashed into the Mont Blanc massif on the slopes of Mont Maudit. There were no survivors.

I spent happy evenings browsing the third-floor library of the Hotel Monte Rosa, avidly reading English stiff-upper-lip tales of the conquest and attempted conquest of the highest peaks in the world, of the Himalayas, as I have mentioned, but also of the Alps, in particular the Matterhorn with even more brusque gratitude for their local guides – the Swiss Sherpas – who risked and often lost their lives for these lords of Albion, some of whom also suffered and died, fearless pioneers scaling vertiginous rockfaces that no man had dared attempt before. Even today, I can give the date when the Swiss north face of the Matterhorn was first conquered (14 July 1865) and the first ascent, three days later, by the Italian south face, as well as the names of those who took part – those who died and those who survived. But I also know the dates of the conquests in the Mont Blanc massif, the Bernese Oberland, the Himalayas and even the Andes, all the way to Monte Fitz Roy in Argentina; I know the names of the eponymous conquerors whose names now grace the most perilous routes, gorges and spurs, I also know the names of those who perished and the circumstances in which they disappeared.

From the hotel in Kleine Scheidegg, where we had stayed the previous winter, it is possible, in summer and with a telescope, to watch climbers roped together struggling up the terrible, hostile, forbidding north face of the Eiger – the name means 'Ogre'. Unlike the Matterhorn, which so fascinated the British, the north face of the Eiger mainly attracted German mountaineers who, after a succession of cruel tragedies, finally succeeded in conquering it in 1938, sixty-three years after the great Edward Whymper reached the summit of the twisted pyramid in Zermatt. For Whymper too there was tragedy, coming immediately after his victory, when five of those in his climbing party died on the descent; only he and two Swiss guides – Peter Taugwalder and his son, also Peter Taugwalder – survived. I read almost everything there was to read about the north face of the Eiger, either in the Hotel Monte Rosa or in the hotel in Kleine Scheidegg. About the Death Bivouac at the summit of the third ice field, the Hinterstoisser Traverse, the Traverse of the Gods, the White Spider, the Schwieriger Riss or Difficult Crack, the Stollenloch or Thief's Hole – via which the rescue team tried in vain to reach Bavarian climber Toni Kurz.

But what I did not know in the early 1950s as I sat next to Castor reading the story of the first successful ascent by two teams – Austrians Heinrich Harrer and Fritz Kasparek and Germans Anderl Heckmair and Ludwig Vörg – rivals at the beginning, knowing nothing about each other, but deciding to band together when they met up at the Death Bivouac, what I did not know was that in 1959 I would spend hours in Paris with Heinrich Harrer, talking to him, questioning him about the years he spent in Tibet as tutor to the Dalai Lama. The interview took place just as the Dalai Lama, together with a group of young monks aged about twelve and a number of elderly lamas, fled the Potala Palace in Lhasa under cover of a sandstorm as Chinese General Tan Kuan-San's troops invaded Tibet. Hélène Lazareff, wife of Pierre, founder and editor of *Elle*, had asked me to write a feature on what she believed was a historic event. This was the first time I had written for *Elle*. I knew nothing about Tibet, Buddhism or the Dalai Lama, but I avidly read *Seven Years in Tibet* by the conqueror of the Eiger, which had been published five years earlier. There was no possible way I could go there, nor could I join the Dalai Lama's cortège as it made its way across the Himalayas and through the jungles of Tibet, playing hide and seek with the Chinese airforce. It was easier to bring Heinrich Harrer to Paris and ask him my questions. I read other, older and rarer books, a number of monographs, I studied photographs and left the rest to my imagination. My long, in-depth article appeared in issue 696 of *Elle* on 27 April 1959. I was, and on rereading it forty-eight years later I still am, proud of this visionary article in which everything was at once totally invented and absolutely true. Thinking back on the years 1958–9, which were crucial in my life as you will see, I now realize that *Shoah* was prefigured in that meticulously documented yet not documentary article, so profoundly empathetic that the twenty-four-year-old Dalai Lama comes alive to every reader:

> Stock-still on his white pony, wearing the simple purple tunic of a monk, unadorned, seemingly impervious to events, the Dalai Lama, the fourteenth reincarnation of the living Buddha, for the last time looks over the holy city and on Potala, his palace. It is nothing, barely a breath, barely a shadow in his handsome godlike eye, but something, for an instant, has troubled the exceptional impassivity of the Buddha's face ... The shadow of a sigh of the Asian man-god at the mountain pass of Gompste La on the scale of western emotions rivals the blast of Roland's Oliphaunt horn at Roncevaux or where Boabdil, the young Muslim king of Granada, fainted at the Moor's last sigh where he wept 'like a woman' when the Catholic King Ferdinand hounded him from the city he loved so well.

I had good reason to be proud. In 1997, the French philosopher Jean-François Revel and his son Matthieu Ricard, a Buddhist monk and friend and interpreter to the Dalai Lama who gave up what would have been a brilliant career as a molecular biologist, jointly published a conversation entitled *The Monk and the Philosopher*. In their introduction, Revel wrote: 'While for a long time, information about Tibet was hard to come by, it was not non-existent. As early as 1959, Claude Lanzmann, the future director of *Shoah*, one of the great masterpieces of cinema and of contemporary history, wrote in the pages of *Elle*, then the flagship of intelligent women's magazines, an article entitled "The Secret Life of the Dalai Lama" in the very year in which the lama was forced into exile in order to escape slavery and perhaps even death.'

At forty-five, Simone de Beauvoir was rational; Castor, however, was madder than I was and it was she who won out. Refusing the gentle – or lazy – itineraries I suggested, she decided that we were sufficiently acclimatized to embark on a long trek, a hike from Zermatt to the Theodul Pass, the boundary between the Swiss and the Italian sides of the Matterhorn, taking the cable car down to Breuil-Cervinia in Italy, where we would spend the night, and return the following day via the same cable car, to the Theodul Pass. At that point, depending on how we felt, we could either take the Swiss cable car back or descend the Theodul glacier on foot, across the high ice fields and steep rutted meadows, plunging down into the valley and the paths – which to tired muscles seemed endless – leading to Zermatt, a distant, constantly disappearing mirage on the horizon. The weather promised to be 'magnificent' and so it proved. We set off at sunrise like true mountaineers, but wearing espadrilles once again and carrying no creams or ointments, nor anything to cover our heads. The first part of the ascent went well, I wept with love before Castor's headstrong courage, her steady pace, the forbidding majesty of the Matterhorn, which constantly revealed new and beautiful facets as the sun, arcing around it, flared on the rockfaces and the crests, throwing others into shadow. It began to get hot, I decided to expose my back, my chest, my arms, my shoulders to the heavenly body's life-giving rays. My legs were already bare, as I was wearing only a pair of lightweight shorts. I forgot to mention that neither Castor nor I were wearing what were popularly called 'sunglasses', I am not even sure that we knew such things existed. All our wisdom was contained in two aluminium flasks attached to my belt, which jangled softly like the bells on the cows we passed in the high mountain pastures. The ascent between Zermatt (1,600 metres) and the Theodul Pass (3,301 metres) is spectacular. We had planned to stop at the Gandegghütte (3,029 metres) for lunch. But the slope was sheer, tiredness crept up on us as it does in the mountains and our hopes of reaching the cabin, which we had glimpsed a dozen times, were constantly disappointed. We finally arrived, famished, red as peonies, bathed in sweat. What a haven – the window-boxes of geraniums on the terrace, that feast, the exquisite white wine – a humble Fendant Les Murettes, which I will remember to my last breath! I readily exhorted my love to drink with me and the droplets of sweat that pearled on her upper lip so moved me that I devoutly drank them down. We drank, we ate, the sun wheeled in the sky, we dusted ourselves down and prepared to set off again, oblivious to the fact we were embarking on the most difficult stretch, a long hike across the Theodul glacier more than 3,000 metres above sea level, while the sun faded and the temperature quickly dropped just as the glacier rose steeply, the air becoming rarefied, our espadrilles damp and slippery.

While Castor had forged ahead until we reached the Gandegghütte, since she had the maps, knew how to read them and had a good sense of direction, I now took the lead, my overheated body suddenly cold, constantly turning back to make sure she was still behind me, watching the gap between us increase, even though I did not feel I was walking any faster. We were behind schedule, we had stopped too often and for too long to contemplate the wonders of nature; we had arrived late at the Gandegghütte, had had too much to eat and drink, set off again too late. I knew that the last cable car to Cervinia left the Theodul station at seven o'clock precisely and had stupidly calculated that if the Gandegghütte was at 3,029 metres and the

Theodul Pass at 3,301, we would make short work of the final 272 metres. What a fool! Tragedy suddenly loomed in the mountains in this 'magnificent' weather just as, years later, in the sea off Caesarea, it almost cost me my life. Veteran climbers, roped together wearing crampons, quickly made their way down the glacier, which we were struggling to ascend. I asked one of them how far it was to the pass. He looked at his watch and said that we would certainly miss the cable car. Castor was exhausted, her heart hammering in her chest; even if we slowed our pace considerably she would not make it to the top. We had a quick, urgent conversation. I made her lie on the snow close to a rock that still retained some warmth and, though I was not in much better shape, set off to find help. When I finally arrived, the last cable car to Italy had indeed already left, night was drawing in, and with it the cold; the Swiss all seemed to have been struck deaf and it was the Italian *Bersaglieri*, whom I promised to pay whatever it took, who showed their human side. Castor had to be saved, I was worried about her heart, all this I explained in bad Italian, making little drawings to indicate where I had left her. Three *Bersaglieri* strapped on their skis, put on helmet lamps and disappeared into the darkness, dragging a sled equipped with blankets and duvets. They were cheery, earnest, sturdy, seasoned. As I waited for them to return, I negotiated with their comrades and by phone with their superior officer, explaining to him what a shining light to the world Signorina de Beauvoir was. I must have been convincing because he agreed – exceptionally – to send a cable car back up to the pass. It arrived just as Castor showed up, somewhat revived by the kindness of her Italian rescuers, the warmth of the sled and the fact that her heart was beating normally once more. But we were a long way from getting back to the Hotel Monte Rosa. As soon as we got to Breuil-Cervinia, I saw a doctor; I was seriously burned and shivering with fever, I had to be taken by ambulance to the hospital in Aosta, where I was immediately admitted, suffering first-, even second-, degree burns. I spent three days in hospital, watched over by a fretful Castor.

So many images from our trips are jumbled together in my memory, in no apparent order, but always as though time had ceased to exist. We are driving to Salamanca, or from Salamanca to Madrid, across the high desert plains of the Province of León, through what once was Castile, endlessly commenting, she and I, our minds agreeing, sometimes competing, about the wonders of the world, the measureless skies, the infinite gradations of yellow and ochre of the arid ground that itself seemed boundless. Me behind the wheel, we talked for hours and hours, never tiring, of what we had seen, what we would see, of the books we had both read and those one of us had read. My capacity for wonderment, my childlike freshness, rekindled hers. Midnight in Toledo, the *promenade des cigarrales* that snakes above the deep gorge of the River Tagus and the city on the far shore, close-packed houses huddled around the cathedral and the Alcázar. We spent hours attempting to understand the nature of a fortified town; which principles of fear, defiance, defence caused it to be built, to thrive, coming back to gaze on it every night we spent there. But the Alcázar was also a part of recent history – this was the height of Francoism – when, some twenty years earlier, in 1936, in a defiant gesture, Colonel Moscardó held out for seventy days at the Siege of the Alcázar against the 'Reds' who had captured his son, a boy of sixteen, telephoning Moscardó and giving him ten minutes to surrender or they would shoot his son and putting the boy on the phone to convince him they were serious. There ensued a heroic conversation that the colonel himself recounted in a letter he sent to his wife that, after Franco's victory, was taught in every Spanish school: 'I regret to inform you that I spoke to our dear son on the telephone. "Father, they say they are going to shoot me, but I do not believe them." I answered him: "To save your life, they would take my honour. I shall not surrender the Alcázar." All I could do was to tell him to commend his soul to God if the worst were to happen and cry out before the firing squad, "*Viva España*".' The boy was indeed executed a month later, and his father greeted the senior officer of

Franco's Nationalists who came to relieve the fortress with the words, 'All quiet at the Alcázar, sir.' Francisco Franco y Bahamonde, the Generalissimo, promoted him to general – it was the least he could do. Another man to die by firing squad, Robert Brasillach, who, as I had said, preceded me at the Lycée Louis-le-Grand, wrote a book in praise of Moscardó, *Les Cadets de l'Alcazar*.

Catalonia, Barcelona, the Barrio Chino, a maze of narrow streets in the heart of the city running parallel to the Ramblas and down towards the sea. The Barrio Chino and its dark alleys with that nightly throng of lonely souls in the doorways of the brothels with their red lights lining the narrow streets. When first encountering an unfamiliar foreign city, we always have a sense of the centre and where it is; invariably, it proves not to be where we thought. The centre is elsewhere, at least it was when we were young; it is not the museums, the universities, the monuments or the governmental buildings, but those things that are hidden, censored, the red light districts. The true centre was that of sex, just as for foreigners coming to Paris the centre remains a series of stops on the métro: Clichy, Blanche, Pigalle, Anvers, a boulevard of many names that today is home to the dreary line of neon-fronted sex shops and peepshows. Unembarrassed, Castor wanted to see everything and missed nothing of the Barrio Chino, which fascinated her as much as it did me. The only difference was that she was not allowed to go upstairs, not even just to look, as I did once or twice. I say 'just to look' because never have I witnessed a trade in sex so terrifyingly raw and unvarnished, except perhaps once in Mexico. To understand what I am saying you would need to see the photographs taken of a brothel in Alicante by the young Cartier-Bresson. But we stood in the streets outside the most frequented bordellos and watched those going up and those coming down meet on the stairs, those leaving still adjusting their clothes, while strange men in white coats spattered with purple, carrying heavy syringes filled with potassium permanganate, which they brandished like an obscene solicitation, waved those arriving into a little office situated on the ground floor of every whorehouse marked *Enfermería*. Together with syphilis, gonorrhoea was the most common STD back then. The 'nurses' with their thin waxed moustaches then plunged a needle into the patient's urethra and, with a single, painful, life-saving thrust, administered 10cl of their purple liquid. The Barrio Chino no longer exists, there are no alleys, no *enfermerías*, no permanganate, no brothels, everything is bright, refurbished, the mystery is elsewhere. Is it?

Not content with daring to go to Franco's Spain, we hurtled in a single day in a crazed diagonal across the country from Huelva on the Atlantic coast of Andalucía near the Portuguese border, to València on the Mediterranean coast much further north. Shame on us, shame on Castor and of course on me, since as her 'husband' I immediately and without query, but with enthusiasm and a willingness to learn, embraced her passion for bullfighting and *corridas*. A passion so real that she scorned the political correctness of the time, which, as you might guess, cared little for tourism in a Fascist country, the mass slaughter of bulls being considered symbolic of Franco's barbarity. At Lycée Louis-le-Grand, Cau, who hailed from Carcassonne and who slipped off to Catalonia whenever he could, had told me about the bullfights and instilled in me the desire to see one. I had also read Hemingway's *Death in the Afternoon*; I was ready. Why that exhausting day, in the sweltering heat of August, on poor and dangerous roads? Because Castor had decided that for several weeks we would follow the greatest *toreros* of the day on the summer tour they call the *temporada*. *A las cinco de la tarde* [at five in the afternoon], Miguel Báez – 'El Litri' – and Julio Aparicio had fought in the bullring in Huelva together against black Miura bulls, the most feared and formidable beasts, and against the trade winds that made perilous the difficult passes with the *muleta* before the *estocada*. In spite of these gusts, which would suddenly lift the *muleta* to reveal the ornate gold embroidered uniform of the *torero* to the eyes of the bull, El Litri and Aparicio had dazzled with their fluidity and their courage – the cardinal virtues of their profession – and were presented with the ears and tail of the beast, which they brandished as they made five laps of the bullring. The audience applauded and threw flowers. In fact, *The Ears and the Tail – Les Oreilles et la queue* – is the title of another great book extolling the virtues of bullfighting, a book much loved by the Spanish for its humour, its poetry and its technical accuracy. It was written by my friend Cau in the 1960s.

We stopped at Albacete, a city famous for its knives, a Castilian version of Laguiole, but one that to me is also associated with the name André Marty, a senior member of the *Parti communiste français*, appointed by the comintern as political commissar of the International Brigades during the Spanish Civil War. He was nicknamed the 'Butcher of Albacete' by the anarchists in the Confederación Nacional del Trabajo and the Trotskyites in the Partido Obrero Unificación Marxista, since he was a Stalinist disciplinarian who cared little if he had to shed blood.

We drove and drove past the harvested fields, bleached yellow from the heat only to plunge – literally, since the road dipped steeply and suddenly towards the Mediterranean – into the verdant *huerta* of València like a refreshing oasis. But València, where El Litri and Chaves Flores were to fight six more Miura bulls the following afternoon, was suffering from something else. While the *huerta* exuded a subtle perfume, València reeked. There was not a drop of water in the whole city, the ageing pipes had burst and it was impossible to wash or even to flush the toilet. Under Franco, València had been allowed to go to rack and ruin. The hotel we had booked into – because the *toreros* and their *cuadrillas* were staying there – stank so badly that their managers, the *apoderados*, had immediately moved them to houses out in the *huerta*, which had been spared this plague. Castor and I walked for hours, exhausted after the long drive, drinking – to forget, to numb ourselves – heavy Spanish wines, the only liquid to be found. It was just as well: we stumbled into bed, dead drunk and therefore oblivious to the stench. By morning there was water again, a cholera or typhus epidemic was avoided, and the *corrida* went ahead. It must surely remain unforgettable to all those who were there: here too, El Litri and Aparicio proved themselves to be at the height of their art, making passes that brought the beasts' sharp horns within millimetres of their stomachs, their thighs, their vital arteries constantly threatened by the long, agile necks of the bulls. But Chaves Flores was gored when his second bull made a sudden upward thrust with his head, piercing the *torero*'s groin then attempting to toss him into the air, which served only to aggravate the 'very serious' wound, according to the medical report posted that evening by the arena *enfermería*.

In Spanish, a passion for bullfighting is called an *afición* and its devotees are known as *aficionados*. Surely I have recounted here our holiday in the summer of 1955. Our *afición* became such that the spectacle alone was not enough: we needed to take home material proof to allow us to dream during the winter months, so wherever we went we bought posters of the *temporada* to take back to France. In fact, we would use them to paper the high walls of the studio Castor had just bought at 11 *bis* rue Schœlcher with the money from the 1954 Prix Goncourt she had won for *Les Mandarins*; we could think of nothing better to decorate the vast, dreary walls of this new residence. Later, coming back from my trip to North Korea and China, I would bring her precious offerings: Korean drums formed from two cones, whose points meet, and two identical heads of animal skin on which the drummer beats. Rarer still, and to me more poignant, a war drum from the Chinese People's Volunteer Army, those who fought like devils, like lions, in the bloody assaults on Hill 1211, captured a dozen times, lost a dozen times. It was painted red, streaked with white lines made by the hail of bullets; it was round, bulbous at the centre, with rings that buckle so the drum could be strapped over the drummer's belly while, on the other side, the drumskins were held in place by three rows of gilt tacks, like those used to upholster English leather armchairs. The atelier at 11 *bis* was also a single room, but it was much bigger, high-ceilinged and in one corner there was a narrow mezzanine entirely occupied by the bed and the wardrobes, which received scant sunlight from two small decorative windows that opened onto the studio below. Access to the mezzanine was via a spiral staircase that led to a suspended balcony. The bedroom was on the left and on the right was a small bathroom with a window that overlooked the street, but was set so high that it was possible to see all the way to the great mausoleums of Montparnasse cemetery. Castor and I were together when we first set foot in the studio – the only property she ever owned – and we had a sexual housewarming in which we explored the new possibilities afforded by the breadth and height of the space. As I write, 11 *bis*, which many would have liked to see become the Musée Simone de Beauvoir, has been sold and resold, but a commemorative plaque was recently affixed to the wall outside that reads: 'Simone de Beauvoir, writer and philosopher, lived here from 1955 until her death in 1986.' I had crossed the threshold with her, spent five crucial years of my life there, and even after we separated, I spent at least two evenings a week there since we remained, to the end, bound by an unbreakable friendship, a relationship of equals based on love and mutual respect, on complicity, work and our mutual struggles.

During the twelve difficult years when I was making *Shoah*, I went to see her whenever I could, I needed to talk to her, to tell her of my certainties, my uncertainties, my fears, my disappointments. I always came away from these evenings together if not serene, at least strengthened in my resolve. It was not so much what she knew and what she shared – how could she have known about the horrors I was discovering? It was I who told her about them – but the unique and intensely moving way she had of listening, serious, solemn, open, utterly trusting. She was transfigured by the act of listening, her face became pure humanity, as though her ability to focus on other people's problems relieved her of her own fears, of the weariness of living that never truly left her after the death of Sartre. On several occasions I brought her to the LTC studios in Saint-Cloud where *Shoah* was being edited to show her sections of the film in progress. She wanted to be present at all the screenings I had to organize while the film was still in production. In 1982, when François Mitterrand asked to see the first three hours of the film, she came with me to the private screening room of the Elysée Palace. All I could show him was a rough, well-worn, black-and-white copy with no subtitles, meaning that I had to shout the translations from the aisle. We know that after *Shoah* was released, Simone de Beauvoir wrote a front-page article for *Le Monde*, a piece that was decisive for the future of the film, a wonderful text that now serves as the preface to the book *Shoah*, published all over the world. But six months earlier I had screened the whole film – nine and a half hours – in a private screening room in Paris. The film had not yet been subtitled and I gave a simultaneous translation before an audience of 200, including Castor. Knowing *Shoah* by heart, every lull, every sigh, every silent shot, I knew precisely when to speak and in fact, without intending to, I occasionally mimicked the rhythm and the intonation of the protagonists. The problem was my voice: would it hold out for such a long period? My assistants had prepared bottles of freshly squeezed lemon juice, which they handed me whenever the strain in my voice began to show. I persevered to the end. There were those who said that my presence, my voice, the obvious fact that I was utterly caught up in the film, added to the screening. The following day I got a call from Castor: 'I don't know if I'll still be alive when your film is released,' she said. 'I want people to know what I thought of it, what I would have thought of it, what I think of it. I've written a few lines, I'll send them to you.' This is the first time I have mentioned those lines. Here they are:

I consider Claude Lanzmann's film to be a great work; I would go so far as to say a genuine masterpiece. I have never read nor seen anything that has so movingly and so grippingly conveyed the horror of the 'final solution'; nor anything that has brought to light so much evidence of the hellish mechanics of it. Placing himself on the side of the victims, of the executioners, of the witnesses and accomplices more innocent or more criminal than others, Lanzmann has us live through countless aspects of an experience that, until now, I believe, had seemed to be inexpressible. This is a monument that will enable generations of mankind to understand one of the most malign and enigmatic moments of their history. Of those who are still alive today, the greatest possible number should be part of this discovery.

Seated next to the President of the Republic, Castor attended the première of *Shoah*. I was not invited to the unveiling of the commemorative plaque at 11 *bis* rue Schœlcher.

As at the rue de la Bûcherie, we each had our own desk, but now they were bigger and more practical and the vast space in the atelier meant I did not feel guilty when I was not working. Truth be told, I worked a great deal and wrote a lot at the rue Schœlcher, both for *Les Temps modernes* and *France Dimanche*. I was the link between these two apparently contradictory activities, it was the same man who wrote the articles, with the same anxiety as he began each article, the same seriousness, the same scrupulousness, the same attention to detail ensuring that famous unity of self. We could write for four or five hours at a time without speaking to each other, but I would unhesitatingly interrupt Castor to read her a passage from something I was writing for *France Dimanche* and ask her opinion. In addition to rewriting, I was asked to write about a number of difficult criminal investigations and frequently accepted. It amused and interested me, I learned much: how to question, be cunning, to take risks – it was here I learned the lessons that would repay me a hundredfold during the making of *Shoah*, which in many respects can be considered a criminal investigation. A man named Bobine, who had barricaded himself in a farm in the Cévennes in a siege situation, threatened to shoot me even as I negotiated with him. He dashed from one window to another, aiming his loaded hunting rifle at me, then suddenly fired, missing me only by some miracle. The bullet ripped through the shoulder pad in my anorak. Bobine was suspected of having murdered three people. On another occasion – Castor and Sartre were in Switzerland on the first leg of their summer holiday – I was sent with a young photographer to Villeneuve-sur-Lot to investigate a murder. We arrived after a terrible overnight train journey and at Villeneuve station I rented a car, a convertible Renault 4CV, to drive fifty kilometres along winding roads with treacherous bends to the crime scene. At three o'clock we wrapped up our inquiry and, eager to return to Paris as fast as possible, I headed back. The Renault 4CV was the standard French car of the time, it was a narrow four-seater and was skittish, but cheap. The tyres on the one I had rented were bald – I had forgotten to check them before we set out – and I may also have been driving a little fast along the twisting road. The car suddenly skidded, nothing serious, this had happened to me before, all I needed to do was steer into the skid then gently correct it. But my passenger, the photographer, panicked and did the worst thing possible, throwing himself across me, grabbing the steering wheel and jerking it violently the other way. The car rolled, bouncing onto the roof, back onto the wheels, the roof again, until it finally came to a halt, like a stunt in a movie. Back then, safety belts did not exist and I was catapulted out through the roof and knocked unconscious. When I came to, I felt a terrible pain all over my body, I was lying face down, my feet, legs, my belly in the deep ditch on the verge, my chest and my head lying on the tarmac. There was a crowd of people around me, I could see the crazy photographer – I won't give his name, though I will never forget it – bounding from one side to the other, taking photographs of me from every conceivable angle and it was impossible to guess whether he was doing this as a joyful, conscientious professional or to cover himself in case of an investigation.

A large crowd had gathered, drawn by the accident. Through my mounting pain I heard imperious voices say, 'Whatever you do, don't move him, don't turn him over, his spine is probably broken.' Other voices: 'Don't give him anything to drink.' It was the day of the annual fair in Villeneuve-sur-Lot, a Sunday of festivities that mobilized firemen, ambulances and police. As a result, I spent four hours lying in the ditch because, even after they had been alerted, the rescue services could not reach me, their sirens and flashing lights proving utterly ineffective at clearing the roads that would lead them to me. I was admitted to the religious hospital in Cahors only late in the afternoon and was not examined until the following morning. I had no broken bones, neither spine, nor ribs, hand nor foot, arm nor leg nor skull, but my body was covered with spectacular bruises and contusions that would cause me great pain for some time and took several weeks to fade. The pain was such that the doctors prescribed Palfium, another name for morphine. I have happy memories of Sister Apollonie hovering over my motionless body with a thermometer, because I was running a high fever, her blue and white wimple framing her fresh face, and saying, 'Go ahead, stick in the bayonet.' At about five o'clock – just at the time bullfights usually begin – she would administer the Palfium and in that moment I experienced ecstasy, happiness greater than I have ever known in my life. All pain vanished as I lay there revelling in pure time, spending a blissful night, a faint anxiousness as night wore on, faint at first then mounting because suddenly, at dawn, the pain would return, all the more excruciating since the memory of that blissful peace I had just experienced did not fade. I rang the bell, called out to my friend Sister Apollonie, who never failed to come, and asked her for more Palfium. She tried to make me understand that it was important I did not become dependent, I was given painkillers that had no effect, placebos that I recognized as such, every fibre of my being waiting for that return to ecstasy, that blessed hour when I would be given my drug.

Since it had been agreed that I would join Castor and Sartre in Basle, I had the hospital send a message that as a result of *force majeure* I was unable to come. Castor panicked and before long both of them were at my bedside, having cut short their holiday, changed their plans to be with me. Castor spent the afternoon in my room with her 'knitting' – by which I mean a book – while I hurled curses and insults at Sister Apollonie who was immovable as to the time I was given my Palfium. Sister Apollonie and Castor, a lapsed Catholic famously educated at Cours Désir, became as thick as thieves, siding against me. By the time Sartre joined us in the evening, I would already be in a state of bliss. I was touched by his affection for me and, though I tried in vain to persuade them to continue their holiday as planned, they stayed in Cahors until the pain finally subsided and I was discharged. Travel plans were seriously revised, Castor having decided, with her constantly renewed enthusiasm, that the three of us should explore the Lot and Limousin, visiting Gordes and the Lascaux caves. This unforeseen parenthesis was to end at Toulouse where we would go our separate ways.

I often travelled with Sartre, both in France and abroad. I remember a Paris–Athens drive, leaving La Coupole on the boulevard Montparnasse after an early breakfast in the joyous spirit of adventure of Paris–Dakar, Sartre chirruping like a bird, somewhere between six and eight stopovers scheduled, as well as a number of 'specials' planned by Castor who always insisted on deviating from the shortest route in her determination not to miss some wonder of nature or art. Turin or Milan, Venice, Trieste, Belgrade, where Sartre would be received by Serbo-Croatian writers and possibly by Josip Broz Tito himself, Skopje and the Macedonian writers, these were the planned stopovers, and finally, the Parthenon as the supreme pleasure. It was a long trip, with no motorways – they barely existed at the time – except for a section between Croatia and Belgrade christened the *autoput*, commissioned by Tito, a 300-kilometre stretch built by brigades of young volunteers – who sang as they worked – drawn from the various peoples of the Federation of the Yugoslav nations, united by the partisans' war they waged against the Nazis and, as we know, doomed fifty years later to slaughter each other. The *autoput* had nothing in common with the slick, smooth, well-signposted motorways of today: workers' songs are no compensation for skill and expertise. Arriving at night in some unfamiliar foreign town was like something out of vaudeville, or some scholastic *disputatio* that sometimes led to violent arguments and lengthy sulks. The guiding principle that ruled Sartre's heart and his actions demanded that he be dependent on no one but himself in a profound ontological mistrust of others – 'Hell is other people', the famous line from *Huis clos*, was, I can attest, lived and personified by him in everyday life. To find the hotel, in dimly lit streets with unreadable signposts, with me at the wheel, Castor in the passenger seat beside me armed with a map, and Sartre, with another map in the back seat, each devising a route that rarely coincided. Voices were raised, each was determined to be right, I kept driving, following conflicting orders, round and round in circles, so close to our goal yet hopelessly lost as exhaustion set in, something that made Sartre particularly cantankerous. During one of our first trips, when I naïvely said to Sartre, 'I'll ask someone,' he was beside himself at the very idea. So I said nothing for a while; then, with Castor's support, I decided to ask anyway. I rolled down the window and uttered the magic word *centrum*, intelligible in any language. The answer quickly put an end to our peregrinations but Sartre scowled, his face and his mood that of a bulldog.

His Cornelian determination to be dependent on no one led him to extremes: I would watch him suffer for days with a vicious toothache resulting in abscesses and gumboils, and still he carried on writing, claiming he could master the pain, since it was unthinkable that he should ask anyone – even a dentist – for help. In conflating his body's misadventures with his sovereign liberty, it was logical that the cure, too, depended entirely on him. When we travelled, he always carried an enormous sum of money in his back pocket, money for the journey but also as guarantor of his autonomy. This should not be mistaken for avarice, or as some penchant for hoarding. It was quite the contrary: he was always the most generous of men, throwing his *sous* ('*le sou*', as we have seen, being his favourite use of litotes) to the four winds and to anyone who asked. He never owned anything, never bought an apartment and died renting a spartan two-room flat. It would be wrong to think that it was easy for him to refuse the Nobel Prize, he was in desperate need of money and the prize money would have been a godsend, alleviating his financial worries for quite some time. Knowing how much it would have helped, I urged him to accept since, as I told him, he would be stuck with the Nobel whether he accepted or refused. But he did not give in to my tempting sophisms. 'I might,' he said, 'have accepted the Nobel Peace Prize for what I did to help the Algerian people.'

I spent two days with them in Toulouse and the end of that curious jaunt that resulted from my accident. Sartre was in dreadful shape; I had never seen him like that, and Castor herself seemed terror-stricken. He would sit for hours at a café table on the place du Capitole, his good eye almost as dead as the bad, absent from the world, from others, from himself, staring fixedly at the leg of a table, like Roquentin in *Nausea* staring at the root of a chestnut tree when *contingency*, the one truth in the universe, is suddenly, brutally, revealed to him. Sartre's usual gaiety and hyperactive optimism had suddenly sunk into a chasm of meaninglessness, the obvious, irrefutable fact that 'man is a useless passion'. Existential angst, whatever Sartre may have said when showing off – 'I have never suffered from nausea,' he maintains in his *Carnets de la drôle de la guerre* [*War Diaries*] – was not merely a philosophical concept but a reality. While in Sartre it manifested itself by gloom and inactivity, in Castor – since it was something they shared, and this was not unimportant in their relationship – it translated into an utterly unpredictable explosion. Sitting, standing, or lying down, in the car or on foot, in public or in private, she would burst into violent, convulsive sobs,

her whole body racked with gasps, with heartrending cries punctuated by long howls of incommunicable despair. I don't remember
the first time, it happened many times during the seven years we
spent together, but thinking about it now as I write, it was never
associated with some wrong done to her nor some misfortune. On
the contrary, she seemed to break on the rocks of happiness, to be
crushed by it. When I witnessed these attacks, which hardened her,
shut her away completely, I felt utterly helpless: no word, no gesture
could help or soothe her. Awkward, terrified, I tried to hold her in
my arms, to press my hands to her temples, to kiss her lips, to talk
to her. Nothing worked, the convulsive overpowering dread had to
progress through every stage until, after a considerable time, she
would manage to calm herself, but always at the cost of an acute,
excruciating awareness of the fragility of human happiness, of the
mortal fate of what mortals call 'happiness', whose very nature is
always threatened, compromised. The very thought of Sartre's death,
that he might die before she did, or that our relationship would
one day end, something that, from the beginning, she insisted was
certain, might trigger a violent attack. So violent that it involved and
altered her whole body and its function: her usually sweet breath,
'fragrant with long vegetal and rose-rich honeys', as Rimbaud says
in 'Les Chercheuses de poux', suddenly became putrid and I had to
force myself even to get close to her. Fear showed itself in her in other
ways: she was haunted by the obsessive belief that recounting every
detail, of a day, a dinner, a week, was always and everywhere possible.
Everything had to be said, everything immediately recounted with
almost breathless haste, as though to defer the right moment or to be
silent condemned to nothingness anything that was not immediately
spoken. It truly entailed an inaugural, almost military, account
of one's activities, her desire to know everything and her fear of
forgetting what was yet to be detailed made it impossible to linger
on this or that significant event. She was in such a hurry to move on
to the next point that she often did not hear what was said to her,

or became muddled. The accounts, oral or written, she later gave, to Sartre for example – because, as in the shimmering, shifting whispers in Saint-Tropez I mentioned earlier, the first story became the story of a story of a story – are evidence of this confusion, an unambiguous symptom of neurosis. In the time that we lived together, it was not really obvious to me, since living with her meant I was spared the majority of these accounts. It was later, after our separation, when I came to see her twice a week, to take her out to a restaurant, that her fervent need to tell me everything the moment we met became unbearable because, having difficult or important things to say, I needed to impose my own timescale on our conversations; this was crucial to me. There would be a scene almost as soon as we met, I was incapable of producing the detached, quick-fire account she expected, I told her as much and she closed in on herself, her face took on an offended, sullen expression; only wine could harmonize our temporalities at which point we would spend long, happy hours, her fears now allayed, and her wonderful ability to listen that I mentioned earlier was given free reign.

Chapter 13

1958, I am thirty-three. For me, this is the year of 'Le curé d'Uruffe', of Général de Gaulle's return to power, of my trip to China and North Korea and of the presentiment, which quickly became obvious, that my relationship with Castor had to take a new form. What links these moments in my life is something much deeper than mere chronological confluence.

In Uruffe, an ordinary parish in Lorraine, the curate put a bullet through the neck of Régine Fays, a member of his flock, a girl of twenty, pregnant by him and about to give birth; then, having murdered her, he cut open her belly, delivered the baby and put out the child's eyes with a penknife although not before, in an expeditious abridgement of the liturgy, he had baptized the baby and given it the last rites. It was a crime the like of which occurs once in a lifetime and *France Dimanche* asked me to cover the trial, which opened before the *cour d'assises* of Meurthe-et-Moselle on 24 January 1958, a cold morning, with all of Nancy shrouded in snow and ice. I will not recount here the disturbing life of Guy Desnoyers, the 'murderer of Uruffe' as *Le Figaro* had the audacity to call him in its issue that first day, with an adept sleight of hand managing simultaneously to extricate the curate from the Church and the Church from the curate. I followed the whole trial, including those parts of it that were held *in camera*, and I was present for the passing of the lenient sentence, which allowed the curate, guilty of double murder and a thousand sins, to escape the death penalty, the result of mitigating circumstances that were never stated during the two-day trial conducted by a prosecutor anxious above all to avoid raising any difficult questions.

I wrote an article for *France Dimanche* that I would delight in rereading today; it was satisfactory, to my mind, for what it contained, but unsatisfactory because considerations of space made it impossible for me to do an in-depth analysis. *France Dimanche* – the unity of self is found here – was like a pilot-fish, like the first stage of a rocket; I decided that I could not leave it at that, that I wanted to write another article, free of all constraints, for *Les Temps modernes*, a publication that had always afforded news items a status and a dignity every bit equal to that of literature and philosophy. Sartre and Castor eagerly devoured anything to do with human passions in the newspapers, they read crime novels, and at *Les Temps modernes* we never baulked from publishing accounts of the most deviant acts if we felt them to be revealing. So I set to work at my desk on the rue Schœlcher early in February, but Castor was determined not to miss out on her sacrosanct winter holidays and had planned that we would go skiing in Courchevel. I explained to her again that I could not juggle skiing and an article that was taking up all my time. In the end I forewent skiing, something that surprises me to this day, I wouldn't have thought myself capable of doing so, given how much I loved hurtling down the pistes: in the two weeks we were in Courchevel I did not spend a single hour skiing. Castor went out on her own, while I barely left the dark room, writing from morning to night, not even going out for a breath of the pure, rarefied mountain air; every evening I gave her what I had written. I was taking mild doses of amphetamine at the time, one tablet of Corydrane could switch on, in Sartre's words, 'a sun inside my head'. One tablet was not enough for him, he needed a huge sun and took fistfuls of Corydrane, chewing them to a bitter paste, consciously ruining his health in the name of what he referred to as the 'full employment' of his brain. Corydrane helped me when I was writing several articles simultaneously, but it was important to measure the dose, the effects were short-lived and it was impossible to avoid the muscles stiffening in the lower jaw and the depression that followed the effects. I gave up a long time ago, even before amphetamines in all their forms were banned (RAF bomber pilots who had to make long flights to reach their targets stayed awake thanks to Benzedrine). My article was published in April 1958, in issue 146 of *Les Temps modernes* under the title 'The Curate of Uruffe and the Church Interest' – 'the Church interest' in the sense we talk about the 'national interest'. I was immensely proud of this long piece, which immediately won praise from all who read it and has remained in their memories like a beacon; people still comment on it today. What is called 'word of mouth' was very influential, the article did not simply reach readers of *Les Temps modernes*, but also the judges, the barristers and – surreptitiously, of course – the Church. Great lawyers such as Georges Kiejman, who worked on several famous cases, asked me to do for them what I had done for the Uruffe murder case. One Sunday afternoon, when I was alone in the atelier on the rue Schœlcher, the doorbell rang unexpectedly. I opened the door to find Jean-Jacques Servan-Schreiber and Françoise Giroud, the owners of *L'Express*. This was the first time I had met Jean-Jacques, but I had regularly bumped into Françoise in the offices of *France Dimanche*, where she was something of a star, with her own weekly column profiling personalities who, starting out with little or nothing, had 'made a success of themselves'. Jacques-Laurent Bost had viciously mocked her in an unattributed article for *Les Temps modernes* titled 'From Pickled Herrings to Caviar', which I was wrongly thought to have written, and which proved to be a turning point in Françoise's career and in her life. She was so hurt by the piece that she stopped writing the column and quickly joined the serious press, in this case *L'Express*, where, at

Jean-Jacques' behest, she proved a brilliant editor. They both worked Sundays and holidays and were utterly focused on consolidating the newspaper's success, building on its eruption into the media world. Mauriac and Sartre had written for them and Françoise later got her revenge on Bost when she hired him. They had read my piece on the curate of Uruffe and had come to ask me, in a very formal manner, to join the editorial team of *L'Express*, offering terms that were difficult to refuse. Instead of leaping at the opportunity, however, I asked for some time to consider their offer, something that seemed to surprise, indeed to irritate them. And although their offer was flattering and tempting, in the end I said no. Something deep within me insisted I refuse; I did not want to lose the freedom I had and did not want to be a professional journalist. I could never have written 'The Curate of Uruffe' for *L'Express* as I had for *Les Temps modernes*. I was a lone wolf, I wanted to remain so, and limiting my range of options was becoming increasingly impossible.

Ten years ago, in 1998, Philippe Sollers, who had not seen the article when it was published, discovered 'The Curate of Uruffe' and to my immense pleasure, reprinted it in *L'Infini*. The article found new readers, many of whom were as struck, forty years after the event, as the original readers had been. It has not become outdated any more than my films *Shoah* or *Pourquoi Israël*. I do not eviscerate women, do not put out the eyes of newborns, nor do I consider myself, in any sense, a man of the Church. Yet I remember that I spent the whole trial as close to the curate of Uruffe as possible, two metres behind him, staring fixedly at that scrawny neck that, I was sure, was destined for the guillotine. I did not simply watch, I listened, taking in every one of his words, rare and invariably trite, and of course listening to the testimony of the victim's parents, of his parishioners from Uruffe and from Blâmont and Rehon, other villages in Lorraine where he had served, listening to the evidence of the policemen and detectives who had interviewed him. I can attest – though this can only be understood by reading the article

– that I slipped into the skin, the belly, the heart, the mind of the murderer. When she finished reading my article, Castor expressed her astonishment at how I had penetrated the dark soul of this apparently model priest, a man capable of throwing himself into his parochial duties right after being masturbated, his cassock hiked up, by girls of thirteen, ejaculating hurriedly in the sight of God; capable of raising the alarm after he committed a double murder, a mad monk swinging from the bell rope, as he attempts to divert the legitimate concerns of his parishioners. I laughed, and parodying Flaubert, told her, 'Le curé d'Uruffe, c'est moi.' Of course he is not me, but the quip had some substance. A year later, I wrote the long article for *Elle* I mentioned about the flight of the Dalai Lama. I worked on these articles in the same way I worked on my films: in-depth research, distancing myself, forgetting myself, entering into the reasons and the madness, the lies and the silences of those I wished to portray or those I was questioning, until I reach a precise, hallucinatory state of hyper-alertness, a state that, to me, is the essence of the imagination. It is the one rule that makes it possible for me to reveal other people's truth – to flush it out if necessary – to make them real and alive for all time. It is my rule, at least. I consider myself a seer, and I have recommended that anyone who wants to write about cinema integrates this concept of 'foreseeing' into their critical arsenal.

One evening in January, shortly before the trial in Uruffe, I heard from Armand Gatti, whom I knew slightly and liked enormously: for the way he rolled his eyes like Harpo Marx, for the extraordinary range of his talents as playwright, filmmaker, poet, for his history as a militant anti-Fascist and the suffering he endured, for his talent as a leader of many, his ability to mobilize vast projects, whether theoretical, practical, social, revolutionary, literary or all of these combined, creating spaces in the suburbs of Paris or Marseille for every *Iliad* and *Odyssey* that welled up in his child-like mind, for his infinite capacity of wonderment and the self-belief that made it possible for him to ignore cultural institutions or use them only to subvert them. Gatti rang me to ask whether I would consider joining the first Western delegation to North Korea, five years after the end of the Korean War. I enthusiastically accepted: because it meant travelling far away and I had never been to Asia; because after Korea we were to spend a month in China and it was an unhoped-for opportunity to understand what the war had been about. We were due to set off at the end of May, a month after the publication of 'The Curate of Uruffe'. In addition to filmmakers such as Gatti, who, with Bonnardeau, planned to make a film there someday, and Chris Marker, who had been to China with Gatti the year before to make a short film called *Sunday in Beijing*, the delegation included a singer, Francis Lemarque, a sweet Jewish boy of Polish origin with a cheeky Parisian wit who had first become famous in dancehalls of the *banlieues rouges* – the Communist-controlled suburbs – for songs he wrote and performed, accompanying himself on the guitar. The delegation was led by Raymond Lavigne, a journalist from *L'Humanité*, and also included a freelance journalist from *Le Figaro* and three others from left-wing provincial papers, of which I remember only the *Courrier Picard*. It was a baroque and disparate group, the result of Gatti's whims and the PCF's policy of openness – neither Gatti, Chris, Bonnardeau nor I were members of the Party. We had two meetings to prepare before the trip at which Gatti and Chris, who had already been to China, advised us to bring presents: exchanging gifts was a customary obligation in the factories, Party secretariats, military posts, universities, schools and theatres likely to be on our itinerary. I asked what sort of presents and was told: large rectangular postcards of the monuments of Paris – the Arc de Triomphe, the Eiffel Tower, Notre-Dame, Concorde, the Louvre – and small books about French painting, especially the Impressionists. I didn't much like this idea; it felt a little like giving beads to native tribes. It is true that globalization was still a long way off. Chris Marker approached the matter differently, which I only realized after we had arrived. Having edited a book entitled *Giraudoux par lui-même* [*Giraudoux in His Own Words*] for a series published by Les Éditions du Seuil, he simply packed a hundred copies of this annotated anthology, which he liberally dispensed to factory workers after our visits. It hardly mattered, the staunch Korean workers could not read a word of French and, had they been able to, it's far from certain they would have appreciated Giraudoux's stylistic affectations!

We almost did not go. The French generals in Algeria were in open revolt against the Pflimlin government, a military putsch seemed inevitable and, in the face of this threat, Général de Gaulle sought to return to power: 'I began the process . . .', this was the first line of a speech he made on the radio that signalled his intent. Suddenly, de Gaulle seemed to be siding with the putschists. We were on tenterhooks: the war in Algeria had been going on for four years now; *Les Temps modernes* was among those supporting the Algerians and spearheading the independence movement; Francis Jeanson, from our editorial group, had gone underground to set up an extraordinarily efficient support network for the FLN; the periodical had been censored several times and impounded on at least one occasion. The putsch brought back de Gaulle, who claimed to be the one to resolve it, this was how ambivalent things were. I attended the famous press conference given by the Général at the Palais d'Orsay where, as he spoke, his long arms hewed the air. It was not so much de Gaulle who was frightening, but those who swarmed around him, the arrogant, triumphant sneering of those who, having been so long in the wilderness, realized their hour had come: the SAC for example, *Service d'action civique*, a polite term for what was in fact a brutal militia. I remember Claude Bourdet abruptly asking the General how he reconciled his professed democratic values with the fact that his return to power was due to an imminent putsch, and the latter's evasive answer: 'Monsieur, it is not my universe.' It was as true and as profoundly political on de Gaulle's part as his 'I have understood you', said only weeks later to the crowds of Algerian *pieds-noirs* who, for their part, understood it to mean what they wanted it to mean. But Castor and I and many others thought at the time that Fascism would follow in de Gaulle's wake; that whatever happened, it would outflank him and prove too strong for him. The last Sunday before my departure Castor and I went for a drive in the country. It was a magnificent May day and we thought that the beauty of the world – the lush green of the meadows so poignant, the fresh scent of the apple blossom so delicate – would never again be the same. We had decided that there was no reason for me to abandon the trip to Korea, my being in Paris would change nothing. Our reaction testifies first and foremost to the violence of the times, our loathing of colonial wars that had begun in Indochina, or even before that, with the Sétif massacre in 1945 and the ruthless repression in Madagascar. De Gaulle was not, and had never been, a Fascist, and he proved stronger than the generals leading the putsch, forcing them to toe the line. I truly believe he was a great man, a great statesman and a great politician; also a great writer. As I have already said, I read and still reread his books. But this was in May 1958 and the Algerian War was to last another four years.

Late in the day, we boarded an Aeroflot Tupolev destined for Prague, where we would spend the night, taking off the following day for Moscow, where we would spend a week before the great leap to the Far East. As we landed in Prague, I thought my eardrums would burst. At the time, Soviet pilots – all of them military – did not, as is common in the West, set down a plane gently in a gradual landing procedure, they merely put the plane into a nose-dive, heedless of the fierce changes in air pressure from the sudden loss of altitude that often left passengers screaming in agony. In the cockpit, the pilot and co-pilot permanently wore black oxygen masks: if there was a problem with cabin pressure, they, thanks to their personal oxygen supply, could resolve it by inhumanly diving to a more human altitude. Problems with cabin pressure were common in Tupolevs, which is probably what had led the pilots to behave with such savagery. In Sheremetyevo, the Moscow equivalent of Orly, there was a second violent nose-dive. I didn't know the city, the weather was warm and beautiful, it was June. On the eve of our departure for Korea, our guides had planned a visit to the USSR Agro-Industrial Exhibition, an immense asphalted area with huge hangars filled with tractors, bulldozers and all sorts of machinery attesting to Soviet might and ingenuity. The tour lasted a long time. In the end, weary of diagrams, of standing around listening to the guides' explanations, I felt the need, as soon as we were back out in the fresh air, to do something with the eager blood coursing through my veins, so I suddenly said to Gatti, 'Come on, I'll race you.' He was not the type to say no: he rolled his eyes and we ran as fast as we could, neck and neck across the Stalinist tarmac. I was determined to win; so was he, and we pushed and jostled. He fell, fracturing his left forearm. I was mortified and worried, because though he should have gone straight to hospital to have it set, he categorically refused, worried that the doctors might not allow him to fly the following day as arranged. The guides took us to a chemist, then to a doctor who put his arm in a splint, strapped up a sling and gave him some painkillers.

At last, we finally embarked on the great journey, with me sitting next to Gatti, watching over him like a mother, eaten up with remorse, cursing myself, telling him how wretched I felt. He was in pain, but he was tough. I promised that as soon as we arrived at Pyongyang I would get him to a hospital. It had been 30°C when we left Moscow but on the brief stop in Omsk to refuel when we got out to stretch our legs in our lightweight shirts, it was –6°C. We were at the end of the runway, far from the airport buildings; while the plane was being refuelled, an elderly *babushka*, completely muffled up, stood under the wing of the plane selling vodka by the ounce and I discovered for the first time something I would later come to be familiar with during the long winters filming *Shoah* in

Poland: the cold-banishing properties of this divine grain alcohol. Shooting a film in the snow and the cold among the standing stones of Treblinka, wearing leaking boots and too few layers of clothing, unable, since the days were short and every hour of daylight was precious, to go back to the cars where I might have found a change of clothes, I was saved from pneumonia for the first time by Pavel, my Polish sound-engineer, a tall, bearded, anti-Semitic and likeable guy who hunted bears in Masuria. He handed me a litre bottle of two-thirds vodka to one-third cognac and, whenever I started to shiver, I took a long draught straight from the bottle, thus holding out until it was dark, having used every second of useful light without losing consciousness or even tottering for an instant.

After Omsk, there were brief layovers at Irkutsk, on the shores of Lake Baikal, and at Ulan-Ude and Chita on the borders of Mongolia. A plane from the Democratic People's Republic of Korea was waiting for us, a little yellow twelve-seater with the hammer and sickle proudly painted on the tail. We were saluted by two young military pilots with very slanted eyes who were to fly us across the Gobi desert and Manchuria, expecting to land in Pyongyang at dusk. It was a very long journey, and I could see that the pain in Gatti's arm was worse. I tried to re-secure his splint, gave him something to drink and some tablets, but I knew we had to get him to a hospital as quickly as possible. When the plane finally came to a halt on the runway at Pyongyang airport, I saw that a huge crowd was waiting for us, thronging the space between the plane and the main terminal. A multitude of children and teenagers, girls and boys, lined up in concentric circles according to age, pioneers, red scarves, long plaits that came down to their waists, young breasts uniformly compressed by the smocks of their national dress. Pale with exhaustion, we staggered down the plane's narrow ladder, me going down backwards so I could use my body to protect Gatti should he fall. A dozen beauties, their fiery gaze filtered through the narrow slit of their dark eyes, stood waiting for us, arms laden with flowers.

Everyone applauded. There were also officials with hats and brachy-cephalic faces, helmeted figures that seemed to glide rather than walk as they moved, and photographers, flashbulbs, TV cameras. Our arrival was clearly a much anticipated event and treated as such. A small, slight, smiling man, wearing a hat and a light-coloured suit, introduced himself: 'Ok, Tonmou. I will be your interpreter.' He explained that 'Ok' was his name, *tonmou* means 'comrade'. There could be no Ok without *tonmou*, we had to call him 'Comrade Ok'. He spoke a musical, old-fashioned French that I found charming. We left the airport, taking the main roads, which had been devastated in the bombing raids – the neat piles of rubble and boulders on the hard shoulder reminded me of the piles of bricks made by the *Trümmerfrauen* in Berlin ten years earlier – until we came to a large, newly rebuilt avenue running parallel to the Taedong, the river that flows through the city. This was where we were to stay, in the only hotel appropriate for esteemed foreign visitors, the Taedonggang Hotel, to be precise. I did not take the time to settle in, but explained to Ok that I had to get Gatti to the hospital immediately. Later in this account, we will see the importance of my initiatory journey to the hospital of the capital of the Democratic People's Republic of Korea on my first night in the Far East, crossing the recently inaugurated bridge with its soaring metal arches only to be astonished by an Asian throng that seemed to form and reform as we drove past. Though travelling through the city for the first time, I mentally photographed the route from the hotel to the hospital. This also proved overcrowded, but Comrade Ok worked wonders, and Gatti's arm was set in plaster. The visit could begin.

There were two of us to a room. I shared mine with a journalist from *Le Figaro* who, if I remember rightly, had to leave early, meaning I had the room to myself. Chris Marker shared with Francis Lemarque, but Chris imposed his rules, his universe, plastering the walls and the ceiling with pages torn from the American comics he liked. It may have been an attempt to provoke our hosts, or his way of dealing with culture shock, to place himself at the centre of the world. I would establish which later in Beijing: in order to receive post from France, we had given to those who wanted to write to us complicated addresses with long, pompous names; instead, Chris had told his correspondents to write to him at 'Chris Marker, Beijing' and not one letter went astray. By that time he and I cordially hated each other, we never exchanged a word. Prognathism of the lower jaw made it difficult for him to articulate, he spoke through clenched teeth and accompanied his few words with an arrogant, ironic tilt of his head that turned his every pronouncement into an enigmatic maxim. I can say this with a clear conscience because later on our trip Chris and I became firm friends. I admire his films and somewhere in Tokyo in the *yakuza* district there is a dark narrow bar, called 'La Jetée' in homage to Chris's film, that has a bottle of Chivas Regal with my name scrawled on it. I bought it from the *mama-san* one night; now it is part of the furniture.

The itinerary for the Korean trip was interesting, sometimes frightening, exhausting, even backbreaking. Two or three factory visits a day, presentations, welcome speeches, farewell speeches, responses, the exchange of presents – including Chris's *Giraudoux par lui-même*, the mother of all gifts. The responses given by the delegation were made either in French by Raymond Lavigne from *L'Humanité* – christened Sur Chung, or 'Lush Springtime' in Korean – and translated by Ok, or, more often, in English by myself, as a number of Korean officials understood the language. Sometimes I had to speak three times in a day. Like China at the time, North Korea aspired to complete self-sufficiency, planning to construct vast steelworks and factories, and I think I sensed even then that Kim Il-sung, with whom we dined twice at formal state receptions, was already contemplating a nuclear arsenal. We were taken to places far from Pyongyang that appeared on no maps, to underground facilities guarded by soldiers, where everything seemed to be top secret. During one of our dinners with the Great Leader and his ministers, all from the anti-Japanese resistance movement, I dared to raise the subject of certain dissidents plucked from public life, whose disappearance had been mentioned to me in Paris. Hardly had I mentioned the names than the broad smiles on the faces of Kim and his Praetorian guard vanished. Suddenly, there was a granite hardness in their eyes, I was meddling in the internal affairs of the People's Republic, showing myself to be a dissident. The Great Leader uttered a single phrase, haltingly translated by Ok: 'They are enemies of the people.' To persist, to argue, was out of the question. The entertainment was supplied by the National Theatre, the Opera and the acrobatic athletes of North Korea, the best in the world, who invariably performed to packed houses mostly made up of soldiers, this was always immediately followed by speeches in the actors' dressing rooms and an exchange of gifts. In the streets, the trains, the buses, we never saw a Korean woman with a European man, it was simply unimaginable and the only 'long noses' to be seen were 'experts' from other People's Republics – mostly Polish, East German and Czechoslovak – come to support a brother country. They were always on their own or accompanied by their wives – fat, flabby Soviet bloc creatures – and indeed they lived in an enclosed neighbourhood. Among the pleasures of the country – and by no means the least – was the national dish known as *sinseollo*, 'Soup of the Mountain Gods', an elaborate fondue of subtle flavours and spices topped with ginseng, a dish from the ancient Korean royal court that supposedly enhances sexual desire and prowess, a peculiar contra-indication to the ascetic life in store for us. During these dinners, the so-called Asian impassiveness was shattered. I persuaded a number of young officers and soldiers aged between twenty-five and thirty to talk about the war that had ended five years earlier. Each of them became animated as I asked questions, before dissolving into tears. Heroes decorated for bravery were racked by heartrending sobs as they spoke of the terrible slaughter that had so recently seen the narrow strait separating China from the Nippon archipelago run with blood.

I had left Paris already exhausted from my hard work on the 'Curate of Uruffe' article and since, as I've said, I was only thirty-three, I believed in health. There are fads in medicine. The fashion at the time, the one that most interested me since I believed in its regenerative powers, was for intramuscular injections – in the buttocks – of 1000μg of Vitamin B12. It was my friend Louis Cournot, who had a practice on the rue de Varenne opposite the Musée Rodin, who first prescribed the treatment to me. 'If you feel run down while you're there, take some.' I had brought seven doses with me, together with the prescription. After a month of North Korean Stakhanovism and ten days before we were to leave for China (in fact, the delegation was to split into two: Gatti and the others were staying in Pyongyang, I was heading for Beijing via Manchuria with my enemy Chris), I decided I needed invigorating and I confided in my dear Ok, explaining to him that, so as to avoid any complications, I would go to the hospital by myself if he could simply tell me to which department I should go. That would not be necessary, he told me, someone would come to my room and give me the injection. The procedure, I was solemnly informed, would take place the following morning, Monday, at eight. When the knock on the door came, I was already up, in pyjamas, the windows were open, it was hot, it was summer. I open the door and am greeted not by a male nurse, but a stunning female nurse in traditional dress, her breasts restrained but still visible beneath her smock, her long black hair in two plaits, her eyes slanting and aglow with fire, though she keeps them lowered. I step aside and, taken aback, gesture for her to come in with a sort of *Grand Siècle* bow. Behind her stands Ok, who also steps in, behind Ok a man in a peaked cap, behind the man in the peaked cap another man in a peaked cap, and a third and a fourth and a fifth: all told there are six men standing in my hotel room, ready to observe every detail of the procedure, meticulously. I hand Ok the box of magic phials together with Louis Cournot's prescription, which he translates for the nurse with the lowered eyes. She does not say a word, but takes a syringe, a needle, alcohol, from her case; in a shaft of sunlight she watches carefully as she draws the 1000µg of Vitamin B12 into the syringe. I stand next to her, ready to slip my pyjama trousers down slightly to reveal a buttock, but Ok and the five men in peaked caps – whom we had long since recognized as members of the Korean KGB, silent phantoms that moved through the corridors of the hotel and followed us wherever we went – have not moved, show no signs of moving, but stand in a circle watching us. I tell Ok, 'I'd be grateful if you could leave, please ask them to go outside. In France we do not have injections in public.' He seems very annoyed, says a few words, and they all step back a metre, but no more. I raise my voice, pretending to be angry, protesting about their evident mistrust of me, a government-invited official and a guest of the Great Leader. They move back now, though only as far as the door. I grab the nurse by the arm, and leading her to a blind spot in the room where I cannot see them, nor they me, I now present my naked flesh to this impassive beauty. Her movements are perfect, precise, clean, without brutality, I feel no pain as the needle goes in and she begins the procedure, which is usually uncomfortable, very slowly injecting into the muscle thereby avoiding any suffering. Picture the scene: the spacious hotel room, the door open on to the corridor, the everyday noises of the hotel, Ok and the men in caps huddled, waiting, an idle and frustrated crack team; a surreptitious intimacy born out of transgression – in moving to the blind spot – is established between the nurse and me without a single glance, a flutter of eyelashes, without the least sign of complicity being exchanged. My pyjama trousers pulled up, I reappear in the middle of the room as she puts away her instruments. I say, 'You may come in now, messieurs.' This they do, though slightly less assertively than on their arrival. An appointment is made for the same time the following morning. To the nurse, I say nothing other than, 'Thank you, mademoiselle'; to Ok, who puffs out his chest and translates to the others, 'She is a consummate professional, there are not many like her in the West!'

The procedure was repeated exactly the following day with the sole exception that there were not five men in caps this time, but four. And I did not have to ask them to withdraw; of their own volition they did not cross the threshold. The nurse and I went to the blind spot, as though it were the most natural thing in the world, our haven, like the bull's *querencia* in the bullring. I never heard my nurse's voice. How could she speak to me? We had no common language, and in any case the men in caps were all ears. On the third day, there was one less cap again. Then, nothing changed until the sixth day, when only three people showed up: one cap, Ok and the nurse. The final injection was to be the following day, which was Sunday. I asked if the time could be pushed back to ten o'clock, say, rather than eight as I wished to make the most of the Lord's Day to sleep in. Ok reminded me that the delegation was scheduled to go on a picnic to the country, a favourite pastime among Koreans, leaving between nine and half-past nine. I said that I had decided not to go, that having met so many people and spent so much time talking over the past month, I wanted to spend some time alone, which would be the best way to get some rest, and I hoped he understood. Besides, I did not much like the lakes where they took us for picnics, man-made expanses of water from which rocks poked up here and there rather like those mawkish unimpressive landscapes in Japanese prints. The appointment was therefore set for ten. I assumed that, in the absence of Ok, the nurse would be accompanied by one or more men in caps. Nothing was as I expected. At ten o'clock precisely there came a knock at the door. I opened it: no caps, no one but her, transformed, barely recognizable, dressed in European clothes, a light print skirt, her unrestrained breasts filling out her blouse, the braids gone and her hair piled up in a chignon with a curl falling over her forehead, her mouth red with lipstick, an insolent, an intriguing beauty. All this I observe in a single glance, I am so astonished that I stand frozen on the threshold, not even thinking to let her in, heedless of the men in caps who must surely be about to appear. She does not look down this time, but straight at me. The situation demands a response, I act quickly, reflex and reflection merging into one, leading her to the blind spot in the room and leaving the door open as I had done every day. I am filled with an almost unbearable sense of imminence. Something is about to happen, cannot not happen, I do not know what or when. I am trembling inside; I have not touched a woman since Paris. Pyongyang is particularly hot that morning, beads of sweat appear on her upper lip, further accentuating the sensuality of her mouth, the irresistible sexual magnetism that emanates from her body, her face. As she gives the injection, she moves with infinite slowness, breaking down her every gesture and time itself, as though it would never, could never, end. The injection now administered, as she packs her case she finds ways to slow, to defer her every movement. The door is still open, I cannot bring myself to believe that the caps will not suddenly appear, something that intensifies the feeling of imminence, of anxiety. Everything is done, I have no idea how to take my leave of her; I tell myself she is probably waiting for me to pay her and remember that I have the huge bundles of crisp new won, the Korean currency, which had been given to each member of the delegation the day after our arrival, to pay for incidental treats and expenses. Aside from the drums I was planning to bring back to Castor, there was nothing to buy here. I gesture for her to wait, take one of the bundles from the wardrobe and offer it to her. She vehemently refuses, shocked. I rush to my suitcase – before leaving Paris I had bought a number of pretty shirts, which are still wrapped in tissue paper; I think they might suit her, or she might have some use for them. I offer them to her. She categorically refuses. We are no longer in the blind spot but standing in the middle of my room, in full view of the door, the caps are forgotten, suddenly insignificant compared to what is about to happen, to the devastating power of the inexorable. I don't know which of us moved first, I never did know. We fall upon one another, kissing each other fiercely, our tongues wrestling with a passion, a strength, an eagerness, a ferociousness that is immeasurable and uncontrollable. We are in plain sight, making no attempt to hide, but it is impossible to leave things like this, I want more, I want it all, *we* want it all, so I act with extraordinary decisiveness: bringing her back into the blind spot, taking off my watch and resetting it to read two o'clock. I tap my watch several times with my fingernail to make sure she understands. I am not asking if she agrees, this is a command, an order. I lead her to the window overlooking Pyongyang Avenue and, leaning out, I point to a spot about two hundred metres away where the avenue meets the river. The watch in my hand now reads a little after two. With an imperious gesture I remind her of the time of the rendezvous while pointing repeatedly to the bridge where we are to meet. I am suddenly seized by panic: the caps are bound to show up and if they see she's still here it will be disastrous for her. She presses herself against me, oblivious to danger, completely overcome, but I refuse to be moved, refuse to kiss her again, I throw her out without even checking to see if the coast is clear, I close the door, preferring to lose everything at that moment so that I might gain everything later.

I am alone, I consider things, tell myself this is madness, the regime is terrifyingly Stalinist, the indoctrination of everyone by everyone allows for no freedom or – which amounts to the same – no deviation. What does the sudden transformation of the nurse with the downcast eyes mean? Does she come from South Korea? I convince myself that she will not show up for the meeting, that she will not come because she cannot, because she will realize the enormity of the risk. Besides, how would we communicate? She speaks Korean, Russian, perhaps Chinese, languages that are utterly alien to me . . . If she were mad enough to meet me at the bridge, we will have to invent our own language. I get some paper, two notebooks and some pencils. I suggested meeting her by the bridge because the previous Sunday the delegation had walked along the towpath by Taedonggang past a place where boats could be rented. As I pointed to the place where we should meet, I was thinking we could walk as far as the pier, she would know where it was, rent a boat and let it drift downstream through the city and out the other side, ending up in the countryside where we could make love, out of sight, in a rice field whether desiccated or waterlogged, in the grass, in some meagre forest, in the boat itself.

I didn't have to worry, didn't have to wait for her. When I arrived she was already there, leaning against the bridge, dazzling, her lips red, as the crowds crossing the bridge in their Sunday-best gazed at her, undressed her with their eyes. When she saw me, the flicker of a smile lit up her face. I did not approach her but simply nodded towards the towpath and mimed rowing a boat. She immediately understood and walked on ahead in the direction I had indicated. She walked quickly, and I hurried to catch up with her. She stared fixedly ahead, either quickening her pace when she felt me drawing near or deliberately dropping back if I insisted in trying to keep pace with her. Below us to our right the river, some three metres below the towpath. To our left a two-metre-high embankment, and above, close enough to touch us, in an unbroken line that stretched all along the route, were the singing brigades of reconstruction workers. They wore lightweight work clothes, in different colours depending on the section they belonged to, but they were all white with dust since their almost Sisyphean task was to clear away the ruins and the rubble piled high since the end of the war: it was impossible to conceive that they would ever finish. Armed with a megaphone, a political commissar controlled the rhythm of the work like the leader of a coxed eight on the Cam. Or rather he barked hoarse orders that, as one, the red pioneers of Pyongyang duly obeyed, having sacrificed their day of rest to rebuild the nation's capital. To maintain the harsh rhythm imposed, these young men and women sang at the tops of their voices, poignant airs of radiant tomorrows to the glory of the Great Leader, celebrating victory over imperialism or the triumph in every heart of *Juche*, the ruling dogma in North Korea, the product of the prodigious brain of Kim Il-sung, whose subtlety may be gleaned from a few trenchant quotes: 'The North Korean is master of his own destiny', 'He will overcome every obstacle', 'For disciples of the Great Leader nothing is impossible', a more inflexible version of Mao's *Little Red Book.* But *Juche* did not preclude astonishment or shock. For me, having to walk ten paces in front of or behind this woman I was taking for a walk was unbearable; I could not understand what crime I would be committing in her eyes and the eyes of others simply by being close to her, by trying to talk to her, even if she didn't know what I was saying. I could not imagine walking four kilometres with my conquest without a word or a smile, without brushing against her hand, her arm, just as Cau and I had done on the Champs Elysées. But the moment the singing pioneers realized we were together, the moment I flaunted the fact – against her will – that I was with her, the brigade fell silent, stopped working, stopped in mid-stroke, leaned on their shovels and picks and stared until we had passed, only for the next brigade to do the same. Now, she quickened or slowed her pace so noticeably that it seemed to me like the admission of some terrible crime, proving them right, confessing the offence, presenting us to be judged. But she was the one who was right, as an insider she had anticipated everything, the brigades' reactions, their thoughts, their comments, she knew what she had to do; it was I who was being improper, inappropriate, who was dangerously compromising us with the pathetic idealism of a French Don Juan, following his own narrow navel-gazing rules. We could not be together, it was as simple as that. By the time we had walked a kilometre, we no longer were. I was beginning to wonder how we would be able to get into the same boat.

We reached the place where the boats were rented, a wooden pier down the bank to the left. There was a queue at the ticket office, which she joined, and I quickened my pace and joined it behind her, clutching my sheaf of won, because a French lover does not allow his lady friend to pay for herself. She ignored me and when she reached the counter she opened a white embroidered purse the size of a lady's clutch bag, took out a banknote and exchanged it for a pair of tickets. Without looking at me she walked along the path and down the steep bank to the river where the empty boats were moored. Before boarding, shoes and socks had to be removed and handed in at a small wooden hut in exchange for a ticket; boating could only be done barefoot. I forgot to mention that the bank was teeming with people, those who planned to row and some who were happy to watch since the boats were unstable, frequently capsizing as I had seen the previous week when Francis Lemarque had tipped his boat-mate into a deep stretch of river, where he floundered, yelling, 'The camera! The camera!' (The camera was saved in the nick of time.) When we finally climbed aboard before hundreds of incredulous eyes – there was no way for us to avoid being seen together now – I admired her courage, and I was beset by a single, obsessive thought: 'Don't capsize.' The tall, strapping chubby-cheeked men in dark overalls who helped us aboard and handed me the oars seemed less than friendly, but I moved off impeccably and, as I did so, I noticed what had not previously occurred to me: our bare toes and the soles of our feet were now touching and could communicate.

I rowed vigorously towards the middle of the river, extricating myself with some difficulty from the mass of lazy, circling boats. Had I not been terrified by the thousand staring faces and the certainty that we would capsize, I would have launched myself at that mouth, those thighs, those breasts, those eyes, but first I had to complete phase one of my plan: to float downriver, out of the city and into the countryside. I left the other boats upstream, having gauged the speed of the current and expecting to move downstream quickly. An inhuman howl erupted from behind me and I saw fear in my beloved's eyes: she could see what I could only hear – 'Tonmou!' A

single strangled 'Tonmou!', and the boat could no longer be manoeu-
vred, an iron hand had gripped the bow and was attempting to turn
it back upstream. There could be no question of going any further.
I had crossed some invisible barrier, attempted to escape a high-
security area. The guard in his boat monitored everything. Farewell,
countryside! But I do not give up easily. Again I began to row, against
the current this time, fully expecting another 'Tonmou!' to halt my
progress at any moment. I rowed through the well-ordered circle of
the other boats – 'They're going round in circles,' I said to myself,
'they're going round in circles' – to me the circle seemed the very
image of prison, the convict endlessly circling the prison yard, his
cell, cut off from his plans, from his future. It was not long before
my worst fears were confirmed. 'Tonmou!' The second shout was even
more thunderous than the first. The warder upstream had obviously
witnessed my attempted escape downstream, had watched me turn
and prepared himself to capture me. He did not have to grab the
bow; with a brusque sweep of my oar, I turned around and let the
boat float until we melted into the crowd of boats – she trembling at
the vehemence of the prohibition, I realizing and cursing the extent
of my naïveté – rowing around in circles with everyone else while I
tried to think.

All of a sudden I noticed, in the middle of the river, close to
yet outside the circle, a sand bar I had overlooked in my initial
impetuousness. Gradually widening the circumference as I rowed,
I allowed the boat to drift towards it until it ran aground, the
bow wedged firmly in the sand. The language of entwined toes, of
looks and shrugs and sighs was no longer enough. I took out the
notebooks and pencils I had brought and, chatting all the while to
her in French as much to dupe any rowers who came close enough
as to spur myself on, I sketched a crude map of the Korean peninsula with a line through the centre representing the 38th parallel
– in fact, I wrote 38 next to it. With a large black dot I indicated
Pyongyang, saying 'Pyongyang' aloud and gesturing broadly around

us. With another black dot on the far side of the line, I marked Seoul. Since I hadn't understood her sudden transformation, her make-up, her hair, her dress, I suspected, as I've said, that maybe hailing from South Korea she had kept some of its customs. With the pencil I pointed to Seoul on the sheet of paper, my finger pointing at her. Her feet arched violently, almost in protest, against mine. She took my map and drew a larger map that extended as far as the Yalu River on the border with China. She made a black dot close to the river. Then she drew a house and pointed to herself, and sketched fighter squadrons dropping bombs in the sky above the house. She glanced around quickly, to ensure that no one in the other boats could see what she was about to do, then she unbuttoned her blouse to reveal a pair of high, firm, tanned breasts and, beneath her left breast, a deep, terrible burn scar that slashed across her torso, and uttered one word in Korean, a word that is universal: napalm. This ghostly slash, this apparition, immediately vanished as she began to do up her blouse. Terrified, overwhelmed, frozen like a statue by the situation, I suddenly found myself swearing undying love like a chivalric knight, promising to take her suffering upon myself and find the Holy Grail. But chivalrous though it might be, the love I felt for her was not platonic and I did not have time for a lengthy courtship; my carnal desires had not abated, I wanted to hold her, to kiss her, I wanted to possess her and be possessed by her. On the pad, in a crude complicated sketch she nonetheless understood, I drew the route from the Taedonggang Hotel across the metal bridge to the hospital where she worked via the streets I had mentally photographed on my first night when Ok and I had taken Gatti there. She smiled, seeming surprised at my precise knowledge of the city. Though I did not have any coloured pencils, I traced a cross over the hospital, touching my finger to her lipstick to indicate 'red'. I then drew a room with a bed and two people entwined on it and reinforced this childish signifier with a more adult one, my arms embracing the empty air beneath the eager gaze of other rowers who, without our noticing, had begun to crowd round us. She laughed openly, took the notepad and drew another room, longer and narrower, with twenty beds in it and a shelf above each bed: a dormitory. It was hopeless. Where could I be alone with her? Here she was, willing, within my grasp, yet out of reach, the textbook definition of the torment of Tantalus.

Then I remembered a park we had been taken to visit at the beginning of our stay, a park famous in Pyongyang and throughout all of North Korea, since it had a theatre carved out 100 metres underground, where plays had been staged at the height of the bombing raids to galvanize the audience. This was *Juche* at its acme. I was not able to challenge Gatti – in his plaster cast – to race me up the 350 steps that led outside, but I challenged myself, only to stop halfway, exhausted and out of breath. I thought I remembered that the park had bushes, trees and benches.

Whatever the case, we had to move, it was pointless to stay beached here. She, like me, realized it was time to go. I rowed gently, calmly, back to the jetty above which, along the steep embankment, hundreds of pairs of eyes all stared at us with the same lack of kindness. I drew alongside perfectly. She got to her feet; the men in overalls did not offer her a hand, she stumbled, slipped, tried to right herself and, suddenly, inexorably, the boat capsized just as Francis's had the week before. The turbid water was at least four metres deep and, when she did not surface but carried on sinking, I dived as hard as I could, managing to catch hold of her and bring her to the surface. Now people offered to help, but I could see she was panicked, staring at the water, distressed, her little white handbag gone. I dived back in and, by some miracle, spotted something white against the mud. I rescued the bag, gave it to her and saw a fleeting flicker of pleasure in her distraught face. We were hustled, dripping wet, into the hut with the shoes where she collapsed and lay, motionless as though dead. I knew I had to do something, that action was our only salvation. I raised her up, gripping her hard to show her there was no way out, that I was in charge and that I did not care what the Koreans thought. I dragged her, literally, up the embankment between the double row of staring faces, back to the towpath by which we had come. Just then, a military vehicle appeared, driving slowly, and she spoke to the driver, probably asking for a lift; he stared, spat at us contemptuously and drove off.

I did not feel able to walk back the way we had come, censured by the singing brigades, and I chose the craziest solution, but one that would afford us privacy: we would walk through the rubble of the ruined city back to my hotel. So began a long march, me pulling her along when she refused, climbing over mountains of rubble, hills of stones, stumbling down slopes of gravel and scree, our clothes sodden and white with dust, our faces pale as pierrots, her beautiful hair a mess. There were falls, injuries, trickles of blood on chalk-white shins and thighs. It was long, exhausting, demoralizing, but we did not encounter anyone, my sense of direction was good and we reached the avenue. It was still early on that sweltering Sunday afternoon, there were few people about. I let go of her hand and walked on ahead, turning back more and more often as we approached the hotel. Then, what I expected happened: she stopped dead and, like a mule, refused to take another step. I went back to her, aware how much we looked like clowns. People were stopping to stare at us as I talked to her in my gentlest, most persuasive voice, carefully articulating the French words as though she might somehow read my lips. We were about a hundred metres from the hotel. I managed to convey to her I was going to investigate, that she should wait, that I would be right back. By some miracle the lobby, usually patrolled by the whispering men in caps, was completely deserted, as was the sweeping central staircase up to the landing where it split into two flights leading to the first floor. My room was on the second floor. I rapidly sized up the situation and went back to where she stood, frozen, her eyes vacant. I took her hand, almost wrenching it from its socket until finally she followed me. As soon as we reached the lobby, I let go and made a dash for the stairs, turning back on the landing to make sure she was behind me. I thought that by some extraordinary stroke of luck we had made it when two thunderous roars of '*Tonmou!*' rooted us, each to a different stair. The shouts came from the porter's glass lodge, which I had mistakenly assumed was empty. She stopped, resigned to the worst, and walked back towards the lodge where I saw her attempting to placate the furious porter who was already on the phone. I rushed down the last few steps, dashed towards the lodge, shouting abuse in French and waving my fist at the dumbfounded doorman. Then I did something the like of which no one had ever seen in the Taedonggang Hotel. Anger having given me the strength of ten – though my panic and the shots of B12 may have had something to do with it – I swept my petrified princess into my muscular arms, carried her to the second floor, opened the door to my room, locked it behind us, turned on the light in the bathroom, ran the shower, took from my suitcase some of the shirts I had tried to give her that morning, together with a pair of lightweight trousers, and handed them to her, taking her ruined handbag to dry it on the windowsill. Then I left her on her own in the bathroom.

I had barely had time to recover my breath and my composure when I heard footsteps in the corridor and a knock at my door. I threw it open: there was Ok, and behind him the rest of our group back from the picnic, inquisitive, mocking, jealous; the caps followed behind, one by one, more and more of them, appearing from everywhere, like rats summoned by the Pied Piper of Hamelin. In a loud voice, I recounted my tall tale: I had gone for a walk by the river to the jetty we had seen the previous week where, completely by chance, I had encountered my nurse and asked her to go for a boat trip with me; my unforgivable clumsiness had capsized the boat and I had brought her back to the hotel through the ruins because she was so ashamed of the state she was in. At this point in my story – which clearly no one believed – she suddenly stepped out of the bathroom, an unforgettable apparition, an Asian version of a Botticelli Venus, my shirt knotted above her bellybutton, the new pair of trousers, which suited her perfectly, turned up at the ankles because they were too long. I asked Ok to repeat my hastily invented story to the caps. She had to hear it if we were to get our stories straight. He did as I asked. But there was nothing to be done, the caps escorted my beloved and Ok to an office upstairs. It was a trial. I took a shower, gradually making myself human again, marshalling every ounce of courage because I knew I would have serious need of it. The other members of the delegation had gone back to their rooms, I was the only person in the corridor, hesitating as to whether to await the outcome of the trial or intervene. It went on and on, seemingly never-ending.

I brutally intervened, throwing open the office door to find it really was a trial: she was sitting next to Ok on one side of a long table, facing twelve judges lined up on the other side. I interrupted the session with a solemn, measured political statement, asking Ok to translate each of my words for the caps. What was happening here, I said, would force me to revise everything I had thought about the Democratic People's Republic of Korea, would undermine the opinion I had formed during the course of my trip about this proud nation, this heroic people, the prodigious achievements they had made thanks to *Juche*, which I promised to report faithfully to Western Europe in my articles. But perhaps the word 'democratic' in describing the regime was going too far; at the very least, what I was now witnessing gave me pause for thought. Ok translated and I waited until he had finished each sentence before continuing. I then repeated in detail my account of how I had met the nurse, whose name I did not even know, my friendly, innocent suggestion that we go boating as a way of thanking her for the excellent care she had given me. If anyone was guilty here, it could only be me, and yet I could not see what my crime, or hers, or ours, might be; why a leisurely boat trip on the Taedong should justify this tribunal with its sinister overtones. I was far from convinced that the Great Leader, who had invited me and whose breadth of vision and diplomatic skill I had witnessed at first hand, would approve of such behaviour. Since I was a guest in this country, surely the customs of my country should prevail? In France, when a man wrongs a member of the opposite sex, even inadvertently, he makes amends. This I now intended to do, by taking the young woman back to the hospital where she worked, stopping by my room to pick up her shoes and her handbag, which I hoped would be dry by now, and her clothes, which I would parcel up.

Hardly had Ok translated my last word than I took the nurse by the hand. She meekly followed me, we went back to my room leaving the door open, then we calmly walked down the stairs past caps who, to the shock of the other members of the delegation alerted I know not how, fell into step behind us. When we reached the street I turned towards the bridge, still holding her hand, which I squeezed tightly, trying to communicate impossible feelings. After about a hundred metres, she suddenly steered me left towards a new building of about a dozen storeys with a narrow spiral staircase. She led the way and we slowly climbed the steep stairs; at every landing I leaned over the banister and saw the men in caps silently following us with the same inexorable tread. On the eighth floor, she stopped and knocked on a door: a woman immediately answered, at which she turned to me and by a desperate look implored me to leave her. I waited for a moment in the doorway, watching the caps who, having come to a halt, now looked like herons perched on one leg. Then, with a heavy and wounded heart, I headed back to the hotel.

Over dinner, as we were enjoying our last 'Soup of the Mountain Gods', which I found unbearably aphrodisiacal, Ok told me the name of the woman: Kim – not Il-sung, but Kum-sun – Kim Kum-sun. I asked Ok to write out her name in Korean characters, telling him I wanted to leave her a note, apologizing again. In fact, I was afraid that, through my fault, she would now be caught up in an endless spiral of problems with potentially severe consequences. I felt wretched and cut myself off completely, I did not speak to anyone and no one dared ask me about my day or question my version of events. I was due to leave Pyongyang with Chris only two days later for Shenyang, formerly Mukden, the capital of Manchuria, the immense province in northern China. It would be a long train journey, part of it along the Trans-Siberian railway. That night I barely slept: the thought of leaving without seeing her again, after such a disaster, such a romantic fiasco, was abhorrent and made me despise the undiluted Communist totalitarianism that I was now experiencing. I could not bear the thought that she should suffer on my account. And though ours had been only a brief encounter, I loved her, I would have loved her, an infinity of possibilities lay before us. I was distraught, spending the whole night fomenting wild, meticulous detailed plans to see her again. That is how I am, it is difficult to make me give up. During my years in the Resistance I had learned several techniques to avoid being shadowed, I resolved I would use them to visit her the following day, I would not leave without holding her in my arms again. I would shake off the caps, outsmart anyone who tried to tail me.

The following day at about noon, I arrived at Pyongyang central hospital without having taken a single wrong turn, or hesitating for even a moment. I went inside and found myself in a long corridor full of stretchers, I heard whimpers and moans. I spotted an elderly woman with an air of authority wearing a white coat with a stethoscope around her neck, clearly a doctor. I showed her the piece of paper on which Ok had written Kim Kum-sun's name and asked her, in English, where I might find her. She did not seem surprised, did not ask any questions, but simply pointed to a door nearby. I knocked, opened the door, and saw her with two other nurses grouped around a patient whose bloody hand they were bandaging. All three of them were wearing the national costume, the smock and the braids she had worn the first times I had seen her. She looked up, rushed towards me, taking my hand and dragging me into the courtyard where, in a small alcove, she embraced me with a fierceness I reciprocated: we picked up the wild kiss we had begun the day before, tongues wrestling, mouths crushed together, panting for breath, our time together even more threatened. Now it was she who pushed me away, holding me at arms' length, gazing at me passionately, desperately, before heading back to the building where she worked without turning back.

It was late August 1958. One December morning in Paris, I received a large brown envelope mailed by standard post. Inside was a large postcard depicting a temple half-hidden by the snowy branches of trees in flower. On the other side, in Korean ideograms, in a confident hand was a message that filled the entire space. With it, on a sheet of thin paper bearing the letterhead of the Ministry for Foreign Affairs of the Democratic People's Republic of Korea, was the translation, also handwritten. This is it:

친애하는 꿀로쌔. 반구라 쓰에게
(Sarang laumia clearka)

동지께서 이사야를 내쓰면서 보내주신
편지를 저는 실로 감명 깊게 받아 보았습니다.
지금 뿐은 이국 타국에 계신 동지에게 진정
정으로 인사를 보냅니다. 또한 저 나라에서
전쟁을 반대하며 평화를 위해 투쟁하는 전체
모성들과 어린이들에게 힘있이 동하고 따거운
심정으로 뜨건 증의를 축복합니다. 동지는 지난날
우리나라 평양 대동강 빨은상에서 저와 함께 빼
진것에 대하여 미안하다고 썼지요. 아니 그것은
우리들에게 그 얼마나 빛해간 추억으로 남겠습니까!
저는 동지와 인상 깊은 모습과 함께 그날 있은
뜻깊은 사변을 항상 가장 귀한곳에 간직하려고
합니다. 평화를 위하여 투쟁 하시는 그래
한 벗. 꿀로쌔. 반구라 동지! 부디 건강
하여 사업에서 높은 성과를 걷으세요. 비록
저 나라와 이곳라는 수만리 떨어졌지만 전세
계 평화라와 함께 반드시 목쌍한 동지들라 상봉
하리라는 꿈을 저의 신념을 확신해 주세요
—— 조선 정심지 병원 총향 진료소 강 종녀 ——

Dear M. Lanzmann,

It was with great pleasure that I read the letter you addressed to me when leaving our country. By now, you must be back in your own country, I send you my warmest greetings. With all my heart I wish a great victory for all mothers and children who struggle against war and for peace.

I remember how upset you were about the accident – which was rather funny – when I fell into the Taedong during our boat trip. Don't be, it is an amusing memory that we will have for a long time to come. As for me, I will keep it deep in my heart together with the memory of your noble profile.

Dear sir and noble friend, you who fight for peace, I wish you good health and great success in your work. France is far from my country, but once world peace has been established, all those who love peace will meet each other, I am sure.

Kim Kum-sun
Red Cross General Hospital of Korea

Chapter 14

The few days I spent hazardously strolling in Shenyang were a revelation, even if the highlights of the trip were supposed to be Beijing and Shanghai. After North Korea, where everything had been inhuman tension, strictness, discipline, submissiveness, the triumph of the impossible, the empty colour of life, after all this, my first Chinese city seemed like a paradigm of freedom, human inventiveness, happiness and the joy of the possible. I remembered Sartre who, three years before me, in 1955, had, with Castor, made the trip to China, though not Korea. Of the Chinese, he wrote: 'industrious without industry'. I will come back to the subject of industry, but there can be no doubt they were industrious: the range of notebooks, pencils, inks, made the stationery shops in Shenyang magical places. I wanted to buy everything, bring everything back to France, even though Chris recommended I wait until we got to Beijing, the metropolis, where all those things that delighted me about the Manchurian capital would be multiplied a hundredfold. Not to mention how tall the northern Chinese were, how big their teeth, revealed every time they burst out laughing, something culturally considered polite. Sartre was not alone in writing about China; Castor quickly capitalized on the six weeks she had spent in the Middle Kingdom, launching into a book 500 pages long for which, once again, I came up with the title: *La Longue marche*. For I did not arrive in China with absolutely no knowledge. The Communists had come to power ten years earlier, forcing Chiang Kai-shek and the Kuomintang into exile in Formosa, which, given the intensity of the Cold War, immediately became a bastion of the other camp. With the same passion I had devoted to reading about Richard Hillary and the Battle of Britain, I had devoured every book that traced this legendary, epic retreat-turned-victory of the Eighth Route Army as it travelled from south China to north with a sweeping detour west, famously known as the Long March; books by great reporters as only Americans can be, in particular Jack Belden's *China Shakes the World* and Edgar Snow's *Red Star over China*. To me the finer work is Belden's, which is less ideological, but both had been published in French with beautiful crimson covers in Gallimard's Collection Rouge, an imprint that no longer exists and which no one at the company seems to remember. Another book in the same collection, a thrilling 500-page masterpiece entitled *Eastern Approaches*, by the British diplomat Fitzroy Maclean, kept me reading through the night. Fitzroy Maclean was a man of remarkable intelligence and unimaginable daring that took him from Paris to Moscow, from Moscow to Soviet Central Asia, where no Westerner before him had been. His accounts of the Moscow show-trials, especially that of Bukharin, his intense understanding of the accused, the extraordinarily accurate portrait he gives of Bukharin facing down his judges and the prosecutor Vyshinsky, his description of the moustached face of Iosif Vissarionovich Dzhugashvili – alias Stalin – peering out from a small window high up under the ceiling of the courtroom, if one rereads them today, say much more about the horror of the Soviet regime than many works of history or *post hoc* so-called philosophical explanations. But, to add to his intelligence and daring, Fitzroy Maclean also had considerable courage, an acerbic sense of humour and an all-consuming sense of adventure. During the war, he was to be found in the desert of Cyrenaica in Libya with the raiders of the British Eighth Army who operated far behind Rommel's lines, often at the loss of close friends whom he salutes in an unforgettably understated manner. The same indomitable death-dodger was then sent by Churchill to Yugoslavia to represent the interests of the British empire to Tito in his stubborn and painstaking attempt to encircle Hitler's armies. Here again the lively, funny portraits sketched by this diplomat daredevil Lawrence of the Balkans are those of a born writer and it is easy to understand why they were published in Gallimard's Collection Rouge, an imprint that should be revived to bring these forgotten, flawless treasures back to light.

China Shakes the World is a scrupulous and moving account of the 12,000 kilometres and the twelve months of the epic and murderous gesture that was the Long March, which Jack Belden witnessed at first-hand, following Mao Zedong's shabby soldiers on their long trek to the caves of Yan'an. Fewer than a quarter of the 130,000 men who set out on the march survived. What moved me when I read the book was how these illiterate soldiers were taught to read and write during calmer periods on the long summer march: every day, a single ideogram in huge script was posted on the back of every cart so that those following behind could immerse themselves in its form, its every brushstroke. The following day there would be another, and then another, until the troops, during the group lessons held whenever the march halted, could identify and reproduce each one.

Chris had brought a copy of *Sunday in Beijing*, the film he had made on his first trip, the year before. He wanted to show it to Chinese officials, hoping to get logistical and financial support for his great project, a feature film based on the popular legend of the Monkey King. In Shenyang, in the lobby of our hotel, he organized a screening for the city and Party officials. *Sunday in Beijing* is about thirty minutes long with a commentary by Chris, devoted almost entirely to what remained of pre-revolutionary Beijing, that timeless Beijing that the new rulers scorned, consumed instead by the idea of destroying it. He gave a brief introduction, which was translated by an interpreter, and the screening took place in deathly silence. The officials did not understand what they were watching, but rejected it nonetheless, getting up without applauding and leaving without a word. The following day we set off for Beijing where the film was scheduled to be screened in the main hall of the Sino-Soviet Friendship building, which held at least 500 people. I advised Chris that if he really wanted the support of the Ministry for Light Industry, which oversaw filmmaking, he would do better to cancel the Beijing screening. Though disheartened by the response in Shenyang, he was still hopeful and did not follow my advice – the hostility between us had not yet disappeared, but I felt sorry for him and truly wanted to help. What I had feared did in fact transpire: the same leaden silence, the same rushed exit, no accolades, only this time to the nth degree, and in the capital of the empire. Chris never managed to get his interview with the ministerial department in charge of cinema and the legend of the Monkey King was never filmed by him. Two days later, at dusk, he said something that broke my heart. We were sitting in the back seat of a huge Zim Soviet limousine on our way back from a moving visit to the Great Wall when suddenly, through clenched teeth, Chris broke the silence: 'This is what I love, collusion.' I squeezed his arm and that was the beginning of a genuine friendship, a friendship that has been unfailing and unshakeable and constantly renewed by our personal and professional admiration for each other.

I am not going to recount here for the umpteenth time my trip to China as was then the fashion for the rare few who travelled there. I will mention only one or two milestones: what they called the 'Rectification Campaign' was at its height. Following the Hundred Flowers Campaign, in which many people had recklessly dropped their masks, naïvely embracing the inconceivable freedom to speak the truth, came the period of fierce, ruthless criticism, of everyone accusing everyone else, heralding the mad excesses of the Red Guards and the populist communes, extraditions to the countryside for purposes of 're-education', the triumph of rural purity over urban decay. In every factory and university on our itinerary, every wall was covered from floor to ceiling with *dàzìbàos*, huge handwritten posters, statements of bitterness and hatred that dripped with a terror no one could or would escape. A Shakespearean question of deadly seriousness recurred again and again in these *dàzìbàos*, that of the 'Red experts'. Who, they asked, should be favoured, those with expertise or those who fervently adhered to the Party line – though it was rather a jagged line during those years. Red *or* expert, Red *and* expert, that was the question. I remember sitting in the office of the head of the department of Romance Languages at the University of Beijing, a private office plastered with *dàzìbàos* and posters criticizing him by students he could not prevent from coming in even while I was sitting there, to jeer at him with a violence that terrified me. One of his younger colleagues had posted a *dàzìbào* that he translated as: 'I shall be Red with all my heart and expert with all my mind.' As we know, red blood would flow, prevailing over expertise. When I asked the head of department, in French, what they were criticizing him for, he burst out laughing, baring his teeth like the northern Chinese he was, answering in a thin, reedy voice, 'Oh, pride! Pride!' A year later, this pride saw him dispatched to a remote, enforced retirement where he was to spend ten years, something that utterly broke his pride, his expertise and him. Today, leaders of the Communist Party of China, the Central Committee and the Politburo, are likely to be qualified engineers, such as Hu Jintao, the current General Secretary, a hydraulic engineer. They are undeniably experts, but the most rigid dichotomy is still practised: under the cloak of this expertise, the old Red Guard still controls, with an iron fist in a velvet glove, the hearts and minds of one and a half billion people.

The 'friendship' between the peoples of China and the Soviet Union were increasingly strained at the time, foreshadowing their break-up. Contrary to what Sartre wrote, China was doing everything it could to build up industry: in the 200-metre-long workshop of a machine tools factory, its walls covered with *dàzìbàos*, black or blood red, all the machines in the production line were Soviet, but what rolled off the line was a Chinese machine tool, born to patriotic cheers, hostile to the USSR, immediately stamped with the national flag and with proud ideograms. These brand new machine tools would be used to equip other factories throughout the region. As in North Korea – though it was actually Kim Il-sung who was imitating his Chinese comrades – the idea that the great industrial complexes, the old Manchurian steelworks for example, would not in themselves be enough to satisfy the needs of a vast country, had taken root. They had to be replaced with rural steelworks, unsuited to producing specialized or high-quality steel, but capable of supplying less tempered metal, sufficient for everyday junk. Together with the ubiquitous *dàzìbào*, the rivalry and one-upmanship between rural villages over steelwork production figures, the promised productivity in future months, was the second revolution to galvanize the Red Chinese. Now we know that the rural steelworks were a folly that turned out to be a disaster. But at the time they were a banner in the populist communes and a decisive weapon for Mao in the unprecedented civil war, the general unrest, the confusion he was determined to unleash so he could consolidate power and, having eliminated countless suspects at every level of society, rule unchallenged. The Rectification Campaign I witnessed was the forerunner to that evil upheaval.

When we arrived in Beijing, we were asked what we wished to do. I said I would like to meet President Mao in person, or Zhou Enlai, the Premier at the time. Every night I was told to be patient, leading me to hope that something might happen. While I waited, I explored Beijing, though I was never able to visit the Forbidden City, the Imperial Palace or the Temple of Heaven. The Forbidden City, I discovered, truly was so. I became aware of the level of indoctrination and the stupidity of the lower echelons of the Party, whether guides or interpreters. One day at dawn, at about five o'clock, I am walking with my interpreter, a graceless young woman, along a *hutong* – one of those crudely cobbled narrow Beijing streets lined by low, single-storey houses around a central courtyard. In the distance, three figures are approaching, two women and a man, waving a red flag firmly attached to a pole. In the deserted dawn street I ask my guide, 'What's going on? Who are they?' She replies, donnish and dogmatic, 'They are the masses.' In Shanghai, the itinerary includes a visit to happy, domesticated capitalists who declare themselves freer in business matters since the revolution, laughing and showing their teeth after every sentence. These teeth no longer bite, but perhaps they sense that there are better days ahead for capitalism and that, in the end, it will prevail. This was fifty years ago. Our most unpleasant duty was a visit to a re-education camp for prosti-tutes, a revolting attempt to break women who were unbreakable: this was clear from their defiant stares during the indoctrination sessions, in their refusal to lower their eyes while evil-looking female 'instructors' accompanied by prostitute *kapos* slowly passed them in review, examining each in turn, by the way they stared at visitors, a mixture of supreme arrogance and almost sexual provocation. Some, even in these intolerable circumstances, still had a mesmerizing beauty. Castor, like Sartre, was charmed by the intellectual fluidity of Chinese Communists, who had not banned prostitution as one might have expected them to. There were so many prostitutes, the authorities had argued, that putting them out of work would only create social problems much more serious than the moral problem of tolerating the flesh trade. But times had recently changed and, in this domain, 'rectification' was ruthless: they had now begun to be re-educated, but were still resisting.

Still in Shanghai: I am alone for the afternoon on the Bund, the embankment of the Huangpu River where, before the revolution, there were skyscrapers – banks and multinational companies, historic hotels built by Iraqi Jews in the late nineteenth century, the Sassoons and the Kadouris, who were at the heart of the rapid capitalistic expansion of this incredible city. The Bund was famous for its opulence, and for its heavy traffic, both on the river and on land. It was also a place for wheeling and dealing of all kinds. But on this afternoon in 1958, ten years after the Red Army marched into the city, the Bund and the river are completely deserted. Not a car, not a boat, not a living soul. The skyscrapers are intact, neither destroyed nor inhabited, vestiges of a world that has vanished never to return. But wait, there *is* a living soul. A man. A funny little Chinese man in a cap who appears to be watching me intently, constantly advancing towards me only to retreat again. I try to ignore him, to embrace in a single glance the roaring Huangpu, Pudong on the far shore upstream, and here, where I stand, the spectral skyline of useless towers. The man does not give up; he smiles, he circles me, I notice he seems to be juggling something with his hands, moving something swiftly from one to the other. Behind me is a stone bench, a remnant of yesteryear, I go and sit down; the man becomes bolder, approaches, retreats again, I now see that he is shuffling cards, fanning them out then snapping them together, glancing around furtively. I smile at him, what does he want to sell me? Pornographic photos, perhaps? This is what I imagine. A shabby imagination. He is beside me now, nearly touching me, and the images he flashes before my eyes with the speed and skill of a conjurer are of the Bund. They are postcards of the exact spot where we are, but long ago, thronged with cars and elegant pedestrians, umbrellas, bowler hats, frock coats, liveried porters and, on the river, boats and ships of every conceivable tonnage, long barges filled to overflowing. Because of his act of resistance, the dangers and fear of getting caught, because we had to act quickly, I bought every postcard, showering the hawker with yuan.

Back in Beijing, guides and interpreters whispered to me with greedy, conspiratorial expressions that I had to be prepared and to stay at the hotel: I might be summoned at any moment. Impossible to say who might summon me, Mao, Zhou, they themselves did not know, but the Castle would certainly get in touch. I spent a sleepless night. Beijing had been at fever pitch for forty-eight hours: American marines had just landed in the Lebanon and the Chinese demonstrated spectacular support for Arab countries, of Gamal Abdel

Nasser, President of the ephemeral United Arab Republic (the union between Egypt and Syria), who, two years earlier, had nationalized the Suez Canal and forced the Franco-British allies of Israel to end their military intervention. After the official speeches made from the famous balcony on Tiananmen Square, immediately translated into Arabic for the ambassadors and their wives, it was time for the people to express their solidarity. From Tiananmen and Chien-Men, on each side of the avenue that divides the Tartar city from the Chinese, for as far as the eye could see, 500,000 Pekinese, a caviar of black heads, marched past for hours, brandishing fists, flags and streamers, improvising brief, violent open-air theatrics on the subject of the American landings. Led by Death himself (a tall, thin Chinese man wearing a black cape over his shoulders, his face and body made up to look like a skeleton), the Arab people in chains advance into a circle of spectators. The Arab people: two women in gypsy skirts made up as Chinese women never were and two swarthy men in rags with black painted sideburns. Heavy chains bind their arms. An American in uniform – sunglasses, beard and moustache – and an Arab sheik in a turban follow them, brandishing whips. The clash of a Beijing Opera gong. Drums roll. The sheik, miming hatred and fear, raises his whip and rushes at his own people. But the people do not retreat, and twice they knock the sheik to the ground. The American then orders the sheik to get up and strike them. The sheik, a rictus of terror on his face, lashes out at one of the chained men until he falls to the ground. Clash of cymbals: the people suddenly throw off their chains and pick up guns – real guns – given to them by the audience. The sheik and the American, ashen with fear, throw themselves on the ground, pleading, while the people, resolute and determined, trample them underfoot. The American screams hoarsely. To the sound of aeroplanes, well imitated by drums, two Chinese men wearing false noses and sailors' berets divide the crowd, pushing papier-mâché models of US gunships before them. The people retreat twice around the circle before one of the Arabs shouts in Chinese,

'Americans! Leave Lebanon, leave Korea, leave Taiwan, leave the Philippines, leave Japan!' The audience picks up the chant and the Arabs have only to advance for the American marines to turn and flee, scurrying away on all fours ashamed.

The call when it came was not from Mao, nor from Zhou Enlai, but from Chen Yi, the Foreign Minister and Vice-Premier, one of the five great heroes of Chinese Communism, a hero of the Long March. After thirty years, first fighting in the Revolutionary Army then leading it, he was the first man to enter Beijing, Nanjing and Shanghai. The interview took place in the former Imperial Palace on the banks of Lake Zhonghai (the Central Sea) to which I was driven in a limousine with drawn blinds – I could not know then that I would have to wait until 2006 to discover the wonders of the Forbidden City. At fifty-eight, Chen Yi seemed to be in rude health. When I arrived he said, 'We have three hours ahead of us, so we may speak calmly and weigh our words.' In fact, the interview lasted precisely five hours, but I will not give an account of it here. Chen Yi was surrounded by assistants and secretaries feverishly jotting down his every word, my every question, and by diffident interpreters whom he corrected himself, for he spoke perfect French – he had, like a number of senior members of the Chinese Communist Party, worked as a labourer in the Renault factory in Billancourt – and we could have spoken without intermediaries had he chosen to. Of the five hours I spent with him, my host devoted an unquantifiable but to my mind significant period of time to the ceremony of spitting: two large golden spittoons sat on side tables to left and right of his armchair and, as the conversation led him to lean one way or the other, he dispatched the product of his expectorations with extraordinary precision, a Chinese method of pausing for thought. In general, his lengthy responses masked rather than revealed the keen intelligence I sensed in him. He gave me a world tour in geo-strategic waffle, but he was also sending a message to France and to Général de Gaulle who had made overtures to China.

'The Chinese,' Chen Yi essentially told me, 'will not accept recognition until you dismiss Chiang Kai-shek's diplomats. The same goes for the UN, we will not be a part of it until he is excluded. This does not mean we cannot forge amicable commercial and cultural ties with France. We greatly respect the French people and admire its considerable revolutionary tradition.' In conclusion, he added that it would be more sensible for France not to intervene in the Middle East.

These pronouncements could not wait. I retired to my room in the Beijing Hotel and was given everything I could possibly need, secretaries, typists. Locked in, I wrote all through the night – my second sleepless night – and the whole of the following day, relating what I had seen in Tiananmen before giving an exact account of the interview itself. My text was carefully reread by Chen Yi in person who gave it his approval. It was essential that it appear in *Le Monde*, and, though I no longer knew anyone there, I sent it, in a long telex paid for by the Chinese government, to the editor-in-chief together with the necessary explanations, recommending that, if he were not prepared to publish it, he forward it to *L'Express*. This was indeed what happened. *Le Monde* pussyfooted while *L'Express* published the piece in its entirety, considering that Chen Yi's pronouncements constituted 'essential information, crucial to understanding the current situation'.

When I returned to France I wrote a number of theoretical articles about China that prompted calls from all over Europe, especially from Italian leftists who were very excited by the idea of the rural steelworks. I wrote nothing about North Korea, although it had been our host country. I thought about Kim Kum-sun, I worried about her and, though reassured by her letter, never in the intervening fifty years have I stopped thinking about her. I could not imagine her growing old, going grey; the memory, when I bring it to mind, is frozen in time. Long before, I had seen a British film by David Lean called *Brief Encounter*, starring Trevor Howard and Celia

Johnson, and I never thought of Kim without thinking of that film. Astonishingly, I saw the film again with Sartre in a small arthouse cinema in Montparnasse, and we both left the cinema in tears. We were both hopeless romantics. In fact, on another occasion, we watched Howard Hawks's *Only Angels Have Wings,* starring Cary Grant, Rita Hayworth and particularly Richard Barthelmess, a film that completely satisfied my passion for flying and my taste for love stories. For Sartre, the film was a touchstone; he had seen it many times and never tired of it. On that occasion too we both cried. I sometimes told friends about my brief encounter with Kim, but it only made sense to do so if I could tell the whole story at length; it cannot be condensed. This happened rarely, and those who heard it said, 'What a wonderful film it would be!' When I began making and directing films myself, Kim was still very much in my mind, but *Pourquoi Israël, Shoah* and the others were a far cry from Taedong and the amorous wrestling of bare feet.

In the long years that preceded the ascetic retreat necessitated by the making of *Shoah,* I never felt any desire to go back to China; other countries, other continents were calling me. For me to return would have required a major event such as the one that presented itself twenty years after the release of *Shoah.* Over the years, Chinese cinephiles had had the opportunity to see the film only at festivals or in cinemas in Europe, America or even in Japan where, after all sorts of surprising events, the film had finally arrived ten years earlier. Some had succeeded in getting hold of video copies, and *Shoah,* though it had never been released in China, had a considerable reputation there. In September 2004, I was invited to screen it in Beijing, Nanjing and Shanghai: a brilliant translator, Chang Xien Ming, had single-handedly taken it upon himself to translate the subtitles. I had met him the previous May at the Cannes Film Festival and doubted that he could finish the work before September for the opening of the first documentary film festival held in China, at which *Shoah* was to be screened. He did so. To perfection, probably, though I had no way of gauging the accuracy of his work. It was he who interpreted for me – consecutive rather than simultaneous interpretation – during the conferences I gave while there. I spoke for twenty minutes while he took notes, he then translated for a similar period, I'd recognize the proper names that he was obliged to leave in French; I had the feeling that he left nothing out. His sole mistake, albeit serious, and one of which I was not immediately aware, was to have translated into Chinese the untranslatable title, *Shoah*. This is an issue I will address in some detail later on. I confess that I was moved when I saw the Chinese ideograms appear on the screen beneath the words of Simon Srebnik, Filip Müller, Abraham Bomba or Rudolf Vrba, in vast, crowded theatres with film people and representatives – mostly female – from far-flung provinces brought to Beijing, a city they were seeing for the first time, together with students of both sexes and every possible discipline.

To those who, when discussing the Chinese and the Japanese, would say to me *ad nauseam* that they could never understand a film like *Shoah*, as it was not part of their experience, their world, I always stubbornly responded, 'But why? There is only *one* humanity. If it is possible for me to be profoundly moved by a film like Ozu's *Tokyo Story*, I don't see why someone Japanese or Chinese might not be similarly overwhelmed by *Shoah*.' It is always what is most particular that attains the universal, this is what is referred to as '*l'universel concret*'['the concrete universal']. I remember my emotion, my admiration when I saw the Turkish film *Yol* by Yılmaz Güney, which, hour by hour, follows prisoners from an Ankara prison on a week's home leave as they return to the snowy, glacial mountains of Kurdistan. For these men, so different from me, I felt a closeness, a kinship, even though they had been educated according to rigid traditions that lead to the tragedy that concludes the film. Never have I been made so aware that humans are human only because they have the capacity to transform that which oppresses them into something of value, and to sacrifice themselves for it. It is the very essence of humanity, but could also be called tradition, or even more, culture.

At the screening in Nanjing, the former imperial capital, forever marked by the terrible 1937 massacre I mentioned at the beginning of this book, I took questions late into the night from film students at the university. They had watched *Shoah* over the preceding two days, and I was struck by the subtlety and precision of their comments, by their unerring ability to remember the film, the places and the protagonists, something that is not always the case. Suddenly, a female student asked, 'What advice would you give me if I wanted to make a film about the massacre committed in this city by the Japanese?' Her question was so broad that, for a moment, I thought I would not be able to reply, but I quickly recovered my wits and immediately responded, 'Go to Japan!' This seemed to enlighten all of them, none of them had thought of that, had been able to think of it. I then explained at length, translated by Chang, what had happened to me in Germany, in Poland. These young people were my friends by the time I left Nanjing for Shanghai, where I wanted to see the Huangpu River and the Bund once more. Almost fifty years after my first visit, China's transformation was staggering and filled me with enthusiasm, but I will say nothing of it. Except for this: in Shanghai, I took a boat downstream on the Huangpu to its confluence with the Yangtze Jiang, where both become a boundless sea. During the three-hour trip, one feels physically the strength of China, the sense that it has of its own power and the pride with which it shows it. Though I have known Rimbaud's 'Le Bateau ivre' all my life, it was only that afternoon, sailing down the Huangpu, which grew wider and wider as it approached the estuary, as part of an extraordinary flotilla of ships, private and military, merchant and tourist, of every conceivable shape and size, floating past immense shipyards whose streaming red pennants like tongues of flame seemed to be competing with one another; it was only then that I truly understood the last lines of the poem:

Je ne puis plus, baigné de vos langueurs, ô lames,
Enlever leur sillage aux porteurs de cotons,
Ni traverser l'orgueil des drapeaux et des flammes

I can no longer, bathed in your languors, O waves,
Obliterate the cotton carriers' wake,
Nor cross the pride of pennants and of flags

Beijing, its ten ring roads, its skyscrapers built at dizzying speed, transforming the cityscape so much in a few short weeks that the Beijingers seem like strangers to their own city, which has become the epicentre of globalization. Beijing, the dazzling sight of the Forbidden City and the Temple of Heaven, finally open to all. Beijing by day, Beijing by night, with its restaurants, its bars, its Mongol prostitutes, sturdy and devastatingly beautiful.

But it was Kim Kum-sun I was thinking about, and whether there was a possibility, however remote, of my getting from Beijing to North Korea; I should seize the opportunity. No, not that: I did not want to see Kim again, as an old woman; I had long avoided that kind of face-to-face meeting. Besides, I would not want to bet on life-expectancy in North Korea: she might well be dead. I had been told so often 'It would make a wonderful film!' that I had considered it, telling myself that if one day I were to make what is called a fictional film, I would tackle this part of my personal history and weave it into the great course of history. In my own 'brief encounter', there were many episodes that could be powerfully cinematic: the nurse's first appearance with Ok and the caps, her transformation on Sunday, the voracious kiss, the long march along the towpath, the dizzying whirl of boats, the language of bare feet, the sketches, the napalmed breast, the shouts of *tonmou*, the capsizing, the agonizing walk back through the ruins. The prospect of having to film such sequences did not frighten me; on the contrary it excited me. The serious and crucial problem to me was the city, ruined and being rebuilt, the singing brigades, the climate of fear; in other words how to create a truthful reconstruction of the time, of a totalitarian world, of the curious Western sympathizers we were. It would require thousands of extras, sets, a huge, Hollywood-style budget. I was not sure either that I was capable of filming a fictional version nor, deep down, was I even sure I wanted to. I was beset by these many certainties and this one doubt, and as soon as I reached Beijing, I inquired about the possibility of going to North Korea. Only small numbers of tourists, I learned, were granted a visa for four days, or a week at most, and then only on payment of an exorbitant sum in hard currency. I decided that I wanted to be clear in my own mind, to see what changes there had been since 1958, hoping that this return to the distant past would help me make the right decision about my prospective film. Assuming that those who had been in charge during my first visit would long be gone, I imagined that no one would remember and that all records would have disappeared; on the form, I declared that I had never been there. To get from Beijing to Pyongyang, one went either by rail or by air: the first entailed a forty-eight-hour journey with a stop of indeterminate length at the Sino-Korean border before travelling north at a snail's pace through the septentrional regions of North Korea since there had recently been a catastrophic explosion that had destroyed a railway station and two trains, resulting in countless victims. I feared borders more than anything else, marked by the terrifying memory of something that had happened to me in 2000, four years earlier, at Brest-Litovsk when, during the filming of *Sobibór*, I wanted to travel with my equipment and crew from Poland to Belarus. We waited for eight hours on the way out as cameras and film were seized in order to be examined; I had no idea to whom I could protest, I was sent from one official to another, forced to respect their breaks for lunch and dinner while we had no way of getting anything to eat or drink. The return journey from Minsk was even worse: we spent a whole night and the following morning stranded in a car park reserved for Belarusian customs, forced in the freezing cold to keep the engine running to stay warm until we ran out of petrol. In principle, taking the plane to Pyongyang obviated such torments but it required a certain fatalism on the part of the passenger since the planes were ancient, patched-up Ilyushins that, it was rumoured, periodically crashed. In the end, of course, I decided to fly and found myself at Beijing international airport with a tiny group of Anglo-Saxon tourists – about ten in all, including Scots, Englishmen from Hong Kong, an American couple and their two children – all of whom were clearly making the visit in sympathy with the hard-line Communism they expected to find when we landed. My criticisms, when I dared to voice them, found no echo among them. Hardly had I taken my seat on the plane when I was enveloped by the characteristic smell, the greenish colour, the shabbiness typical of People's Democracies, all of which, with a shudder of fear, immediately transported me back in time to the GDR, to Bulgaria, to Poland, to Czechoslovakia, to Cuba, even before we had left the ground.

Unsurprisingly, Pyongyang airport did not look remotely familiar. Since it is in the middle of nowhere, a dead end, there were few tourists, and so whole flocks of uniformed officials threw themselves carnivorously upon every passenger, fastidiously examining passports, visas, faces, waving additional forms to be filled in, trying to confiscate my PDA and my cellphone – which in any case were useless in this far-flung place – carefully counting every dollar I was carrying with me, although the entirety of my stay had been paid for in advance in Beijing. The other tourists suffered this hellish procedure with beatific smiles and not a murmur of complaint. After two hours, we were finally loaded onto a minibus where two trained, tame interpreters, a young man and a young woman, delivered the same speech, she in English to everyone else, he in French, to me alone. I told him that I understood English and he did not need to bother, but he followed the orders he had been given. In any case, both their French and English were barely intelligible, their vocabulary was poor, their syntax faulty. Interpreters such as Ok in

1958, with his delightfully archaic French, no longer existed. What did become clear from their mumbo-jumbo was that the Korean people had no desire to meet foreigners, that we were forbidden to go off on our own, that the only space where we were free to wander was our hotel, and that we were to follow our itinerary to the letter. The itinerary stated that we would first go to our hotel and as soon as we had registered and settled in, we were to be taken to the Pyongyang Grand Theatre, because the performance would start on the dot. Afterwards, back to our hotel, dinner and nighty-night. As the minibus drove through Pyongyang, I ignored this prattle and scrutinized the cityscape, looking for some landmark I might recognize, some vestige of the past by which I might get my bearings and find lost time. Pyongyang looked to me as though it had been completely rebuilt; there were broad avenues devoid of traffic and indeed pedestrians. I thought I recognized the avenue along which Kim and I had walked after crossing the ruins, but I could not see the Taedonggang Hotel. The hotel we were staying in was some distance upriver, far from the bridge I had crossed when taking Gatti to the hospital and the scene of my fateful rendezvous with Kim. We crossed a bridge that had not existed in 1958, one that connected the riverbanks, arching over Yanggakdo Island, which could be accessed by a slip road. Our hotel, a fifty-floor American-style skyscraper, towered above the river from the centre of the island. From the bridge to the hotel was a distance of about two kilometres and there was only one road. The forecourt in front of the hotel was utterly deserted; I asked the interpreter whether there were any taxis and he answered, 'It is forbidden.' The vast lobby was also empty, the only living souls, sitting or standing, stationary or walking, were the caps. I recognized them at once, although they no longer wore caps: the uniform had changed, but not their function. My room, on the fortieth floor, had no view of the city. I went back down to the lobby and asked if I might change it, and for a considerable supplement for the four-night stay, this was done, but I did not even have time to see the new room, as the interpreters were already vociferating that we had to get to the theatre.

We arrived late, just as the houselights were dimmed; every one of the thousands of seats was filled. Following our guides, we groped our way through the darkness to our reserved seats, thereby protecting the delicate eyes of the public from foreign contamination. Almost no one saw us. Almost 90 per cent of those in the theatre were young soldiers in uniform. The acrobats and trapeze artists were as marvellous as those I had seen years ago, vying with each other in daring to the rather apathetic applause of the troops who appeared to have seen the show several times before. I hoped I might see some faces when the curtain went down, but we had to get up some seconds before the end and make a dash for the nearest vomitorium; once outside, we were piled back into the minibus. Dinner, too, took place in complete isolation: a small private dining room had been reserved for us; no one saw us and we saw no one, with the exception of two silent, thin-lipped waitresses. The food was inedible, thin slivers of cold mystery-meat, swimming in some acrid, purplish liquid that burned my throat, which I pushed away after the first mouthful. To drink we had a pale locally made sparkling drink every bit as vile as the main course. While the Anglo-Saxons – doubtless disciples of Chomsky – cleaned their plates with angelic smiles, I went in search of the kitchens, planning to bribe someone to make me an omelette. I needed wine too, or at the very least water. The French interpreter rushed to block my way: clutching my stomach as though in serious pain, I told him I felt sick and that I needed eggs. My acting proved effective, he got them for me. I also casually mentioned that in a hotel like this for the élite *nomenklatura*, surely there was someplace where, in exchange for dollars, wines and spirits might be obtained. (My frequent visits to Eastern Europe had taught me that much.) This proved to be the case and he led me to the basement where there were bars offering every possible kind of drink, casinos with no gamblers, massage rooms, and so on; all were absolutely deserted. For a small fortune, I bought a mediocre Spanish Sangre de Toro, which I took back with me and savoured, to the quizzical and disapproving stares of my British comrades. As they all headed back to their respective rooms, I went out on to the forecourt to get some fresh air and walk around in authorized, circumscribed circles. It was clear to me that the hotel was an Alcatraz, from which there was no escape.

The following afternoon, while the Chomskyist faction led by the English-speaking guide scrupulously adhered to the itinerary, I told my guide I had a sore throat and said I would stay in my room until evening. Two hours later, I went downstairs again, firmly resolved to go into the city on my own and convinced that by now he would have left the lobby. A grave error on my part; as soon as I stepped out of the lift I saw him sitting on a bench, staring at me. He had been waiting for me: he would have waited all day and all night, those were his orders. I went outside, he was right beside me, there was a lone taxi waiting. I wanted to take it but he said, 'It is not for us.' 'Let's walk, then,' I said, and set off briskly in the direction of the bridge, determined to wear him out. He was at least sixty years younger than me but I noticed he quickly became breathless, he was struggling. I continued to quicken my pace. After about a kilometre, he begged for mercy. I said, 'The taxi we saw must be free, otherwise it would have passed us by now, there's only one road.' He suggested going back to get it, no longer objecting to taking it. At this point I told him that I was a film director by profession and that I needed to get a feel for the city, for North Korea, for which I felt a profound sympathy, that I was considering making a film celebrating the glories of his country and would be happy for him to accompany me. So he headed back towards the forecourt of Alcatraz, while I lay on the grass and waited; it was a long wait. Then suddenly, to my surprise, I saw him arrive in the taxi. I climbed in and explained that I wanted to head down the left bank of the Taedong to the next bridge. He translated for the driver, who did as

I asked. I recognized the bridge where I had rendezvoused with my beloved. I suggested we get out, asking my guide to come with me and make the taxi wait for us. Things that had been crucial to my brief encounter had vanished: there was no bank now, no towpath, but instead a large flagstone promenade that seemed to stretch out forever. In the distance I saw a number of small boats circling. The embankment from which the singing brigades had so intently watched Kim and me was now a line of tall buildings overlooking the waterfront. In fifty years, the city had had time to change. And yet I still needed to locate the Taedonggang Hotel. We got back into the taxi and I pointed to the road I wanted to take, indicating to the driver to go slowly. Though I looked carefully, I could not see the hotel, something that completely baffled me. I told the interpreter that some decades ago, a friend of mine had stayed in a hotel that bore the name of the river, which, from what he had told me, should be around here somewhere. He had never heard of it but asked the taxi driver, who said that the remains of the Taedonggang Hotel, which had burned down in 2001, were behind the fence we were just driving past. It was not my memory that had been at fault.

Time had stood still in North Korea at least twice: in 1955, at the end of the war, and in 1994, after the death of Kim Il-sung, the Great Leader. Kim Il-sung is not dead, he cannot be dead, he is here for eternity. As all infrequent tourists do, as all the children, the pioneers and the citizens of the People's Republic have a duty to do several times a year, I had to profess my respect and admiration, participate in the cult of his immortal personality. At the entrance to the park, on the brow of a hill, where the colossal, twenty-metre-high bronze statue of Kim Il-sung was erected, teenage girls dressed in white arrived carrying small bouquets of flowers – also white – that, having reached the summit, they had to lay at the feet of the man-god. The gleaming sculptured bronze of the statue reflects the sun so intensely that one has to squint if one wants to take in the vertical panorama, to contemplate him in his full stature. The statue is flanked, to left and right, by two grey bas-relief statues of men and women fused together, armed with rifles, sickles, hammers, with every tool devised by man, and all leaning forward, so accustomed are they to the sublime fervour that propels them towards the radiant future. There are statues, portraits, photographs and posters of Kim Il-sung all over the country, in every town and village, infinitely multiplied. It might be said that his son, Kim Jong-il, based his authority on the reverence paid to his father's authority rather than daring to claim it for himself. But war is as eternal as he who declared and waged it: the Korean War is not over, it has lasted for fifty years and is being fought still. The whole country is in a constant state of frantic alert, a veritable hothouse atmosphere without which it would collapse. Everywhere – on television, on the cassettes sold in the basement of the hotel – the North Korean army marches endlessly, company by company, unit by unit, goose-stepping past the grandstand where Kim's chubby-cheeked son stands, surrounded by his ministers and his generals, ghosts of bygone ages. On other stands are the veterans, the Party leaders, the wealthy élite of the regime who are its bedrock, who perpetuate it, in spite of the sacrifices inflicted generation after generation, on the youth, on a whole people. As in 1958, I was again taken to Panmunjom on the 38th parallel where the armistice that brought hostilities to a close was signed and where I was exposed not only to South Koreans, braggarts in sunglasses photographing the Chomsky faction and me across the famous immaterial line, but also to the officers of the Korean People's Army in Soviet kepis with broad peaks and large epaulettes, giving the same speech they have given every day for fifty years, the same commentary on the same photos, the same diagrams, feigning anger as though it had all happened yesterday. The weariness of these valiant men is evident in only one respect: they smoke like chimneys, chain-smoking foul-smelling cigarettes. Half a century of mobilization, half a century of being ready for action with not a single shot fired, is something that cannot be, cannot continue, without some powerful consolation: tobacco. In spite of the parades, the goose-stepping and the sabre-rattling, the Korean People's Army is on its last legs. This is immediately confirmed by the meagre angle of elevation of their extended calves, pitiful when compared to how the Nazis performed their goose step, throwing the leg high, perpendicular to the pelvis.

On the far bank of the Taedong, directly aligned with the giant statue of Kim Il-sung, and almost as tall, is the *Juche* Tower, culmination of the theory of 'self-reliance'and as immutable, more crucial now than ever. There are no means of transport in North Korea, trains, like buses, are rare and slow, cars, motorbikes and bicycles non-existent. On our 250-kilometre drive, Noam's friends and I encounter only three official limousines. The only means of transport: walking. This is where the *Juche*, which makes man the master of his own destiny, fully comes into its own. For on the same 250-kilometre drive, we pass or encounter countless people walking. As they set out, they walk briskly, energetically, arms swinging, each, even if alone, attempting to be his own singing brigade. They start out intending to walk five, ten, twenty, even thirty kilometres, but as we have seen, they quickly become breathless and they are hungry, very hungry. In truth, these fanatical disciples of *Juche* tire quickly, their progress slowing to a crawl; they stop frequently, hunkering by the side of the road, waiting to gather their strength. Traffic in the city flows so freely it seems unreal, Pyongyang is the city of the 'as-if' personality, and there is something almost comic about watching the slim, almost diaphanous young policewomen in Soviet caps perched on pedestals shaped like drums at every major crossroads directing the exclusively pedestrian traffic with the jerky movements of wind-up toys. Their robotic gestures, the unearthly solemnity of their faces are infinitely more effective than all our road markings and traffic lights: no one would dare to try and cross at the wrong time, though it would entail only one risk, the greatest risk of all, that of breaking the rules.

My guide worked hard to come up with plans that I did my best to thwart, but I knew I had to give in to him if I wanted something in return, that something being nothing less than a sliver of freedom – supervised freedom, of course, but enough to allow me, with him by my side, to retrace the steps of a past I could not help but try to rediscover. So I agreed to taking the Pyongyang metro, which, according to him – and he was right – dwarfed those of Moscow and Beijing by the vastness and the opulence of its stations, the numbers of commuters, and the unbelievable depth of its tunnels, which even offer shelter in the event of nuclear war. In fifty years, the masters of Korea had succeeded in making their capital at once monumental and desolate. Pyongyang was clean, there were no shanty towns, no slums, but the living moved like shadows. As the days passed I felt increasingly hungry, since I did not eat anything that was offered, anxiously waiting to board the plane again. And yet Kim Kum-sun was engraved on my memory and I stubbornly kept thinking about the impossible film, which hunger and my revulsion for the food made seem even more impracticable. My 'bodyguard', increasingly baffled by the demands I made of him – he was beginning to realize that I knew Pyongyang – agreed to take me by taxi to the scene of my shipwreck with Kim, which I tried to locate precisely, pacing up and down the promenade, talking to myself and gesticulating wildly. But the area was barely recognizable: everything had vanished, the ticket booth, the steep bank down to the river, the hut where we had left our shoes and, most of all, the boats. The only place to find them was across the bridge, past the Tower of the *Juche* Idea, where a few small boats circled in the distance while a dozen others were moored along the quay waiting for the following Sunday. The Pyongyang of today, sleek and with no past, offered me no purchase. Since we were now on the far bank, I explained to my guide that I wanted to follow a particular route, that he needed only to translate my directions to the driver. After that, I promised, we would rejoin the rest of the group for a dance performance in a 'traditional' restaurant to which we had been invited.

I had got it into my head, as a sort of ultimate test, to try to find the hospital. So I gruffly gave directions, as though I knew exactly where I was going: 'right, left, straight ahead, keep going', to my young guide's mounting astonishment, my commands all the more brusque because I was not at all certain I knew where I was going. Suddenly, I shouted – almost yelled – 'STOP!' The hospital, set back in its large courtyard appeared before me like a mirage, unchanged, the only complex of buildings in the whole city that was exactly as it had been. I had helped Gatti across this very courtyard on our first night here, had crossed it with Kim the day before I left, it was here we had passionately kissed, our tongues meeting, oblivious to everything, in a hopeless embrace. I was speechless, staring at the building, then I heard myself unexpectedly say, 'I know this city very well.' I could no longer keep my guide on tenterhooks and, in a sense, I was happy to be able to tell him the truth. I told him I had been treated at this hospital, that I had been to Pyongyang long before he was born, probably before his father was born, that I had been a member of the first delegation of Westerners invited to North Korea after the war, and, most importantly, that I had seen the Great Leader Kim Il-sung in the flesh many times, I had had dinner with him twice, that if he wanted to check he had only to read the newspapers of the period, which had daily reported our thoughts and our comments. Talking to him in the car, still parked in front of the hospital, I witnessed an extraordinary metamorphosis: since I had broken bread with the Great Leader, I therefore shared something of the nature of him; a veritable transubstantiation was taking place, making me sacred. The young man closed his eyes, he reached out, touched me, and an expression of rapture I had never seen before came over him. He was so eager to share the good news that I did not want to keep him hanging around any longer. I said – in Spanish for some reason – 'Vamos', which he nevertheless understood perfectly. On the way back, I told him that I had said I'd never been to North Korea before because I thought that no one from my visit fifty years earlier would still be around and I would have had to leave China long before I got through the bureaucratic red tape. I was thinking about making a film in praise of North Korea and I wanted to face my past dispassionately before officially declaring myself. He told me that he would have to refer the matter to his boss, who would probably want to meet me. I asked if he could do so as soon as possible: the flight back to Beijing was leaving the following day and I could not prolong my stay. I did not tell him the real reason I could not stay: I was starving.

That evening, when we got back from the show, the Deputy Minister for Tourism and a high-ranking Party official was waiting for me at the hotel. He was a slim, elegant man of about fifty with a pleasant face and a perfect command of English: he had clearly lived abroad. Here, too, transubstantiation played a role: he showed great deference as I talked on and on about the Great Leader, his comportment, his authority, his wisdom, his political audacity, the exquisite 'Soup of the Mountain Gods' I had once shared with him. The Deputy Minister did not question anything I said. What most impressed me was that he joined me when I ordered a whisky from the bar, and then he ordered a second, for me and for him. I said nothing about the real reasons I wanted to film in Korea, giving him instead other reasons he would find convincing, just as I had with Polish bureaucrats in order to get permission to film freely in Poland, including in the places where Jews had been exterminated, by persuading them that telling the truth would be the best way of doing justice to their country. I realized the Minister was not opposed to such a project, indeed that he was interested, even fascinated. He did not suggest that he would have to take it to a higher authority but seemed sufficiently high-ranking to make the decision himself. I told him that, for my part, I would need some time to think about it, that it would take considerable preparation and a number of return visits to Korea. He gave me his address and every modern means of getting in touch with him. We took leave of each other on friendly terms, he believing that he could trust me, that such a film would help Korea break out of its isolation, I believing that perhaps things were not as bad as I have just painted them. Sometimes, all it takes is one man.

My real problem, one that I have not resolved to this day, was – my 'brief encounter' will probably never be filmed – what film? I felt profoundly repelled, almost outraged, at the thought of making fiction. Anyone other than me would have decided to shoot the film using actors in South Korea or some other Asian country by some other river without a constant police presence, without having to charter a plane to ship in food for the cast and crew. It's even possible to imagine it being shot in a studio in a purely Hollywood style: Universal, Paramount or Spielberg's DreamWorks are designed for such productions and would not baulk at the scale of the project or at potentially despoiling the truth by reinventing it. The result might even be a magnificent film – something they have proved time and again they are capable of. As for me, it's not completely impossible that I might one day write a screenplay based on this true story. But, leaving Pyongyang after what I had experienced over those four days, my natural inclination and my filmmaker's instincts suggested something else, an insane desire to tell the truth, which, if successful, would have exploded the traditional documentary/fiction dichotomy: I would direct a documentary about the North Korea of today, powerfully depicting everything I have said above about the city – the emptiness, the monumentalization, the permanent mobilization, the tobacco, the universal weariness, the hunger, the fear, the way time has been suspended for fifty years – showing how everything yet nothing has changed, how everything has got worse. And over the shots of modern Pyongyang, a voiceover – my voice as it is today, no actors, no actresses, no reconstruction – would recount, as I did in the previous chapter, the 'brief encounter' between Claude Lanzmann and Kim Kum-sun. It would require sensitive, highly meticulous work on image and text, on words and silence and their positioning in the film, the points at which the account of the past is inserted into the present of the city, the discordance and concordance culminating in a single temporality where word reveals itself as image and image as word.

Chapter 15

Never was a September in Paris more glorious than the one that greeted me when I returned from Asia. I was supposed to leave the city almost as soon as I arrived: Castor and Sartre were waiting for me in Capri, eager to see me, hungry for stories of my trip. It had been arranged that we would extend our holiday in Italy until the beginning of October. But I couldn't leave; something held me there, I needed to be alone, to stroll around Paris on a whim, to enjoy the new-found strength I felt coursing through me, the new and strange sense of freedom. I was not the same man, the fabulous day I had spent with Kim Kum-sun had profoundly changed me, something I only fully realized in the atelier on the rue Schœlcher. In Capri, Castor was fretting, less than convinced by the excuses I invented to defer my departure. I had brutally cancelled a first arrival date by telegram on the pretext that I had to do an interview about China. The truth was that I had just fallen head over heels for an aristocratic woman with a double-barrel name, younger than Castor, although not as young as she claimed. When I finally got to Capri, I tried to allay suspicion, giving an account of my trip to China and Korea, but saying nothing about Kim Kum-sun. Together, the three of us explored the Amalfi coast all the way to Ravello, pushing on as far as Paestum beyond Salerno, experiencing very happy days.

The break-up with Castor was long and painful; it took almost a year before we separated, because she was so compassionate, so understanding; she had always foreseen what she considered to be an inevitability. Back in Paris, I had not ended my relationship with the beautiful aristocrat, I saw her often and began to arrive home at the rue Schœlcher increasingly late. One night, having quietly crept up to the low-ceilinged mezzanine that was our bedroom, I found Castor awake, sitting up straight in bed, a sullen pout across her unhappy face. 'I want to know,' she said. To go on lying was out of the question. I sat down next to her, took her in my arms and confessed everything. An immense relief spread over her features; truth was her business – in fact, lying to her had been absurd and criminal on my part – and immediately her optimism and sense of action took over. She began by interrogating me about 'the other woman', perfectly prepared to accept that she was in love with me and I with her; Castor wanted to meet her and concur with all the good things I said about her. 'There's no reason for her to suffer,' she went on, 'there's no reason you should cut short your nights together,' and she suggested sharing me: I would spend three days and nights with one, four days and four nights with the other and the reverse the following week. I was overwhelmed, transfixed with love and admiration; I was little more than a virgin, I knew nothing about women, I thought the aristocrat would jump for joy at the prospect of such an arrangement. But an 'arrangement' was exactly what she would not agree to, she wanted to win, to triumph, she wanted to deliver a death blow, especially if her rival's name was Simone de Beauvoir. Her face contorted with mute fury and pain when I told her the plan. Still, she had no choice but to accept, yet every time I insisted that she meet Castor as agreed, she evaded the issue, something Castor rightly interpreted as a sign of open hostility. So began for me an agonizing period of being torn apart. Because sharing requires punctuality and discipline. If Castor, having spent the evening with Sartre, was expecting me at the rue Schœlcher at midnight, I could not turn up at one o'clock, something her rival did her best to make happen. The moment I was about to leave, already running late, the moment I reached her door, marshalling all the charms at her disposal, she'd say, 'Surely you can stay five more minutes?', hoping I would give in, which I did. Such games of love are familiar and I won't dwell on them.

It took more than a year before I summoned the courage to put an end to this double life with a savage break and at the cost, both for the beautiful aristocrat and for me, of terrible heartache. At that point, I left the rue Schœlcher and did not see Castor again until the following September, when we had to begin to build a friendship. The situation at Les Temps modernes, harried by lawsuits, censorship, threatened with distraint, actual seizure of goods, the escalating violence of the war in Algeria and, in France, the mounting climate of suspicion, of civil unrest, the impossibility of deciphering the intentions behind the hysterical, contradictory statements of Général de Gaulle; all this forced personal matters into the background. There was never the least trace of bitterness or resentment between Castor and me, we ran the publication just as we always had, we worked together, campaigned together. In the early months I rented a room from an elderly lady on the first floor of a vast mansion above the Café de Flore. Life was hard there: night after night, I barely slept a wink. Eventually, I found an apartment nearby, on the rue des Saints-Pères, which belonged to an actor, Peter van Eyck, a tall, well-built man with piercing blue eyes and a great shock of silver-white hair who had a fine and honourable career chiefly playing Prussian officers. He was a peaceable man and the most accommodating of landlords; cancer took him far too young.

In the spring of 1954, in the first flush of passion, Castor and I had travelled to Algeria and Tunisia, taking a ferry from Marseille to Algiers with our car, the Simca Aronde, not knowing by which port we would return. In the end, after numerous setbacks, we came back via Tunis. The Aronde was an ordinary saloon car; it could just about cope with main roads, yet we forced it to scale huge sand dunes such as those between El Oued and Tozeur. Countless times we got stuck in the sand; to make headway across the dunes requires a technique only acquired through long practice, specially equipped vehicles and a wealth of rescue and survival equipment. But she and I were as reckless in the south of Algeria as we had been in the Swiss Alps and had it not been for the local man who agreed to be our driver – also getting stuck in the sand a number of times – we would have died of thirst, of heatstroke, or of the cold desert nights. Speaking to him and to the people he introduced us to with some difficulty, I realized that the country was on the brink of an explosion. Although I was well aware of the living conditions of the Algerian working class in France – I spent hours outside the gates of the Renault factory in Billancourt, watching spellbound as North African workers, Algerians mostly, were bussed in from distant suburbs at dawn or taken home in the dead of night when their eight-hour shifts were done; seeing the impenetrable, exhausted faces of these lonely men heading back to the shanty towns, the grim dormitories of these modern-day slaves, terrified and appalled me – I had no idea what the real Algeria was like. It was as though our innocence, our stubbornness, our tourist's obsession with the beauty of the desert, the grandeur of the landscape, had veiled the connection between Billancourt and colonial oppression, or the massacres of Sétif and Guelma, news of which reached us only faintly, belatedly.

Our interests were inexcusably folkloric. I was obsessed with the South and insisted that I wanted to cross the Sahara in the Aronde. Castor insisted we go to Laghouat to see the Ouled Naïl belly dancers, prostitutes who wore upon their bodies in gold and precious stones everything they had amassed in a lifetime of work. Then, pushing further south, I stopped, dazed with wonder by Ghardaïa, a key city on the deadly trans-Saharan route, capital of the M'zab, a region remarkable not only for its architecture but for its skilled, resourceful merchants who plied their trade all over Algeria. In the streets of Ghardaïa, standing before the market stalls, the shops, I was preoccupied by a single question: how could camels and dromedaries be compossible with piles of tinned sardines? Never for a moment did it occur to me that the tins might have been carried there by caravan, which was the predominant method of transportation at the time. The tinned sardines seemed illogical, their banality was incompatible with the nobility of the striding camel and the austere – meagre as it turned out – imaginative world it conjured. It took me years to let go of stereotypes, to reconcile myself to the reality, the complexity of the world.

This was the spring of 1954. Ahmed, our guide through the dunes, knew everything and it was he who informed us, on one of our stops, that the Battle of Dien Bien Phu had begun in Indochina. One after another the fortified positions, each bearing a beautiful woman's name, Éliane, Béatrice, Huguette, Dominique, and so on, were attacked and surrounded. The battle lasted from March until May and 'Gabrielle', which, Ahmed told us through clenched teeth, his face etched with pain, had been defended by a valiant Algerian infantry battalion, was one of the first to fall after heavy artillery fire and an extremely violent struggle. There were serious losses. Dien Bien Phu fell a month after we returned to Paris. For France, in any case, the war had long since been lost; maintaining the illusion of a colonial empire in Asia had long involved turning a criminally blind eye, entailing lies, a failure of nerve, political racketeering and corruption raised to the level of government policy. Dien Bien Phu, a strategic folly, was merely the culmination of this madness. When it fell, it marked the end of the war in Indochina, or of the French war, at least. Paratroopers were still being dropped into that hell three days before the defeat: though France could no longer win, and knew it could not win, Frenchmen still gave futile, heroic demonstrations of their willingness to die with honour.

The contrast between the empty, bombastic declarations of prime ministers and commanders-in-chief that followed, and the sacrifices imposed on the troops, death for honour, masking colonial folly and negligence, was so intolerable to us and to our friends that when it was all over we cracked open the champagne. We put our hopes for a new kind of politics in the new Prime Minster, Pierre Mendès France, who alone was capable of accepting defeat and of negotiating peace with Ho Chi Minh. He did so in precisely thirty days in Geneva, and was never forgiven for it. For the remainder of his brief tenure, he granted Tunisia home rule. Algeria, however, was to become the real combat zone, and though during our trip Castor and I did not know when or where it might begin, we foresaw everything. The attack on 1 November 1954 in which the teacher Guy Monnerot was murdered and his wife seriously injured is generally accepted as the *casus belli* of the Algerian War. I sometimes said to Castor, 'If we'd gone six months later, that could have been us.' But we were protected by our innocence, our ignorance, by the fact that we were the epitome of naïve tourists. Perhaps, too, because Ahmed, our guide, realized that we understood him, that he had opened our eyes once and for all.

In the end, everything happens quickly. Six years later comes not only the publication of the Manifesto of the 121, asserting the right of conscripts to refuse to fight, but also the Jeanson trial. These things are part of objective history so I will not dwell on them. I was one of the ten signatories of the Manifesto who was prosecuted and called to give evidence at the trial, which took place in the courtroom of Cherche-Midi prison in Paris on the corner of the rue du Cherche-Midi and the boulevard Raspail, which has since been demolished and replaced by the École des hautes études en sciences sociales. I was interrogated twice at length by Braunschweig, the examining magistrate, a man of impeccable courtesy and an impassive face to whom I explained my reasons for firmly supporting those who refused to serve in Algeria, doing my best to avoid any bombast. Coming out of the magistrates' chambers, I encountered Jean Pouillon, also a member of the editorial committee of *Les Temps modernes*, and another of the accused, awaiting his turn. In the Jeanson trial, I was called as a witness for the defence of Jean-Claude

Paupert, a member of the Jeanson network, although I barely knew him. He was a young man of few words who lived his life according to his ideals, breaking with his family and making a moral choice, one that he owed in part to my family, to my mother and to Monny. His father owned a bistro, Le Métro, on the boulevard Garibaldi on the corner of the place Cambronne. Paulette lived on the other side of the square, in the well-to-do area that was already part of the 7th *arrondissement*, and Monny crossed the boulevard every day to have his coffee at Paupert's bistro. The taciturn boy was fascinated by Monny's way with words and quickly became a regular visitor to the apartment on the rue Alexandre-Cabanel and almost a son to them. All this I discovered much later: at the time I was not living in Paris. He refused to work behind the counter of Le Métro but continued his studies and developed a visceral hatred of the war. He became a member of the Jeanson network, one of the '*porteurs de valises*', the 'suitcase carriers' who delivered money and papers to the FLN, and he went underground until the arrests from which, as we know, Jeanson was one of the few to escape. I sat for hours in the witness room, and when I was finally called into court, I arrived in the middle of a violent argument between the magistrates and the lawyers. Jacques Vergès, at the head of his 'collective' defending the FLN, was leading the offensive, challenging the competence of the court; also involved was Roland Dumas, future Minister for Foreign Affairs and future president of the *Conseil constitutionnel*, of whom Vergès said, rubbing his hands together as he left the hearing, 'He is our *harki*'. I was questioned by the presiding magistrate and then by the lawyers. I told them what I knew about the life of Jean-Claude Paupert and said that I entirely supported his position and his actions. I added that, as a signatory of the Manifesto of the 121, I considered that my place was in the dock with Paupert and his comrades and not on the witness stand. The legal correspondent for *Le Monde*, Jean-Marc Théolleyre, laid considerable emphasis on my testimony in the paper the following day.

Sartre, who was in Brazil at the time, wrote a long letter to the tribunal that was read out, I think, by Vergès, or maybe by Roland Dumas. It was said that I had drafted Sartre's statement together with Marcel Péju, then editor-in-chief at *Les Temps modernes*. In her *Memoirs*, Simone de Beauvoir gives credence to this version of events, but in fact it came about very differently: I managed, with great difficulty, to get a call through to Brazil and explained the situation to Sartre who, with Castor, had long since left Paris. It goes without saying that he gave us permission to speak in his name. Nonetheless, I did not write a single word of that letter, nor did I know anything about it until it was made public during the tribunal. Péju wrote the letter alone, and he did not ask me to read it, because he knew that there were several statements in it that I would never have supported. Nor indeed would Sartre, as he told me on his return, but by then there could be no question of making public this profound disagreement. In phrases marked by hollow rhetoric, Péju linked victory in the Algerian revolution with that of the impending revolution in France, which he heralded, associating the destinies of the two peoples: 'The left is powerless, and it will remain so unless it accepts that it must unite its efforts with the only force that is today truly fighting against the common enemy of Algerian and French freedoms. That force is the FLN.' He denounced the left 'mired in a miserable prudence' and emphatically concluded, 'the ephemeral power that is preparing to judge [the accused] already represents nothing'. If he thought it just, Sartre was capable of resolutely defending a cause, but in doing so he never gave up his freedom. He was a radical but a realist; he was not naïve and he never made prophecies. Péju – and there is ample evidence for this – became, quite literally, the FLN's man at *Les Temps modernes*, something so intolerable to the editorial committee that, during a particularly painful meeting attended by Sartre and Castor immediately after Algeria was granted independence, having questioned him and given him an opportunity to defend himself, we voted to dismiss him from the journal: the evidence we brought against him was damning, there is nothing more to say. He left immediately. The members of the network received long prison sentences. I met Paupert again many years later, when he had become the chief accountant at Éditions Odile Jacob and he was more taciturn than ever.

After the trial, Péju suggested we go together to Tunis. The headquarters of the provisional government of the Algerian Republic, the newspaper *El Moudjahid* and the diplomatic and propaganda wings of the FLN were based there. I agreed and was immediately struck by the cheerfulness of those who welcomed us; their jokes, their extraordinary, exhaustive knowledge of the situation in France and the principal political players in France and in Algeria. I was especially struck by their optimism, their conviction that they had won the war, that independence was within their grasp and, after six years of bitter fighting, it would be theirs within a year or two, perhaps within a few months. They all spoke impeccable French. I remember Mohamed Yazid, a lawyer from one of the great Blida families, who had taken up the role of Minister for Information and was later the first Algerian ambassador to France, and I remember Mohammed Benyahia, later Minister for Foreign Affairs, a short, thin and frail man of powerful intelligence, who spent his time dreaming outlandish strategies worthy of a chess-player, each more daring than the last, which had him in fits of uncontrollable laughter. He died suddenly, which was a great shock to those who knew him, and a great loss for Algeria.

But the encounter that really shook me, unsettled me, captivated me and that was to have a profound effect on my own life was my meeting with Frantz Fanon. A native of Martinique, born in the same year as me, Fanon had signed up to fight the Germans in Europe, had been wounded in combat and been awarded the Croix de Guerre. His life had been turned upside down, as had mine, though very differently, by Sartre's book *Réflexions sur la question juive*. It was through reading the book on his return to Martinique after the war to pass his *baccalauréat* that Fanon became acutely conscious of being black. He came back to France, studied medicine in Lyon while simultaneously taking courses in philosophy – in particular those of Merleau-Ponty – and psychology. His first book, *Peau noire, masques blancs* [*Black Skin, White Masks*], might be regarded as his response to Sartre, his '*Reflections on the Black Question*', in which, while acknowledging his debt to Sartre and the giant leap the writer had helped him make, he clearly distinguishes himself from Sartre in a radical attempt to force everyone to drop their masks, beginning with those white people who, for all their compassion and their good intentions, made no attempt whatsoever to experience the *flavour* of black life: for them, it was enough to believe in the abolition of slavery, the recognition of *négritude*, for example, as sensible and necessary steps towards reconciling all of humanity. Fanon is infinitely more violent and demanding: just as Jews are not the creation of the anti-Semite – as I had told Sartre and Simone de Beauvoir when I returned from my first trip to Israel – so blacks will finally be free of the white masks glued to their skin only through struggle, by becoming the sole authors of their own freedom. In 1953, Fanon was named head of department at the Blida psychiatric hospital, in Algeria, where – incurring the hostility of his colleagues and the authorities – he practised a true ethno-psychiatry, long before the term existed, refusing to see the sick merely as a collection of symptoms and linking mental illness to colonial alienation. In the early stages of the uprising in Algeria, he was contacted by the officers of the ALN (*Armée de la libération nationale*) and the political wing of the FLN. He unhesitatingly joined them, resigned his post as a doctor, was deported from Algeria in January 1957 and joined the FLN in Tunis where he began working with *El Moudjahid*.

My abiding memory of the first afternoon I spent with Fanon in El Menzah, a suburb of Tunis, in the apartment where he lived with his wife and son, is the absolute emptiness of the place – nothing on the walls, not a stick of furniture, no bed, nothing. Fanon was lying on a sort of pallet, a mattress on the floor. I was immediately struck by his fiery dark eyes, black with fever. He was already suffering from leukaemia, which he knew would prove fatal, and was in terrible pain. He had just come back from Accra in Ghana where he had been sent by the Provisional Government of the Algerian Republic – as ambassador to Nkrumah. It was in Accra that he had been diagnosed with leukaemia and repatriated to Tunis where he was now waiting to leave for the USSR to be treated. He had only just arrived in Tunis, which explained the emptiness of the apartment. Péju and I sat on the floor next to the mattress where Fanon lay and listened to him talk about the Algerian revolution for hours, stopping several times when the pain became unbearable. I put my hand on his forehead, which was bathed in sweat, and awkwardly tried to dry it, or I held his shoulder gently as though by mere touch I might ease his pain. But all the while Fanon spoke with a lyricism I had never before encountered, he was already so suffused with death that it gave his every word the power both of prophecy and of the last words of a dying man. He questioned me about Sartre, about Sartre's health, and I could sense the affection, the admiration he felt for the man. *Critique de la raison dialectique* had been published in April, and Frantz had managed to have a copy sent to Ghana where he began reading it. He had recently finished it, something that had required considerable effort and concentration for a man suffering from leukaemia, though his philosophical acuity was still dazzling.

He talked to us about the ALN, the *djounoud* [combatants], explaining that the men from the interior were more true, more pure. This dialectic between interior and exterior I grasped only dimly at the time; it would be years before I fully understood it, but it has existed in most liberation movements. Fanon esteemed those of the interior so highly they became polymaths who not only fought the French by force of arms with utter purity and self-denial, but also studied philosophy. The men over there, he told us in a confiding tone that brooked no argument, had begun reading *Critique de la raison dialectique*. This was not true, as we will see later, but in that room in El Menzal, Fanon's passionate words made it impossible to doubt the existence of these peasant-warrior-philosophers. He talked with the same conviction, the same persuasive power about Africa, about the whole continent, about African unity and brotherhood. Before being appointed ambassador to Ghana, he had gone to Accra in 1958 as leader of the FLN delegation at the first All-African People's Conference. Among the other delegates was Patrice Lumumba from the Congo, Holden Roberto of the Union of Peoples of Northern Angola, Félix Moumié of the *Union des populations du Cameroun*, representatives of the ANC (African National Congress) from South Africa, who, after *Les Damnés de la terre* [*The Wretched of the Earth*] was published, were lucidly to choose the path of violence. Lumumba and Moumié, as we know, were murdered two and three years respectively after the congress. Dr Omar's speech was a sensation. Contrary to the 'positive action' advocated by Nkrumah, Fanon saw a generalized armed struggle as the only hope for the emancipation of the African continent groaning beneath the weight of the various colonial powers, and cited Algeria as a model, as the spearhead in a struggle that would have to be ruthless: 'And in our struggle for liberty,' he concluded, 'we should plan actions that will strike at the heart of the imperialists – we will have to act with force and, truth be told, with violence.'

All this I would learn later, but in the apartment in El Menzah, as he propped himself up on his elbow and announced like a visionary that Africa, the Africa of his dreams, would not experience the Middle Ages as Europe had, one could not but be carried along by his words, could only subscribe to his glorious utopian ideal. I know that when I returned to Paris I was still completely carried away by this man whom I believed to be the keeper of the truth, and of the truth as a secret. There was a secret in truth, and he held it. All this I told Sartre and did so in such terms that he felt he too had to meet Fanon, something unusual for him.

After that first time, I met Fanon alone several times, always in Tunis, though not always in the El Menzah apartment. He seemed much better, he had periods of remission from the leukaemia. One of his closest friends was Omar Ousedik, a Kabyle or Berber from the north, a likeable man whom Frantz trusted completely and in front of whom he could speak freely. By questioning Fanon more closely, I learned that his relationship with the Algerian people and theirs with him were not as simple as I had first believed. He was one of them and yet was not, because he was Martiniquais and black. His loyalty was unconditional, but he constantly had to reaffirm it, to prove it. He knew about the rivalries, the often fierce power struggles within the FLN, but when he talked to me about them, he constantly used the word 'secret', 'secret', repeating it ten times in the course of a conversation. I realized that Fanon himself was afraid. Abane Ramdane, one of the worthy leaders of the FLN and a close friend of Fanon, had just been murdered in Morocco, having fallen into a trap set by Boussouf, Ben Tobbal and Krim Belkacem, members of the FLN's all-powerful central committee, the *Comité de coordination et d'exécution*. Abane Ramdane was determined to maintain the primacy of political authorities over the ALN and that of the *wilayahs*, or provinces, over the *Armée des frontières*, something that the colonels in the ALN profoundly disagreed with. The image of a united front that the FLN liked to project to the outside world, particularly to those who supported it, was merely a façade, a pretence. There were bloody purges, savage executions. Amirouche, for example, the leader of Wilayah III, brainwashed by the French secret services into believing he had been betrayed, had decimated his own troops, subjecting them to excruciating tortures and summary executions – a massacre known by the name '*Bleuite*'. They called themselves brothers, but it was what Sartre in *Critique de la raison dialectique* referred to as fraternity-terror: each brother was a potential traitor to the others.

It should be understood that, from a purely military stand-point, the French army had done an efficient job. The Moriceline, running along the Tunisian–Algerian border, left the inland *wilayahs* completely isolated; they were equally hemmed in along the border with Morocco and any attempts to supply them with weapons or provisions failed, resulting in terrible losses. As for the FLN itself, it had been widely infiltrated. Many people talked, and not only under torture. The French had numerous informants with a variety of reasons for their betrayal: fear, revenge, power, money. There were also rivalries between clans and tribes, the conflict between the Kabyles and the Arabs. Ousedik, Fanon's Kabyle friend, who was very light-skinned, whispered or put a finger to his lips when he spoke, and even then only in code. I didn't care, I was not there as a journalist, what was important to me was to maintain their trust and hear as much as they wanted me to hear. It was during this period that Fanon began to write *Les Damnés de la terre* – not writing, in fact, but dictating. He read a number of passages to me with one thought in mind: he wanted Sartre to read it and write the preface.

Every time I visited, he said, 'You're never going to learn anything about the Algerian revolution here in Tunis; everything here is corrupt, you need to go there,' *there* being what Fanon referred to as 'the interior', the men reading *Critique de la raison dialectique*, the pure warrior-philosophers. In fact, the men he referred to were not from the interior at all, they were the *Armée des frontières*, whom the people of the interior despised, but I did not know that then. The *Armée des frontières* was made up of veteran combatants from the 'interior' who had crossed over, first to Morocco and later to Tunisia, and created an influential organization that alone wielded power and whose political influence would make and unmake successive Algerian governments. Most of the members had joined the FLN years earlier and were now high-ranking officers. This *Armée des frontières* was first and foremost a political army. The true 'interior' – the Algerian *wilayahs* themselves – had been bled dry and were incapable of mounting any significant attacks against the French. From a military standpoint the French army had clearly won the battle, an argument often used by the generals who spearheaded the Algiers putsch to justify their break with de Gaulle.

Fanon organized my trip into what he called 'the interior' and, on the eve of my departure, invited me to dinner at his place in El Menzah with a thin, self-effacing man from Blida called Benyoucef Benkhedda, a pharmacist by profession, who had just been appointed head of the Provisional Government. He was a compromise candidate and shortly after independence he stood down. Over dinner, Fanon gave me his final recommendations: 'You absolutely must ask to meet with Colonel Houari Boumediène. Oh, you're so lucky! How I'd love to be going with you!' Fanon left for Moscow two days later where doctors were waiting for him.

An FLN driver came to pick me up at five o'clock in the morning to take me from Tunis to Ghardimaou on the Algerian border. It was here that the ALN had their headquarters. The driver visibly took pleasure in terrifying me, driving at top speed on appalling roads to impress me, to test me, maybe to kill me. After a few hours, we arrived in the courtyard of a large sunlit barracks where young men in civilian clothes were wandering around. A number of them immediately gathered around me; they were friendly and spoke excellent French. They led me to a large room with a long, broad table, a real conference table. They had me sit at one end as more and more men filed in and casually sat down around me, taking the chairs facing me and to my right. Slowly, the table filled up, mostly with men in civvies, then, finally, a tall, pale, red-haired man who came and sat on my left at the head of the table – the only empty seat. He did not say a single word during the discussion but kept a transistor radio pressed to his ear from beginning to end. The men began gently questioning me about recent events in France. They knew everything – there had been a tentative initial attempt at negotiations at Lugrin, but they had just broken down. While knowing exactly who I was and what we had done for them, they blamed the French people as a whole, me included, as though I had some role in it. I told them they were talking to the wrong person, that there was no point saying these things to me.

The discussion went on for some time; they meticulously reviewed everything that was going on in France before asking why I had wanted to meet them, why I had wanted to come here. I answered, 'Dr Fanon told me that until I met you, I would never understand the Algerian revolution, never understand your struggle.' They continued to interrogate me, eventually asking me exactly what I wanted. I gave my answer: 'I want to spend some time with ALN units.' Four or five people only had been asking questions, the others had said nothing. One of the five now asked, 'Do you like danger?' I replied that I didn't like danger for danger's sake, but that I had found myself in many dangerous situations and had been forced to deal with them, that I too had been a Resistance fighter, a *maquisard*, that I had fought in the war. I added, 'Dr Fanon strongly advised me to meet your leader, Colonel Boumediène.' He was on a mission, they said, and they did not know when he would be back; they added that I would not be staying there in the barracks but would be taken out that afternoon. Did I have the physical stamina, they asked; I told them I had. Could I hike for hours in the mountains, they asked; now beginning to feel a little worried, I said, 'I think so.' As I left the table after the frugal lunch I had barely had the opportunity to eat, the questioning having been so relentless, I asked again, 'Is there a chance I can meet Colonel Boumediène?' It would not be easy, I was told: 'The colonel is out on an inspection detail at the moment. We'll see when you get back, but it's not very likely.'

We set off that afternoon. My guide was a young man of about twenty-five who moved along the steep paths as sure-footedly as a goat, never stopping for an instant. I followed him for eight hours into the mountains, seeing and hearing the French planes droning over the whole area. At night, exhausted, I was led into a blockhouse built deep underground. By the light of the sooty lamps, I saw several disturbing faces. These were ALN fighters and their leaders, true battle-hardened fighters who would slit the throat of a sheep or a man, who had a long record of fighting against France. I was the first Frenchman to reach this place. I stayed with them for a week, holding out under the brutal and very precise French bombing raids. I questioned them for hours and they told me about the battles, the ambushes; told me appalling stories of cruelty, barbarity and oppression. I encouraged them to talk about their lives and succeeded in striking up tentative friendships with one or two. They had all started out fighting in the *wilayahs* in the interior, but later had left the country – it was impossible to cross the Moriceline, they explained, every attempt to bring weapons or provisions across the line had failed, resulting in terrible losses. They even took me there: hiding a few hundred metres away, I was able to observe the formidable French defence network and its sophisticated alarm systems. I made copious notes. By the time I left, our goodbyes were heartfelt. I started back, guided by another *djoundi*.

Arriving at the barracks, I was given a warm welcome: I had proved myself. A young ALN captain with magnificent blue eyes, one of those who had questioned me that first day, took me under his wing; he told me in almost poetic terms how moved he had been by the beauty of the dawn as the first shot of an ambush was fired in south Algeria. Knowing I was Jewish, he added, 'After independence, we will have to send units to Israel.' Seeing my astonishment, he explained, 'Oh, there is much we can learn from the Jews.' 'What sort of things?' I asked. 'Oh, the kibbutzim, the irrigation, afforestation, improving the soil.' This captain who guided me for the rest of my stay was Abdelaziz Bouteflika. As we know, today he is President of the Republic of Algeria.

I spent a week at the ALN headquarters, living with these men, eating at the same table, talking late into the night. They all spoke to me, and with remarkable candour, confiding private thoughts and secrets they barely dared speak of with their comrades. I was a midwife. Some of them took me aside to explain why polygamy was absolutely necessary, because so many of their brothers had been killed during the seven or eight years of the war: 'You have to understand that we cannot leave our sisters in need, so each of us must take several wives.' When I told Simone de Beauvoir about this later, she was absolutely horrified. The great hope for all of them was Ben Bella, imprisoned on the Île d'Aix, whom they were counting on being freed. On the eve of my departure, I spent the whole afternoon talking with two of the negotiators from Lugrin – one of whom would later briefly be Minister of Finance – when a third man joined us, the tall, pale, red-headed man with the transistor. We talked about what the Algerian political regime would be like, about Marxism, and so on, and I soon realized that their knowledge of *Critique de la raison dialectique* was limited to a seminar that Fanon had just given. That night, they organized a leaving party for me, an open-air feast with *méchoui* – whole sheep barbecued on spits. There were 300 men present. Obviously, I don't speak a word of Arabic and there was a traditional Algerian storyteller acting out a great ALN victory against the French. Every time he pretended to be the French, 300 men burst out laughing. It was very violent. Afterwards, I found myself alone with Bouteflika who, eager to assess how my visit had gone, began, 'As Colonel Boumediène told you this afternoon ...' I couldn't believe it: the tall red-haired man with the transistor 'on an inspection detail' was *him*. He had not thought it appropriate to introduce himself, although I had seen him on my first day, then at every meal since I had returned from the mountains.

I had planned to write about the trip on my return to Paris, although I don't know where I would have published it. In *Le Monde*, perhaps, or *Les Temps modernes*. But I never wrote the piece. It rapidly became known that I had been there and I gave two lectures in praise of the *Armée des frontières* at 115 boulevard Saint-Michel, headquarters of the North African Students Union, which was essentially run by Algerians. Ahmed Ghozali, later Minister for Oil, was present. Afterwards, I was quickly contacted by the men from Wilayah IV, the region of Algiers, who had heard about my trip to Ghardimaou. One of them unexpectedly showed up at my apartment, a luminous, intelligent, likeable young man from the deep interior, determined to open my eyes: 'You have to hear us out, our story is different to theirs. They deserted us for purely political reasons. They want to keep power for themselves.' He proved uncannily accurate: in fact, barely had independence been declared than Wilayah IV led a brief, doomed revolt against the new Algerian authorities. Events moved rapidly and quickly overtook me; in the end I told myself that I had no right to take sides in this civil war, that a period of reflection was necessary. The *Armée des frontières* had presented a unified front, which masked the internecine struggles and savage rifts. There was nothing extraordinary about this, it was born out of the circumstances in which the FLN had formed, its violent struggle with the MTLD (*Mouvement pour le triomphe des libertés démocratiques*) to be the sole representatives of their cause, born out of the betrayals, out of French oppression. None the less, to us they seemed the most unfortunate of all, victims of racist attacks, of torture, and of the Paris massacre of 1961 – the CRS riot police had lain in wait for them at the entrances to métro stations after a peaceful demonstration in favour of Algerian independence that had included women and children; some were beaten to death with truncheons, others dragged off in police vans and thrown into the Seine. That night I witnessed a number of such atrocities. It was hardly surprising that we idealized these people, that we regarded them as our purity. But the revelation of their brutal violence, the hatred these 'brothers' bore each other, suddenly forced me into silence. And so I kept the story to myself and wrote nothing.

When Fanon returned from the USSR, his health was worse. He was given little time to live, but it had been agreed that he would be admitted to Bethesda Hospital in Washington, where specialists hoped to do better than their Russian counterparts. It was easy for me to persuade Sartre to see Fanon, and it was I who organized their meeting in Rome in 1961, which coincided with a stormy, historic meeting of the CNRA (*Conseil national de la révolution algérienne*) in Tripoli at which the decision was being taken whether or not to continue negotiations with the French. Simone de Beauvoir and I went to meet Fanon at Rome airport; we had booked a room for him at our hotel and the three of us had dinner with Sartre on the first night. At this point something unthinkable, something unheard of happened: Sartre, who spent every morning, every afternoon writing, whatever the circumstances or the weather (he wrote in Gao in Mali in 50°C heat), who never compromised about his work schedule – he would never deviate from his schedule, nothing justified his not working – now Sartre stopped work for three days to listen to Fanon. Simone de Beauvoir did likewise. They felt as I had done in El Menzah. Fanon communicated a sense of urgency to all those he spoke to: he was literally in the grip of death and he knew it (leukaemia would take him six months later), there was a feverishness in the way he spoke, his words burned like flames. And he was also a gentle man whose delicacy and warmth were contagious. So he began to talk about the Algerian revolution, and about Africa, as he had done with me, in precisely the same terms. I will not recount it again. He was persuasive, convincing, it was impossible to raise objections, in the face of his words every objection seemed trivial. It is impossible to object to a prophet's trance. We now know that the real Africa is not the Africa of Fanon's dreams, that it has not managed to bypass our Middle Ages. The real Africa is Rwanda, the genocide of the Tutsis, it is the Congo, Liberia, Sierra Leone, Darfur and others. Horror seems to slowly pervade the whole continent, not sparing Algeria. The French may have become a constituent in the identity of Algerians, even as they fought against France. Once the French had left, the Algerians found themselves completely hobbled on the inside. Hobbled and lame.

The fact remains that, for three whole days, Sartre did no work. We listened to Fanon. He talked about Angola, about Holden Roberto, the head of UNITA who was supported by the Americans and later was assumed to have been a CIA agent, a traitor, a sworn enemy of the MPLA (Popular Movement for the Liberation of Angola), which rules the country today. Fanon liked Holden, they were friends. But he also talked about Aimé Césaire, Caribbean literature, and of his experiences as a doctor in the psychiatric hospital in Blida. Those three days were exhausting, physically and emotionally. I never saw Sartre as charmed, as captivated by a man. It went without saying that he would write the preface for *Les Damnés de la terre*, the manuscript of which Fanon had brought to give him. Then he left us, heading for Washington.

We wrote to each other and, realizing that his health was not improving, I decided to go over and see him one last time. I had talked with his wife Josie on the phone. He was very ill, she said, the doctors were giving him one transfusion after another but his pain was worse, there were moments when he almost succumbed to psychosis, accusing the doctors of transfusing white blood to hasten his death. I had my ticket for Washington, I was supposed to take the plane at ten the following morning when I got a call from Josie in the middle of the night to say, 'There's no point in your coming now; he has just died.' It was 6 December 1961. I was in such denial about his death, I think, that I decided to go anyway. I arrived in Washington to a memorably cold winter and spent two days talking to Josie, two days walking with her along the banks of the frozen Potomac.

Fanon's remains were repatriated to Tunisia and, six days after his death, he was interred in a provisional grave between Ghardimaou and the Moriceline – where I had been – as an ALN squad fired a salute. Everything moved very quickly: the Évian Accords were signed shortly afterwards and it became possible, with the consent of the administration, to visit Algerian prisoners in jail. This was how I came to spend a whole afternoon in Fresnes Prison with Mohamed Boudiaf, one of the 'historic leaders' whose plane had been hijacked in mid-air by French forces. This exceptionally intelligent man was assassinated in Bône in 1992 when, after years of exile, he was asked to return as head of state. I spent another afternoon with Ahmed Taleb Ibrahimi, a man of great charm but an intractable Islamist, future Minister for Education and later Minister for Foreign Affairs. The prisoners enjoyed considerable autonomy within Fresnes Prison. After they were freed, we took them in for several days. Taleb, as I have mentioned, stayed with my sister Évelyne; others stayed with me. Simone de Beauvoir attempted to persuade them to abandon polygamy, and they let her talk.

The ceremony of independence took place in Rabat and I was among those invited. The whole of revolutionary Africa was in attendance: Dos Santos from Mozambique, representatives from Angola, Amílcar Cabral from Portuguese Guinea, Vergès, obviously. Ben Bella and Boumediène reviewed the troops. The former made a very short speech to the *djounoud*: 'You are our blood.' It was clear that in this fractured, complicated brotherhood, everyone was keeping a watchful eye on everyone else. Indeed, it was not long before Boumediène, the tall redhead, deposed Ben Bella. The latter was very friendly towards me, calling me 'my brother'. But a few short weeks later, in one of his first speeches as head of state, he suddenly announced that the newly created Algerian Republic was planning to send to the Middle East, not emissaries as Abdelaziz Bouteflika had assured me, but 100,000 troops to liberate Palestine. For me, it was over: I had thought it was possible to believe both in an independent Algeria and the state of Israel. I was wrong.

Before Ben Bella's thunderous pronouncement, I had wanted to see Josie Fanon once more and had travelled to Algiers to do so. (I have never since set foot in independent Algeria.) Josie gave me a warm welcome. She was living with a high-ranking official in the Algerian security services who was madly jealous but seemed to make her happy, to make her laugh. She had become his mistress during Fanon's long stays in hospital: as I had learned in Ghardimaou, 'sisters' could not be left without a man. I stayed for three days, but it was impossible for me to have a private conversation with her since he never left the apartment for a moment. The weather was very hot, the sea nearby was tempting, and I suggested we go for a swim. We piled into his car and, teeth clenched and eyes spitting fire, he drove at breakneck speed. When we got to the beach and Josie started changing into her swimsuit – I took great care to turn away – I saw out of the corner of my eye that he stretched out his arms to form a windbreak, thereby shielding from view every inch of the white flesh of his concubine. Back in Paris, I recounted my brief trip to Castor, telling her that Josie Fanon was being held captive by her Algerian lover. Naturally, it was impossible for us to continue to be in touch. Later I learned that the chief of the Algerian security services had stolen Josie away from his subordinate and that she had promptly adopted the view of her new lover, that Israel had to disappear. When Maspero wanted to republish *Les Damnés de la terre*, she insisted that Sartre's preface be removed because he had, at my insistence, signed a petition supporting Israel in the turbulent weeks that preceded the Six Day War in June 1967. Although Maspero largely agreed with the swing of opinion of much of the left against Israel following the Israeli army's speedy victory and the sight of barefoot Egyptian soldiers fleeing across the Sinai, he held fast to his professional code of ethics as a publisher and did not give in to Josie Fanon's ultimatum and so the book was not republished. At least, not then and not by him.

Two or three years after the release of *Shoah* – in 1987 or 1988 – to my complete surprise, I received a long letter from Josie in Algiers in which every line seemed to be a cry for help. She said nothing about the past, but seemed to be profoundly lonely and all but destitute. She talked in friendly terms about Sartre and Castor, told me she was reading or rereading them, she said how much she regretted not having seen *Shoah* – in Algiers it would obviously have been impossible – and added that the few issues of *Les Temps modernes* she had managed to get her hands on were like an 'iron lung' to her, and asked me if I could arrange a free subscription for her (which of course I immediately did). She ended the letter with a postscript that was calmly informative and all the more distressing for that: 'Did you know I made a serious attempt to commit suicide five months ago?' How could I have known? I wrote back to her, suggesting we renew our old friendship and promising to do everything in our power to help her. I think I received two more letters in which it was clear that she was not telling me everything; they were evasive, she was obviously not free to write what she wanted.

In 1990, barely four years after Simone de Beauvoir's death, her unedited letters to Sartre were published by her adoptive daughter. Many of the letters included references to people who were still alive; I know that Castor would never have published them nor allowed them to be published like that. I know this because she told me so, because she states as much in her introduction to the edition of Sartre's letters published in 1983, and because I shared her life. Although she might at times have thought ill of those closest to her, the idea of hurting them was unbearable to her: I never knew her to miss an engagement with her mother, with her sister, with interlopers if she had agreed to meet them, or with pupils she had known long ago out of loyalty to some shared idea of a past. I understand the shock, the disbelief, the revulsion some may have felt when reading these letters they were never meant to see, in which, in the arrogant competitive letter-writing of their younger days, Sartre and Castor had ripped those closest to them to shreds. This did not preclude either delicacy or courtesy. In this, I subscribe completely to the distinction made by my friend Michel Tournier between 'effective language' and 'ineffective language': to say behind someone's back, 'He's a stupid bastard', has no consequences. To say to his face, 'Fuck off, you stupid bastard', is something very different. In one of her letters written in 1960, which I discovered in 1990, when the two volumes of her letters to Sartre were published, Castor, idly gossiping, told him about my brief stay with Josie Fanon and her jealous lover.

This became: 'Poor Lanzmann has just got back from Algiers where he was held captive by the Fanon woman'. About this, I would make three points: 1) as I mentioned earlier, in her neurotic rush to say everything, hear everything, recount everything immediately, Castor, anxious to move onto the next point on the agenda, didn't listen or misunderstood what was said to her. I caught her out in mishearings and misrepresentations like this a thousand times. I had said: 'Fanon's wife is being held captive by a jealous Arab'; this becomes: 'Poor Lanzmann . . . was held captive by the Fanon woman'. 2) Is 'poor', referring to me, part of effective or ineffective language? I am not saying one way or the other, I am simply observing that the letter was written in 1960, that we had just broken up and that anything that could be held against me might have been considered positive. I tend to think that in this case 'poor' was intended as compassionate. Twenty-three years later, in 1983, she would dedicate to me the two large volumes of Sartre's letters to her: 'To Claude Lanzmann with all my love. Simone de Beauvoir.' 3) The casual 'Fanon woman' and the confusion of roles in the captivity are much more serious. I was caught in a difficult dilemma: I knew how fragile Josie was, I knew that she read *Les Temps modernes,* read everything by and about Sartre and de Beauvoir. Should I stay silent, hope that she might not notice this minor reference or, on the contrary, alert her and by my words neutralize the pain an absurd letter written thirty years earlier might cause her? Aware that either course of action was a serious responsibility, I weighed the two. For too long. Some weeks later a friend, a member of the editorial committee, who had just come back from Algeria, asked me, using almost exactly the words Josie herself had used in her letter to me after her long silence: 'Did you know Josie Fanon just committed suicide?'

Chapter 16

The early 1960s were a critical time for me in both my personal and my professional life. Though I was working hard at *Les Temps modernes*, I had become something of a star journalist in the Lazareff group, the most important press group in France at the time. After my article on the Dalai Lama, Hélène Lazareff had asked me to write a monthly column for *Elle*, a background piece on world events, or on books, writers or actors. I was given complete freedom, I decided which articles I signed my name to and which I wrote under the pseudonym – chosen on a whim one night while putting an article to bed – in a brutal surge of Christianization: 'Jean-Jacques Delacroix', Jean-Jacques almost certainly after Servan-Schreiber, and Delacroix after St John of the Cross, or perhaps after the painter Eugène. But whether I was Delacroix or Lanzmann, I worked with the same meticulousness, the same conscience: I am not ashamed of any of the pieces I published under the name J-JD; in most cases, I could have swapped the names round, although some articles – typically psycho-sociological reports about love and sex, such as the Kinsey Report – could only have been written by Delacroix, in spite of the effort they cost me and my alter-ego. On the other hand, more than once, articles commissioned by *Elle* and considered a little too hard-core for the average female reader were published by *France Observateur* where, after I agreed to some cuts, they were given the entire back page. I'm thinking of, for example, the speech Malraux made at the Acropolis: in spite of my genuine admiration for him, I wrote a rather vicious article mocking the preposterous idea behind this *son et lumière* at the Parthenon, with the impatiently oracular voice of an orator seeming to unite Général de Gaulle and Piero della Francesca. It was Hélène Lazareff herself who took me to Athens in the first Caravelle that Air France put into service. I was surprised, when we arrived, to be greeted by pretty and comely young maidens, all from the upper echelons of the French aristocracy, who dragged me off forthwith to meet 'the prince', whose title was whispered with a deference worthy of the *ancien régime*. And prince indeed he was – it was Jean de Broglie, a rotund corpulence, clearly a political schemer, this *son et lumière* being but the tip of an extremely shady iceberg. Some years later, the prince was assassinated in the middle of Paris in broad daylight, which caused a terrible scandal. '*Plus jamais Agadir*', which also appeared on the back page of *France Observateur*, was another example of my adherence to my one rule. At three o'clock on the night of 29 February 1960 the phone rang and the anguished voice of Hélène Lazareff woke me with a start: 'Claude, there's been a terrible earthquake in Agadir, they're saying there may be tens of thousands dead, you have to get on the first plane.' I left for Casablanca that morning – it was my first visit to Morocco – hired a car and, by following the Atlantic coast, managed to cover the 600 kilometres of unfamiliar roads to Agadir at breakneck speed. The ground was still shaking with after-shocks from the quake when I arrived. It was truly terrifying, the whole city had crumbled and dozens of the surrounding villages been reduced to rubble, which had already begun to stink in the heat of the day. I joined a patrol of French marines from the escort ship *La Baise* who, with grapnels and makeshift tools, were trying to free those buried from the vice-like grip of the stone. The crown prince, Hassan II, had set up a huge royal tent in the middle of a field far from the buildings and was leading a number of Moroccan army units with forceful authority, while the French colonials bewailed their fate, conflating two disasters, political and natural: the sultan's return from his exile in Madagascar, heralding as it did the end of the good years of the French protectorate, and the earthquake. '*Plus jamais Agadir!*' – 'Never again Agadir' – they raged, muttered and shouted defiantly around the prince's tent. I spent three days there, then, heading north, I stopped on the coast some thirty kilometres outside the ruined city, stripping off, unable to bear the stench of my clothes and my body any longer, running into the sea where I tried in vain to purify myself. I was almost naked as I drove back to Casablanca where I might find a hotel room, a bath, soap, shampoo and clothes to buy. When I got back to Paris, I wrote '*Plus jamais Agadir*' for *Elle*, only for it to be published by *France Observateur*, to the great regret of Hélène: she had given in to the pusillanimity of the editor who stupidly felt the article was too political.

A week before the earthquake, Sartre and Simone de Beauvoir had left for Cuba at the invitation of Carlos Franqui, editor of the weekly *Revolución*, Cuba's largest-circulation magazine. They stayed there until 20 March. The previous year, Castro and the *barbudos* had seized power, forcing the dictator Fulgencio Batista to flee the country. It was impossible not to love Cuba then – all those who made the trip, everyone from Kouchner to Ania Francos, were equally enthusiastic – and Sartre was no exception. I remember his return, his seriousness, his feeling of kinship with all the Cubans he had met, from twenty-five-year-old ministers to illiterate peasants cutting sugar cane, and Castro himself, of whom he spoke as he would of himself four years later at the end of *Les Mots*, the book that won him the Nobel Prize that he declined: 'A whole man, composed of all men and as good as all of them and no better than any.' But what I remember most was Sartre's clear-sightedness: his friendship and admiration, his approval for what was happening in Cuba, did not blind him. He told me that he had said to Castro, despite his energetic denials, on several occasions, 'The terror lies ahead of you.' Let us not forget: in that important year of 1960 (the Manifesto of the 121, the Jeanson trial, Sartre's meeting with Fanon, his trip to Brazil in August followed by a second, brief, trip to Cuba in October), he published *Critique de la raison dialectique,* with its trenchant analyses of the fleeting, liberating moment in every revolution – what he calls *'la groupe en fusion'* ['the group-in-fusion'] – followed ineluctably by *'fraternité-terreur'* ['fraternity-terror'] – which in turn disintegrates to become institutionalized suspicion, bureaucracy and dictatorship. And yet Sartre wanted to help the Cuban revolution and make it known to as wide a public as possible. He decided he wanted to write about it not for his own publication, *Les Temps Modernes,* nor for a weekly, but for a popular daily newspaper with a large circulation. He settled on *France-Soir,* and I was asked to negotiate with Pierre Lazareff. *France-Soir* had never previously contemplated publishing Sartre, but it did so superbly, making no attempt to censor his piece, contenting itself with stating, in an introductory note, that the newspaper did not necessarily share all of the opinions of the author, all the while boasting that it had been chosen by the 'illustrious writer' to publish 'Hurricane over Sugar' (the title was Sartre's). Pierre Lazareff, who knew his job, told me he had rarely read a piece of such power, and this too won him over. With his permission, and that of Sartre, I edited the piece into sixteen instalments that appeared daily as full-page (sometimes double-page) articles from 28 June to 15 July 1960. I chose the headings and the subheadings, always with the approval of Sartre and the editor of *France-Soir.* I don't know whether such courtesy, such collaboration and such freedom would be possible nowadays. For the reasons I gave in issue 649–50 of *Les Temps modernes* (April–May–June 2008), Sartre's reportage never became a book and remained buried for forty-eight years, until a researcher undertook to transcribe the newspaper's microfiche copy in the Bibliothèque Nationale. Reading it again I was struck, as I had been the first time, by its literary elegance, its depth, its intelligence, its honesty. I decided to republish it.

Listing all the actors and actresses about whom I wrote articles for *Elle* during those years would be tedious unless I went into detail.

The simplest thing would be to reread the articles – perhaps I will publish them in an anthology one day. With Sophia Loren, born Sofia Scicolone, at six in the morning in the kitchen of her apartment in Rome, the only hour when it was possible to avoid the prying, jealous presence of her mentor, Pygmalion, lover and soon-to-be-husband, Carlo Ponti; with Lollobrigida and her dazzling smile in her beautiful home on the via Appia Antica; or a forbidding pilgrimage across the paddy fields of the Po, with Silvana Mangano, who had agreed to return and face the attacks of the most ferocious mosquitoes on the peninsula, I celebrated Italian women. But I celebrated Americans too, and all the French actresses.

Every Sunday, on their vast estate in Louveciennes, the Lazareffs gave an elaborate lunch, inviting the jet-set, politicians, and a number of contributors to the various magazines and newspapers in the group. Hélène, like Pierre, was truly in touch with what was happening in the world, and more than once lunch was interrupted when it was decided I should leave immediately on some bizarre assignment. Pierre's nickname was 'Pierrot les bretelles' – 'Pierrot in braces' – since at the table he rarely wore a jacket. I can still see him, thumbs hooked into his braces, fingers drumming on his puny chest, glasses pushed up onto his balding pate, suddenly leaping from his chair like a demon, dashing from the table because someone had whispered some piece of news that had just come in, then coming back with a smile on his face – his greatest pleasure was to be first with an important scoop, to be able to announce it. One day he came back to the table, his face like that of a serious child, and at the top of his voice proclaimed, 'There's a Russian orbiting the earth!' The man sitting on my right said curtly, 'That's just propaganda.' This was Georges Pompidou, future Prime Minister, future President of the Republic, but at the time senior executive of the Rothschild Bank; nowadays he would be called its CEO.

At the end of one of these lunches, Hélène came up to me and said, 'Claude, you're the only person who can do something, you need to leave at once for Saint-Paul-de-Vence, Simone Signoret is all alone there at the hotel La Colombe d'Or and desperately needs help, we need to launch a counter-attack, to convince everyone in Hollywood that there's nothing going on between Montand and Marilyn Monroe, that they're friends with a great professional regard for each other, nothing more.' A tough brief, Mission: Impossible, barely compensated for by my delight at returning to La Colombe d'Or, a paradise I had discovered shortly before on another assignment for Hélène when, overnight, all the paintings in the prestigious *auberge*, the Picassos, the Mirós, the Légers, the Braques, had been stolen by professional thieves intimately familiar with the comings and goings there. Paul Roux, who had founded the establishment, had been a friend to painters and a painter himself, creating this unique collection through donations, purchases, exchanges – he had provided hospitality for unknown, undernourished geniuses, who thanked him with paintings. Paul Roux passed away before my first visit, so I never got to meet him, but I was welcomed by his very elderly wife, Titine, who always dressed in black like a Sicilian widow and sat by the stove at the entrance, keeping an eye on everything. But I particularly remember her son, Francis, a jumble of qualities: intelligent, handsome, open and cunning, with a formidable sense of dynastic responsibility; he not only proved to be an unrivalled negotiator with the thieves, succeeding in recovering the stolen paintings, but he also oversaw the expansion, development and modernization of the *auberge* without sacrificing any of its original charm. The dynasty still exists and it is now his son, François, who brings to the task all his father's virtues together with his own; he has the same kindness, the same sense of organization, which, though it appears casual, runs like a well-oiled machine, his is an iron fist in a velvet glove, smiling and stoic when the family was struck by tragedy. Even now, after so many years, it is always a great pleasure to go back there, for a reason as simple as it is rare: there is no distinction between the guests and the numerous staff, all express an easy kindness, which is like a sense of family. I spent two days with Signoret, her face haggard, listening as she effortlessly lied to me; I spent the whole night writing, claiming that I knew from an employee at the telephone exchange in Saint-Paul that there had been a constant stream of phone calls from Bungalow 20 at the Beverly Hills Hotel in Los Angeles to Room 3 at La Colombe d'Or, day and night, because of the time difference. All in all, I did what I could for Simone, and I too lied through my teeth so that she would not lose face. After that, she thought of me as a friend, I became her favourite writer; in fact, when I got back to Paris I had to fob off Hélène, who was determined to send me to Hollywood to be near Marilyn and Montand. Over the decade, I must have written a dozen articles about Simone Signoret, and I will never forget the week that I spent with her at the Savoy Hotel and the Royal Court Theatre in London. Alec Guinness had persuaded her to play Lady Macbeth in English before the most snooty traditionalist audience in the world. It was clear to me from the first rehearsal that she was heading for disaster: aside from her French accent, which her efforts to overcome simply magnified, she just did not have what it took to play Shakespeare. I made no attempt to hide my sense of foreboding, I begged her to cry off, but she was brave and stood firm. Indeed, the disaster unfolded – never were reviews so vicious; it took her some time to recover.

I met them all, wrote about them, and I can say without vanity that I helped some of them to make a qualitative leap in their careers. Bardot confided in me her eternal, undying love for each new boyfriend; Jeanne Moreau lounged by an emerald swimming pool in Cuernavaca in Mexico that some hopelessly besotted American lesbian strewed with fresh rose petals every morning; Ava Gardner in Madrid, still sublime but already an alcoholic, on the set of 55 Days at Peking; Richard Burton and Liz Taylor in Sardinia for a Joseph Losey film, who retired each evening to a yacht, their shouts and death threats booming around the decks until dawn as they chased each other – they were truly Shakespearean – each vowing that the other would not live to see another day; Gary Cooper in his Bel Air villa, tall, handsome, poignant, marked and almost mute, already eaten up by cancer. How could I forget Martine Carol, Michèle Morgan, Juliette Gréco, Madeleine Renaud, Edwige Feullière, Delphine Seyrig? And the men: Michel Piccoli – whose best man I was at his wedding to Juliette Gréco – Sami Frey, François Périer, Curd Jürgens, Lelouch, Aznavour, Gabin, Belmondo, Antoine, Gainsbourg – and that's not the half of them. I wrote about almost every subject: the Pope's first visit to the Holy Land; the discovery by a Dutch–American archaeological team of Çartan, a forgotten, Biblical city in the Jordan Valley complete with a queen's diadem and jewels (the piece began: 'The queen had been waiting for three thousand years, so with no time to lose I jumped on the first flight'). I wrote about the riddle of Tutankhamun's treasures; tragic events in Alpine ascents; mime and Marcel Marceau – who was effusive once you got him to open his mouth; and the great Raymond Devos, with his huge barrel chest and his way of throwing his arms up wide then bringing them forwards slowly, a movement he learned when using cheesewire to cut slabs of butter in his first job, in a dairy.

One day Pierre Lazareff called me into his vast office on the rue Réaumur and asked if I would be the famous Captain Cousteau's ghostwriter, and assist him in writing a book about his experiment in underwater living off the coast of Marseille. Needless to say, only Cousteau's name would appear. My role was strictly confidential and I would receive no royalties. When the job was done, I would be paid a bonus in addition to my salary. It was a paltry sum, as I recall, but I agreed to everything. I boarded the *Calypso* in Marseille – the first *Calypso* – where I was greeted by Madame Cousteau – the first Madame Cousteau – and introduced to the divers, who were devoted to their master body and soul. He himself eventually arrived, trailing a pack of photographers and TV reporters in his wake. After they had left, I introduced myself; he was friendly but cold. The experiment, he explained, was to begin the following day: a test house had already been built thirty metres underwater. Falco, the main diver, and his team had already made several dives transporting everything that was needed for a stay of a week, perhaps two, including oxygen tanks that ensured a constant supply of air. Eventually, Cousteau asked me if I had ever been scuba diving before and when I said, 'No, only free diving', but that I was eager to try, he entrusted me to Falco, a friendly, stocky man from southern France who had already made several deep dives to test gases other than oxygen, including sophisticated mixtures. The following day we made a twenty-metre dive; before we did so, he explained to me that it was vital I stop on my way back to the surface, respecting the necessary decompression stages. I found diving easy and a little intoxicating, captivated, perhaps, from my first attempt by the call of the deep. But I disregarded Falco's advice and shot back to the surface without stopping, like an arrow, which resulted in bleeding from my nose and ears. Luckily, Cousteau was not aboard at the time and I set myself to studying the decompression tables. I spent a whole day and two nights in the undersea house, while Cousteau, a great communicator, made two brief visits, but for the most part spent his time on the deck of the *Calypso* surrounded by cameras and microphones, being filmed from every angle, discussing science with Falco in terms easily comprehensible to the layman, asking him how comfortable we were, since the purpose of the experiment was to prove that it was possible to live for long periods in a pressurized environment, moving easily about the house, entering through a series of airlocks, so there was no need for oxygen tanks. I must admit that I did not sleep a wink on either of the two nights I spent in the underwater paradise and, when I came back to the surface, I was exhausted and suffering from violent headaches. The experiment over – and utterly conclusive according to Cousteau, who immediately sent out press releases to that effect – I had to begin writing. Cousteau set me up in a house he owned in Sanary. I was alone there. He assigned me a small study where I worked like a maniac, day and night, surrounded by scholarly tomes. I had become an expert on decompression tables, stops, gas mixtures, and since I

361

have a naturally epic writing style, I tried to make the story, which was really nothing more than a publicity stun, into a heroic adventure, inspiring and full of promise. Cousteau, who was living nearby in another of his houses, kept a close eye on me, came over every evening to see how I was getting on, and had me read aloud what I had written. 'It's much too good,' he said over and over, 'it's not my style.' I had to convince him that the style of the article would only enhance his reputation. One evening, unable to bear being cooped up any longer, I slipped out through a ground-floor window and went to spend the night with Castor, who was waiting for me in Saint-Tropez. I planned to get back by the following morning.

Excerpts from the book were published in *France-Soir* and I quickly forgot that episode of my life. I ran into Cousteau several times after that; he never said hello, his long thin face was accustomed to surveying the horizon, and he simply did not notice me. When I accepted Pierre Lazareff's proposal, I had not realized that Captain Jacques Cousteau was the brother of Pierre-Antoine Cousteau, a Nazi collaborator who had been tried after the Liberation and only narrowly escaped facing a firing squad – there was undoubtedly a family resemblance. This was something I discovered only later at a session of the *Académie française* to which I had been invited by Erik Orsenna, who, having been chosen to take the seat held by the late Captain Cousteau, paid tribute to his predecessor before, in turn, tributes were paid to him. Accolades were the order of the day, not a word of misgiving was spoken, no one put his foot in it. As I left the *Académie*, the evening papers were just out and I bought a copy of *France-Soir*, which carried a despicable letter from Cousteau to his wife, written in the spring of 1942, in which he told her, in the crudest and most vulgar terms, 'Don't worry about the apartment, the Jews have all been swept up in the raids, we'll be spoilt for choice now.'

But I also wrote about other writers: Sartre, for a start, the Sartre who wrote *Les Mots*; about Claire Etcherelli and *Élise ou la vraie vie* [*Élise, or the Real Life*]; about Françoise Sagan on several occasions; about Albert Cohen's *Belle du Seigneur* [*Her Lover*] and later, *Les Valeureux* [*The Valiant*]. Albert and I became such firm friends that once a month I used to fly to Geneva, where he lived with Bella, his last wife, at 7 avenue Krieg. The apartment was divided into two halves, his and Bella's, connected by a large central living-room-cum-dining-room that they shared. I usually arrived at about ten o'clock to be greeted by Albert in his dressing gown, clutching an amber rosary that he fingered constantly. He showed me into his study, an extraordinarily bare room with stainless steel furniture and mirrors, and drawers that silently slid home on runners, locking automatically. He was seventy-four at the time and his greeting was always the same: 'Give me a cigarette.' He never had any; he suffered from bronchitis, and when I arrived, Bella, who had strictly forbidden him to smoke, always reminded me that cigarettes would kill him. So I would always start by firmly refusing, but I smoked; he would promise not to inhale, and to limit himself to one cigarette. So then we smoked together as he reeled off a list of celebrities who had called to tell him how much they admired him: 'François Mitterrand wants to set up a committee in support of my nomination for the Nobel Prize,' or 'Brigitte Bardot asked me to promise she could play Ariane, but Catherine Deneuve called to ask me the same thing . . .' At one point, on my first visit, he suddenly began to tremble and it was clear I had made some unforgivable mistake and, in retrospect, I can only agree with him: there were two ashtrays set out in front of us, one ordinary, the other a revolving, free-standing model. The first was for the ash, the most noble of substances, all the more so for us Jews, he said, given what was done to our people. But the cigarette butts, the quintessence of all that is foul, were not to be casually stubbed out in an ashtray, they had to disappear, to vanish into this revolving receptacle conceived for the purpose. I never committed such sacrilege again, yet every time I visited him I gave in to his pleading, and handed him a lethal cigarette. You must understand that Cohen was very isolated, he took no part in Parisian literary life, published a book once every ten years and desperately needed to be reassured of his genius: on my visits he read to me or had me read letters from admirers, articles paying tribute to him; I considered this normal, fair and touching precisely because I believed him to be a man of genius. Afterwards, we moved into the living-dining-room where Bella was waiting with a light, delicious lunch of smoked salmon. At this point, Albert would ask me what I had been doing, worry about my material needs, wonder whether I would have enough money to live on in my old age.

After lunch, he and I went back to the study with the sliding steel drawers and he gave me letters to read, from Sigmund Freud or from Chaim Weizmann, the first President of Israel, whose personal representative he had been when de Gaulle was in London during World War II. On one occasion he told me how, with considerable difficulty, he had managed to organize a meeting between Weizmann and de Gaulle in Carlton Gardens. Weizmann and Cohen were kept waiting rather too long: de Gaulle was late and Weizmann, impatiently checking his watch, said, 'If he isn't here in ten minutes, we're leaving!' Cohen had explained again how difficult the meeting had been to arrange, but Weizmann was adamant. After ten minutes, he got to his feet and announced, 'One does not keep the Jewish people waiting, they have suffered enough.' Who could have understood such overweening pride better than de Gaulle? But at that moment Albert began to tremble, just as he had when I had made the *faux pas* with the ashtrays: he could not bear for a document or a letter to be left lying around a second longer than was necessary, everything had to be put back immediately in its file and the file returned to the steel drawer. He himself best described this neurosis in *Belle du Seigneur*: 'A mania for order that took the place of happiness.' The remainder of our afternoons together, until I caught the last plane back to Paris, were spent in the most peculiar fashion: I read his works to him. This was not laziness, we both agreed that any commentary debased perfection and became paraphrase and, having an excellent memory,

I already knew whole passages of his books, learned by heart while reading to him. He would beam with pleasure, suggest a passage from another novel he wanted to hear, his hands moving ever faster over his prayer beads, signalling his happiness.

When he came to Paris to receive the *Grand Prix du roman de l'Académie française* – which cost him the Goncourt – I was determined that Simone de Beauvoir should meet him. I had persuaded her to read *Belle du Seigneur*, which she loved as much as I did. At the time I barely knew Albert, though I had written an article about him two weeks earlier. The meeting took place in his room at the Hôtel George V. He opened the door wearing an extravagant dressing gown, clutching his rosary. Castor complimented him warmly on his book even as it became clear that he had not read a word of any of hers. We cracked open the champagne. As we were about to leave, he opened the door of the bathroom, to which he had confined Bella, ordering her not to come out. She appeared for an instant to curtsy to Simone de Beauvoir, who was as dumbfounded as she had been when the FLN were defending polygamy to her. Years later – just before he turned eighty – the City of Geneva celebrated his birthday in a handsome museum belonging to a Jewish billionaire. Cohen sat next to Bella in the front row, toying with his beads, preparing to savour every word that the speakers would address to him. They were Marcel Pagnol, his childhood friend from Marseille, Jacques de Lacretelle, author of *Silbermann*, Jean Starobinski, an influential critic, Jean Blot, born Alexandre Blok, a Jewish novelist of Russian extraction, a translator with UNESCO who spoke several languages fluently and, first and foremost, Albert's dear friend, a Swiss man whose name I forget and, lastly, me. Pagnol, speaking of their shared childhood, was funny and spirited, the others, clearly more familiar than I was with the discreet charms of Jewish high society in Geneva and perfectly fluent in the emasculated language of the symposium, expurgated all mention of anything unseemly in his work, painting a portrait of Cohen that I entirely failed to recognize.

I was last to speak, and although I had prepared a speech, I decided not to read it and announced, by way of preamble, the subject of my address: 'I am going to speak to you about the role and function of the toilet, what is still referred as the WC, in *Belle du Seigneur*.' A shudder of horror ran through the audience, but I saw a twinkle of malicious pleasure in Cohen's eyes, who was sitting directly in front of me. I kept strictly to my topic, sprinkling my speech with examples and quoting extensively from the passages I mentioned earlier as evidence. Among a hundred possible examples: in the WC of Members B of the League of Nations, Adrien Deume dreams of one day reaching the dizzying heights of the marble urinals of the WC of Members A; it is sitting at home on the throne that the heartbreaking realization of his misfortune comes to him; in the final pages of the novel in which relentless cruelty is matched with great compassion, the lovers, imprisoned in an opulent palace on the Côte d'Azur, and each disposing of a private shitter, conceal their matter like some shameful sickness, each for the other attempting to be the embodiment of some perfect, perfumed idealism. Albert, I knew, hated idealism more than anything. The following day a number of newspapers mentioned my speech, bandying words such as 'scandal'; one or two approved of my intervention. Cohen told me, 'You are the only one who talked about me as I would have wished.'

Élise ou la vrai vie by Claire Etcherelli was a revelation to me. I remember the first line of the article I wrote for *Elle*: 'Claire Etcherelli has come to us from another world.' It was the world of the assembly line in a car factory, the story of an impossible love between a female factory worker and an Algerian man during the War of Independence. I also persuaded Simone de Beauvoir to read this book and we talked about it to anyone who would listen, campaigned for it, and shortly afterwards Etcherelli won the Prix Fémina. Etcherelli the factory worker was a born writer; she lived in poverty with her two sons in a room on the rue du Chateâu and, when I first visited her, had barely enough to keep the place warm. Michel Drach, a film director married to the actress Marie-José Nat, immediately wanted to adapt the book, with his wife playing the lead role, and he suggested that I write the screenplay. I told him that I thought it would be difficult and I would need some time to think. The plot was undoubtedly strong, well constructed and would make a real tear-jerker of a film. But to me the great strengths of the book lay elsewhere: how a factory worker, in order to describe the tedium, the mindlessness of factory work, becomes a writer; how, in order to tell the truth, one must, in a sense, become a false witness, since her colleagues, male and female, consider their lot to be in the nature of things and feel no need to rebel. It is this change in status, as much as the story itself, that seemed to me to be the true subject of the book and hence the film. But Drach was in a hurry. 'The next meeting of the *Centre national de la cinématographie* financial support committee is a month from now,' he said. 'You've got one month to write the screenplay, but after that there's all the time in the world to do rewrites.' So I wrote the first draft to his deadline, sticking as closely as possible to the book, but Drach had no intention of keeping his word: he shot the film the moment he got the grant. It is a good, moving film, with an actress of considerable talent, but what is most important in the book is missing on the screen. After a screening he arranged for me on the eve of its release, I asked him to take my name off the credits. He refused, we quarrelled, but I think my name is still there in the credits.

As soon as the secretary of *Les Temps modernes* retired, we suggested to Claire that she take over. She managed this crucial position ably and tactfully, while she went on writing her books, but when we co-opted her to the editorial committee she still had a tendency to consider us as tough factory 'management', and preferred to return to the workers on the 'shopfloor' as the periodical's secretary, which put her in the best possible position since now she knew us from within and without. When she was not mistrustful, she was the most adorable of women, but her suspiciousness grew back like the Hydra's heads, forcing us into an endless series of decapitations.

Theatre too was like a drug to me during those years. I had always loved it, but this addiction was a very different thing, it meant seeing the same play with the same actress every night for as long as the play ran, not wanting to see any other play. This brings me back to Judith Magre, my first love, as I have mentioned, whom I had lost fifteen years earlier and met again by accident on the rue des Saints-Pères while I was renting the apartment of the German actor Peter van Eyck. Hélène Lazareff was sending me on an urgent assignment to Madrid to spend a few days with Ava Gardner, and Judith insisted on coming with me. After a week of shared Spanish passion, she once again insisted – drastic measures and ultimatums were her way of relating to people – that I sort out my life within a week or never see her again. I did as she ordered, although it was very painful for the woman I left, as it was for me. My life with Judith was thus strained from the first by the weight of my guilt, which I assuaged by going to the theatre every night to see her act – usually the Théâtre National Populaire at that point in time. I always observed a very precise ritual: I first went to her dressing room in the bowels of that massive grim edifice via a labyrinth of stairs and corridors, usually running into Georges Wilson, the director who had succeeded Jean Vilar as head of the TNP, who was constantly cursing the vastness of the theatre and of the stage and threatening to resign, none of which prevented him continuing to stage magnificent productions there for years. I sat with Judith as she put on her make-up and costume, her stage-fright mounting until it was almost hysteria. This was how she psyched herself up for her entrance, which I watched, heart pounding, sitting in the stalls at the dress rehearsal alongside the most fearsome critics in Paris, whose pronouncements decided the fate of the piece, made or broke careers. I admired Judith as an actress, her edgy bearing and perfect diction, her abrupt shifts of tone and rhythm, her irony and tragic power, a unique combination that would later earn her three separate Molières for best actress. I watched her with both the eye of a lover and of a professional, since I not only helped her learn her lines, but sometimes analysed them for her, or with her. At school, I had loved doing critical analysis in the French style – before the advent of the lobotomy of structuralism – and I taught Judith what I had learned. Then when I went backstage to her dressing room on her evenings of triumph, when I had added my own praise to the thunderous applause of the audience, she would regularly greet me with a gloomy, unconditional, 'I was shit, wasn't I?' This was the verdict she invariably gave after performances where she had been truly outstanding: *Mr Puntila and His Man Matti*, *King Lear*, Euripides' *The Trojan Women*, which Sartre, at my request, had adapted for her, *Turandot*, *Nicomède*, *Children of the Sun*. To me Judith was equally exhilarating on television, in *Bajazet* where she played Roxane, in *La Double Inconstance*, *Antony and Cleopatra* or *Huis clos*.

I don't know whether I answered the question I had been asking myself: why this addiction, why this need to see her every night, to jump up and rush to her dressing room at the intermission if her performance was not as good as the previous night, to subject her to my valid criticisms so that in the second act she could reach the sublime heights I knew her capable of? Every performance of a play is different from one night to the next, differences that only I and the actors were aware of, but to which I had become so attuned that even an infinitesimal difference in a gesture, a tone of voice, became absurdly important, and I was transformed, at once without my knowledge and with complete lucidity, into an implacable yet bedazzled spectator. This is the very definition of addiction. I loved the actors and the actresses, the world of the theatre, which was revealed to me anew every day. Everyone became so accustomed to me trailing in Judith's wake, to my comments and my thoughts, that sometimes a sort of mutual aid developed between me and the directors. Perhaps I was taking the first steps in the career I was to follow later, in a different field. I have happy memories of the Festival d'Avignon. Judith, who had played Cassandra in both the *Oresteia* and *The Trojan Women*, now played the role again, directed by Jean Vilar

369

in Giraudoux's *La Guerre de Troie n'aura pas lieu* [*The Trojan War Will Not Take Place*]. The central courtyard of the Palais des Papes under a starlit sky, the actresses' dressing room where I would go during the interval to congratulate them, captivated by the beautiful thighs of Claudine Auger, the exquisite food – tapenade, anchovy paste, rosé wines from Provence – the *mas* where we stayed at Villeneuve on the far bank of the Rhône, the joyful sound of constant backfire from the Triumph convertible I had bought on a whim especially for the trip; today, all these things constitute a single memory in which every detail inextricably conjures and signifies every other.

My marriage to Judith meant becoming part of a real French family. I had always envied other people's families, proper families, which to my mind implied order and beauty, *luxe, calme et volupté*. Judith and I married in a mad rush, almost secretly, at the town hall of the 6th *arrondissement*. At some point I had to be introduced to my in-laws, the Dupuis family, industrialists in the Haute-Marne, inventors of agricultural machinery, owners of a large factory, a family of good Catholic stock, with six children – four girls, two boys. In order to welcome the young bridegroom of thirty-eight summers, they all gathered for a Sunday lunch, and Clotilde, Judith's mother, tall, slender, pious, on almost cheerfully intimate terms with death, and an unrivalled cook, had prepared a sumptuous yet down-to-earth wedding feast. I played my part as the son-in-law, a role that I played more easily as the hours passed and I became increasingly fond of them; my initial play-acting soon gave way to naturalness. It was my father-in-law René who showed me around Montier-en-Der, the family mansion, and took me on a tour of the factory as though it were mine, seemingly ready to show me the books, introduce me to the managers and the factory workers, talk to me about his plans, his problems. The mansion had a billiard room and René, a gifted player, taught me the game over the course of countless frames, without ever patronizing me. He played billiards in all seasons; in autumn and winter he hunted in the immense wooded estates of nearby Colombey-les-Deux-Églises; in summer he went to Chamonix, since he had climbed every peak and continued to climb. Aside from the billiard lessons, of which I remember nothing, I owe to him the pleasures of waiting, of imminence, standing *'ventre au bois'* – the rifle-stock against my belly – on a frozen trail, waiting for a herd of boar to charge, bewitched by the infinite, precise, poetic language of hunting – never fire at a wild sow 'followed by a singular of striped shoats'. I owe to him too my introduction to abseiling when I was over forty and the shift from theoretical mountaineering – at which, as we have seen, I excelled – to a genuine mastery of heights, learning not to tense my muscles crossing the slopes of Les Gaillands. These steep rocks are required training for budding climbers, and are difficult even for experienced climbers, and me, given my technical rating at grades 5 or 6. Over several summers, with René and his son, my brother-in-law François Dupuis, I climbed some of the easier *aiguilles* in Chamonix. The first was the Aiguille de l'M with its twin peaks: I remember the early morning hike from the cableway stop at L'Aiguille du Midi and my excitement as I reached the foot of l'M, touched the rockface already caressed by the rising sun, looking up to try and make out the summit I had to conquer. It was a wonderful conquest, so easy it felt somehow undeserved. My victory was put into perspective, however, on the ridge leading to the summit, when René showed me how simple my climb had been compared to his own conquests over the unforgettable craggy façade of rocks that towered over the valley, rolling out peak after peak. As I stood, absorbing its true measure, René, with the respect of the seasoned climber, recited the names of the peaks and the difficulties each of them posed: Petits Charmoz, Grands Charmoz, Le Grépon, the Charmoz-Grépon traverse, Le Peigne, and so on. Yet this did not lessen my euphoria and I split my head open on the way down: heroes always bleed.

My kinetic energy levels are high, probably excessive. A few months after this episode, Judith persuaded me to buy her an expensive dress in a shop on the rue François-Ier. We went there together and, since there were no parking spaces, I double-parked. While she was trying on the dress, asking my opinion so I would get my money's worth, I saw, out of the corner of my eye, a police van brake suddenly and the officers piling out and pouncing on their prey – my car – traffic tickets in hand. I headed for the door, intent on stopping them – I didn't run, I walked – but what I took to be the open door of the shop turned out to be a plate-glass window. I walked straight through it and as it shattered into a thousand razor-sharp slivers, my iliac artery was neatly severed by a shard of glass. My blood spurted out in cadenced pulses, Judith was running and screaming, the cops grabbed me and rushed me to the hospital, sirens blaring. This conjunction of police thoroughness, a gift to my wife and my boundless kinetic energy cost me dearly; I spent forty days in hospital, and ever since my left leg has always been weaker than my right.

The year after I climbed l'M, René Dupuis gave up mountain climbing. He had gone with a guide to scale the famous Peigne, a peak he had conquered many times, and one that has a number of dangerous sections that can only be crossed by a single leap, mustering every ounce of courage and physical strength. The climb took much longer than planned. 'Without the guide,' he told me when he got back, 'I would never have made it. There were several moments when he literally had to drag me. Mountaineering is over for me, I'm too old.' He made the announcement calmly, stoically, while the man he had hired every summer for years nodded gravely. He and I still went for long hikes up to the mountain huts, but it was not the same. With Claude Jaccoux, who was president of the National Union of Mountain Guides, I went on some classic climbs, some easy, such as the Arête des Cosmiques, others more arduous, such as the Tour Ronde or even the Midi-Plan – classed AD, *assez difficile* – a gruelling ascent over ice, snow and rock, negotiating steep seracs, glacial ridges, which he insisted we descend in a single, non-stop dash since the sun was beating down on the ice, which, weakened, crumbled behind us in a roar like a bomb blast, forcing us headlong onwards.

Midi-Plan runs from L'Aiguille du Midi to the mountain refuge of Le Requin. I had arrived from Paris by car late the previous evening and met up with Jaccoux near midnight in a bar in Chamonix. I was very fond of him, having known him mainly through literature and *Les Temps modernes* rather than mountaineering: he had given up teaching literature to devote himself entirely to skiing in winter and climbing in the Alps or the Himalayas in summer. He was extraordinarily handsome and his female clients fought over him fiercely. They rushed to see Claude returning from a day in the mountains, his pure face, his blond curls, his broad chest slung with ropes, pitons and karabiners. In the bar he told me, 'I'm setting off with an American tomorrow morning to do the Midi-Plan. If you like, I'd be happy for you to come along.' I said yes, not actually knowing what he meant by the Midi-Plan, not telling him I had no training, thinking only about the fact that Jeremy, the rich American, would be paying for the expedition. It was an unremitting seven-hour trek before we reached Le Requin, famished. Barely had we finished eating than Jaccoux left, some other clients having come up from Montenvers via the Vallée Blanche: he was taking them up a rockface where they were to bivouac for the night. It was summer, high season, and Jaccoux was fully booked. Jeremy and I left the mountain lodge to head back down the Vallée Blanche, climbing the steep slope of Montenvers to catch the train back to Chamonix, if we arrived in time; otherwise we would have to walk back – another seven kilometres' hike. We had no idea of the ordeal we were about to endure: aching and stiff from our climb to Le Requin, we headed down, slaloming between the crevasses of the Vallée Blanche, when we were caught in a terrible storm, the wrath of the gods, the sky like lead, the rain torrential, jagged lightning flickering all around, raging thunder booming and echoing throughout the valley. Drenched and blinded by the rain, surrounded by lightning, I suddenly realized that our ice axes might attract the lightning and I yelled to Jeremy, 'Alpenstock, alpenstock!', throwing mine as far from me as possible so he would do the same.

We reached Montenvers at nightfall; it would take us another three hours to reach the Hôtel Mont Blanc, where I was staying. My body ached so much that every movement was agony; I did not get up the following day, nor the day after; it was a week before I was back to normal. The weather was magnificent, and from my bed I saw Mont Blanc glittering through the window. I spent my time reading and my memory of those long hours of enforced rest is one of physical and mental release – the feeling of relief in my bones – spoiled only by news of the invasion of Czechoslovakia, Soviet tanks on the television, cruelly marking the end to the Prague Spring. It was August 1968.

A year later, July 1969; it is night, I am in a cramped, uncomfortable hotel room in Aber-Wrach in Brittany, writing an article about Jaccoux for *Elle* – a piece I had proposed. I have to finish by dawn no matter what, so that I can dictate my copy to the magazine before setting off for Chamonix where the whole Dupuis family is waiting for me with Jaccoux, who is determined to take me on some new adventure. But this night is like no other: tonight, on a tiny, crackling old TV set, barely visible through the interference, I watch the first moon-landing in history. I forget about *Elle*, about Jaccoux, about all the mountain peaks on earth, as the dialogue – clipped, devoid of emotion, technical, an exchange of numbers, codes, coordinates – between Neil Armstrong, whose voice sounds so close across the infinite void of space, and the flight director at NASA in Cape Canaveral in Florida eclipses everything, relegating earthly matters to the background. Apprehension mounts as the lunar module, like some curious gallinaceous bird with four spindly legs of flexible steel wire, carries two human pioneers towards the unknown, towards who knows which Sea of Tranquility. With each passing minute the tension grows more unbearable, a primal urgency gives the lie to the apparent calm, the detachment of the only two voices that can be heard. As Armstrong and his co-pilot engage the reverse thrusters, allowing them to reduce the moon's weak gravity to zero and delicately land the module, as they count down the number of feet separating them from the lunar surface, it is imminence itself. My heart stops beating. When, after a pause that seemed endless, after a long stationary shot of the module, Armstrong appeared in his white spacesuit and began to climb down the scant few steps of the ladder, setting his right foot on the surface of the dead satellite, when he said in his clear American accent the famous phrase, prepared and rehearsed so that he could plant it like a victory flag, 'That's one small step for man, one giant leap for mankind', I shed tears in tribute to the genius of humanity. Then I left my hotel room for the white sand of the deserted beach, plunging into the ocean. I swam with all my might. My article on Jaccoux and mountaineering was delivered on time.

Chapter 17

I realize, rereading the joyful chapter I have just completed, in the moment that I begin this one, that for a whole decade, between 1952, the year of my first trip there, and 1962, when the war in Algeria ended, Israel disappeared from my thoughts, or at least it faded into the background. I was completely occupied by my life with Simone de Beauvoir, travelling, discovering the world, earning my living, the anti-colonial campaigns, *Les Temps modernes*. Although I did not belong to a party – the committee meetings and responsibilities of professional political activism bored me to death – I was passionate about French politics, politics in the essential sense of the word that will doubtless be considered antiquated and outmoded today, now that the triumph of technocracy and expertise has blurred everything, masking the ineluctable reality of mankind's materiality. Back then, the class war existed, and having felt even as a child that to lose one's status could result in being abandoned by all one's friends, that there comes a moment when no one will help you, that it is possible to die of starvation, of cold, of loneliness, I was extraordinarily sensitive to anything that, to my eyes, concerned naked necessity, anything that exposed the violence underpinning all human relationships. When, a few short hours before going to the guillotine, Julien Sorel tries to calm his fears, quiet his emotions, contemplate life and death, he comes up with a phrase of sublime simplicity: 'Men who frequent salons never get up in the morning with the urgent question – What will I eat for dinner?' And a few lines further on, Stendhal allows Sorel to comment, 'There is no such thing as *natural right* . . . there are no *rights* until there is a law forbidding something or other on pain of punishment. Until there is a law, there is nothing *natural* but the lion's strength or the needs of someone who is hungry, who is cold – in a word, *necessity*.'

In June 1955, working-class riots at the Chantiers de l'Atlantique in Saint-Nazaire were brutally suppressed and many were injured. I decided to cover the story for *Les Temps modernes* and I spent an entire week there, rapidly developing a close bond with the supposed ringleaders among the union workers, those whom the management of the shipyard, adopting shock tactics, had suspended, leaving them penniless and isolating them from their comrades. Saint-Nazaire was a rather bleak town, completely destroyed during the war and then hurriedly rebuilt to the plan of a soulless grid. But I felt at home there, I liked these men, I lived a frugal existence, learned about the history of the shipyard, interviewed the labourers, the foremen, the engineers, wanting to find out everything there was to know about shipbuilding, amazed to see the way a vast seagoing vessel could grow, day by day, in the dry dock as hundreds of workers beavered away on every deck. It was clear that jobs here were insecure, and not just labouring jobs, but those of skilled craftsmen who took pride in their profession. Orders were scarce or non-existent, because of competition from Asia, and there were heavy redundancies, with many labourers thrown out of work. In spite of promises made, there had been no rise in salaries at the shipyards for a long time. Angry shopfloor workers circumventing the union had staged sit-ins in management offices. The unions declared a general strike in support of the grassroots movement. After a month the government resolved to break the strike by any means necessary. The union backed down and a number of workers who had fought heroically against the CRS invited me into their homes with their wives and their children, knowing they had been stigmatized for life. Their defeat was infinitely sad, it made my heart bleed.

My departure for Saint-Nazaire coincided with a special issue of *Les Temps modernes* published in May, entitled 'The Left'; I had written a very long article for it called 'The Man of the Left', which was preceded by a piece by Simone de Beauvoir on 'Right-wing Thought Today'. I had spent some time studying the Canut revolts, the uprising of the Lyon silk-workers in 1834, and I had been forcibly struck both by the overwhelming expression of the power of human need and the diffidence and indirectness of the workers' demands, and the incredible respect they showed to their oppressors and their representatives. No sooner had the slightest concession been made than they would shout, 'Long live the *Préfet*! Long live our father!', but any concession was just a sop to get them to drop their guard, allowing the right-wing owners to call in the army and mercilessly crush them. Fifty years ago the long march towards working-class consciousness and the formation of workers' organizations were not merely academic subjects – as the events in Saint-Nazaire attest – they were news, our reality, even if the seeds had already been planted for the strange and depressing world we know today in which man's inhuman indifference to man seems to be a fact of life, accepted as such, where casting the weak into the abyss of history seems to be taken for granted.

In spite of everything I knew, and everything I know now, of the black and bloody face of real Communism, in spite of my own experience of the cynicism and treachery of the PCF during the Resistance, in spite of my loathing for the show-trials in Moscow and Prague, for a long time the Soviet Union remained like a sky above my head, as it did above those of many men of my generation. This stems from the German invasion of 1941, from the extraordinary sacrifices made by all the peoples of the USSR, the victory of the Red Army at Stalingrad, which marked the decisive turning point in the war. We owed our freedom, in large part, to the USSR and, in spite of everything, to our minds it remained the cradle, the future, the assurance of mankind's emancipation. We discovered Marx in 1945, we were serious and passionate, history had to have a meaning, otherwise what point was there to living? What Sartre wrote in *Les Mots* about his atheism, 'a cruel, long-term business', I can use for the 'sky above my head': it was a long time before I gave up on utopia. I confess that Stalin's death brought tears to my eyes, not for the demise of a bloody dictator who had always left me cold, but because, reading his obituary in *France-Soir*, amid the litany of regrets and lamentations, I came upon a phrase that moved me deeply: 'The Soviet marines dip their battle flags . . .' Perhaps what I felt had to do with the words themselves, with the battle flags, I don't know. It was both real and fleeting.

The bellicose and, to me, astonishing pronouncements of Ben Bella not only forced me to break with Algeria, a country in which I had invested so much hope for brotherhood and reconciliation, but brought to the foreground the danger that Israel would have to face for a long time to come. What many people were content to dismiss as Arabic cant and rhetoric were words and threats that I took very seriously, believing that there would be no end to the hatred and irredentism until the Arabs' declared goal – the destruction of the Jewish state – had been attained. This appalling, malign fact was one that I had shied away from for so long, one that, extraordinarily, had not occurred to me on my first visit ten years earlier when my preoccupation with the metaphysical, or more accurately ontological, questions posed by its improbable existence had blocked out the properly existential threat to the young nation, which suddenly loomed large. The idea of a special issue of *Les Temps modernes* about the Arab–Israeli conflict was suggested to me by Simha Flapan, an Israeli leader of Hashomer Hatzair and a member of the kibbutz Gan Shmuel, a bastion of left-wing Zionism. Simha, a man of uncompromising gentleness, had been born in Poland and arrived in Palestine before World War II, and he devoted all his energies to fostering understanding between Israelis and Palestinians. The exodus of Palestinian Arabs when the state of Israel was declared in May 1948,

379

the attacks by Arab countries, the War of Independence, had all profoundly marked him; he was extraordinarily aware of the rights and wrongs on both sides. Skilfully handling people with a resolute calm, he devoted himself – through his journalism and his talent at the Israeli national sport of fundraising – to muster both goodwill and money to achieve his goals. He had just been named chief representative of Hashomer Hatzair in France and was revitalizing the Jewish pro-Israel left-wing, the *Cercle Bernard-Lazare* for example; he travelled widely, forming alliances with Arab journalists. Flapan truly was what one might call a man of influence. He introduced me to Ali el Saman, an Egyptian correspondent who charmed me with his vitality, his acerbic wit, his uncommon political astuteness and the warm friendship he professed for me. We became very close. Once Sartre approved the idea of a special issue of *Les Temps modernes*, Flapan organized an investigative trip to Israel for me to select the contributors for the Jewish section. Had I followed Flapan's wishes, I would have chosen entirely from the Israeli left, better yet from Hashomer Hatzair and its workers' party, Mapam; he was blind to everything else. But I realized that Flapan and his people represented a tiny minority in the country and that for such a project, on such a subject, all groups, including right-wing groups, should be able to express their opinions. In any case, as far as Israel is concerned, I have always been more susceptible to what unites Israelis than what divides them, to consensus rather than dissensus.

So I took a second trip and discovered an Israel that I did not know. I also managed to persuade Flapan to concede the validity of my position. Ali would be responsible for the Arab contributors. After long and finicky negotiations, it was agreed that the issue would be just a receptacle rather than a forum for discussion: Arabs agreed for the first time to appear alongside Israelis in the same publication, but only on condition that they would have the final say over the choice of contributors, their subjects and that there be no exchange of views. The issue would have an Arab section and a completely separate Israeli one, what Sartre, in his introduction, called 'passive contiguity'. In my own introduction I explained that even this contiguity had cost us considerable sweat and tears. I did not go into detail, but an Algerian writer, Razak Abdel Kader, who, on his own initiative, had sent me a remarkable article, was rejected for publication by Ali and the Arab contingent for coming too close to embracing the 'enemy' point of view. It was a case of take it or leave it; we capitulated and took it. By the same token, Maxime Rodinson, a French Jew of Polish Bundist origin, a Communist, a theoretical and visceral anti-Zionist, a scholar of Islam by profession, offered an eighty-page article to the Arab section entitled 'Israel, a Colonial Reality?' The Arabs insisted that this article should lead their section, and therefore the issue, since they had been allowed to fire the first shot.

This unprecedented project took two years to complete: with the exception of two articles, the issue, entitled 'The Arab–Israeli Conflict', was almost ready at the beginning of 1967. It ran to 1,000 pages and, against all odds, I had succeeded in ensuring that in each segment the number of articles, if not of pages, was equal. Apart from Rodinson's contribution, the Arabic articles – Palestinian, Egyptian, Moroccan, Algerian – were much shorter than those of the Israelis.

What I had intuited while we had been working together turned out to be true: Ali, too, was a man of influence, and his involvement in launching and realizing the project was like the fulfilment of a political mission entrusted to him by the Egyptian authorities. He told me that to celebrate the forthcoming release of the issue (his own article, he informed me, would be ready just before publication), Sartre, Simone de Beauvoir and I were invited to Egypt by Mohamed Hassanein Heikal, editor of *Al-Ahram*, the largest daily newspaper in Cairo, and a loyal personal friend of the *reis*, Gamal Abdel Nasser. The two-week trip was scheduled for March and was more or less an official visit, since it could not have taken place without Nasser's personal approval, which indicated the extent of Ali's influence. But this invitation, which pleased me, prompted one from Israel. The difference was that there was no Israeli Nasser, and Sartre would agree to go only at the invitation of the Israeli left, meaning Flapan and his friends.

I will not dwell on the Egyptian trip here – Simone de Beauvoir has told of it – which was both touristy and political, except to give a few brief impressions: the indescribable chaos of the Cairo Museum, the City of the Dead, the dazzling beauty of Luxor and the Valley of the Kings, the most exquisite tombs, closed to ordinary visitors, opened especially for Sartre; Aswan and its waterfalls, the formidable dam on the Nile planned and constructed by the Soviets, that high, broad wall of stone and earth – an 'embankment dam' – graceless but indestructible, which specialists contrast with an 'arch dam', whose ethereal grace can prove deadly if the planning engineers make the smallest error in calculation. And our flight upriver from the dam in a Cessna four-seater provided by the *reis* across the vast reservoir named Lake Nasser, so shimmering and inviting beneath the harsh southern Egyptian sun that I longed to dive in until the pilot told me that swimming was forbidden since the waters were infested with bilharzia. We landed at Abu Simbel, gateway to the Sudan, where the wonders of Aswan were being reinstalled, having been moved to make way for the dam. Aboard a felucca-restaurant moored on the banks of the Nile in Cairo, the most famous belly-dancer in Egypt whirls around our table as we dine with the editor of *Al-Ahram*, she takes my hand and leads me to the middle of the stage where I stand stock-still like a totem pole, Sartre, Castor and Ali watch as she gyrates her hips wildly, thrusting herself at me, offering herself, only to retreat. It goes on for a long time. After she finishes, she bows to Heikal, referring to him as '*Effendi*'. She is pure poetry.

Our audience with Nasser lasted several hours, causing a commotion in security, bustling and deferential whispers from the guards who led us through a labyrinth of doors to his offices. The 'free officer' who had deposed King Farouk, nationalized the Suez Canal, transformed the Tripartite Aggression of France, Britain and Israel into a political victory, proclaimed a United Arab Republic with Syria, and compelled most Egyptian Jews to leave the country – this 'free officer' turned out to be a tall, timid man who impressed by his soft voice and his dark handsome eyes, which seemed to sound his own depths even as they gazed searchingly at his interlocutor. In other words he seemed to meditate, confer with himself as he spoke, never repeating what he said. One knows when one is in the presence of a statesman. Nasser was one, certainly. I remember he gave a general overview of the situation, considered the terms of the conflict, the various possible solutions and why each in turn was impossible. He concluded with a hypothesis, formulated as a four-word question, 'So, war then?' And answering himself, 'But war, this is very difficult . . .' He congratulated us on the issue of *Les Temps modernes*, and Ali, who had a naturally dark complexion, flushed bright red with pride. I saw that his career had just taken a great leap forward. The *reis* was aware of everything, he knew exactly who I was, knew of my connections to Israel and several times – there could be no doubt about his ulterior motives – looked at me, addressing himself to me alone.

During our stay in Egypt, Sartre was clearly beset by an inner conflict. He had a very full itinerary – a plenary session at Cairo University, press conferences, meetings with writers, and so on – and he relaxed in the evening by drinking too much. We were staying at Shepheard's, a famous old hotel, and on more than one occasion Ali and I had to hold Sartre upright as he staggered back to his suite. He could not bear to be dependent on us and one night as we were carrying him back, even more drunk than usual, he started to insult us, his voice slurred, calling us 'queers', insinuating that we were the prime example of how to resolve the conflict. Ali, who was unfamiliar with Sartre's cantankerous, drunken ravings, could not believe his eyes or his ears. Since I was used to such behaviour, I reassured Ali that everything would be fine in the morning and that the great man would not remember a thing. Yet I did not like what I had heard. I spoke to Castor about it and she, like me, had noticed that Sartre was torn between his affection for our Egyptian hosts – who welcomed us with charm and sumptuous ceremony – his support for the Arab cause in general, and the unspoken anxiety aroused in him about our impending departure for Israel. I understood that I was a constant reminder of what was to come, like a statue of the Commendatore, a guardian of Israel, preventing him from truly enjoying the seduction of the Arab world and forcing him to maintain a certain objectivity.

The grand finale of this suppressed turmoil occurred during a visit to Gaza, then under Egyptian rule. Nasser had afforded us the use of a plane, which was filled with officials and journalists poised to note down our smallest reaction or comment on the horrors that were the reason for this side trip: the Palestinian refugee camps. The plane made a stopover at El Arish military base on the Mediterranean coast of the Sinai. There was no apparent reason for this stop, since the plane could easily have flown from Cairo to Gaza without refuelling. We were there for about half an hour, just long enough to witness a training flight of an Egyptian airforce MiG 21: this was clearly the motive for our stopover. It was a virtuoso display. I was struck by how tall and aristocratic the pilots looked. Who would have imagined, at that moment, that three months later, in a few short minutes, that very airfield, these very runways, those very planes would be destroyed together with most of the Egyptian air fleet and much of the Sinai and the Nile Valley, in a lightning strike by the Israeli airforce, launching a war that would last just six days, but change forever the face of the Middle East? In Gaza we were welcomed by the assembled Palestinian élite, whose leader at the time was not Yasser Arafat but Ahmad Shukeiri, who lost not only face but power as a result of the Six Day War. After that we were taken on a tour of the neat, clean streets of two refugee camps, mobbed by photographers, cameramen and microphones, deafened by the briefings of political commissioners in soft hats and the lamentations of Palestinian mothers as we passed. Sartre enjoyed the banquet that followed, which was as astonishing for the number of Egyptian and Palestinian guests – notables and landowners and all the well-heeled inhabitants of Gaza were in attendance – as for the number of dishes served. This meal, at which there was no alcohol, was truly a feast, and contrasted starkly with the wailing women we had seen that morning. A number of people spoke, each of the Palestinian speeches a call to arms, clearly implying that a war, even a world war, was preferable to any negotiated settlement. Sartre dared to respond with an extraordinary sincerity born of the indignation inspired in him by the camps, the banquet, the incendiary speeches. He spoke about the vastness of the Arab countries, the extraordinary wealth of some of them, his disbelief that they could leave the people of Jabailya or Dar El Bayla to rot, surviving on handouts from the United Nations Relief and Rehabilitation Administration – the product, he noted, of the very American imperialism they purported to despise – instead of marshalling Arab solidarity and doing something concrete, dealing with this cancer, whatever the eventual outcome of the conflict. I was completely in agreement with Sartre, yet I did not say so publicly, nor privately: I feared that such an expression of solidarity from me, rather than serving to appease, might make relations between us even more strained. But Ahmad Shukeiri's Palestinians in their trilby hats insisted that we travel closer to the enemy. When the banquet and the speeches were over, we were taken to the demarcation line of the 1948 armistice and shown the Israeli guardhouse. I felt oddly disoriented for I had been at that same guardhouse not long before, on the other side of the line, staring out at Gaza. I was the only person there who knew these places and could not resist pointing towards the horizon and naming the borderland kibbutzim we could see in the distance. I still have a photograph of the scene: in it I am standing next to Ali, behind Sartre and Castor, surrounded by Shukeiri's men, playing my role as guide to the hilt.

But there was no way to cross this border to go to Tel Aviv, barely sixty kilometres away, where people were waiting for us. To get to

Israel, we had no choice but to fly via Athens where we were to have dinner and spend the night. We arrived there from Cairo in the late afternoon. Sartre had brought only one book with him about Israel, which he obstinately leafed through during the meal in spite of my and Castor's shocked reproof: it was *Fin du people juif?* [*The End of the Jewish People?*] by the sociologist Georges Friedmann, who specialized in industrial relations. Eighteen months earlier Friedmann had published this radically anti-Zionist book, whose central thesis was that Israel had brought an end to Jewishness, which could only thrive and be expressed by the diaspora. The least that can be said is that Sartre was setting out on the second leg of what was intended as a journey of reconciliation with a very prejudiced bias. The balance of his affections was not equal. I told him this, Castor agreed with me, and at that moment I decided I would spend only a few days with them in Israel.

On our arrival, we were welcomed by joyous, democratic, congenial chaos. The Israelis who had invited us had done their best, but the means at their disposal were not equal to those of the Egyptian government. I became overtly angry with Sartre as Flapan attempted to outline the itinerary of our visit. An unimpeachable left-winger, Flapan had arranged a meeting with the army, a visit to a military base, a discussion with officers and soldiers. Sartre refused point blank: there could be no question of him meeting anyone in uniform, even a woman. It was an obstinate refusal even to try to understand Israel, and the vital role played by the conscript army in such a country in education, the melting pot of immigrants from around the world, the formation of a national identity, to say nothing of its primary, primordial mission: defence. It amounted to accepting a drastically reduced view of the country. I said as much to him, asked him who his judges were, what he was afraid of, but he clammed up and, to my distress and to the genuine sorrow of many officers who were both intellectuals and his readers, it was impossible to get him to change his mind. On the second day, the plan was to visit the Weizmann

Institute of Science and lunch with scientists of all disciplines. As we stepped into the vast laboratory in the biology department, its head, Michael Feldman, welcomed Sartre with the words, 'Monsieur Sartre, there are at least ten people in this room who would not have refused the Nobel Prize.' Here again, the atmosphere was strained; though these were not soldiers, according to Sartre they spoke English with a rather too-perfect American accent, a clear sign of a consubstantial imperialism.

I returned to France while Castor and Sartre continued the trip at their convenience with their guide, Ely Ben-Gal, a French Jew from Lyon, a member of the kibbutz Bar'am and of Hashomer Hatzair, and without me as a mentor daring to tell them what to think. It was the end of March 1967 and the issue of *Les Temps modernes* was about to be put to bed, but events began to overtake us, with every passing day Nasser's pronouncements became more bellicose. The man who, thinking aloud, had said, 'So, war then? But war, this is very difficult...' seemed to have forgotten the difficulties and had now embarked on a worrying escalation, ordering the withdrawal of the UN troops who had been stationed in Sinai since the Suez expedition of 1956 to create a buffer zone between Egypt and Israel, mounting a blockade of the Straits of Tiran, an act of open hostility to Israel, as it cut off access to the Red Sea. Having begun this escalation, Nasser had no choice but to persist if he were to be taken seriously, each new stage seemed inexorable, like a spiral that no one could control: military alliances negotiated with Syria and Jordan, the deployment of troops in Sinai almost on the borders of Israel. Israel was in danger, in our hearts alarm bells were ringing, every day the news was more disquieting, many of our Israeli friends were terrified and their fears became our fears. The European diaspora mobilized, particularly in France, organizations and individuals normally hostile to one another rallied to present a united front. During a hastily convened meeting on the place Saint-Germain-des-Prés in Paris, I was surprised to see Professor Pierre Vidal-Naquet, of the École des hautes études en sciences sociales, hardly an ardent Zionist, suddenly appear. But like the rest of us he felt that Israel was in mortal danger and that was something he was not prepared to tolerate. French governmental policy merely served to heighten our apprehension: de Gaulle had met the Israeli Foreign Minister, Abba Eban, who wanted to know what position the French government would take if Israel, considering itself legitimately threatened, took pre-emptive action to break this vice grip; if, in other words, Israel attacked first. The General informed him that Israel was not sufficiently 'established' to resolve its problems alone, that any solution should be left to the major powers, and ordered him, 'On no account should you fire the first shot,' and threatened an arms embargo – France was Israel's principal arms supplier at the time. This was no idle threat: de Gaulle announced the embargo on 2 June 1967, an act that, in all likelihood, actually hastened the war, which erupted three days later. My speech to the meeting on the place Saint-Germain-des-Prés was impassioned: I declared that, after Auschwitz, the destruction of Israel was unthinkable and that, if by chance it should happen, I for one could not bear to go on living. I ended my speech by calling for the formation of 'international Jewish brigades, or brigades of the International Jewry, whichever you prefer!', which was met with enthusiastic applause.

Let me be clearly understood: I never considered Israel as the redemption for the Shoah, the idea that six million Jews gave their lives so that Israel might exist; such a teleological argument whether explicit or implicit is absurd and obscene. Political Zionism long pre-dates World War II, even if the Zionist leaders who met at New York's Biltmore Hotel in 1942, highly aware that European Jews were doomed, considered the 'Jewish National Home' and the future state of Israel as the only salvation: good would come out of a catastrophe. The end of Steven Spielberg's *Schindler's List* is set in Israel, with the survivors saved by Schindler walking past the tomb of their benefactor to lay small stones on it, according to Jewish tradition. In contrast, the last scene of *Shoah* shows a goods train moving endlessly through the twilight of the Polish countryside. But there was no need to believe in any redemption or final salvation to be repelled by the prospect of a second bloodshed of the same people twenty-five years later. For it is also true that the state of Israel was born of the Shoah, that a causal relationship connects these two key events in the history of the twentieth century, and that a core of Israel's population is made up of survivors and refugees weary of suffering.

During these anxious weeks, I finally received the article from Ali, who had remained behind in Egypt. It did not beat about the bush. I was furious, I felt I had been betrayed by a friend, but at least now things were out in the open: the concluding section of his article for a special issue that saw peace on the horizon, however distant, was a candid anti-Zionist imprecation and, in the final analysis, a call for war: 'May I say in conclusion how much *I hate this Zionism that separates Arab from Jew?*' (The italics are his.) A petition in support of Israel was circulating, and I was asked to obtain Sartre's signature. Outside his apartment, on the pavement of the boulevard Raspail, I gave it to him to read and he agreed to sign it, half-heartedly, as I have said, but he signed. He liked the issue of *Les Temps modernes*, which he had read in part. He wrote his introduction just before we went to press, and his last sentence began, 'Even if blood should flow' and later in the same piece, he said, 'Let us not forget that these Israelis are also Jews', so clearly Georges Friedmann had not led him completely astray. I then wrote my foreword, which he warmly approved. The issue appeared on 5 June 1967, the first day of the war. Israel had launched the first strike. The success of 'The Arab–Israeli Conflict' issue was unprecedented, we had to reprint several times, and the huge 1,000-page issue sold 50,000 copies, even today it remains a work of reference; some of the articles are as topical now as they were then, while others give a glimpse of the remote and obscure roots of the conflict and how the road to peace, if it should one day come, is steep and rugged.

Contrary to what has been claimed over the past forty years, the Six Day War was not a walkover. The casualties of Tsahal, the dead and the wounded, were numerous and deeply painful to a people forced into war. The extent of the victory did not compensate for the loss. But Israel's generals had demonstrated unparalleled strategic brilliance, and Jewish combat units displayed a courage and a self-sacrifice that could only have been inspired by the keen awareness of the mortal danger of the country felt, to his core, by each soldier citizen. The conquest of the entire Sinai Peninsula by three divisions that relentlessly breached Egyptian lines, as tank commanders stood in open turrets, being decapitated by enemy shells; the assault on the Golan Heights by armoured bulldozers detonating the mines that riddled the area beneath their caterpillar treads to clear a path for the front-line troops, who defeated the Syrian infantry in hand-to-hand combat; the capture of Jerusalem at great cost, since it meant defeating the Arab Legion of Glubb Pasha (its chief and founder, a British soldier who had converted to Islam), intensively trained and lying in ambush behind the crenellated walls of Suleiman the Magnificent – these theatres of war were a heroic gesture that would forever transform, for better or worse, how the world saw that narrow stretch of land on the eastern Mediterranean known as Israel. Among French Jews, the anxiety that lasted until the very end, because of the absolute secrecy Israel maintained over the operations, changed once victory was assured and its scale known into an explosion of relief, of joy, of pride that is difficult to understand today. Those who, until then, had been indifferent, or wanted nothing to do with Israel, became extremely curious about the country: some considered settling there, serving the country, studying or teaching at an Israeli university. I remember a lunch with Pierre Nora at which he and François Furet – my close friends at the time – decided in front of me to visit Israel on a reconnaissance trip. I listened, sceptical, convinced that there were a thousand things about the reality of Israel that would offend rather than captivate them and that their professional tendencies would win out in the end. I was not entirely wrong; they returned after a short trip full of fine feelings, but convinced that postgraduate studies in Israel could not compare with those in France and that Paris still remained the seat of excellence.

Be that as it may, the time for rejoicing, for optimism born of a crushing victory, illustrated by the cover of *Life* magazine with its photo of a smiling Yossi Ben Hanan – the young officer who had been first to reach the Suez Canal near the El Fridan bridge and had dived in fully clothed, deliriously happy because he thought the war was over – that time of optimism was short-lived. Neither the national pride of Egypt nor of its Soviet ally – at the height of the Cold War – was prepared to tolerate such a defeat. Egypt was very quickly rearmed by airlift and by naval convoys. The Red Army sent instructors, missile batteries, completely new weapons systems that proved their worth in the 1973 Yom Kippur War. But while it took Egypt another six years before it renewed hostilities, as early as 1968 – barely a year after Israel's establishment along the length of the Suez Canal – the Egyptian artillery positions on the other side began shelling the *maozim*, the bunkers hastily constructed by Israel every ten or twenty kilometres to protect the units stationed there. This was the beginning of what would later be known as 'the war of attrition', which went on for almost two years and proved to be extremely bloody. I arrived there, dispatched by *Panorama*, the French television programme directed by Olivier Todd, having crossed the Sinai from east to west with a small crew. About a kilometre from the Canal, in a sort of transit camp that seemed to be in total chaos, a Tsahal officer, surprisingly young, calm and elegant, introduced himself: 'I am Lieutenant Ami Federman.' His name has remained engraved on my memory because, as he spoke those words, three black Tupolev aircraft from the Egyptian airforce appeared, flying low, strafing the compound and dropping bombs. The Israeli anti-aircraft defence was composed entirely of reservists manning obsolete equipment. The bombers risked nothing. Ami shrugged, 'It's always like this, they take us by surprise, they make a single pass and don't come back.' But the one pass was enough to leave dead and wounded in its wake. Field ambulances quickly arrived, the drivers' heads protected by nothing more than *kippahs*, their equanimity impressive. Federman – I later learned that he came from an illustrious family – explained that the Orthodox, who believed that their destiny was in the hands of the Almighty, had the singular courage of fatalism. We headed towards the Canal and the bunkers, whose concentric walls, made of stones and boulders piled high and ringed with barbed wire, surrounded a central courtyard with trenches leading to rooms deep underground capable of resisting intense shelling. The bunkers, crudely planned and built once it became clear that the Egyptians were not about to allow the Israelis to play tourist on the banks of the Canal and go swimming in peace, were improved over time until they became modern fortified castles, with slits in the walls making it possible to spray the far bank with bullets, and all surmounted by Israeli flags that floated on the breeze like an act of defiance. I stayed for several days, moving from one bunker to the next, spending the nights in blockhouses several metres underground that shuddered whenever a large-calibre shell exploded in the courtyard, devastating it. The muffled sound of bombing is the background to almost every interview I did. But the Israelis were not passive, they retaliated: one day, through the loophole on a bunker, I witnessed a retaliatory airforce raid made up mostly of Vautours, outdated French aircraft that were slow and vulnerable, flying at low altitude and dropping clusters of bombs on the Egyptian fortifications. The stretch of Canal where I was at the time was not even a hundred metres wide and the noise was so infernal it sounded like we were being strafed. Some Israeli army veterans consider that this war of attrition was the hardest they ever fought: you had to be constantly alert, you could never drop your guard, anyone who left the claustrophobic bunker to get some air had a good chance of being picked off by an Egyptian sniper. During my relatively short stay there, I saw a number of soldiers killed like that. I mentioned it in another chapter: every morning, the newspapers published the photographs of those killed the previous day, which meant the whole country was in a permanent state of fear and mourning, an atmosphere accurately reflected in the film we shot for *Panorama*, combining interviews with the men on the Canal and interviews with mothers, wives and children behind the lines. Dov Sion, the Israeli military attaché in Paris and husband of Yael Dayan – the daughter of General Moshe Dayan – sent me a huge crate of Jaffa oranges. My decision to one day become a filmmaker is doubtless connected to this documentary. When I got back to Paris, I would have liked to have done the editing myself, but that did not suit the pace of television: yet I know it would have been a better film if I had been at the helm from beginning to end.

This was something I had felt before, though I had not fully understood it. I was no longer a novice when it came to television. During these years, on Channel One – there were only two television channels at the time – there was a very good programme called *Dim', Dam', Dom'*, which regularly employed the best journalists and directors. The producer was Daisy de Galard, the editor at *Elle*. I conducted a number of memorable interviews for *Dim', Dam', Dom'*: an interview with five nuns, for example, who answered my questions with good grace and intelligence; another, with the permission of the prefecture, interviewing five policemen, ranging from an ordinary policeman to a high-ranking officer, in which my probing questions unsettled them to such an extent that their responses were overly revealing and the segment was almost cut. The interview was meticulously scrutinized at three separate screenings by the highest echelons of the Ministry of the Interior and I was asked to make cuts, which I refused to do. Daisy – an aristocrat of great courage – supported my decision completely. This interview caused a great stir.

I also interviewed actresses, sports personalities, singers and celebrities for *Dim', Dam', Dom'*, but every time I regretted not directing every stage of the process leading to the birth of a film. I also did a long and rather savage interview with the great couturier Pierre Cardin on the subject of 'designer labels'. How had he made his fortune? He became more and more ill at ease under my tenacious questioning, as I forced him to talk about his origins, his child-hood, his activities under the Vichy regime. When our interview, filmed in his *hôtel particulier* on the quai Voltaire, came to an end he was visibly relieved. The programme, which neither he nor I had watched, was scheduled for broadcast on the evening of 10 May 1968. Cardin had the good taste to invite Daisy de Galard, the director Guy Seligmann and me to dinner that night on the quai Anatole-France. Nicole Alphand, who ran his shops, was also there, together with her husband the ambassador. I personally thought the programme rather caustic about Cardin, I would have preferred not to be there, but since his friends showered him with compliments, he decided to seem pleased, going so far as to thank me and congratulate me on my talent. I had another reason for not wanting to be there: it was 10 May 1968 and, just before the programme was broadcast, there had been a newsflash about clashes between police and countless demonstrators on the place Edmond-Rostand, on the boulevard Saint-Michel and around the jardin du Luxembourg that seemed likely to degenerate into pitched battles. I left the dinner as early as I could and rushed to the Senate (at the time Judith and I were living nearby on the rue de Tournon). The great night of May '68 – the night of the barricades – was beginning.

I took part in numerous demonstrations, I was beaten up by the police, I was with Sartre in the main lecture hall at the Sorbonne when he was summoned to appear before the student body, acting as a people's assembly, where, to his delight, he was heckled and addressed as *tu* by twenty-year-olds who thought they were the Revolutionary prosecutor Fouquier-Tinville. Although I never for a moment tried to hang back, present at many flashpoints, spending whole days in the Sorbonne, which was occupied by students, listening for hours to the long-winded orators at the Théâtre de l'Odéon, commiserating over the death of Gilles Tautin, killed in the fields surrounding the Renault-Flins factory, hating viscerally, almost instinctively, the sight of breastplated troops of riot police, truncheons raised, the mist of tear gas that enveloped Paris from grenades thrown at point-blank range, although I was constantly present, I must confess that, truthfully, I experienced May '68 from the outside, like a curious, disinterested spectator, never believing in the realization of the incredible Second Coming in the history of mankind promised by the creative, poetic, sometimes powerfully moving slogans, most of which I subscribed to. I was of another generation; at a much younger age I had devoted myself, body and soul, to other battles, and as an adult had campaigned for other causes; in my profession, having no boss, I was unreservedly a loner, little concerned with the anti-institutional struggle that had triggered the revolt. But mostly, at the same time, something was happening within me that pushed everything else into the background. My relationship with Judith was in trouble, and I had been asked to direct a film about Israel. A millionaire's daughter had set herself up as a film producer and, ever since she had seen my footage about the Suez Canal, she had been bombarding me with bullying messages, urging me to act.

For me it was a dark dive into the turbulent waters of my life: just as I had eighteen years before, I set off from Marseille for Israel by boat, on a bleak November evening in 1970. I needed time to think, to work out whether I truly wanted to make this film and to decide whether I felt capable of working in cinema, never having studied filmmaking. Furthermore, and though it pained me too much to admit it even to myself, I no longer felt as close to Sartre as I once had. He still retained, until his death a decade later, my affection, my admiration and, I believe, my very real loyalty, especially after I took over as editor of Les Temps modernes – steering the journal according to what I called a 'course of non-disloyalty' – but after 1968, I can no longer claim to be an accurate witness to his life. I played no part in the 'Mao' period, I did not know his new friends, or had seen them only fleetingly, and it was difficult for me to see Sartre and Simone de Beauvoir selling *La Cause du peuple* on street-corners and being carted off in police vans as flashbulbs popped, even more to watch the impact of Sartre's sartorial *tabula rasa*: thrown out were the suits and the ties, now replaced by tatty cardigans and shabby jackets that encouraged fifteen-year-olds to heckle him in the most aggressive way.

Now editor of *La Cause du peuple* and of *Libération*, Sartre became on the one hand increasingly indifferent to his own journal or, on the other, attempted to use it as a propaganda tool in the service of his new passions. He insisted that *Les Temps modernes* publish an interminable article by Philippe Gavi about the Bruay-en-Artois affair that, without a shred of evidence and based entirely on the ideology of 'class war', claimed that wealthy notary Pierre Leroy and his mistress were guilty of murdering the sixteen-year-old daughter of a pit worker, Brigitte Dewèvre. This was 1972, a year in which I spent almost all my time editing *Pourquoi Israël*, although Jean Pouillon and I took turns editing *Les Temps modernes*. It was my turn when Gavi's article arrived and I read it with bewilderment: it was entitled 'Only a Bourgeois Could Have Done This?' and contained at least twenty possible grounds for lawsuits, all of which we would have lost. I discussed the piece with Sartre, showing him the actionable passages. He agreed with me and then said in his usual offhand manner, 'Correct it yourself.' I did so; Gavi threw a tantrum and went to Sartre, who would not be moved. No one to this day knows who killed the miner's daughter, and the case has long since gone cold. In 1974 a book was published called *On a raison de se révolter* [*It is Right to Rebel*], written by three authors, Gavi, Pierre Victor and Jean-Paul Sartre. Sartre was challenged by Gavi and Victor, who could not understand why he was wasting his time writing about Flaubert – a book about a bourgeois for the bourgeois. Sartre began by acknowledging the criticisms levelled at him, but he did so tenaciously, cleverly and with a wit that his opponents, devoid of humour, did not notice, slyly returning to the attack, telling them in short, 'Let me do the only thing I am capable of, I can't even attend the street demonstrations any more. What do you want? You want me to be carried on a sedan chair like a figurehead? I'm too old, too old to change. If I tried to write a revolutionary novel, it would be bad, etc . . .' It is Sartre's standing up to his juvenile inquisitors that makes *On a raison de se révolter* a book that is not just funny, but strange, in which the writer's refusal to drink from the Maoist fountain of youth as his co-authors suggest reminds me of the incredulous refusal of the old Boaz, in Victor Hugo's poem 'Booz endormi' ['Boaz asleep'] when he is visited by a dream that promises him youth and descendants:

Je suis seul, je suis veuf, et sur moi le soir tombe,
Et je courbe, ô mon Dieu!, mon âme vers la tombe,
Comme un boeuf ayant soif penche son front vers l'eau

I am alone, am widowed, and evening falls upon me,
And I lean, O God, my soul towards the tomb,
Just as an ox, when parched with thirst, bends his head
to the water

And so Sartre fought every inch of the way to go on writing the fourth volume of *L'Idiot de la famille*, devoted to *Madame Bovary*, until his failing eyesight finally forced him to give up, made it impossible to write by himself.

For my part, I was completely consumed by *Pourquoi Israël*, consumed by the discovery of the staggering possibilities that filmmaking offered me, and afterwards by the immense preparatory work for *Shoah*. I did not read *La Cause du peuple*, and ignored most of the numerous interviews Sartre gave during this period to compensate for the fact that he could no longer write. I did not, therefore, read his response to the massacre of the Israeli athletes in Munich: 'In this war, the only weapon the Palestinians have is terrorism. It is a terrible weapon, but the oppressed have no other [. . .] The principle of terrorism is that one must kill.' No one mentioned it to me, not even Castor, who later confessed that she was so shocked that she had deliberately contrived a memory lapse. Thinking about it now, Sartre's comments are hardly surprising: this was how the Algerian War had been triggered, by an attack on civilians, and though we deplored it, we did not express our indignation at Algerian terrorism, but considered it a response to secular colonial oppression, to institutionalized torture, to the killing by French forces of the prisoners known as 'corvées de bois', to the death of mathematician Maurice Audin, to the inhuman torture suffered by Henri Alleg recounted in his memoir La Question, to the guillotine working overtime in the prison yards of France and Algeria. Indeed, it was Sartre who, in a splendid, irrefutable and courageous article entitled 'A Victory', wrote the preface to La Question in 1958.

I feel somewhat responsible for another preface, the one he wrote for Les Damnés de la terre, since I had organized the encounter between Sartre and Fanon. By the time he met Fanon, Sartre was already morally committed to writing it. I have already told of the three days Sartre, Fanon, Simone de Beauvoir and I spent together, and of Fanon's irresistible charisma, only increased by fever and his awareness of the approach of death. Sartre was much criticized for that preface, but my feeling, rereading it forty years later, is that in agreeing to write it, Sartre did not make a free choice but rather was forced by circumstances. I witnessed on many occasions how, when he had to write something that was not his idea, he resorted to what came most easily: rhetoric. The preface is too long, at times bombastic, at times tedious; the call to violence and its glorification ring false, he clearly intended to please Fanon, using formulas such as 'the patience of the knife', or others that sound excessive or irresponsible when one reads them today, in the light of all the 'nights of the long knives' that still bathe independent Algeria in innocent blood. I did not get a chance to discuss it with Fanon, but I am not sure that he was enthusiastic about Sartre's preface. He had wanted it because he had read *Critique de la raison dialectique* with the magisterial analysis of colonialism that concludes that book: a magnificent chapter of concrete philosophy, luminous without being excessive, in which Sartre marshals all the concepts elaborated in the course of this immense work, thereby attesting to their profound truth.

But for Sartre, the pen, when necessary, replaced the sword: it is largely thanks to him that even the most extreme factions in France – all too ready to imitate their German or Italian counterparts – never progressed to actual violence. Sartre was both their supporter and their moderating influence; Alain Geismar summed up Sartre's approach to me: 'I'm on your side, but only up to a certain point. Don't mess around. There is a boundary, do not cross it.' It is true that Sartre acceded to the lawyer Klaus Croissant's request and visited Andreas Baader, the instigator of terrorism in Germany, in Mannheim Prison. Sartre justified this visit as humanitarian, considering that solitary confinement, the silence and the blinding whiteness of Baader's cell, amounted to torture, but he insisted, during the ensuing press conference, that his presence did not amount to an endorsement of the bloody acts perpetrated by Baader and his gang. Yet it is true that, carried away by the logic of his preface to *Les Damnés de la terre*, he did support Palestinian terrorism, the taking hostage of the Israeli athletes and their assassination in Munich being but a forerunner to a long series of bloody actions – the hijacking and blowing up of airliners, the appalling culmination of which took place in Entebbe, where Jewish passengers were parodically segregated by Germans enlisted under the Palestinian banner. I don't know what I would have done had I known about Sartre's pronouncements when they were first published. Please believe me, I found out only much later, so late that any reaction on my part would have been meaningless. In any case, I was in an entirely other world. Today, I blame myself for my irenicism: I should never have allowed the issue of *Les Temps modernes* on the Arab–Israeli conflict to open with Rodinson's article, 'Israel, a Colonial Reality?', for I do not believe that this is, or has ever been, the case: in my films and in my writings, I have striven tirelessly to reveal the complex reality of Israel. Rodinson's simplifications, though dressed up as 'science', did much harm, beginning with Sartre himself – as was already apparent during our trip to Egypt – and at times justified the worst.

But in November 1970, on the boat from Marseille to Haifa, and in spite of my gloomy outlook, I could not imagine Munich or Entebbe. Nor did I even imagine *Pourquoi Israël*, since I did not know yet whether I would succeed in making the film. I did not speak to a single person during the trip, there were few passengers, and I heard on the radio that de Gaulle had died, a 'mighty oak felled', in Colombey, struck dead by a ruptured aneurysm. I had admired the man, fought against him, misjudged him, and his death marked the end of a world, the end of an era and, as I sailed towards the country that sheltered 'an élite people, self-assured and domineering', as he had referred to Israelis in a press conference three years before, I felt a very real sadness. It was tinged with joy too, when, out on the open sea, I remembered the famous cartoon by Tim in *L'Express* depicting a member of this 'élite people', wearing the striped pyjamas of Auschwitz and a forage cap, leaning in debonair fashion on the barbed-wire fence. And I realized that my boat was now following the same course as the Boats of Cherbourg, which, less than a year earlier, on Christmas Eve 1969, had made France a laughing stock by cunningly and daringly breaching the arms embargo de Gaulle had announced in the run-up to the Six Day War. The Israeli government had paid cash for twelve missile boats, but at the time of the embargo only seven had been delivered; the others were detained in Cherbourg harbour with their Israeli maintenance crews. It has to be said that the Jewish marines who piloted the boats for six days and nights from Cherbourg to Haifa, observing a complete radio blackout in order to elude the French navy, could not have carried off their coup without the help of French soldiers. In retaliation for this slight, de Gaulle had immediately declared *persona non grata* Admiral Mordechai Limon, who was responsible for Israeli arms procurement, and who had remained in France after the embargo. I was invited to a party thrown by the admiral on the eve of his departure, where I saw a number of high-ranking French officers and industrialists exchanging smiles of complicity: champagne flowed and, all in all, Limon's send-off was a truly joyous one.

Jerusalem was at its lowest ebb when I arrived that November night: heavy clouds lowered above the rooftops, an icy rain chilled me to the bone, the wind and the cold leached into the houses. I was staying at the American Colony Hotel in the Arab quarter of the city; the hotel was as bleak as my soul and I asked myself what I was doing here, why I was even thinking about making the film, the pretext for my trip. On the second day, I fell ill, I was coughing, flu-ridden and running a temperature and had no hope of light, or even a wisp of blue winter sky. I decided not to stay in bed but to have dinner at Fink's, a restaurant-bar in the Jewish city, its walls plastered with crude, vulgar German slogans, bordering on the obscene – 'only happy farts [*frölicher Furze*] are permitted in this establishment' – where they served wine, *pommes sautées* and red meat. The owner was a tall Westphalian Jew who had arrived in Israel as a child; his first name was Dave and his last name, although he was not related to the Frankfurt bankers, was Rothschild – something he was proud of. I had been invited there once before while working on the special issue of *Les Temps modernes*, but the entrance was so inconspicuous I had trouble finding it again. I stepped inside. Only one table was occupied, and I immediately recognized Uri Avnery, a member of the Knesset and editor of the weekly magazine *Ha'olam Ha'zeh*, whom I had first met in 1952. He too was a German Jew, wounded during the War of Independence, a staunch advocate of Arab–Israeli reconciliation who systematically opposed every Israeli government and also one of the contributors to our special issue. Avnery was not alone, there was a woman sitting next to him who he introduced in German, then we quickly slipped into English. He invited me to join them and I accepted, despite my red nose, my cold and my cough. I had not quite caught the name of the woman whom I assumed to be Avnery's mistress, he had hissed it inaudibly, but it hardly mattered, from the moment I set eyes on her, she fascinated me, her presence here in Fink's, in Jerusalem, in Israel, was a mystery to me. Such matchless beauty does not exist there, nor in France, nor anywhere. I could not connect her with anything, not to the most beautiful Jewish women I had ever met, who had never evoked such a feeling of strangeness, nor to any of the women I had met in other countries. Faced with this utterly enigmatic woman, who to me had no name, no origin, no history, I truly felt in *terra incognita*, with no landmarks that might lead me to her. She said little, a word or two in German from time to time, in a gravelly voice that electrified me, and she proved to speak impeccable English. I was in no condition to sustain a conversation with Avnery, who I liked a lot, but whose sarcastic way of pulling his country to pieces until there was not one stone standing on another had always irritated me. For him, it was a sort of existential trick that made it possible for him to go on living here, an extreme incidence of Hegel's 'unhappy consciousness', happy in its own unhappiness. Israelis are particularly adept at this subterfuge, and although Uri was one of the best at it, he was not the first I had encountered and, as it was not something I really needed to hear while preparing to make a film about Israel, I took my leave of them, resolving to penetrate the mystery of this unknown woman, whose stern but noble face and the intimation of her sylph-like body tormented me all night. I wanted desperately to see her again but the only information I had gleaned over dinner was that she was currently living in Jerusalem. I wondered how to track her down: finding a woman whose name I did not even know would be an impossible task and I had to face the fact that Avnery was the only person who could help me. I phoned him, thanked him for dinner and frankly confessed that I was obsessed with this mysterious woman and wanted to see her again. He had the good grace to give me her name, her phone number and some information about her. She was from Berlin, her mother was Jewish and her father a member of the Prussian *haute bourgeoisie*; after living for several years with a Bavarian baron, an architect by profession, she had left him the day after their wedding to move to Jerusalem where she had encountered friends of her mother who had known her as a child and who had fled Germany in 1936 or 1938. Angelika Schrobsdorff was a writer who had published a merciless but hugely successful novel about men, *Die Herren* [*The Men*], and was considered to be the most beautiful woman in Germany. My cold cleared up, I called her, we met, and in my rough and ready way, I swept her off her feet by the intensity and sincerity of the passion I felt for her from the moment I first set eyes on her. It was mutual love at first sight and I believe that, ill-disposed towards happiness, she was happier at the beginning of our relationship than she had ever been. Hardly had she married the baron than she had told him that making their relationship official had been a mistake and she wanted a divorce.

There was no longer any need to think about whether or not I would make a film; it was obvious that I would. I stayed in Israel for about a month, crisscrossing the country, sometimes by myself, sometimes with her, alone as little as possible. She gave me the priceless gift of meeting her friends, Berlin Jews, her mother's friends in fact, who thought of her and treated her as their own daughter, admiring her for her beauty and because to them she represented all that was great about the German language, the critical freedom, the inventiveness and the mordancy of pre-Hitler Germany, for which they had retained an incurable nostalgia. Handsomely bound editions of the *Sämtliche Werke* [Complete Works] of Goethe, of Schiller, of Hölderlin, of Hegel, of Kant, lined the bookshelves of the *Yekke* – as German Jews were known in Israel – in the quiet, shady neighbourhood of Rehavia I mentioned earlier, causing my eyes to well with tears, though I did not really understand why. Israel, Germany, the two years I had spent there, the Shoah, Angelika, connected within me at unsuspected depths. And I began to feel an affection for the bankers, the doctors, the lawyers, the teachers, the pernickety law-makers who comprised the majority of Israel's Supreme Court, an admiration that overshadowed the friendship I felt for Flapan's friends, the kibbutzniks of Hashomer Hatzair. I have already mentioned how dazzled I had been by Gershom Scholem's library, that glorious Aladdin's cave of Jewish culture, but I became immensely fond of Scholem on the first occasion that he and his wife Fania invited Angelika and me to dinner. This great scholar was no priggish pedant, he was generous with his knowledge if he felt that the person he was talking to was genuinely interested. He was a pioneer, a land-clearer, curious about everything, a thinker, a philosopher, a polemicist, plain-spoken and extraordinarily witty. I liked his face too, his big, commanding nose, his pale blue eyes that still held a glimmer of childhood. He was a Berliner like Angelika, with whom he had a close friendship; he took us both under his wing and four years later he was a witness at our Jewish wedding when Rabbi Gotthold married us under the *huppa* in Jerusalem on a warm October afternoon. There is no such thing as a civil wedding in Israel, but the Yom Kippur War had taken place in October the previous year, and to marry like this was for Angelika and me a tribute to this country that we thought we had lost and that we both loved.

I returned to Paris and informed the producer that I would direct the film, consumed by a single thought: seeing Angelika again, going back to be with her as soon as possible. But Mademoiselle CW had no intention of taking shortcuts. Though she was rich, she did not intend to finance the project personally. Producers, as is well known, rarely risk their own money. Since she wanted to play at being a producer, she now had to prove herself by behaving as they do, and so she asked me to write a treatment – a word and an activity I despise – of about a hundred pages that she could use to raise the necessary funds. This delayed my reunion with Angelika, something that upset her as much as it did me. We wrote long letters to each other every day in English (for many years, until she learned French, it was our shared language), I loved her cynical, pessimistic style, she never lied to herself, the worst, as far as she was concerned, was a foregone conclusion. I loathed the idea of writing a screenplay, scene by scene, with dialogue and directions like 'EXT.-DAY' or 'EXT.-NIGHT'. But I set myself to work and produced seventy pages distilling my essential thoughts about the normality of Israel, which for me was in fact the abnormality, with indications of shots and sequences. CW and her assistant declared themselves delighted with my work and some days later informed me that, according to their calculations, I would need to film for forty-eight days, eight nights, four dawns and three dusks. I realized I was dealing with grotesque amateurs and that I would never get anywhere with them. But I agreed to go back to Israel with CW, who, armed with my screenplay, planned to raise the money for the film there; my only plan was to rush straight into Angelika's arms and spend every night with her while we were there. Finally, I grew tired of CW's endless quirks and procrastinations and put an end to our collaboration and set about trying to find alternative funding for the project. The budget for *Pourquoi Israël* was very small; I managed to raise modest sums from various sources, which I offered like a dowry to a production company recommended to me by Claude Berri. If I seem to be making much of this it is only because I want to make it clear that the love of a woman was the decisive motivation for the film. In fact, *Pourquoi Israël* is dedicated to Angelika Schrobsdorff, and the key scenes are peopled by the German Jews that I met through her. Gert Granach, whose contributions open and close the film and whose deeply moving Spartacist songs, accompanied by his accordion, punctuate it, is a close friend of Angelika's. She herself can be seen in a long shot panning from left to right, but there is another shot – a more subtle way of marking her presence – a shot of a stone balustrade in Jerusalem with her cat, a beautiful tortoiseshell Persian named Bonnie, replaced, after she died, by Deborah, the cat I was chasing in our garden in Paris when I broke a bone in my foot.

When I first met her, Angelika had not written for several years; she was obsessed by her family's painful past, which she knew she had to face, to relive, if she were ever to regain her creative freedom. I managed to coax the story from her in snatches, the story she has since told in her books after I managed to convince her (with the reciprocity of love) to write again, to persuade her that she would come through her crippling bouts of depression only if she faced what was hardest for her to face. But it was not until she gave me the magnificent, heart-wrenching letters written by her half-brother, Peter Schwiefert, to their mother that these fragments came together for me into a coherent whole and I understood the tragic uniqueness of those lives crushed by history. It was the only solution to the enigma posed by Angelika that first day, the enigma was her life. After reading Peter Schwiefert's letters, I knew which questions to ask and how to ask them. In the vibrant, uninhibited Berlin of the 1920s, Else, their Jewish mother, beautiful, frivolous, at once carefree and anguished, did as she pleased; she had three children by three men, all gentiles, the last of whom she married. Bettina was the daughter of the first man; Peter was the son of the second, a fashionable playwright named Fritz Schwiefert; the father of her youngest child, Angelika, was Eric Schrobsdorff, the son of wealthy developers who owned a number of properties in Berlin. Eric married Else in spite of his family's fierce disapproval. His mother joined the Nazi party after Hitler came to power and forced Eric to divorce: his marriage to a Jew was bringing shame on the family. But Else loved Berlin, she could not imagine living anywhere else, she did not take the Nazi threat seriously. Rather than leave the country for Palestine while she still could, as her friends had done – the friends I had met who were the reason for Angelika's presence in Jerusalem – she waited until the last moment. It was too late. Eric, who was still very fond of her and had provided for her financially, found a Bulgarian who agreed, in return for a hefty fee, to participate in a marriage of convenience and to convert to Judaism. Since Bulgaria was one of the rare Balkan allies of the Axis powers not to lapse into anti-Semitism and, thanks to King Boris, protected its Jews, Else moved to Sofia with her daughters, Bettina and Angelika, where she spent the war years unworried. It is only fair to say that during the war Eric Schrobsdorff, in his *Wermacht* uniform, visited his wife and daughter, and helped them out during their exile.

But what of Peter, the son? He abhorred Nazism: in spite of the fact that he was protected by his father's status as a non-Jew, and though his mother begged him to stay – he was not yet twenty – he left Berlin and Germany for Portugal without a penny a few days after *Kristallnacht* (9–10 November 1938). There he lived in abject poverty, learning the language, giving lessons, and beginning an extraordinary correspondence with his mother: while she stubbornly refuses to leave what she still refers to as her homeland, he deliberately chooses the Jewish part of himself, going to the German consulate in Lisbon to declare himself a Jew and consequently being forbidden from returning to Germany. And, in letter after letter, it is this half-Jewish son who, often in coded terms, pleads with his mother to accept who she is, imploring her to recognize the consequences. He demands that she do something, that she live up to the Judaism of her forefathers, yet he understands the difficulties and the contradictions with which she is struggling, his compassion invariably prevailing over his intransigence. For he is devoted to his mother, and once he learns that she is in relative safety in Sofia, he devises lunatic schemes to get to her from Greece – where he is now living – organizes daring meetings that inevitably come to nothing. In 1941, the letters suddenly stop: Peter Schwiefert has left for Egypt where he has enlisted in de Gaulle's Free French Forces. He fights against Vichy troops in Syria, in Cyrenaica in Libya with the British Eighth Army, he is one of the heroes of the battle of Bir Hakeim; he crosses Italy from south to north, is wounded in the Battle of Monte Cassino and again north of Rome; he arrives in Saint-Tropez where he fights until he reaches the Vosges where, for the first time in three and a half years, he writes to his mother, having heard that Sofia has been liberated by the Red Army, telling her that, for all this time, he had lost the ability to write or even to speak: 'The bird has no wings any more,' he writes. A long, absolutely admirable letter, a ruthless condemnation of the Germans who supported Hitler to the end and who are obeying him still. He vows to march into Berlin and settle scores with Germany and with his own family. It is he who tells his mother and his sisters of the enormity of the crimes committed by their country. This letter, like all of his letters, reveals a lucidity, an honesty, a nobility of thought, a sensitivity that are unique and can be read only with tears in one's eyes and with profound admiration. But Peter Schwiefert never made it to Berlin. He was killed on 5 January 1945 during Generalfeldmarschall von Rundstedt's counter-offensive, known as the Ardennes Offensive, or the Battle of the Bulge. By the time his mother Else received his last letter in Sofia, he had already been dead for six months. He is buried in the military cemetery of Strasbourg-Kronenbourg and his grave, when I visited it with Angelika, had a cross over it. This was something that had to be put right. I did so. Peter's letters were published in 1974 by Gallimard under the title *L'Oiseau n'a plus d'ailes* [*The Bird Has No Wings*], in the collection 'Témoins', edited by my friend Pierre Nora. I wrote the preface and the linking texts and corrected or rewrote the transla-tion. The book met with unanimous praise by the critics and earned the success it deserved. It was my wedding present to Angelika. By this time, I had been working on *Shoah* for a year.

Chapter 18

*P*ourquoi Israël met with a curious fate. Shooting was brutally interrupted one day by an uncompromising female producer who considered I had already amassed sufficient 'material' to edit the film and refused to allow me to buy the film stock I knew I still needed. My cinematographer, William Lubtchansky, who refined and deepened my cinematic education, was as distraught as I was. The same producer then reoffended during the editing process after a screening that thrilled those invited to attend, who explained their enthusiasm in terms that were new to me: 'It's a *film d'auteur*, a *film d'auteur*.' The following morning, when my editors, Françoise Beloux and Ziva Postec, and I arrived, in deepest darkest Neuilly, feeling animated and enthusiastic, I was refused entry to the stuffy box-room that served us as a cutting room. I was told that the production had no more funds and that editing had been stopped *sine die*. This meant sorting things out by myself; the producer wasn't taking the slightest risk: she knew this was my first film and that I would be ready to do whatever it took to complete it. She was not wrong, I found the money, brought it to her, the cutting room was reopened. In order to devote myself to *Pourquoi Israël*, which cost me almost three years' work, I had asked Pierre Lazareff if I could take unpaid leave and he had agreed. Being inexperienced and madly in love with the film and with Angelika, I had signed the contract imposed on me without negotiating terms – I would have signed anything. Thus, although I had raised some of the funding and made it possible to complete the film, I was paid a bare minimum. Compared to my previous salary, it was a considerable step backwards, and by the time I finished the film I was desperately poor, and the joy I felt at completing it was tinged by anxiety over my future.

The film was, as we know, chosen for the New York Film Festival in October 1973 on the condition, imposed by Richard Roud, the programme director, that I cut it by ten minutes and not a minute less – his way of flaunting and exercising his omnipotence. Honestly, I tried but failed to cut the film even by a minute, to the despair of the producer. I informed Roud that, as he wished, I had cut the running time of the film, convinced he would not notice. I was right. In Israel, the very title of the film put off professional film distributors, who could see no reason to ask what was not a question – there is no question mark in the title *Pourquoi Israël* – still less to answer it. Its running time was the *coup de grâce*. I organized a number of private screenings away from the hesitant commercial network and the ordinary Israeli film audiences. My audiences – intellectuals, writers, artists, journalists, politicians, people who managed vast ministries – responded to the film very favourably. To stand at the back of a cinema, to experience the rapt silence, to wait for the laughs that came exactly when I expected them, or to feel the bureaucrats' shudder of anxiety at certain scenes – because *Pourquoi Israël* is not remotely a piece of propaganda – and then their relief after a difficult sequence was, one might say, 'corrected' by another that complicated matters and revealed the empathy with which the whole film is imbued, all this was a new and exhilarating experience for me. Gershom Scholem's comment, when he rose to his feet after the three hours and twenty minutes of the screening, turned to the audience and shouted, 'We've never seen anything like it!', was, for me, the ultimate accolade, the greatest joy. The film critic Moshe Nathan said the same thing in more detail in a long article in the newspaper *Maariv*, a few short months before he was run over and killed by a bus in Tel Aviv.

It is here that the adventure of *Shoah* begins: my friend Alouph Hareven, director-general of the Israeli Ministry of Foreign Affairs, invited me in and spoke to me with a gravity and a solemnity I had never experienced from him. Having congratulated me on *Pourquoi Israël*, this in substance is what he said to me: 'There is no film about the Shoah, no film that takes in what happened in all its magnitude, no film that shows it from our point of view, the viewpoint of the Jews. It's not a matter of making a film *about* the Shoah, but a film that *is* the Shoah. We believe that you are the only person who can make this film. Think about it. We know the problems you had in making *Pourquoi Israël*. If you agree, we'll help you out as much as we can.' So the idea for *Shoah* is not mine, I had not even thought about it: although the Shoah is central to *Pourquoi Israël*, I had never thought about tackling such a subject head on. I left that meeting stunned and shaking – the conversation took place at the beginning of 1973 – and went back to Paris, not knowing what to think, weighing up the vastness of such a task, the insuperable obstacles, which seemed to me countless, terrified that I would never be equal to this incredible challenge. And yet something powerful, even violent, inside me urged me to accept: I could not see myself going back to my former profession as a journalist; that period of my life was over. But if I said yes I would be turning my back on prudence and security, committing myself to a project with no fixed term, without knowing how long it might take, stepping into the unknown, perhaps into danger. I felt as though I was standing at the foot of some petrifying, uncharted north face, the summit obscured by thick clouds. I spent a whole night, a night like Pascal's *nuit de feu*, roaming through Paris, I steeled myself, telling myself that what was being offered was a unique opportunity, one that would require the greatest courage, and that it would be thankless and cowardly not to seize that opportunity with both hands. I also asked myself what I knew about the Shoah. Nothing, was the truthful answer, I knew nothing, nothing but a statistic, an abstract number: six million of our people had been murdered. And yet like most Jews of my generation, I felt that I innately knew about it, that it was in my blood and hence I did not have to learn about it, to come face to face with the terrifying reality. I had been absolutely contemporary to the Shoah, I could have been among the victims, but the terror it evoked in me whenever I dared to think about it had consigned it to a different time, almost to another world, light years away, beyond human time, to some quasi-legendary *illo tempore*. This thing could not have happened in my time, terror required distance. I am simplifying now, and I regret it, the confusion of thoughts I struggled with throughout that night so much like Pascal's. In the morning, exhausted, before sinking into dark and peaceful sleep, I phoned Alouph Hareven to tell him I would do it.

It took me time to define my subject. I spent the summer of 1973 with Angelika in Jerusalem, waiting for the screening of *Pourquoi Israël* at the New York Film Festival. We lived in an apartment facing the walls of the old city in Mishkenot Sha'ananim, a foundation for intellectuals and artists from around the world. I divided my time between reading Reitlinger and Hilberg, furiously making notes without knowing where they might lead me, and the archives and the library of Yad Vashem, most of whose staff were survivors – by this I mean the old, simple, unassuming and poignant Yad Vashem that appears in *Pourquoi Israël*, not the more recent creation, a gigantic Americanized stone city, a triumph of the museum-builders' art, the result of an arrogant competition between architects from around the world, a multimedia confection that promotes forgetfulness rather than memory. I had hired Irène Steinfeldt, a young student, the daughter of one of Angelika's friends, to assist me; in addition to speaking Hebrew, she also spoke German, English and French fluently and she proved to have a unique talent for simultaneous interpreting, which was very useful to me during the exploratory work for *Shoah*, in particular during my German escapades. I had no idea where I was going, I made wild stabs in the dark, took random samples. In the tiny office that Yad Vashem put at my disposal, I gradually made headway in reading *The Destruction of the European Jews,* Hilberg's unrelentingly dry book, in the first American edition – 1,000 pages of close print, two columns per page, overviews spanning 1933 until the end that traced, albeit with a rigorously deconstructed chronology, each of the phases of the Final Solution (definition, branding, expulsion, ghettoization, putting to death) with a plethora of notes that seemed important to me as they contained the names of the Nazi protagonists. On whiteboards, I drew up charts, endlessly erasing and redrawing, which I thought might help me to articulate this unthinkable 'thing' that I was discovering, this 'thing' about which, believing I knew everything, I knew nothing. Hilberg's sources were primarily German and I already knew, knew very early on, that I would not make this film unless the killers appeared in it.

I had absolutely no idea how I would proceed, the sheer effrontery I would need to summon, the dangers I would have to expose myself to. I also knew from the start that I would not use archive images. The most powerful and most luminous reason for this refusal did not occur to me immediately, it became obvious only when I understood the nature of the film I had been called to make. But I had already seen films that used archive footage, such as Frédéric Rossif's *Le Temps du ghetto* [*The Witnesses*], which had infuriated me because it did not cite its sources, said nothing about the provenance of the archive footage used, much of it filmed in the Warsaw Ghetto by the PK – *Propaganda Kompanien*, the *Wehrmacht*'s propaganda companies – to show the world, and Germany, how good life was there: the PK 'directors' had organized sham cabarets, dances featuring Jewish women in outlandish make-up, selected for this farce. No one is denying that in the ghettos, especially at the beginning, there was a class structure – I showed as much in *Shoah* – but it is reasonable to wonder what the uninformed viewer will make of such footage, which seems to be irrefutable documentary evidence. I remember spending three mad days in London with an obsessive, poignant, haunted Jew named Kissel who had stopped the clock in ghetto time and lived in an apartment, every room of which was filled with black-and-white photographs of all sizes, most of them taken in the Warsaw Ghetto. Strewn over the floors, the tables, the armchairs, the beds, piled in boxes and pinned to walls were not only these fake photographs of 'happy times', but also horrifying photographs – since the PK had filmed everything – of corpses in the streets covered with newspapers, carts piled with bodies being dragged by skeletal figures, morgues swarming with enormous black flies, all attesting to the powerful fascination the death and suffering of the Jews exercised over those talented professionals trained in Joseph Goebbels' schools. Kissel could find his way unerringly through this invaluable, grisly chaos, dashing from one box to another, the meticulous curator of a buried world, the stalwart companion of the agony of his people – all the more so, he told me, as he felt his own days drawing to a close (he was suffering from cancer of the larynx) – capable of proposing such things as I had not even imagined, racing to dig out a print from this or that series, constantly making copies, since this was also his profession: the countless films made around the world about the ghettos all used his archives, each time with a different commentary. People in Jerusalem had talked to me about Kissel and, not knowing which way to turn, I had decided to visit him: 'It's very important for your film,' they told me. They were not wrong: the three days I spent with him were to put me off archive material forever. On the other hand, since I was making a film and was looking for characters, I thought that Kissel might be one of them, that he and his clutter might make an interesting opening scene. It was a bad idea. One that his death spared me having to confirm.

As my reading progressed, as the months passed, my film, if I can put it this way, was pieced together in the negative, by trial and error. My work was interrupted for several months by the Yom

Kippur War of 6 October 1973, which coincided with the screening of *Pourquoi Israël* in New York, and its release in Paris on 11 October. It was made clear to me by the Israelis that what had almost been a catastrophe for the nation, forcing a change of government and the resignation of a Prime Minister as irremovable as Golda Meir, had inevitably relegated the interest they had expressed some months earlier in a film about the Shoah. This meant that at some point I would have to struggle on alone and that I would not be spared the problems they had hoped to spare me. The day after the New York screening, Angelika took the first plane back to Tel Aviv, unable to bear being elsewhere while Israel was in danger. I joined her a week after the release of the film in France; the fighting was still going on, although the initial stranglehold had been broken. A few hours after the ceasefire, Ariel Sharon, the great victor of the war – who, after the terrible Battle of the Chinese Farm and in spite of intense bombing by Egyptian artillery, ordered armoured units to cross the Suez Canal on pontoon bridges – invited me aboard his military plane. We touched down on a crude landing-strip near the Canal and crossed one of the bridges the tanks had taken, making straight for Suez, then advancing on Cairo, where the armistice hastily requested by the Egyptians had stopped them at Kilometre 101. It was a truly Napoleonic stroke of genius, completely turning the tables, cutting off the Egyptian Third Army and trapping them in Sinai, making it impossible for them to retreat. One of the terms of the ceasefire was that Israel was to allow supplies through to the enemy Third Army and there was something comical in seeing small boats full of Egyptian officers and soldiers shuttling back and forth to their own bank of the Canal to get food and water from ironic but friendly Israeli troops.

Unlike the special issue of *Les Temps modernes*, which had benefited from a publication date coinciding with the first day of the Six Day War, the coincidence between the start of the Yom Kippur War and the screening of *Pourquoi Israël* at the New York Film Festival did not help the film. Despite uniformly excellent reviews, it was a very bad time to distribute the film in the United States: day and night Israel was on every television network. Despite this there were a number of distributors willing to take the risk, but the producer insisted on an advance against receipts that they all considered excessive, and I agreed with them. In France, on the other hand, in spite of similar circumstances and my hasty departure for Israel the day after its release, the film was a critical and commercial success. In addition to reviews by the film critics in the newspapers and weekly magazines, Claude Roy, François Furet, Pierre Nora and Philippe Labro also wrote enthusiastic articles. Truth be told, the film had been ready since the spring and the release had been pushed back because it had been selected for the New York Film Festival in October. There had been a number of private screenings in Paris. After one of them, Philippe Labro called me to say he had given my phone number to Jean-Pierre Melville, who had been enthusiastic about the film and very much wanted to meet me. Melville's actual surname was Grumbach, and he was a Jew, something I did not know, nor had I seen all his films. It was the beginning of a close friendship, cut short all too soon by Jean-Pierre's death in August that year. He lived in an astonishing, rather gloomy building in the 13th *arrondissement* that he had converted into a mansion, installing an editing suite and a state-of-the-art private cinema that seated a hundred people. When I first encountered him, he remained seated, hulking, motionless, a stetson covering the bald pate of his enormous head, his eyes unfathomable behind dark glasses, the room was only softly lit. He spoke little except about the film, which he talked about passionately, the eye of the great *cinéaste* had noticed everything. I realized he had a Jewish sensitivity, which perhaps explained his need for masks. *Pourquoi Israël*, I feel sure, liberated him, and he lit up when we talked about Jerusalem. Every time I visited him, it was the same ritual: fraternal conversation punctuated by long silences in his dim study – but then people rarely speak in his films either – then the ceremonial descent into the cavernous basement garage, the showcase for his gleaming, understated Rolls-Royce Silver Shadow, an expensive jewel that deeply impressed me. Melville would get behind the wheel, never taking off his sunglasses, not even at night, and drive up the ramp, heading south for the motorway via the Porte d'Italie. We always drove for twenty kilometres or so in the regal silence of the Rolls, without exchanging a word, then we would turn and head back. He would then invite me to dinner at a brasserie in Gobelins, where he was known and worshipped; he was the first man I ever saw pay by credit card – American Express, I think – something that impressed me almost as much as the Silver Shadow. The highlight of these evenings began after dinner in his private cinema, just the two of us. Sitting next to him I watched all of his films, more than once, sometimes two films a night – he slept little – and also *Pourquoi Israël*, which he insisted on, which pleased me immensely. I told him all about the adventure I had just embarked on and he approved and asked me to be sure to talk to him about it again. His sudden death put paid to all of that. I was told that he died completely penniless, that the Silver Shadow was leased . . .

After the Yom Kippur War and before I went back to work, I decided to try to release *Pourquoi Israël* in the USA by myself. Arthur Krim, chairman of United Artists, organized a screening in the private cinema of his opulent mansion on Long Island Sound. Krim liked and wanted the film very much, but here again the producer asked for too much money. A second screening took place in another palatial mansion on Long Island, the home of New York tycoon Larry Tisch, the owner of the famous Tischman Building at 666 Fifth Avenue. Larry was a tall, very pale, red-headed man and the numerous photographs of him and his wife shaking hands with presidents and ministers, Americans and Israelis, showed they were serious donors and fervent Zionists. We were joined by a couple of their friends, and a remarkably frugal, non-alcoholic snack was served, then we went into the theatre: the armchairs and sofas were so soft and deep you almost disappeared into them, you had to lean forward and crane your neck to see the person next to you. As soon as the screening began with Gert Granach's Spartacist songs, I realized, trying to sink even deeper into my seat, that this was neither the place nor the audience for my film and that what was about to happen would be torture. The first resonant, unselfconscious snore came within about ten minutes; I turned round, and Larry, mouth hanging open, was fast asleep. He was quickly followed by his wife. Only his friends didn't sleep or snore, and when the lights went on again three hours later, they gave me complicit smiles, their eyes bright and shining, looking at Mr and Mrs Tisch and shrugging their shoulders. Larry must have felt bad because three days later he arranged to meet me in his office on the sixty-sixth floor of 666 Fifth Avenue, which offered a 360° panorama that took one's breath away. But he did not care about the view, he was engrossed in something else: I watched him for forty-five minutes before he even registered my presence so captivated was he by the dozens of televisions and computer screens listing stock exchanges around the world, by the machines and the telephones and the modern gadgets I could not even name, into which he relentlessly barked orders to sell, to buy. Watching this made up for everything, I completely forgave him: he was a genius. He finally noticed me, smiled, thanked me for coming and congratulated me on my film, as though he had not missed a single second of it. As I sat there, he phoned a business partner, recommending he meet me and even arranging a time and a place for us to meet again. Because Larry – and this was something I had not known – owned chains of cinemas across the entire country. I realized to my astonishment that he was prepared to distribute *Pourquoi Israël*. But it was the same story all over again with the producer. I'd had enough, I gave up, deciding to go back to Europe, back to work.

I had seen *Nuit et brouillard* [*Night and Fog*], had read Primo Levi, Antelme, Rousset and a hundred other books and monographs, I had spent hours with people who had survived, who had escaped, some of whom I knew, others of whom someone had said 'You absolutely have to hear what they've got to say', getting them to talk more by putting myself in the position of an attentive listener than by questioning them. I later learned that one needs a vast body of knowledge before questioning someone. At the time I really didn't know enough. All the stories, all the witness accounts I collected, even the most harrowing, fell silent when it came to something central that I could not quite grasp. The beginnings: the arrests, the roundings up, the traps, the 'transports', the overcrowding, the stench, the thirst, the hunger, the deception, the violence, the selection process on arrival at the camps – these were all the same and we quickly came to the horrifying routine that was life in the camps. There could be no question of my film not dealing with these things, but what was most important was missing: the gas chambers, death in the gas chambers, from which no one had returned to report. The day I realized that this was what was missing, I knew that the subject of the film would be death itself, death rather than survival, a radical contradiction since in a sense it attested to the impossibility of the project I was embarking on: the dead could not speak for the dead. But it was also an epiphany of such power that when this obvious fact was revealed to me I immediately knew that I would carry this thought to the end, that nothing would persuade me to give up. My film would have to take up the ultimate challenge; take the place of the non-existent images of death in the gas chambers. Everything had to be created from scratch: not a single photograph exists of Belzec extermination camp where 800,000 Jews were asphyxiated, nor any of Sobibór (250,000 deaths), nor of Chełmno (400,000 victims of the gas vans). Of Treblinka (600,000), there is one image, of a distant bulldozer. The case of Auschwitz, that vast factory, both concentration camp and extermination camp, is not radically different: there are numerous photographs taken before the killings, by SS officers on the ramp, mostly of Hungarian Jews waiting for the selection, but there are none of the frantic struggles to snatch a breath of air, to go on breathing a few seconds longer that took place in the huge gas chambers of Birkenau in which 3,000 men, women and children were asphyxiated at a time.

Two things I read proved to be very important to me: the transcripts of the Treblinka trials held in Frankfurt in 1960, in which I found statements from two people who were to appear in my film, SS officer Franz Suchomel and Richard Glazar, a Czech Jew who survived the uprising in the camp, and also the German state prosecutor, Alfred Spiess, who later agreed to meet me and became himself a protagonist of *Shoah*; during the same period I also read *Into That Darkness* by Gitta Sereny, a British journalist of Hungarian origin, who, in addition to Suchomel and Glazar, had interviewed the second commandant of Treblinka, Franz Stangl, at length in his prison cell. Sereny's subject is undoubtedly death, but her approach seemed to me purely psychological: she wanted to think about evil, to understand how a husband and father can calmly take part in mass murder, the central subject of many later literary-historical works. From the beginning of my own research, by contrast, I was so astonished that I braced myself with all my might against the refusal to understand. Sereny later wrote a book about Albert Speer, Hitler's chief architect and, during the war, Minister for Armaments, a defendant at the Nuremberg trials who was sentenced to twenty years. On his release, he wrote a memoir, which went on to be a bestseller. Sereny fell for his charm and that of his family, his wife, his daughters, and, carried along by the niceties proper to psychology as a means of inquiry, wrote her massive tome in tribute to them. She understood everything. She understood too much. I myself met Speer after his memoirs were published; he invited me to his seigniorial manor in Heidelberg near the Schloss on the hill overlooking the Neckar Valley. The conversation began at three in the afternoon and, despite the long years of incarceration that should have liberated him to the truth, from the first he seemed to me incredibly evasive and stilted, more worried about his pose and his posture than about giving honest answers to my questions. I questioned him about architecture, about the Führer's talents as an architect and the monuments of frozen geometry he built to the Thousand Year Reich. I talked to him about the Éxposition Universelle in Paris in 1937, where Hitler's pavilions had faced those of the USSR. It was there I had seen my mother for the first time since she left home, she showed me the giant marble statue of an Aryan couple facing an equally gigantic Soviet couple, the woman scything the air with her sickle, the man brandishing a fearsome steel hammer. Speer had not been the architect of the marvel I had mentioned, but he went off and got a portfolio of drawings and I was forced to look at his work as he commented on the cost and the scale of those that had been built. Night drew in as we talked, he sat back down in a large armchair, I sat in another. He did not turn on the lights, made no move to do so, so we went on talking in utter darkness: he did not offer me anything to eat or drink, I left him at midnight with no desire ever to see him again.

A scientific committee chaired by Yehuda Bauer, professor of contemporary Jewish history at the Hebrew University of Jerusalem, had been set up, to which I was supposed to give a broad overview of my work and a progress report. After a few months, the meetings of the committee became more infrequent and I talked about the difficulties I was facing with Yehuda Bauer alone. It was by now clear to me that the Jewish protagonists in my film had to be either the *Sonderkommandos* – the Special Units, to use Nazi terminology, who worked at the final stage of the destruction process and hence, with the killers, were the only witnesses to the deaths of their people, the only witnesses to the last moments of the lives about to be lost, asphyxiated in the gas chambers (I have already talked at length, in Chapter 2, about Filip Müller, who was part of the Auschwitz *Sonderkommando* for almost three years, and who miraculously survived the five *Sonderkommando* purges) – or those men who, having spent long periods in the camps, ended up holding crucial positions, making them particularly able to describe in detail how the machinery of death functioned. Bauer perfectly understood what I wanted to achieve and agreed with me; he was of Czech extraction and had known the antecedents and the various stages of the Final Solution in Czechoslovakia – of all the Jews in Europe, perhaps because of their geographical proximity to Auschwitz, the Czechs and the Slovaks were the first to be deported there. It is hardly surprising that three of the most important protagonists in *Shoah* are Czech, like Glazar and Filip Müller, or Slovak, like Rudolf Vrba: it was through Yehuda Bauer that I first heard of these last two. Finding them and persuading them to appear in the film was a very different matter. But there was yet a further reason to include them: aside from the fact that all three were exceptional in their intelligence, in their remarkable survival, their heroism and their ability to articulate their experience, I could only speak to them in a foreign language; this estrangement – another term for the distance I spoke of earlier – was for me, paradoxically, a necessary condition to approach the horror. There was no question of what would have happened had I met a French Filip Müller – it could not have happened, there could never have been such a voice of bronze, with that resonant and reverberating timbre that hung in the air long after each of his frank, dramatic utterances, never such profound intelligence, a unique meditation on life and death forged by three years in hell.

I met almost all of the surviving members of the Auschwitz *Sonderkommando*, having set about tracking them down as soon as I realized how essential they were to my project. None rivalled Filip Müller, and I knew they would not be in the film, apart from Dov Paisikovitch, a butcher in Hadera, a little town in Israel. He was the most taciturn man I have ever met, a slab of silence. A native of Transylvania, he had been deported to Birkenau with his family in May 1944; the extermination of the Hungarian Jews was at its height: as the furnaces were unable to cope with the thousands of corpses that daily came out of the gas chambers, pits had been hastily dug in which those for whom there was no place in the white-hot maw of Crematoria IV and V were burned. Beaten and whipped as he climbed down from the goods train, separated from his family, Dov, not yet eighteen years old, was forced with truncheon blows and dog bites to one of the pits where, along with others, he had to douse the corpses in petrol, pounding with wood or concrete poles the large bones that did not burn, collecting the boiling Jewish fat in buckets. He carried out his harrowing task for as long as he had to, surviving Auschwitz by a mixture of luck and extraordinary courage. He could not be compared to Filip Müller, but I liked him and visited him at his butcher's shop several times, convinced that his youth, his absolute silence deserved a place in the tragedy that the film had to incarnate. Silence, too, is an authentic form of speech. The only thing I managed to learn from his own lips was that he liked to fish in the Mediterranean, near Caesarea, at twilight casting ledger lines from a long, heavy fishing rod firmly fixed in the sand and then waiting with infinite patience for the rush of the reel that indicated he had a bite. Since I too had a fondness for fishing, for waiting, for imminence, I thought, 'We won't speak, we'll fish together in silence and I will tell his story in voiceover.' Dov agreed to my proposal but, sadly, died of a heart attack before I could film the scene. I felt great regret. And grief.

Just as *Shoah* is a film impossible to master, offering a thousand ways by which to enter it, so it makes little sense to attempt to recount day by day, year by year, how it came to be made. From the moment I became convinced that there would be no archive footage, no individual stories, that the living would be self-effacing so that the dead might speak through them, that there would be no 'I', however fantastical or fascinating or atypical an individual fate might be; that, on the contrary, the film would take a strict form – in German a *Gestalt* – recounting the fate of the people as a whole, and that those who spoke for them, forgetting themselves and supremely conscious of their duty to pass on their memories, would naturally express themselves in the name of all, considering the question of their own survival almost as anecdotal, of little interest, since they too were fated to die – which is why I consider them as 'revenants' rather than as survivors – from the moment I made that decision I began to fight, not randomly, but as I needed to, on each and every front. A few more words about self-effacement, about the implacable discipline we imposed upon ourselves, the 'revenants' and I, because one of my regrets is that I make no mention of it in the film. In the film, there are two survivors from Vilnius, Motke Zaïdl and Itzhak Dugin, members of a commando of young Jewish men who were forced to dig up the immense mass graves in the Ponary forest, to exhume the corpses without the use of tools, with their bare hands; among the thousands of bodies buried there they recognized those closest to them, whom they were forced to refer to as *Figuren* or *Schmattes* – puppets or rags. If they dared use the words 'corpse' or 'victim' they were savagely beaten. What I do not recount in *Shoah* is the extraordinary escape attempt made by the young men of this commando, among them Zaïdl and Dugin. Digging a long, deep, airless tunnel in the sand that led to the depths of the forest beyond the barbed-wire fence, Dugin and Zaïdl managed to make it to the other side. The SS, having learned of the escape attempt, set their dogs after them. It is Dugin who speaks: 'We were so exhausted that the dogs caught up with us, and we were convinced they would tear us to pieces. Then suddenly they started to whine, circling around us, whimpering in terror, and trembling, they lay down. We smelled so strongly of death, having had to wade through the pits for weeks, that the stench was enough to frighten off the dogs.'

Thinking about it today, some of my research methods seem obscure, even incomprehensible. I was obsessed by the last moments of those who were to die, or by their first moments in the death camps – for most of them it was the same thing – by the thirst, the cold – what did it mean to be waiting, naked, in temperatures of –20°C for one's turn to enter into the gas chamber at Treblinka or at Sobibór? I asked myself these questions over and over, they haunted me, yet it never occurred to me to set out for the places where the extermination had happened, although logic would have dictated that I start precisely with them. I could not bring myself to go to Poland, something deep in me made it impossible. I thought there was nothing to see, nothing to be learned there, that Poland was a non-place, that if the Holocaust – that was the word at the time – existed somewhere, it was in the minds and the memories of the survivors and of the killers, and could therefore be talked about in Jerusalem, in Berlin, Paris, New York, Australia or South America.

Finding the members of the *Sonderkommando* was not difficult in itself. There were not many of them, and they were known, some had testified at Eichmann's trial. The problem was not in knowing how to contact them, but in persuading them to speak, to speak in front of a camera and a film crew. Were they to accept, they would be paying a terrible price, forced to relive it all. It was an almost impossible task. The Eichmann trial would be of no use to me. Reading the transcripts, it became clear to me that the trial had been conducted by ignorant people: the historians at the time had done too little research, the president and the judges were poorly informed; Hausner, the chief prosecutor, thought that pompous moralizing flights of rhetoric compensated for what he lacked in knowledge – he made hundreds of mistakes, for instance confusing Chelm and Chełmno; the tearful witnesses gave a kind of show, making it impossible to recreate what they had truly experienced; and the shocking way in which the trial was directed unjustly put much of the responsibility and the blame for the extermination on the *Judenräte*. This became the subject of a bitter dispute between Gershom Scholem and Hannah Arendt, who followed the trial and, in her book *Eichmann in Jerusalem*, showed a partiality, a lack of compassion, an arrogance and a failure of comprehension for which he was right to reproach her.

Abraham Bomba, the Barber of Treblinka and one of the heroes of my film, did not give evidence at Eichmann's trial. But people at Yad Vashem had mentioned him to me, I knew he had been a member of the Treblinka *Sonderkommando*, that he had cut the hair of women actually inside the gas chambers, that he had managed a daring and extraordinary escape and that when he went back to the ghetto of Częstochowa, the Polish town where he had been born, no one had believed the unbelievable things he told his brothers; instead he was accused of spreading panic, with some wanting to turn him in to the police in order to silence him. Having escaped in the spring of 1943, Bomba had no choice but to return to the ghetto in his home town; he had no chance of surviving alone among the Polish people. It should be said that the Germans never cleared a ghetto in a single 'action'. The liquidation of the Częstochowa ghetto took months and Bomba astonishingly escaped a second 'transport' to Treblinka. Such a man was crucial to me, but all I knew was that he lived in New York, where he still worked as a barber; no one knew his address. Once before on a short visit, I had already tried to locate him when, at my request, I was attending – as an observer, not as a participant – a symposium of specialist historians of the Holocaust, but I could find no mention of him in either the personal or business directories for Manhattan.

This international symposium took place in early 1975 and it was then that I first met Raul Hilberg. The curtness of his tone, the lack of emphasis and pathos in his voice and his often mordant wit, all this contrasted sharply with the manners of his colleagues. Yehuda Bauer had suggested to him that we meet, and I saw him on his own one evening, talked to him about his books, which I had read and assimilated completely, but also about my film project, asking him if he would be willing to appear in it. I saw him on a number of occasions at his home, in Burlington, Vermont, we became friends, and he agreed to appear in the film. The other contributors at the symposium – many eminent scholars in their fields – struck me by their cheerfulness. The symposium was bursting with life, people congratulating each other, laughing, something that seemed to me to be at odds with the subject of the meeting. For my part, I was so haunted by death that I found it difficult to comprehend the palpable frivolity of the academic approach. I mentioned this to Yehuda Bauer one day, who suggested I try to enjoy myself: 'It's impossible to think about this twenty-four hours a day, it would drive you mad.' Perhaps that is what was happening to me, I was thinking about it increasingly frequently, it became very serious, to the point where I imagined everyone was dead, not just the victims but the killers. Every time I discovered someone still alive, I was absolutely stunned, it felt almost like something unearthed during an archaeological dig, my find appeared to me as a sign, a vestige of the immensity of the catastrophe.

In the end I found an old address for Abraham Bomba somewhere in the Bronx. On one of my trips to New York, having yet again trawled through the phone directories in vain, I decided to go out there in person. I found a ramshackle building with no lift, the walls black with soot from a recent fire, as were a number of the surrounding buildings. It sometimes happened that the property owners, who lived in more upmarket areas and were often reluctant to carry out necessary repairs, set the fires themselves in order to collect on the insurance. Perhaps Bomba had lived here, but if so, it had been many years earlier. Having checked the mailboxes without finding his name, I took the stairs and knocked on every door; the tenants I encountered were all Hispanic, most of them Puerto Rican. Dismayed but refusing to believe that Bomba, who was crucial to the film, was lost forever, I started walking, wandering in circles for hours around that dreary neighbourhood. Suddenly, I stopped in front of an unlikely cobbler's shop. Through the window, I saw a man tacking a sole on to a shoe, and from his old-fashioned trade and his facial features I knew at once the cobbler was Jewish. I am rarely mistaken: I would have excelled at facial profiling. Not only was he a Jew, but a Polish Jew with a thick Yiddish accent, an isolated and lonely sentinel of Zion and of Eastern Europe in this utterly Hispanic world. It goes without saying that he too had been in the camps. And of course he had known Bomba who, he told me, had moved to a different part of the Bronx twenty years earlier, to Pelham Parkway, a middle-class neighbourhood whose residents were primarily Jewish. I rushed over there and started wading through the phone directories of Pelham Parkway, but Bomba was not in any of them. Since he was a barber, I thought, I might have better luck asking his competitors. So I went from one hairdressing salon to another, stopping off in every barber shop in between. It happened on my fifteenth try, in a salon for women; I don't know how she overheard me, but all of a sudden one of the customers, like a tortoise, popped her head out from under a hood, her hair bristling with curlers and hairpins from what I believe is called a 'perm', and she called out, 'I know him, I know where he lives. It's not far.' She was right, it was not far. Bomba lived in a little suburban house identical to thousands of others. I rang the doorbell. No answer. I decided to wait. It was getting dark, when a teenager arrived. I asked her if Bomba lived in the house. 'He's my father,' she said. 'What do you want with him?' As soon as I said the word 'film', the young girl's eyes opened wide: 'Hollywood . . . ?' she murmured in curiosity. Her parents, she told me, would be coming back together but not before nine o'clock, so I had at least another two hours to wait. Bomba, she told me, worked as a barber on the lower concourse of Grand Central Station, but even if I hurried I wouldn't catch him before he closed up. So I decided to stay put, and the charming girl suggested I come inside. The instant, powerful warmth I felt for Bomba the moment I set eyes on him was equalled only by the irritation and later the exasperation I felt for his wife: she clearly meant no harm, but she hardly let the man get a word in edgeways. She anticipated his every answer, making conversation impossible. Deeply annoyed, I took Bomba by the arm and said, 'Why don't we go outside? I need a walk.' There, I told him that I had been looking for him for years; I gave him an overview of the film I was working on and explained why his time at Treblinka was crucial to my project. I needed to spend time with him, I said, just the two of us, we needed to come up with a way to make it work. He immediately understood what I meant; he told me that he had a mountain lodge in upstate New York and that he could be free the following Saturday and Sunday if I could get a car, since he did not have one.

I hired a car, extricated him from his terrible wife early on Saturday morning, and we crossed the Hudson River and its primeval banks at Tarrytown and headed north towards Albany. I had no means of recording our conversations, no camera, not even a tape recorder, barely a pen and a notebook. My hands were empty but my intuition was that it had to be so. I spent Saturday afternoon, most of the night, and all of Sunday with Bomba, before driving him back to Pelham Parkway. Those two days proved critical, not simply because of what he told me, things I didn't know, that nobody knew, things that made him a unique witness, but because what he told me then gave me the key to how I was to deal with the Jewish protagonists in my film. In his rough, imperfect English, Bomba the barber was a magnificent speaker and during the forty-eight hours we spent together he spoke to me as I believe he had never spoken to anyone; as though he were doing so for the first time. No one else had ever listened to him, shown him such thoughtful and companionable attention, which, as I encouraged him to rack his brain for every detail, forced him to plunge ever deeper into the unspeakable moments he had spent inside the gas chambers. I realized that in order to be able to film him, and people like him, I had to know everything about them in advance, or to know as much as possible – one can never know everything. Because to trigger such a reawakening meant being able at any moment to come to their aid, by which I don't mean offering some sort of compassion and support, but having the necessary confidence and the knowledge to dare to interrogate, interrupt, get the speaker back on track, ask the right questions at the right time. By the time I left Bomba, one of those questions had been resolved: the matter of confidence. He knew that he could count on me, knew to whom he would be talking. On the way back, I asked if he would be willing to be filmed, although I couldn't say whether that would be in a year or two or even three, since the financial problems had not yet been resolved. He consented solemnly and I think joyfully, having understood the need to bear witness. I told him I would get in touch with him again as soon as I could set a date.

This I was in a position to do two years later. I phoned for days without getting an answer, I wrote, but the letters were returned to sender. But I could not postpone the American shooting schedule, as I had already arranged to film others, such as Vrba and Jan Karski. Once in New York I decided to visit Pelham Parkway just to check. I rang the doorbell, and someone other than Bomba answered, a new tenant or perhaps the owner, I don't know. In answer to my questions, the man could only say that Bomba and his family, whom he had never met, had left the United States and were now living in Israel. He had moved without giving a forwarding address, without contacting me, although I had given him my details in case he needed to get in touch. But it was most likely my fault. I had left him too long without any news and he probably thought the film would never get made. In the summer of 1979, I arrived in Israel. A shooting schedule was planned, but my first priority was to find Bomba. I set about it by the simplest and most obvious means: since, in Israel, every Polish town has its own Survivors' Association and since Abraham came from Częstochowa, the home of the famous Black Madonna visited by so many popes, I simply presented myself to the association of the town's elders. Bomba, I discovered, had recently joined. And so I found him; he had come to think the film was a mirage; now, the fact that I had searched for him around the world was to him another indication of my determination and of his importance to my project. He was living in Holon, a suburb of Tel Aviv, where once again I met his daughter and his wife, who seemed calmer now. But, being afraid he might disappear again and fearful of the difficulties I would encounter while filming him, I decided to change my plans completely and start the shooting schedule with him. I filmed him facing the Mediterranean, on the beautiful terrace of an apartment in Jaffa that Théo Klein had loaned me. Once again, as Abraham Bomba described his deportation from Częstochowa, the hellish thirst suffered during the journey by his first wife and their baby, both of whom were sent to the gas chambers as soon as they arrived in Treblinka, he displayed the oratorical talent, the capacity to embody his account that had so captivated and seduced me in the mountains of upstate New York. The sun was setting quickly, as it invariably does in the eastern Mediterranean, and Dominique Chapuis, my cinematographer, said, 'We have to stop, I don't have enough light.' But I didn't care about the light, I was so caught up by the scope and the magic of the barber's words, I said, 'No, let's keep going, his face will fade away and he will go on talking in the dark.' It was stupid of me, the film was unusable, and in fact we did not use it. I mention this to show how captivated the whole crew was by this man.

But as filming continued, I sensed a nervousness overcome Bomba that echoed my own anxiety. We both knew that the hardest part was still ahead of us and that soon we would have to speak about the cutting of Jewish women's hair inside the gas chamber, the culmination of the horror, and the essential reason for our undertaking. On several occasions, on the days leading up to it, he took me to one side: 'This is going to be very hard,' he warned, 'I don't know if I can do it.' I wanted to help him, to help myself. There could be no question of having him talk about this on that sunny terrace facing the blue sea. It was I who thought of using a barber shop. Bomba was no longer a barber, he had retired and his retirement had been the main reason for his *aliyah*, his 'ascent' to Israel. But the idea appealed to him

431

and he set about finding a salon himself. This immediately posed an ethical problem: it couldn't be a ladies' hairdressing salon. We both realized that would be horrendous and obscene. So he found a genuine barber shop with an owner surrounded by a staff of young men who worked without uttering a word as customers came and went. Abraham wore the yellow jacket from his life at Grand Central Station, a proud relic of a profession he loved. The Israeli barbers, who spoke only Hebrew and worked around him in their usual blue-and-white check shirts, did not cast a single glance at the crucial scene of which he was the focus. It was Abraham, too, who chose his customer, a friend of his, probably from Częstochowa, whose hair he cut, working away with his scissors for almost the whole sequence, that is to say, at least twenty minutes. Or rather, he pretended to cut the man's hair: if he had really been cutting, the 'patient' would have ended up completely bald. But Abraham, on his own initiative and without receiving from me any other indication than 'Just make it look *as though* you are cutting his hair', became an actor and succeeded in giving the illusion of a genuine haircut, ensuring we heard the constant clicking of the blades, now and then actually snipping a hair, stepping back to inspect his work, then returning to perfect it while recounting his hell, compelled by my questions to describe every little detail. Why the barber shop? The familiar motions, I thought, might serve as a support, a crutch to the feelings, easing the task of speech and actions he needed to perform before the camera. Of course, they were not the same actions, a barber shop is not a gas chamber, pretending to cut one man's hair is nothing like the tale he had told me in the mountains of New York: how, naked, terrified after having been whipped by the Ukrainian guards, the Jewish women were forced into the gas chamber, in batches of seventy at a time, where the seventeen professional hairdressers waiting had them sit on long wooden benches and, in three or four snips of their scissors, cut off all their hair. When, while filming, I ask Abraham to re-enact the actions of the barbers in the gas chambers, he grabs the head of his friend, his fictitious client, brandishes the scissors and, moving quickly around his skull, demonstrates what he did: 'We just cut like this . . . here and there . . . and there . . . this side and this side . . . and it was all finished.' Two minutes per woman, no more. Without the scissors, the scene would have been a hundred times less evocative, a hundred times less powerful. And perhaps it might not have been filmed at all: the scissors allow him to incarnate what he is saying and to carry on, but also to catch his breath and gather the strength to tell his impossible and harrowing story.

In fact, there are two moments in that long sequence: as he begins his account, Abraham adopts a neutral, detached, objective tone, as though what he is recounting does not concern him, as though the horror might emerge without his involvement, almost harmoniously. My questions make it impossible for him to carry on as he would wish; initially, these are topographical, demanding details relating to logistics. I ask a question that is incongruous, absurd: 'There were no mirrors [in the gas-chambers], no?' – knowing perfectly well, since I had seen the gas chambers at Auschwitz and Majdanek, that there was nothing but bare walls. However, the walls of the barber shop in which we are filming are lined with mirrors and his movements are infinitely reflected in them. These questions make it possible to recreate as precisely as possible the place, the situation, but they also allow me to engage in the most difficult interrogation, which triggers the second moment in the sequence: 'What was your impression the first time you saw arriving these naked women with children, what did you feel?' Abraham avoids, dodges the question, the conversation continues with other details about the process of cutting the hair, designed to deceive these women in the last minutes of their lives, making them think, by the use of scissors and combs rather than clippers, of a man's haircut as it would be performed by an ordinary barber. At that moment, I became aware of something in Bomba's face, in his voice, in the silence between his words: a visible, palpable tension welled up in the room, I did not know what or

433

when, I was not sure, but I sensed that something was about to occur, that something might happen, something crucial.

I was standing just behind the cameraman and could see the counter indicating how much film stock was still in the magazine: five minutes. It is a lot, it is so little. Following a brutal intuition, I said to Chapuis in a low voice, 'Let's cut there and reload now.' With the Aaton 16mm camera, magazines had to be changed every eleven minutes. We had full magazines ready, the reload was done instantly and the conversation continued as though no interruption had occurred. Bomba hadn't noticed. After a moment, I repeated the question he had left unanswered. His answer was magnificent and overwhelming, he made no attempt to sidestep the issue: 'I tell you something . . . to have a feeling over there was very hard, to feel anything or to have a feeling, because working there day and night, between the people, between the bodies, man and woman . . . your feeling disappeared, you were dead, with your feeling, you had no feeling at all.' Then he added, 'A matter of fact, I want to tell you something that happened at the gas-chamber, when I was chosen in, over there to work as a barber, some of woman that came in from a transport from my town from Częstochowa, and from the woman, from the number of woman, I know a lot of people . . .' At that precise moment, this man dead to feeling was submerged by such intense feeling that he could not go on, indicating by a little gesture of the hand both the pointlessness and the impossibility of continuing to speak, and also the impossibility, the futility, of understanding. The scene is famous. Abraham wipes away the tears welling in his eyes with the corner of a napkin, lapses into silence, still clicking his scissors around his friend's head, trying to recover his composure, chatting in a low voice to his friend in Yiddish; he and I begin to talk, a conversation between two supplicants, he pleading with me to stop, me gently urging him to continue because I believe it is our common task, our shared duty. All of this happens at precisely the moment when, had I not reloaded the camera when I did, there would have been no film left. And the loss would have been irreparable: I could never have asked Bomba to start crying again as one might if rehearsing a play. The camera kept turning, Abraham's tears were as precious to me as blood, the seal of truth, its very incarnation. Some people have suggested some sort of sadism on my part in this perilous scene, while on the contrary I consider it to be the epitome of reverence and supportiveness, which is not to tiptoe away in the face of suffering, but to obey the categorical imperative of the search for and the transmission of truth. Bomba hugged me for a long time after we finished shooting, and again after he had seen the film: we spent several days together in Paris, and he knew that he would forever remain an unforgettable hero.

From Chełmno, where 400,000 Jews had been murdered with carbon monoxide emitted by the Saurer truck engines, there were two 'revenants': Michael Podchlebnik and Simon Srebnik. Both were living in Israel, the former in Tel Aviv, the latter in Ness Ziona near Rehovot and the Weizmann Institute, both equally unforgettable protagonists of *Shoah*. I went to see Srebnik first, the younger of the two, who had survived the second period of extermination at Chełmno (extermination there took place in two periods: between January 1941 and the summer of 1942, then, after a 'dead season', between July 1944 and January 1945). He was forty-four years old – in Chełmno he had been thirteen and a half. We talked, or rather tried to talk, since I barely understood anything he said. Every time he uttered the name of one of the SS officers in Chełmno, he preceded it with the title *Meister*, 'master'. It seemed to me that, though now over forty, he was still the terrified child he had surely been back then. I forgot to mention that his father had been butchered before his eyes in the Łódź Ghetto, that his mother, with whom he had been deported to Chełmno, eighty kilometres north-east of Łódź, had been gassed as soon as they arrived, and that he himself had been executed with a bullet through the back of the head on the night of 18 January 1945, two days before the Red Army arrived to liberate that area of

Poland. By some miracle the bullet missed his vital brain centres and he survived. We talked in rudimentary German, and as he spoke, I could make out words such as *Kirche* [church], *Schloss* [castle], and proper names such as Narva [the River Ner], but I could not understand the sense, nor could I connect them to one another. I left Srebnik filled with doubts about the way I was going about things, feeling I lacked the objective knowledge necessary to question him. And besides, it seemed to me thoughtless to pretend to understand how extermination using gas vans in Chełmno had worked without ever having seen the place. In my mind, it was becoming increasingly important that I make a trip to Poland: I could not understand Srebnik or make myself understood until I had seen Chełmno. When Bomba had talked to me about Treblinka in his mountain cabin, I had completely understood what he was telling me, and the idea of comparing his account with the place itself had never occurred to me: he brought the place to life with his words. The snatches of conversation I had recorded with Srebnik were disjointed memories of a world that was exploded, both literally and in the terror it had instilled in him. It was only much later that I realized how accurate my sense of an exploded world was: nothing was more difficult than the filming of Chełmno, with two periods of killing and the destruction of the sites where it took place. But there could be no question of abandoning Srebnik, of sidelining him: he was to play a crucial role in my film, and it was up to me to work and to adapt in order to be able to understand him.

With the first of the two 'revenants', Michael Podchlebnik, there was no such problem: everything could be read in his face, a splendid face of smiles and tears, his face *is* the site of the Shoah. And every time I see him on the screen, sensing my hand pressing on his shoulder to help him to find a voice for his most gruelling account – that of discovering his wife and children among the corpses when he opened the doors of the first gas van – the moment when his face changes, his courageous smile giving way to discreet tears, I can do nothing but weep with him. Heroic and rigorous, Michael Podchlebnik who, in his first appearance in the film says, 'Let's not talk about that,' just after Srebnik's words, 'No one can represent to oneself what happened here'; the heroic Podchlebnik, who says nothing about his extraordinary escape because, according to him, his personal story is not important. Nor does he say anything about the courage and the cunning he had to marshal, the suffering he endured: he escaped at the beginning of the first period of extermination in Chełmno and was forced to survive in German-occupied Poland for almost four years.

I will talk more about Poland later, but I can say now that I read a lot before going to Chełmno; once there, I paced the narrow road that runs through the village, the paths that lead down the Ner, below the banks of the river, which, though it looks idyllic, reeks; I saw the church, still intact, the same church that appears in the 15 August procession in the film; I saw the 'castle', now a coal depot; I paced the road that leads from the church to the mass graves in Rzuszow forest, walking at the speed of the gas vans, that is, slowly, anxiously wondering how to film these many sites of death. Then, though I had not come up with a solution, I returned to Israel to see Srebnik. Straightaway I told him that I had just come back from Chełmno, I had prudently brought paper and pencils so that we could both sketch our memories of those places. Just as Kim Kum-sun and I had done twenty years earlier in North Korea, Srebnik and I invented a common language. He corrected me, I corrected him. In some sense, I knew more than he did, since I had roamed these places as a free man, whereas he had been forced to march in shackles, suffering the hunger, the beatings, the humiliation and the constant fear of death, which might come at any moment. And yet there was a new and intense joy in the way that through these drawings, we shared, exchanged and compared what each of us knew; we began to talk, I knew now what to ask, he wanted to speak. It was during this conversation that I learned that he sang for his SS guard in a flat-bottomed

437

boat on the river. I immediately asked him to sing what he used to sing back then and, beneath the arbour in his garden in Ness Ziona, his lyrical voice soared: '*Mały biały domek w mej pamięci tkwi* . . .' ['A little white house sticks in my memory . . .'] Then, at my request, he sang the chorus of the old Prussian military song that the elderly SS guard had taught him: '*Wenn die Soldaten durch die Stadt marschieren, öffnen die Mädchen die Fenster und die Türen. Ei warum? Ei darum! Ei darum!*' ['When the soldiers march through the town, the young girls open their windows and their doors . . .'] Such are the obscure and unforeseen paths to creation: in that garden in Ness Ziona, at that very minute, I knew for certain that this man singing would go back with me to Chełmno, that I would film him singing on the River Ner, that this would be the opening sequence of *Shoah*. There was no doubt about it, there were many obstacles still to be overcome before it could happen, not the least being to convince Srebnik and his wife, but my desire, it was dazzlingly clear, would prevail over everyone and everything.

Much later, in the years when I was editing the film, someone gave me a cassette of Marlene Dietrich, whose voice, whose life, whose songs I loved. Driving to Saint-Cloud, to the LTC editing studios, I put it into the cassette deck in the car and, to my shock and amazement, I heard Marlene sing the song that the SS man in Chełmno had taught Srebnik. Hearing it gave me a lift that lasted several days. Later still, only a few years ago, invited to a screening of *Shoah* followed by a discussion at the celebrated film school in Łódź, I fell into an astonishing trap. I had experienced every possible dirty trick from the Poles when it came to *Shoah*, but I could not possibly have imagined that a fat red-haired fishwife, dripping with make-up and accompanied by her lawyer, would stand up at the end of the session to scream at me, demanding that I pay her royalties for 'Mały biały domek' ['Little White House'], the Polish song at the beginning of the film that Srebnik, in shackles, sang on the River Ner for his SS guard in 1944. Apparently, this monster's father had written the lyrics!

It was while shooting on the Ner one rainy afternoon, listening to that singing child, now a forty-seven-year-old man, that I found the solution to the problem that had seemed to me insoluble: how to film Chełmno, this long peasant village of low houses stretched out on either side of a single street. I had the idea of travelling through it on a horse-drawn carriage, a tracking shot taking in the wet road, the houses, the church, the rump of the horse, its tail sweeping through space like the pendulum of a metronome, the regular clatter of its hooves making all the more terrible the words of Frau Michelson, the wife of the Nazi schoolteacher in Chełmno, the woman who had witnessed the ceaseless comings and going of the gas vans and who could no longer remember how many Jews had been asphyxiated, 4,000, 40,000 or 400,000. When I tell her it was 400,000, she says simply, 'I knew it had a four in it.'

Chapter 19

Heart pounding, I arrived in Ludwigsburg, near Stuttgart, to meet Adalbert Rückerl, director of the *Zentralstelle für Landesjustizverwaltung*, the German federal agency responsible for locating, pursuing, hunting down and, when possible, prosecuting Nazi war criminals and those responsible for crimes against humanity. The rendezvous with this courteous and highly cultured man had been arranged in Jerusalem. I had a list with me of 150 names, drawn up during the course of my reading, all of whom seemed to me essential to my project. Rückerl and his assistant had no legal obligation to help me, yet they agreed to do so, although they were rather taken aback when they found out how many people I was trying to trace. They began by saying that many of those on the list were now dead, others had disappeared without trace; for the rest, I would have to give them time to try to track down the addresses – by now probably out of date – of those with whom the agency had had dealings. When I met them again, the winnowing had been considerable – of the 150 names I had given them, they could only locate about thirty possible leads. And there was no guarantee that even these would prove useful, since the details they had on file dated from investigations or trials carried out during the 1940s and early 1950s, after the great Nuremberg trials – what were collectively known as the 'subsequent trials', like those of the *Einsatzgruppen*. As they gave me what information they had, they wished me luck but they were looking at me with that mixture of sympathy, astonishment and pity one might feel when faced with a naïveté bordering on idiocy. As he took his leave, Rückerl said, 'Alas, I fear you won't get very far.' I did not know, as I left, that this first trip to Germany was to be followed by countless others; that it was the beginning of something that, during the long nights I spent in bars and hotel rooms in far-flung towns and cities, crushed and disheartened after countless setbacks, feeling ready to give up, I would come to think of as a senseless Calvary.

To begin with, not a single address proved useful. I was determined, for example, to track down a man named Wetzel from the *Ostministerium*, the Nazi Ministry for the Occupied Eastern Territory, a high-ranking bureaucrat who, in an appalling letter, had suggested using gas to swiftly liquidate Jews in the Baltic countries. He had paid with only a few years in prison and, according to the information I had, was living in Augsburg in southern Germany. I arrived there one day with Irène, but the tenants at the address I had informed me that he had left Augsburg fifteen years previously and they did not know where he had gone. Fortunately, there exists a unique agency in Germany known as the *Einwohnermeldeamt*, where citizens are required to register any change of address. The *Einwohnermeldeamt* in Augsburg told me that Wetzel had moved to northern Germany, to a little town in Schleswig-Holstein whose name I've forgotten. From Augsburg to Lübeck, the principal city in Schleswig-Holstein, is a long and expensive trip and it began to dawn on me that organizing my schedule was going to be very difficult. When I arrived in the town where I expected to find Wetzel, I was met with suspicion and hostility – many former Nazis had chosen to live in northern Germany – but I was told that Wetzel had left this idyllic paradise some ten years earlier. My only resource was the Lübeck *Einwohnermeldeamt*. Wetzel clearly had itchy feet – he had headed south again, this time to Darmstadt in southern Germany. It was becoming clear that this switchbacking from one *Einwohnermeldeamt* to another could scupper the film before it had even begun. The other possibility was to write to the *Einwohnermeldeamt*, something that took considerable time, entailed much dispiriting bureaucratic wrangling and even then did not always result in an answer. I therefore decided that I would have to go in person or send one of my assistants, either Irène or, later, Corinna Coulmas, a brilliant and courageous young woman, daughter of a Greek father and a mother who was a member of the *Bundestag*. Having decided to convert to Judaism, Corinna had an astonishing command of Hebrew and a broad knowledge of the Torah and the Talmud.

Occasionally I would track down a Nazi, only to arrive a day late, in time for the funeral. Fortunately, however, this was not generally the case. In the beginning, in the pitiful naïveté of my inexperience and transparency, I proceeded as follows: I telephoned, gave my name and the reason for my call – namely, that I was making a film about the extermination of the Jews. I rarely got the chance to say any more. Either the phone was slammed down or, in the rare cases where they spoke to me, despite my placid tone and my feeble German, which I deliberately pretended was worse than it actually was, the person I was speaking to stalled for time, telling me I had the wrong number or the wrong person – and all the while in the background I would hear some shrew screaming, 'Don't talk to him! *Ruf die Polizei an!*' ['Call the police!'] Former Nazis, those who had been up to their necks in it, were invariably as meek as lambs with their wives. Because it had been the wives who kept the families together while the husbands were on the run or in prison, they made the law and wore the trousers. If it happened that the wife, rather than the husband, answered the phone, I was rudely interrogated and, having explained the reason for my call, I was threatened and insulted. So, after a number of setbacks, I decided not to phone but to turn up unannounced, alone or with Corinna or Irène, on the doorstep of the person I was looking for. As you can easily imagine, this approach required not only considerable nerve but also meant that the old problem of having to resort to the local *Einwohnermeldeamt* increased. If no one answered the door when I arrived, I could not know whether my target was out shopping or on holiday for a month. I therefore had no choice but to wait and if I were ever to draw up a 'stake-out' table, enumerating the number of hours I spent watching and waiting during the making of the film, the total would be enormous. The random nature of these encounters and my inability to stick to a work schedule made these trips to Germany exhausting. But sometimes it happened that all obstacles were overcome, that the door was answered by the person I was looking for. Once I had introduced myself, the conversation often came to an abrupt end on the doorstep, without my ever having been asked to come inside. To Germans, my name was obviously Jewish, something that did little to help things along.

There were, however, two exceptions: Perry Broad and Franz Suchomel, whom I have already mentioned. Perry Broad, who had been an SS officer in Auschwitz, was extremely intelligent. Born in Brazil to an English father and a German mother who moved with him back to Berlin when he was five. In 1941 at the age of twenty he enlisted in the *Waffen* SS as a foreign volunteer. Later posted to Auschwitz, he became a member of the *Politische Abteilung*, the grim Political Department that ran Block 11 (the 'death block') that inter-rogated, tortured, almost always pronounced the death penalty and executed the prisoners with a *Genickschuss* (a bullet in the back of the neck) in the courtyard. Filip Müller, who had been a prisoner there in cell 13, gives an account of it in his first appearance in *Shoah*. Captured by the British army shortly before the end of the war, Perry Broad, on his own initiative, wrote an impressive report about his experiences in Auschwitz and the operation of the gas chambers, which he had witnessed. He was released in 1947 only to be arrested by the German authorities in 1959, and released again a year later on bail of 50,000 Deutschmarks; he was questioned again in 1964, during the Auschwitz trials in Frankfurt where he was one of the defendants. He was found guilty of supervising the selections on the ramp at Birkenau and of having participated in the interrogation, torture and execution of prisoners in the Political Department. He was sentenced to four years' hard labour, though he did not complete the sentence: he was forty-four years old. He himself opened the door when I arrived unannounced and rang the bell at his Dusseldorf apartment. He was polite, asked me to come in and sit down. I told him that I had read his 1945 report, and praised its honesty, its literary quality and its considerable historic importance. He was a tall, thin man, moderate in his language, who looked much younger than his years; he travelled a lot in Germany since he worked as a sales rep. I tried to persuade him to testify in my film, to appear as the author of the report and to repeat for the cameras what he had written of his own accord. He replied that writing the report, the existence and contents of which he did not contest, was the greatest regret of his life. In the eyes of his SS comrades, he was a traitor, he had been stigmatized when he came to trial and later in prison; there could be no question of him doing so again. His wife, much younger than he, extremely pretty and clearly very much in love with him, appeared at this point. I introduced myself and repeated my request in front of her, stressing that for him to accept would be proof of great courage, that times had changed and that all humanity would be forever in his debt. I added that I would make clear the great moral strength it had required for her husband to appear before the cameras and tell the truth. She was not impervious to my arguments and I sensed that she might be an ally. Because I had no intention of abandoning Perry Broad, I was not prepared to give up easily. In the months that followed, I phoned him and saw him several times. I invited them to dinner and twice, at about four o'clock in the morning, after much alcohol, I thought the goal was in sight. His wife took what I said very seriously: the truth would be redemptive, and the light of day was preferable to the clandestine lives they had been forced to endure. With tears in his eyes, he would say yes, but fifteen minutes later he was back to no. I tried so often, did everything I could, and I finally became convinced that Perry's were just drunken tears; I was going to have to find another way.

Franz Suchomel was living in Altötting in Lower Bavaria, near the Austro-German border, on the German bank of the River Inn. I arrived one morning with Corinna, unannounced as was by now my rule. I told him I had read the evidence he had given at the Treblinka trial and what he had said to Gitta Sereny. I had not come, I added, out of psychological interest, nor was I a judge, a prosecutor or a Nazi-hunter; he had nothing to fear from me. But, I told him, I believed that *we* desperately needed his help – without explaining precisely what I meant by 'we'. '*We* don't know,' I continued, 'how to raise *our* children. The young generations of Jews do not understand how this immeasurable catastrophe could have happened, how six million of our people could have allowed themselves to be massacred without response. Did they really die like sheep in a slaughterhouse?' This way, I was putting Suchomel in the position of teacher and myself in the position of student, impressing on him the historic role that would be his were he to explain the various stages of the process of mass extermination in Treblinka. I knew that Suchomel was a native of the Sudetenland, on the edges of Germany, on the border with Czechoslovakia; I also knew that he had participated in the ultra-secret *Aktion-T4*, a codename that referred to Tiergartenstraße 4, the address of the Berlin office where a man named Victor Brack secretly planned the euthanasia of mentally and physically handicapped German citizens in five castle-hospitals throughout the Reich: Schloss Hartheim, Schloss Sonnenstein, known as '*Die Sonne*' ['the Sun'], Schloss Grafeneck, Schloss Hadamar and Schloss Brandenburg. The elderly residents of Hartheim I spoke to still had fear in their eyes at the mere mention of the long black SS vans driving up to the castle. No one dared say anything, but the rumours that children were being put to death in bathrooms converted into 'infirmaries' were rife throughout Germany. They were entirely justified; the rumours were true. It was in these bathrooms that gassing was first experimented

445

with, a prelude to the extermination of the Jewish vermin. Suchomel, who was a gifted liar ('If you lie enough,' he said to me in *Shoah*, 'you end up believing your own lies'), claimed that his only role in *Aktion-T4* was as a photographer. But the Catholic Germans were very attached to their citizens with goitre, with Down's syndrome, with club-feet, their children with harelips. In August 1941, the Bishop of Münster, the Count von Galen, ascended the pulpit of his cathedral, where he forcefully and courageously denounced the crimes being committed against the weak, the needy, the destitute. Hitler, who could not handle an internal front, immediately capitulated and gave orders that T4 was to be stopped. For a while Suchomel and his colleagues became inoperative, on half pay, but between the spring and the summer of 1942, they were again called up to active service and posted – with no apparent scruples on their part – to the extermination camps of Belzec, Sobibór, Treblinka and Majdanek, where they were able to make full use of their expertise. Suchomel was tempted by my offer of the role of lead witness; to make it more attractive, I offered him money, considering it appropriate, I told him, that he be reimbursed for his time and effort. Thus began between us, between Paris and Altötting, a long correspondence, as well as numerous trips by train, by plane. I visited him several times, spent long hours with him, tried to get his consent; twice I believed I had succeeded, just as I had with Perry Broad, the difference being that I had never offered Broad money, believing that this would not work with him. Suchomel, on the other hand, cared about money more than anything and the sum I was offering – although doing so felt like stabbing myself in the heart – was considerable, the equivalent of €2,000. Then, one night, having sat up with me until three in the morning, in spite of the angina he was constantly complaining of, he said, '*Jawohl, ich werde es machen*' ['All right, I'll do it']. I didn't waste a second but left immediately, knowing that time, as Jankélévitch put it, 'is the organ of denial'. Telling him I would be back as soon as I could get a camera crew together, I drove to Munich, took the first plane to Paris and, when I arrived, found a telegram already waiting for me: Suchomel had gone back on his word, his son-in-law was threatening to divorce his daughter if he went through with the filming. My heart skipped a beat; I took the first Lufthansa flight back to Munich, hired a Mercedes and raced back to Altötting. It was dusk when I rang the doorbell. He opened the door, clearly not expecting me. Terrified, he took a step back, and brought his finger to his lips. But it was too late. I heard furious footsteps on the stairs and then a Bavarian maniac, heavy-set and about thirty years old, hurled himself at me, roaring, '*Raus! Weg!* Leave us in peace! Enough of this old shit!' He pushed me towards the door, but I shouted back, in French, pushed back at him and forced him to retreat. Suchomel's wife and daughter stood screaming on the first-floor landing, calling back the son-in-law, while Suchomel, like a referee in a boxing ring, tried to separate us, forcing me into a rather despicable collusion by telling me, 'Leave it, leave it, he can't understand . . .' I remained with him in the ground-floor room for some minutes, he begged me to leave, I told him I needed to think, that I was not about to give up on him, that I would phone. He said, 'Not you, anyone but you! Get your assistant to call, tell her to say it's Fraülein Diesler calling from Frankfurt.'

Thus, with the help of Corinna, I made him one last offer: I agreed not to film him, but I wanted to record an exhaustive oral statement; on the matter of money, the arrangement was as before, he would get the sum proposed. We needed to arrange a time and a place, since clearly we could not record at his home. I still have all of Suchomel's letters – I received about one a month for a year. Each time, he made a new suggestion as to where we might meet, each time something cropped up with his health or his family preventing him from honouring his commitment. His letters are a mixture of fear, an inability to deliver, and a staggering obsequiousness. He wanted the money with all his heart, but there were times when I did not have a penny, when I did not know if I would be able to go on with the film.

In one of his letters he complains that I cancelled a meeting because I had to go to the United States. This was true; the Israeli government, having given up funding me, had organized several fundraising tours to visit rich Jewish-Americans. This, however, proved to be a complete disaster: I flew from Baltimore to Chicago, Chicago to Los Angeles, making speeches to businessmen, to local versions of Larry Tisch, then on to Boston, to El Paso, to Miami, to Denver, and every time it was the same dreary conversation. I would persuasively outline the reasons why such a film should exist, I presented the extent of my knowledge and the work I had already done. When I had finished, the questions began, and inevitably in every city I visited, everywhere I went, from the mouths of a hundred different people, came the same question, one that meant OK, we've listened to you, now let's get down to the facts: 'Mr Lanzmann, what is your message?' Each time, I remained silent, I was incapable of answering such a question; I still am. I don't know what the 'message' of *Shoah* is. I never thought of it in those terms. If I had said, 'My message is: Never again!' or perhaps 'Love one another', wallets would probably have sprung open, but I was a sorry fundraiser: of the budget for *Shoah*, not one single dollar came from the USA.

My proposal to Suchomel – that I wanted his oral testimony – was serious. At the time I did not know how I would proceed, thinking I would have to make do with second-best, editing it as a voiceover, over footage of Treblinka as it is today. This was not really a satisfying solution, but what he had to say was so important that the question of form was secondary. We continued to write to each other; he made a further request that I had no intention of respecting, even as I told him that I would: he wanted to remain anonymous.

Mankind, Marx says, sets itself only such problems as it is able to resolve. While I was grappling with impossibilities on every front, an engineer from Grenoble, Jean-Pierre Beauviala, the inventor of the Aaton camera, had created a small wonder that was to change radically the conditions under which I could film in Germany and led me to choose the path of deception, subterfuge, secrecy and maximum risk. Adalbert Rückerl had been right when he looked at me pityingly. Frankness and honesty had been repaid with resounding failure; I had to learn to deceive the deceivers, it was my bounden duty. The 'Paluche' was a cylindrical camera about thirty centimetres long and not very wide that could be pointed by hand (hence the name, meaning 'paw') without needing to look through a viewfinder. It worked using a high-frequency video system; there was no film or tape inside, instead it transmitted a signal that could be received within a limited radius – by a VCR that recorded and stored the footage. I demonstrated in *Shoah* how the footage was received by a minivan parked on the street in front of the house or the apartment building of the person I was surreptitiously filming. We tested the process in Paris from the upper floors of high-rise buildings, with the van parked at the foot of the building. When the system worked, it was truly miraculous, and considerably opened up the field of the possibles, to put it in Leibnizian terms. But this was not always the case. If there was a television transmitter nearby, or if there were too many powerful electrical devices in the apartment itself, the footage was blurred and unusable. In addition, it was essential that the Paluche be directly in line with the minivan. If the minivan was parked on one side of the building, and I was forced to interview on the other, the footage was not received. Sometimes I would arrive in a house or an apartment entirely unknown to me, only to be brought into a living room at the back of the building while the minivan was parked in the street by the kitchen – in such cases, I had to work out the layout of the apartment and come up with an idea on the spot, taking my interviewee firmly by the arm and leading him, for instance, into the kitchen, as though I had decided on a quick, informal conversation, wanting to avoid disturbing anyone. Sometimes it worked. Not always.

Once I became confident with the Paluche, I completely changed tack, and started everything again from scratch. The most pressing thing now was to equip myself with a new identity. I hope I will be forgiven for not divulging the names of the people involved, but I promised secrecy: I acquired a fake passport, which I promised to return as soon as filming was completed. Now I was Claude-Marie Sorel, born in Caen – all records in that Norman city having been destroyed during bombing raids. My second decisive step was the creation of a 'Centre d'études et de recherches sur l'histoire contemporaine' – a Research Centre for the Study of Contemporary History – attached to the University of Paris. I housed my Institute at 26 rue de Condé, Paris, the address, then and now, of Les Temps modernes, where I could easily receive mail. A printer in Évreux made up some letterhead paper and envelopes, on stock of an impressive weight and texture, clear signs of authenticity.

Aside from Suchomel and Perry Broad, I drew up a list of about thirty people whom I knew to be still alive, a mix of criminals and Nazi bureaucrats whom I knew I could question effectively because I had read widely about them. Hence, for example, Professor Laborde, the director of the Centre d'études et de recherches sur l'histoire contemporaine, wrote a long letter to Walter Stier, the head of Büro 33 of the Reichsbahn (the German Reich Railways), which had been specifically responsible for the 'transport' of the Jews to the death camps. A number of attempts had been made to indict Stier but he had always managed to disappear, escaping to live with his daughter who had married a Syrian and was living in Damascus. When I tracked him down, he was living in Frankfurt; no one bothered him any more. I had read a number of books glorifying the Reich Railways, justifiably proud of its achievements; in spite of bombings, the destruction of tracks, stations and installations, the Reichsbahn tirelessly continued to convey troops and provisions to all fronts, promptly, selflessly and with great discipline, repairing and restoring the lines. And it had transported not just troops, but also civilians. For all these many reasons for justifiable pride, the books are notably silent on the subject of transport of the Jews. This is an injustice since, even in the most difficult military periods, these transports were often given priority over all other tasks the *Reichsbahn* had to handle. But it should be said that, in the case of the Jews, such trains made a profit, since, like ordinary holidaymakers, they were transported on a 'group fare' basis and were responsible for paying for their last journeys themselves. So Professor Laborde contacted Stier to inform him that a research assistant from his Institute, Claude-Marie Sorel, Ph.D., was to be in Germany from such-and-such to such-and-such a date and would telephone him to try to arrange a meeting, the reason given being that Dr Sorel was making a study of the extraordinary way in which the *Reichsbahn* managed to carry out its mission during the war, a subject about which little was known in France. Professor Laborde elucidated the premises of Dr Sorel's research in terms that would gratify a self-important Nazi, adding that Walter Stier, a decorated, high-ranking former official of the *Reichsbahn*, seemed admirably qualified to assist Dr Sorel with his research, and offering a sizeable sum of money to compensate him fairly for his time. The word 'Jew' obviously did not appear in the letter.

In response to the thirty letters I sent, requiring much effort, a great deal of reading, mental contortion and spiritual exertion, I received ten replies: five positive, five negative. Stier, as one can see from *Shoah*, was among the former. Of the twenty who did not reply, the greatest loss to me were the members of the *Einsatzgruppen*. I knew everything about them, had read everything, studied the diagrams and the detailed organization charts published by Hilberg, their biographies, their adherence, and the theatres where their bloody crimes were committed. I had also read the transcripts of the *Einsatzgruppen* trial held in Nuremberg after the main Nuremberg trials. Three had been sentenced to death: Otto Ohlendorf, their leader; Paul Blobel, who, over three days, had had 50,000 Jews from Kiev machine-gunned in the ravine at Babi Yar; and Heinz Schubert (related to the composer), who had been responsible for the massacres in the Crimea. Ohlendorf and Blobel were hanged, Schubert's sentence was commuted at the eleventh hour by John McCloy, US High Commissioner in Germany. Nahum Goldmann, president of the World Jewish Congress, managed to get me an interview with McCloy during my investigations in America. In his office on the top floor of a skyscraper on Wall Street, he greeted me with these words of rare elegance: 'Ah! You've come about this Jewish business!' I could only nod. Nowadays, people refer to the killings committed by the *Einsatzgruppen* in the Ukraine, Belarus and the Baltic countries as the 'Shoah by bullet', suddenly 'discovering' what has been known for more than sixty years.

During my various trips to Germany before I had acquired the Paluche, in my period of innocence, I had managed to meet with three members of the *Einsatzgruppen* and also with Bruno Streckenbach, who had trained the first commandos in Pretzsch and in Düben, readying them for action from the beginning of Operation Barbarossa, the massive invasion of the Soviet Union in June 1941. They had agreed to speak with me, attracted by the breadth of my knowledge and the accuracy of my information about them, but the moment the word 'film' was mentioned, they became tongue-tied. Those who received subsequent letters from Professor Laborde were, naturally, not those who had met me as Claude Lanzmann. A long letter was addressed to Schubert, who had been condemned to death and then pardoned. This letter remained unanswered.

The Paluche had its first outing with Suchomel in late March 1976, two years before the actual shooting of the film began. He was ready, we had exchanged I don't know how many letters, and I didn't want him to go back on his word again. Besides, he was complaining of heart problems and I was afraid that if I waited too long he might die. (In fact, he did die four years before *Shoah* was released.) He had the surprising idea of meeting me, not in Germany, but in Austria, on the other bank of the River Inn, at Braunau am Inn more precisely, the birthplace of one Adolf Hitler. From Alfred Spiess, the prosecutor at the Treblinka trial, I had managed to obtain a plan of the extermination camp, which I had had enlarged by a specialist company in Paris to the size of a school blackboard. William Lubtchansky, my cinematographer, was to pose as the sound-engineer. We had commissioned a large leather bag with two side pockets. When opening the bag, one could see only a Nagra, the standard professional sound-recording equipment. The Paluche lay in one of the pockets, with a hole cut in the leather for the lens. However, William had made a foam cover to make the lens look like a microphone. In the other pocket was a tiny video monitor, allowing him to frame the shot. We left for Braunau two days before the scheduled meeting; I rented rooms at the Hotel Post, one of which we converted into a recording studio, pinning the map of Treblinka to the wall, choosing where William would sit – at some distance from Suchomel so that he wouldn't suspect anything. In his last letter, Suchomel had informed me that he and his wife would arrive at nine o'clock at Simbach, the small German border town opposite Braunau – one had only to cross the river. He also added, 'I am delighted that you have not gone back on the promised amount of *Schmerzensgeld* [pain money]. I have one last request: that it be paid to me in German currency. Please forgive this request. I am not doing this deliberately.' On the eve of their arrival, I bought a fishing rod, which I cut in half to create a *baguette de magister* – a schoolmaster's pointer.

When Suchomel, whom I had fetched from the station at Simbach, stepped into the studio and found himself face to face with the huge map of Treblinka and saw William with all his equipment at the other side of the room, he took a step back. I calmed him down, gave him the pointer, and said, 'I am your pupil, you are my teacher, you will instruct me.' We broke for lunch, to which I had also invited his wife; I remember they stuffed themselves with duck, followed by whipped cream, while William, whose father had been gassed at Auschwitz, shot me murderous looks. By the time we began again, my 'teacher' had been completely won over, twice I persuaded him to sing the song the Jews of the *Sonderkommando* were forcibly taught the moment they arrived; and the cruelty in his eyes at that moment shows how completely he was caught up in the grip of his past as an SS-*Unterscharführer*, and what a ruthless man he had been when he held the power over life and death. It was a gruelling and exhausting day. I was horrified by what I learned, and yet I knew that this was extraordinary testimony since no one had ever described in such a detailed manner – urged on by my precise questions, which sounded purely technical and devoid of all moral implications – the killing process of Treblinka extermination camp. And during the long hours of complex and concentrated shooting, I feared that at any moment he might discover the subterfuge, that he might see, as I did, the sunlight glinting on the lens of the Paluche. When we had finished, I counted the 100 Deutschmark notes slowly in front of him and his wife, the price for his 'pain'. He was so happy, so sure of himself and of me by now, that he suggested we might do it again: he had, he claimed, many more things to reveal. I said yes, but I never followed up; it was he who pestered me with more letters, he was clearly interested in my money. In Treblinka, he had been the head of the *Goldjuden*, the Gold Jews, a commando responsible for finding any money, gold or jewellery hidden in the clothes, for pulling the gold teeth from the jaws of those who had just been gassed. That same evening, in a Munich restaurant, William and I had a fierce argument. He was at the end of his tether, as shocked as I was by the risks we had run and the horrors we had heard, but what he could not accept was my extending a lunch invitation to Suchomel, my lack of emotion and, worst of all, my paying him. I understood William's point of view, he was right, but without my self-imposed iron discipline there would not have been a single Nazi in the film. My coldness and my calm were an integral part of my deception.

Like Suchomel, Perry Broad didn't know Dr Sorel, since I had introduced myself to him under my own name back when I still had faith in mankind. Now that I had the Paluche, I phoned him one day in 1979, in the middle of a hectic shooting schedule in Germany, and told him that I would be coming to see him with Corinna, my German assistant: I hadn't given up hope of persuading him. The approach was different this time. William, who was working on another film, was not my cinematographer at this point; Dominique Chapuis had replaced him and together we worked out a more efficient and less obvious way of using the Paluche. In any case, the approach we had taken with Suchomel could not work since I could not explain to Perry Broad that I was just going to record his voice, and there could be no possible reason for me to be accompanied by a so-called sound-engineer. It was here that I made a qualitative leap in my deception. We bought an ordinary linen bag, the sort any woman might carry, and decorated both sides with little stars and circles of silver paper. The bag had two pockets, one on either side, in which we placed open packs of cigarettes, ready to be smoked. The Paluche lay at the bottom of the bag in a foam cradle, and where the lens was, we cut a circular hole in the linen and replaced it with a disc of a silver paper that allows light to pass through. Once the Paluche, the transmitter and the antenna were in place, we filled the bag with a variety of items – newspapers, books – that were all readily visible. I had already been to Perry Broad's apartment so even before we arrived I knew the position of the armchair where he usually sat, and the sofa facing it where he would seat Corinna and myself. I also remembered a low table between us where Corinna could put her bag, with the lens of the Paluche pointed at Perry Broad. The sound-recording was done as it would have been for any television recording; I had a high-frequency transmitter in my pocket and an ultrasensitive microphone clipped under my tie, meaning I had to wear a suit and tie and a thick shirt even in the sweltering heat. But we needed to make sure that this system would work, by which I mean that the minivan would receive both sound and image. So, shortly after we arrived, I pretended to rummage through the bag for a document I couldn't find, turned to Corinna and said, 'I must have left it in the car, could you get it for me?' The minivan had tinted windows so that from the outside nothing could be seen, neither the recording equipment, nor the engineers fiddling with monitors and recorders as a covert interview was going on. But we had agreed a code: a piece of green cardboard on the windscreen meant the signal was coming through loud and clear, red meant that it wasn't working. When Corinna came back, she winked to let me know that everything was fine, and I began to speak to Perry using the conditional mood: 'If you should agree to be filmed some day, this is what I would ask you.' I read out excerpts of his celebrated report, formulated certain objections, asked him to clarify certain things, expressed my astonishment. He was reticent in his answers, but he replied, having no idea of the trap I had set. I carried on, but my triumph was short-lived. To make things look natural, as I've said, the bag had been stuffed full of papers and files. Too full as it turned out: suddenly, as Perry Broad was speaking, wisps of white smoke began to rise from the bag as in a fairy tale, or at the election of a pope. Perry saw the smoke too, of course, but his astonishment, and his Teutonic slowness, meant his reactions were not as quick as mine. I leapt to my feet, snatched up the bag, shouted to Corinna, 'Come on!', grabbed her hand and we dashed down the stairs before he caught up with us. And he never did catch us. We jumped into the minivan and took off in a screech of tyres, like in a cop film. But the Paluche was completely fried. This was a catastrophic setback that compromised the entire German shooting schedule. It also represented a financial loss as the Paluche was an expensive piece of equipment. Still, two weeks later I managed to get a brand new Paluche. Dr Sorel would finally be able to go to work.

Depending on our mood and the difficulties we anticipated, we used either the leather bag and the 'sound-engineer' approach that had worked three years earlier with Suchomel, or the linen bag version, though the bag was no longer stuffed with paper as it had been at Perry Broad's apartment: the Paluche needed to breathe. It took great nerve for Corinna to agree to be alone with me with the 'targets', all deeply suspicious by nature. What is not clear in the film is that these people were invariably surrounded by extremely nosy family members. The shoot with Stier, 'strictly a bureaucrat' as he described himself – who, to me, is one of the most despicable Nazis to appear in *Shoah* – is a perfect example of this. Some will remember a moment in the interview when the camera goes crazy, veering around wildly. What happened is this: Dominique Chapuis, the cinematographer 'sound-engineer', felt that Stier's wife and two of her friends were taking an unhealthy interest in his equipment and, fearing they would notice the video monitor in the side pocket, he began to shake the bag. It is true, too, that I felt more confident when I had a man with me rather than a delicate young woman.

Armed with our second Paluche, we were like a circus or like the *Illustre Théâtre*, Molière's strolling players, touring the towns and the *Länder* of Germany, continually finding new prey. It was a truly crazy time because it always worked; my interviews went on for hours and by the time they were finished everyone was exhausted, but by hook or by crook, I got my footage – in addition to those who accepted Dr Sorel's request, I also visited some who had declined and even some who had not replied – and in the evenings, in the Steinberger hotels, only a bottle of fine red wine could revive our spirits, steeling us to sup with the devil again the next day. Euphoria and a feeling of omnipotence began to set in for me and for the troupe of strolling players, I lowered my guard, my vigilance was dulled.

On that morning, I sensed something dire was about to happen, but instead of trusting my intuition I stubbornly carried on, as I have so often in my life when I have taken up a challenge, simply so as not to seem cowardly. Chapuis and I had spent the previous night filming until late in Mölln, at the home of Hans Gewecke, who had been *Gebietskommissar* in Shavli, also known as Šiauliai or Schaulen, the second largest city in Lithuania. *Gebietskommissar* was a post more or less equivalent to that of governor. Gewecke was not the worst of the *Gebietskommissars*, his colleague in Slonim, in Belarus, had earned himself the nickname the *'blutigen Gebietskommissar'* ['the bloody governor'] of Slonim. Gewecke was more like a kindly grandfather than a killer and we said our goodbyes, he and I, almost with regret. I had decided for geographical reasons – we were in northern Germany and were using Hamburg as our base – but mostly because I desperately wanted one of the leaders of the *Einsatzgruppen* in the film, that the following day we would tackle Heinz Schubert, the man condemned to death and reprieved by McCloy, the man who had been responsible for the terrible slaughter in Simferopol in the Crimea. Schubert hadn't thought it worth while to answer Professor Laborde's letter informing him of Dr Sorel's visit. I knew a great deal about him, about what he had done and what his defence had been during his trial. He lived in Ahrensburg, an efficient, sanitized, well-to-do little town in northern Germany. There was only one possible approach: Corinna, her linen bag and me. On that sweltering day, we had four vehicles – aside from the minivan and the car I was driving, there were two others. The reason for this was that there was a lot of footage we had already shot that couldn't be sent to Paris until the next day and moreover because an American assistant had joined us to talk to me about another fundraising campaign in the USA. When we arrived in Ahrensburg, we parked all the vehicles in a public car park in the centre of town and Chapuis, Corinna and I went to scout the location. Schubert lived in a large villa on a narrow street, the opposite pavement had a cycle path and what I discovered greatly concerned me: parking was impossible on both sides of the street. This was an upmarket residential neighbourhood and every house had its own garage. Though there were few bicycles, it being the middle of August, there were signs everywhere clearly stating that parking was strictly forbidden. But to ensure good reception, the minivan had to be parked outside Schubert's house, not right outside, since that would be too obvious, but at the most a short distance away on the opposite side. Chapuis pointed out that to do this we would have to block the cycle path. And where would I park my own car? The minivan was too cramped to hold us all and, besides, I couldn't risk anyone in the villa seeing Corinna and me getting out of this strange, illegally parked van with tinted windows. As we drove past the house again, I noticed a cul-de-sac a hundred metres further on that ran perpendicular to Schubert's street and where, it seemed, parking was possible. None of us was particularly confident, common sense suggested giving up. I knew there was someone in Schubert's villa because Corinna had telephoned that morning and, when someone answered, pretended to have dialled a wrong number. Back at the car park, I reluctantly stood while Bernard Aubouy, the genuine sound-engineer, clipped the microphone behind my tie and concealed the transmitter. Usually, I made some joke about this bizarre ceremony of being put in harness, but this time my heart wasn't in it: the nearer the time came, the more disaster seemed certain. But I gave my instructions, instructions I would quickly come to regret: no one, I said, under any circumstances, was to be visible in the driver's cab of the minivan, everyone was to stay in the back, make as little noise as possible and keep the sound being transmitted at the lowest possible volume. If anything were to go wrong, they had orders to make a quick getaway, to save the earlier footage waiting to be dispatched to Paris. We were to meet up in Hamburg later. They left first, planning to park in the spot we had decided on. Corinna and I arrived about fifteen minutes later, drove slowly past the minivan, checked that all was well, then turned around and parked in the cul-de-sac. Corinna, her bag, the Paluche, the silver stars and I stepped out onto the street, walked past the minivan and Schubert's villa; I was sweating from the heat and from anxiety and wanted my heart to stop hammering before ringing the doorbell.

The door was opened almost immediately by an imposing matronly woman. 'Frau Schubert?' I asked. She nodded. I introduced myself: 'Doktor Sorel, a letter was sent to Herr Schubert, but I'm afraid we did not get a reply. Since I happened to be in the area and have your address but, unfortunately, no phone number, I took the liberty of calling on you unannounced.' She was well aware of my letter and did not seem in the least surprised. She said, 'You're lucky to have caught us in, we are going on holiday tomorrow.' 'Where?' I asked. '*Südtirol*,' she replied. It was, I knew, a holiday spot much favoured by former Nazis. I went into raptures: 'Ah! You're so lucky! Bolzano, Misurina, the Tre cime di Lavaredo, I adore the Tyrol myself, both the Italian and the Austrian.' Corinna smiled broadly as Dr Sorel went on about what an honour it would be, and what a boon to his research, if Herr Schubert would agree to answer a few questions. She told me that he would be there in a moment, invited us in and showed us to a living room that overlooked the sunny garden. She gestured for us to sit in the two armchairs facing the sofa. Between the sofa and the chairs there was not a stick of furniture, not even a coffee table.

Schubert appeared, he had probably been pottering in his garden since he was wearing clogs and a dusty pair of trousers. He was a thin man, who looked younger than his age and very much like the photographs taken of him during the *Einsatzgruppen* trial. He vanished for a moment and then reappeared wearing town shoes and a clean pair of trousers. He sat on the sofa, facing us, and Corinna had no choice but to hold the big bag with the Paluche on her lap, the lens trained on Schubert. But before we could do anything, we needed to be sure that the minivan was picking up the signal, something that was far from certain since we were on the garden side. I asked Corinna to go to the car and get the Hilberg organization chart of the *Einsatzgruppen*. She went out, leaving her bag on the chair, and I noticed Frau Schubert looking at it curiously. Corinna came back with the document, winked to let me know that all was well, sat down and placed the bag on her lap. Frau Schubert suddenly asked what the bag's silver stars and circles meant. Not in the least flustered, Corinna said, 'Oh, it's a recent fashion in Paris, it's all the rage. The bags aren't expensive, you can get them in any department store.' Herr Schubert and I then struck up a conversation, he seemed staggered by the extent of my knowledge. Like many of his peers, he had frozen time itself, and it was I who refreshed his memory, explaining to him how much work had been done, since these tragic events, by professional historians, and that we now possessed new analytical tools of understanding, enabling new perspectives, and that today the time had come to reconsider the facts, the role of the *Einsatzgruppen*, for instance, in a more objective, less rancorous manner than at the time of the trial, which, as needed to be stressed, had been decided on and conducted by the victors. Abruptly, Frau Schubert grabbed Corinna's bag and set it on the ground, so now we were filming only feet and ankles. Unruffled, I carried on, dividing in order to rule, by explaining to Schubert that to lump together a vicious brute such as Blobel, who was responsible for the massacres at Babi Yar, with Schubert, who had not been an active participant but had simply happened to be in Simferopol (this had been his defence at the trial), was inadmissible these days, something I planned to make clear in my study. And in fact, I said – at this point I asked Corinna to get the document from her bag, which entailed shifting the focus of the Paluche from ankles to face – Herr Schubert had only ever used the word *besichtigen*, 'to visit [as a tourist]': he vehemently agreed, so vehemently that he inadvertently gave himself away, changing the prefix of the verb so that *besichtigen* became *beaufsichtigen*, 'to supervise'. This triggered a howl from his wife: 'Shut up, you idiot, it was because of the "*auf*" that you were sentenced to death,' and as she said this, her arm shot out like a spring, seizing the bag and setting it once more on the floor. Things were going wrong. Suddenly, the phone rang in the hall and she got up to answer it; when she came back after a moment and sat down, she again picked up the bag, only to set it down when the phone rang once more. The call was longer this time, and meanwhile I went on talking to Schubert, Corinna did not even attempt to pick up her bag. Frau Schubert reappeared and sat down next to Corinna, foaming at the mouth, her eyes almost literally blazing. Then four hulking young men suddenly appeared behind me, and the first of them barked, 'Open that bag!' Corinna, a model of *sang-froid*, used this as an excuse to pick up the bag, hugging it to her as the hefty brute informed Schubert, who was clearly his father and was sitting dumbfounded, 'We can hear your voice from a minivan across the street, everything you're saying is being recorded.' I leapt up and shouted, 'I don't know what you're talking about, I came here on my own with this young woman,' then, to Corinna, 'Come on, let's get out of here.' While she clutched the bag as they tried to pull it from her, I dragged her by the arm towards the door. But they began to rain blows, lashing out with fists and feet at our faces, our bodies; before long both she and I were bleeding and – shame on me – I did not have the presence of mind to call out to the team in the minivan to help us, who, although they didn't understand a word of German, must have been alarmed by the fracas being broadcast to them. Like Charlemagne, who in Hugo's poem 'Aymerillot' cries out, '*Eustache, à moi!*', I should have cried out, '*Bernard, Dominique, à moi!*' But I had given my instructions and, blindly, in true Germanic fashion, they obeyed. Corinna and I, covered in blood, managed to make it to the street, pursued by the baying pack, just as I saw the minivan making a quick getaway. Dragging Corinna, who was still desperately trying to cling on to the bag, I dashed towards the cul-de-sac; they were gaining on us, still oblivious to what exactly was hidden in the bag; we had to get away, to avoid the police; I snatched the bag from Corinna's hands and threw it as hard as I could at our pursuers. This stopped them in their tracks for a moment, they had to pick it up, while I pulled Corinna, still bleeding, into the cul-de-sac, and we leapt into the car, which was parked facing the wrong way. I made two swift, vicious manoeuvres – reverse gear, forward gear – then floored the accelerator and drove straight towards the entrance to the cul-de-sac, now blocked by a human barricade. Our aggressors had been joined by neighbours and I had only one chance of getting away from them, of getting away from the police and the disastrous consequences that would ensue: I could not slow down, I had to force my way through, crash straight into them. They realized that I was prepared to injure or even kill rather than be caught, my determination was so obvious that the wall of people parted like the waters of the Red Sea before Moses. As I drove past, they thumped and kicked and spat at the car; I wheeled into the street at top speed and drove frantically, aimlessly, around Ahrensburg, unable to find the turnoff for the Hamburg motorway, begging Corinna to find some tissues so we could wipe the blood from our faces before someone noticed and stopped us.

Losing the second Paluche was a disaster; I did not know how I would be able to carry on. It was also obvious that someone had probably logged the French number plate of the minivan and the number plate of my hired car: I needed to return it before the police caught up with us. Once on the motorway to Hamburg, I drove as fast as I could to the hotel where we had stayed the previous night and which was a headquarters of sorts, but neither the minivan nor the other cars were there: we were the first back, and there was every reason to believe that the others had been stopped and arrested by the police. I was desperate to know what had happened, how the hulking brutes had been tipped off. One thing was clear, we had to get out of Hamburg as quickly as possible. Corinna, whose father lived in a large house in Cologne, suggested we head there; we could drive through the night and then stay there long enough to heal our wounds and consider our next move: I would have to change all my plans. Finally, the others arrived and, seeing we were battered and bruised, explained that they had had to look after themselves as best they could. My orders that everyone stay inside the minivan had been reprehensible and impracticable: the van got so hot they thought they would suffocate and, eventually, unable to bear it any longer, the sound-engineer slid back the partition between the van and the cab and climbed into the driver's seat with his Nagra. My voice and those of Schubert and his wife had been distinctly heard by neighbours and passers-by, who started to hover around the suspicious vehicle. They had phoned the Schubert house and Frau Schubert had alerted her sons. Not wanting to show up at the car-rental office covered in cuts and bruises, I gave the rental contract to Chapuis and asked him to return the car. We paid our hotel bill and headed off in convoy towards Cologne, the minivan leading the way.

Obviously, this was not to be the end of the matter. The Schuberts had called the police and handed over the bag and the Paluche, hired a lawyer and, on his advice, pressed charges. Though I had a passport in the name of Dr Sorel, I did not have a driver's licence: Sorel was a phantom, it had been Lanzmann who had rented the car. We changed our plans and bravely went on with our shoot, out in the open this time. We would arrive at people's houses all smiles, as I did in Munich with Franz Grassler, the deputy to the Nazi commissioner of the Warsaw Ghetto, who had repeatedly refused to be filmed, telling him I had not come to talk about him at all, that it would be very brief, employing a gentle pressure to which he could not but yield. The German police investigation took some time, it was even a while before they worked out that the Paluche was a camera; we were filming in Berlin with a standard camera when I was informed that a summons had arrived at my Paris office, stating that legal proceedings had been initiated against me. I called Spiess, the prosecutor in the Treblinka trial, to ask his advice; I was quite open with him about my methods. He did not reproach me in any way, saying he was prepared to help me, advising me, however, not to evade the law but to hire a lawyer. I did so, picking a name at random out of the Hamburg telephone directory and arranging an appointment. I got it. And I travelled from Berlin to Hamburg, outlined the facts for the lawyer, unable to discern whether he was sympathetic to or horrified by what I had done. The most serious charge, apparently, was that I had made unauthorized use of *die deutsche Luft*, German airspace, German radio frequencies, German air. According to my lawyer, there was a risk that the sentence passed on me would not be symbolic, but serious. I was forced to spend considerable time and energy fighting these charges. In the end, after an intervention from Spiess, I wrote a long letter to the public prosecutor of Schleswig-Holstein. I explained to him that I was working in the service of history, of truth; that, as a Jew making a film about the extermination of my people, I needed the testimony of Nazis. I explained how for years I had been honest and straightforward and that it had been the perpetrators' abject cowardice that had forced me, like them, to resort to deception and subterfuge in order to break through the wall of silence that was poisoning Germany. It was a very beautiful letter – I regret not keeping a copy of it, but at the time I was not thinking about such things. It turned out to be very effective too, because the public prosecutor, a man of genuine rectitude, wrote back to say that he was persuaded by my arguments and would not pursue the matter. Furthermore, he told me that after the interval of a few months imposed by law, the bag, the Paluche and the silver stars would be returned to me, which indeed they were – Corinna went to pick them up.

There are six Nazis in *Shoah*. Of those, three were filmed without their knowledge, the other three with a standard camera. But I filmed five others who do not appear in the film for reasons relating to the structure and composition of the film. What they had to say is in a safe place. The greatest loss in the Schubert affair is that no members of the *Einsatzgruppen* appear in *Shoah*. This was crucial to me. I had tried everything with the *Einsatzgruppen* executioners and I had failed. The footage I obtained by violating Ahrensburg airspace could not be used, both because the terms of my agreement with the prosecutor precluded it and also because most of the footage was of feet and ankles. As to the substance of the interview, we were still at the preliminary stages, I had barely had time to bring Schubert out of his shell. Not prepared to give up entirely, I hoped I might be able to film one of the *Einsatzgruppen*'s victims whom I had located in Israel, a woman named Rivka Yossilevska. She was a tall, very thin woman with a deeply sorrowful face, her whole being was pain. With several bullets in her body, she had found herself still alive, buried under a pile of bloody corpses in a mass grave in Liepāja, Latvia, and had managed to drag herself from a pit perfunctorily covered in earth.

Nothing in the world would persuade her to tell her story in front of my camera, she did not have the strength and would not give in to my pleas.

One of the reasons why, in spite of my reservations, I was kind to Jonathan Littell's novel *Les Bienveillantes* [*The Kindly Ones*] was because, in the first part at least, he depicts the *Einsatzgruppen* with a precision that the breadth of my work allowed me to understand. I met, in the flesh, many of the people he writes about, people he had never met; for the others we had read the same books, principally Hilberg, and I found his fictional re-creation of Babi Yar, for instance, of the forced march of the Jews of Kiev to the ravines of death, utterly convincing, as I did the monologues he attributes to Paul Blobel, one of the two men hanged after the trial. The same Blobel who one day, driving past the mass grave while the soil was still shifting from the gas released by the corpses, proudly said to his passenger, '*Hier sind meine Juden begraben*' ['This is where my Jews are buried']. Having read the passages about the *Einsatzgruppen* in *Les Bienveillantes*, I said, 'Only two people are capable of understanding it all the way through: Hilberg and me.' This, needless to say, was misunderstood and stupidly attributed to some sort of conceited outburst. The important part of the phrase was '*all the way through*'. To Hilberg and to me the names Streckenbach and Pretzsch and Düben, which I mentioned earlier and which appear in the novel, are not fictional, interchangeable names, or real but abstract names, they are the echo of an immense objective study that grounds them and gives them life.

This was not the only case of spite and unwillingness to understand, far from it. The photographic image, it seems to me, has become a new idol: people need images, need them of everything and of everywhere, they alone are the measure, the only witness to truth. It is commonly agreed that there were no photographs of the gas chambers, by which I mean images of men, women and children actually being gassed inside them. Some free-thinkers still claim that, with time and a good investigator, they will be flushed out. Why not?

The fact is that people died in darkness and in the sixty-five years since the events, not one image has been found. A few years ago, in a blaze of publicity, there was an exhibition of photos at the Hôtel de Sully in the heart of the Marais, in Paris, an exhibition that claimed to assemble everything, to gather together the entire experience of the camps, and was indeed entitled *Mémoire des camps*. The exhibition was accompanied by a huge catalogue of images and texts written by a 'historian of photography', a 'director of photographic heritage', a photographer, an 'art historian' and a simple 'historian'. The exhibition itself was a confusing ragbag that purported to be exhaustive – though every photograph here had been seen a thousand times before – and it haphazardly conflated the various periods of Nazism, the killers and the victims, the piles of corpses and the living. Two photos of beaten, swollen faces were exhibited side by side, one of a prisoner beaten by an SS officer, the other of a Nazi killer with a black eye given him by a prisoner who had just been freed after the liberation of a camp. Obviously, there was nothing on the extermination camps in Poland: Treblinka, Belzec, Sobibór or Chełmno: no images there.

Even if one is prepared to grant that the motives of those organizing the exhibition were pure, there was, in the very principle of this exhibition, something profoundly shocking that made one extremely uneasy about its realization: the tangible subconscious pleasure that had gone into the selection and the display of the photographs in the various rooms. Outrage rumbled and finally exploded, for me as for many others, when I discovered that this jumbled collection was intended to showcase, like precious stones, 'four photographs, ripped from hell itself'; these were presented in the special, final room where lighting effects, sweeping spotlights panning slowly over the subjects, an immoral attempt at deconstruction with pedagogic pretensions, like some silent *son et lumière* in Birkenau, intended to pierce the visitor's heart at the end of his tour. The four photographs in question had all, of course, been known for years, and not just

467

by specialists, but by numerous others, as they had been frequently exhibited. They were taken by members of the Auschwitz-Birkenau *Sonderkommando* and depict, in the sweltering heat of the summer of 1944, Jews in shirtsleeves and caps outside Crematorium V, burning the bodies of those who have just been gassed because there were so many victims that the furnaces alone could not cope. Another photograph showed a sparse thicket of birch trees in Birkenau with naked women waiting their turn to go into the gas chamber. Here the panning spotlights went to town. These photographs were taken, at great risk, by a number of men in the *Sonderkommando*: I have met some of them, including David Szmulewski, who worked as a *Dachdecker* – a roofer – which, together with that of locksmith, was one of the most prized positions in Birkenau since it meant one could move about the camp with relative freedom. In the exhibition catalogue, the psychic novice who took it upon himself to comment on these photographs declares, without a shadow of proof, that they were taken from inside the gas chamber of Crematorium V. This claim was presented as a remarkable discovery: there are images of death from inside the gas chambers! Let us dispel once and for all this fantasy that photographs were taken from the inside of the gas chamber of Crematorium V – the real *raison d'être* for the exhibition at the Hôtel de Sully. To do so, one only need refer to the remarkably precise account given by Filip Müller in *Shoah*[2]: the gas chamber of Crematorium V did not open to the outside. In order to reach it, it was necessary to go through the huge *Auskleideraum* [undressing room], where the victims had to undress before going into the death chamber, a room that was used, after the gassing, as a morgue or repository for corpses awaiting incineration. The photos could have been taken only from the door of this undressing room, which looked

---

[2] *Shoah: le livre* (Gallimard), Folio no. 3026, p.224.
Shoah: The Complete Text of the Acclaimed Holocaust Film (Da Capo Press), pp. 145–6.

out on to the grassland where bodies were burned. Or, in the case of the photograph of naked women, it could only have been taken by a camera held at hip level on the roof of the same building. But our commentator is a trickster: if these four photographs were taken from inside the gas chambers it is possible, by twisting the truth and confounding the readers through association, deviation, confusion and distortion of meaning, to lead people to imagine that there exist photographs of death in the gas chambers, as is suggested by the title given to these remarks: 'Images, malgré tout' ['Pictures, despite everything'].

There are many who, like this commentator, demand images. After the release of Steven Spielberg's Schindler's List, and in order to testify, by a reductio ad absurdum, to the uncompromising stance of Shoah, I observed that if I had discovered a hypothetical silent film shot by an SS officer showing the deaths of 3,000 people in a gas chamber, not only would I not have included it in my film, I would have destroyed it. Outrage! Attacks from all sides! 'He wants to destroy the evidence!' Were those who denounced me insinuating that, perhaps unbeknownst to themselves, such evidence was necessary? I did not make Shoah in response to revisionists and Holocaust deniers: one does not debate with such people. I have never contemplated doing so. A vast choir of voices in my film – Jewish, Polish, German – testifies, in a true construction of memory, to what was perpetrated.

Chapter 20

After four years of work, I finally arrived in Warsaw, yielding to a necessity more pressing than all my misgivings. Marina Ochab was waiting for me at the airport. She was not the blonde athletic Polish woman my simplistic imagination had been expecting. She was short, with incredibly dark, piercing, intelligent eyes and, like my mother, her nose unmistakably marked her out as a Jew. Clearly, not all Polish Jews had perished. Marina's mother indeed proved to be Jewish, her father, Edward Ochab, had been President of the Council of State – the highest authority in the People's Republic during the Gomułka period – until the anti-Semitic clashes of 1968, a few months after Israel's victory in the Six Day War and just before the Soviet tanks put an end to the Prague Spring in August of the same year. After that, some Polish intellectuals became dissidents, left their country, as did the last remaining Polish Jews, those who had been brought back to their birthplace in Red Army trucks, those who, in October 1939, had been lucky enough to escape the Nazis, fleeing to that area of Poland already under Soviet occupation. The majority of the Polish Communist *nomenklatura*, including Ochab, had spent all or most of the war in Soviet-occupied Poland, but he had clashed with Gomułka when the Jews were once again made scapegoats, and he resigned. Marina, who was very charming and spoke perfect French, was unable to be of any real help to me since she knew nothing about the fate of the three million Polish Jews who, unlike her mother, had been unable to survive in Moscow or Uzbekistan. When I told her, within minutes of our first conversation, that I was planning to go to Treblinka as soon as possible, I realized she had never been there, had never thought of going there, had never really known what had happened there. The same was true of Sobibór, Belzec, Chełmno, the principal sites of Jewish death in Poland. She knew something about Auschwitz (Oświęcim, she called it) because at school, in the history books she had studied, Auschwitz subsumed everything else, all lumped into a category much favoured by Communist regimes: 'the victims of Fascism'.

The following day, I rented an old Russian jalopy and we set off for Treblinka, by which I mean the site where the camp had stood. It was cold, there was still snow on the ground, though it was grey rather than white, and there was not a soul to be seen among the fields of standing stones and the granite memorials bearing the names of the *shtetls* and the Jewish communities that had been annihilated, or, on the great imposing boulders that looked prehistoric, the names of the countries ravaged by the whirlwind of extermination. As we walked, Marina and I, among these symbolic tombs, I felt nothing and yet I waited, my mind and my soul alert, for some reaction to this place, to these vestiges of the catastrophe that, I wanted to believe, could not fail to move me. But what I saw seemed completely unrelated to what I had learned, not only from books but most of all from the accounts of Suchomel that I had filmed, and that of Abraham Bomba in the forty-eight hours we had spent together in the mountains of upstate New York. Distraught, attributing my lack of emotion to my stony heart, I went back to the car after two hours and began to drive slowly, aimlessly, trying to stay as close as possible to the boundaries of the camp, which was marked out by triangular stones placed at 300- or 400-metre intervals. But the road did not follow the boundary line and instead led me to neighbouring villages whose names, since that first day, have been forever inscribed in my memory:

Prostyń, Poniatowo, Wólka-Okrąglik. Children and teenagers, men and women of all ages lived here and, stopping the car to think, to look – more watched than watching in truth because every passer-by stared back at me – I could not help but think: 'Between July 1942 and August 1943, while the camp at Treblinka was in operation, while 600,000 Jews were being exterminated, these villages existed!' That these were long-established villages was clear from the muddy dirt-tracks, the architecture of the farms, the dark, massive presence of one or more churches towering over each settlement. And I thought: a man who was sixty in 1978 would have been twenty-four in 1942, someone who was seventy now would then have been in the prime of life. A fifteen-year-old boy in 1942 would now be about to turn fifty. This was a shattering revelation to me, a shock born of logic. I have said many times, the terror and the horror the Shoah inspired in me had forced me to banish the event from human history, to a time other than my own; now, suddenly, I realized that many of these Polish farmers had lived through it. In Prosty, in Poniatowo, in Wólka-Okrąglik, I didn't speak to anyone, attempting to postpone that moment of understanding. I set off again, driving slowly. Then I saw a sign: black lettering on a yellow background that indicated, as though nothing had happened, the name of the village we were approaching: 'TREBLINKA'. Although I had remained impassive before the snowy wasteland of the camp, the standing stones, the memorials, the central blockhouse that purportedly marked out the place of the gas chambers, the sight of this simple road sign utterly devastated me. Treblinka existed! A village named Treblinka existed, dared to exist. It seemed impossible to me; such a thing simply could not be. Though I had wanted to know everything, learn everything, about what had happened here, though I had never doubted that Treblinka had in fact existed, the curse that, to me, hung over the name also entailed an almost ontological taboo; it was then that I understood that I had consigned it to the world of myth, of legend. The conflict between the 'perseverance in being' of this accursed village, stubborn as the millennia, between the dreary contemporary reality and the terrifying human memory of it could only be explosive. The explosion occurred some minutes later when, still behind the wheel of the car, I unexpectedly came upon a long convoy of goods-train wagons coupled together, standing at a platform that was nothing more than a dirt ramp. I drove on to the ramp and stopped dead. I was at the station. At Treblinka station. I got out of my car and began to walk, crossing the tracks to the main platform where the station building stood bearing a sign, in proud, high letters, 'TREBLINKA'. Beneath it, a scroll on which, in Polish, were the words 'Never Again', the only reminder of what this place had once been. At the end of the platform, at right-angles to the tracks, nailed to two posts set into the concrete, was a signpost bearing the name Treblinka on either side so travellers could see it from either direction. Treblinka was nothing but a ghost station: as I stood petrified on the platform, attempting to come to terms with the enormity of what I was witnessing, trains passed, some hurtling straight through, others stopping to load and unload passengers. As for the goods wagons, they had not been placed there as some sort of memorial, but had simply been shunted on to a siding waiting to be put back into service.

I had not wanted to come to Poland. I arrived full of arrogance, and convinced I was coming only to confirm that I had not needed to come, so I could swiftly return to what I had been doing. In fact, I had arrived there fully primed, crammed with all the information amassed in four years spent reading, interviewing, even filming (Suchomel); I was a bomb, though a harmless bomb – the detonator was missing. Treblinka had been the detonator; that afternoon I exploded with sudden, devastating violence. How else can I put it? Treblinka became real, the shift from myth to reality took place in a blinding flash, the encounter between a name and a place wiped out everything I had learned, forced me to start again from scratch, to view everything that I had been working on in a radically different way, to overturn what had seemed most certain and, above all, to allocate to Poland, the geographical heart of the extermination, the crucial place it deserved. Treblinka became so real that it could not wait; I was gripped by a powerful sense of urgency that day, one I would continually live with from that moment on: I had to film, to film as soon as possible, that was the order I received that day.

It was already late in the afternoon. On foot, Marina and I covered every inch of this village whose centre truly was the train station and the tracks. I stopped at a farm whose farmyard afforded spectacular views of the passing trains. It belonged to the farmer in the reddish shirt with the cheerful potbelly, an unforgettable figure to those who have seen *Shoah*. It was cold, he invited us in and I understood from the way he looked at Marina that he had identified her as a Jew, something she had felt herself and later confirmed to me. The gloomy room in which he lived smelled of sour milk, cabbage, slurry and an unidentifiable odour of mildew that immediately turned our stomachs. But what was most frightening was the monster, his son, paralysed, mentally handicapped, wracked by uncontrollable spasms in his chair, head always turned to one side, tongue hanging out. Czeslaw Borowi and his wife had conceived him in the August stench of 1942, as the trains bringing Jews from Warsaw waited at the station for their turn to arrive at the extermination camp. From that very first conversation, Borowi, who, given the smell of his house, must have been immune, nonetheless insisted on talking to me lyrically about the futile efforts and the methods employed by the inhabitants of Treblinka to get rid of that stench, which, for months, day and night, enveloped every house in the village – as Suchomel had said to me, 'It depended on the wind' – holding their noses, closing doors and windows, stopping up every opening, every crack and crevice. The peasants who lived near the camp struggled heroically not to smell. They ate and they made love in the unbearable stench of charred flesh, of bodies being burned in pits to eliminate any trace of the extermination and in the even more intolerable stink of putrefaction from mass graves. Dusk and daybreak, Borowi told me, when dew settles at morning and evening, were the worst, because the smell did not rise, did not drift, but hung in the air at ground level, leaching into every corner of every house, into even the least delicate nose. Borowi seemed to be an expert on the subject of smell, his olfactory memory had a truly poetic refinement. As I listened to him more than attentively, I fulminated on the inside, harangued, cursed and reproached myself. How could I have thought even for an instant of making this film without the man sitting opposite me, without all those I had seen that same day, without the places that seemed to me exactly as they had been thirty-five years ago, without the permanence that could be read in the stones of every building, the steel of the railway tracks, without the fearsome plunge into the heart of the past I was discovering in these old farms?

The journey to Poland was like a journey through time. If by 1978 in Western Europe, it was all but impossible to imagine what the countryside and what life in the country had been like in the nineteenth century, the profound socio-economic changes having wiped out virtually all traces of the past, it certainly was not the case in Poland. Here the nineteenth century existed, one could touch it. The persistence and the disfigurement of places coexisted, wrestled with each other, impregnated each other, chiselling perhaps even more finely, more heartrendingly, the presence of what remained of the past. My sense of urgency was suddenly overpowering. As though I were trying to recapture all those wasted years, the years without Poland, I went on asking questions, oblivious to the night drawing in, to the hunger we must surely have felt as we had not eaten since Warsaw, but I was in a trance, spellbound, in thrall to the truth being revealed to me. I left Borowi and, in the mud and the darkness, I talked to people whose faces I could barely make out, aware that they seemed pleased to have found a stranger curious about a past they remembered with extraordinary exactness, yet one that they spoke of as if it were legend – something I understood

475

only too well – a past both incredibly remote and yet very close, a past-present etched forever in their minds. Marina, who was hearing accounts of the massacre for the first time, stared at me, stunned by my relentlessness, thinking it would have been better not to dig up all this, but faithfully, patiently translating every question, every answer. I discovered that an engine driver who had driven the death trains for the duration of the camps' existence was now living in a village called Małkinia, about ten kilometres from Treblinka. I decided to go there right away, heedless of the lateness of the hour and of common politeness. I could not wait. We left Treblinka by the narrow road that meets the railway line as it crosses the River Bug, which runs parallel by the same bridge. All the trains that had transported victims had clattered in the opposite direction over this bridge, which spanned the wide river whose powerful waters I could sense in the darkness, not knowing that some months later, illuminated by a magnificent sunset, I would be drifting down it on a motorboat with my cameraman, on what would also be the first day of shooting in Poland.

At eleven o'clock that night Małkinia was asleep. I found Henrik Gawkowski's small farm only with great difficulty and, as I knocked, the peals of midnight rang out from a church as immense as a cathedral. At first no one answered; I knocked harder, there was a sound of swift feet on stairs and a female voice struck up a conversation with Marina. Then the door was opened by a little woman with a round, kindly face, her hair tied up in a scarf. She turned on the lights, had us sit down and went to wake her husband, who shuffled downstairs rubbing his eyes. I liked him immediately, I liked his child-like blue eyes still heavy with sleep, his air of innocence and loyalty, the lines of pain etched into his forehead, his evident kindness. Though I apologized for showing up so late, he seemed so unsurprised by my urgency that it was as though he shared it. He had neither forgotten nor recovered from the horrifying past in which he had played a role, and he found it entirely just that he should have to answer any demands made on him at any hour. In fact, I was the first person ever to question him; I had arrived in the night like a ghost, no one before me having troubled to hear what he had to say. He went to fetch a bottle of the wonderful vodka drunk by Polish farmers, miraculous, blessed rot-gut, and after we had downed the first shot, I ventured that we were famished. He and his wife bent over backwards, ransacked a mesh-panelled meat-safe like the one my grandmother Anna had had, providing us with a cornucopia of food, of cold meats and bread and the vodka that unlocks mind and memory. Listening to Henrik I knew, just as I had felt that afternoon with Borowi, that the preliminary research was over, that it was now time to act and begin filming as soon as possible. I needed not just to film, but first and foremost to staunch the flood of words my questions had unlocked, these memories, as precious as gold, as blood, that I had rekindled. We talked about how the unloading had operated on the ramp, the chaotic rush, the beating, the truncheons, the screams of people who would be dead within an hour or two. When I said, 'When you pulled the wagons up to the ramp' he stopped me dead. 'No, no, that's not how it happened, I didn't pull them, I pushed them,' and he balled his fist and made a pushing gesture. I was devastated by this detail, floored by this truth, by which I mean that this trivial confirmation told me more, helped me more to imagine, to understand than any pompous reflection on evil doomed to reflect only on itself. It was clear to me that it was vital that I stop questioning Gawkowski: unlike the Jewish protagonists about whom, for reasons I've mentioned, I needed to know as much as possible before shooting, in this case it was essential not to sully anything. I was the first person to return to the scene of the crime, to those who had never spoken and, I was beginning to realize, wanted so much to speak, to speak torrentially. It was vital, it was imperative to preserve this purity, this spontaneity; this Poland was a treasure not to be squandered. Already, after one day and one crazy night, I knew that during my stay here I would visit the sites, pace them and survey them as I was later to do at Chełmno, but I needed to say as little, to ask as few questions, as possible; to remain on the surface, to move lightly over the land of extermination. But if I was to wait until filming began before daring to go deeper, I had to act fast. This detail, powerfully moving in every sense of the word, that Henrik Gawkowski had pushed the wagons with his engine rather than pulling them was the occasion of a moral lapse I committed during filming, one I readily admit to, one that shames me every time I think about it. Before the cameras, though I already knew what he would say, I asked him that question and, like an actor, I feigned surprise at his answer. I did so because I thought it was important not only that the audience know such operational details but also that they realize how revealing this discovery had been for me. But I blame myself for deciding to pretend that this was the moment I learned it for the first time.

What a night I spent with Henrik! He proved to be devastatingly honest, he wept from the emotion, and doubtless the vodka. I myself had tears in my eyes and we hugged each other several times. I make no mention of this in *Shoah*, but the picture he painted of Treblinka and the surrounding villages during the thirteen months when the gassings were taking place defied any tale. The most voracious prostitutes from Warsaw, regulated by their pimps, had set up shop and did brisk business with camp mercenaries, with the Ukrainian and Latvian guards and with the local farmers, all with the knowledge and complicity of several SS officers. What was at stake in these encounters, which went on every single day, was the money taken from murdered Jews: most of them, not knowing they were about to die but having always prepared themselves for the worst, had brought their money with them, sewn into the lining of their clothes and were to leave it when they stripped off to go into the gas chambers. If they were not concerned to keep count of the number of Jews murdered there, the statisticians of *Aktion Reinhardt* (the codename given by the Nazis to the extermination in the three camps, Treblinka, Belzec and Sobibór) calculated to the last penny the sums – in dollars, drachmas, florins, francs, and currencies of every kind – discovered by the *Sonderkommandos* that Suchomel, chief of the *Goldjuden*, was in charge of, as they ripped the linings from the coats, the jackets, the corsets of the victims or ripped the heels off their shoes. Some of the money, however, went unreported to the accountants of the WVHA (*Wirtschafts-Verwaltungshauptamt*, the Economic and Administrative Main Office of the Nazi SS). Instead, it found its way into the pockets of those who laboured in this business of death, the SS, the Ukrainians, the Latvians, or it was buried by Jewish members of the *Sonderkommando*, to be used in the infinitely unlikely event of an escape. This was the money that the villagers and the prostitutes were given in exchange for vodka, pork and pleasure. Henrik, in tears, confessed to me that in one night, playing poker between trains, he lost $50,000 – a fantastical sum at the time. He added, 'Ill-gotten gain never prospers.' I saw him again when I came back to film, singing at the top of his voice in the church choir. Sometimes even money and jewels were too abstract: again, I make no mention of this in *Shoah*, but Jan Piwonski, a colonel in the Polish army and former assistant pointsman at Sobibór railway station, told me that while on guard one night, someone knocked loudly on the window, a Ukrainian who looked to him like a giant, demanding a litre of vodka and offering in return a heavy, stinking parcel crudely wrapped in newspaper. He had no choice but to accept, he told me, and as soon as he opened the parcel, he vomited: inside was a bloody jaw complete with gold teeth ripped from a freshly gassed corpse.

By the time I left Henrik at dawn I had made my irrevocable decision. I had to start filming that year, by summer if possible – this was February – but before I could do so, I needed to get permits from the Communist government. Back in Warsaw and before continuing this first trip, for which I had allocated a month (I was determined to spend time in Chełmno, in Auschwitz and in each of the camps, since none, to my mind, could take the place of any other), I got in touch with the relevant authorities to inquire about permits to film in Poland. I was asked to write a memorandum explaining my intent, the places I wished to visit, the proposed duration of the shoot, and so on. The senior civil servant I dealt with was not unpleasant and I already knew the party line: once dead, those three million Polish Jews had once again become full Polish citizens, taking the total number of Polish victims to six million. The Polish chimera was constantly attempting to match the sacrifice of the Jews. And though it is true that the Poles suffered heavy losses during the Nazi invasion, the deportations, the Soviet massacres such as Katyn, the Polish resistance movement of the *Armia Krajowa* (the Home Army) and the Warsaw Uprising of 1944, such losses never amounted to the three million claimed in patriotic fantasy.[3] At the root of this astonishing and macabre feat of accountancy was a determination to negate the singularity and enormity of the extermination of the Jews: six million cancels out six million! At this point, I had not fully realized the extent of Polish anti-Semitism. There was, after all, a large avenue in Warsaw named after Mordechaj Anielewicz, the commander of the Jewish Combat Organization and a hero of the Warsaw Ghetto Uprising; there was a famous monument built to honour the Ghetto Heroes on one of the huge city squares, and a memorial plaque at Miła 18 beneath which was buried, deep underground, the headquarters of the Jewish Combat Organization, etc. All of these points I stressed in the memorandum I wrote feverishly at the desk in my hotel room before continuing my Polish journey. I remember that it began in this way: 'Poland is the only country where one can see signs along the road marked *"Obóz zagłady"* [extermination camps]'. In short, my film was to be a homage to Poland, was to do justice to the country and redress anti-Polish prejudice. I lied as and when it became necessary. I was given permission to film in

---

[3] Today, a number of Polish historians have revised this figure downwards: 1.5 million Nazi victims and 500,000 Soviet victims.

Poland under supervision: a sort of delegated spy from the Security Service of the Ministry of Internal Affairs was with me constantly. Or he was at first, since he quickly grew discouraged, tired by the rigours of the shooting, and the whimsical or nocturnal schedules I imposed. Quickly, I discovered that he was rather fond of strong liquor and I constantly dreamed up reasons for him to celebrate, making him an ally. After that, he rarely appeared.

The other issue I had to deal with urgently was Marina. I liked her a lot, but I quickly saw that she would be an obstacle in my getting to the truth, which would inevitably require ruthless, even aggressive questioning on my part. With brutal frankness, I told her that her beautiful face was too Jewish for Poles to feel able to speak freely in front of her. She agreed. I replaced her with Barbara Janicka of good Catholic stock, a wonderful interpreter who none the less caused me other problems. On more than one occasion she threatened to leave the shoot not only because she knew what was at stake, because what she heard filled her with dread, but also because, given that she could only work for me with government approval, she had to report back to the authorities and she was too honest to lie to them. Each time, *in extremis*, I managed to persuade her to stay, assured her of the integrity of my intentions. She then took it upon herself to moderate everything, both the forthrightness of my questions and the often incredible violence of the Polish responses. When they talked about the Jews, the Poles almost always used the word '*Żydki*', a pejorative term meaning 'little Yid'. Barbara translated this as 'Jews', which is pronounced '*Żydki*', a word that was almost never used. One day, I organized a discussion in the church in Chełmno between the priest with the hooked nose, Srebnik, the child singer and me. Barbara's distortion of everything that was said – my questions, the priest's hypocritical pronouncements and Srebnik's words, a reflection of his shyness and his visceral fear – made the scene unintelligibly comical and, inevitably, unusable. Sometimes – having spent hours on end listening to Polish, in time I was able to understand a little and I was sensitive to the gestures of the people I was interviewing – sometimes I caught her red-handed toning down what was said and immediately confronted her. When this happened, she stopped mistranslating and instead took an almost malicious pleasure in the pitiless details, inflecting every phrase she translated as though to say, 'You asked for it, you've got it!', as if she agreed with what was being said. It is a constant failing of female interpreters – even the best of them, especially the best – they give in to their fears, their emotions.

When, in Israel, I managed the amazing feat of getting a few words from 'Antek' (Yitzhak Zuckerman), the deputy commander of the Warsaw Ghetto Uprising, the tragic beauty of his words was mangled by Francine Kaufmann, my well-regarded Hebrew interpreter, something I only realized later during the edit. It happened in Galilee, at the kibbutz Lohamei Ha Geta'o, (the kibbutz of the Ghetto Fighters), where everyone seemed determined that I should neither meet Antek nor get him to talk. Antek, the hero, was a drinker with a puffy drunkard's face. I respected this man, I liked his face, I understood that he liked to drink and I loathed the bureaucrats of the kibbutz, who were determined to fly in the face of truth in order to preserve their irenic vision of what a ghetto fighter should be like, doing everything they could to conceal Antek's existence and shut him out. I fought them every inch of the way, promising I would not make him talk but insisting that he be present, even if only in the background of the shot while Simcha Rotem, known as 'Kazik', recounted how he had escaped from the ghetto and returned via the sewers. But I had no intention of keeping my word, I knew that I would do everything in my power to get Antek to speak, realizing that once he began it would be impossible to stop him. A terrible storm was raging outside, the electricity went out on several occasions, it was late afternoon just before the beginning of Shabbat and Francine, an observant Jew, wanted to get home before it began. Antek had already interrupted once to say, 'Claude, if you could lick my heart, it would poison you.' After a pause, he went on and I listened as the interpreter's voice translated: 'I started drinking after the war . . . *It was very difficult . . .*' But he had said something very different, and I never got over the fact that it does not appear in *Shoah*: 'I started drinking after the war *when I climbed up onto that huge tomb!*' This, clearly, has a very different ring. During editing, I spent a long time wondering whether I should subtitle the latter part of his sentence in French, even if it meant overruling the interpreter, since we would still hear her say 'It was very difficult', which would be impossible to remove without cutting the footage. In the end, I did not do so for ethical reasons, just as I allowed Barbara to translate 'Żydki' as 'Jews', something for which all Jews of Polish origin who see *Shoah* invariably reproach me.

My first trip to Poland had taken place in February 1978. When I got back, I made a brief trip to Israel to see Srebnik again, having now been to Chełmno; then I launched into the complex preparations for the shoot, which was to take place in a number of countries. Shooting began six months later, around 15 July, in Treblinka and from that moment, gripped by the same feeling of urgency, and I spent three years on one shoot after another – in Corfu, the United States, Israel, Germany, Switzerland, Austria, until late 1981. I returned to film in Poland four times. I still wonder sometimes what *Shoah* would have been like had I begun my explorations there as logic dictated, instead of first roaming all over the rest of the world. What I do know is that I was obedient to an altogether different law, one that was restricting, obscure to me, and of another order: the law of creation. I am convinced that Poland would have remained a film set, I would never have experienced the explosion that blazed in me that first day which had me imagining the scenes I needed to film and beginning – with stubbornness, conviction and resourcefulness – the difficult process that would allow me to film them. I instinctively knew that Gawkowski, who had not driven a train since the end of the war, would get back into an engine car identical to the one in which he had transported Jews from Warsaw and Białystok to Treblinka, sickened by the pleas he heard coming from the wagons behind him, able to endure it thanks only to the officially sanctioned triple-ration of vodka. In 1978, the country still had steam engines, which had not changed since 1942. Not only did I have to convince him, something I knew I could do, but I also had to persuade Polish Railways – a more difficult enterprise – to rent (for a steep fee) an engine that spat out red-hot grit, to let me keep it as long as necessary, to adapt their timetables and to allow me to film the arrival of the train at Treblinka station as often as I needed. The literal hallucination I was gripped by also spread to the protagonists. Just as, in the mirrors of that hair salon in Israel, Bomba would see himself again cutting women's hair in the Treblinka gas chambers, so Henrik Gawkowski – who, in one of the wagons he drove to the Treblinka station, had probably transported Bomba, his wife and their baby – is completely hallucinating when, under the eye of the camera, he leans out of the window of his engine and looks onto the fifty imaginary wagons he is shunting to the place of death. There are no wagons, there is only the engine: renting a whole train would have been impossible, futile and exorbitant. It is Henrik, his body wracked with remorse, his eyes wild, repeating a gesture of slitting his throat, his face gaunt, transfixed with pain, who gives life and reality to the phantom train and makes it exist for all those who witness this stupefying scene.

From the inside of the goods wagon parked at Treblinka, through the window that had once been fitted with barbed wire, I zoomed in slowly on the station sign, on the name that so terrified me, but which had meant nothing to the wretches who, for hours or days, had been cramped together inside it – filming it as I imagined they first saw it, terrified and suspicious. Inside the wagon, standing stationary on the tracks, they would wait, sometimes for a very long time. Gawkowski was a man of all trades: from Warsaw, from Białystok, from Kielce he drove the trains to Treblinka station where they were uncoupled into sections of ten wagons, then shunted each section forward to the ramp of the camp, and that was the end of the journey. We filmed in Treblinka in all seasons, the four seasons of death (according to Richard Glazar, there was even a 'dead season' – '*die Flaute*' – during which for a time no trains arrived), and I filmed and re-filmed that slow zoom of the sign twenty times so determined was I to see through the eyes of those who were about to die. Inside the camp itself, I filmed the slabs and the stones for days, from every conceivable angle, unable to stop, running from one to another, looking for some new angle, with my cinematographer, Dominique Chapuis, climbing onto the slippery stone roof of the tall blockhouse symbolizing the gas-chambers, trying to get a 360° panorama to give a sense of the whole site at sunset, without realizing that our shadows and that of the camera were in the shot. They are still there, I didn't cut anything. Chapuis, or before him Lubtchansky or Glasberg, would say to me, 'Why are you still filming stones? You've already got ten times too much footage.' I never had too much, in fact I hadn't shot enough footage, and had to return to Treblinka to film more. I filmed them because there was nothing else to film, because I could not invent, because I would need this footage for when Bomba, when Glazar, when the farmers, or indeed when Suchomel, were speaking. These steles and these stones became human for me, the only trace of the hundreds of thousands who died here. The hard-heartedness I had felt in those first hours on that first day had melted in the face of the work of truth.

The railway station at Sobibór is unlike that at Treblinka, it is almost a part of the camp itself, and every time I see the sequences I shot there again, I tell myself it is the same haunted urgency that forces me to adopt the strange gait of a surveyor – so I can understand and make others understand – crossing and recrossing the tracks with Piwonski, the assistant pointsman in 1942. I can see myself, can hear myself saying to him, 'OK, so here is life still. I take a single step and already I'm on the side of death.' As I say it, I take the step, make the leap, and he nods in agreement. Twenty metres further on, I clamber onto a grassy embankment and he tells me, in the slightly sententious voice of a Communist colonel, 'Here, you are standing on the ramp where the victims destined for extermination were unloaded.' Running alongside the ramp, two blue steel tracks, impervious to the passage of time. 'And these are the same tracks?' I ask. '*Da, da!*' he answers. The weather is beautiful, a beauty that unsettles me, plunges me into disarray and helplessness. I ask him, 'And I suppose there were days when the weather was as beautiful as it is today?' He murmurs, 'There were days when the weather was much more beautiful than today.' I truly think that it is possible that I was in the grip of a sort of madness, and not some gentle madness, either: in each of the places of death, I wanted to make the last journey, descending with Chapuis, camera in hand, the steps to the vast underground rooms of Crematoria II and III in Birkenau, unable to walk straight among the ruined, snow-covered blocks, both of us falling flat on our faces, trying as best we could to protect the camera, but it was good to fall, it was right to feel pain, to have to reheat the camera motor when it was −20°C so that we could continue, absurdly, to pan slowly from left to right, right to left, filming the connection between what remained of the undressing room, which Filip Müller calls the 'international information centre', to the immense gas chamber and vice versa. Still in Birkenau, though with Lubtchansky this time, Lubtchansky assisted by Caroline Champetier, we spent almost a whole night in the bitter cold, filming a panning shot that required an absolutely steady hand, one that could not tremble in the slightest, could not have the least change in pace, a panning shot of the scale model depicting 3,000 plaster figures going down into the death chambers, undressing, then, after the long, inevitable hiatus that, in the shot, separates the undressing room and the gas chamber, coming upon them, a tangled mass of lifeless bodies. What was there to film but the stones in Treblinka, the models in Birkenau? In Chełmno, with Chapuis, retracing the seven kilometres from the church to the forest at the constant, measured pace of the gas vans that asphyxiated victims during the journey, ending this hallucinatory tracking shot on a muddy path stippled with puddles of rain that I refused to skirt around, at the place of the graves, of the pyres, the place where Srebnik says the flames rose as high as the sky. Yes, as the sky.

It was the last day of our last shoot in Poland, December 1981, four days before General Jaruzelski decreed a 'state of war'. There were three of us, me, Chapuis and Pavel, the sound-engineer, though there was no human voice to record since I was not interviewing anyone, there was nothing but the song of the forest, the wind and the rivers, but this too I would need. Before Chełmno, we had spent four days in Treblinka, filming the stones of the camp again and again, filming the steam engines crossing the bridge over the River Bug, headlights punching a hole in the darkness. Chapuis was lying, camera in place, almost on the tracks, I was hugging his chest tightly so that he could not move or fall. On his Nagra, Pavel recorded the thunderous roar of the train. All of Poland had ground to a halt, with hundreds of cars queuing outside every petrol station; our hotel, the only hotel in Małkinia, was lit by oil lamps and church candles because of the constant power cuts. Chapuis and I were sharing a long, narrow room where we couldn't move since all our equipment was stored there too. In December, in eastern Poland, the days are very short and the daylight hours numbered. At four o'clock, we were lying on our beds waiting for dinner, a word as hollow as our stomachs since there was almost nothing to eat, the peasants deliberately refusing to supply Intourist, on which our hotel was dependent for food. Chapuis, lying on his bed, was able to listen to music on his Walkman; I did not even have a book, and I was brooding. It would have been worse still had I known that Dominique – our work together meant we became very close – was to be carried off by cancer twenty years later. He was a great cinematographer, a filmmaker to his very soul. Most of the protagonists in *Shoah* are dead now. Death never ceases. Aside from Chapuis, I should mention the grief I felt when the marvellous Sabine Mamou, who did the sound editing for *Shoah* and was the overall editor on *Tsahal* and did much of the work on *Sobibór, 14 octobre 1943, 16h*, was brutally taken by the same disease.

It had been announced that there would be a delivery of beer to our hotel in Małkinia and about a hundred farmers had invaded the ground floor feverishly waiting for the cans to arrive. It proved not to be a tall tale, the beer did arrive and, by the dim light of the candles, I witnessed an incredible session of collective drunkenness, everyone downing bottle after bottle, at least a dozen each, until they staggered off or collapsed where they sat. For dinner, we had nothing but some disgusting borscht until it occurred to me to flash a ten-dollar bill at the waitress. Things moved quickly then: she led me to the window and pointed to a house on the far side of the street, exchanging a few words to Pavel. Suddenly, organized famine was transformed into a fabulous feast: the people opposite, who were retired, had apparently just killed a pig and, for a staggering sum in dollars, we were treated to black pudding, sausages, ham, bacon and lard, which we wolfed down with the same heedless greed as the beer drinkers. And we were invited to return the next morning for breakfast before we set off for work at Treblinka, taking with us a copious pork-based lunch. The God of the Jews, I know, has forgiven us. In the face of great adversity, strict observance must compromise.

In Chełmno, in the Rzuszow forest, we were shooting the last scene in the biting cold. It was getting dark, and I had a feverish urge to be finished when a boy, a messenger, came running up and said something to Pavel, who translated: the mayor had killed a pig and, in celebration of our departure, had invited us to dinner. I thanked the boy and accepted, although I found this generosity surprising since I had already had dealings with the mayor. Anyone who has seen *Shoah* will remember him in the scene in the church in Chełmno, after the procession. Speaking to a group of farmers gathered on the square in front of the church, I ask, 'In your opinion, why did this thing happen to the Jews?' At that moment, a face with a pointed chin comes forward and answers, 'Because they were the richest,' and the others nod their heads in agreement. That was the mayor. He did indeed provide a wonderful dinner, washed down with vodka. I got to my feet to thank him and take my leave quickly, since we were setting off on icy roads for Łódź where we were to spend the night before heading towards Auschwitz and Czechoslovakia. But the invitation to dinner turned out not to be an invitation. I was handed a bill, not in zlotys but in dollars, and it was not cheap: $150. I paid, cursing silently, but once in the van I was overcome by a surge of rage. I was sitting in the back with Pavel, the Masurian bear-hunter. He had been sound-engineer on Wajda's *The Promised Land*, a film about the town of Łódź and about the Poznańskis, a rich Jewish family in the textile business, which contains long, profoundly anti-Semitic passages. Pavel agreed that both the film and the mayor were anti-Semitic, there could be no other motive for his sham invitation: I was part of the 'rich', and so it was completely normal that money should be extorted from me. And at that instant, as the car drove on through the night, Pavel said something magnificent: 'Thankfully, there are no Jews left in Poland, otherwise there would be appalling anti-Semitism.'

I had filmed in Auschwitz several times already and, during my first, exploratory trip, I had walked alone along the railway tracks, through the blocks, the crematoria, the lake of ashes, the ramps, the museum; I had seen the watchtowers, the piles of suitcases, of spoons, of glasses and pince-nez, the chamber-pots, the lone, charred, twisted tree framed against the white sky next to the Little Farm House, which had been turned into an experimental gas chamber; I had allowed it to seep into me, to imprint itself on me. This time it was Auschwitz the town that I wanted to see again, I wanted to film the old Jewish cemetery with its tall tombstones carved with Hebrew letters, the cemetery where, before the war, before Hitler, the Jewish citizens of Oświęcim, who were lucky enough to die at home of natural causes, had been buried. In fact, the town of Auschwitz – I had not known this but learned it on my first visit to Poland – had been 80 per cent Jewish. I did not realize how precious the few graves that had survived the passage of time and the vandalism eradicating all traces of the Jews in Poland would be to me during the editing phase. As I had decided there would be not one word of commentary, the editing of the film is the key to its intelligibility, it is what makes it possible for the story to move forward and the viewer to understand. There is no voiceover to say what is about to happen, to tell the audience what to think, to connect one scene to the next. Such facile expedients, commonplace in what are classically called documentary films, are not permitted in *Shoah*. This is one of the reasons why the film defies and eludes the categories of documentary or fiction. The editing work was a long, serious, delicate, subtle process. On many occasions I found myself completely blocked, unable, as when climbing a mountain, to find the path that would allow me to carry on, to climb higher. Usually, there is only one, not two – just one right path. I refused to carry on until I had found it, which could take hours or days, on one occasion I am not likely to forget it took three weeks: it was about thirty-five minutes into the film, I was looking for a way to have Birkenau appear on screen for the first time, the great gateway of Birkenau, that sinister bird of death beneath which clattered the death trains heading for the gas chambers. I had begun by showing Oświęcim, this town that had once been 80 per cent Jewish, and I could not see how to engender Birkenau out of the scenes I had shot in the town, to have it rear up at once as a scandal and a fatality, as a startling and surprising proof, to make it appear naturally and of itself, so to speak. All the attempts I had made were unsatisfying, then the radiant solution suddenly came to me: to bring to the screen this cemetery with no tombs, no skeletons, that is Birkenau. To allow Birkenau to appear for the first time in the film, I had to use the ancient tombstones, those of the Jews who had once lived in Auschwitz, who had died and been buried there before the calamity. So I speak to Madame Pietyra, a Polish woman born in Auschwitz, who lived there all her life, and ask her, 'Was there a Jewish cemetery in Auschwitz?' She nods vehemently, happy to be able to teach me something I did not know. I press her, 'Does it still exist?' She nods immediately and over footage of the splendid tombstones, lopsided but proud still, we hear Madame Pietyra's voice as she continues, 'It's closed now.' 'Closed? What does that mean?' 'They don't bury there now.' A few moments later I ask again, 'What happened to the Jews of Auschwitz?' 'They were resettled,' she gives me an almost pitying smile at this preposterous question. 'In what year?' 'It began in 1940, which was when I moved in here. This apartment also belonged to Jews.' 'Where were they deported to?' At first she says she does not know and I say to her, 'According to our information, they were "resettled", since that's the word, not far from here, in Będzin and Sosnowiec in Upper Silesia.' 'Yes, yes, that's right, because these were Jewish towns too.' 'Do you know what happened to the Jews of Auschwitz later?' Another pitying smile at my naïveté: 'I think they all ended in the camp.' 'You mean they returned to Auschwitz?' On the 'yes' that ends this conversation, naturally, harmoniously, so to speak, the first tracking shot appears, bringing us towards the entrance of the camp. I remember I pushed the mobile platform, on which Lubtchansky was standing behind the camera, along that single railroad track that ended the journey. And as we reach the accursed gatehouse, we hear Madame Pietyra's voice, off-screen this time, lamenting, 'There used to be all sorts of people here, from all over the world, they came here, they were sent here . . . All the Jews came here. To die.'

During the five years that it took to edit the film, I only obeyed my own rules, not yielding to the constraints of time or money, or to those people who, not understanding why it was taking me so long and giving up hope I would ever complete it, pressed me to finish. But that was how I was. I filmed with Jan Karski in the United States in 1979, the great Karski. He was professor of political science at

Georgetown University in Washington and I had thought that he, too, was dead. Finding him alive, after a sequence of events it would be pointless to relate, excited me deeply and I accepted what Karski requested of me: as is customary in America, he wanted to be paid. We signed a contract in which he agreed not to appear in any other film (or television programme) until mine had been released. He had, of course, the right to give as many spoken interviews and to write as many articles or books as he wished.

Then I forgot about Karski, having other pressing matters to deal with. What was important to me was that I had filmed him even if I did not yet know how he would appear, how I would use the footage in the film. It was he who got in touch with me about two years later in a long, courteous, tentative letter. He was surprised that the film was not yet finished since, according to him, he had given me all the time I needed. My slowness surprised him all the more because other people, now aware of his existence, were impatient to hear him speak and could not understand why he had signed such a one-sided contract with no specified term. The photocopies of letters he sent to me were from prestigious institutions such as the BBC and Channel 4 or from major American television stations. I replied in great detail, in the most civilized manner I could, I explained to him for the first time, I think, the unique dimension that I wanted to give my work, trying to convey a sense of what was extraordinary and even revolutionary about such a project, which attempted to encompass everything, to show everything that had happened from the point of view of the Jews themselves. I said again that his part in the film was irreplaceable and asked him, with all the conviction I could muster, to trust me. I liked Karski, I knew what courage he had shown under torture and I guaranteed him that, however long it took me to finish the film, and however protracted he found it, he would not regret it. In the end, the film would be a success, I had more faith in myself than in all the radio and television professionals in the world, first and foremost for one compelling reason: I had the strength to take my time.

I have to say, in Karski's defence, which is another way of under-
lining the absolute respect I have for him, that he felt bound by the
contract he had signed and had no intention of going back on his
word. Day after day, I struggled to move forward, solving one after
another the problems thrown up by the film. Five hours were now
complete, of which I knew I would not change a single frame, but
Karski had still not appeared, he was far from my thoughts and I
still did not know myself where, how and at what moment he would
appear. After another two years – and I was so panicked by then
that I barely dared to open my post – I received not one letter but a
whole sheaf of letters, all arranged by date and by the importance of
his correspondents, detailing his exchanges with people attempting
to persuade him to have done with me. I have to say that he fought
heroically not to abandon me and that the sums he had been offered
would have swayed less steadfast souls. He concluded by asking me
the one question I could not answer: when will the film be finished,
will it ever be finished, do you have the right to get us involved
in this interminable project? It was the old story of the guillotine
again, I could only stay true to my own law, I had nothing to offer
the blade but my poor, oft-endangered neck. I exploded and wrote an
exasperated, ironic letter to Karski, doubting that he would grasp all
the implications both good and bad: 'Dear Jan Karski,' I wrote, 'Five
hours are now complete, that is to say more than half of the film.
Everyone says they are very good, and you have not yet appeared.
According to the most accurate calculations I can make right now, I
have planned things such that you will appear in another two hours,
thirty-seven minutes and twenty-two seconds. This is the best I can do
and all that I can promise at the moment. I would add that your part
will be a long one and decisive for the film and for history. But I beg
you, do not bother me again, let me work as I see fit. Otherwise, the
film will be made, but without you. I realize that the film needs all
of its protagonists, but at the same time it can manage without any
one of them. That is surely the mark of a great work.'

The first screening Karski attended, in a cinema in Washington, moved him so much that he wrote me ten breast-beating letters, he was my most ardent supporter and I remember, with an emotion that even now I find hard to contain, the three days we spent together for the première of the film in Jerusalem.

Not all Poles are Karski. The release of *Shoah* in Paris in April 1985 unleashed a huge tsunami in Warsaw. The French *chargé d'affaires* in Poland was immediately summoned by the Minister of Foreign Affairs, Olechowski – there was no French ambassador at the time, nor properly speaking any diplomatic relations – who, in the name of the Polish government and of General Jaruzelski, demanded that the film be immediately banned and all planned screenings cancelled. National honour had been impugned, and the only possible reparation was to consign to oblivion this perverse, anti-Polish work, which attacked all that Poland held sacred. For my part, I was much too busy trying to find the exorbitant sum to print another copy of *Shoah* to pay attention to the truckloads of calumny that, I was told, appeared every day in the Polish press; lies that grew off one another with every passing day since no one there had actually seen the film. And, to tell the truth, this explosion produced by *Shoah* rather amused me. I had never thought of *Shoah* as an anti-Polish film; there were among the protagonists in the film people I loved and respected enormously, even if others were utter scum. As to Polish anti-Semitism, it was not something I invented: the opinions expressed by some of the villagers of Treblinka and Chełmno were enough to make you shudder, but I had not solicited them, they had had no problems expressing themselves and I had found it difficult to believe what I was hearing. And yet, while I may have been amused, I did not realize that the Polish lobby disposed of some heavy artillery. Compared to their firepower, the Jewish lobby was barely capable of a skirmish. To my astonishment, some of those who defended *Shoah* in France, essentially among the intellectuals, and recognizing all the strengths of the film, found it nonetheless tainted, alas, by an anti-Polish bias that seemed to echo the way Poland had been abandoned by Western Europe at crucial points in the country's history. At the request of François Furet, the president of the *Fondation Saint-Simon*, I had organized the first full screening of the film in the large, beautiful theatre of the LTC laboratories, where I had spent every day during the last five years editing *Shoah*. I was very moved: first screening, first unseen, virginal print, and an assembly of big names from the Foundation whom I didn't know. Simone de Beauvoir was present, as was Jean Daniel, editor of the *Nouvel Observateur*. We were not close friends but I had the greatest respect for him, though he did not perhaps know it. Beginning at nine in the morning, the screening lasted all day, with only a short intermission for lunch in the LTC cafeteria. At the end of the film the spectators, stunned and profoundly moved, came up to me and, though it is difficult to find something to say after *Shoah*, each of them said a few words. I remember Jean Daniel's words as he shook my hand powerfully and with great eloquence said, 'That justifies a life.' And yet, early the following morning, after a short night, the telephone started ringing. It was some of those who had been in the audience the night before: Furet, Jean Daniel and a number of others, each began by telling me again how much they admired the film, but then quickly turned round to criticize it: the film was unfair to the Poles, it did not show what they had done to save the Jews, and I sensed that they had spent quite some time consulting one another and their friends in Warsaw. The Polish lobby had acted quickly. I had no wish to argue and referred people to those scenes in *Shoah* that refuted what they were saying. 'You're making a snap judgement,' I told them. 'Watch the film again, then we'll talk.' The international countercheck to the French screening was to take place in Oxford some months later, in September.

Meanwhile, some Poles had begun to travel, had come to Paris specifically to see *Shoah* and, returning to Warsaw, took it upon themselves to contest the calumnies, writing to assert that the film did not lie and beginning, individually, an examination of conscience that was to encompass all of Poland, one that would go on for years, including certain episodes to which I shall return. These people added that Poland was not the subject of the film and confessed to having been intensely moved by something they recognized as entirely new and as a major event.

One morning, about a month and a half after the release of *Shoah*, to my astonishment I got a phone call from Warsaw. A clear, laughing and trilling young woman's voice asked for me in English of crystalline purity. Assured she was indeed speaking with me, she introduced herself: 'I am calling from PolTel – Polish Television – and we were wondering if the rights to *Shoah* were free.' Incredulous and almost laughing myself, thinking this was a practical joke, I answered, 'Yes, they are in fact, but why do you want to know?' 'We are thinking about buying the film and showing it on Polish television!' I struggled not to burst out laughing, saying, 'My dear lady, I'm afraid I don't understand. How do you expect to buy and broadcast a film that all of Poland – the newspapers, the radio, the government and every official authority – has bombed day and night with your rocket launchers?' She replied, 'We think that these are people who have not seen the film.' Then she added quickly, 'If you like, I can put you through to my boss, the director of PolTel, Lew Rywin.' He spoke impeccable American English and said, 'Would it be possible to get a video of *Shoah*?' 'I'm sorry,' I replied, 'I don't have any, I didn't have any made, it didn't occur to me, and I can't see why you would want one.' 'I intend to have your film seen by all the governmental and military organizations concerned. Since they are very busy people and have little time, they need to be able to watch the film at their own pace, otherwise we'll get nowhere.' Lew Rywin's voice had the mellow tone of a crooner and I could not resist. I promised to send him the videos, which, alas, I would have to have made at my own expense. 'I'll get back to you,' he said. We left it at that. I fulfilled my part of the deal, sent off the videos and, two months later, having had no news from Warsaw, I called Lew directly. He answered immediately: 'I know it's taking a long time but be patient, I'll call you soon.' The years I spent working had been very hard, I was exhausted, I decided go on holiday to Corsica. While there, I received a call from my secretary that I didn't understand at all. She told me, 'Someone phoned this morning, but I'm afraid I can't remember his name.' (I was used to this, she could never understand foreign names.) I was the first to think of Rywin and we stumbled from Rywin to Rewan, Rowan, Ravon. I decided it had to be Rywin. I was urgently to call a number in northern Greece (Macedonia) and key in a complicated sequence of numbers. It was indeed Rywin: 'Monsieur Lanzmann, will you be in Paris between 25 July and 1 August?' I replied, 'If necessary, I can.' 'Could you book a hotel room near your home?' He gave me a price range. 'Can you give me your solemn word that no one besides you and me will be told about this meeting?' I gave my word. 'Especially not the Polish Embassy,' he added. 'That's hardly likely, I don't know anyone at the embassy.' My secretary found a hotel near my apartment that suited Lew's requirements. She was given details about when this courier from the Vistula would arrive and a meeting was arranged at the hotel. In the week preceding his arrival, Rywin's laughing Polish secretary called my assistant daily to ensure that arrangements had been respected to the letter and that, above all, there had been no leak to Polish officialdom.

At ten o'clock in the morning, when I arrived at the hotel, the man was already waiting. He was about forty, not very tall, heavy-set and plump with a moustache and dark eyes that sparkled with extraordinary shrewdness and intelligence. I immediately realized who I was dealing with, a long career studying facial features assured me that I could not be wrong: Lew was Jewish. As I led the way to the restaurant, I subjected him to a skilful, rapid interrogation, he told me that he had been born in the USSR to a Jewish mother and a staunch Russian father. All of this confirmed the immediate sympathy I had felt the moment I saw his face. The restaurant was the Balzar on the rue des Écoles and his first words, whispered, were to ask whether I had a VCR. I said, 'No.' If necessary, however, I could perhaps find a solution. 'I've got a film I want to show you,' he said. From the start, the tone and the atmosphere between us were conspiratorial, which, with all the racket in the restaurant, made conversation difficult. He began very solemnly, 'Monsieur Lanzmann, whatever the outcome of our meeting, I want your word that you will not mention it to anyone. I am here in an official-unofficial capacity representing General Jaruzelski personally. I have, as I promised, shown *Shoah* to all of the authorities in Poland: Mr Olchowski, the Minister for Foreign Affairs [the person who had led the campaign against me] is ready to have you summarily executed. A number of our most important generals are of the same opinion and have ordered an inquiry into how permission was given for a man like you to be given free rein to rummage around in our back alleys and paint such a negative picture of Poles and their relationship with the Jews. Only one man supports you, General Jaruzelski. He has not seen the film in its entirety, but has given it several hours of serious consideration: "*Shoah* does not lie," the general said. "It is a mirror held up to Poland and what it reflects is the truth."' Lew then explained at length the power struggles taking place in the highest echelons of the Polish government and how, much as he would like to, in current circumstances it would be impossible for the general to authorize a broadcast of *Shoah*. A meeting of the Central Committee had been convened for October; Jaruzelski's position was at risk; it would be him or Olchowski; I only half-understood the subtleties Lew used to convince me of I did not yet know what, but it sounded as if the fate of Poland was in my hands. All would become clear once I had seen the film he had prepared for me with the approval of General Wojciech Witold Jaruzelski. If I agreed, Poland would be eternally grateful to me.

The film, completely concocted out of Lew's lawless, twisted mind, was absolutely shocking. The fact that anyone imagined a creator could consent to such a bastardization of his work showed to what depths of intellectual decline and dishonest compromise 'real' Communism had sunk. The film, which bore the title *Shoah*, ran for about two hours, Germany was mentioned for about five minutes: Suchomel speaking incomprehensible German. What he had to say was summed up by the sentence: 'An SS officer from Treblinka tells his story.' But Suchomel was not the only one; every one of the protagonists of *Shoah*, Jew or SS, appeared for a few seconds. The Poles, especially in the group scenes, were allowed to speak uncut, and obviously translation was not an issue. Lech Wałęsa, the president of Solidarity and future President of Poland, having seen a few minutes of the expurgated scene at the Chełmno church, said to the press: 'A meeting should not be held in front of a church!' When I realized that hundreds of copies had been made of this bowdlerization of Rywin's, I became furious, told him that there was no point carrying on with our conversation, that I would never dream of sanctioning such a travesty and that we should leave it at that. He left, simply saying, 'This is not our last word on the subject.'

Two months later, I was out in the countryside when I got a panicked call from Angelika: 'You have to phone Warsaw urgently, they have a proposal they want to make to you.' Barely had I hung up when the phone rang again: it was not Warsaw, but Paris, the foreign editor of *Le Monde*. 'Monsieur Lanzmann, we just want to confirm something. Jerzy Urban, a spokesman for the Polish government, has just held a press conference announcing that you have reached an agreement.' I said, 'I would like you to refute it in the strongest possible terms. There is no agreement, I have broken off all contact with the Poles.' But that was just the beginning. The spokesman for Jaruzelski's government was not to be refuted; our 'agreement' had been announced *urbi et orbi* and I finally discovered what I was being offered: *Shoah* would be shown in its entirety in two cinemas in the Warsaw suburbs. And in exchange, I was to give permission for Lew Rywin's film to be shown on Polish television at a date to be agreed.

By now, in any case, *Le Monde* had already announced that an agreement had been reached: the Polish lobby was so active, so powerful, that no one took any notice of my objections or reservations. All of this posed considerable problems: how to ensure that the film was screened in its entirety, that the translation and the subtitling were faithful. I didn't have the means to deal with such problems, it would have required an established production company capable of paying lawyers and investigators. I was in no position to do so. I was suddenly faced with a thousand other problems that I had not foreseen, such as those that would result from the American release of the film. *Shoah*, I decided, would have to succeed on its own merits as, in fact, it had already begun to do; for my part I needed my inner freedom, which was what mattered above all else.

If I decided to forget about Warsaw, Warsaw did not forget about me. In early September 1985, I received an invitation from Oxford University to an uncut screening of *Shoah*, to be followed by a debate, the following day, in which the most renowned Polish, American, English and Israeli authorities on the subject would participate. The host was an institute for Judeo-Polish studies and its journal *Polin*, a pioneering organization that comprised two robust departments, one in Oxford, the other in Poland. They seemed to have buried their previous differences and formed a united front on the subject of *Shoah*. Among the big names invited were members of the Communist Party, Jaruzelski's men, but also the most respected Polish Catholic journalists and writers such as Jerzy Turowicz, editor of *Tygodnik Powszechny* in Krakow, and Professor Józef Gierowski, rector of Jagiellonian University in Krakow. The most surprising thing about 4 August, this night of reconciliation, was the inclusion of dissident Polish intellectuals, such as the philosopher Leszek Kołakowski and Professor Peter Pulzer, who had both fled their country after Gomulka launched his official anti-Semitic campaign.

I arrived in Oxford in the afternoon, a little nervous, with a fighting spirit, having no idea what would happen nor why I had been summoned to appear before this tribunal. The screening had started at ten o'clock that morning, I popped my head around the door, the cinema was packed, the silence had a powerful presence and I decided that rather than attending the formal dinner to which I had been invited, I would eat on my own in a local restaurant. I wanted to avoid wasting my energy and my nerves on polite small-talk in order to remain battle-ready for the debate the following day where – I knew – it would be me against everyone else. It is impossible to go into detail here about the debate, which lasted for seven hours, but it began with a joint *mea culpa*, all of the participants apologizing to me for the vicious official campaign against *Shoah* in Poland, a campaign that was still in full force. Though there were points they wished to criticize about the film, they all agreed that it was a work of art, faithful to its own rules, not a piece of reportage about how the Poles had been the closest witnesses to the extermination of their Jewish compatriots. After the Oxford debate, numerous articles were published around the world, in the United States, Britain, Germany, Israel, even in Poland; for example, there was Timothy Garton Ash's article in the *New York Review of Books,* which was twenty pages long, Neal Ascherson's in the *Observer* and Abraham Brumberg's in the *New Republic.* All of them paid tribute to *Shoah* and to the way that my knowledge of history and the preparatory work that had led to its realization had utterly routed those who, at first, had put themselves forward as my fiercest enemies, having proved to them that their weapons, like their criticisms, were hollow and empty. Some, such as the philosopher Leszek Kołakowski, wrote to me after the screening to tell me that their admiration had far outweighed any reservations they had had, and that if *Shoah* did not tell the whole story, its overwhelming power of suggestion and its originality revealed the truth as never before.

In Poland, reactions to the Oxford debate were, as one might expect, a tissue of contradictions, but *Shoah* had started out on a long road and it would take another fifteen years – and many contracts brutally cancelled at the last moment with no reason given – before the film was broadcast there on a cable channel in October 1997 and on Polish national television in February 2003.

During all that time, one man prospered. When, in a private screening room in Paris, I watched the première of *Schindler's List*, I discovered that the Polish co-producer – in capital letters in the credits – was none other than Lew Rywin. He had gone far; providence moves in mysterious ways. In 1996, thanks to Brigitte Jacques, I was invited to a symposium in Vilnius, Lithuania. *Shoah* was to be screened there in full for the first time and I was asked to respond to the address by the President of Lithuania in a large university lecture hall. When I arrived, my heart was thumping. I had spent so many sleepless nights reading and rereading so much about Vilnius, about the Ponary massacre, about the appalling things that took place in Lietūkis Garage during the Kaunas (Kovno) pogrom where Lithuanians, their white shirts stained red with blood – this was during the heatwave of June 1941 – battered Jewish women and children to death while German soldiers stood by laughing, that it kept me awake at night. Moreover, Vilnius and the two heroes of the exhumation of the Ponary mass grave, Motke Zaïdl and Itzhak Dugin, appeared in the first minutes of *Shoah*. Since I had been asked to speak, I had no intention of remaining silent about these things and was wondering how best to go about it. I glanced around the huge lecture hall and suddenly I saw, sitting in the centre of the stage, surrounded by an entourage, Lew Rywin. He had put on a lot of weight, his face was jowly, he had a paunch and his moustache was blacker than ever. My heart skipped a beat, I walked up the steps and, as I drew alongside him, I said, 'You owe me reparation.' He nodded and suggested doing something about it the following week: 'I'm the head of Canal+ Poland, and I will broadcast *Shoah* on my station.' Canal+ certainly knew how to pick its employees. I said, 'Why should I believe you?' 'I will be in Paris next week,' he replied, 'one of my assistants will get in touch and arrange a meeting and together we will work out how the film should be broadcast.' I wasn't sure whether or not to trust this new proposal from such a shark. As it turned out, the following week I did indeed receive a call in Paris from a very polite Frenchman to arrange a meeting with the Polish TV tycoon. He was determined that Canal+ Poland would broadcast *Shoah* as soon as practicable, a contract was drawn up and signed and I stipulated only one condition: that there should be a press conference in Warsaw before the screening so that I could explain myself to those Poles who wished to listen, and answer their questions. This condition I made a *sine qua non*. Yet two days before the broadcast, the polite Frenchman rang once more to explain that the press conference would not take place and that the film would be broadcast with no special announcement, like any other programme.

To chronicle the later episodes in the struggle for *Shoah* to exist in Poland would be tedious. Only one event warrants comment. Four or five years later I received a very official, very charming letter from Polish National Television, advising me that their programming adviser had finally decided to broadcast *Shoah* on one of the two national networks. They would send a team of their finest technicians and the journalist who was to interview me, so that each of the proposed four segments (the film was to be broadcast over four consecutive nights) would be preceded by a discussion in which Poles could explain their long hostility to *Shoah*. For my part, I was offered the opportunity to make an inaugural speech, explaining what I had hoped to achieve in making the film and how unjust I found it that my work was considered anti-Polish. I accepted.

The journalist was a man called Ludwig Stomma. The moment I opened my door and he saw me, he broke down in tears, threw his arms around me and, hugging me long and hard, told me how much *Shoah* had moved him when he first saw it, and how it still did every time he watched it again. Compared to him, the director and the technicians had classic, slightly pinched Polish faces, but their work was sincere and was completed within a day. After that, everything happened with almost magical simplicity. The first day of the broadcast was set and the Polish press announced it as a major event. A few hours before it was due to go out, with extraordinary harshness, I got a call to say the broadcast would not be going ahead. I called Warsaw but could not get hold of any of my contacts, only the cruel voice of some female bureaucrat who said, 'A television station is never obliged to broadcast a programme, even one it has paid for.' I forgot to mention that they paid very little for the rights – I didn't care.

I have no proof of what I am about to suggest, but at the time, another scandal was at its height: a Polish-American historian by the name of Jan Gross had just published a book about the Jedwabne pogrom of 1941 in which the Polish population had massacred their Jewish neighbours. This caused uproar in Poland between pro- and anti-Semitic groups, the mayor of Jedwabne fell to his knees as a sign of repentance, the wounds were savage and deep. The occasion would have been an ideal opportunity to broadcast *Shoah*, but all my requests went unanswered. Having to travel again to Poland in 2001 for the shooting of my film *Sobibór, 14 octobre 1943, 16h*, I turned to Adam Michnik, himself a Jew, editor of *Gazeta Wyborcza*, a well-known newspaper in Poland, whom I had met several times. Several weeks later, Michnik told me that he had made inquiries: according to him, the organized Jewish community in Poland had itself intervened to request that the broadcast of *Shoah* be cancelled. They feared a new surge of anti-Semitism and demonstrated scant courage. I don't think Michnik was lying. Because *Shoah* never compromises with truth, it is in a sense the epitome of transgression.

In 1986, I had experienced something similar without realizing all the implications during the four screenings of *Shoah* at the Berlin Film Festival. Leaders of the Jewish community had been officially invited, not only to the screenings, but to a meeting with the mayor of Berlin and members of the government. Not one of them showed up. My pigeonhole at the hotel desk was stuffed with letters from Germans who had seen the film, many of their comments profound, some of them heart-wrenching, but I had not one word of apology from the dignitaries representing the Jewish community. Clearly, if the Shoah happened, there can be no Jews in Germany, and if there are Jews in Germany, the Shoah cannot have occurred. Things, happily, have changed since then but that was the shameful reality that prevailed at the time.

Chapter 21

The question of what title I should give the film arose right at the end of those twelve years of work, in April 1985, a few short weeks before the première took place in the vast Théâtre de l'Empire on the avenue de Wagram – attended, as we know, by the President of the Republic, François Mitterrand. In all those years I did not have a title, constantly postponing the moment when I would give the matter serious thought. Given its sacrificial connotation, *Holocaust* was unacceptable; moreover it had already been used. The truth is that there was no name for what, at the time, I did not even dare call 'the event'. To myself, almost in secret, I said 'the Thing'. It was a way of naming the unnameable. How could there be a name for something that was utterly without precedent in the history of mankind? If it had been possible not to give the film a title, I would have done so. The word 'Shoah' occurred to me one night as self-evident because, not speaking Hebrew, I did not understand its meaning, which was another way of not naming it. But for those who speak Hebrew, 'Shoah' is just as inadequate. The term occurs several times in the Bible. It means 'catastrophe', 'destruction', 'annihilation'; it can refer to an earthquake, a flood, a hurricane. After the war, rabbis arbitrarily decreed that it would designate 'the Thing'. For me, 'Shoah' was a signifier with no signified, a brief, opaque utterance, an impenetrable, unbreakable word. When Georges Cravenne, who took it upon himself to organize the première, wanted to print the invitations and asked me for the title and I said *Shoah*, he asked, 'What does that mean?' 'I don't know, it means "Shoah".' 'But you have to translate, no one would understand.' 'That's exactly what I want, for no one to understand.' I fought to impose the title *Shoah*, not knowing that in doing so I was performing a radical act of naming, because almost as soon as it had been named the title of the film became, in many languages, not just in Hebrew, the name for the event in its utter singularity. From the first, the film was an eponym, people began to use the word 'Shoah', the word supplanting 'Holocaust', 'genocide', 'the Final Solution' and others. These have become common nouns, while Shoah is now a proper noun, the only one, and hence untranslatable.

The screening at the Théâtre de l'Empire, which, with necessary breaks, ran from 1 p.m. until 2 a.m., made everything worthwhile. No one, not a single person, left the packed cinema, even when it got late, as though they all wanted to support each other, to see through to the bitter end this terrible journey, which I prefaced with a few words that quavered with emotion. Actually, I'm mistaken, at the end of the section *'Première époque'*, the chief rabbi, René-Samuel Sirat, leapt to his feet, caught sight of me and shouted, 'This is appalling,' before rushing out. I remember his broad-brimmed hat flying down the aisle towards the exit; I remember thinking, 'I wonder if he'll come back to watch the *"Deuxième époque"*?' He never came back, never saw it: *Shoah*, the Shoah, was over for him. I have long felt a great respect and admiration for Sirat, who was born in Algeria. He is a scholar deeply committed to Judeo-Christian inter-institutional relations. I realized that for him, as for many others, I had committed a serious transgression: this film, with no corpses, no individual story, whose sole subject is the extermination of a people rather than their survival, is probably an outrage. The Shoah should remain entombed in a deathly silence for all eternity. Even if we constantly commemorate it, we cannot make death speak. Shortly after the release of *Shoah* in

Paris, solemn symposia were organized to which I was invited. I went to the first one, my conscience clear, unaware of the trap I was about to fall into: bearded intellectuals, thirty-somethings in *yarmulkes* quickly paid tribute to *Shoah* – because I was present – only to dismiss it, on the pretext that it was art, so they could get to the heart of the matter. It was time to stop this unhealthy fixation with the past, time to forget these Jews mired in negativity, obsessed by misery – as they undoubtedly considered me – and move on to what was important: study, Jewish culture, observance. They puffed themselves up in their conceited certainties, proud of their conviction, they were brutal in their attacks, with no respect for basic decency. I stayed only for the initial bout. Though I am not religious – something of which I am neither proud nor ashamed, it is simply how I am, the path my life has taken – I have always felt an almost philosophical astonishment and an unfailing admiration for the Jewish religion. I understand the horror Rabbi Sirat felt, I am grateful to him for having dared – unlike others – to brave *Shoah*, I know many people who so dreaded the pain that seeing the film would cause them that they decided never to see it. The story of Rabbi Sirat should not be generalized. There were other reactions. Having stared in disbelief at the endless queue on the corner of Broadway and 68th Street in front of the studio cinema at Lincoln Center where *Shoah* played for months, I went to the cinema myself where Dan Talbot, the owner and the film's US distributor, asked me to wait with him in the foyer until the audience came out and the next showing started. Every one of them – not just those from Manhattan, but those from far-flung suburbs in New Jersey and from New York state, where there would be no chance the film would ever be shown – everyone rushed over to me the moment they recognized me, hugged me, kissed me. Then suddenly, while the cinema was being cleaned between showings, a tall beanpole of a man, the rabbi of a thriving congregation in Orange County, New Jersey, asked a curious favour of Dan, one that he found impossible to refuse. And so the rabbi and a number of his congregation went back into the cinema and began to say Kaddish, transforming the cinema into a house of prayer.

In Paris, I got a call one day from Radio Nôtre-Dame – a station I did not even know existed – asking for an interview. I was happy to agree and asked, 'Have you seen *Shoah*?' 'Um, no . . .' 'See it, there's no point interviewing me until you've seen it.' 'We'll get back to you.' They called back a week later and we had the identical conversation. I was a little angry and said, 'Don't call back until you've been to a screening, otherwise it's pointless'. Determined – it was a different voice this time – they called back again and I realized that seeing *Shoah* was an impossible task for them. They were merely obeying their superiors. Then there was the newly appointed Cardinal Archbishop of Paris, Monsignor Jean-Marie Lustiger, himself a Jew, whose story we know. I had met him twice, having been invited to lunch with him at the home of Théo Klein, an eminent lawyer and president of the *Conseil représentatif des institutions juives de France* who organized official talks with the Prime Minister and held an annual dinner that brought together members of government and senior Jewish representatives in France. Théo was beaming, thrilled to have the Cardinal Archbishop of Paris at his table, imagining in his heart of hearts that the man would soon be Pope and he himself would be Cardinal Secretary of State or maybe Camerlengo at the Vatican. He is a sweet man who has always been enamoured of politics and glory. For my part, I liked the look of the new cardinal, we were of similar ages and had in common many memories of France recent and ancient, and those of Germany and Poland. I talked to him a little about *Shoah*, which I was editing at the time, and told him I would invite him to the première, if he would do me the honour of attending. We promised to keep in touch.

In 1987, in *Le Choix de Dieu*, a book of interviews with the cardinal – a fascinating book in many respects – I discovered the key to Radio Nôtre-Dame's contradictory stance. I had received a copy of the book inscribed in the monsignor's elegant hand:

For Claude Lanzmann
Fraternally
† Jean-Marie Cardinal Lustiger

In it, one of the interviewers, Jean-Louis Missika, asks the cardinal, 'Even Lanzmann's film, *Shoah*, you don't want to see it?' to which he replies, 'I cannot see it! Lanzmann talked to me about it when he was finishing work on the film. He invited me to the première . . . I declined. It's not possible. No, I can't do it. Although I promised him I would see it one day.' 'Is this work really necessary?' 'He did it, and it is good that someone did it. Yes, someone had to do it. I don't know whether he did it well, whether it's fair, whether it's partisan, I don't know [. . .]' Let us not forget that Pope John-Paul II was Polish. But, astonishingly, Jean-Marie kept his promise. He phoned me one day, years later, and invited me to dinner at the Archbishop's Palace on the rue Barbet-de-Jouy. I arrived, my heart beating a little faster, and a young Vietnamese girl led me through the dark archway to be relayed by a black teenage boy, showing me upstairs to the first floor, where he opened the door to a small drawing room and said, 'The Cardinal sends his apologies, he will be a little late.' The reason for his lateness was blatantly obvious, I could hardly believe it – the floor, the tables, the two sofas were all littered with videos of *Shoah*, a chaos that betrayed both the viewer's urgency and his inability to make sense of the film. I was attempting to reconstruct the order of the film in my mind when the cardinal threw the door open, pointing his finger with such vehemence at the *corpus delicti* that I could not even kiss his ring, as I had been advised to do. 'I've watched it, you see? I've watched it!' he repeated over and over, extremely agitated. I felt I had to believe him, and we were led down to the basement, this time by a young black girl, to a small dining room where a table had been laid. The conversation was effortless, we had so much in common, we discovered that we agreed on many things. At one point, we argued about the difference – crucial to him – between Christian anti-Semitism, whose perversity and capacity to harm he staunchly denied, and Nazi anti-Jewishness, which was, he claimed, a product of the Enlightenment. I replied, 'And the scene at the church?' He didn't know what I was talking about. I dared to press him and then I realized that, despite the videos scattered around the drawing room on the first floor, he had not seen *Shoah* at all, and he confessed: 'I can't do it, I just can't, I've managed to watch about a minute of it a day. Please forgive me . . .' I forgave him. Later, when Sollers republished in *L'Infini* the article I had written in 1958 for *Les Temps modernes*, 'The Curate of Uruffe and the Church Interest', that atrocious story that the future cardinal was only too familiar with since it had occurred in 'his time', I sent it to him with a very kind note. He made the same tireless and tiresome reply: 'I can't read this.' What is the relationship between faith and truth? The reactions of Rabbi Sirat and of the cardinal are strangely similar: evil does not exist.

These are only examples of the thousands of questions that were raised when *Shoah* began its career. I had not thought about it, I had not imagined how such a film, which to my eyes should unite people, would instead create so many enemies among the very people for whom I had made it: the Jews, my own people. Even some of those who had been in the camps violently threw themselves at me: 'I don't need to see your film, I know it all by heart, I was in seven different camps, Monsieur!' To which I replied, 'Bravo, you were lucky. If you had been in only one you would not be here to tell me so.' Others, young people, publicly complained in the newspapers. I remember a certain Pierre-Oscar Lévy in *Libération*: 'Monsieur Lanzmann has said all there is to say, shown all there is to show, left nothing for us. What are we supposed to do?' he wrote with as much resentment as admiration. He was wrong, I have not done all there is to do, but it is true there will not be two *Shoahs*. Happily – and this is the law of time – Pierre-Oscar Lévy later went on to make a film, forgetting about the existence of *Shoah*, which was the best thing to do. I acknowledge his pioneering courage. This is the source of the stupid, persistent myth that Lanzmann somehow considers that he owns the Shoah. I remember Michel Polac asking me for permission to show on one of his television programmes ten minutes from *Shoah* alongside *Nuit et brouillard*, which he intended to screen in its entirety. Polac, who had lost one of his parents in the catastrophe, was reacting just like the cardinal, but he had the honesty to say to me, 'I haven't seen *Shoah*, I will never see it, it is impossible.' *Nuit et brouillard* is a very important film, Resnais is a great filmmaker and Jean Cayrol's commentary is very beautiful. But I have never understood how those, like Polac, who have shed bitter cathartic tears watching the thirty-five minutes of the carts piled with corpses, of the lines of latrines in Birkenau in *Nuit et brouillard* can claim, in all good conscience, that they cannot bring themselves to watch *Shoah*. Is it a mystery; am I incapable of thinking about, of contemplating evil? There are piles of bodies of those who died of typhus at Bergen-Belsen that, when the camps were opened, were filmed by the Allied news services, footage that appears in *Nuit et brouillard*, but there were no gas chambers in Bergen-Belsen, in Dachau, in Sachsenhausen or in Buchenwald. *Nuit et brouillard* is a beautiful, idealistic film about the deportations, the word 'Jew' is mentioned only once during its long litany, and the tears it elicits are the sign of its formidable powers of consolation. Yes, *Nuit et brouillard*, in spite of the corpses, of the horrifying conditions of the camps suggested by the images, is a film about the living, about the survivors, a film that makes it possible for life to go on as it must after great grief, when tears have dried. I have said this on more than one occasion and I am grateful to Alain Resnais, when his film was recently issued on DVD, for asking that my observations be included.

During a conference in Paris organized to celebrate the launch of Rachel Ertel's great book on Yiddish poetry written during the Shoah, a woman heckled me with such bitter violence that I was left speechless: 'What we need,' she shouted from the floor, 'is a French *Shoah*!' What did she mean? What was *Shoah* if not that? One need only visit the Mémorial de la Shoah on the rue Geoffroy l'Asnier and slowly walk along the walls on which, reverently engraved into the stone thanks to the tireless efforts of Serge Klarsfeld, are the names of the 76,000 men, women and children gassed, deported from France. Of these, 95 per cent were Polish Jews with names that are difficult to pronounce. Most of them were not French. Thinking about it, she was reproaching me for not talking about Drancy, about Compiègne, about the role of the French in the deportations. What she wanted was not a film but a trial, like those of Barbie or Papon, trials that advocates insist have an educational benefit much greater than that of any film, *Shoah* being first and foremost. Later, when it was too late, I realized I should have said, 'You need a Le Pen to direct it.' In any case, it was a complete misinterpretation of what I had been trying to do: the subject of *Shoah* is not the raids, the roundups, the arrests (I made no mention of Belgium, or the Netherlands, or Westerbork, or Prague, or Berlin and the German cities); it is not about the point of departure but about the last leg of the journey, the last junction, when it is too late, when what cannot be undone is about to be done. I understand that those who have lost family members might be angry that their deaths are not mentioned in *Shoah*. They are wrong, they have completely misunderstood: *Shoah*, in a sense, is entirely about them, even if I make no mention of the responsibility of the policemen who arrested them. Nor do I mention anything about the handful of Polish nuns who hid Jews in their convents. It was the peasants who lived closest to the extermination camps who made it possible for me to understand and to help others understand what had happened.

But others who should have rejoiced felt, on the contrary, their mandarin prerogatives and their status threatened: a number of professional historians. At the end of a symposium held at the Sorbonne in 1992, Professor Pierre Vidal-Naquet scandalized his colleagues in attendance when he claimed that history was 'something too serious to be left to historians'. According to Lucette Valensi, herself a historian, commenting on this public statement in the scholarly publication *Les Annales*, Vidal-Naquet, in order to illustrate his contention, continued by 'citing three major works that did more to enhance our knowledge of the extermination of the Jews than the work of professional historians: the work of Primo Levi, that of Raul Hilberg, and Claude Lanzmann's *Shoah*'. Comically, barely had she written this than Madame Valensi urged, 'Let us not dwell on these names.' This symposium, astonishingly, spread panic among certain historians, as though such works disqualified the professional: 'We came close to thinking so in front of the power of the witnesses, the truth and the authority of their testimony.' A Canadian historian, Michael Marrus, felt hounded from his kingdom. Happily, he compensated for it in malice. It was I who gave a speech celebrating Raul Hilberg's retirement party in Burlington, Vermont. Marrus was at my table at lunch: his dark beady eyes glared poisonously at me throughout the meal. In 1987, another historian, a Frenchman, Henry Rousso, an ambitious young graduate, published a book in which he dismissed *Shoah* in a few hurried lines full of factual errors, attempting to demolish what he saw as the unwarranted sanctification of a work that, if it were not challenged, would eclipse all others, in particular his own book *Le Syndrome de Vichy* [*The Vichy Syndrome*]. In doing so, he seemed to feel he might check the reputation of *Shoah*. A number of his teachers, including Vidal-Naquet and François Bédarida, condemned his short-sightedness in no uncertain terms. I attacked him myself at every chance I got. And on 30 January 1990, three years after *Le Syndrome de Vichy* was published, I received a letter of apology from the author, informing me of a forthcoming paperback edition correcting his foolish remarks in the original. In substance, he admitted that he had made a value judgement about *Shoah* that he later realized was absurd. His criticisms, he acknowledged, were neither explained nor substantiated. He reproached himself for not attempting to stand back and take stock of his negative reaction on first seeing the film. He added – and this was the crux of the letter – that he had been more irritated by the way in which the film had been sanctified on its release than by the film itself. Whether or not there was a new edition, the damage was already done and though his decision to apologize was gracious, however much Rousso agreed that I was right in principle, he nonetheless stubbornly continued to argue for the dangers, according to him, of confusing the Shoah with a single representation of it, even one whose greatness he now recognized. I replied politely, and seven years later he wrote to me again to refine his reservations further. He told me that in his previous letter he had not really understood the nature of the malaise he had felt when he first saw *Shoah*: the film had made him understand how estranged he was from this tragedy, though at the time he felt he was directly concerned by this 'memory', doubly so since he was both a historian and a Jew. *Shoah* had made him feel 'repudiated' by that which mattered most to him. He ended the letter by assuring me that, in hindsight, *Shoah* had offered him a remarkable opportunity to reflect – and not only as a historian – on memory, on how it is passed on, on the weight of the past, a past, he said, that one has to accept, to come to terms with, including that part of it which is suffering. Even if he had not always agreed with me on incidental things, he agreed on the essential. He concluded by saying that he had learned much from me.

I am grateful to Henry Rousso for having sent me these letters, especially the second, which, sadly, I cannot quote in its entirety. This is the heart of the matter, we have touched on a crucial issue. Rousso, an Egyptian Jew who was not deported to the camps, nor were any members of his family, felt 'repudiated' by *Shoah*. He is not alone in this: there are those who were deported who felt an identical sense of negation. They are not present, they are not in the film, not as they think they should be or would want to be present. And yet, as I said earlier, *Shoah* is all about them. I am not speaking here of Belzec, of Treblinka, of Sobibór or Chełmno. In those camps, there was no question as to who would live or die: everyone was condemned to die and knew it; those few survivors, those I refer to in my film as the 'revenants', having miraculously survived, were themselves dead men granted a stay of execution. No, I am speaking of Auschwitz, that vast, unique camp that had a double function, being both a concentration camp and an extermination camp. In Auschwitz, when the trains arrived, an Angel of Death – either Mengele or another – was waiting on the ramp and decided who would be sent immediately to the gas chambers, and who would be sent to the concentration camp where, despite the horrors camp prisoners endured, there was a chance, however small, that they would survive. I have been known to say something that has not always been understood and has shocked those whose opinions are cut and dried: 'No one was in Auschwitz!' It is true that the phrase is provocative and impossible to accept. And yet it attested to a profound truth, something graven on the paradoxical heart of the tragedy that took place there. One need only look, with tears in one's eyes – it is impossible to do so otherwise – at the Auschwitz Album made by the Germans themselves, which shows the convoys of Jews, mostly from Hungary and Transylvania, arriving and disembarking on the ramp at Birkenau in the spring of 1944. After days and nights spent in harrowing conditions, they are herded out of the carriages with truncheons and batons and, waiting and screaming, they are lined up to wait for a verdict to be given as to their fate, the faces of the women, the children, of the few men accompanying them frantic with fear and disbelief. They sense the worst, know nothing about this place where they have come, they understand that they will die, do not know how and refuse to believe it. Moments later, whipped on by *kapos*, escorted by heavily armed Germans and police dogs, their bared fangs goading them on, they jostle each other, rushing down into the underground chambers of Crematoria II and III where they are forced to undress and step naked into an enormous room, 3,000 of them crammed in together, into which the greenish crystals of Zyklon B will be thrown as soon as the doors are closed. The lights are shut off, in the darkness, what Filip Müller calls 'the struggle for life, the struggle for death' takes place as each person fights for one more breath of air so they can live one second longer. These scenes were repeated day after day for years and the wretches who were its victims had no knowledge, no intimation of their own deaths: until the last moment, until with whips and clubs and truncheons they were hounded into the death chamber; and even troubled by a terrible sense of foreboding, they knew nothing of Auschwitz, neither the name nor the place, nor even the means by which their lives would be taken. They ended their days in darkness, enclosed by four walls of smooth stone, in a true 'non-place' of death.

But what of the others, those in the concentration camp who also witnessed the convoys arriving, the march to the crematoria, and who watched for hours and hours as wreaths of thick black smoke rose from the squat chimney of the building where mass murder was being committed? There can be no doubt that they were in Auschwitz, they knew everything there was to know about it. Everything, except the gas chambers. Anne-Lise Stern, deported from Paris to Auschwitz in the spring of 1944, who, from the first, was one of the most ardent and insightful admirers of *Shoah*, who never felt herself excluded by the film, understood what I meant when I dared formulate the almost unthinkable paradox of this camp where she survived for a year, this camp whose principles are implacably explained by Rudolf Vrba, in the '*deuxième époque*' of *Shoah*: 'The more the conditions in the concentration camp improved, the greater the number of new arrivals were sent to the gas chambers.' Vrba needs to be seen again, listened to again. Anne-Lise was too intelligent not to agree with what he said and what I made my own in perhaps a more brutal phrase. Over the years, I have sometimes felt Anne-Lise withdraw, come back, come closer, withdraw again. Doubtless the paradox of Auschwitz became too abstract, too theoretical, it did not take account of her personal experience, which needed to be put into words. This she did magnificently in 2004 when she published a book for which she invented the splendid title *Le Savoir-Déporté* [*Deported Knowledge*].

I read it with admiration, at times deeply moved, certain passages are forever engraved in my memory. The fundamental argument it presents, the experience it documents, are irreplaceable. For my part, I did not experience 'deported knowledge'. For twelve years I tried to stare relentlessly into the black sun of the Shoah, I forced myself to get as close as I could. It is a different approach, I do not believe the two approaches to be antagonistic, nor, I know, does Anne-Lise.

Shoah brought me, and still brings me, many friends both non-Jewish and Jewish, some of whom have become intimates. To make a list of them would be impossible, it would be tedious and would be hurtful to those I would inevitably forget to mention. I am thinking of Didier Sicard, who, in 1985, sent me a long letter that began: 'Monsieur, you have made the most beautiful film I have ever seen.' How could we not have become friends, and remained so? Michel Deguy who, in 1990, published *Au Sujet de Shoah. Le film de Claude Lanzmann*, an anthology of the most powerful articles published around the world about *Shoah*, including his own. And of course I cannot help but mention the magisterial hundred-page article that Shoshana Felman devoted to *Shoah*, which I spent a whole summer translating myself, or the seminars she asked me to give at Yale, where she was then a professor. Also I cannot ignore the profound and acutely nuanced pages devoted to *Shoah* by Gérard Wajcman in his book *L'Objet du siècle*, where I find myself in the curious and flattering company of Marcel Duchamp and Malevich. Wajcman is someone for whom, in spite of his fickle nature, I feel an unshakeable friendship. I also feel it for Arnaud Desplechin, one of the great younger figures in cinema, who published an admirable article in *L'Infini* about *Shoah* and my other films, telling of his shock when he first saw them. In his second term as Minister for Education, Jack Lang asked me if I would agree to a DVD being made for schools, not an abridged version of *Shoah* but a collection of extracts running to about three hours to be given free to secondary schools. I said yes. The DVD was made up of six sequences – each separated from the next by a black screen – and was accompanied by an 'educational booklet' explaining the film as a whole and giving a scene-by-scene commentary on each of the sequences included. Jean-François Forges, professor of history in Lyon, was given the responsibility for the project and did a superb job, something I am struck by every time I am asked to present in person a section from the DVD to a class.

I omitted to mention that, of all the tributes paid to me, one of the first, the most phenomenal and unquestionably the boldest, was that of Max Gallo, who in 1985 was editor of *Le Matin de Paris*, a newspaper that no longer exists; while other newspapers serialized witty little thrillers or love stories as summer reading, *Le Matin de Paris* decided to offer their readers, daily, the unexpurgated text of the film. People said that Max Gallo was crazy. It's true; he was crazy about *Shoah*.

It was through *Shoah* that I met Bernard Cuau. I employed him on the editorial committee of *Les Temps modernes*, and his death in 1995 left me inconsolable. He never slept and I could phone him at all hours of the day or night, something I did when I felt anxious; his mellifluous voice was like a drug to me, I will always miss it. Bernard taught film studies at the University of Paris VII and spent a month holding seminars about *Shoah*. His oeuvre, whether on the page, on film or for the theatre, are among those rare works paid for with one's life and which are not called part of literature because they are literature itself. When I say 'oeuvre', I include the articles he wrote during his ten years at *Les Temps modernes* and his earlier books – *La Politique de la folie* [*The Politics of Madness*], an implacable denunciation of psychiatric brutality, *L'Affaire Mirval* [*The Mirval Case*], with a preface by Michel Foucault and Pierre Vidal-Naquet – and his plays and the dozen films of touching power and subtlety he directed. The latter are mostly known only to students since they were directed through and for the university circuit: Bernard had no real interest in reaching a wider public. Power stratagems and media ploys were alien to him, self-effacement was his law. The multifarious works he produced throughout his life were ordained by a single burning locus; a vigil to absolute suffering, Bernard situated himself deliberately on the side of what was irreparable, the incurable, the sole setting for his words and his actions: madness, exclusion, prisons. He gave weekly lessons at the prisons of La Santé, Melun and Fresnes. One day he had the extraordinary idea of suggesting a screening of *Shoah* for the inmates of La Santé, followed by a seminar, which he would lead. His suggestion was greeted with whistles, jeers and insults, with a brutal and definitive refusal: his students were Arabic and black and wanted nothing to do with Jews. But Bernard, with inflexible gentleness, did not give up and, over a period of weeks, brought them round to the idea. For six months in La Santé he taught a course on *Shoah* and, at the request of his class, asked me to spend a day there. I arrived at nine in the morning and the discussion proved so intense, their knowledge of the film so precise, their questions so surprising and intelligent, that the inmates asked the wardens if they could skip lunch so we could go on talking. The wardens agreed and the discussion went on until five. I have rarely encountered an audience with such an in-depth knowledge of *Shoah*, or such an intense understanding of the issues raised by the film. Some of them wrote to me for a long time afterwards.

The friendship Bernard-Henri Lévy has shown me, generously offering me his hospitality so that I could have somewhere to write in peace, needs to be stated and restated here. But it is impossible in three lines to do justice to a man of such talents, he deserves much more, I will talk about him one day. People always forget to mention his courage, his madness, his wisdom, his remarkable intelligence, these are the things about him that matter most to me.

The further I got in the making of *Shoah*, the more the mounting financial difficulties began to smooth themselves out. It was possible for me to show scenes already filmed and even an edited section of the work in progress. I have spoken of the debt I owe the Israeli government. The help given to me, especially towards the end, by the French government, thanks to François Mitterrand and to Jack Lang, was also very precious to me. But it is individuals – some of them already friends of mine, others not yet – who made it possible for me to carry on during the lean times, when I surveyed the immensity of what remained to be done and the dire straits I was in. The film was saved many times by my very dear friend André Wormser, whom I first met at the Lycée Blaise-Pascal in Clermont-Ferrand, and by his brothers, Marcel and Jean-Louis, who, like him, were bankers. (I write these lines only a few short months after André's death.) I also managed to persuade Alain Gaston-Dreyfus and his wife, Marianne, of the need for such a film, and they brought together a group of donors, many of whom preferred to remain anonymous. To my great sorrow, Alain died from bone cancer. The work was taken up – and how! – by Thérèse, André and Daniel Harari, the latter two brilliant ex-students of the École polytechnique, inventors whose high-tech innovations are famous the world over, men of great humility and generosity, they will never know the extent of my gratitude. Charles Corrin, who had been deported to the camps, rallied the merchants of Le Sentier – I sometimes encounter strangers who tell me, 'I helped you with your film' – but his heart, which had known such trials and hardships, suddenly stopped beating; he was sixty-eight years old. Rémy Dreyfus actually went round making collections from impoverished friends – ten francs, fifty francs, the record was a hundred francs – making it possible at the time for me to buy more film stock. I have not forgotten the historian Georgette Elgey, nor my dear friends Gilberte and Adolphe Steg, who supported me from the beginning of my mad project. Nor have I forgotten the men and women who helped at the end, when the film was complete. For finishing the film did not mean that my problems were over: with conviction and generosity, Simone Veil headed up a small group who rallied to help me out of a difficult situation about which I will say a few words.

Nahum Goldmann, the first president of the World Jewish Congress, a statesman and a man of culture who negotiated German reparations with Chancellor Adenauer, aware of the considerable financial difficulties I faced in trying to complete the film, promised to help me. He would have done so had he remained in power but unfortunately he was forced to leave office and was replaced by Edgar Bronfman of the famous Canadian family of distillers whose founder, Samuel Bronfman, had a reputation as a successful bootlegger during Prohibition. The Bronfman family was impeccably respectable but Edgar, too occupied with his countless business concerns, appointed as his deputy, specifically responsible for Jewish affairs, Rabbi Israel Singer, who was primarily interested in politics. He was a young, sinuous man who seemed to glide when he moved, his eyes were invariably hidden, even at night, behind tinted glasses that added to his air of secrecy, which flourished together with his considerable power. Nahum Goldmann's friends in the World Jewish Congress had begged Singer to watch the first hour of *Shoah*. At the time I was at a critical stage in the making of the film: Parafrance, the distributor, had just gone bust. I was in need of money for the post-production work, which would require substantial sums. The French government had helped me as much as it could and I did not dare ask for more funds from the dear friends I have named who had already demonstrated such generosity. An organization as rich and powerful as the World Jewish Congress would surely contribute to ensuring that a film about the destruction of European Jewry could see the light of day. It was its bounden duty. A meeting was arranged and I hired Club 13 on the avenue Hoche so that Singer could see the film at its best. It cost me a lot of money, but I was very hopeful and, together with Nahum Goldmann's old friends, I invited a number of key figures. When we were due to start, Singer had still not appeared. I asked everyone to wait. By 8.30 he had still not arrived and I could no longer rudely expect my other guests to wait, all the more so since the room had been rented only for an hour and had to be free for another screening at nine. Singer finally arrived at 8.45, slipping along the row like a ghost, his eyes hidden behind his glasses, and slumping into the seat reserved for him, where he crossed and uncrossed his legs impatiently throughout the fifteen minutes he spent watching the film. Failure, humiliation, it was arranged that I meet with him briefly two days later in a hotel bar. He said only one thing: 'It's too long. It's not for the Americans.' In the summer of 1985, while spending a week with Dan Talbot in Watermill, at his charming Long Island home, the two of us would get together every morning in his study and, in a joyful almost warlike mood, attempt to come up with a strategy for the American release of this strange unidentified object known as *Shoah*. I learned from Dan that Singer, the august representative of the World Jewish Congress, was already fiercely negotiating with the Polish lobby before the film was even released – backslapping, effusive speeches, kosher banquets, junkets, the restoration of the Yiddish theatre in Warsaw, and more. With the skill of a practised diplomat, he was promoting a veritable policy of reconciliation with the Eastern bloc countries and paradoxically, *Shoah* – a film he had given no help to, it had been beneath him – deserved some of the credit. Israel Singer's triumph was yet to come: he became almost a world power in his own right, succeeding in forcing the Swiss banks and others to pay considerable, hard-won and much-deserved reparations to Jewish organizations. But he is no longer with the World Jewish Congress. He and Edgar Bronfman appear to have fallen out. For good, it would seem.

It is impossible to tell everything at once and I have not been able to talk about it until now, but the death of Sartre cast a terrible pall over the last years of the struggle – 1980 to 1985 – that would finally bring *Shoah* to completion. Castor's grief was spectacular and uncontrollable, people will remember the photographs taken of her at Montparnasse cemetery: she had to be held back or she would have fallen into the grave. Death invariably entails much work and I was the one who discussed with the police the route the funeral cortège should take. They did not want it to be a long procession and they did not want Sartre's remains to pass through the centre of

Paris, determined to contain the whole thing within southern Paris, within the 14th *arrondissement* where he had lived and where he had died at the Hôpital Broussais. The route I was forced to agree to was therefore relatively short: from the rue Didot, the boulevard Brune, along the outskirts of Paris, Porte d'Orléans, Denfert-Rochereau, the boulevard Raspail, the boulevard Montparnasse – from the junction at Raspail to the station, for which I had to argue fiercely since the police feared some sort of public outburst as Sartre passed the pavements he had strolled along so often – finally, the boulevard Edgar-Quinet and Montparnasse cemetery. The route, it is true, was very short, but the people of Paris, inconsolable, knew that with Sartre's passing they were saying goodbye not simply to a great man, but to a whole era, and thronged into the streets in such numbers that the cortège could move only in fits and starts, its progress blocked in front and to either side by people who did not know how to express their solidarity, their grief. A brief disagreement between those closest to him had occurred the night before the funeral: President Giscard d'Estaing had asked if he might come and pay his respects at the graveside. Some present were vehemently opposed to the idea. I was not. He came.

With Sartre dead, nobody had any real hopes for Castor's failing health or thought she would long outlive him. The doctors decided that she should be hospitalized and she was admitted to the Hôpital Cochin where she was treated for several weeks and recovered. She moved back to the rue Schœlcher and things returned to normal. Together we wrote an editorial explaining that *Les Temps modernes* would continue to be published. It was Castor's wish, our wish, and besides a journal belongs as much to its readers as to its founders. I have already talked about how close I was to her during the last years of her life, the evenings I spent discussing *Shoah* with her and all the screenings she attended. I remember the period before her death in 1986 as almost a happy time, she was still planning to travel in the far north and was sad when she was forbidden from doing so.

In 1986, the doctors ordered that she should urgently be admitted to the intensive care unit of Cochin, where she remained until the end. Her body was too frail, she was kept alive only artificially and it was painful to sit next to her, holding her hand when she could not speak or even move her head since she was intubated. A large tube passed through her mouth into her body, only her eyes were still alive, but they stared fixedly ahead of her and keeping her up to date with what was happening in the world seemed meaningless to me: her enforced silence rendered me mute also. I could only communicate my feelings by squeezing her hand, touching her body. According to the doctors, she was terminally ill, there was no possibility of saving her, but they could not say how long they would be able to keep her alive: if they took her off ventilation she would die. I was in an awkward position: *Shoah* was a major event in the United States and I had been invited to tour several cities and universities. I had told Dan to decline all invitations, that I could not possibly leave Paris. But a ceremony of great solemnity and importance for Americans had been organized in Los Angeles months earlier: the B'nai B'rith (whose Anti-Defamation League is one of the most powerful and aggressive anti-racist organizations in the United States) was to present me with their Torch of Liberty Award, and the date could not be changed. So as not to be away from Castor too long, I arranged to fly directly from Paris to Los Angeles, arriving on the day of the award ceremony; I planned to write my speech on the plane, and to leave again the following day. The doctors told me, 'She'll still be here when you get back.' When I landed in Los Angeles, the party that had come to meet me were in shock: a telegram had just arrived from Paris to say that Castor was dead. I was in an appalling state, wracked with guilt; heartsick, I attended the banquet in my honour, the organizers were kind enough to inform the guests of the sacrifice I had made to be with them and why – in spite of a thousand requests – I could not stay longer. I read the speech I had written on the plane, passed a sleepless night and flew back the following morning, arriving in Paris at dawn in order to organize Castor's funeral, just as I had Sartre's. She was no longer in the intensive care unit, but in the hospital morgue.

Once again, *Les Temps modernes* was faced with the decision of whether to wind down or carry on. If we decided to carry on, we needed an editor, the responsibility of which could only fall to the old hands. It was either Jean Pouillon, who had all but founded the journal, or me. I was ten years his junior. Pouillon spoke in favour of me: ten years is nothing, he said. We voted, I was chosen and, though I had never felt a desire to run a journal, to spend all the time necessary to do so, I agreed. One of my unspoken reasons was that the reputation I had made through *Shoah* would help me to protect the journal and ensure that the publisher, Claude Gallimard – who, six years earlier, after Sartre's death, had launched another journal, *Le Débat,* run by Pierre Nora with the considerable support of Les Éditions Gallimard, next to which *Les Temps modernes*, with no advertising and no modern equipment, looked like an antiquated relic – would support us. I did not know him but asked to meet him then, and he agreed, promising to support *Les Temps modernes*. I have been the editor now for twenty-two years, we have gone from strength to strength, and Antoine, Claude's son, now considers *Les Temps modernes* one of the most important journals that Gallimard publishes.

*

Why have I suddenly decided to give my book the curious title *The Patagonian Hare*? For a long time I had thought of calling it *La Jeunesse du Monde – The Youth of the World –* with no conflict between the world and myself, between my own youth and my age now. It has never occurred to me, in all the years I have amassed, to dissociate myself from the present, to say, for example, 'In my time . . .' My time is the time I am living right now and even if I like the world less and less – with good reason – it is mine, absolutely. No retirement, no retreat, I don't know what it means to grow old and it is first and foremost my youth that guarantees the youth of the world. One day, in circumstances I will never know, time stood still for me. This suspension of time was of implacable rigour during the twelve years it took to film *Shoah*. Or, to put it another way, time has never ceased *not to pass*. How, if time were passing, could anyone work for twelve years to produce something? This formulation 'time has never ceased *not to pass*' simultaneously denotes the inexorable flow of what Immanuel Kant called 'inner sense' as well as its interruption. And although time has started, very slowly, convalescent, to pass again, I still find it difficult to believe.

Along with capital punishment, incarnation – but is there a contradiction here? – has been the abiding obsession of my life. Though I know how to see, though I am gifted with a rare visual memory, the spectacle of the world, or the world as spectacle, always relates for me to an impoverishing dissociation, an abstract separation that forbids astonishment, enthusiasm, de-realizes both object and subject. When I was twenty, as I said in this book, Milan became true only when, as I crossed the piazza del Duomo, I began to recite the opening lines of *La Chartreuse de Parme* to myself. It is one example among thousands. There was an incredible shock in Treblinka, with its endless consequences, triggered by the meeting of a name and a place, by the discovery of this accursed name on ordinary road signs and train stations as though, over there, nothing had happened. There were the tears Abraham Bomba held back in the hairdressing salon in Tel Aviv. I have thought about hares every day as I was writing this book: those hares in the extermination camp at Birkenau that slipped under those barbed-wire fences impassable to man; those countless hares in the great forests of Serbia as I drove through the darkness, careful not to kill them. Lastly, the mythic animal that appeared in the beam of my headlights just outside the Patagonian village of El Calafate, piercing my heart with the obvious fact that I was in Patagonia, that at this very moment Patagonia and I *were true together*. This is incarnation. I was almost seventy years old, but my whole being leapt with a wild joy, as it did when I was twenty.

A Note About the Author

Claude Lanzmann is a French writer and the director of a number of films, including the nine-and-a-half-hour classic *Shoah* (1985), which was described by *The Washington Post* as "the film event of the century" and is regarded internationally as a historical and cinematic breakthrough. Lanzmann is chief editor of *Les Temps Modernes*, which was founded by Jean-Paul Sartre and Simone de Beauvoir.